AF772397

HANDBOOK OF LEARNING ANALYTICS AND ADAPTIVE LEARNING IN SCHOOLS

ELGAR HANDBOOKS IN EDUCATION

Elgar Handbooks in Education present a comprehensive analysis of the latest scholarly research in education. Edited by prominent experts, each *Handbook* features a wide range of chapters covering the latest international developments in the field. Often widely cited, individual chapters offer an overview of the current state of research in education, whilst also creating a forum for challenging current perceptions, and offering new perspectives of how research may develop in the future. *Handbooks* in the series often take an interdisciplinary approach, assessing the relationship between education and research areas as diverse as technology studies, social policy, public policy and environmental studies. These *Handbooks* will form a vital reference point for all researchers and students of education, creating a comprehensive and overarching guide to the field.

For a full list of Edward Elgar published titles, including the titles in this series, visit our website at www.e-elgar.com.

Handbook of Learning Analytics and Adaptive Learning in Schools

Edited by

Cathrine E. Tømte

Professor, Department of Information Systems, University of Agder and Adjunct Professor, Centre for the Science of Learning & Technology (SLATE), University of Bergen, Norway

Linda Barman

Associate Professor, Department of Education, Stockholm University, Sweden

Barbara Wasson

Professor and Director, Centre for the Science of Learning & Technology (SLATE) and AI LEARN, University of Bergen, Norway

ELGAR HANDBOOKS IN EDUCATION

EE Edward Elgar PUBLISHING

Cheltenham, UK • Northampton, MA, USA

© The Editors and Contributing Authors Severally 2026

Every effort has been made to trace all the copyright holders but if any have been inadvertently overlooked please notify the publisher.

All rights reserved. No part of this publication may be reproduced, stored in a retrieval system or transmitted in any form or by any means, electronic, mechanical or photocopying, recording, or otherwise without the prior permission of the publisher. Without limiting the author's and publisher's exclusive rights, any unauthorised use of this publication to train generative artificial intelligence (AI) technologies is expressly prohibited.

Published by

Edward Elgar Publishing Limited
The Lypiatts
15 Lansdown Road
Cheltenham
Glos GL50 2JA
UK

Edward Elgar Publishing, Inc.
William Pratt House
9 Dewey Court
Northampton
Massachusetts 01060
USA

Authorised representative in the EU for GPSR queries only: Easy Access System Europe – Mustamäe tee 50, 10621 Tallinn, Estonia, gpsr.requests@easproject.com

A catalogue record for this book is available from the British Library

Library of Congress Control Number: 2026934098

This book is available electronically in the **Elgar**online
Sociology, Social Policy and Education subject collection
https://doi.org/10.4337/9781035330676

MIX
Paper | Supporting responsible forestry
FSC® C013604

ISBN 978 1 0353 3066 9 (cased)
ISBN 978 1 0353 3067 6 (eBook)
ISBN 978 1 0353 9463 0 (ePub)

Printed and bound by CPI Group (UK) Ltd, Croydon, CR0 4YY

Contents

List of contributors vii

PART I INTRODUCTION

1 Why do we need a handbook on learning analytics and adaptive learning in schools? 2
Cathrine Edelhard Tømte, Barbara Wasson, and Linda Barman

PART II UNDERSTANDING LEARNING ANALYTICS AND ADAPTIVE LEARNING: DEFINITIONS, PRINCIPLES AND SCOPES

2 Learning analytics in schools: provocations and pointers 10
Paul Prinsloo and Mohammad Khalil

3 Adaptive learning systems: leveraging generative artificial intelligence for optimal adaptivity 21
Sima Caspari-Sadeghi

4 Designing multimodal collaboration analytics: challenges and opportunities 35
Daniel Spikol, Morten Misfeldt, Zaibei Li, and Viktor Holm-Janas

5 Integrating the Science of Learning with EdTech solutions: from frameworks to models of practice 51
Natalia Ingebretsen Kucirkova

PART III ETHICAL CONSIDERATIONS AND PRIVACY CONCERNS

6 The General Data Protection Regulation's right to explanation of algorithmic decision-making in the context of using AI-powered learning analytics in compulsory education 64
Małgorzata Agnieszka Cyndecka

7 Smart predictions, unseen bias: navigating the promises and pitfalls of predictive analytics in compulsory education 77
Lin Li

8 When categories matter: attendance data practices in an upper secondary classroom 96
Fride Haram Klykken

PART IV PEDAGOGICAL POSSIBILITIES AND CHALLENGES

9 Teacher development with learning analytics: a design narrative 113
Fabio Campos, Ha Nguyen, and June Ahn

10 Multi-case teacher inquiry to inform dashboard development 127
Merike Saar

11 Understanding the interrelated nature of academic, social, and emotional competencies through learning analytics 137
Jae H. Paik, Igor Himelfarb, Seung Hee Yoo, Jongtak Lee, Hoyong Ha, and Yurim Park

12 Using learning analytics to explore pre-service teachers' lesson planning 157
Kjersti Nedland Røneid, Gleb Belokrys, and Kristin Børte

13 Teaching Learning Analytics as formative assessment for pre-service teachers: report from a first trial 176
Cathrine Edelhard Tømte and Maria Wasmuth Grønvold

14 EssayCritic: enhancing student essays with locally trained AI feedback 191
Anders Mørch and Irina Engeness

15 Adaptive learning in primary mathematics: teachers' practices and insights 210
Kjetil Egelandsdal

16 Operationalising science competencies to support teachers' formative assessment and instruction with Inq-ITS AI 230
Janice D. Gobert, Amy Adair, Jessica A. Owens, and Rachel Dickler

PART V PROMOTING IMPLEMENTATION

17 Navigating learning analytics: challenges, opportunities, and recommendations 248
Marte Blikstad-Balas

18 Implementing learning analytics and adaptive learning in Norwegian schools: lessons learned 259
Barbara Wasson and Cecilie J.S. Hansen

19 Bridging the data divide in Swedish school education: challenges and opportunities in data standards 276
Italo Masiello and Zeynab (Artemis) Mohseni

20 The paradoxes of AI promises in schools: Insights from a multi-sited ethnography 295
Katarina Sperling and Linnéa Stenliden

Index 309

List of contributors

Amy Adair, PhD (Learning Sciences, Rutgers University), is a Postdoctoral Fellow in the Graduate School of Education at Rutgers University, advised by Dr Janice Gobert. She was an NSF Graduate Fellow (DGE-1842213) during her doctoral program, working with the Inq-ITS team on the development and use of AI for STEM instruction, learning, and assessment. Prior to graduate school, she taught high school mathematics and robotics.

June Ahn, PhD, is a Professor of Learning Sciences and Research–Practice Partnerships at the UC Irvine (UCI) School of Education. June is also a Senior Associate Dean at the UCI School of Education. He conducts research at the intersection of participatory design, technology, education, and community partnerships.

Linda Barman is a Associate Professor at the Department of Education at Stockholm University, and Deputy Director of CeUL, Centre for the Advancement of University Teaching at Stockholm University, Sweden. Her research interests include digital technologies and educational change, professional becoming and collegial learning.

Gleb Belokrys is a Senior Engineer at the Centre for the Science of Learning & Technology (SLATE), University of Bergen, Norway. His research centres on knowledge management, semantics-driven software, and graph-based modelling for intelligent systems. He explores the integration of AI and human–machine interaction through adaptive cognitive interfaces and lifelong learning infrastructures.

Marte Blikstad-Balas is a Professor in the Department of Teacher Education and School Research, University of Oslo, Norway, and Adjunct Professor at NTNU. Her research interests include literacy, reading, writing, digital media, classroom research, Norwegian didactics, research methodology, and video studies.

Kristin Børte, PhD, is a Senior Researcher at the Centre for the Science of Learning & Technology (SLATE) at the University of Bergen. Her research interests are technology use in education, learning design, student active learning, research and data use, teacher education, school leadership, and professional learning.

Fabio Campos, PhD, is a Brazilian researcher affiliated with Columbia University's Transformative Learning Technologies Lab (TLTL). His work lies on the intersection of critical pedagogies, citizenship education, design, and human–computer interaction, with special attention to marginalized youth from Brazilian *favelas* (slums).

Sima Caspari-Sadeghi is Associate Professor in ICT and Learning at Østfold University College, Norway. She holds a Habilitation and Alexander von Humboldt Postdoctoral

Fellowship from Germany. Her research focuses on Artificial Intelligence in Education (AIED) and Mathematics education, particularly the validation of AI-driven learning systems.

Małgorzata Agnieszka Cyndecka is Professor of Law at the University of Bergen (UiB). She is also affiliated with the UiB's Centre for the Science of Learning & Technology (SLATE). In addition, she is a member of the Norwegian Privacy Appeals Board (Personvernnemnda) and the Council of Europe's expert group "Artificial Intelligence and Education". She works mainly with EU/EEA law, in particular rules on data protection and State aid, and their interactions with new technologies.

Rachel Dickler, PhD (Learning Sciences, Rutgers University), completed her doctoral work under the supervision of Dr Janice Gobert. Rachel has an interdisciplinary research background spanning AI in Education, collaborative learning technologies, and formal/informal science education. Rachel is the Community Research and Evaluation Manager at the Denzer Zoon, where she conducts social science research.

Kjetil Egelandsdal is Associate Professor of Education at the Department of Education, University of Bergen. He holds a teacher education degree and a Master's in Education with a specialization in educational leadership from NLA University College. He completed his PhD in Education at the University of Bergen and subsequently held a postdoctoral position at the Centre for the Science of Learning & Technology (SLATE) at the same institution. His research interests lie at the intersection of teaching and technology, assessment practices, and educational philosophy.

Irina Engeness is a Professor at Østfold University College, Norway, with a research focus on digital education, artificial intelligence in learning, and teacher training. Her work draws on cultural-historical theory to explore how technology can support learning and development. She has authored two books on Galperin's legacy (Springer) and has led several national projects on digital competence in teacher education. Currently, she leads two Norwegian Research Council-funded projects – AI4AfL and AI-EXCAfL – which investigate how AI can enhance formative assessment and support deeper learning in schools.

Janice D. Gobert, PhD (Cognitive Science, University of Toronto), is Distinguished Professor of Educational Psychology and Learning Sciences at Rutgers Graduate School of Education. She has created and evaluated many technology-based science learning and assessment tools, and has expertise with quantitative data (log, performance, and classical assessment data) and qualitative data (think-aloud data, students' explanations, models/drawings). Janice is the lead inventor on three patents on Inq-ITS' underlying algorithms and methodology, and also holds three other patents for eye-tracking technology.

Maria Wasmuth Grønvold is a PhD Research Fellow at the Department of Information Systems, University of Agder. Her research interests include education, technology, social inclusion, learning, and gaming.

Hoyong Ha is an Education Supervisor at the Gyeongsangnam-do Office of Education in South Korea. From 2019 to 2023, he oversaw development operations for learning management system (LMS) platform, i-TokTok, an AI-powered education platform focusing on big data and AI integration. He continues to support digital transformation in public education through educational technology and research initiatives.

Cecilie J.S. Hansen is a PhD Research Fellow at the Department of Education, University of Bergen, Norway. Her research interests include teacher inquiry, professional development, data literacy, digital competence, learning analytics, artificial intelligence (AI), higher education, academic cultures, and the teaching–research nexus.

Igor Himelfarb is a distinguished professional in the field of psychometrics and research, with a career that spans across academia and industry. As the Director of the Department of Psychometrics and Research at the National Board of Chiropractic Examiners, Dr. Himelfarb oversees critical operations including scoring calibration, equating, linking, and scaling and communication with key stakeholders. Dr. Himelfarb earned his M.B.A. in Marketing and Data Analytics from Colorado State University, a Ph.D. in Education with an emphasis on Research Methodology and Quantitative Methods in Social Science from University of California Santa Barbara, an M.A. in Statistics from the same institution, an M.A. in Education Psychology and a B.A.in Psychology from California State University, Northridge. His research interests are intesting, psychometrics, learning, data analysis, and machine learning.

Viktor Holm-Janas is a PhD student at the Department of Computer Science, Copenhagen University, where he works at the Center for Digital Education and Human-centered Computing. He has a background in physics from the Niels Bohr Institute, but has mainly worked within the field of Physics Education Research, focusing on blended teaching methods and scenario-based didactics. In his PhD, he is working with Multimodal Learning Analytics in real classroom settings, with a focus on human-centric data analysis and meaningful feedback for stakeholders as part of a research effort called Collaborative Courageous Science, which studies how students can use each other to maintain groupwork when faced with adversities.

Mohammad Khalil is Associate Professor of Artificial Intelligence and Education at the Centre for the Science of Learning & Technology (SLATE), University of Bergen, Norway. His research interests probe the intersection of AI, learning analytics, and data-driven educational innovation, with a particular emphasis on privacy-enhancing and security-conscious solutions that empower human learning.

Fride Haram Klykken is a Postdoctoral Research Fellow at the Centre for the Science of Learning & Technology (SLATE), University of Bergen, Norway. Her research interests include sociomaterial and relational approaches to teaching, learning, education, and technology, as well as research ethics, game-based strategies for data literacy, and issues of trust in artificial intelligence within educational contexts.

Natalia Ingebretsen Kucirkova is a Research Professor affiliated with the University of Stavanger, Norway, and The Open University and University College London, UK. Natalia's research takes place collaboratively across academia, commercial, and third sectors. She co-founded and currently directs the International Centre for EdTech Impact that connects EdTech academia and industry. Natalia is widely published on topics of EdTech evidence in leading journals, including *Nature* and *NPJ Science of Learning*. Her research on personalized learning, early literacy, and digital books is highly cited and has been covered in *The Guardian*, *Newsweek,* and *The Washington Post*. Her latest book is *The Future of the Self* (Emerald Publishing 2021).

Jongtak Lee is the CEO of FOX EDU and the Co-CEO of Grow X Education. He is also the Vice President of DATAEUM. He leads the development of scalable, data-driven educational platforms that enhance teaching and learning across diverse environments. He holds a M.A. in Computer Engineering and a B.A. in Applied Software Engineering from Kongju National University. His research interests include AI, robotics, and their integration into personalized learning ecosystems, with a broader focus on digital education infrastructure and learner-centred innovation.

Lin Li is a Doctoral Researcher and Assistant Lecturer at Monash University, Australia. Her research lies at the intersection of algorithmic bias, artificial intelligence, and social impact in education. She investigates how bias and unfairness in machine learning can be effectively measured and mitigated to ensure equitable support for students from diverse backgrounds.

Zaibei Li is a PhD student at the University of Copenhagen, Department of Computer Science and Science Education. His research interests include multimodal learning analytics: educational data mining, learning analytics, and human-AI collaboration; ubiquitous computing: Internet of Things, system design, and mobile computing; and dashboard: data visualization, user interface design, and human-computer interaction.

Italo Masiello is Professor of Educational Technology at the Department of Computer Science and Engineering and head of the same department at Mälardalen University. He has a background in medical education, behavioural sciences, and digital technology. Italo's research focuses on digital technology-enhanced learning, an interdisciplinary field of research and development where educational, technical, behavioural, and design sciences meet.

Morten Misfeldt is Professor and leader of the Center for Digital Education (CDE), Department of Science Education (DSE), and Department of Computer Science (DIKU), University of Copenhagen. His research is placed on the intersection between digitalization of teaching and learning and mathematics education. He has published on game-based learning, learning analytics, the role of digital tools in mathematics education, and the influence of tools and representations on mathematical thinking. Recently, Misfeldt has worked with implementation studies in relation to the digitalization of infrastructure for teaching, as well as with the interaction between technology education and mathematics education.

Zeynab (Artemis) Mohseni is a Postdoctoral Fellow in the Department of Theory of Signal and Communications and Telematic Engineering at the University of Valladolid, Spain, and a member of the multidisciplinary research group GSIC/EMIC. She earned her PhD in

Computer and Information Science from Linnaeus University, Sweden. Her research focuses on generative AI, machine learning, data analysis, visual exploration of educational data, and visual learning analytics.

Anders Mørch is Deputy Head, Director of Studies, and Professor at the Department of Education at the University of Oslo. His research interests centre on educational technology and human-centred artificial intelligence in classrooms, makerspaces, and virtual 3D environments. By utilizing mixed methods research and theory-based design, Mørch seeks to inform and enhance his research outcomes. He is currently involved in the Norwegian Research Council-funded project LAT (Learning in the Age of Algorithms).

Ha Nguyen, PhD, is an Assistant Professor in Learning Sciences and Psychological Studies at the University of North Carolina, Chapel Hill. She uses design and learning analytics methodologies to explore how technologies can support collaborative learning and instructional improvement in STEM education. She is also interested in how educators, students, and researchers can collaborate with emerging AI technologies for teaching and learning.

Jessica A. Owens, MA (Higher Education, Geneva College), is a doctoral student under the supervision of Dr Janice Gobert. Jessica's interests are in collaborative learning technologies for science and the analyses of logfile data and discourse data to better understand and support collaborative science inquiry processes. Jessica is also the Academic Success Assistant Director in the School of Medicine at the University of Pittsburgh.

Jae H. Paik is Professor of Developmental Psychology at San Francisco State University, California. With over 20 years of research experience working with global school communities, Jae H. Paik is committed to advancing holistic education. Applying cutting-edge research on social, emotional, and cognitive development, she enjoys collaborating with schools to create and implement evidence-based learning experiences to support student learning and success in both online and offline environments. She holds a Ph.D. in Developmental Psychology and Cognitive Science from Indiana University.

Yurim Park is the Head of Business Development at Grow X Education, an EdTech company specializing in social-emotional learning (SEL). She holds a M.A. degree in Global Governance with a focus on International Development Cooperation from Kyung Hee University. Her work centres on integrating learning analytics with SEL to design data-driven platforms that support personalized learning and foster students' cognitive and emotional growth. She is passionate about bridging data science and pedagogy to enhance educational outcomes and student well-being.

Paul Prinsloo is Professor Emeritus at the University of South Africa (Unisa), and his research interests include, inter alia, Artificial Intelligence in education, learning analytics, student data privacy, and student success.

Kjersti Nedland Røneid is a PhD candidate at the Centre for the Science of Learning & Technology (SLATE) at the University of Bergen, Norway. Her main research interests are technology-enhanced teaching and learning, student active learning, lesson planning, and teacher education.

Merike Saar, PhD, is a researcher in the field of learning and teaching analytics at the School of Digital Technologies at Tallinn University. Her research centres around teacher professional development and technology-enhanced learning. She is actively involved in different European Erasmus+ projects involving teachers and schools to explore technology (including AI) adoption and constructive use in education. In addition, she is also a teacher of English, a teacher-trainer, and an educational technologist at the Tallinn French School.

Katarina Sperling holds a PhD in Pedagogical Work at the Department of Behavioural Sciences at Linköping University, Sweden. Her research focuses on the intersection of data-driven artificial intelligence (AI) and teacher practices. In particular, Katarina is investigating the use of AI-based educational technologies in K–12 classrooms. She is also involved in two major research initiatives around AI literacy in Swedish K–12 education and teacher education.

Daniel Spikol is an Associate Professor at the University of Copenhagen. Learning and play are central to human development, providing individuals with opportunities to understand how the world functions. Crucially, play allows people to safely explore boundaries and take risks, fostering mistakes that encourage learning through trial and error. However, both learning and play face challenges today, as children and adults increasingly spend time in front of screens and in digital environments that offer controlled, risk-free, and manufactured experiences. Consequently, it is essential to discover innovative ways to reconnect individuals with authentic play, integrating it into education and everyday life for the benefit of society. My research addresses this challenge by investigating how interactive digital tools can be thoughtfully designed to provoke diverse forms of play, learning, and well-being. Ultimately, my goal is to create new types of environments and experiences that encourage exploration and discovery.

Linnéa Stenliden is Professor in Educational Sciences at the Department of Behavioural Sciences at Linköping University, Sweden. Her research interest focuses on teaching and learning in relation to Digital Media and Artificial intelligence. She is, among others, the director of the WASP-HS project: "AI Literacy in Swedish Teacher Education – A participatory design project" and the sister project "AI Literacy for Swedish Primary Education: A Co-Design Approach" funded by the Swedish Research Council (SRC).

Cathrine Edelhard Tømte is a Full Professor at the Department of Information Systems at the University of Agder, deputy director of CeDIT, Centre for Digital Transformation, and visiting professor (professor II) at SLATE, Centre for the Science of Learning & Technology, University of Bergen. Her research interests include technology, society, and education.

Barbara Wasson is Professor and Director, Centre for the Science of Learning & Technology (SLATE), University of Bergen, Norway and Co-Director of the national AI Centre for the Empowerment of Human Learning (AI LEARN). She is a member of the Council of Europe's expert group on AI and Education, the expert group on Policy in Higher Education, and a member of the Norwegian Ministry of Education's expert group on AI in Higher Education. Her research interests include AI and education, learning analytics, data and AI literacy, and governance of AI in education.

Seung Hee Yoo is an Associate Professor in the Clinical Program at the Wright Institute in Berkeley, California. Research examines the connections between emotional intelligence, cultural values, and self-compassion and their impact on academic performance, interpersonal relationships, and psychological well-being. She received her Ph.D. in Social Psychology from Yale University.

PART I

INTRODUCTION

1. Why do we need a handbook on learning analytics and adaptive learning in schools?

Cathrine Edelhard Tømte, Barbara Wasson, and Linda Barman

WHY THIS *HANDBOOK*?

The widespread use of digital tools in classrooms generates a wealth of data on student engagement, progress and learning behaviours. However, without proper guidance, this data often remains unexplored.

Learning analytics (LA) refers to the use of digital technologies to understand and enhance learning. While educators have always assessed students' learning processes to adapt their teaching, LA introduces a new, data-driven dimension. It involves the systematic collection and analysis of digital traces left by learners to gain insights that can inform educational practice. Unlike traditional assessment, analytics implies the use of digital tools to sort, interpret and derive knowledge from data. Here, the digital nature of both the data and the analysis is used to improve learning.

In 2025, the International Society for Learning Analytics Research (SOLAR) updated the original 2011 definition of LA (SOLAR, 2025) to:

> Learning analytics is the collection, analysis, interpretation and communication of data about learners and their learning that provides theoretically relevant and actionable insights to enhance learning and teaching.

This new definition emphasises that LA is both an academic field of research and a field of educational practice, and that the insights provided by LA need to be theoretically grounded.

As digital technologies are increasingly becoming embedded in everyday educational practices, the key questions are no longer whether to use digital technologies for teaching and learning, but how these technologies may be aligned with LA. This includes considering which aspects of teaching, leadership and educational management technology should support, transform or challenge.

Despite its potential, in schools, there remains uncertainty around the use of student data in general and around the educational potential of LA and adaptive technologies. Teachers may raise concerns about how LA may provide insights into student learning and help tailor instruction more effectively. Parents may expect greater transparency and support for their children's progress, while school leaders may get a better opportunity to monitor more closely how data can be used to improve learning outcomes.

This *Handbook* is designed to support educators in enhancing their knowledge of how to interpret and apply LA effectively, thereby enabling informed, data-driven decisions that enhance teaching and learning. Moreover, the use of adaptive learning technologies can potentially personalise education by adjusting the content and pace to meet individual student needs. This *Handbook* will support teachers in integrating these tools into their practices, ensuring they are used purposefully and in alignment with curriculum goals. LA can also help identify students who may be struggling or at risk, allowing for timely and targeted interventions. Furthermore, many educators lack formal training in digital and data literacy (Sandoval-Riós et al. 2025). This *Handbook* bridges this gap by providing clear explanations and practical examples. LA also involves ethical considerations of data use that are addressed in the book, offering best practices for ensuring privacy, consent and responsible interpretation. Finally, this *Handbook*, based on the most recent research, serves as a state of the art in the field of learning analytics and adaptive learning in schools, and in this way informs future avenues of research.

This *Handbook of Learning Analytics and Adaptive Learning in Schools* thus equips researchers, educators and policymakers with updated knowledge about learning analytics and adaptive learning in the context of compulsory education. It offers a holistic understanding of LA, exploring its origins, definition, scope and key components. This approach includes elaborations of the collection and analysis of data, collection and analytics of data from administrative systems and learning platforms and tools, and the sharing of this analysis through the creation of visualisations, dashboards and other forms of feedback. Furthermore, the *Handbook* addresses ethical considerations and privacy concerns associated with LA, empowering readers to responsibly navigate these complexities. Closely related to LA is the concept of adaptive learning technologies. In this *Handbook*, you will be introduced to its principles, models and strategies related to adaptive learning in compulsory education. The concepts of personalisation and differentiation in compulsory education are explored, and adaptive learning technologies and tools, such as intelligent tutoring systems and adaptive features within learning platforms and tools, are introduced.

Recognising the interplay between LA and adaptive learning, the *Handbook* highlights how LA can enhance adaptive learning by providing insights into learners' progress and needs, while adaptive learning contributes to data collection and analysis to inform instructional decisions. Moreover, taking the perspectives from governance and policymaking, the *Handbook* also addresses how concepts such as LA and adaptive learning are recognised in broader debates associated with 'platformisations' and 'datafication of education' (Kovanovic et al. 2021; Mertala et al. 2025; Sergis and Sampson 2017; Williamson et al. 2023).

Finally, the *Handbook* provides empirical contributions that address challenges and limitations to support successful implementation. Contributions emphasise the importance of professional development for educators and educational leaders, collaboration among stakeholders, and the need to address ethical, privacy and regulatory concerns. With this comprehensive approach, the *Handbook of Learning Analytics and Adaptive Learning in Schools* serves as an invaluable resource for researchers, educators and educational leaders seeking to leverage these transformative approaches to improve learning outcomes and enhance educational experiences for all students.

OVERVIEW OF THE CHAPTERS

While there is a substantial body of research on LA and adaptive learning within higher education, less exists in the context of primary and secondary schooling. As editors, we are therefore very pleased to provide the readers with updated research that touches upon the various perspectives that comprise LA and adaptive learning for children and teenagers in schools. The *Handbook* comprises contributions from researchers from around the world, all contributing to unpack LA and adaptive learning, and to critically assess their possibilities and challenges in schools. After the introductory part, which contains this introductory chapter, the *Handbook* comprises four further parts that address these issues. Part II unpacks the concepts of LA and adaptive learning by introducing principles, definitions and scopes. Part III addresses ethical considerations and privacy concerns, Part IV explores various perspectives with regard to pedagogical possibilities and challenges, whereas Part V explores perspectives that touch upon the implementation of LA and adaptive learning in schools. In the remainder of this chapter, we elaborate on the sections and their contributions.

Part II brings together four distinct yet interrelated contributions that explore the evolving role of data, LA, artificial intelligence (AI) and adaptive technologies in contemporary education. Together, these chapters offer a multifaceted perspective on how digital tools are reshaping pedagogical practices, learner experiences and educational governance – particularly within pre-school, primary and secondary education.

In Chapter 2, Prinsloo and Khahil address the legal and sociological dimensions of LA in early and compulsory education, with a particular focus on the vulnerabilities of children in digital learning environments. The chapter highlights the dual potential of datafication: while it may enhance the personalisation and effectiveness of teaching, it also raises significant concerns regarding privacy, consent and the protection of minors. Through a layered analysis of children's decisional, social and constitutive vulnerabilities, the chapter offers critical guidance for policymakers, educators and researchers navigating the ethical complexities of data use in schools.

Chapter 3 provides a comprehensive overview of Adaptive Learning Systems (ALS), tracing their development over the past four decades and examining their current capabilities and limitations. Here, by drawing on advances in AI, particularly machine learning and natural language processing, Caspari-Sadeghi outlines the architecture of ALS and explores how these systems tailor instruction to individual learners. She also considers how emerging generative AI technologies, such as large language models, may address persistent challenges in affective modelling and learner engagement.

In Chapter 4, the focus shifts to Multimodal Learning Analytics (MMLA) and the analysis of collaborative learning in both educational and professional contexts. By integrating data from wearable sensors, audio tools and digital traces, Spikol and colleagues present the open MMLA system as a theoretically grounded approach to capturing and interpreting group dynamics. Through case studies in science outreach programmes, the authors demonstrate how MMLA can bridge the gap between scalable data collection and the nuanced understanding of human interaction.

The last chapter in this section, Chapter 5, turns to the quality and impact of EdTech data in LA. Here, Kucirkova argues for the adoption of multidimensional evidence standards, embodied in the 5E framework, that encompass not only efficacy and effectiveness but also ethical, equitable and environmental considerations. By linking the Science of Learning with practical evaluation tools, the chapter advocates for a shared 'evidence mindset' among EdTech developers, educators and researchers to ensure that digital tools genuinely enhance student learning.

Together, these contributions illuminate the promises and perils of data-driven education. They underscore the importance of interdisciplinary approaches that combine technological innovation with ethical reflection, pedagogical insight and commitment to equity.

Part III brings together three chapters that critically examine the ethical, legal and socio-material implications of data-driven technologies in compulsory education. As LA, AI and digital data infrastructures become increasingly embedded in educational systems, these contributions offer timely and necessary reflections on the risks, responsibilities and regulatory challenges associated with their use.

In Chapter 6, Cyndecka interrogates the legal foundations of the *right to explanation* under the General Data Protection Regulation (GDPR) in the context of AI-powered LA. While the GDPR is often referred to as the world's most comprehensive privacy framework, its application to algorithmic decision-making in education remains contested. This chapter explores the ambiguities and limitations of the right to explanation, particularly in relation to children as data subjects, and raises critical questions about the extent to which this right can be meaningfully exercised in educational settings.

Chapter 7 turns to the ethical and fairness concerns surrounding predictive analytics in primary and secondary education. As machine learning models are increasingly used to forecast student outcomes and inform pedagogical decisions, Li reviews the current landscape of predictive practices and highlights the risks of bias and discrimination. It offers a conceptual and methodological toolkit for identifying and mitigating predictive bias and concludes with practical recommendations for ensuring that predictive systems align with ethical principles and promote educational equity.

Chapter 8 adopts a sociomaterial perspective on the datafication of education, focusing on the production and use of attendance data in schools. Through empirical examples and theoretical analysis, Klykken illustrates how digital attendance systems are not merely passive tools but active participants in shaping classroom practices and institutional norms. By situating attendance data within broader assemblages of educational measurement and governance, the chapter contributes to a deeper understanding of how digital infrastructures enact power and agency in everyday school life.

Together, these chapters underscore the importance of critically engaging with the ethical, legal and material dimensions of AI and data use in education. They call for a more reflective and responsible approach to educational technologies – one that foregrounds the rights and well-being of learners, particularly those most vulnerable to the unintended consequences of datafication.

Part IV of the *Handbook* brings together chapters that explore the pedagogical implications of LA and adaptive learning technologies in schools. These contributions examine how such tools can support teaching and learning, while also addressing the practical, methodological and conceptual challenges that arise when integrating data-driven approaches into everyday educational practice.

In Chapter 9, Campos and colleagues discuss the human-centred design of LA tools. Drawing on a seven-year design-based research project centred around the development of Edsight, a visual analytics suite for middle school mathematics teachers in the United States, the chapter reflects on the limitations of existing design practices in contexts where learning management systems (LMS) are not widely used. It proposes three key design principles – long-term design partnerships, designing for sensemaking and leveraging cultural forms – as essential for developing effective and context-sensitive LA tools for school settings.

Chapter 10 investigates the role of teacher inquiry in the development and use of Learning Analytics Dashboards (LADs). Through a multi-case study, Saar examines how science-of-learning strategies and digital tools can be adapted by teachers to support evidence-based decision-making. The chapter highlights how teacher-led inquiry into pedagogical practices can inform the design of LADs, particularly in environments where data is not readily available from LMS platforms. It also demonstrates how such inquiry can enhance teachers' confidence and competence in using data to improve student learning outcomes.

In Chapter 11, Paik and colleagues address the integration of social and emotional learning (SEL) into LA and educational data mining (EDM). Recognising the growing importance of SEL in promoting academic success and student engagement, the chapter explores how predictive models can be developed to capture the complex interplay between social, emotional and academic factors. Using data from Korean elementary students, it illustrates how behavioural indicators, self-reports and activity logs can be used to build models that track learning trajectories over time. The chapter advocates for a more holistic and interdisciplinary approach to LA, one that incorporates robust psychometric foundations and reflects the multifaceted nature of student development.

Chapter 12 investigates how LA can support teacher educators in assessing pre-service teachers' lesson planning competence. Drawing on data from the ILUKS planner, a digital tool designed to scaffold lesson design and facilitate peer and instructor feedback, Røneid and colleagues analyse the planning trajectories of pre-service teachers and the types of feedback they receive. It highlights both the potential of LA to provide insight into pedagogical development and the challenges of capturing the nuanced processes involved in lesson planning.

Chapter 13 continues the focus on teacher education by examining how pre-service teachers are introduced to LA through the lens of formative assessment. Framing LA as a process of producing, interpreting and responding to data, Tømte and Wasmuth Grønvold present a pilot study in which teacher educators implemented a structured lesson and assignment to familiarise pre-service teachers with LA concepts. The findings offer practical guidance on how to prepare future educators to critically engage with data and adopt LA as part of their professional toolkit.

In Chapter 14, there is a shift to the classroom context, introducing EssayCritic, an AI-based writing tool designed to provide automated feedback to upper secondary students in English as a second language. Through a case study in a Norwegian school, Mørch and Engeness demonstrate how locally trained language models can support collaborative learning and improve writing outcomes. They propose three metaphors to help educators conceptualise the use and potential misuse of AI tools, and discuss the pedagogical implications of using smaller, context-specific models versus large, general-purpose ones.

Chapter 15 explores teachers' experiences with adaptive learning systems (ALS) in primary mathematics education. Drawing on sociocultural theories and the notion of teachers as designers of learning environments, Egelandsdal presents findings from a mixed-methods study that reveals that while ALS can effectively support individualised practice and progress monitoring, they often fall short in fostering conceptual understanding. The chapter underscores the critical role of teachers in mediating between system-generated adaptivity and broader pedagogical goals.

Chapter 16 forms the final chapter in Part IV. While students worldwide continue to struggle with STEM competencies, the Next Generation Science Standards (NGSS) aim to guide educators. Here, Gobert and colleagues argue for the need to provide teachers with real-time, formative and actionable data to guide instruction aligned with the NGSS. Consequently, they present Inq-ITS (student platform) and Inq-Blotter (teacher dashboard), which generate fine-grained assessments of students' science practices and help teachers identify what support to provide, to whom and when. They argue that by operationalising complex practices into measurable components, educators can better foster students' ability to apply scientific thinking in real-world contexts – skills vital for addressing global challenges such as climate change and pandemics.

Together, these chapters underscore the pedagogical potential of LA and adaptive learning technologies, while also emphasising the need for thoughtful design, teacher involvement and a broader conceptualisation of learning that includes emotional and social dimensions. They offer valuable insights for researchers, developers and educators seeking to harness the power of data to enhance teaching and learning in meaningful and equitable ways.

The final part of the *Handbook, Part V,* brings together four chapters that examine the practical realities of implementing LA and AI in school systems. These contributions address policy frameworks, technical infrastructures and professional dynamics that shape how data-driven technologies are introduced, integrated and experienced in educational contexts. Together, they offer a critical and constructive perspective on the systemic conditions necessary for responsible and effective implementation.

Chapter 17 presents the findings and recommendations of a Norwegian government-appointed Expert Group tasked with evaluating the use of LA in the national education system. Drawing on interdisciplinary expertise in education, technology, ethics and law, the group assessed both the opportunities and the barriers to LA adoption in schools. In this chapter, Blikstad-Balas highlights key ethical and pedagogical considerations, including privacy concerns and the need for clear regulatory guidance. While grounded in the Norwegian context, the chapter's insights are broadly applicable to other countries navigating the digital transformation of education.

In Chapter 18, Wasson and Hansen focus on the results of an eight-year Norwegian R&D project that began by investigating how to design and develop an LA dashboard that leverages student activity data from across vendor platforms and presents teachers with insights into student learning and progression. Such an approach to implementing LA in Norwegian schools introduced technical, ethical and legal complexities. This chapter presents the Norwegian AVT project's experience in developing and implementing an LA system, outlining the infrastructure, practical challenges, solutions for responsible data handling and concludes by sharing the lessons learned.

In Chapter 19, Masiello and Mohseni focus on technical infrastructure and data interoperability in Sweden, detailing the development of a standardised data model and pipeline to integrate educational data from municipalities and EdTech providers. Guided by principles from implementation science, the chapter emphasises stakeholder collaboration, GDPR compliance and transparency. It identifies both the progress made – such as improved dashboard visualisations and teacher engagement – and the persistent challenges, including inconsistent data quality and varying levels of digital competence. The chapter positions Sweden's efforts within a wider Nordic and European context, offering a model for scalable and ethical data integration.

Chapter 20 adopts a critical lens to examine teachers' experiences with AI-supported technologies in schools. Drawing on three field studies involving different AI and LA tools, Sperling and Stenliden explore how these technologies are introduced into educational settings and how they affect teachers' professional agency. Rather than enhancing autonomy, the findings suggest that AI systems may constrain teachers' decision-making and pedagogical flexibility. This contribution raises important questions about the assumptions underpinning AI implementation in education and calls for a more teacher-centred approach to technological innovation.

Collectively, these chapters underscore that the successful implementation of LA and AI in education requires more than technological readiness. It demands thoughtful policy, robust infrastructure and a deep understanding of the professional and ethical contexts in which these tools are deployed. They offer valuable guidance for policymakers, system leaders and practitioners seeking to navigate the complex terrain of educational data use.

REFERENCES

Kovanovic, V., C. Mazziotti and J. Lodge (2021), 'Learning analytics for primary and secondary schools', *Journal of Learning Analytics*, **8** (2), 1–5. https://doi.org/10.18608/jla.2021.7543

Mertala, P., Fagerlund and L. Palsa (2025), 'Experts' discourses of children in the context of datafication of education', *Childhood*, **32** (4), 482–501. https://doi.org/10.1177/09075682251346331

Sandoval-Ríos, F., C. Gajardo-Poblete and J.A. López-Núñez (2025), 'Role of data literacy training for decision-making in teaching practice: A systematic review', *Frontiers in Education*, **10**, 1485821. https://doi.org/10.3389/feduc.2025.1485821

Sergis, S. and D.G. Sampson (2017), 'Teaching and learning analytics to support teacher inquiry: A systematic literature review', in A. Peña-Ayala (ed.) *Learning Analytics: Fundaments, Applications, and Trends* (Studies in Systems, Decision and Control). Cham, Switzerland: Springer, vol. 94, pp. 25–63 https://doi.org/10.1007/978-3-319-52977-6_2

SOLAR (2025), 'Reimagining learning analytics. Report from the SOLAR Executive Committee Task Force.' https://www.solaresearch.org/wp-content/uploads/2025/06/Reimagining-Learning-Analytics-V3-002.pdf

Williamson, B., F. Macgilchrist and J. Potter (2023), Re-examining AI, automation and datafication in education. *Learning, Media and Technology*, **48** (1), 1–5. https://doi.org/10.1080/17439884.2023.2167830

PART II

UNDERSTANDING LEARNING ANALYTICS AND ADAPTIVE LEARNING: DEFINITIONS, PRINCIPLES AND SCOPES

2. Learning analytics in schools: provocations and pointers

Paul Prinsloo and Mohammad Khalil

INTRODUCTION

Learning analytics (LA), since its emergence as a distinct research focus and practice in 2011 (Siemens 2013), has initially been mainly focused on higher education but has increasingly been deployed in primary and secondary (K–12) educational contexts (Culbreth et al. 2025). As digital media finds its way into pre-schools and nurseries, the collection and use of pre-school children's data will become as mainstream as data collection in other educational contexts (Bradbury 2020; Culbreth et al. 2025). There is also evidence of the increasing use of Multimodal Learning Analytics (MMLA) in educational contexts, widening the scope of concerns and potential for harm, especially for minors (Prinsloo, Slade and Khalil 2023).

While schools have always collected a range of data, this has intensified due to the advent of educational technology (Lupton and Williamson 2017) and further accelerated after COVID-19, resulting in 'new data infrastructures and algorithmic capabilities' that allow for analytics of an 'unprecedented complexity and scope' (Parks 2014, p. 356; also see Jarke and Breiter 2019). Though linkages between privacy, online surveillance and governance are not new, concerns about students' privacy have been on the increase (Culbreth et al. 2025). Schools have the moral obligation and fiduciary duty to act as guardians 'through the mechanisms of data governance, choosing apps and vendors that limit use of children's data to school activities, and, in some nations, producing self-regulatory codes of conduct intended to provide assurances to teachers and parents' (Rennie et al. 2019, p. 87).

Feldstein (2020), in the context of Monitoring Applications (MA) to protect students' safety in online environments, points to concerns that the collection of personal data from children 'can bring significant consequences when children become adults (not to mention that children's data are often mixed in with adult data)' (p. 3). A UNICEF report (2019) titled 'Faces, fingerprints and feet' points to key challenges in collecting biometric data from children such as, inter alia, lifelong data risks – 'more data will be collected on children over their lifetime than ever before, and the future use, applications and impact of this data on their lives is unpredictable' (p. 19).

PROBLEM STATEMENT

While issues pertaining to ethics and privacy have been part and parcel of LA, much of the theoretical and empirical research has focused on the central roles of consent, the role of students' choice and agency, often in tension with higher education's fiduciary duty to design and provide effective, appropriate and quality learning experiences to students as mandated by legislation and their charters (Khalil, Slade and Prinsloo 2024; Liu and Khalil 2023). Except for the fact that the notion and practice of consent are often seen as problematic and fragile (Andrews 2020; Prinsloo and Slade 2016; Prinsloo, Slade and Khalil 2023), what about legal subjects who cannot give consent – such as children under a particular age? And even when consent is provided by children's parents and guardians, how do we understand and protect children's specific vulnerabilities in digital environments?

With evidence that LA is increasingly being operationalised in pre-primary, primary and secondary school contexts, this chapter briefly maps selected legal approaches to protect children and then uses a sociological lens for understanding children's 'vulnerability' in online, platformed learning environments. We start by briefly introducing the collection, analysis and use of children's data before summarising legal and sociological/socio-digital understandings of vulnerability. This is followed by a discussion, before concluding with some pointers or recommendations and a conclusion.

LITERATURE REVIEW

This section will briefly outline current research on LA in schools before looking at the discourses surrounding children's digital vulnerability and safety.

Learning Analytics in Schools

Aguerrebere et al. (2022), in their report on LA in K–12 education, state that while it is an emerging phenomenon, 'what is clear is that the adoption of learning analytics within K–12 education represents a complex endeavour' (p. 223), partly due to the fact that '[s]chool systems are highly heterogeneous in their cultures, practices and attitudes toward technology and data and they occupy a politically charged position within society' (p. 223). The authors provide an overview of the benefits and concerns related to the deployment of LA from 'the *perspective of six researchers*' who are working in five global contexts, namely China, Finland, South Africa, Uruguay and the USA (p. 223; italics added). It is important to note that *perspectives* shared by researchers from these five global contexts do not necessarily provide a comprehensive investigation into LA in these contexts, but in a sense, provide glimpses of developments based on the perspectives of the researchers.

In China, for example, the terminology 'Learning Analytics' or 'Educational Data Mining (EDM)' is not used, and research focuses on the notion of 'Big Data' in education. The authors note that in the case of China, 'data security, privacy, and ethics are important challenges' (p. 224). In Finland, '[e]ach city and municipality has the freedom to choose the web services (eLearning solutions) that will be integrated in the school context, making 'the collection of learning data a challenging task' (p. 225). The South African report does not deal with the collection, analysis and use of student data but rather focuses on 'Operation Phakisa in Education (OPE) – a project to fast-track the delivery of computer devices to learners' (p. 225) which would have included 'surveillance for pedagogical and administrative activity' (p. 226) and resulted in a 'colonisation' by Big Tech transnationals. In the context of Uruguay, authors report details on progress with 'Plan Ceibal', which would deploy 'a Big Data platform for learning analytics'. Concerns about student privacy would be addressed by a committee 'for ensuring user privacy, whereas an inter-institutional ethics committee is in charge of establishing the ethical guidelines that govern educational research' (p. 227). Concerns about 'high student dropout and grade retention problems' in the context of Uruguay 'motivated the development of a national learning analytics initiative focused on tracking the trajectories of Uruguayan students during upper secondary education' (p. 227).

The section on LA in the context of the USA reports that '[t]here has been no comprehensive empirical assessment of the use of learning analytics in schools', resulting in an unclear picture regarding 'how many schools and to what extent they are utilizing new forms of data to impact learning' (p. 227). Despite the lack of empirical research on LA in schools, 'the work of Digital Promise lays out a detailed framework for embedding sound data processes and analytics research into teaching practice' (p. 227). The authors conclude that 'LA currently has limited ascertainable impact in K–12 education' (p. 228), despite the fact that the USA 'has one of the most active education technology sectors in the world' (p. 228) resulting in, inter alia, 'growth in partnerships by the ed tech sector and school districts' (p. 228). After presenting these five country snapshots, the book's authors conclude that there remain two main concerns, namely 'a) that data utilization is a task of far greater complexity than data collection and b) that governments are playing catch-up with respect to understanding how analytics are being used in K–12 education' (p. 228). Of particular interest in the context of this chapter is the fact that the five country snapshots by Aguerrebere et al. (2022) do not discuss, at all, the problems of consent, age or legal frameworks in these respective contexts.

Tzimas and Demetriadis (2021), in their review of ethical issues in LA research, found very little empirical research on LA in schools. Discussing the notion of transparency, they state that 'a K–12 school must inform the parents about collecting and analysing their children's data to consent' (p. 1112), and with regard to algorithmic fairness, they report on one study that found that 'wealthy schools typically have computerised education, so the data and insights extracted from learning analytics may not accurately reflect the general population' (p. 1114). In the context of data ownership and privacy, the authors report on one study that concluded that 'a school's data must not be sold, and analytics should not be the only source of decision-makers' prediction' (p. 1117). The review found no discussion on the ethics of specifically using LA in schools and the complexities of the age of consent, differences in vulnerability, etc. The lack of any research on privacy and data protection in the context of schools was also found in the systematic review by Liu and Khalil (2023).

In a recent review by Paolucci, Vancini, Bex II, Cavanaugh, Salama and de Araujo (2024) on opportunities and challenges of LA for K–12 education, they found that

> many see the educational benefits of learning analytics (for example, more equitable instruction, individualized learning, enhanced assessment for learning); others remain unconvinced by a lack of evidence of improved outcomes and [are] concerned about persistent challenges and potentially harmful impacts (for example, infringement on users' privacy, misuse or misinterpretation of data by educators).

While the authors (Paolucci et al. 2024) discuss, in general, ethics and consent, there is no dedicated discussion on, for example, the legal and regulatory implications of collecting children's data or the complexities that younger children may be more vulnerable to than older children. The lack of any comprehensive consideration about, for example, the differential implications of children's ages ranging from pre-school to K–12 or the different vulnerabilities children may experience, is also found in the recent study by Tzimas and Demetriadis

(2025) on 'K–12 Teachers' Acceptance and Resistance Perceptions of Learning Analytics Adoption'.

The Use of Children's Data in Schools – A Broader Perspective

Due to a seeming paucity of research on LA in the context of schools, and specifically the legal and sociological implications of collecting, analysing and using children's data, we briefly explore a selection of other literature that provides insights regarding the complexities of using children's data.

Hope (2015), in a study on e-safety in schools, makes the very interesting distinction that international law must define children as being under the age of 18: 'What might be labelled as an e-safety issue for a 5-year-old could be perceived as unproblematic for a 15-year-old' (p. 345). While older kids are deemed to explore more risky digital behaviour, younger kids are more vulnerable, and therefore it is necessary to differentiate between children's age groups, as a one-size-fits-all approach would not be appropriate. Children are anything but a homogeneous group, and the complexities in the nexus between students' online engagements, age and contextual factors make it impossible and even dangerous to generalise. Hope (2015) furthermore points to the fact that in much of the discourse about childrens' digital wellbeing, their e-safety is much more prominent than their privacy, and childrens' right to privacy is only part of strategies to protect their safety.

Rennie et al. (2019), in their research on the use of applications in 148 Australian primary schools, found that teacher decision-making in the selection of apps was far from uniform, 'making individual guardian consent *an inadequate approach* to the protection of children' (p. 78; italics added). The authors conclude that '[t]he failure of consent leads to other legal and self-regulatory approaches through which the state and technology companies together recreate the school's role as administrator over the conduct and formation of future digital citizens' (p. 78). While '[s]chools have a function in both constraining and protecting the child, as well as cultivating civic capacities' (p. 81), the use of technology in schools, and the increasing influence of educational technology companies in education result in 'new geographies of power' where platforms 'generate and enforce their own forms of sovereignty' (p. 82). Rennie et al. (2019) cite Bratton (2015, p. 5), who sees 'planetary-scale computing as largely unaccountable, a consolidation and alignment of political and technical systems into 'an accidental megastructure' (p. 82). As such, schools and platforms 'respond to and legitimise each other' (p. 82). Interestingly, Rennie et al. (2019) state that '[t]eachers and schools are therefore required to enact privacy protections on students' behalf' (p. 85).

Lastly, Culbreth et al. (2025) report on MA in the context of K–12 contexts during the COVID-19 pandemic. In the context of the USA, legislation includes the Children's Online Privacy Protection Act (COPPA) (Office of the Federal Register 1998) and the Children's Internet Protection Act (CIPA) (Office of the Federal Register 2000). Though children as young as 13 could give consent, COPPA established that websites 'must provide a privacy policy that outlines the data collected, how it is collected, what it is used for, and a description of parental rights. They must also maintain reasonable procedures to protect the privacy, integrity, and confidentiality of the data that they collect' (Culbreth et al. 2025, p. 191). COPPA was updated in 2013 to include the need to declare the inclusion of 'persistent identifiers (for example, cookies and hardware addresses) and geolocation' (Culbreth et al. 2025, p.

191). CIPA (2000) contains directives that '[prevent] minors access to obscene, pornographic or otherwise harmful media' (Culbreth et al. 2025, p. 191).

Children's Vulnerability – A Legal Perspective

In the recent publication by DiPaola and Calo (2024) on socio-digital vulnerability (see the later discussion), the authors refer to vulnerability as 'a state of being that renders people and groups less powerful or open to harm' (p. 2). They link vulnerability to being vulnerable to manipulation or to being exploited for 'self- or institutional interest' (p. 2). The law considers vulnerability as a special status or as binary – you are either vulnerable or not, for example, children under the age of 13 in the context of the Children's Online Privacy Protection Act (COPPA) and the moment you turn 14, the special protection falls away. In the interest of protecting vulnerable individuals, DiPaola and Calo (2024) propose to move away from seeing vulnerability as a binary to 'highlight the importance of context in making the decision of who is vulnerable at any given time' (p. 3). Referring to the work of Luna (2009) (see the later discussion), the authors agree that vulnerability is layered and dynamic and 'can be influenced, including deliberately by design' (p. 3). In the context of digital environments, digital mediation 'furnishes pervasive opportunities to 'vulnerabalise and manipulate' (p. 4) individuals and/or groups of individuals. Socio-digital vulnerability takes on particular forms – decisional, social and constitutive. Decisional vulnerability 'involves interference with the formation or exercise of preferences' (for example, through interface design, predictive algorithms, recommender systems); social vulnerability refers to 'susceptibility to the deliberate shaping of our social interactions, including by social mimicry' (for example, the anthropomorphic understandings of algorithmic decision-making systems and/or Large Language Models; chatbots); and constitutive vulnerability addresses the 'malleability of human identity and sense of self' (for example, how socially mediated environments shape human identity and sense of agency) (seeDiPaola and Calo 2024, p. 4; for a further discussion on socio-digital vulnerability, see the next section).

Regarding the legal implications of moving away from seeing vulnerability as binary, DiPaola and Calo (2024) propose seeing vulnerability as 'a state that can be created and manipulated toward particular ends' and explore two sets of rules to address the legal aspects of socio-digital vulnerability, namely 'harm rules' and 'power rules'. Harm rules 'anticipate harm and seek to deter it – and, in the case of torts, to try to restore the victim to the status quo ex ante' while power rules could 'make the potential victim more powerful' or 'could make a potential perpetrator weaker' (p. 10). The authors suggest that 'harms caused by socio-digital vulnerability are often subtle and hard to identify, making it even more important to reduce the power imbalance upfront' (p. 11; for a full discussion see DiPaola and Calo 2024).

In terms of the protection of children under the General Data Protection Regulation (GDPR), Lievens and Verdoodt (2018) state that 'the text of the GDPR offers little clarity as to the actual implementation and impact of a number of provisions that may significantly affect children and their rights, leading to legal uncertainty for data controllers, parents and children' (p. 269). Lievens and Verdoodt (2018) mention several concerns, such as the fact that the GDPR does not define who qualifies as a 'child' in terms of age, and second, even if a specific age is specified, this would not protect younger children who need different, if not more, protection. A second issue raised by Lievens and Verdoodt (2018) states that the GDPR 'is fundamentally built on the notion of the informed data subject, who agrees in a freely given, specific, informed and unambiguous manner', which is more complex when it comes to children and their parents or guardians. According to the GDPR, children above the age of 16 can provide legal consent – 'Where the child is below the age of 16 years, such processing shall be lawful only if and to the extent that consent is given or authorised by the holder of parental responsibility over the child' (Article 8, GDPR). Recital 38 (GDPR) states

> [c]hildren merit specific protection with regard to their personal data, as they may be less aware of the risks, consequences and safeguards concerned and their rights in relation to the processing of personal data. Such specific protection should, in particular, apply to the use of personal data of children for the purposes of marketing or creating personality or user profiles and the collection of personal data with regard to children when using services offered *directly to a child*. The consent of the holder of parental responsibility should not be necessary in the context of preventive or counselling services offered directly to a child. (italics added)

According to Lievens and Verdoodt (2018), there is no clarity on whether educational institutions would fall under the provisions of Section 8, and second, what the implications are of the phrasing 'directly to child'. Article 8 furthermore allows for Member States to lower the age to 13, which means that providers of digital online educational services offer these services, considering possible differences between Member States. Many of these services originate from Silicon Valley and are therefore covered by COPPA, which 'requires that websites and services that are specifically targeted at children or service providers who reasonably should know that they are collecting personal data of children under 13, obtain prior parental consent' (Lievens and Verdoodt 2018, p. 272). According to these researchers, the Netherlands adopted 16 as the age of consent, while the age of consent in Spain and Austria is 14, and in Belgium, 13. The authors refer to the research by Livingstone and Olafsson (2017), who researched the notion of commercial literacy of children and found that this increases between the ages of 12 and 15 years. 'This implies that younger children require more protection by their parents or regulators, in particular against privacy-intrusive data processing practices such as profiling (infra)' (p. 273; for a full discussion see Lievens and Verdoodt 2018).

A further issue raised by Lievens and Verdoodt (2018) relates to the GDPR regulation that the controller 'shall make reasonable efforts to verify in such cases that consent is given or authorised by the holder of parental responsibility over the child, taking into consideration available technology' (article 8, para. 2 GDPR). The GDPR does not include criteria for what is regarded as 'verifiable consent' and 'reasonable effort'. Once again, Lievens and Verdoodt (2018) refer to COPPA, which 'provides that parental consent can be obtained by any means, if the method can reasonably ensure that the person providing consent is the parent of the child' (Lievens and Verdoodt 2018, p. 274; also see Slabu 2017).

UNDERSTANDING CHILDREN'S VULNERABILITY – A SOCIOLOGICAL PERSPECTIVE

According to Mackenzie, Rogers and Dodds (2014), the notion of 'vulnerability' is under-theorised. Vulnerability is furthermore a key ontological dimension or characteristic of all human life on earth, but some humans are more vulnerable than others. Vulnerability, furthermore, is contingent on a range of often mutually constitutive factors and, therefore, in its essence, relational. It is possible to distinguish between three types of vulnerability, namely inherent, situational and pathogenic (Mackenzie, Rogers and Dodds 2014). *Inherent* vulnerability refers to human 'corporeality, our neediness, our dependence on others, and our affective and social natures' (p. 7). In the context of this chapter, children, due to their nature of being children, have an inherent vulnerability – not only in relation to their abilities and/or stage of development (cognitively, physically, socially or emotionally), but also due to their specific dependence on others. *Situational* vulnerability refers to vulnerability that emerges due to contextual or situational factors, such as, for example, in contexts where there is a higher risk of physical or emotional violence and/or abuse or in contexts where their basic psychological, social and physical needs cannot be met, but may be met if the situation changes. A subset of situational vulnerability, according to Mackenzie, Rogers and Dodds (2014), is *pathogenic* vulnerability 'when a response intended to ameliorate vulnerability has the paradoxical effect of exacerbating existing vulnerabilities or generating new ones' (p. 9). Pathogenic vulnerability can arise from interpersonal relationships and/or institutional structures or a combination of both.

Linked to, and expanding an understanding of vulnerability as intersectional, is the proposal by Luna (2009) to understand vulnerability as *layered*, and not as a 'label'. Luna (2009) maps her proposal of vulnerability against the backdrop of the operationalisation of designating certain subpopulations, for example, females, as vulnerable in the context of research (for example, the Belmont report). She states that understanding vulnerability as such – as linked to a specific characteristic such as gender – suggests 'a simplistic answer to a complicated problem' (p. 124). She justifies her proposal of vulnerability as 'layered' by stating – 'The metaphor of a layer gives the idea of something 'softer', something that may be multiple and different, and that may be removed layer by layer' (p. 128). Not only does seeing vulnerability as 'layered' allow for overlaps between different layers, but it also allows flexibility that binary understandings of vulnerability lack.

A layered understanding of vulnerability may be illustrated by starting with a phenomenon such as poverty, and then considering how poverty affects different races, genders and cultural groups differently. A female and a male may be equally poor, but in a specific context, gender may afford either of them some amelioration or worsen their vulnerability. Add to this scenario the impact of race and the impact of a particular context, such as a slum in New York or Nairobi, in a time of social unrest or a pandemic, and it is clear how different layers of vulnerability will interact and shape individuals' options and agency. Should the unrest be resolved or the pandemic be short-lived, a layer of these individuals' vulnerability will be removed, while the other layers may remain intact or may have morphed/mutated during the unrest or pandemic.

Earlier, we referred to another type of vulnerability, namely *socio-digital* vulnerability, which DiPaola and Calo (2024) define as '[s]ocio-digital vulnerability refers to the susceptibility of individuals and groups within mediated environments to decisional, social or constitutive interference' (p. 1). Pertaining to *decisional* vulnerability, the authors point to the reality that digital technologies have introduced vulnerabilities 'into human decision-making processes by exploiting limits to our cognitive abilities' (p. 4) in specifically interface design, manipulating users to increase revenue and in 'channelling attention or selectively presenting information on the basis of algorithms' (p. 5). With minors' lack of awareness and digital literacy regarding how these interfaces are designed, children's vulnerability is exploited to establish compulsive and addictive online engagement.

Social vulnerability refers to the anthropomorphic effects of chatbots, social robots and voice assistants and the emotional and social dependence created by these personalised, always-on and available technologies. For children in particular, research shows their increased vulnerability in sharing secrets and depending on these technologies. Constitutive vulnerability points to the impact of recommender systems and personalised services based on search histories and online behaviours – which impact on individuals' self-determination and choice. Ironically, most of the educational recommender systems are premised on the promise of self-regulated learning, while, in fact, individuals' behaviours are increasingly regulated by commercial and surveillance algorithms. As such, it seriously hampers children's freedom of choice and authentic self-regulation.

DISCUSSION

The purpose of this chapter was not to provide an extensive overview of first, the deployment of LA in pre-primary, primary and secondary (K–12) schools, but rather to introduce a snapshot of LA as an emerging phenomenon. What has become clear, however, is that it would seem as if the meagre research on LA in these contexts has not considered the complexities of the age of consent, the problematics of informed consent by parents or legal guardians or evidence that 'children' are anything but a homogenous group and that their vulnerabilities to a range of possible biases, discrimination and exploitation, to mention but a few, are either ignored or not explored.

As such, based on the literature review, as well as the brief discussion of two perspectives on children's vulnerability (legal and socio-digital), we conclude with a number of pointers that also act as provocations.

1. Even though different legal and geopolitical jurisdictions may define the age of consent differently, this chapter provided some indications that children's age is a very poor indicator of children's capacity to understand consent as fragile and complex, and second, as an indicator of their vulnerability in socio-digital contexts (DiPaola and Calo 2024; Lievens and Verdoodt 2018).
2. Vulnerability is not a label, but layered and comprises several intersecting inherent, situational and pathogenic variables and relationships. Algorithmic decision-making systems use classification or labelling systems that create assumed stable clusters of individuals who share a particular conglomeration of variables. Vulnerability, like children's identity, is dynamic, relational and constantly developing. The dangers of locking children into particular profiles, such as 'vulnerable' or 'at-risk', are not only heightened among children, but the impacts of these classification systems will have lifelong implications (DiPaola and Calo 2024; Luna 2009; Prinsloo and Slade 2016; Prinsloo, Khalil and Slade 2024a).
3. Evidence furthermore suggests that not only is the number of data brokers, analytical services, and educational applications and platform providers increasing, but the legal agreements between these and schools are often, if not mostly, outside of the scrutiny of parents and school governing bodies (Prinsloo, Khalil and Slade 2024b).
4. Children, no matter which side of the age of 13 or 18 they fall, deserve the right to develop their interests and learning trajectories without being held captive in 'filter bubbles' consisting of recommender systems and predictive algorithmic decision-making systems (DiPaola and Calo 2024).

5. Evidence suggests that many apps and learning services/platform providers are used outside of the formal governance policies and processes in schools. Schools should be held accountable for the introduction and use of any application that has not been signed off by parents and approved by the school management committee (Prinsloo, Khalil and Slade 2024b).
6. Interface design and manipulation of user behaviours are of particular concern, impacting on children's decisional vulnerability. The use of this digitally mediated learning and support also raises important concerns regarding children's social vulnerability. Self-regulated learning is the dominant learning theory in LA (Khalil, Prinsloo and Slade 2023), and ironically, children's decisional and social vulnerabilities culminate in a constitutive vulnerability where their ability to make authentic and personal choices is increasingly steered by algorithmic decision-making systems, impacting their autonomy, selfhood and future (Prinsloo, Khalil and Slade 2024a).
7. Finally, LA systems should only be operationalised for children younger than 13 with the utmost care, stringent, transparent, accountable processes, and oversight systems in place. If these are not in place, LA should not be deployed under any circumstances.

LIMITATIONS

This chapter provides *an initial* and anything but comprehensive exploration of LA in the contexts of schools through the use of the notion of socio-digital vulnerability as a heuristic.

CONCLUSION

This chapter has explored the promises and tensions of applying LA in school contexts. While LA offers valuable insights into student learning and teaching practices, its use in schools requires careful consideration. The chapter has pointed to the importance of aligning LA tools and approaches with educational values, involving educators meaningfully in the process, and ensuring that data use supports, not replaces, professional judgement.

Schools are complex environments where data must be interpreted in light of pedagogical intentions, local needs and ethical responsibilities. We argue that LA should not be treated as a neutral or purely technical solution, but as a set of tools and approaches embedded within educational systems and shaped by human choices and institutional priorities. We also argue for prioritising human-centred approaches that foreground human agency rather than relying primarily on technology-centred solutions.

We conclude this chapter by inviting educators, researchers and policy makers to engage more thoughtfully and carefully when working with LA in the context of K–12 education. When approached with care, collaboration and a focus on what truly matters in K–12 education, LA serves as a catalyst for reflection, dialogue and improvement, rather than a means of control or standardisation. The challenge lies not only in developing better tools but in fostering the capacity to use them wisely in the service of meaningful learning.

ACKNOWLEDGEMENTS

This chapter has been funded by the Trond Mohn Research Foundation, project 'EduTrust', no. TMS2023TMT03.

REFERENCES

Aguerrebere, C., H. He, M. Kwet, M.J. Laakso, C. Lang, C. Marconi, … and H. Zhang (2022), 'Global perspectives on learning analytics in K–12 education', in C. Lang, A. F. Wise, A. Merceron, D. Gašević and G. Siemens (eds), *Handbook of Learning Analytics*. The Society for Learning Analytics Research (2nd ed., pp. 223–31). doi:10.18608/hla22.022

Andrews, L. (2020), 'The fragility of consent', *Loyola Law Review*, **66**, 11–22. Retrieved from https://heinonline.org/hol-cgi-bin/get_pdf.cgi?handle=hein.journals/loyolr66&section=6

Bradbury, A. (2020), 'Datafied at four: The role of data in the 'schoolification' of early childhood education in England', in J. Jarke and A. Breiter (eds), *The Datafication of Education*. Abingdon, UK: Routledge (pp. 8–22).

Children's Internet Protection Act (CIPA) (2000). Retrieved from https://www.fcc.gov/consumers/guides/childrens-internet-protection-act

Children's Online Privacy Protection Act of 1998, 15 U.S.C. 6501–6505 (1998). Retrieved from https://www.ftc.gov/legal-library/browse/rules/childrens-online-privacy-protection-rule-coppa

Culbreth, D., R. Davis, C, Meral, F. Martin, W. Wang and S. Foxx (2025), 'K–12 monitoring applications in the pandemic: Safety, datafication, and the student experience', *TechTrends*, **69** (1), 189–200. doi:10.1007/s11528-024-01021-5

DiPaola, D. and R. Calo (2024), 'Socio-digital vulnerability'. Retrieved from https://papers.ssrn.com/sol3/papers.cfm?abstract_id=4686874

Feldstein, S. (2020), State surveillance and implications for children. UNICEF. Retrieved from https://www.unicef.org/innocenti/media/1136/file/UNICEF-Global-Insight-data-governance-surveillance-issue-brief-2020.pdf

Hope, A. (2015), 'Schoolchildren, governmentality and national e-safety policy discourse', *Discourse: Studies in the Cultural Politics of Education*, **36** (3), 343–53. doi:10.1080/01596306.2013.871237

Jarke, J. and A. Breiter (2019), 'The datafication of education', *Learning, Media and Technology*, **44** (1), 1–6. doi:10.1080/17439884.2019.1573833

Khalil, M., P. Prinsloo and S. Slade (2023), 'The use and application of learning theory in learning analytics: A scoping review', *Journal of Computing in Higher Education*, **35** (3), 573–94. doi:10.1007/s12528-022-09340-3

Khalil, M., S. Slade and P. Prinsloo (2024), 'Learning analytics in support of inclusiveness and disabled students: A systematic review', *Journal of Computing in Higher Education*, **36** (1), 202–19. doi:10.1007/s12528-023-09363-4

Lievens, E. and V. Verdoodt (2018), 'Looking for needles in a haystack: Key issues affecting children's rights in the General Data Protection Regulation', *Computer Law & Security Review*, **34** (2), 269–78. doi:10.1016/j.clsr.2017.09.007

Liu, Q. and M. Khalil (2023), 'Understanding privacy and data protection issues in learning analytics using a systematic review', *British Journal of Educational Technology*, **54** (6), 1715–47. doi:10.1111/bjet.13388

Livingstone, S. and K. Olafsson (2017), 'Children's commercial media literacy: New evidence relevant to UK policy decisions regarding the GDPR', LSE Media Policy Project Blog. Retrieved from https://blogs.lse.ac.uk/medialse/2017/01/26/childrens-commercial-media-literacy-new-evidence-relevant-to-uk-policy-decisions-regarding-the-gdpr/

Luna, F. (2009), 'Elucidating the concept of vulnerability: Layers not labels', *IJFAB: International Journal of Feminist Approaches to Bioethics*, **2** (1), 121–39. doi:10.3138/ijfab.2.1.12

Lupton, D. and B. Williamson (2017), 'The datafied child: The dataveillance of children and implications for their rights', *New Media & Society*, **19** (5), 780–94. doi:10.1177/1461444816686328

Mackenzie, C., W. Rogers and S. Dodds (eds) (2014), *Vulnerability: New Essays in Ethics and Feminist Philosophy*. Oxford, UK: Oxford University Press.

Paolucci, C., S. Vancini, R.T. Bex II, C. Cavanaugh, C. Salama and Z. de Araujo (2024), 'A review of learning analytics opportunities and challenges for K-12 education', *Heliyon*, **10** (4). https://doi.org/10.1016/j.heliyon.2024.e25767

Parks, M.R. (2014), 'Big data in communication research: Its contents and discontents', *Journal of Communication*, **64** (2), 355–60. doi:10.1111/jcom.12090

Prinsloo, P. and S. Slade (2016), 'Student vulnerability, agency and learning analytics: An exploration', *Journal of Learning Analytics*, **3** (1), 159–82. doi:10.18608/jla.2016.31.10

Prinsloo, P., M. Khalil and S. Slade (2024a), 'Vulnerable student digital well-being in AI-powered educational decision support systems (AI-EDSS) in higher education', *British Journal of Educational Technology*, **55** (5), 2075–92. doi:10.1111/bjet.13508

Prinsloo, P., M. Khalil and S. Slade (2024b), 'Learning analytics as data ecology: A tentative proposal', *Journal of Computing in Higher Education*, **36** (1), 154–82. doi:10.1007/s12528-023-09355-4

Prinsloo, P., S. Slade and M. Khalil (2023), 'Multimodal learning analytics: In-between student privacy and encroachment: A systematic review', *British Journal of Educational Technology*, **54** (6), 1566–86. doi:10.1111/bjet.13373

Rennie, E., K. Schmieder, J. Thomas, S.K. Howard, J. Ma and J. Yang (2019), 'Privacy and app use in Australian primary schools: Insights into school-based Internet governance', *Media International Australia*, **170** (1), 78–89. doi:10.1177/1329878X19828368

Siemens, G. (2013), 'Learning analytics: The emergence of a discipline', *American Behavioral Scientist*, **57** (10), 1380–1400. doi:10.1177/00027642134988

Slabu, E. (2017), 'Protection of personal data of children, according to the GDPR Provisions', *Public Administration & Regional Studies*, **10** (2), 66–74. Retrieved from https://www.ceeol.com/search/article-detail?id=1014053

Tzimas, D. and S. Demetriadis (2021), 'Ethical issues in learning analytics: A review of the field', *Educational Technology Research and Development*, **69**, 1101–33. doi:10.1007/s11423-021-09977-4

Tzimas, D. and S. Demetriadis (2025), 'K–12 teachers' acceptance and resistance perceptions of learning analytics adoption: A mixed-methods approach', *TechTrends*, **69** (2), 385–399. doi:10.1007/s11528-025-01045-5

UNICEF (2019), 'Faces, fingerprints and feet'. Retrieved from https://data.unicef.org/resources/biometrics/

3. Adaptive learning systems: leveraging generative artificial intelligence for optimal adaptivity

Sima Caspari-Sadeghi

INTRODUCTION

The concept of Personalized Learning (PL), also called *adaptive, customized, differentiated* or *individualized* learning, being more efficient (that is, reduced time to reach mastery) and effective (that is, better learning outcomes) than conventional mass education is not new. It has been practiced in various forms throughout human history, such as one-on-one tutoring, apprenticeship, mentoring or self-regulated learning (autodidactic). PL involves dynamically adjusting instruction—such as the sequence, difficulty, and pace—to the learner's individual knowledge, skills, preferences, needs and other characteristics (Shemshack and Spector 2020; US Department of Education 2017). However, it is impossible for a classroom teacher to simultaneously personalize instruction and cater to the needs, strengths and weaknesses of every individual student. Over the past decades, significant technological developments, coupled with the emergence of digital environments and big data, have revived the hope that PL can be offered on a large scale at low cost—which traditional education failed to deliver (Luan and Tsai 2021). In this chapter, the term Adaptive Learning Systems (ALS) (San Pedro and Baker 2021) is used to refer to educational technologies with varying degrees of adaptivity, which can provide PL in smart learning environments. Instances of these systems include Intelligent Tutoring Systems (ITS) (Koedinger and Corbett 2006), Adaptive Instructional Systems (AIS) (Sinatra et al. 2023), Adaptive Educational Hypermedia (AEH) (Brusilovsky 2001), neuro-fuzzy recommender systems (Sevarac, Devedzic and Jovanovic 2012), adaptive pedagogical games (Meluso et al. 2012), and others. ALS employs artificial intelligence (AI) and other advanced technologies, such as Educational Data Mining (EDM) and Learning Analytics (LA), to help users learn more effectively and efficiently (AIS Consortium 2021; Baker and Siemens 2014).

The historical evolution of these systems can be categorized into three distinct generations, each reflecting broader advancements in AI (Nkambou, Bourdeau and Psyché 2010). The first generation (1970–1990) laid the foundation of early ITS, that is, SCHOLAR, which incorporated limited AI elements into Computer-assisted Learning (CAL). The second generation (1990–2010) witnessed the integration of more advanced AI techniques into domain-specific ITS, resulting in the development of several rule-based expert systems that used statistical or classical Machine Learning (ML) models. The third generation (2010–present) has been significantly shaped by developments in ML, that is, deep learning and transfer learning. These advancements enabled ITS to provide more adaptive and personalized learning experiences, leading to the modern ALS (Xie, Hwang and Wong 2021). For instance, SquirrelAI utilizes a large adaptive model framework to provide personalized learning paths by linking learners' profiles, content knowledge graph, and a study-path planning recommendation system (Li et al. 2024).

Empirical studies, some involving hundreds of thousands of students, have been conducted to evaluate the effectiveness of such systems compared to teacher-led classrooms. Cognitive Tutor, Auto Tutor, ASSISTments, Crystal Island, CogBook, Smart Sparrow, Squirrel AI and ALEKS are among the well-known and successful examples of ALS in compulsory education (Caspari-Sadeghi 2022 2025).

This chapter aims to offer a detailed overview of ALS from a techno-pedagogical perspective by addressing the following questions:

1. What are the key components or modules of ALS?
2. How does adaptivity function within ALS?
3. What are the primary limitations of current ALS?
4. How can ALS benefit from advancements in GenAI?

The chapter is structured into four main sections. To begin, we provide an overview of the architecture of a robust ALS, detailing its modules and components. We will also discuss the need to transition from a rigid to a more flexible, interoperable design. Following this, we explore the operational aspects of adaptivity in ALS, focusing on what, how, and when a system adapts to learners. In the third section, we address the current limitations and challenges of existing ALS, including the lack of non-cognitive modeling and authoring tools. Lastly, we discuss how recent developments in Generative AI, such as Large Language Models (LLMs) and Generative Diffusion Models (GDMs), could potentially address some of these enduring challenges. Especially LLMs such as OpenAI's ChatGPT, which are trained on extensive text corpora and capable of producing human-like content in response to user prompts, have transformative potential for ALS.

ARCHITECTURE: COMPONENTS OF ALS

Although there are variations in the interfaces of different systems, such as in visualization, most ALS consists of three main modules or components in addition to the interface module, all of which are interdependent; that is, the output of one module serves as the input to update and optimize the others. Below, we provide an overview of these modules as well as the recent shifts in the architecture of ALS.

Domain Module

This component, also known as the expert or content model, represents all structured knowledge and content of a specific subject matter or target domain. The domain module is the result of domain modeling, a process that involves specifying subject-matter knowledge along with its relationships and structure, such as the particular order or prerequisite that specifies the trajectory toward mastery of content. Domain module can be extracted from three primary sources: textbooks (theoretical know-that), experts (practical know-how) and common misconceptions and errors associated with specific knowledge components. Domain modeling can be performed using various extraction techniques: manually by experts; semi-automatic through learning factor analysis; or fully automated using Natural Language Processing (NLP) techniques, such as Information Extraction. NLP, a subfield of AI that allows the processing, understanding, and generation of human language, is widely used for tasks such as sentence classification, topic modeling, and text annotation in educational technologies. As students interact with ALS, the initial domain module is continuously refined and updated (Rus et al. 2020).

Learner Module

The learner module, also called the student model or profile, contains all learners' characteristics, including knowledge, competencies, motivation, attitude, and more. Traditional learner modeling primarily focused on cognitive aspects, that is, inferring knowledge and competencies, whereas the current models aim to capture and represent non-cognitive aspects, such as emotion and engagement. Earlier ALS relied on Cognitive Diagnostic Models (CDM) to build profiles. CDM is a subset of multidimensional latent variable models that can diagnose students' proficiency level based on their performance on several skills and attributes in a specific domain (Williamson 2023). In recent years, the development of robust probabilistic models (for example, Bayesian Knowledge Tracing) and ML techniques (for example, Graph Neural Networks) has significantly increased the accuracy and efficiency of representing what a learner knows and can do (Pelánek 2017).

Instructor Module

This module, also known as the pedagogy model, refers to analytic and predictive algorithms that adapt instruction and content to the learners' characteristics and performance. It defines what, how, and when adaptation should be implemented. It utilizes both initial domain-learner models and real-time assessments of learners' performance to customize several aspects of learning experiences, including the content's sequence and complexity, visual interface (modes and formats of instruction), scaffolding and coaching, feedback, conversational agents and the types of tasks or practice activities necessary to reach mastery (Arroyo et al. 2014). Different approaches, such as cognitive models (for example, Adaptive Control of Thought by Anderson) and ML techniques (for example, gradient-boosted decision trees), are employed to provide personalized instruction (Sense et al. 2022).

From Standalone to Modularized ALS

In their recent paper, Colby, Tucker and Siggins (2024) criticized the rigid, inflexible, and non-interoperable four-component architecture of the existing ALS as a critical limitation. This architecture results in siloed research and domain-dependent systems, narrowing their usability in broader educational contexts. The authors call for a shift from standalone ALS to a services-based, modular ecosystem. In such a system, ALS will be a part of a reusable, interoperable, and scalable infrastructure. This approach facilitates the integration of emerging technologies via authentication services, that is, Google, and reduces the cost associated with replacing or upgrading individual components (p. 5).

Colby, Tucker and Siggins (2024) also indicated two approaches toward modular ALS, both of which are in the experimental or prototyping phase:

1. *Augmentation*: This approach involves enhancing existing ALS by improving the flexibility of modules. For example, Cognitive Tutor has recently added an authoring tool that enables educators to add students' variables. This makes student modeling more modularized and adaptive; therefore, enhancing the system's overall flexibility.
2. *Generalized Intelligent Framework for Tutoring (GIFT)*: This approach supports domain independence, allowing ALS to adapt to diverse contexts and learner profiles. For example, STATS (SoarTech Adaptive Training Services) incorporates the GIFT framework to make the components or modules more interconnected and adaptive. It uses LLM for content production, learner modeling or domain representation, which increases its applicability and effectiveness.

FUNCTIONING OF ALS: WHAT, HOW AND WHEN TO ADAPT

The central premise of ALS is that instruction is most effective when it adapts to the diverse learners' differences. Adaptivity is defined as meeting learners where they are. However, learners differ on numerous variables or factors, such as background knowledge, learning pace, and motivation. This section builds on the work of Shute and Zapata-Rivera (2012), Aleven and colleagues (2017), and Plass and Pawar (2020) to further explore the concept of adaptation in ALS by addressing the following questions:

1. To which learners' differences or variables should a system adapt (what)?
2. When is the optimal time for adaptation (when)?
3. What type of adaptivity is most effective in improving learning outcomes (how)?

What to Adapt

The choice of the variable to which the system adapts can be based on empirical evidence, theoretical foundations, and the designer's priority. The selected variable should be relevant to the intended learning objective and exhibit sufficient variability to justify adaptation. Learners can differ in the following aspects:

- cognitive variables (for example, prior knowledge, current proficiency, learning rate, learning styles, learning strategies);
- meta-cognitive variables (for example, self-regulated learning, cognitive load);
- affective variables (for example, emotion, self-efficacy attitude);
- motivational variables (for example, extrinsic vs. intrinsic, personal interest, task value, growth mindset);
- socio-cultural variables (for example, social context, values, social agency, relatedness); and
- demographic variables (for example, age, gender, socio-economic status).

Most ALS use cognitive variables, such as the heterogeneity of knowledge—including background knowledge, current proficiency, and learning rates—to adapt to learners' needs. This approach is partly driven by empirical evidence showing that incoming knowledge is the most significant predictor of academic achievement and performance in both traditional and technology-enhanced learning environments.

It should be noted that the discussion on which variable a system should adapt to is still an active area of research and discussion. For example, despite its intuitive appeal and extensive literature, adapting to learning styles, as measured by models like the Felder-Silverman Learning Style (LS) or Fleming's (2001) VARK (Visual, Auditory, Read/Write, Kinesthetic), has faced criticism due to several issues, that is, lack of a coherent theory, unclear explanatory structure, and scant empirical evidence supporting the notion that adapting to learning styles improves learning outcomes (Barbosa et al. 2024).

When to Adapt?

VanLehn (2006) suggests that ALS can perform adaptivity in two ways: (a) the outer loop, which involves automatically adjusting the sequence, difficulty or complexity of the next content, task or activity based on real-time assessments of the student's performance; and (b) the inner loop, where the system uses fine-grained, detailed activity data from learners' problem-solving to provide automatic scaffolding during the activity, such as hints, feedback or meta-cognitive advice.

Aleven et al. (2017) further propose that adaptivity can be performed at three different times or phases: the design loop, task loop and step loop. Design loop adaptivity involves data-driven decisions made by designers during the creation of the system, such as using empirical evidence from similar learners to sequence the content and activities within the ALS. By contrast, task loop and step loop adaptivity occur while the system is running and rely on real-time data from a particular learner. Task loop adaptivity involves selecting the next pedagogical task, activities, interventions or learning experiences, such as a worked example to tutor problem-solving or through demonstration or analogy. Step loop adaptivity is the most granular form, occurring during problem-solving itself. It requires monitoring step-by-step individual strategies, errors, and misconceptions to provide adaptive scaffolding as the learner performs the task. The finer the granularity of the adaptation level (for example, step loop), the more computationally expensive and complex the process becomes.

How to Adapt? Personalization Techniques

The approaches to adaptation in ALS depend on selected variables as well as the timing of adaptation. Over the last five decades, advancements in AI have significantly enhanced the accuracy and efficiency of adaptive algorithms. Below, we provide a brief overview of methods used to adapt to 'knowledge growth' in both the outer loop (task loop) and inner loop (step loop). Our choice of knowledge as the variable for adaptation is due to two reasons: (a) all ALS rely on the learners' knowledge as the key component of their adapting engines, and (b) knowledge tracing models represent the most robust area of research and development in adaptive systems (Caspari-Sadeghi 2023; San Pedro and Baker 2021).

Knowledge tracing refers to quantifying a learner's knowledge states or mastery levels by monitoring dynamic changes in their learning process, such as their past and sequential records on tasks and exercises in an online environment (Corbett and Anderson 1995). Measuring any underlying constructs or latent variables with statistical approaches comes with certain assumptions that pose challenges to current knowledge tracing methods. These include (a) the unidimensionality of underlying constructs, (b) independence of performance on each task, and (c) accounting for the decay of knowledge, that is, forgetting (Abdelrahman, Wang and Nunes 2023).

Existing knowledge tracing methods can be broadly categorized into three groups: (a) statistical models, (b) probabilistic models, and (c) ML models. These methods are extensively compared and evaluated in terms of model parameters, model inferences, and temporal analysis (Duan et al. 2024). Below, we present a brief overview of the most commonly used algorithms in ALS.

Statistical Models

A prominent knowledge tracing method is the Factor Analysis family, such as performance factor analysis and item response theory. These methods use a logistic regression function to estimate the probability of correctly answering an item related to a specific skill. For example, performance factor analyses (Pavlik, Cen and Koedinger 2009) employ the expectation maximization algorithm to fit three parameters for each skill: skill/item difficulty (β); the effect of prior successful attempts (γ); and the effect of prior failed attempts (ρ). However, it has been criticised for ignoring item-level differences and lacking a temporal dynamic—specifically, how learning evolves over time. The major issue with performance factor analysis is that it predicts performance on a particular item rather than making inferences about the underlying latent constructs, such as students' knowledge and ability (San Pedro and Baker 2021).

Probabilistic Models

Bayesian Knowledge Tracing (BKT) and its variants, that is, Dynamic Bayesian Networks, use probabilistic graphical models, like the Hidden Markov Model, to monitor and track changes in students' knowledge state as they practice a particular skill. It's based on the concept of Mastery learning, which requires (a) knowledge and skills should be organized hierarchically, and (b) students should master lower-order skills before moving to the higher ones (Corbett and Anderson 1995).

BKT uses a four-parameter model: (a) initial state: probability of mastery before the practice p(L0); (b) learned state: probability of learning p(T); (c) slipping: probability of making a mistake while having knowledge p(S); and (d) guessing: probability of getting the correct answer without knowledge p(G). It uses two algorithms, namely expectation maximization and grid search, to calculate parameters from the training data.

Although being the most popular model in most of ALS, BKT has two underlying assumptions that become problematic when used for tracing the progress of learning. First, it does not consider Forgetting (the probability of transiting from a learned state to an unlearned state is zero). Second, it assumes all items within a skill have the same level of difficulty (Abdelrahman, Wang and Nunes 2023).

Machine Learning Models

Machine Learning (ML) is a subfield of AI that enables algorithms to autonomously solve a task by learning from training data without being explicitly programmed. ML approaches, especially a large family of Deep Knowledge Tracing (DKT) models, have shown remarkable accuracy in predicting learners' performance in ALS. DKT leverages artificial neural networks and deep learning to automatically learn hierarchical, high-dimensional feature representations from data. This allows modeling and predicting learners' knowledge state over time by analyzing the sequence of their interaction in real time (Piech et al. 2015). This family includes various techniques such as sequence modeling (for example, Long-Short-term Memory, a variant of Recurrent Neural Networks), memory-augmented methods (for example, Dynamic Key-value Memory Network), graph-based models (for example, Graph Knowledge Tracing), interactive models (for example, Deep Reinforcement Learning) and transformer-based models (for example, Relation-aware Self-attentive Knowledge Tracing). For example, Graph Knowledge Tracing represents knowledge relations as a graph and treats knowledge tracing as a time-series node-level classification problem within a graph neural network (Duan et al. 2024); or Deep Reinforcement Learning, due to its ability to select optimal policies based on interaction, is particularly useful for inner-loop adaptivity, such as providing feedback, hints or coaching during problem-solving steps.

Despite the remarkable performance of deep learning models (Nakagawa, Iwasawa and Matsuo 2019; Sutton and Barto 2018), existing ALS typically use older models such as BKT. This could be partly due to the following issues: (a) the trade-off between prediction accuracy and computational efficiency of neural-based models; (b) the lack of interpretability of their structure; and (c) although DKT models are highly accurate in predicting performance on the next task or exercise, their effectiveness diminishes when predicting the transfer of learning outside of ALS, such as on standardized achievement tests or classroom post-tests. This suggests that contemporary advanced algorithms like DKT are better at estimating performance (for example, correctness on the next problem) than ability (latent construct). This is a significant weakness, as most stakeholders, such as teachers or policymakers, are more interested in knowing about a student's ability—what they know and can do—than their performance on the next exercise in ALS (Scruggs et al. 2023). Furthermore, (d) DKT is unable to model epistemic uncertainty in the learner's knowledge state (Christie, Cook and Rafferty 2024). Epistemic uncertainty, akin to measurement error, refers to uncertainty that can be decreased by collecting additional observations and data on learner performance. This concept is fundamental to many adaptive educational technologies, that is, Computer Adaptive Testing (CAT).

It should be noted that ALS should also be able to trace and predict decay. According to the Law of Disuse (Thorndike 1914), a learned habit can decay or fade (that is, the forgetting parameter) over time if it's not used continuously. This predictive information is essential for scheduling re-learning to enhance long-term retention. ALS can employ models such as the predictive performance equation (Gluck, Jastrzembski and Krusmark 2019) to estimate the optimal time for re-practicing a particular knowledge component for an individual learner.

CHALLENGES OF ALS

In this section, we examine some weaknesses and challenges affecting existing ALS in terms of their efficacy (including cost, time, and human resources) and effectiveness (in improving learning) (Sinatra et al. 2023). While automation and AI development may hold the key to solving many technological problems, ALS faces challenges—pedagogical or policy-related—which need long-term solutions. For example, it is crucial to create a culture of data-informed decision-making, enhance teachers' data literacy through appropriate professional development programs, and establish trust and acceptance of AI-related technologies among key stakeholders.

Lack of non-cognitive modeling: ALS focus predominantly on modeling the cognitive aspects of learning, such as knowledge growth. However, other important aspects of learning, including affective, motivational, meta-cognitive, and socio-cultural, are often overlooked. This could be partly due to the lack of evidence-based best practices. For example, given the temporal nature of feelings and emotions, if the system recognizes boredom or frustration at a particular moment, it is unclear what the best pedagogical intervention would be: providing hints, introducing a conversational agent, changing the exercise format, moving to the next topic or another approach?

Lack of team modeling: ALS are primarily designed to improve the performance of an individual learner. However, many modern jobs require teamwork, collaboration, interpersonal communication, and feedback—competencies that are quite difficult to capture, assess, model, and coach. Current ALS are not yet mature enough to collect and analyze such a significant amount of multimodal data (for example, eye tracking, log data, bio-sensors, speech, facial expression), nor do they afford the complicated mathematical modeling involved.

Lack of interactivity: While a few ALS, such as Auto Tutor (Nye, Graesser and Hu 2014) or Betty's Brain (Biswas, Segedy and Bunchongchit 2016), can establish conversation through virtual pedagogical agents, the majority of existing systems are text-based and lack interactive elements. Incorporating interactive environments and technologies, such as serious games, simulations, virtual reality and NLP techniques to enable meaningful conversations can enhance both interactivity and improve the engagement and motivation of the learners.

Neglecting ill-defined domains: The majority of ALS are developed for well-defined domains such as Mathematics (for example, ALEKS), Physics (for example, Andes) or Science (for example, Betty's Brain), where the knowledge components and their structural relationships are more straightforward. Domains like law, management, and medical diagnosis are often overlooked. Furthermore, ALS are traditionally designed for formal education settings rather than for job-related training or informal learning environments, such as museums.

Lack of sustainability: The development and maintenance of ALS are costly, complex and time-consuming endeavours that require collaboration among multiple experts, which negatively impacts their scalability. Additionally, the usability of ALS is currently restricted for several reasons: (a) limited accessibility, as they cannot run on smartphones due to their heavy computational load; (b) lack of an authoring tool; (c) low technology acceptance; and (d) lack of interoperability. The latter is particularly problematic because, in the absence of interface and data standards, none of the ALS components are reusable, and updating necessitates either complete replacement or redesign.

OPTIMIZING ADAPTIVITY: INTEGRATING GENAI WITH ALS

Generative AI (GenAI) refers to AI models that create novel content and authentic, human-like outputs, such as images, texts, videos, audios and codes. Although GenAI has its roots in ML, namely deep generative models like Generative Adversarial Networks (GAN), it goes beyond the ability of discriminative ML algorithms to analyze and interpret data automatically. In discriminative models like ML, the goal of data processing is to determine decision boundaries defined by the researcher, that is, classification, clustering or prediction. By contrast, generative models aim to produce new content based on the principles of generativity and variance. Therefore, the output of GenAI is probabilistic rather than deterministic; that is, for the exact same prompt, GenAI produces multiple equally valid outputs, whereas different input prompts can lead to the same output, reflecting the inherent variance principle in its design (Banh and Strobel 2023). By utilizing technologies like LLM or diffusion models, GenAI surpasses state-of-the-art ML algorithms in solving many complex, real-world tasks in NLP and computer vision (Cao et al. 2023; Li et al. 2024).

Several studies have already explored the use of GenAI in different areas of education, such as automated scoring (Xiao et al. 2024), pedagogical chatbots (Dan et al. 2023) and Physics education (Kieser et al. 2023). GenAI opens novel avenues as well as challenges to education. Harnessing its potential needs critical reflection and dialogue among different stakeholders about its appropriate use. For example, teachers and students can jointly examine content or answers generated by LLM for potential hallucinations, for instance, faulty or fabricated information. In this section, we will present examples of how GenAI can be leveraged to optimize and improve ALS by addressing some of the long-standing challenges these systems face.

Authoring Tools

As previously mentioned, the lack of authoring tools for content creation and customization is a critical impediment to the usability and adoption of ALS. GenAI can enhance the sustainability of ALS by empowering practitioners or subject-matter experts to develop adaptive content for individual modules or entire adaptive courses, without requiring programming or data science expertise, that is, the use of the product should not require in-depth technical knowledge. Generative LLMs are already being used to create adaptive curriculum, learning objectives, reading comprehension, quizzes and automated feedback (Dijkstra et al. 2022; Sridhar et al. 2023). According to multimedia learning theory (Mayer 1997), learning is inherently multimodal, and learners construct mental models from different modalities or representations, such as reading texts, listening to lectures, visualizing through flowcharts and diagrams, demonstrating through performance and communicating ideas verbally. Multimodal LLMs, such as PandasGPT or Google Gemini, can be used to enhance both content (for example, learning materials) and environments (for example, animation, simulation, games) by creating multimodal input. For example, instructors can use generative models, for instance, DALL-E and Midjourney, to create real-time, high-fidelity instructional illustrations. These resources support the learning of abstract or complex concepts by reducing cognitive load and improving the efficient organization of knowledge for learners at different proficiency levels (Bewersdorff et al. 2024). This might seem contradictory to what was mentioned earlier about the lack of conceptual and empirical evidence for 'learning styles'. However, it is likely to be safe to assume that offering content in different modalities provides learners with choices in when, where, and how they learn.

Enhanced Knowledge Tracing

Recent works have explored the use of generative LLMs for knowledge tracing tasks (Neshaei et al. 2024). NLP-enhanced models, such as BERT and GPT, outperformed both baseline models—traditional models (for example, BKT and PFA) and DL models (for example, RNN)—irrespective of training dataset, as measured by the area under the curve, the most common evaluation metric in tracing learners' knowledge. Additionally, NLP-enhanced models proved to mitigate another core issue of knowledge tracing, which has long posed a challenge for ALS and other adaptive technologies: the cold-start problem, where scant or no historical interaction data is available from learners' performance (Jung et al. 2024). However, such results should be treated with caution. More studies are needed to examine the effectiveness of NLP models beyond experiments and in real-life application scenarios.

Adaptive Coaching

With their abilities to understand natural language and generate contextually appropriate responses, Gen LLM can serve as embodied pedagogical agents such as chatbots, virtual tutors or learning peers. For example, EduChat (Dan et al. 2023) is a virtual assistant that improves learning experiences by offering emotional support, Socratic teaching, open questions answering, essay assessment, and some other pedagogical functions. Such intelligent assistants can address some of the previously mentioned limitations facing ALS, including:

1. Dialogue-based learner modeling: by engaging in rich conversations with learners, ALS can more accurately infer and represent learners' knowledge, plans and preferences compared to text-based models.
2. Affective modeling: traditional methods of capturing learners' emotions primarily rely on static data, for example, pre- and post-course questionnaires (text-based). Conversational agents can collect real-time, dynamic data about how learners feel during the learning process through verbal communication. This dynamic data is used to continuously update the learner's profile and adjust instruction based on a learner's emotional state.
3. Precise scaffolding: ALS has often been criticized for its overuse of hints and other support strategies (Sinatra et al. 2023). An enhanced understanding of students' questions and misunderstandings through natural interaction allows the system to provide tailored feedback and an optimal level of assistance.

CONCLUSION

ALS use real-time, detailed data about students' performance to infer their proficiency levels and provide automatic, personalized instruction, such as the next topic, task or feedback. In this chapter, we provided an in-depth exploration of ALS from a techno-pedagogical standpoint. We discussed adaptivity in terms of selecting the desirable difficulty and sequence

(Bjork and Bjork 2020) based on tracing knowledge growth. Additionally, we addressed two main challenges faced by state-of-the-art adaptive algorithms: (a) predicting performance on the next task vs. estimating knowledge (latent construct), and (b) predicting decay or forgetting in order to schedule optimal re-learning. We argued that, despite their superior predictive accuracy, DKT cannot model epistemic uncertainty. This limitation has led existing ALS to rely on more traditional models, such as BKT, for monitoring learner progress. Several limitations of the current ALS are discussed, including its adaptation to a single dimension of learner in a single manner (Baker 2016; Caspari-Sadeghi 2025).

We discussed how Multimodal GenAI can contribute to existing ALS by offering authoring tools, enhanced knowledge tracing, and adaptive coaching through NLP-based embodied conversational agents. Despite great excitement surrounding GenAI technologies such as LLM, also called foundation models, their transformative potential as well as their limitations are yet to be explored and validated; that is, due to their lack of common sense, the adaptivity becomes brittle with even slight changes in the context.

We conclude this chapter by proposing Self-improving Systems as a promising area for future progress in ALS. Such systems have the capacity to monitor, evaluate, and improve their own performance based on experience (Brusilovsky and Rus 2019). By using data-driven techniques, such as Reinforcement Learning, sequence mining or other approaches, the next generation of ALS can continuously assess the effectiveness of its chosen actions and use this information to optimize future adaptivity. Nevertheless, until ALS reach their full potential, keeping humans in the loop remains the most practical solution.

ACKNOWLEDGMENT

I would like to express my sincere thanks to my colleague, Professor Ingebørg Krange, as well as the anonymous reviewer for their thoughtful comments and suggestions, which greatly enhanced the quality of this chapter.

REFERENCES

Abdelrahman, G., Q. Wang and B. Nunes (2023), 'Knowledge tracing: A survey', *ACM Computing Surveys*, **55** (11), 1–37. https://doi.org/10.1145/3569576

AIS Consortium (2021), 'Adaptive Instructional Systems defined', in *The Charter of the Adaptive Instructional Systems (AIS) Consortium.*

Aleven, V., E.A. McLaughlin, R.A. Glenn and K.R. Koedinger (2017), 'Instruction based on adaptive learning technologies', in R.E. Mayer and P. Alexander (eds), *Handbook of Research on Learning and Instruction*, 2nd ed., New York: Routledge, pp. 522–60.

B.P. Woolf, W. Burelson, K. Muldner, D. Rai and M. Tai (2014), 'A multimedia adaptive tutoring system for mathematics that addresses cognition, metacognition and affect', *International Journal of Artificial Intelligence in Education*, **24** (4), 387–426. https://doi.org/10.1007/s40593-014-0023-y

Baker, R.S. (2016), 'Stupid tutoring systems, intelligent humans', *International Journal of Artificial Intelligence in Education*, **26** (2), 600–14. https://doi.org/10.1007/s40593-016-0105-0

Baker, R. and G. Siemens (2014), 'Educational data mining and learning analytics', in K. Sawyer (ed.), *Cambridge Handbook of the Learning Sciences*, 2nd ed., Cambridge, UK: Cambridge University Press, pp. 253–74.

Banh, L. and G. Strobel (2023), 'Generative artificial intelligence', *Electron Markets*, **33**, 63. https://doi.org/10.1007/s12525-023-00680-1

Barbosa, P.L.S., R.A.F. do Carmo, J.P.P. Gomes and W. Viana (2024), 'Adaptive learning in computer science education: A scoping review', *Education and Information Technologies*, **29** (8), 9139–88. https://doi.org/10.1007/s10639-023-12066-z

Bewersdorff, A., C. Hartmann, M. Hornberger, K. Sesler, M., Bannert, E. Kasneci, G. Kasneci, X. Zhai and C. Nerdel (2024), 'Taking the next step with generative artificial intelligence: The transformative role of multimodal large language models in science education'. Retrieved from arXiv:2401.00832.

Biswas, G., J.R. Segedy and K. Bunchongchit (2016), 'From design to implementation to practice – a learning by teaching system: Betty's Brain', *International Journal of Artificial Intelligence in Education*, **26** (1), 350–64. https://doi.org/10.1007/s40593-015-0057-9

Bjork, R.A. and E.L. Bjork (2020), 'Desirable difficulties in theory and practice', *Journal of Applied Research in Memory and Cognition*, **9** (4), 475–79. https://doi.org/10.1016/j.jarmac.2020.09.003

Brusilovsky, P. (2001), 'Adaptive hypermedia', *User Modeling and User-Adapted Interaction*, **11**, 87–110. https://doi.org/10.1023/A:1011143116306

Brusilovsky, P. and V. Rus (2019), 'Social navigation for self-improving intelligent educational systems', in A.M. Sinatra, A.C. Graesser, X. Hu, K. Brawner and V. Rus (eds), *Design Recommendations for Intelligent Tutoring Systems: Volume 7 – Self-Improving Systems,* Orlando: US Army Research Laboratory, pp. 131–45.

Cao, Y., S. Li, Y. Liu, Z. Yan, Y. Dai, P.S. Yu and L. Sun (2023), 'A comprehensive survey of AI-generated content (AIGC): A history of generative AI from GAN to ChatGPT'. Retrieved from arXiv:2303.04226.

Caspari-Sadeghi, S. (2022), 'Artificial intelligence in technology-enhanced assessment: A survey of machine learning', *Journal of Educational Technology Systems*, **51** (3), 372–86. https://doi.org/10.1177/00472395221138791

Caspari-Sadeghi, S. (2023), 'Assessment and evaluation in the age of big data: Learning analytics in higher education', *Cogent Education*, **10** (1), 1–11. https://doi.org/10.1080/2331186X.2022.2162697

Caspari-Sadeghi, S. (2025), *Technology-enhanced and Formative Assessment.* Habilitation Thesis, University of Passau, Germany.

Christie, T., C. Cook and A.N. Rafferty (2024), 'Uncertainty-preserving deep knowledge tracing with state-space models', *Proceedings of the 17th International Conference on Educational Data Mining*, pp. 909–14. https://doi.org/10.5281/zenodo.12729995

Colby, B., E. Tucker and T. Siggins (2024), 'Beyond standalone systems: Creating an ecosystem of adaptive training services', in R.A. Sottilare and J. Schwarz (eds), *Adaptive Instructional Systems (HCII 2024).* Lecture Notes in Computer Science, vol. 14727. Washington, D.C.: Springer, pp. 3–14. https://doi.org/10.1007/978-3-031-60609-0_1

Corbett, A.T. and J.R. Anderson (1995), 'Knowledge tracing: Modeling the acquisition of procedural knowledge', *User Modeling and User-Adapted Interaction*, **4** (4), 253–78. https://doi.org/10.1007/BF01099821

Dan, Y., Z. Lei, Y. Gu, Y. Li, J. Yin, J. Lin, L. Ye, Z. Tie, Y. Zhou, Y. Wang, A. Zhou, Z. Zhou, Q. Chen, J. Zhou, L. He and X. Qiu (2023), 'EduChat: A large-scale language model-based chatbot system for intelligent education'. https://arxiv.org/abs/2308.02773

Dijkstra, R., Z. Genç, S. Kayal and J. Kamps (2022), 'Reading comprehension quiz generation using generative pre-trained transformers', in *Proceedings of the Fourth International Workshop on Intelligent Textbooks,*Durham: iTextbooks, pp. 4–17. https://hdl.handle.net/11245.1/a1109043-92d4-4c63-be33-6e238780d3b7

Duan, Z., X. Dong, H. Gu, X. Wu, Z. Li and D. Zhou (2024), 'Towards more accurate and interpretable model: Fusing multiple knowledge relations into deep knowledge tracing', *Expert Systems with Applications*, **243**, 122573. https://doi.org/10.1016/j.eswa.2023.122573

Fleming, N.D. (2001), *Teaching and Learning Styles: VARK Strategies.* Christchurch: Neil Fleming.

Gluck, K.A., T.S. Jastrzembsk and M.A. Krusmark (2019), 'Prospective comments on performance prediction for aviation psychology', in M.A. Vidulich and P.S. Tsang (eds), *Improving Aviation Performance through Applying Engineering Psychology,* London: CRC Press, pp. 79–98.

Jung, H., J. Yoo, Y. Yoon and Y. Jang (2024), 'CLST: Cold-start mitigation in knowledge tracing by aligning a generative language model as a students' knowledge tracer'. Retrieved from arXiv:2406.10296.

Kieser, F., P. Wulff, J. Kuhn and S. Küchemann (2023), 'Educational data augmentation in physics education research using ChatGPT', *Physical Review Physics Education Research*, **19** (2), 020150. https://doi.org/10.1103/PhysRevPhysEducRes.19.020150

Koedinger, K.R. and A. Corbett (2006). Cognitive Tutors: Technology Bringing Learning Sciences to the Classroom. In R. K. Sawyer (Ed.), The Cambridge handbook of: The learning sciences (pp. 61–77). Cambridge University Press.

Li, H., T. Xu, C. Zhang, E. Chen, J. Liang, X. Fan, H. Li, J. Tang and Q. Wen (2024), 'Bringing generative AI to adaptive learning in education'. Retrieved from arXiv:2402.14601.

Luan, H. and C.C. Tsai (2021), 'A review of using machine learning approaches for precision education', *Educational Technology & Society*, **24** (1), 250–66. https://www.jstor.org/stable/26977871

Mayer, R.E. (1997), 'Multimedia learning: Are we asking the right questions?', *Educational Psychologist*, **32** (1), 1–19. https://doi.org/10.1207/s15326985ep3201_1

Meluso, A., M. Zheng, H.A. Spires and J. Lester (2012), 'Enhancing 5th graders' science content knowledge and self-efficacy through game-based learning', *Computers and Education*, **59** (2), 497–504. https://doi.org/10.1016/j.compedu.2011.12.019

Nakagawa, H., Y. Iwasawa and Y. Matsuo (2019), 'Graph-based knowledge tracing: Modeling student proficiency using graph neural network', *2019 IEEE/WIC/ACM International Conference on Web Intelligence (WI),* pp. 56–163, Thessaloniki, Greece.

Neshaei, S.P., R.L. Davis, A. Hazimeh, B. Lazarevski, P. Dillenbour and T. Kaser (2024), 'Towards modeling learner performance with large language models'. Retrieved from arXiv:2403.14661.

Nkambou, R., J. Bourdeau and V. Psyché (2010), 'Building intelligent tutoring systems: An overview', in R. Nkambou, J. Bourdeau and R. Mizoguchi (eds), *Advances in Intelligent Tutoring Systems* (Studies in Computational Intelligence, vol. 308), Berlin: Springer, pp. 361–75.

Nye, B.D., A.C. Graesser and X. Hu (2014), 'AutoTutor and family: A review of 17 years of natural language tutoring', *International Journal of Artificial Intelligence in Educati*on, **24** (4), 427–469. https://doi.org/10.1007/s40593-014-0029-5

Pavlik Jr, P.I., H. Cen and K.R. Koedinger (2009), 'Performance factors analysis – A new alternative to knowledge tracing', *Artificial Intelligence in Education*, **200** (1), 531–38. https://doi.org/10.3233/978-1-60750-028-5-531

Pelánek, R. (2017), 'Bayesian knowledge tracing, logistic models, and beyond: An overview of learner modeling techniques', *User Modeling and User-Adapted Interaction*, **27** (3), 313–50. https://doi.org/10.1007/s11257-017-9193-2

Piech, C., J. Bassen, J. Huang, S. Ganguli M. Sahami, L.J. Guibas and J. Sohl-Dickstein (2015), 'Deep knowledge tracing', in C. Cortes, N. Lawrence, D. Lee, M. Sugiyama and R. Garnett (eds), *Advances in Neural Information Processing Systems* 28 *(NIPS 2015)*, Montreal, Canada, pp. 505–13.

Plass, J.L. and S. Pawar, (2020), 'Toward a taxonomy of adaptivity for learning', *Journal of Research on Technology in Education*, **52** (3), 275–300. https://doi.org/10.1080/15391523.2020.1719943

Rus, V., S.E. Fancsali, D. Bowman, P. Pavlik Jr, S. Ritter, D. Venugopal, D. Morrison and The LDI Team (2020), 'The Learner Data Institute: Mission, framework, & activities', in V. Rus and S.E. Fancsali (eds), *Proceedings of The First Workshop of the Learner Data Institute – Big Data, Research Challenges, & Science Convergence in Educational Data Science*, The 13th International Conference on Educational Data Mining (EDM 2020), July 10–13, Ifrane, Morocco.

San Pedro, M.O.Z. and R.S. Baker (2021), 'Knowledge inference models used in adaptive learning', in A.A. von Davier, R.J. Mislevy and J. Hao (eds), *Computational Psychometrics: New Methodologies for a New Generation of Digital Learning and Assessment*, Switzerland: Springer, pp. 61–77.

Scruggs, R., R.S. Baker, P.I. Pavlik, B.M. McLaren and Z. Liu (2023), How well do contemporary knowledge tracing algorithms predict the knowledge carried out of a digital learning game? *Educational Technology Research and Development*, **71** (3), 901–18. https://doi.org/10.1007/s11423-023-10218-z

Sense, F., R. Wood, M.G. Collins, J. Fiechter, A. Wood, M. Krusmark, T. Jastrzembski and C.W. Myers (2022), 'Cognition-enhanced machine learning for better predictions with limited data', *Topics in Cognitive Science,* **14** (4), pp. 739–55. doi:10.1111/tops.12574

Sevarac, Z., V. Devedzic and J. Jovanovic. (2012), 'Adaptive neuro-fuzzy pedagogical recommender', *Expert Systems with Applications*, **39** (10), 9797–806. https://doi.org/10.1016/j.eswa.2012.02.174

Shemshack, A. and J.M. Spector (2020), 'A systematic literature review of personalized learning terms', *Smart Learning Environments*, **7** (1), 33. https://doi.org/10.1186/s40561-020-00140-9

Shute, V.J. and D. Zapata-Rivera (2012), 'Adaptive educational systems', in P.J. Durlach and A.M. Lesgold (eds), *Adaptive Technologies for Training and Education*, Cambridge, UK: Cambridge University Press, pp. 7–27.

Sinatra, A.M., A.C. Graesser,, X. Hu, G. Goodwin and V. Rus (eds) (2023), *Design Recommendations for Intelligent Tutoring Systems: Volume 10 – Strengths, Weaknesses, Opportunities and Threats (SWOT) Analysis of Intelligent Tutoring Systems.* US Army Combat Capabilities Development Command – Department of Defense (DoD).

Sridhar, P., A. Doyle, A. Agarwal, C. Bogart, J. Savelka and M. Sakr (2023), 'Harnessing LLMs in curricular design: Using GPT-4 to support authoring of learning objectives'. Retrieved from arXiv:2306.17459.

Sutton, R.S. and A.G. Barto (2018), *Reinforcement Learning: An Introduction* (2nd ed.), Cambridge, MA: MIT Press.

Thorndike, E.L. (1914), *The Psychology of Learning*. New York: Teachers College.

US Department of Education, Office of Educational Technology (2017), *Reimagining the Role of Technology in Education: 2017 National Education Technology Plan Update.* https://files.eric.ed.gov/fulltext/ED577592.pdf

VanLehn, K. (2006). 'The behavior of tutoring systems', *International Journal of Artificial Intelligence in Education,* **16** (3), 227–65.,

Williamson, J. (2023). *Cognitive Diagnostic models and how they can be useful.* Cambridge, UK: Cambridge University Press & Assessment. https://doi.org/10.17863/CAM.110853

Xu, K. Zhang, Y. Wang and Q. Fu (2024), 'From automation to augmentation: Large language models elevating essay scoring landscape'. Retrieved from https://doi.org/10.48550/arXiv.2401.06431

Xie, H., G.J. Hwang and T.L. Wong (2021), 'Editorial note: From conventional AI to modern AI in education: Re-examining AI and analytic techniques for teaching and learning', *Educational Technology & Society*, **24** (3), 85–8. https://www.jstor.org/stable/27032857

4. Designing multimodal collaboration analytics: challenges and opportunities

Daniel Spikol, Morten Misfeldt, Zaibei Li, and Viktor Holm-Janas

INTRODUCTION

Over the last decade, research in Multimodal Learning Analytics (MMLA) has emerged as a distinct field within Learning Analytics (LA). MMLA combines many disciplines to investigate and support learning processes using diverse sensors, data streams and systems for collection and analysis (Ochoa and Worsley 2016; Yan et al. 2025). However, practical challenges, such as providing easier-to-use systems deployed in diverse and complex learning situations to capture learning in authentic situations (Chejara, Andrade et al. 2024a), the infrastructure and costs of the equipment, the performance of the system in real-world settings that include diverse lighting, high levels of audio, along with reliability and generalisability, underscore the need for further research in how to develop systems and technologies for this area (Chejara et al. 2023).

Now, the rapid development of powerful and accessible AI frameworks (for example, OpenAI, Azure, Meta, Whisper, Llama) allows for the development of new tools that, in real time, can transcribe speech to text and describe and analyse physical interaction between people through interpreting video (Schneider et al. 2026; Yan et al. 2024). These new tools offer innovative methods for capturing and analysing multimodal data across physical and digital learning environments, featuring new forms of interaction and feedback for learners and teachers (Cukurova et al. 2020; Snyder et al. 2024). Designing, developing and deploying new MMLA systems that enable emerging technologies across various learning contexts has been an elusive goal for researchers. Currently, the need for available systems and the generalisability of how these platforms and software perform in diverse and authentic learning environments have impeded the adoption of these tools (Chejara, Andrade et al. 2024a). Developing a system that incorporates both hardware and software, considering the context and complexity of education, as well as the vulnerability of children, learners and teachers, requires distinct approaches.

This chapter reports on our ongoing research, design and development of an MMLA system investigating group work. Our focus is on collaborative learning, driven by the educational benefits of collaboration and the need to support group work. The system aims to provide insights and, in the future, real-time feedback into group dynamics and individual contributions. However, the chapter presents our current progress on the platform from a systems perspective, capturing the relevant interactions of learners and the current accuracy.

Research Aims

A primary challenge for MMLA is designing and developing a general platform that supports collaboration across different contexts (Chejara et al. 2024b). Additionally, this platform needs to be open, adaptable, flexible, usable and relatively affordable to allow diverse research and practitioner use. More importantly, the MMLA system needs to support how people (teachers, students and researchers) understand the learning process while being transparent in its analysis. The aim is not to replace human judgement but to support how we understand learning. Therefore, creating this platform requires more than tools (sensors, data pipelines and inference); it needs to be grounded in collaborative learning theories that leverage human interaction modalities, such as speech, movement, proximity and behavioural interactions. These tools and components must function within a configurable platform in real-world learning situations. The chapter raises the following research aim: How do we design an MMLA system theoretically grounded in people and learning while leveraging technology?

Chapter Organisation

The chapter is organised as follows: the next section presents a brief background on collaboration and MMLA systems, providing research opportunities and the foundation for the design requirements for the tool and the platform. In the third section, we present the system and, following that, an evaluation. The final section presents a discussion and considers the next steps for this work.

BACKGROUND

MMLA

Multimodal Learning Analytics (MMLA) began to be defined around 2013 in response to the need to collect multiple streams of data from learners' behaviours in the field of multimodal interaction, which specialises in collecting diverse data streams from sensors of human interactions (Blikstein 2013). Through the collection and analysis of multiple streams of data, including computer logs, video and computer vision, audio, proximity, eye tracking and biosensors (such as skin conductivity, heartbeat and EEG), researchers can gain insights across multiple dimensions of interaction and social interaction (Blikstein and Worsley 2016). Challenges remain in the field due to the diverse types of data, including high dimensionality, varying resolutions, missing and noisy data and the need for data fusion, all of which are compounded by the choice of models and techniques (Chejara et al. 2024b; Di Mitri et al. 2018; Lahat et al. 2015). Over the last decade-plus, researchers have explored how to build MMLA systems that capture multiple data streams in learning contexts ranging from group work with mathematics (Oviatt and Cohen 2013) to nursing education (Yan et al. 2025).

The rapid advancement of new artificial intelligence (AI) techniques, including generative AI that combines large language models (LLMs) with large multimodal models (LMMs), provides researchers with new tools and challenges to analyse and capture (Whitehead et al. 2025; Yan et al. 2024). Even with these new tools, we face an observability gap between the somatic and cognitive/emotional evidence that MMLA can capture and the internal drive that initiates, directs and sustains students' learning behaviours (Di Mitri et al. 2018).

Additional research with MMLA explores alternative methods for utilising the insights generated by these systems. Holstein and colleagues' (2018) paper presents a system that utilises augmented reality (AR) in conjunction with an intelligent tutoring system (ITS) to enable teachers to visualise the analytics of their students' learning and metacognition. The teacher can observe the student and intervene at more optimal moments through the AR headset's simple graphics, which display the student's progress. Cohn and colleagues (2025) introduce a hybrid AI approach that integrates the needs of teachers with researchers and AI-enabled MMLA to provide actionable insights, enabling teachers to make informed interventions based on MMLA data through an AI-generated multimodal visual timeline. Combining human and AI MMLA tools creates new avenues for using interaction analysis to gain insights from multiple data streams beyond traditional video analysis, allowing new ways to visualise (Echeverria et al. 2025; Fonteles et al. 2024). Researchers are developing methods to enhance the ecological validity and impact of MMLA (Schneider et al. 2024) by conducting research in authentic settings. Still, diverse challenges from specialised systems, data processing, AI, ethics and privacy provide opportunities and barriers (Alwahaby and Cukurova 2024).

Collaboration, Persistence and Optimal Learning Moments in Education

To investigate the collaboration using MMLA, we need a theoretical formulation of the central phenomenon. Our literature review reveals that research on MMLA to explore collaboration often lacks a foundation in learning theory (Nøhr et al. 2024). This is rare despite an extensive theoretical literature focusing on conceptualising the nature of collaboration and its cognitive, social and emotional dimensions. Technological development and application of tools to capture collaborative interactions often occur without a strong theoretical foundation. This divide suggests a need for greater integration between theory and technological design. Doing so could enable more meaningful analyses of collaborative processes with effective learning support.

In our project, we draw on a combination of psychological approaches that span a continuum, from viewing motivation (Ryan and Deci 2000) as a relatively situated phenomenon to understanding persistence and perseverance as more stable individual traits (Eskreis-Winkler et al. 2014). While these constructs offer valuable insights into student engagement and learning, we aim to reframe them within a more situated and social perspective. Rather than treating motivation and perseverance solely as internal dispositions, we are interested in how these qualities emerge through interaction, context and collaborative dynamics. Our understanding of collaboration builds on Gerry Stahl's construct of group cognition with three dimensions: (1) temporal sequence; (2) shared problem space; and (3) positioning and interaction space (Stahl 2010). This theory has the potential to guide methodological approaches, allowing us to use temporal segmentation and spatial distinctions to map key aspects of group work. Hence, one way of examining our ambitions is to apply and augment Stahl's framework to include shared reflective persistence (Misfeldt et al. 2024) in student group work within science education.

Optimal Learning Moments

One approach that focuses on the internal drive of students is to study when students reach optimal learning moments (Schneider et al. 2016; Shernoff et al. 2014). To gain insights into what 'motivates' students, the Experience Sampling Method (ESM) has been used (Csikszentmihalyi and Larson 2014) and other types of surveys. Researchers argue that MMLA needs to shift from lab-like settings and research interventions to supporting real-world learning while providing meaningful and actionable insights (Schneider et al. 2024). The challenge for technologies is to concentrate more on diverse learning theories, which the field of learning analytics has struggled with, particularly MMLA, which has predominantly centred on technology (Wise and Shaffer 2015) over the last decade. In this chapter, we can utilise optimal learning moments, starting from engagement, which Schneider and colleagues identify as three critical properties: interest, skill and challenge. They describe engagement as a state of involvement in a learning task, characterised by above-average levels of individual interest, skill and challenge, measured relative to the sample mean. This work emphasises emotional enhancers including enjoyment, success, happiness, confidence and activity (Fredricks et al. 2016; Schneider et al. 2016).

Gaps

There is a gap that warrants further investigation through analyses of MMLA for research purposes and to provide feedback to students, teachers and other stakeholders. This can be achieved by looking beyond dashboards and utilising tools like narrative reports based on the systems and surveys. Combining adaptive surveys that utilise concepts like experience-based sampling to gain deeper insights into non-behavioural aspects that drive or hinder learning has the potential to bring real-world value from MMLA.

METHODOLOGICAL APPROACH

Context

The educational activities under investigation occur outside an urban area at a Science Activity Centre. The centre provides free transportation for classes for middle and high school students, making it an accessible and attractive destination for teachers. Teachers consistently highlight three main reasons for booking visits: the availability of buses, access to well-equipped laboratories and specialised technologies and cost-free participation.

When asked about the activities' aims, facilitators at the centre emphasised two key objectives: first, to provide pupils with an enjoyable and engaging science experience, and, second, to ensure that the activities align with specific curriculum goals, thereby offering tangible value for teachers and their ongoing instruction. The centre delivers a range of activity programmes tailored to different school years. This study focuses on an activity for 8th-grade students, structured around four main components: (1) a conceptual introduction covering topics such as conductivity and microorganisms; (2) programming an automated water pump; (3) conducting bacterial growth experiments; and (4) microscope work focused on identifying microorganisms. The latter three components are hands-on, collaborative activities conducted

Source: Authors.

Figure 4.1 *Group of students working with technology as part of the science activity*

in a lab environment, utilising instruments and technologies unfamiliar to most students (see Figure 4.1).

The time spent at the centre varies depending on logistical factors, such as travel distance, traffic and scheduling constraints related to after-school commitments. Within the lab, students are organised into teacher-assigned groups based on the availability of eight lab stations. While the centre's facilitators lead the activities, classroom teachers remain present throughout the visit, supporting and observing their students' engagement. The project creates knowledge about how groups of students learn in situations characterised by ambiguity, difficulty and doubt. The central idea is that engaging together in uncertain, challenging and unknown areas is essential to scientific work and education.

Design Approach

The development of the system is guided by a broad design science approach that uses pragmatic approaches to sketching with technology and agile development (Buxton 2010; Hevner et al. 2003; Vaishnavi and Kuechler 2015). Generally, design science involves identifying

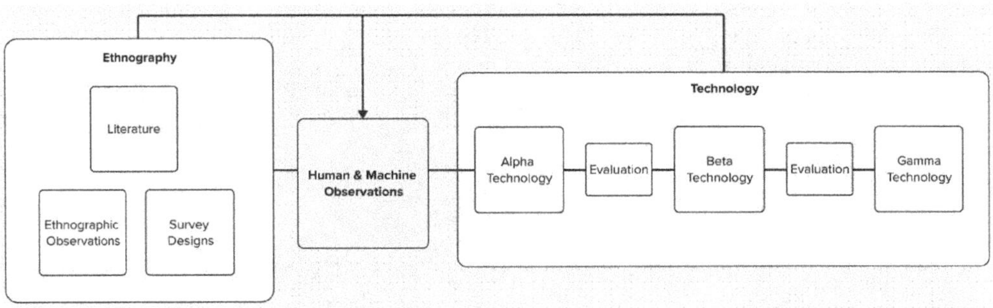

Source: Authors.

Figure 4.2 *A linear illustration of how the project combines human field work (ethnography) with technology development by keeping in focus human and machine observations*

the different requirements for the technology (Gregor et al. 2020), following the iteration of cycles: (1) Awareness of the problem; (2) Suggestions; (3) Development; and (4) Initial reflections on the different outputs and the interplay between approaches. We use the fourth step of this process to provide an initial evaluation of the system and the data collected. However, learning is a complex endeavour, and learning analytics has leaned on the technological deterministic approach. We wanted to ensure that our data and analysis are grounded in learning theories (Wise and Shaffer 2015). Therefore, at the centre of the approach is the desire to create a system that leverages the distinct affordances of human and machine observations, resulting in a hybrid approach that fosters greater transparency and enables the creation of stronger ground truths for evaluating how the system will assess student work (Holm-Janas et al. 2024). This human-machine hybrid approach enables the closer integration of observation data collected by trained observers and system data, providing a rough 'ground truth' through a mixed approach that offers new insights for MMLA (Martinez-Maldonado et al. 2024).

Figure 4.2 illustrates the design process for the project, which began with a literature review and was followed by ethnographic studies at the science centre, investigating: (1) how students engaged in the specific activity with a focus on group work and how they used the different tools and instruments and (2) to create a conceptual framework for creating a post-activity survey that explores cultural context, education settings and the group dynamics from an individual level connected to how the student interacted (from the MMLA system) (Nøhr et al. 2024). At the same time, an emerging framework is being developed to create a human-machine hybrid approach that will help guide the technological development of the MMLA system (Holm-Janas et al. 2024).

MMLA SYSTEM

The following section outlines the latest version of the MMLA system and its new directions. For earlier versions (alpha and beta), see the following (Li et al.2024, 2025; Spikol et al. 2024).

Current System

The MMLA system is a modular and extensible system designed to advance MMLA by integrating diverse data sources to enhance insight generation in educational settings. The system consists of two core components: the MMLA System Toolkit, which enables developers to build customisable analytics pipelines using reusable modules (including different types of sensors, analytics and AI services); and the MMLA System Platform, a full-stack solution for real-time multimodal data collection, processing and visualisation. Through a shared dashboard, the platform supports individual- and group-level analytics, providing real-time, actionable insights to teachers and learners, as well as for post-hoc reflection via a dashboard (Li et al. 2024).

The architecture follows a layered Internet of Things (IoT) and client-server model, addressing key design principles such as privacy, flexibility and scalability. It separates sensing, processing, analytics and presentation into distinct layers, allowing efficient data handling from wearable and environmental sensors. Sensor data flows through base stations and processing servers, which are synchronised and transformed into structured features – the key identifiable human activities (speech, movement, physical interaction signals etc.). These features are rendered in real time on the web-based dashboard, supporting diverse learning environments, from mobile classrooms to distributed remote setups. Privacy is maintained through local deployments and customisable data retention policies, ensuring secure and context-sensitive analytics (Spikol et al. 2024).

The platform follows a three-stage design: input, processing and output. In the input stage, raw data from sensors and wearable badges is streamed to base stations or a central server and converted into structured formats for easier handling. During the processing stage, each stream is handled by its assigned base station, which performs basic processing, while more complex tasks are sent to the server for further processing. Data from related bases is then synced and stored in a time-series database, where key features are extracted and analysed. In the output stage, these features are displayed on a live dashboard and combined into indicators to facilitate understanding of group interactions. The platform also produces post-session visuals, logs and reports for real-time and later review (see Figure 4.3).

AI that uses computer vision (CV) and natural language processing (NLP) is central to the system's analytical capabilities. We utilise computer vision to recognise badges with unique tertiary markers for identification and position tracking by transforming detections from four ceiling-mounted cameras into a unified coordinate system. This is to prevent the use of facial recognition for this vulnerable population. Additionally, at selected intervals (5, 10 or 30 seconds), a frame is transmitted from the primary camera to a video-capable large language model (LLM) that describes the interaction between the students and their activities. The NLP services transcribe speech in real time, extract keywords and identify conversational patterns such as turn-taking and speaker dominance. These outputs are integrated with data from other modalities, such as body movement, audio signals and visual tracking, to develop a rich, contextual understanding of group interaction and collaboration. A basic dashboard presents these insights through interactive visualisations, including real-time speaker timelines, social interaction graphs, movement heatmaps and transcribed dialogues (Li et al. 2025). The project focuses on creating a dashboard for research purposes, rather than for students or teachers.

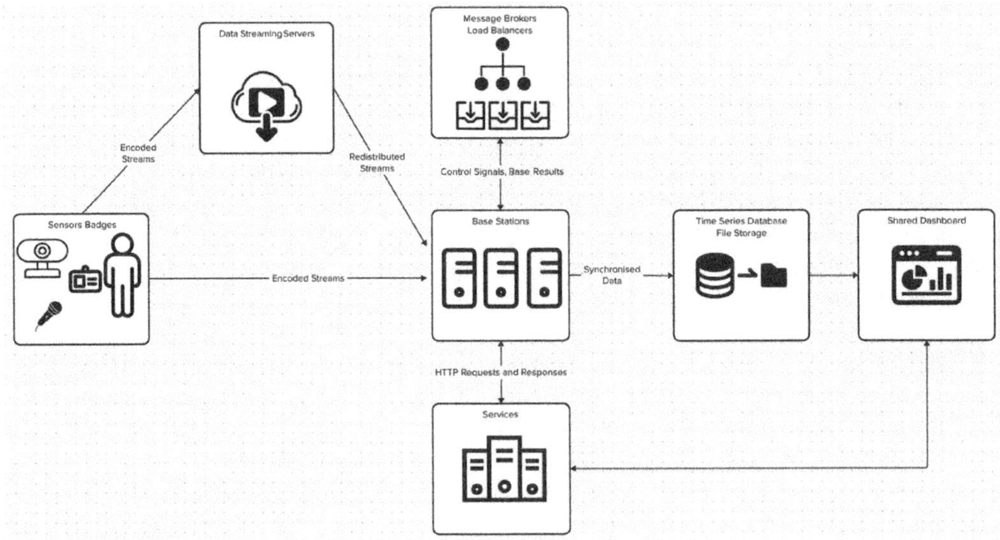

Source: Authors.

Figure 4.3 *The basic MMLA system showing the multiple data streams, services, storage, and processing*

Inferring Learning Constructs

The system is developing a contextualised analytical framework that leverages large language models (LLMs) to generalise across diverse constructs, settings and tasks. The framework maps multimodal behavioural data – such as speech, positions, orientations and actions – onto a structured hierarchy of features, indicators and constructs. This mapping is achieved through unsupervised or self-supervised methods, including rule-based models and few-shot learning with LLMs. Features can be extracted at varying granularities (for example, 1s, 3s, 30s), enabling flexible temporal alignment with behavioural indicators. Each indicator can be modelled using a tailored LLM prompt or classifier to score or classify behavioural instances based on structured and unstructured inputs.

At a higher level, the framework aggregates patterns of indicators into constructs using pattern matching. For example, discrete representations (for example, [0, 1, 2, 0]) may encode distinct configurations of mono-modal indicators that correspond to sub-constructs of interest. This bottom-up approach enables the inference of higher-order capabilities from low-level behavioural traces, supporting robust generalisation across contexts with minimal supervision. By grounding interpretation in pre-defined indicator definitions, the framework ensures interpretability while benefiting from the flexibility and scalability of LLM-based analysis.

For instance, if we have a learning construct we are interested in that looks at the following: (1) Constructing shared knowledge (expresses one's ideas and attempts to understand others' ideas), (2) Negotiation and coordination (achieves an agreed solution plan ready to execute) and (3) Maintaining team function (sustains the team dynamics); Figure 4.4 illustrates how we

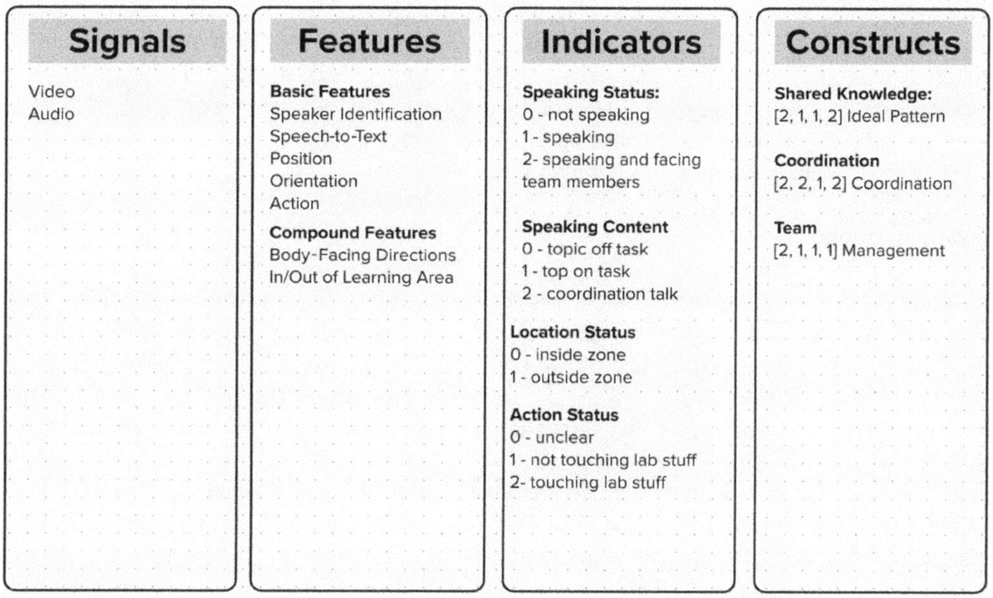

Source: Authors.

Figure 4.4 *The signal, features, and indicators are observable, while the CPS facets are represented as multimodal composite vectors mapped to different codes*

can extract the video and audio signals to determine the following basic features of speaker identification: speech text, position, orientation and actions. Additionally, consider the compound features of where the student faces and whether they are around the lab table. We then create indicators for speaking status, including whether the speaker is speaking or not, speaking and facing team members, the content of the speech, and whether the speech is on target for work or off-topic, as determined by the speech-to-text. We also create an action status indicator to indicate whether the individual is working with the lab materials, which is either true or false. By aggregating the codes, we can create vector representations of the constructs around participation and communication.

The system's signal, feature and indicator levels represent observable data. At the same time, the collaborative problem-solving (CPS) facets – such as knowledge construction, negotiation and team maintenance – are treated as multimodal composite vectors inferred from those observations. One example of an observable signal is location status, encoded as 0 or 1, where 1 indicates proximity to collaborators. For constructing shared knowledge (expressing one's ideas and attempting to understand others'), ideal behavioural patterns include speaking while facing teammates and discussing relevant content, for example, (2, 1, 1, 2). Variants such as speaking without facing others (1, 1, 1, 2) or omitting action data (–1 or 0) still reflect the process of knowledge construction. For negotiation and coordination (achieving a shared plan), patterns like (2, 1, 1, 2) are ideal, involving speech, mutual orientation and action relevance. In some cases, action signals can be omitted without losing interpretability. Lastly, maintaining team function (sustaining dynamics) is inferred from patterns indicating presence, task engagement or interaction, such as facing others while in the zone (2, −1, 1, −1), speaking in the zone (1, −1, 1, −1) or being engaged with relevant work (−1, −1, 1, 2). Each combination encodes how observable signals map onto underlying collaborative behaviours. Figure 4.4 shows how we map the signals to the constructs.

Survey Approaches

Different theories and methods guide survey design; generally, surveys start with a large item pool, where, through iterative testing and refinement, the responses best model the relationship between a person's latent trait (such as ability, attitude or personality) and their responses to survey items (Gershon 2005). At the end of this design process, the researchers have a balanced survey for the target population. However, if you want to investigate specific constructs within subgroups of the population, it can be challenging with a single, broader survey. Therefore, computerised adaptive testing and survey principles would be helpful (Montgomery and Rossiter 2019). The survey has been designed to integrate cultural and contextual information within the educational setting, considering situational and individual factors, organisational context and group dynamics. This approach creates a layered, multidimensional concept for understanding students' persistence in these science experiences. We have been testing and refining the survey across different activities at the science centre to create a single survey. However, with surveys, you generally create one for the entire population. The concept is to develop several surveys based on how the system assesses the student,

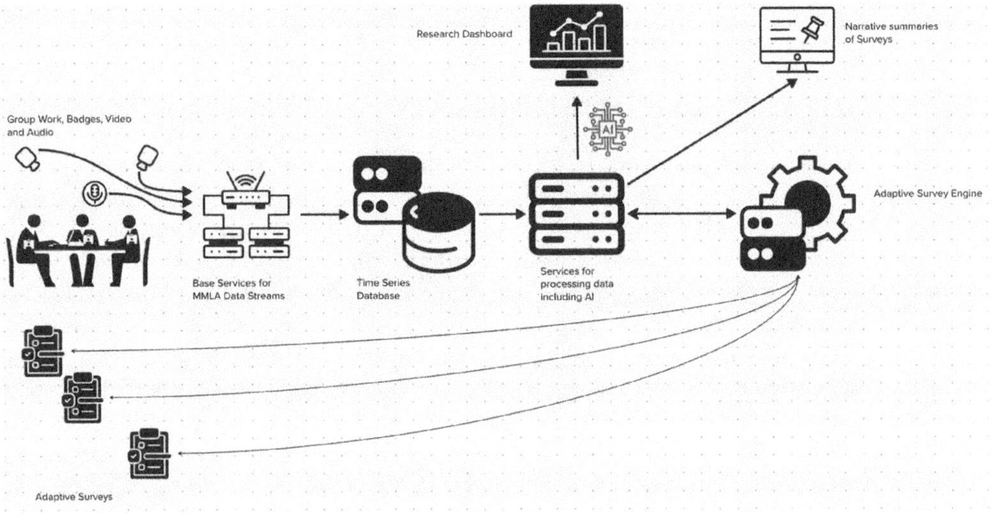

Source: Authors.

Figure 4.5 *Illustrative flow diagram of how the MMLA data and system are used to create the adaptive surveys and the narrative summaries*

allowing us to gain more insight into the student's responses (Parker et al. 2024) based on behavioural patterns (Figure 4.5).

EVALUATIONS

Technical

The MMLA system integrates various technologies to track participants' locations and behaviours in indoor group settings. The system utilises cameras and AprilTags (fiducial markers) to track individuals' positions and orientations within a shared space. This spatial data provides insight into how people move and interact during collaborative activities. The setup utilises web-cameras and low-cost Raspberry Pi single-board computers to capture and transmit data, providing a cost-effective and scalable method for assessing real-time group dynamics.

The system leverages advanced AI models – specifically, large language and vision-language models – to analyse video frames captured every 30 seconds to interpret non-verbal behaviours. These models recognise gestures, postures and interactions by linking visual cues to identified participants and classifying behaviours into meaningful categories. Different types of data are then combined, either at the feature level (for example, fusing image-based embeddings with textual descriptions) or decision level (for example, merging audio and video insights), to enhance the understanding of social interactions, such as who is speaking to whom.

Field tests showed promising results: the positioning system had an average localisation error of just 8 cm, and the audio analysis pipeline achieved high coverage and reasonable accuracy in challenging environments. The system's use of UDP for streaming data showed minimal packet loss, suggesting it is reliable for real-time communication. Still, there are areas for improvement, such as better eye gaze tracking to measure attention more directly, understanding how wearing badges may affect natural behaviour and improving video quality. Future work may involve integrating smartphones or more advanced wearables to enhance data quality and flexibility, as well as expanding analytical tools to uncover richer insights into collaborative learning (Li et al. 2025).

Human

Concurrently with the technical development, the team has been focused on developing MMLA indicators based on a human coding scheme for analysing participation in small-group experimental classroom settings. The coding scheme was inspired by the framework from Hesse et al. (2015), emphasising three key elements of group participation: actions, interaction and task perseverance. Using video recordings of student activity from the MMLA system, researchers identified observable actions and created definitions for three levels of task perseverance: active, passive and non-participation. Verbal interactions were coded based on complexity, from basic acknowledgements to facilitating communication, and categorised by topic (assignment, task, topic or other) and target audience (group members, teacher or others). The chosen observables aimed to be machine-measurable and straightforward enough for consistent human annotation. These included the student's speaking status, location, objects they were touching, gaze direction and topics of conversation. Listening behaviour was also coded using pre-defined keyword lists derived from earlier observations (Holm-Janas et al. 2024).

To generate MMLA indicators from these observables, the researchers implemented straightforward rule-based mappings from sensor data. For example, if students touched a Micro:bit, iPad or paper, they were assumed to be taking notes; if they handled experimental tools, they were labelled as experimenting. Verbal interactions were inferred based on timing: responding occurred when a student spoke immediately after another at the exact location, while initiating communication required speaking for over five seconds following a five-second silence. These simple, transparent rules created meaningful alignment between sensor-based data and the human-coded participation framework (see Figure 4.1).

DESIGN, DISCUSSION AND NEXT STEPS

Design

The chapter presents current work on the design of the MMLA system, which aims to strike a balance between theory, technology and the complexity of learning. One of the challenges of MMLA has been to move beyond the research into real-world classroom settings and provide actionable insights for people. We are nearing the development of lower-cost technologies and new AI tools enabling insights into learning and group work. However, creating meaningful data for students and teachers is a challenging task. In many situations, the complexity of learning and the social dynamics are challenging to generalise for MMLA. For instance, sound quality in diverse classrooms, varying lighting conditions and physical spaces, combined with the need to instrument the space with sensors, present a challenge, not to mention the privacy and ethics concerns associated with using these technologies with students. These quandaries lead us back to the research aim of the chapter: how do we design an MMLA system that is theoretically grounded in people and learning while leveraging technology? Indeed, the technical design, development and initial deployments of the MMLA system show technical prowess, but diverse data collection, processing and analysis without a theoretical grounding is not the aim of MMLA in our opinion (Khalil et al. 2023; Lang et al. 2022; Wise and Shaffer 2015).

Discussion

For MMLA to be effective in the Northern European environment, we need to understand the social contexts of learning, the regulations, laws, and the didactics. Therefore, our approach has been to develop a four-pronged approach that focuses equally on ethnography, technology, survey development, and a hybrid human–machine observation supported with AI.

The ethnographic research conducted at the start of the Courageous Collaborative Science (CCS) project highlights how students engage in doubt. This doubt is highlighted with the tools and instruments in the science activity, for instance, using the microscopes and programming the micro:bits microcontrollers across the two different activities. Additionally, how the students prioritise the tasks and organise their cooperation impacts their engagement with the activities.

The project's motivation for including a post-activity survey is to gather richer insights into the students' contexts. These contexts bring together cultural and demographic aspects, situational aspects related to science, and the intra- and interpersonal aspects related to persistence in these science technologies.

MMLA faces challenges in terms of ethics and privacy when working with children in classrooms. In the case of the system presented in this chapter, video and audio recordings are captured and then processed to create metadata; however, the processing relies on different AI techniques, and the richness of human interactions is reduced for interpretation at best, and, at worst, the system provides erroneous predictions and raises ethical concerns with this vulnerable population (Khalil et al. 2023). Researchers have systematically reviewed different approaches and are developing guidelines and recommendations (Alwahaby and Cukurova 2024; Yan et al. 2022), but without clear technical standards or larger-scale experiments/interventions that are human-centric, MMLA runs the risk of quantifying and optimising what makes compulsory education different from skills-based training (Skaar 2024).

As we develop the technology, we are keenly aware of how to design an MMLA system that captures meaningful data about learning in the context of group work in a science lab. Ultimately, what drives the technology is the goal of creating a human-AI hybrid approach, which leverages MMLA technology to support how people perceive learning situations. Education requires flexibility that can accommodate the differences among people and learning situations, while supporting the agency of learners and teachers.

Next Steps

One challenge for the future is to consider how we, as researchers, can communicate actionable insights back to students and teachers. Currently, we use dashboards, which one can argue may not be sufficiently aligned with the focus on observable features, leaving a significant need to integrate the concept of optimal learning moments and adaptive surveys based on observations to gain insight and provide feedback. Combining the MMLA system with an adaptive survey engine presents new challenges, first for MMLA and second for surveys. The MMLA system is designed as a platform where different pipelines process and analyse the data to create meaningful insights. These pipelines use different AI techniques, ranging from supervised machine learning to generative AI for analysis. Di Mitri (Di Mitri et al. 2018) argued that this data falls within the realm of observability, and the context of the different environments influences the data (Chejara et al. 2024b). Therefore, creating a validity challenge ensures that the MMLA system provides actionable insights. Then, if we use this analysis to generate adaptive surveys based on individual and group work, how do we ensure that surveys are effective (Tourangeau 2021)?

REFERENCES

Alwahaby, H. and M. Cukurova (2024), 'Navigating the ethical landscape of multimodal learning analytics: A guiding framework', in S. Caballé, J. Casas-Roma and J. Conesa (eds), *Ethics in online AI-based systems*, Elsevier, pp. 25–53. https://doi.org/10.1016/b978-0-443-18851-0.00014-7

Blikstein, P. (2013), 'Multimodal learning analytics', *Proceedings of the Third International Conference on Learning Analytics and Knowledge – LAK '13*, 102–6. https://doi.org/10.1145/2460296.2460316

Blikstein, P. and M. Worsley (2016), 'Multimodal learning analytics and education data mining: Using computational technologies to measure complex learning tasks', *Journal of Learning Analytics*, **3** (2), 220–38. https://doi.org/10.18608/jla.2016.32.11

Buxton, B. (2010), *Sketching user experiences: Getting the design right and the right design*, Morgan Kaufmann.

Chejara, P., R. Kasepalu, L.P Prieto, M.J. Rodríguez-Triana and A. Ruiz-Calleja (2024a), 'Bringing collaborative analytics using multimodal data to masses: Evaluation and design guidelines for developing a MMLA system for research and teaching practices in CSCL', *Proceedings of the 14th International Conference on Learning Analytics and Knowledge*, 800–806. ACM. https://doi.org/10.1145/3636555.3636877

Chejara, P., R. Kasepalu, L.P. Prieto, M.J. Rodríguez-Triana, A. Ruiz-Calleja and B. Schneider (2024b), 'How well do collaboration quality estimation models generalize across authentic school contexts?', *British Journal of Educational Technology*, **55** (4), 1602–24. https://doi.org/10.1111/bjet.13402

Chejara, P., L.P. Prieto, M.J. Rodríguez-Triana, A. Ruiz-Calleja and R. Martinez-Maldonado (2023), 'Build vs buy: A decision framework for multimodal learning analytics solutions in authentic educational settings' [Conference Proceedings]. *Proceedings of the 14th International Conference on Learning Analytics and Knowledge*, 185–95. https://doi.org/10.1145/3636555.3636869

Cohn, C., C. Snyder, J.H. Fonteles, T.S. Ashwin, J. Montenegro and G. Biswas (2025), 'A multimodal approach to support teacher, researcher and AI collaboration in STEM+C learning environments', *British Journal of Educational Technology*, **56** (2), 595–620. https://doi.org/10.1111/bjet.13518

Csikszentmihalyi, M. and R. Larson (2014), 'Validity and reliability of the experience-sampling method', in M. Csikszentmihalyi, *Flow and the Foundations of Positive Psychology*, Springer Netherlands, pp. 35–54. https://doi.org/10.1007/978-94-017-9088-8_3

Cukurova, M., R. Luckin and C. Kent. (2020), 'Impact of an artificial intelligence research frame on the perceived credibility of educational research evidence', *International Journal of Artificial Intelligence in Education*, **30** (2), 205–35. https://doi.org/10.1007/s40593-019-00188-w

Di Mitri, D., J. Schneider, M. Specht and H. Drachsler (2018), 'From signals to knowledge: A conceptual model for multimodal learning analytics', *Journal of Computer Assisted Learning*, **34** (4), 338–49. https://doi.org/10.1111/jcal.12288

Echeverria, V., G.F. Nieto, L. Zhao, E. Palominos, N. Srivastava, D. Gašević, V. Pammer-Schindler and R. Martinez-Maldonado (2025), 'A learning analytics dashboard to support students' reflection on collaboration', *Journal of Computer Assisted Learning*, **41** (1), 186–200. https://doi.org/10.1111/jcal.13088

Eskreis-Winkler, L., E.P. Shulman, S.A. Beal and A.L. Duckworth (2014), 'The grit effect: Predicting retention in the military, the workplace, school and marriage', *Frontiers in Psychology*, **5**, 36.

Fonteles, J., E. Davalos, T.S. Ashwin, Y. Zhang, M. Zhou, E. Ayalon, A. Lane, S. Steinberg, G. Anton, J. Danish, N. Enyedy and G. Biswas (2024), 'A first step in using machine learning methods to enhance interaction analysis for embodied learning environments', in A.M. Olney, I-A. Chounta, Z. Liu, O.C. Santos and I.I Bittencourt (eds), *Lecture Notes in Computer Science*, Springer Nature Switzerland, pp. 3–16 https://doi.org/10.1007/978-3-031-64299-9_1

Fredricks, J.A., M.-T. Wang, J. Schall Linn, T.L. Hofkens, H. Sung, A. Parr and J. Allerton (2016), 'Using qualitative methods to develop a survey measure of math and science engagement', *Learning and Instruction*, **43**, 5–15. https://doi.org/10.1016/j.learninstruc.2016.01.009

Gershon, R.C. (2005), 'Computer adaptive testing', *Journal of Applied Measurement*, **6** (1), 109–27. http://europepmc.org/abstract/MED/15701948

Gregor, S., L. Chandra Kruse and S. Seidel (2020), 'The anatomy of a design principle', *Journal of the Association for Information Systems*, **21** (6), 162252. https://aisel.aisnet.org/jais/vol21/iss6/2/

Hesse, F., E. Care, J. Buder, K. Sassenberg and P. Griffin (2015), 'A framework for teachable collaborative problem solving skills', in P. Griffin and E. Care (eds), *Assessment and teaching of 21st century skills,* Springer, pp. 37–56. https://doi.org/10.1007/978-94-017-9395-7_2

Hevner, A.R., S.T. March, J. Park and S. Ram (2003), 'Design science in information systems research', *MIS Quarterly*, **28** (1), 75–105. https://doi.org/10.2307/25148625

Holm-Janas, V., O. Caro Miya Marshall, Z. Li, J. Bruun and D. Spikol (2024), 'Design framework for multimodal learning analytics leveraging human observations, in R.F. Mello, N. Rummel, I. Jivet, G.

Pishtari and J.A. Ruipérez Valiente (eds), *Technology enhanced learning for inclusive and equitable quality education*, Springer Nature Switzerland, pp. 106–12.
Holstein, K., B.M. McLaren and V. Aleven (2018), 'Student learning benefits of a mixed-reality teacher awareness tool in AI-enhanced classrooms', in *Lecture Notes in Computer Science*, Springer International Publishing, pp. 165–68. https://doi.org/10.1007/978-3-319-93843-1_12
Khalil, M., P. Prinsloo and S. Slade (2023), 'The use and application of learning theory in learning analytics: A scoping review', *Journal of Computing in Higher Education*, **35** (3), 573–94.
Lahat, D., T. Adali and C. Jutten (2015), 'Multimodal data fusion: An overview of methods, challenges, and prospects', *Proceedings of the IEEE*, **103** (9), 1449–77. https://doi.org/10.1109/jproc.2015.2460697
Lang, C., A.F. Wise, A. Merceron, D. Gašević and G. Siemens (2022), 'What is learning analytics', in *The Handbook of Learning Analytics*, The Society for Learning Analytics Research, pp. 8–18.
Li, Z., M.T. Jensen, A. Nolte and D. Spikol (2024), 'Field report for platform mBox: Designing an open MMLA platform', *Proceedings of the 14th Learning Analytics and Knowledge Conference*, 785–91.
Li, Z., S. Yamaguchi and D. Spikol (2025), 'OpenMMLA: An IoT-based multimodal data collection toolkit for learning analytics', *Proceedings of the 15th International Learning Analytics and Knowledge Conference*, 872–9.
Martinez-Maldonado, R., L.P. Prieto,D. Spikol and D. Gasevic (2024), 'Lessons learned from using multimodal learning analytics in authentic educational settings', *Proceedings of the International Conference on Learning Sciences*, 452–9.
Misfeldt, M., L. Nøhr, I. Laug, V. Holm-Janas, Z. Li, A. Traxler, J. Bruun, D. Spikol and R.M.Kristensen (2024), 'Addressing shared reflective persistence through three different lenses', *International Conference on Quantitative Ethnography Conference Proceedings Supplement*, 199–205.
Montgomery, J.M. and E.L. Rossiter (2019), 'So many questions, so little time: Integrating adaptive inventories into public opinion research', *Journal of Survey Statistics and Methodology*, **8** (4), 667–90. https://doi.org/10.1093/jssam/smz027
Nøhr, L., V. Holm-Janas, A. Traxler, J. Bruun, D. Spikol and M. Misfeldt (2024), 'Critical reviews with quantitative ethnography: Theory use in literature on quantified group work in educational settings', in Y.J. Kim and Z. Swiecki (eds), *Advances in quantitative ethnography*, Springer Nature Switzerland, pp. 74–88.
Ochoa, X. and M. Worsley (2016), 'Augmenting learning analytics with multimodal sensory data', *Journal of Learning Analytics*, **3** (2), 213–19. https://doi.org/10.18608/jla.2016.32.10
Oviatt, S. and A. Cohen (2013), 'Written and multimodal representations as predictors of expertise and problem-solving success in mathematics', *Proceedings of the 15th ACM on International Conference on Multimodal Interaction*, 599–606. https://doi.org/10.1145/2522848.2533793
Parker, M.J., C. Anderson, C. Stone and Y. Oh (2024), 'A large language model approach to educational survey feedback analysis', *International Journal of Artificial Intelligence in Education*, **1** (1), 1–25. https://doi.org/10.1007/s40593-024-00414-0
Ryan, R.M. and E.L. Deci (2000), 'Intrinsic and extrinsic motivations: Classic definitions and new directions', *Contemporary Educational Psychology*, **25** (1), 54–67.
Schneider, B., J. Krajcik, J. Lavonen, K. Salmela-Aro, M. Broda, J. Spicer, J. Bruner, J. Moeller, J. Linnansaari, K. Juuti and J. Viljaranta (2016), 'Investigating optimal learning moments in U.S. and Finnish science classes', *Journal of Research in Science Teaching*, **53** (3), 400–21. https://doi.org/10.1002/tea.21306
Schneider, B., R. Davis, R. Martínez-Maldonado, G. Biswas, M. Worsley and N. Rummel (2024), 'Stepping outside the ivory tower: How can we implement multimodal learning analytics in ecological settings, and turn complex temporal data sources into actionable insights?', *Proceedings of the International Conference of the Learning Sciences*, 152–9.
Schneider, B., R. Martínez-Maldonado, M. Worsley and G. Biswas (2026), 'Implementing multimodal learning analytics in authentic settings: A roadmap for ecological impact', *Learning and Instruction*, **104**, 102341. https://doi.org/10.1016/j.learninstruc.2026.102341
Shernoff, D.J., M. Csikszentmihalyi, B. Schneider and E.S. Shernoff (2014), 'Student engagement in high school classrooms from the perspective of flow theory', in M. Csikszentmihalyi, *Applications of flow in human development and education,* Springer Netherlands, pp. 475–94. https://doi.org/10.1007/978-94-017-9094-9_24

Skaar, Ø.O. (2024), 'A call for bildung: Addressing the challenges of a digitalized education', *Nordic Journal of Digital Literacy*, **2**, 101–11.

Snyder, C., G. Biswas, L. Jacobs and J. Fonteles (2024), 'Exploring AI-supported teaching and learning in STEM environments: Recent advances and new directions', *Educational Technology Research and Development*, **72** (1), 143–65. https://doi.org/10.1007/s11423-023-10295-0

Spikol, D., Z. Li, A. Nolte, A. A. Ohsaki and K. Rapur (2024), 'Investigating hackathons with collaboration analytics', *Proceedings of the 8th International Conference on Game Jams, Hackathons and Game Creation Events*, pp. 1–8.

Stahl, G. (2010), 'How to study group cognition', in S. Puntambekar, G. Erkens and C. Hmelo-Silver (eds), *Analyzing interactions in CSCL: Methods, approaches and issues*, Springer, pp. 107–20.

Tourangeau, R. (2021), 'Science and survey management', *Survey Methodology*, **47** (1), 3–29.

Vaishnavi, V. and W. Kuechler (2015), *Design science research methods and patterns: Innovating information and communication technology, 2nd Edition*, CRC Press.

Whitehead, R., A. Nguyen and S. Järvelä (2025), 'Utilizing multimodal large language models for video analysis of posture in studying collaborative learning', *Journal of Learning Analytics*, **12** (1), 186–200. https://doi.org/10.18608/jla.2025.8595

Wise, A.F. and D.W. Shaffer (2015), 'Why theory matters more than ever in the age of big data', *Journal of Learning Analytics*, **2** (2), 5–13. https://doi.org/10.18608/jla.2015.22.2

Yan, L., D. Gasevic, V. Echeverria, Y. Jin, L. Zhao and R. Martinez-Maldonado (2025), 'From complexity to parsimony: Integrating latent class analysis to uncover multimodal learning patterns in collaborative learning', *Proceedings of the 15th International Learning Analytics and Knowledge Conference*, 70–81. https://doi.org/10.1145/3706468.3706476

Yan, L., L. Zhao, D. Gasevic and R. Martinez-Maldonado (2022), 'Scalability, sustainability, and ethicality of multimodal learning analytics', *LAK22: 12th International Learning Analytics and Knowledge Conference*, 13–23. https://doi.org/10.1145/3506860.3506862

Yan, L., R. Martinez-Maldonado and D. Gasevic (2024), 'Generative artificial intelligence in learning analytics: Contextualising opportunities and challenges through the learning analytics cycle', *Proceedings of the 14th International Conference on Learning Analytics and Knowledge*, 101–11. ACM. https://doi.org/10.1145/3636555.3636856

5. Integrating the Science of Learning with EdTech solutions: from frameworks to models of practice

Natalia Ingebretsen Kucirkova

Learning analytics are part of Educational Technology (EdTech) that collect data to improve educational outcomes. Through EdTech, learning analytics can improve educational outcomes and provide data-driven insights into student performance and engagement. So that these data can enable personalized learning and support teachers to tailor content and interventions to individual students' needs, EdTech needs to be of high-quality design and use. The data that EdTech collects, for example, teachers' feedback or students' performance on various digital quizzes, can be used for predictive analytics to support at-risk students and proactive interventions. For these predictions and interventions to work, however, the data need to come from high-quality EdTech or EdTech with demonstrated positive educational impact. Yet, while more than 50 per cent of primary and lower secondary school-aged children worldwide use EdTech, the impact of EdTech on children's learning remains largely unknown (UNESCO 2023). Not surprisingly, the OECD (2023) and other global agencies and organizations have been calling for a comprehensive method to holistically evaluate the impact of EdTech in K–12 classrooms. In this chapter, I provide initial pointers for the conceptualization of a holistic approach that integrates the Science of Learning with an interdisciplinary and system-oriented understanding of impact evaluations. I chose the Science of Learning as the guiding framework for educational impact, based on the latest research on what works for student learning. My goal is to support efforts such as those by the Global Alliance on the Science of Learning for Education (see UNESCO 2024) to integrate the principles of the Science of Learning into classroom technology in a sustainable and holistic manner. More specifically, I aim to build on and expand the guidance for EdTech evaluation routines that advocate for methodological plurality in applying research insights (see Kucirkova, Brod and Gaab 2023) with a framework that considers the impact of EdTech tools not only on immediate learner outcomes but also on the broader educational environment, taking into account the inclusive, ethical and sustainable imperatives of effective digital education.

From a research perspective, impact in EdTech refers to the observable or measurable changes to learning as a direct result of the tools' use (Hollow and Jefferies 2022). EdTech includes hardware (laptops, computers) and software (apps, learning platforms, e-books), and evidence of their impact comes in the form of research studies, as well as various third-party impact evaluations commissioned by government, philanthropic organizations or EdTech certification providers (for example, ISTE, Digital Promise). It is well established that some EdTech tools, such as digital books, can significantly improve learning outcomes for children, but only if they are of high quality (Grimes 2025). The positive impact of high-quality EdTech tools has been documented for children from disadvantaged backgrounds (Poleschuk et al. 2023) and under-resourced communities (for example, Moser-Mercer et al. 2023). Therefore, the research community needs to develop frameworks that not only evaluate existing EdTech tools but also promote aspirational principles for high-quality EdTech design in order to achieve a positive impact on learners. How can the positive impact of EdTech tools be evaluated and determined?

EVALUATION FRAMEWORKS FOR EDTECH

A systematic review of EdTech impact frameworks commissioned by the UK Department for Education (2023) identified 74 various EdTech evaluation frameworks, and a follow-up review by Kucirkova, Cermakova and Vackova (2024) identified 65 different frameworks dedicated to the efficacy and effectiveness of EdTech evaluations alone. While the large number of evaluation frameworks signals a growing interest in understanding 'what works' in EdTech, it also highlights the multiple overlapping dimensions that are being considered by diverse research teams. Furthermore, there is significant variation in how the impact of EdTech is valued and evaluated by national governments. For example, in the USA, the Every Student Succeeds Act (ESSA) Evaluation framework emphasizes efficacy through a tiered system of evidence, with the highest tier being a randomized controlled trial (https://tech.ed.gov/essa). By contrast, India's national evaluation and procurement decisions for EdTech follow the Tulna standards, which focus on the pedagogical alignment between EdTech design and classroom practices (https://edtechtulna.org/standards/).

As stated by the Asian Development Bank: 'because EdTech efficacy depends on the context of the use, there is a need for products to be evaluated with a holistic approach using a range of qualifiers appropriate for a given context.' To develop a holistic approach that addresses both efficacy and contextual variation, it is essential to consolidate the various frameworks into an umbrella model that encompasses multiple areas of impact.

MULTIDIMENSIONAL IMPACT EVALUATION FRAMEWORKS

While research evaluation frameworks typically focus on a specific learning domain or area of impact to allow for sufficient depth of analysis, industry-developed frameworks tend to be broader. A good example is three recently developed frameworks for EdTech: The QESA, ISTE and Triple-S Frameworks. These frameworks capture multiple perspectives and quality components in an integrated manner to allow for a holistic perspective. While research-driven evaluation frameworks tend to be driven by a specific theory or theoretical hypothesis, these frameworks are more driven by the desire to address a gap in holistic impact evaluations (see Westenberg and Koele 1994).

The QESA Framework (Quality, Effectiveness, Scalability, and Affordability) breaks down EdTech impact into four key dimensions, each with three sub-dimensions: (1) Quality is assessed through functionality, pedagogy and user-friendliness; (2) Effectiveness is measured by user satisfaction, evidence and impact; (3) Scalability considers infrastructure, local adaptability and security and privacy; and (4) Affordability looks at investment costs, operational costs and sustainability. The EdTech impact framework developed by the International Society for Technology in Education (ISTE 2024) identifies five essential quality indicators for EdTech products: (1) Usability ensures that products are user-friendly for both educators and students; (2) Safety prioritizes robust data privacy and security measures; (3) Interoperability allows for seamless integration with other technologies within a school's digital ecosystem; (4) Inclusivity ensures that EdTech products cater to diverse learners and avoid perpetuating stereotypes or biased algorithms; and (5) Evidence-based criterion expects EdTech to align with the US Government's ESSA Tiers of Evidence. The third, more academically oriented framework, the Triple-S Framework (Moro et al. 2023), focuses on three impact dimensions: Scalability, Sustainability and Serviceability, and emphasizes the importance of outlining expectations around scalable, sustainable and serviceable practices in the procurement or implementation of EdTech.

While all three frameworks encompass multiple dimensions and represent a progression from previous feature-specific or domain-specific research frameworks, they have not gained traction as internationally recognized standards. Instead, they have remained largely confined to specific regions – ISTE in the US, QESA in Asia and Triple-S in Australia – likely due to the specific focuses they selected in defining EdTech and the impact areas they prioritize. By contrast, the 5Es framework has emerged as an international standard, offering a more globally relevant approach to evaluating educational technology and its broader impact.

THE 5ES FRAMEWORK

Synthesizing existing educational evidence frameworks together with the UNESCO 17 Sustainable Development Goals (SDGs), I proposed that EdTech impact falls into five key areas: Efficacy, Effectiveness, Ethics, Equity and Environment (the so-called Five 'Es'; Kucirkova 2023). These five key impact dimensions are interrelated and differently implicated in the overall impact of an organization. Efficacy and effectiveness specifically relate to the objectively demonstrated impact on learning outcomes for users. Ethics, equity, and environment are framed according to the three main 'universal values' described by the United Nations that connect to contextual fit, demand alignment for implementation studies, and data-based practices with EdTech.

The 5Es model weaves together a lot of interconnected efforts to evolve and capture EdTech evidence over the past decade. This includes globally focused initiatives like UNESCO's advocacy for Greening Education Partnership and the World Bank's emphasis on cost-effective EdTech procurement (the so-called 'smart buys'), which consider the impact of EdTech in relation to the efficacy of tools but also pay attention to the impact of an EdTech implementation and its transferability to other contexts.

The 5Es model is built around five guiding questions for policymakers, EdTech procurement teams, and the EdTech industry (see Figure 5.1). The model approaches educational issues by answering both the efficacy question of 'does EdTech work' and the effectiveness question of 'how could EdTech work', and it expands them with a focus on equitable, ethical, and sustainable practices (see Gottschalk and Weise 2023).

The 5Es model is intended as a guiding approach rather than merely another framework in an already saturated landscape of evaluation frameworks. It overlaps with and expands upon the QESA, ISTE, and Triple-S frameworks, as illustrated in Table 5.1.

In 2024, the 5E model was adopted by the International Certification of Evidence of Impact in Education (Eduevidence.org), which aims to consolidate current standards and certifications of EdTech tools. The adoption of the 5Es by the Eduevidence.org system illustrates the

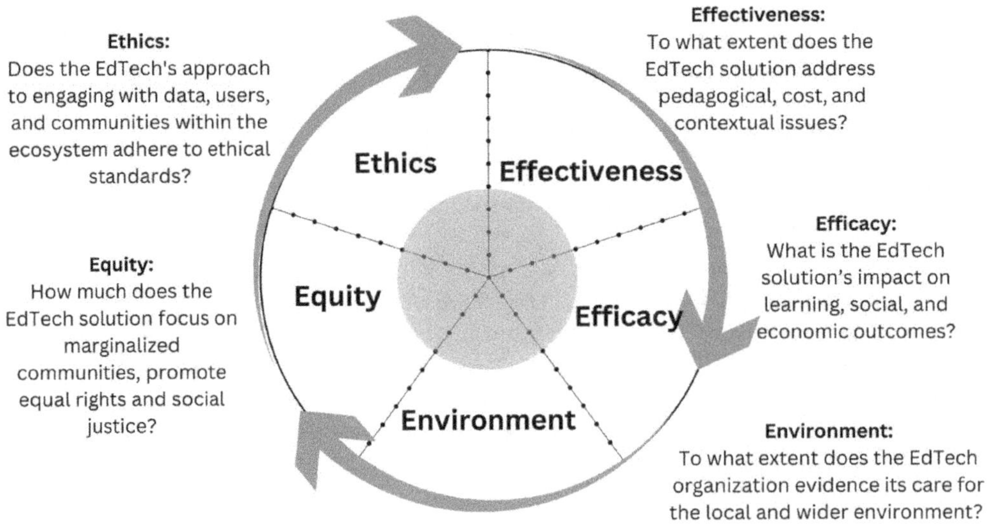

Source: Author.

Figure 5.1 The five dimensions of impact, with accompanying questions

Table 5.1 Points of overlap and expansions between the 5Es model and three prominent EdTech impact frameworks

5Es Model	QESA Framework	ISTE Framework	Triple-S Framework
Efficacy	Evidence	Evidence-based	-
Effectiveness	Effectiveness, Quality, Scalability, Affordability	Usable	Scalability, Serviceability
Ethics	Scalability	Safe, Interoperable	-
Equity	-	Inclusive	-
Environment	Affordability	-	Sustainability

Source: Author.

possibility that the 5E model holds for consolidating diverse approaches, frameworks and criteria concerned with EdTech impact evaluations.

While the 5Es model has been well-received and comprehensive, it remains a dynamic, evolving resource. Ongoing discussions with policymakers, researchers, EdTech providers and other stakeholders continue to refine the model, particularly by enhancing the specific indicators used to evaluate EdTech within each impact domain. As the original conceptualizer of the 5Es model, I have been reflecting on its completeness, especially in addressing the broader scope of EdTech – not just focusing on products, but also on organizations and implementation processes. Drawing from my expertise as a scholar interested in learning and educational outcomes, I propose an expanded version of the 5Es model with attention to the Science of Learning, which I outline next.

SCIENCE OF LEARNING AND THE 5ES

The Science of Learning is, according to a scoping review of 43 unique definitions across 50 documents, including journal articles, theses, conference papers and book chapters, 'the scientific study of the underlying bases of learning with the goal of describing, understanding or improving learning across developmental stages and diverse contexts' (Privitera, Ng and Chen 2023). While traditionally, the Science of Learning (SoL) has been understood as a mono-disciplinary effort focused on cognitive research, more recent definitions of SoL frame it as an interdisciplinary approach that draws on a number of disciplines, including psychology, education, ethnography, digital humanities, philosophy and cognitive science. All these and more disciplines are involved in the study of how people learn.

Insights from the Science of Learning need to be used to not only evaluate but also to describe and improve the underlying bases of learning in diverse contexts (Privitera, Ng and Chen 2023). There is thus a need for an expanded 5E model that would not only focus on the impact of tools and their features but also on the practices surrounding their use that influence both the immediate and broader learning environment.

The Science of Learning further offers a research-based understanding of how learning occurs and, as such, taps into the 5Es. Efficacy, which focuses on whether an intervention can produce the desired learning outcomes under ideal conditions, is grounded in SoL's experimental designs that test cognitive theories in controlled settings. For example, Roberts et al. (2016) tested the efficacy of a computerized adaptive working memory intervention programme for the long-term academic outcomes of children six toseven years of age with low working memory, compared with usual classroom teaching in a population-based randomized controlled clinical trial of first graders from 44 schools in Melbourne, Australia, and found that an adaptive working memory improves the children's visuospatial short-term memory. The study shows that efficacy interventions address specific questions related to learning domains. Conversely, effective interventions are more related to the implementation of SoL approaches or technologies. As such, effectiveness, measuring the practical application of these interventions in real-world contexts, aligns with SoL's emphasis on translating learning principles into classroom practice. An illustrative study is that of Scheffler and Logan (1999), who drew on a suite of implementation studies that investigated effective computer use in various school settings and derived the competencies and standards to guide educational implementations.

In addition to proximal aspects of ethics such as ethical data use and data management, SoL also informs ethical considerations by emphasizing the importance of designing interventions that are transparent and respectful of learner diversity, ensuring the protection of student data and promoting responsible use of technology (Atabey et al. 2024). Moreover, the Science of Learning plays a crucial role in advancing equity and fostering inclusive environments. By identifying evidence-based strategies that support diverse learners, including those from marginalized groups or with special needs, the integration of SoL's principles into EdTech design can create more equitable access to quality education. Equity in this respect extends beyond access to content, encompassing tailored learning approaches that account for individual differences (through, for example, digital personalized learning, see Schmid and Petko 2019). Additionally, the environment of learning is another critical factor, as SoL underscores the influence of both physical and socio-emotional environments on student engagement and achievement, as well as care for the wider environment that all students are part of (Racsko and Troll 2020).

Attention to ethics, equity and the environment is crucial at each level of efficacy and effectiveness studies and is integral to determining their significance. For instance, addressing learner variability and centering marginalized groups is essential for conducting ethical and effective SoL studies (Tare, Pape and Shell 2022). While the Efficacy dimension aligns with national standards of evidence as considered by clearinghouses in Australia, the UK and the USA (for example, the ESSA standards in the USA and the AERO standards in Australia), there is a need to ensure the relationship between the efficacy of EdTech with the pedagogical frameworks implicit in the tools' design as well as the ethics of their use – as made explicit in the publications of the UNESCO Global Alliance on the Science of Learning in Education.

The points of synergy between SoL and the 5Es give rise to an expanded 5E model.

EXPANDED 5ES MODEL

The expanded 5Es model (see Figure 5.2) combines individual quality indicators developed across the five impact strands with three areas where impact can be documented: the product (for example, the EdTech tool and its design), the process of using the tool, and the users (for example, teachers' competencies). The expanded 5Es model signals that some impact dimensions can be assessed at the tool level while others are evaluated at the organizational level.

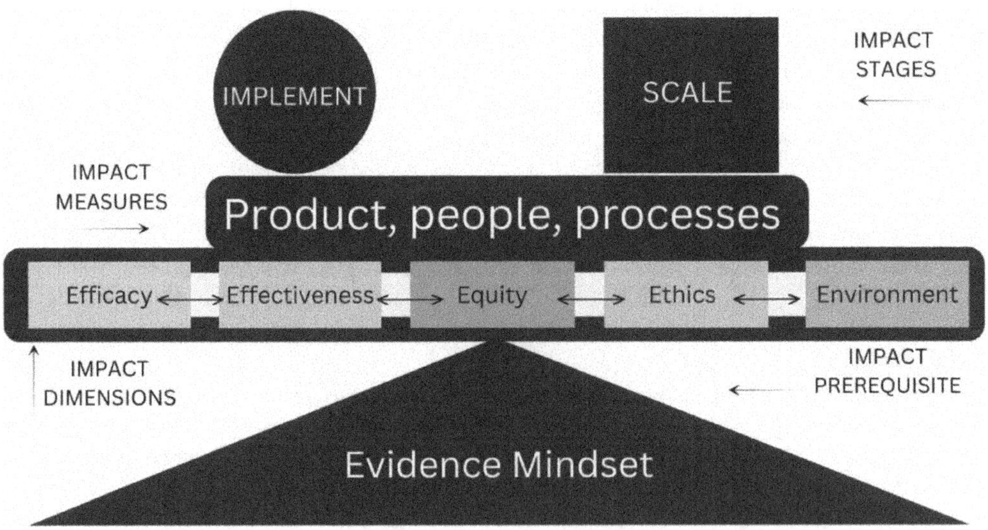

Source: Author.

Figure 5.2 *The 5Es expanded model*

The delineation of specific indicators for products, people and processes is tailored to the nature of EdTech; for example, different quality parameters apply to a learning management system compared to other types of EdTech, such as literacy apps. The weight of the impact generated in different categories will depend on the focus of the evaluation. For instance, ethical considerations may carry more weight when evaluating EdTech interventions for vulnerable populations, whereas effectiveness questions may dominate assessments of learning outcomes. Crucially, it is the aggregated impact across the five dimensions (rather than excelling in just one impact domain) that determines the overall impact of an EdTech approach (depicted with the individual arrows in Figure 5.2).

Figure 5.2 illustrates the expanded 5E model with a depiction of impact stages, mutual dependency among the 5E dimensions, and the evidence mindset underpinning them.

IMPLEMENTING THE EXPANDED 5ES MODEL

The mutually reinforcing effects and multidimensional impact of EdTech require a systems-level perspective to estimate what works. While governments and global agencies have predominantly focused on the efficacy of EdTech and the ethics of AI tools, addressing these dimensions alone – without considering the practices of use and the people involved – will not fully address the systemic changes required in the EdTech domain. This need for a systems-level perspective on EdTech impact is well documented in the literature: based on a meta-analysis of meta-analyses evaluating EdTech impact in the past 20 years, Bernard et al. (2023) found that it is robust teacher training and ensuring alignment between technological tools and pedagogical goals that lead to successful interventions. I propose that a systems-level perspective on EdTech impact necessitates a shift in the current understanding of evidence and should supplement the 5Es empirical validation of EdTech. I frame the shift around the need for nurturing the 'evidence mindset' in the EdTech ecosystem and argue for understanding impact not as a two-way flow of effects between users and tools, but rather as a shared responsibility within an ecosystem with multiple stakeholders (developers, researchers, teachers, investors, users). This proposition builds on and expands earlier calls for a holistic approach to evidence-building in education (for example, Biesta 2007).

THE EVIDENCE MINDSET

The system-level perspective is about bringing together multiple stakeholders or members of the EdTech ecosystem, including researchers, EdTech developers, funders, users, and practitioners around a shared agenda: to improve education through evidence. This perspective implies that a key addition in the expanded 5E model needs to be an element that underlies the shared agenda, and this, I propose, is an evidence mindset. I placed the evidence mindset as the core of the expanded 5E model, not as another dimension or an afterthought after other impact dimensions have been considered, but rather as the backbone of the model. Having an evidence mindset implies prioritizing learning outcomes over mere outputs in the development of EdTech tools and advocating for meaningful engagement with the Science of Learning principles throughout all stages of an EdTech approach: ideation stage, design, implementation, scale, and validation (Looi et al. 2015).

A member of the EdTech ecosystem who has an evidence mindset is someone who understands that evidence is not a quick one-off exercise but rather a commitment to a long-term evidence lifecycle. Adopting an evidence mindset further involves prioritizing effective design together with inclusion (equity) and ethics. It requires balancing various impact dimensions at different stages of the EdTech process and iteratively refining the approach based on not only what works but also what doesn't work, and transparently sharing positive and negative effects as they emerge. These parameters are visualized in Figure 5.2 with the triangle underpinning the five dimensions of impact.

The prominent placing of the evidence mindset in the model aligns with several major frameworks that emphasize the role of people, governance and organizational structure in shaping a product's quality and overall impact. These frameworks highlight that the individuals and teams behind a product, along with the systems and leadership governing them, play a crucial role in determining both the product's effectiveness and its capacity to generate meaningful outcomes. For instance, *Education Digital Transformation: Framework for System Transformation with Education Technology* by UNESCO et al. (2024) features the Coordination and Leadership pillar, which underscores the importance of effective governance in driving digital transformation in education. This governance is fundamentally about the people behind the product – their mindset, culture and capacity to implement, manage and leverage evidence to ensure quality. By focusing on the human element, such frameworks recognize that the success of educational technology depends not only on the tools themselves but also on the leadership and organizational mindset that supports their development and use.

The evidence mindset conceptualization also draws on existing literature around habits of mind: Margolis (1993) discusses how habits of mind govern scientific beliefs and drive action. The evidence mindset is, therefore, the cornerstone of efforts aimed at achieving a holistic understanding of EdTech impact. The evidence mindset invites a reframing of impact, viewing impact not as an intrinsic property of EdTech tools but as a construct co-created by all members of the EdTech ecosystem. It is the systems-level orientation toward evidence as an ongoing process that can adequately support impact aspirations across various stages of EdTech growth that influence the whole child development (cf. Darling-Hammond et al. 2020). Researchers can independently evaluate but also directly collaborate with EdTech developers (Dore et al. 2018) to integrate the principles of the Science of Learning into the design of the tools, thus increasing the potential for positive learning impact these tools can have over time.

NURTURING THE EVIDENCE MINDSET WITH THE 5ES

Nurturing a growth mindset is not a simple task to be completed; rather, it involves a gradual shift in attitudes, deepening understanding, commitment to ongoing self-reflection, openness to being proven wrong, and a willingness to improve while maintaining curiosity. This process likely involves several approaches or techniques, ranging from deliberate practice and mentorship to reflective journaling and feedback loops, but it can also be meaningfully cultivated through the deliberate and systematic use of well-crafted questions. Such questions can guide introspection, challenge fixed beliefs and encourage members of the EdTech ecosystem to reframe narrow understandings of evidence.

Key questions that foster such an evidence mindset, from a 5E perspective, encompass open-ended inquiries addressing all five impact dimensions. These questions evolve to encourage greater commitment over time and collaboration with peers, such as fellow CEOs, leaders or employers within the EdTech ecosystem. Kucirkova and Lewis (2023) proposed 40 such questions to strengthen the capacity of the EdTech field in raising awareness about holistic approaches to impact and advancing evidence. To illustrate, see these five example questions that are currently used in capacity-building workshops with EdTech leaders globally, and are available upon request from the International Centre for EdTech Impact.

Example questions include:

1. How do we ensure that any research/assessment of the impact of our solution is accurate, unbiased, and rigorous?
2. How do we balance the need for rigorous research about the impacts of our solution with financial and logistical constraints?
3. How are we encouraging transparency among our teams, portfolio companies or funded projects, to openly share our data, research findings, efficacy outcomes and/or impact metrics?
4. How are we leveraging multi-stakeholder engagements to bolster community engagement and foster long-term collaborations?
5. How are we aligning our efforts to advance equity in education, ensuring that our solution and approach reach and benefit all children, especially those in underserved areas or from disadvantaged backgrounds?

LIMITATIONS AND IMPLICATIONS

The journey toward a holistic understanding of evidence is not a linear trajectory, and I certainly do not aim to suggest that the use of some evidence mindset questions will resolve the systematic issues in evidence in EdTech, as noted at the beginning of this chapter. Holistic evidence-building encompasses dedicated efforts from assessing product impact to understanding the implementation process and organizational commitment. The expanded 5Es model can guide this process, but to translate it into actionable practice, it is essential to operationalize the model through a suite of practical tools. These might include self-assessment questionnaires that help individuals or teams reflect on their current practices and mindsets, as well as mechanisms for securely and ethically sharing anonymized data generated from these assessments to inform broader learning and benchmarking. In addition, interactive templates, diagnostic checklists, reflective prompts and scenario-based guides could support users in applying the model across diverse contexts. Facilitated workshops, digital dashboards for tracking progress and case study repositories could also enhance engagement and learning. Together, these tools could form a '5Es toolkit', which includes measures for evaluating impact, tools to cultivate an evidence-based mindset within the ecosystem, and a repository that ranks individual solutions based on their evidence level in each of the five impact domains.

At the time of writing, the 5Es model has been operationalized into a suite of self-assessment tools for EdTech companies offered as public goods by EduEvidence, and there is also an ongoing effort to populate the repository of EdTech tools evaluated based on their 5Es evidence levels (see https://certifications.eduevidence.org/). The next step involves verifying the implementation potential of the toolkit across contexts and with attention to integrating the Science of Learning with more EdTech solutions. In addition, a survey is currently being developed by the Global Alliance for the Science of Learning under UNESCO to evaluate EdTech companies' commitment to evidence-building from a holistic perspective. The survey findings will provide systematic insights into how companies approach evidence, moving beyond the current reliance on published reports that often highlight only positive outcomes and completed studies. The survey aims to capture the perspectives of those responsible for evidence, research and impact within EdTech companies, how they plan for evidence generation, their mindset toward evidence, and whether their approach aligns with broader, lifecycle-oriented views of impact, which encompass both immediate and long-term effects.

In conclusion, it follows that nurturing the development of an evidence mindset is not solely the responsibility of EdTech researchers, users (teachers) and developers (the so-called golden trio in traditional understanding of EdTech impact, see Cukurova, Luckin and Clark-Wilson 2019), but also of funders and venture capitalists (VCs), who can incentivize EdTech solutions to prioritize impact over rapid scaling. Policymakers also carry a responsibility in supporting the necessary infrastructure that facilitates effective implementation and testing of tools in classrooms, as well as partnerships between academia, industry, and schools to stimulate the design of impactful and desirable EdTech solutions. In sum, structuring the impact considerations through a systems-level understanding of evidence and along the mindset dimensions allows for a deeper integration of the Science of Learning with EdTech solutions. This approach holds significant potential to transform EdTech into a field driven by educationally meaningful impact.

ACKNOWLEDGEMENTS

The author would like to acknowledge and appreciate her colleagues at the International Centre for EdTech Impact and the UNESCO Global Alliance on the Science of Learning for Education, who have been central in developing the thinking behind the work presented in this book chapter.

REFERENCES

Atabey, A., S.C. Robinson, A.L. Cermakova, A. Siibak and N.I. Kucirkova (2024), *Ethics in EdTech: Consolidating Standards For Responsible Data Handling And Usercentric Design*. Stavanger: University of Stavanger.

Bernard, R.M., E. Borokhovski, R.F. Schmid and R.M. Tamim (2023), 'Gauging the effectiveness of educational technology integration in education: What the best-quality meta-analyses tell us', in J.M. Spector, B.B. Lockee and M.D. Childress (eds), *Learning, Design, and Technology: An International Compendium of Theory, Research, Practice, and Policy,* Cham, Switzerland: Springer International Publishing, pp. 3929–52.

Biesta, G. (2007), 'Why "what works" won't work: Evidence-based practice and the democratic deficit in educational research', *Educational Theory*, **57** (1), 1–22.

Cukurova, M., R. Luckin and A. Clark-Wilson (2019), 'Creating the golden triangle of evidence-informed education technology with EDUCATE', *British Journal of Educational Technology*, **50** (2), 490–504.

Darling-Hammond, L., L. Flook, C. Cook-Harvey, B. Barron and D. Osher (2020), 'Implications for educational practice of the Science of Learning and development', *Applied Developmental Science*, **24** (2), 97–140.

Department for Education (2023), *EdTech Quality Characteristics: Frameworks and Standards Review: A Review to Identify the Quality Components for Educational Technology (EdTech) Design and Implementation.* https://www.gov.uk/government/publications/edtech-quality-characteristics-frameworks-and-standards-review

Dore, R.A., M. Shirilla, B.N. Verdine, L. Zimmermann, R.M. Golinkoff and K. Hirsh-Pasek (2018), 'Developer meets developmentalist: Improving industry–research partnerships in children's educational technology', *Journal of Children and Media*, **12** (2), 227–35.

Gottschalk, F. and C. Weise (2023), 'Digital equity and inclusion in education: An overview of practice and policy in OECD countries', *OECD Education Working Papers No. 299.* https://doi.org/10.1787/7cb15030-en

Grimes, N. (2025), 'Educational technology and the Pre-K–12 environment: Implications for education leaders, teachers, and students', in *Encyclopedia of Information Science and Technology, Sixth Edition*, Hershey, PA: IGI Global, pp. 1–21.

Hollow, D. and K. Jefferies (2022), 'How EdTech can be used to help address the global learning crisis: A challenge to the sector for an evidence-driven future', *EdTech Hub*, September 16.

ISTE (2024), *Coalition of Leading Education Organizations Introduces Five Quality Indicators for Edtech and AI Products.* https://iste.org/news/coalition-of-leading-education-organizations-introduces-five-quality-indicators-for-edtech-and-ai-products

Kucirkova, N. (2023), 'How can philanthropy catalyse a system-wide change in EdTech?' *Alliance For Philanthropy and Social Investment Worldwide.* https://www.alliancemagazine.org/blog/how-can-philanthropy-catalyse-a-system-wide-change-in-edtech/

Kucirkova, N. and M. Lewis (2023), *The Evidence Mindset Cards.* International Centre for EdTech Impact. https://www.foreduimpact.org/evidence-mindset

Kucirkova, N., G. Brod and N. Gaab (2023), 'Applying the Science of Learning to EdTech evidence evaluations using the EdTech Evidence Evaluation Routine (EVER)', *NPJ Science of Learning*, **8** (1), 35–37.

Kucirkova, N.I., A.L. Cermakova and P. Vackova (2024), *Consolidated Benchmark for Efficacy and Effectiveness Frameworks in EdTech.* Stavanger: University of Stavanger. https://ebooks.uis.no/index.php/USPS/catalog/book/270

Looi, C.K., L.W. Teh, D. Hung and L. Wu (2015), 'A synthesis: Expanding the reach of education research and reforms', in C-K. Looi and L. Woon Teh (eds), *Scaling Educational Innovations,* Singapore: Springer, pp. 279–88.

Margolis, H. (1993), *Paradigms and Barriers: How Habits of Mind Govern Scientific Beliefs.* Chicago: University of Chicago Press.

Moro, C., K.A. Mills, C. Phelps and J. Birt (2023), 'The Triple-S framework: Ensuring scalable, sustainable, and serviceable practices in educational technology', *International Journal of Educational Technology in Higher Education*, **20** (1), 7.

Moser-Mercer, B., K.K. AlMousa, R.M. Alhaj Hussein, R.K. AlSbihe, A.S. AlGasem, A.A. Hadmoun and M.M. AlHmoud (2023), 'EdTech in humanitarian contexts: Whose evidence base?' *Frontiers in Education*, **8**, 1038476.

OECD (2023), *Shaping Digital Education: Enabling Factors for Quality, Equity and Efficiency.* https://doi.org/10.1787/bac4dc9f-en

Poleschuk, S., T. Dreesen, B. D'Ippolito and J. Carceles Martinez Lozano (2023), *Unlocking Learning: The Use of Education Technology to Support Disadvantaged Children's Language Learning and Social Inclusion in Italy.* UNICEF Office of Research-Innocenti.

Privitera, A.J., S.H.S. Ng and S.H.A. Chen (2023), 'Defining the Science of Learning: A scoping review', *Trends in Neuroscience and Education*, **32**, 100206.

Racsko, R. and E.M. Troll (2020), 'Our digital education habits in the light of their environmental impact: The role of green computing in education', *Teaching Mathematics and Computer Science*, **18** (1), 69–86.

Roberts, G., J. Quach, M. Spencer-Smith, P.J. Anderson, S. Gathercole, L. Gold, … and M. Wake (2016), 'Academic outcomes two years after working memory training for children with low working memory: A randomized clinical trial', *JAMA Pediatrics*, **170** (5), e154568.

Scheffler, F.L. and J.P. Logan (1999), 'Computer technology in schools: What teachers should know and be able to do', *Journal of Research on Computing in Education*, **31** (3), 305–26.

Schmid, R. and D. Petko (2019), 'Does the use of educational technology in personalized learning environments correlate with self-reported digital skills and beliefs of secondary-school students?' *Computers & Education*, **136**, 75–86.

Tare, M.P., B. Pape and A.R. Shell (2022), 'Understanding and supporting the whole child: Lessons from the Learner Variability Project', in A.L. Betts and K-P. Thai (eds), *Handbook of Research on Innovative Approaches to Early Childhood Development and School Readiness*, Hershey, PA: IGI Global, pp. 165–89.

UNESCO (2023), *Global Education Monitoring Report 2023: Technology in Education: A Tool on Whose Terms?* Global Education Monitoring Report Team. https://doi.org/10.54676/UZQV8501

UNESCO (2024), *Launch of the Global Alliance on the Science of Learning for Education*. Global Education Coalition. https://glhconnect.unesco.org/launch-global-alliance-science-learning-education

UNESCO, UNICEF, ITU and GPE (2024), *Education Digital Transformation: Framework for System Transformation with Education Technology*. Paris, France.

Westenberg, M.R. and P. Koele (1994), 'Multi-attribute evaluation processes: Methodological and conceptual issues', *Acta Psychologica*, **87** (2–3), 65–84.

PART III

ETHICAL CONSIDERATIONS AND PRIVACY CONCERNS

6. The General Data Protection Regulation's right to explanation of algorithmic decision-making in the context of using AI-powered learning analytics in compulsory education

Małgorzata Agnieszka Cyndecka

INTRODUCTION

The development and use of AI-powered learning and evaluation tools in education create both unprecedented opportunities and numerous risks to pupils' privacy and their right to data protection (Colonna 2021, p. 333). Children are vulnerable data subjects, that is, individuals whose personal data are processed, and the use of AI-based tools usually involves the processing of large amounts of personal data. Personal data are defined as 'any information relating to an identified or identifiable natural person ("data subject")' (GDPR, Article 4(1)). In addition, using AI to process personal data may generate new data about data subjects, including 'special categories' or 'sensitive' personal data, that is 'data revealing racial or ethnic origin, political opinions, religious or philosophical beliefs, or trade union membership, … genetic data, biometric data [when processed] for the purpose of uniquely identifying a natural person, data concerning health or data concerning a natural person's sex life or sexual orientation' (GDPR, Article 9(2)). Such inferred data are also personal data (Article 29 Working Party 2007). Although processing vast amounts of pupils' data by using advanced technology in an educational context may have far-reaching implications (Defend Digital Me2024), children and their parents or guardians do not have the possibility to 'opt-out' from such processing. In general, processing of pupils' personal data in an educational context cannot be based on consent. This is simply because any such consent would not be valid due to not being freely given (European Data Protection Board 2020, p. 8).

From the perspective of data protection, one of the most difficult problems raised by the deployment of AI is the lack of transparency (Datatilsynet 2022) and opaque 'black box' algorithms (Malgieri and Comandé 2017, p. 248). Such a combination increases the risk of undetected machine biases that may have serious consequences for both data subjects and controllers. The latter are entities or persons who either determine the purposes of and means used for the processing of personal data or who simply are denoted as controllers by either EU or national law (GDPR, Article 4(7)). Under the General Data Protection Regulation (GDPR), controllers are responsible for ensuring that the processing of personal data is compliant with the GDPR.

In this respect, it has been argued that the GDPR provides for a 'right to explanation of automated decision-making'. The GDPR is an EU Regulation that governs how one may process personal data of data subjects in the EU/EEA, that is, EU Member States and Norway, Iceland and Liechtenstein. The GDPR entered into force in 2018 and replaced the outdated

Data Protection Directive (DPD) of 1995. Importantly, an EU directive must be transposed into national legislation, and Member States have a certain margin of discretion when implementing a directive. However, an EU Regulation is, as a rule, binding in its entirety in all EU Member States. In the case of the DPD, its transposition into national laws resulted in different levels of data protection in the EU/EEA Member States. The GDPR, among other things, provides the same high level of data protection to all individuals in the EU/EEA unless it explicitly allows for national adjustments or requires supplementary national regulations.

While the GDPR is the strongest privacy law in the world, its right to explanation of algorithmic decisions may seem to be very limited. In the educational context, one could even argue for its virtual non-existence. This is because a strict interpretation of the GDPR provides a right to explanation only with respect to fully automated algorithmic decisions, whilst in most, if not all, cases, there is still a 'teacher in the loop' (Colonna 2024), at least in theory. Such an interpretation may open itself up to a widespread deployment of AI-powered tools in education that are not subject to a right to explanation. At the same time, the GDPR stipulates that children 'merit specific protection with regard to their personal data' (GDPR, Recital 38). Moreover, a successful and safe deployment of AI in education depends on (among others) trust, which in turn requires both transparency (van Drunen, Helberger and Bastian 2019, p. 228) and comprehensibility (Edwards and Veale 2017, p. 67). Currently, '[t]he issue of privacy and data protection has come to the forefront of LA challenges' (Liu and Khalil 2023, p. 1716). Moreover, 'the research … indicates that the absence of transparency can undermine trust and thus hinder LA' (link to be included Liu and Khalil 2023, p. 1726, see also Cormack and Reeve 2022, p. 255).

This chapter aims to present the boundaries of the GDPR's right to explanation of algorithmic decisions in the context of deploying learning analytics (LA), on the basis of which one provides adaptive learning in compulsory education. This concerns pupils under the age of 18, that is, children. In this respect, the next section provides an insight into a legal debate on the GDPR's right to explanation and introduces the key provisions on which this right relies. The third section examines in detail a right to explanation derived from Article 15(1)(h), while the fourth analyses and applies Article 22 to cases of using LA for the purpose of providing adaptive learning in compulsory education. The final section provides conclusions.

A LEGAL DEBATE ON THE GDPR'S RIGHT TO EXPLANATION

Shortly after the GDPR was adopted, in June 2016 Goodman and Flaxman argued that one of the reasons why the GDPR could be considered a 'Copernican revolution in European data protection law' (Kuner 2012) was that the Regulation would 'effectively create a "right to explanation", whereby a user can ask for an explanation of an algorithmic decision that was made about them' (Goodman and Flaxman 2016). That almost sensational claim was met with an immediate and intense critique by Wachter, Mittelstadt and Floridi, who claimed that the GDPR did not provide any such right. One could only argue the existence of a 'right to be informed' (Wachter, Mittelstadt and Floridi 2017, p. 89). Those two contributions have shaped the discourse concerning the GDPR's right to explanation, which is based on interpreting Articles 13–15 and 22 and Recital 71 of the GDPR.

Articles 13 and 14 specify the so-called notification obligation. They determine what information a data subject has the right to receive from a controller. In particular, Articles 13(2)(f) and 14(2)(g) oblige a controller to inform a data subject about

> the existence of automated decision-making, including profiling, referred to in Article 22(1) and (4) and, at least in those cases, *meaningful information about the logic involved, as well as the significance and the envisaged consequences* of such processing for the data subject. (italics added)

Under Article 15, a data subject has the right of access to their personal data. Article 15(1)(h) stipulates that a controller must provide a data subject with information concerning

> the existence of automated decision-making, including profiling, referred to in Article 22(1) and (4) and, at least in those cases, *meaningful information about the logic involved, as well as the significance and the envisaged consequences* of such processing for the data subject. (italics added)

Articles 13–15 refer to automated decision-making as it is defined in Article 22. That provision outlines an individual automated decision, that is, an algorithmic decision, as

> [...] a decision based solely on automated processing, including profiling, which produces legal effects concerning him or her or similarly significantly affects him or her.

As a rule, such decisions are prohibited, but there are exceptions. For example, national law may allow using such decisions (GDPR, Article 22(2)(b)).

Recital 71 of the GDPR addresses individual automated decision-making and provides that

> such processing [of personal data] should be subject to suitable safeguards, which should include specific information to the data subject and the right to obtain human intervention, to express his or her point of view, to obtain an *explanation of the decision reached after such assessment* and to *challenge* the decision. (italics added)

Apparently, only Recital 71 establishes a right to explanation that a data subject is most interested in – that is, an *ex post* explanation of an automated decision concerning him or her. The relevant wording is missing in Articles 13–15. This creates a challenge, since recitals in a preamble to an EU legal act are not legally binding (Case C-162/97, para. 54). Although they provide guidance on how to interpret the relevant provisions of a legal text, they cannot constitute an autonomous source of rights or obligations (Baratta 2014, p. 302).

Following an analysis of Articles 13–15 and 22 and Recital 71, Wachter and others proposed the following two distinctions: explanations of 'system functionality' versus 'specific decisions', and *ex ante* versus *ex post* explanations. According to their terminology, 'system functionality' referred to 'the logic, significance, envisaged consequences, and general functionality of an automated decision-making system', whilst 'specific decisions' referred to 'the rationale, reasons, and individual circumstances of a specific automated decision'. According to Wachter and others, the GDPR provided only a right to an explanation of 'system functionality'. As regards the second distinction, 'in terms of their timing in relation to the decision-making process', one could distinguish between an *ex ante* explanation that 'occurs prior to an automated decision-making taking place' and an *ex post* explanation that 'occurs after an automated decision has taken place'. As Wachter and others claimed, 'an ex ante explanation can logically address only system functionality', whilst 'an ex post explanation can address both system functionality and the rationale of a specific decision' (Wachter, Mittelstadt and Floridi, 2017, p. 78). In their opinion, the GDPR could thus only provide a right to an *ex ante* explanation of system functionality, which they named a 'right to be informed' (Wachter, Mittelstadt and Floridi 2017, p. 89). Both these distinctions have been questioned by some legal scholars (Selbst and Powles 2017, p. 239), while others proposed an approach to overcoming the essential distinction between *ex ante* and *ex post* explanations (Malgieri and Comandé 2017, p. 244).

In 2017, the ongoing academic debate was fuelled by some clarifications provided by the Article 29 Working Party (A29WP) in its *Guidelines on Automated Individual Decision-making and Profiling* (Article 29 Working Party 2017). A29WP was an independent European advisory body on data protection and privacy that was set up under the Data Protection Directive. When the GDPR entered into force, A29WP was replaced by the European Data Protection Board (EDPB). Although not being legally binding, the Guidelines from the EDPB carry significant weight. They represent a position taken by the EU data protection authorities and provide general guidance on interpreting the GDPR, which is one of the main tasks of the EDPB.

In the said Guidelines, which were endorsed by the EDPB, A29WP seemed to have supported the view presented by Wachter and others. According to A29WP (2017), 'arts 13–15 right to 'meaningful information about the logic involved' provides a 'more general form of oversight' rather than 'a right to an explanation of a particular decision'. Moreover,

> the controller should provide the data subject with information about the *envisaged consequences* of the processing, rather than an explanation of a *particular* decision. (italics original; Article 29 Working Party, 2017, p. 27.)

At the same time, however, the controller

> should provide the data subject with general information (notably, on factors taken into account for the decision-making process, and on their respective 'weight' on an aggregate level) which is also useful for him or her to challenge the decision. (Article 29 Working Party 2017, p. 27.)

The position of A29WP and now also the EDPB is thus not entirely clear. As noted by Brkan, A29WP's Guidelines could be interpreted as supporting the existence of the right to an *ex post* explanation (Brkan 2019, p. 114). Whether or not that may be the case is discussed in the next section that analyses the scope of the right to explanation derived from the right of access.

THE BOUNDARIES OF A RIGHT TO EXPLANATION DERIVED FROM THE RIGHT OF ACCESS

This section aims to redefine the right to explanation against the distinctions and limitations drawn by Wachter and others. In this respect, it focuses on two questions: first, does Article 15(1)(h) provide a right to only *ex ante* explanation or also *ex post* explanation? Second, does Article 15(1)(h) provide a right to explanation of only system functionality or also specific decisions?

As regards the first question, when Wachter and others excluded the existence of the right to an *ex post* explanation, they interpreted Articles 13–14 and 15 in the same manner due to their identical wording. As they explained, Articles 13–14 suffer from a 'timeline problem', that is, the required information had to be given to a data subject before starting the processing of his or her personal data. Thus, any explanation had to be *ex ante*. There is, however, no such problem with Article 15 (Mendoza and Bygrave 2017, footnote 47; Brkan 2019, p. 113). This is primarily due to the fact that a data subject can exercise his or her right of access at any time – that is, both before an automated decision is made and afterwards. Still, Wachter and others emphasised the use of the term 'envisaged consequences', which in their opinion made any explanation on the basis of Article 15(1)(h) necessarily future-oriented (Wachter, Mittelstadt and Floridi 2017, p. 83).

A number of scholars criticised Wachter and others' point of view (Selbst and Powles 2017, p. 241; Edwards and Veale 2017, p. 52; Hoeren and Niehoff 2018, p. 315). Malgieri and Comandé successfully dismantled the 'timeline problem' by pointing out that Articles 13 and 14 mention 'the purposes of the processing for which the personal data are intended', which clearly indicates a future-oriented perspective, whilst Article 15 refers to the 'purposes of the processing', which makes this provision neutral with respect to time. As regards the term 'envisaged consequences', Malgieri and Comandé noted that it could

> be read as future-oriented, but only because consequences can also occur much later than a decision that has been taken and often they cannot be predicted by the data controller. At the same time, while the adjective 'envisaged' may seem more future-oriented, the reference to the logic 'involved' may be read as more past-oriented. (Malgieri and Comandé 2017, p. 256.)

Moreover, as pointed out by Mendoza and Bygrave, '[t]he fact that one has a right to information about the "existence" of automated decision making suggests that such decisions already take place' (Mendoza and Bygrave 2017, p. 16).

As one may conclude, Article 15(1)(h) also provides a right to an *ex post* explanation of automated decisions.

As regards the question of whether Article 15(1)(h) provides a right to explanation of only system functionality or also specific decisions, Wachter and others relied on their interpretation of the Data Protection Directive of 1995 and its implementation into national legislations in France, the UK, Germany and Austria (Wachter, Mittelstadt and Floridi 2017, p. 85), as well as on Korff's comparative study of 2010 (Korff 2010). The DPD also included the right to explanation, which, however, was not of so much interest nowadays. According to Wachter and others, 'the implementation of the Directive's right of access strongly suggests that the GDPR's right of access will be far from the ex post 'general' right to explanation of system functionality and specific decisions' (Wachter, Mittelstadt and Floridi, 2017, p. 90).

This is a strong claim that should be examined. As Korff emphasised, the DPD gave the Member States discretion in regulating the right to explanation (Korff 2010, p. 86). The examples of national legislation that Wachter and others relied on demonstrated that a right to explanation only concerned system functionality due to a strict interpretation of the protection of trade secrets or intellectual property. At the same time, however, the authors did not mention that other Member States, while also exercising their discretion, chose to extend 'their' right to explanation. As noted by Korff, Greece, Italy and the Netherlands 'extend[ed] this right to all kinds of automated decisions, that is, not just the ones involving an 'evaluation' of a person's 'personal aspects', that is, profiling, which is also mentioned in Article 22. In Ireland, 'the right to information about the "logic" used in any processing by automatic means of data on the data subject [applied] if this processing ... constituted or [was] likely to constitute the sole basis for any decision significantly affecting him or her'. Portugal extended the right in question to 'any automatic processing of data concerning the data subject' (Korff 2010, p. 86). As a result, the implementation and interpretation of the DPD do not provide any final answer as regards the scope of the right to explanation.

Moreover, as mentioned above, A29WP's *Guidelines on Automated Individual Decision-making and Profiling* require that the controller informs a data subject about

> (notably ... factors taken into account for the decision-making process, and on their respective *'weight'* on an aggregate level) which is also useful for him or her to challenge the decision. (italics added)

This requirement has been recently emphasised by Advocate General Pikamäe before the Court of Justice of the EU (Case C-634/21). The case in question concerned SCHUFA, the leading German private credit reference agency. It revolved around the question of whether SCHUFA's automated creation of a credit score, on the basis of which a credit institution decides whether or not to grant a loan to an individual, is an independent automated decision within the meaning of Article 22 GDPR. In this very first judgment on automated decision-making within the meaning of Article 22 GDPR, the Advocate General (AG) clarified that 'the real objective of Article 15(1)(h) of the GDPR is to ensure that data subjects obtain information in an intelligible and accessible form in accordance with their needs' (Case C-634/21, para. 27). In his view, 'those requirements exclude any obligation to disclose the algorithm, given its complexity. The benefit of communicating a particularly complex formula without providing the necessary explanations for it would be questionable'. AG Pikamäe drew attention to Recital 58 GDPR, which requires that information given to a data subject is 'concise, easily accessible and easy to understand, and that clear and plain language' is used. 'This is of particular relevance in situations where the proliferation of actors and the technological complexity of practice make it difficult for the data subject to know and understand whether, by whom and for what purpose personal data relating to him or her are being collected'. As a result, the AG concluded that 'the obligation to provide 'meaningful information about the logic involved' must be understood to include sufficiently detailed explanations of the method used to calculate the score and the reasons for a certain result' (Case C-634/21, para. 57).

AG Pikamäe's examination of Article 15(1)(h) is highly relevant, as he emphasised the perspective of the data subject by drawing attention to what information it is actually necessary to provide in order to provide an explanation that is meaningful. The distinction between 'system functionality' and 'specific decisions', as established by Wachter and others, focuses on the controller's perspective. They argued that an explanation of 'system functionality' included, among others, the 'system's requirements specification, decision trees, pre-defined models, criteria, and classification structures' (Wachter, Mittelstadt and Floridi 2017, p. 78). Such information seems to be hardly 'meaningful' from the perspective of an ordinary data subject who should be able to decide whether he or she will challenge the decision in question. A 'meaningful' explanation will instead require an explanation of how the different factors have been weighed against each other, which is an explanation of a specific decision in terms introduced by Wachter and others.

Interestingly, it appears that the EDPB may have recently modified its stance as regards the distinction between 'system functionality' and 'specific decisions' when compared to

A29WP's position in its Guidelines on automated individual decisions. In its *Guidelines on Data Subject Rights – Right of Access* (European Data Protection Board, 2022, para. 121), the EDPB stated as follows:

> Art. 15(1)(h) provides that every data subject should have the right to be informed, in a meaningful way, inter alia, about the existence and underlying logic of automated decision-making including profiling concerning the data subject and about the significance and the envisaged consequences that such processing could have. *If possible, information under Art. 15(1)(h) has to be more specific in relation to the reasoning that lead* [sic] *to specific decisions concerning the data subject who asked for access.* (italics added)

Finally, Wachter and others limited the right to explanation by referring to trade secrets (Wachter, Mittelstadt and Floridi 2017, p. 89). Indeed, in a legal debate, claims for providing a more specific explanation under Article 15(1)(h) are almost immediately met by the argument of protecting trade secrets and intellectual property that are mentioned in Recital 63 of the GDPR. It provides that the right of access

> should not adversely affect the rights or freedoms of others, including trade secrets or intellectual property and in particular the copyright protecting the software. However, the result of those considerations *should not be a refusal to provide all information to the data subject.* (italics added)

Yet, Wachter and others seem to disregard the latter sentence of Recital 63. Moreover, as noted by Bygrave, 'recitals 34 and 35 of the EU Directive on Trade Secrets (Directive (EU) 2016/943) essentially state that the trade secrets protections laid down therein must not ride roughshod over the data protection rights of persons whose personal data are processed by a trade secret holder, in particular their information access rights' (Bygrave 2020b, p. 19).

As one should add, Recital 4 GDPR emphasises that

> the right to the protection of personal data is not an absolute right; it must be considered in relation to its function in society and be *balanced* against other fundamental rights, in accordance with the *principle of proportionality.* (italics added)

The conflicting rights or freedoms must thus be balanced against each other, which requires a case-by-case assessment. The right to data protection must thus be balanced against the right to intellectual property. This approach is also taken by the EDPB in the said Guidelines (European Data Protection Board, 2022, para.173).

As one may conclude, the distinction between 'system functionality' and 'specific decisions' is not helpful in delineating the boundaries of a right to explanation derived from Article 15(1)(h), as it disregards the requirement of providing 'meaningful information' to a data subject. It should thus be abandoned. While it is difficult to establish what information should be provided in order to be 'meaningful', one may be sure that disclosing an algorithm is not an option. It would not only easily impinge on the protection of trade secrets or intellectual property, but it would also be pointless. This is because it would not amount to providing 'meaningful information about the logic involved'. As a result, the level of detail when providing the information required under Article 15(1)(h) depends on a given case or rather, given processing. In this respect, van Drunen and others argued for a contextual right to explanation (van Drunen, Helberger and Bastian 2019, p. 224). In any case, it is the perspective of a data subject that should be taken into account. That data subject may also possess specific characteristics, such as young age, which need to be considered when providing 'meaningful information'.

ARTICLE 22 AUTOMATED DECISIONS IN THE CONTEXT OF USING LEARNING ANALYTICS TO PROVIDE ADAPTIVE LEARNING

Having shed some light on the right to explanation derived from Article 15(1)(h), it is necessary to clarify what the automated decisions are that are subject to that right. According to Article 22, an automated decision must meet the following cumulative conditions. First, there needs to be an individual decision. Second, that decision must be 'based solely on automated processing, including profiling'. Third, that decision must either 'produce legal effects concerning' a given data subject or 'similarly significantly affect him or her'. This section examines and applies these conditions in the context of deploying learning analytics (LA) to provide adaptive learning. Importantly, a similar exercise with respect to automatic assessment systems was carried out by Colonna, who thoroughly examined the potential of Article 22 (Colonna 2024).

As noted, an Article 22 decision must be an *individual* decision – that is, it cannot concern a group of data subjects (Brkan 2019, p. 99; Colonna 2024, p. 9). In this regard, adaptive learning provides personalised learning by meeting the individual needs of pupils.

As regards the condition of the *decision*, the GDPR does not define this notion. As noted by Mendoza and Bygrave, it 'means essentially that a particular attitude or stance is taken towards a person and this attitude/stance has some degree of binding effect in the sense that it is likely to be acted upon' (Mendoza and Bygrave 2017, p. 10). A notion of decision undoubtedly 'covers official acts of authorities that provide a determination or ruling on a matter with legal effects on those persons covered or targeted by the determination/ruling', but is not limited to such acts. Whilst there is no requirement concerning the form a decision must take, as Bygrave noted, it needs to 'be sufficiently formal to be distinguished from other stages that prepare, support, complement or head off decision-making' (Bygrave 2020a, p. 532). This assumption should be modified given the SCHUFA judgment, whereby the Court of Justice ruled that the notion of decision should be understood as also including a fully automated part of the final decision if such a part plays a determining role in the decision (Case C-634/21, para. 48). This clarification may be considered a game-changer, as it effectively extended the notion of Article 22 decisions to include certain decisions preceding a final Article 22 decision. Although this clarification strengthens a data subject's right to data protection, it may be difficult to implement in practice. In the SCHUFA judgment, the bank 'drew strongly' on the scoring provided by SCHUFA. The question is how to interpret that in a given case.

In a classroom, as a rule, it is the teacher who decides how the process of learning is organised and is responsible for that process, whilst the pupils are supposed to follow the given instructions. In this respect, teachers may choose to use adaptive learning as a decision-support system. This situation mirrors the situation in SCHUFA, where banks to a certain extent rely on the scoring provided by SCHUFA. Given the clarification given by the Court of Justice, the question is to what extent a teacher relies on the 'advice' provided by the given system. Most importantly, however, in order to qualify SCHUFA's scoring as an Article 22 decision, the relevant bank's decision did not have to fall within the scope of that provision (Case C-634/21, para. 63). As a result, one may identify two types of automated decisions that may fall within the scope of Article 22: the one 'made' by an algorithm and the one taken by a teacher.

As regards the requirement of being 'based solely on automated processing, including profiling', it raises two questions. First, must an Article 22 decision necessarily involve profiling? The answer is no. Profiling may be included, but does not have to be (Brkan 2019, p. 96; Bygrave 2020b, p. 16). In practice, however, most Article 22 decisions will involve profiling. In the case of using learning analytics for the purpose of providing adaptive learning, profiling is necessarily involved. Within the meaning of the GDPR, profiling aims to 'evaluate certain personal aspects relating to a natural person, in particular to analyse or predict aspects concerning that natural person's performance' (GDPR, Article 4(4)). This is precisely what happens with personal data when adaptive learning adjusts and personalises the learning process.

The second question concerns the requirement of a decision being 'based solely' on automated processing. According to A29WP, an Article 22 decision must be made without any human involvement in the decision process. As Mendoza and Bygrave specified, 'Even if a decision is formally ascribed to a person, it is to be regarded as based solely on automated processing if a person does not actively assess the result of the processing prior to its formalisation as a decision' (Mendoza and Bygrave 2017, p. 11). Human involvement, however, requires that the controller ensures that 'any oversight of the decision is meaningful, rather than just a token gesture. It should be carried out by someone who has the authority and competence to change the decision. As part of the analysis, they should consider all the relevant data' (Article 29 Working Party 2017, p. 21). Thus, a nominal involvement of a human in a decision-making process is not sufficient to bring a given decision outside the general prohibition stipulated by Article 22 (Wachter, Mittelstadt and Floridi 2017, p. 88).

In the context of adaptive learning based on learning analytics, a decision 'made' by an algorithm fulfils the requirement in question. As regards a decision made by a teacher, one must consider the role and position of teachers. Teachers' formal authority to change a decision is rather undisputed. Yet, as noted by Colonna when discussing automated assessment systems, it 'is unclear who bears the burden of proof to show that formal authority exists to change a grade and what type of evidence is required to meet the burden of proof' (Colonna 2024, p. 11). In this respect, however, it may be argued that the principle of accountability points towards controllers being responsible for proving that the authority exists. However, it remains to be seen what evidence is sufficient in this respect.

Furthermore, given the size of the workload and the lack of time, the question is whether teachers actually have the possibility to critically review a decision that has been 'made' by an algorithm. Such a possibility may rely on both a single teacher's situation in a classroom and the existence of any institutional incentives to review that decision. In the Norwegian AVT project, which explored data protection challenges raised by the use of learning analytics for the purpose of providing adaptive learning, the Norwegian Data Protection Authority (Datatilsynet) stressed the importance of 'developing procedures and training users on how to use the system, how it works and what the system's recommendations are based on' (Datatilsynet 2022). Such training is also crucial in light of the requirement of being able to 'consider all the relevant data'. Teachers must have access to all relevant information and understand how the relevant algorithmic decision-making works (Colonna 2024, p. 12). Importantly, that will depend not only on teachers' competence and confidence in their own assessments but also the transparency of the system that 'makes' decisions.

As regards a decision 'producing legal effects', A29WP clarified that such a decision must affect 'someone's legal rights, such as the freedom to associate with others, vote in an election or take legal action. A legal effect may also be something that affects a person's legal status or their rights under a contract'. In this respect, A29WP referred to the examples of a 'cancellation of a contract; entitlement to or denial of a particular social benefit granted by law, such as child or housing benefit; refused admission to a country or denial of citizenship' (Article 29 Working Party 2017, p. 21). As regards the alternative of having a similarly significant effect, A29WP explained that 'the threshold for significance must be similar to that of a decision producing a legal effect' (Article 29 Working Party 2017, p. 21). Recital 71 provides the examples of 'automatic refusal of an online credit application' and 'e-recruiting practices without any human intervention'. In order to significantly affect a data subject, 'the effects of the processing must be sufficiently great or important to be worthy of attention'. As A29WP (2017) elaborated, 'the decision must have the potential to: significantly affect the circumstances, behaviour or choices of the individuals concerned; have a prolonged or permanent impact on the data subject; or at its most extreme, lead to the exclusion or discrimination of individuals'. Although having difficulties with explaining what would meet the threshold of being sufficiently significant or non-trivial, A29WP (2017) provided the following examples:

> decisions that affect someone's financial circumstances, such as their eligibility to credit; decisions that affect someone's access to health services; decisions that deny someone an employment opportunity or put them at a serious disadvantage; decisions that affect someone's access to education, for example, university admissions.

Interestingly, as A29WP clarified, although online advertising will, as a rule, not have a similarly significant effect on individuals, it is possible that it may do. That would depend on, among other things, 'the intrusiveness of the profiling process, including the tracking of individuals across different websites, devices and services; the expectations and wishes of the individuals concerned; the way the advert is delivered; or using knowledge of the vulnerabilities of the data subjects targeted'. Importantly, it is argued that legal or similarly significant effects should be adverse (Tambou 2023, p. 533).

It is rather uncontroversial to argue that a deployment of learning analytics for the purposes of adaptive learning does not lead to any legal effects that would impact pupils. The question is whether the alternative criterion may be met. Although the example of affecting a data subject's access to education obviously has the potential of having a 'similarly significant effect', the case of learning analytics being used for adaptive learning is far less obvious. Yet, by analogy to the case of online advertising having a strong impact on certain data subjects, one could argue that some pupils may be particularly vulnerable. This could involve pupils with learning disabilities, such as dyslexia or dyscalculia or having substantial learning gaps, for different reasons. In their case, making good progress is particularly important to their further education or even employment opportunities, although it may be difficult to argue a 'similarly significant effect' with respect to every pupil.

Another reason why the use of learning analytics may seem to lack a 'similarly significant effect' in general is that many decisions 'made' by an algorithm may appear trivial – for example, when the system selects the next mathematics assignment to be solved by a given pupil. But what if the algorithm 'makes decisions' about mathematics assignments during a whole month or a semester? Should one assess the significance of such 'decisions' in light of their aggregated influence over time? If adaptive learning can produce many benefits to pupils, it could probably also produce negative results. In this respect, one important factor would be the involvement of AI-based tools in the process of learning for a given pupil, which is decided by a teacher. This would require a case-by-case assessment, which may be challenging.

As demonstrated above, the question of whether the use of learning analytics for the purposes of adaptive learning could amount to taking Article 22 decisions requires a case-by-case assessment. In this respect, the recent SCHUFA judgment might change the business conditions not only for credit institutions but also for educational institutions, such as schools and universities. In this respect, one of the obligations controllers will have to meet would be providing an explanation of algorithmic decision-making.

CONCLUSION

This chapter demonstrated that the GDPR's right to explanation derived from Article 15(1)(h) is not as limited as it would appear. It does cover *ex post* explanations of specific decisions, although what information needs to be provided will depend on a case-by-case assessment. In this respect, one should mention that Article 12 GDPR requires that a controller's communication with a data subject is in 'a concise, transparent, intelligible and easily accessible form, using clear and plain language'. This concerns, 'in particular … any information addressed specifically to a child'. This raises another important question: how one should communicate with pupils in order to provide 'meaningful information' about an algorithmic decision concerning them.

An important limitation to the right to explanation is, however, a strict interpretation of Article 22. Although the recent case law provided for a very welcome clarification and strengthening of the right to explanation, it remains to be seen how the new interpretation of Articles 15(1)(h) and 22 GDPR will work in practice. As one may point out, the Court of Justice of the EU provided its very first interpretation of Article 22 in 2023, eight(!) years after the GDPR was adopted. In the case of learning analytics and using AI-powered tools in an educational context, trust is essential. A proper use of the right to explanation may be the key to a successful deployment of new tools in schools.

REFERENCES

Article 29 Working Party (2007), Opinion 4/2007 on the concept of personal data, WP136. Retrieved from https://www.clinicalstudydatarequest.com/Documents/Privacy-European-guidance.pdf

Article 29 Working Party (2017), Guidelines on automated individual decision-making and profiling for the purposes of Regulation 2016/679, WP251. Retrieved from https://ec.europa.eu/newsroom/article29/items/612053/en

Baratta, R. (2014), 'Complexity of EU law in the domestic implementing process', *The Theory and Practice of Legislation,* **2** (3), 293–308. https://www.tandfonline.com/doi/epdf/10.5235/12050-8840.2.3.293?needAccess=true

Brkan, M. (2019), 'Do algorithms rule the world? Algorithmic decision-making and data protection in the framework of the GDPR and beyond', *International Journal of Law and Information Technology,* **27** (2), 91–121. https://doi.org/10.1093/ijlit/eay017

Bygrave, L.A. (2020a), Article 22. Automated individual decision-making, including profiling, in C. Kuner, L.A. Bygrave and C. Docksey (eds), *The EU General Data Protection Regulation (GDPR). A Commentary,* Oxford University Press, pp. 522–42.

Bygrave, L.A. (2020b), 'Machine learning, cognitive sovereignty and data protection rights with respect to automated decisions', Version 2.0. University of Oslo Faculty of Law Research Paper No. 2020-35. Retrieved from https://ssrn.com/abstract=3721118

Case C-162/97. Nilsson ECLI:EU:C:1998:554

Case C-634/21. SCHUFA ECLI:EU:C:2023:957

Colonna, L. (2021), 'The AI regulation and higher education: Preliminary observations and critical perspectives', in K. de Vries and M. Dahlberg (eds), *Law, AI and Digitalisation*, Juridiska Fakulteten i Uppsala, pp. 333–56.

Colonna, L. (2024), 'Teachers in the loop? An analysis of automatic assessment systems under Article 22 GDPR', *International Data Privacy Law*, **14** (1), 3–18. https://doi.org/10.1093/idpl/ipad024

Cormack, A.N. and D. Reeve (2022), 'Developing a code of practice for using data in wellbeing support', *Journal of Learning Analytics*, **9** (2), 1–12. https://doi.org/10.18608/jla.2022.7533

Data Protection Directive (DPD): Directive 95/46/EC of the European Parliament and of the Council of 24 October 1995 on the protection of individuals with regard to the processing of personal data and on the free movement of such data, OJ L 281, 23.11.1995, pp. 31–50.

Datatilsynet (2022), 'AVT exit report'. Retrieved from https://www.datatilsynet.no/contentassets/e61e90f5d245459d813ad1116ccee887/avt_exit-report.pdf

Defend Digital Me (2024), 'Labels last a lifetime. Commitments for a rights respecting digital environment in state education'. Retrieved from https://defenddigitalme.org/wp-content/uploads/2024/06/Defend-Digital-Me-manifesto-2024-v2.0-1.pdf

Directive (EU) 2016/943 of the European Parliament and of the Council of 8 June 2016 on the protection of undisclosed know-how and business information (trade secrets) against their unlawful acquisition, use and disclosure, OJL157, 15.6.2016, pp. 1–18.

Edwards, L. and M. Veale (2017), 'Slave to the algorithm? Why a "right to an explanation" is probably not the remedy you are looking for', *Duke Law and Technology Review*, **18**, 18–84. https://dx.doi.org/10.2139/ssrn.2972855

European Data Protection Board (2020), 'Guidelines 05/2020 on consent under Regulation 2016/679'. Retrieved from https://www.edpb.europa.eu/sites/default/files/files/file1/edpb_guidelines_202005_consent_en.pdf

European Data Protection Board (2022), 'Guidelines 01/2022 on data subject rights – right of access'. Retrieved from https://www.edpb.europa.eu/system/files/2023-04/edpb_guidelines_202201_data_subject_rights_access_v2_en.pdf

GDPR: Regulation (EU) 2016/679 of the European Parliament and of the Council of 27 April 2016 on the protection of natural persons with regard to the processing of personal data and on the free movement of such data, and repealing Directive 95/46/EC (General Data Protection Regulation), OJ L 119, 4.5.2016, pp. 1–88.

Goodman, B. and S. Flaxman (2016), 'EU regulations on algorithmic decision making and "a Right to an Explanation"'. https://doi.org/10.48550/arXiv.1606.08813

Hoeren, T. and M. Niehoff (2018), 'Artificial intelligence in medical diagnoses and the right to explanation', *European Data Protection Law Review*, **4** (3), 308–19. https://doi.org/10.21552/edpl/2018/3/9

Korff, D. (2010), 'Comparative study on different approaches to new privacy challenges, in particular in the light of technological developments', Working Paper no. 2: Data protection laws in the EU: The difficulties in meeting the challenges posed by global social and technical developments, European Commission, Directorate-General for Justice, Freedom and Security, Centre for Public Reform.

Kuner, C. (2012), 'The European Commission's proposed data protection regulation: A Copernican revolution in European data protection law', *Bloomberg BNA Privacy and Security Law Report*, pp. 1–15. Retrieved from https://ssrn.com/abstract=2162781

Liu, Q. and M. Khalil (2023), 'Understanding privacy and data protection issues in learning analytics using a systematic review', *British Journal of Educational Technology*, **54** (6), 1715–47. https://doi.org/10.1111/bjet.13388

Malgieri, G. and G. Comandé (2017), 'Why a right to legibility of automated decision-making exists in the General Data Protection Regulation', *International Data Privacy Law*, **7** (4), 243–65. https://doi.org/10.1093/idpl/ipx019

Mendoza, I. and L.A. Bygrave (2017), 'The right not to be subject to automated decisions based on profiling', University of Oslo Faculty of Law Research Paper No. 2017-20. Retrieved from https://ssrn.com/abstract=2964855

Selbst, A.D. and J. Powles (2017), 'Meaningful information and the right to explanation', *International Data Privacy Law*, **7** (4), 233–42. https://doi.org/10.1093/idpl/ipx022

Tambou, O. (2023), 'Article 22 Automated individual decision-making, including profiling', in I. Spiecker gen. Döhmann, V. Papakonstantinou, G. Hornung and P. De Hert (eds), *General Data Protection Regulation. Article-by-Article Commentary,* Nomos-Beck-Hart, pp. 525–42.

van Drunen, M.Z., N. Helberger and M. Bastian (2019), 'Know your algorithm: What media organizations need to explain to their users about news personalization', *International Data Privacy Law*, **9** (4), 220–35. https://doi.org/10.1093/idpl/ipz011

Wachter, S., B. Mittelstadt and L. Floridi (2017), 'Why a right to explanation of automated decision-making does not exist in the General Data Protection Regulation', *International Data Privacy Law*, **7** (2), 76–99. https://doi.org/10.1093/idpl/ipx005

7. Smart predictions, unseen bias: navigating the promises and pitfalls of predictive analytics in compulsory education

Lin Li

INTRODUCTION

Predictive analytics refers to the use of statistical algorithms and machine learning techniques to analyse historical data and forecast future outcomes (Larose 2015). In educational settings, predictive analytics typically involves modelling data collected from various sources to predict a wide range of student outcomes, either long-term or short-term, such as identifying at-risk students who might drop out of school or a specific course (Bayer 2021), forecasting future academic performance (Seidel 2017) or even predicting student engagement with learning materials (Hussain 2018). Most commonly available data sources in education include routinely administered data by institutions related to learning and teaching – such as academic records, attendance logs and behavioural indicators – as well as static personal data, such as demographic characteristics like gender and language background (Fischer 2020). Empowered by the advancement of educational technology, richer and more granular data have become increasingly accessible. These include digital learning traces that capture how students navigate and engage with instructional content (for example, video views, page clicks and time spent on tasks) (Pardos 2014; Patikorn 2020), logs of their participation in online discussions and collaborative forums (Hecking 2016; Andresen 2009), as well as their responses and performance in formative assessments administered through digital platforms (Fancsali 2018). Together, these expanded data sources enhance the scope and precision of predictive models, enabling educators and institutions to make more proactive, data-informed and personalized decisions that support student learning and development across diverse educational contexts.

While predictive analytics has found widespread use in higher education and post-secondary settings, its potential within compulsory education, which includes primary and secondary schooling, remains under-explored (Kovanovic 2021). Most of the research and practical applications of predictive analytics in education have been concentrated in higher education, where greater access to data and institutional resources enables the use of more complex models. However, the foundation for a student's future academic trajectory is largely set during their compulsory schooling years (Geary 2013). Early identification of at-risk students – those showing signs of academic struggle, behavioural issues or disengagement – presents a crucial opportunity for timely interventions that can positively alter their educational path. As demonstrated in higher education contexts, predictive analytics has the potential to identify students at risk of falling behind, dropping out or struggling with specific learning challenges at an earlier stage (Baer 2017; Yu 2020). By extending this capability to compulsory education, educators and institutions can be empowered to take proactive steps in supporting students before challenges escalate.

However, the promise of predictive analytics must be tempered with caution, particularly regarding fairness (Caton 2024). Predictive models are only as fair as the data and assumptions underpinning them. When sensitive attributes such as gender, language background or socioeconomic status are closely tied to educational outcomes in historical data, predictive models may encode and reproduce systemic inequities rather than reflect students' actual competencies. This concern becomes especially critical when predictions inform high-stakes decisions, such as resource allocation, academic tracking or targeted interventions. These risks are heightened in compulsory education, where students tend to be younger and more developmentally vulnerable. In this context, biased predictions might deeply affect students' academic identities, expectations and opportunities (Kizilcec 2022). Thus, fairness is not merely a technical concern but a pressing ethical responsibility in the use of predictive analytics in compulsory education.

This chapter examines the evolving landscape of predictive analytics in compulsory education, with a particular focus on understanding the risks of bias and unfairness in predictive models. It begins with an overview of how predictive analytics is being utilized across both primary and secondary school contexts. The chapter then introduces the foundational processes and practical considerations for examining and addressing predictive bias. By reviewing key definitions of fairness in educational prediction and outlining strategies for mitigating bias, it offers a critical lens on how predictive systems can be responsibly measured, designed and applied to support more equitable student outcomes. Together, these sections provide a comprehensive framework for understanding where and how predictive bias arises in compulsory education and what can be done to minimize its impact, ensuring that predictive technologies serve to advance, rather than undermine, educational equity.

PROMISES OF PREDICTIVE ANALYTICS IN COMPULSORY EDUCATION

Compulsory education (Rothbard 1979; Stephens Jr 2014) refers to the period of education that is legally required for children, typically covering primary and lower secondary education. The age range and duration of compulsory education can vary by country, but it generally encompasses the foundational years of schooling, from early childhood education through to the early stages of secondary school (Diffey 2017; Albouy 2009). Given the widespread adoption and demonstrated success of predictive analytics in enhancing teaching and learning across diverse educational contexts, institutions within compulsory education have increasingly sought to harness available data to improve student outcomes. This makes the discussion of its potential and opportunities within compulsory education both timely and increasingly relevant.

It should be noted that within the span of compulsory education, educational goals, pedagogical approaches and data availability can vary significantly across different developmental stages (Eccles 1999). For instance, the early years of primary education tend to focus on foundational literacy, numeracy and social-emotional development, often with limited formal data collection (Bakken 2017; Essa 2019). In contrast, the later years of primary and lower secondary education involve more structured assessments and academic tracking, resulting in richer data sources that are more conducive to predictive modelling (Bastian 2020). As such, any application of predictive analytics in compulsory education must be sensitive to these developmental differences, tailoring methods and objectives to align with the specific needs and contexts of each stage. In the following sections, we explore how predictive analytics is being applied across different stages of compulsory education, with particular attention to the types of data available, the predictive tasks being pursued and the educational objectives they serve. By examining both current practices and emerging opportunities, we highlight how data-driven approaches can be adapted to support diverse learning needs – from early detection of developmental delays in younger children to proactive academic interventions in middle school. This stage-sensitive perspective underscores the importance of aligning predictive strategies with the unique characteristics of each phase within compulsory education.

Data Availability

The types of data available for predictive analytics in compulsory education vary across different stages, reflecting both the developmental needs of students and the growing sophistication of data collection systems. At each stage, educational institutions gather different forms of data, ranging from basic administrative records to more unique and complex data specific to particular educational contexts.

Across all stages of compulsory education, schools routinely collect foundational administrative data of students that form the basis for many predictive modelling efforts (Papamitsiou 2014; Van Barneveld 2012), which typically include the following categories (Innovare SIP 2023).

- *Demographic and Background Characteristics*, including students' age, gender, socioeconomic status, ethnicity and language(s) spoken at home. These attributes help contextualize learning patterns and identify disparities, but they must be used cautiously to avoid reinforcing existing biases in predictive models.
- *Academic Achievement Data*, such as classroom assessments, yearly report grades and standardized test scores. While classroom-level data may vary in consistency and comparability across schools, standardized assessments often provide more structured benchmarks for tracking progress over time – especially in the later years of compulsory education.
- *Behavioural and Social–Emotional Indicators*, which may include documentation of disciplinary incidents, notes on classroom behaviour and teacher observations of social-emotional development. These indicators offer insights into students' non-academic experiences in school, which can be predictive of long-term engagement and success.
- *Engagement Indicators*, are most commonly represented through attendance records, but also include participation in extracurricular activities or school events. These proxies for school connection and motivation are often used in early warning systems to flag students who may be at risk of disengagement.

These basic data types are typically available across all stages of compulsory education and form the foundation of most early predictive models. They serve as a practical and scalable resource, offering essential information for identifying patterns and generating broad insights into student progress, particularly in contexts where more granular, real-time or learning-specific data is limited or unavailable. It is important to note that academic performance in compulsory education is assessed through a combination of informal, observation-based methods and formal, standardized assessments, with the emphasis on each approach varying depending on the educational context and purpose. In the early years of primary education, academic performance data often focus on foundational literacy and numeracy skills, primarily recorded through teacher observations and informal assessments (Bakken 2017; DeLuca 2014). These approaches are more qualitative in nature, emphasizing holistic and developmental perspectives. From around Year or Grade 3 onwards, schools typically introduce standardized assessments, providing more structured and comparable measures of learning progress (Wood 2016; Dowley 2022). By lower secondary education, subject-specific teaching becomes more prominent and students' performance is systematically tracked through formal assignments, exams and projects in subjects such as mathematics, science and languages (Lee 1995).

Except for these commonly administered data in educational institutions, different stages of compulsory education may have additional, more stage-specific types of data available. For example, in the early years of primary education, observational data on social–emotional development, student behaviours and classroom interactions may also be collected to support a holistic understanding of a child's development (Heller 2012). While invaluable for identifying early learning challenges or developmental delays, such data may not readily lend itself to scalable predictive modelling due to its qualitative, subjective and context-specific nature. As students progress, particularly in the later primary years and lower secondary education, the use of digital learning tools becomes increasingly prevalent. In real-world practices, platforms such as *MATHia* (Anderson 1995) and *ASSISTments* (Heffernan 2014) have been adopted in several middle school contexts to support personalized learning and formative assessment. Different from *MATHia* and *ASSISTments*, which are specifically designed to support formal educational settings, there are also platforms such as Khan Academy (Thompson 2011) originally developed as non-profit, open-access resources aimed at supporting student learning outside of the traditional classroom. These platforms have also emerged as supplementary tools that educators and schools can leverage to reinforce instruction, provide additional practice or support individualized learning beyond the constraints of the formal curriculum. Data collection enabled by the use of all these platforms offers opportunities to capture rich, interaction-level data, including time on task, hint usage, response latency and engagement with feedback, that offer deeper insights into students' learning behaviours and cognitive engagement.

However, it is important to highlight that the availability and usage of such technology-derived data can vary significantly across families, schools, regions and countries, depending on differences in technological infrastructure and access (Afzal 2023). For example, intelligent tutoring systems like *MATHia* and *ASSISTments* have been primarily used in US-based schools, while non-profit platforms such as Khan Academy, despite being low-cost and accessible worldwide, still require reliable internet access, which also limits the availability of data, especially those from under-resourced areas. Even within the same region or school, such divides in access to digital learning resources exist between well-funded and poorly funded schools, as well as between high-income and low-income families.

Key Predictive Tasks in Current Practices

With increasing data availability, various predictive tasks have emerged that aim to leverage available data to improve educational outcomes. These tasks are designed to support early intervention, inform instructional strategies and enhance long-term academic success. Below, we discuss some of the key predictive tasks in compulsory education and highlight their current applications at different stages of compulsory education.

One of the most widely used applications of predictive analytics in compulsory education, particularly in the lower secondary stage, is early warning systems designed to identify students at risk of dropping out of high schools (Baker 2020; Roberts 2019). Earlier efforts to identify at-risk students often relied heavily on static demographic characteristics – such as race, gender or parental income, which, while statistically correlated with educational outcomes, frequently proved insufficient or even misleading when used in isolation (Roberts 2019). By contrast, predictive analytics enables a shift towards using more dynamic and behaviour-based indicators. A widely adopted approach in this space involves the use of the ABC indicators – Attendance, Behaviour and Course performance – which have consistently demonstrated strong predictive power for long-term educational outcomes (Roberts 2019). Predictive models trained on these indicators can detect subtle risk signals, such as declining attendance trends or dips in academic performance, well before such issues become visible through traditional monitoring. These predictions form the backbone of early warning systems that enable timely, targeted interventions – ranging from academic tutoring to behavioural support or mentoring – designed to keep students on track. By enabling more proactive, data-driven decision-making, predictive analytics enhances educators' ability to allocate resources efficiently and support students before challenges escalate into long-term consequences. In addition to predictive tasks based on traditional administrative data, the integration of digital learning tools such as *ASSISTments* has opened new avenues for predictive analytics. These tools collect fine-grained, real-time data as students interact with learning content, offering deeper insights into student learning processes. For example, clickstream data, time-on-task, hint request and response accuracy patterns provide rich information that can be used to predict not only academic achievement (Feng 2006; Junker 2006) but also uncover students' learning behaviour patterns (Pardos 2014; Huang 2024). Such data allow for more personalized models that reflect students' day-to-day learning behaviours and cognitive patterns, expanding the potential of predictive analytics beyond summative performance to real-time formative insights.

By contrast, in the primary school setting, predictive analytics remains relatively underdeveloped. Its potential to support and improve student learning outcomes is only beginning to be explored. At this stage, teachers are tasked with cultivating students' foundational skills – such as early literacy and numeracy – while also fostering their social and emotional development (Darling-Hammond 2020). These responsibilities often coincide with high workloads and limited resources, making efficient, targeted support difficult to deliver (Bull 2024; United Workers Union 2021). Predictive analytics presents a promising opportunity to alleviate this burden by offering data-informed tools that assist educators in identifying students who may benefit from additional support. However, to date, most research in primary education has been exploratory and correlational, focusing on identifying associations between student-related factors – such as demographics, executive functioning skills or home environments – and academic outcomes (Pazeto 2020; Ricciardi 2021; Carmichael 2014). While valuable, these studies do not generally employ predictive modelling techniques capable of generating actionable forecasts for classroom use. As such, they fall short of what is typically recognized as predictive analytics.

Emerging Use of Predictive Analytics

In the context of compulsory education, where students' development is both cumulative and dynamic, continuous monitoring plays a critical role. Unlike in higher education, where predictive efforts often target discrete outcomes such as graduation or course completion, compulsory education requires sustained attention to students' ongoing academic and developmental progress. Educators must continuously track growth, detect early signs of learning difficulties and adjust instruction to respond to each student's evolving needs. Consequently, some of the most impactful applications of predictive analytics in this context are those that move beyond static classifications – such as 'at-risk' vs. 'not at-risk' – and instead employ regression-based models that offer continuous, individualized forecasts of student performance.

One particularly promising avenue for supporting such ongoing monitoring is the use of routinely administered student data collected during the flow of everyday instruction. When harnessed through predictive models, these data can generate timely insights that help identify students in need of additional support and flag instructional practices that may be misaligned with students' learning needs. For example, one recent study (Li 2024) demonstrated how predictive analytics can be used to model students' formative assessment performance in the early years of schooling to forecast their outcomes on later high-stakes national assessments. Unlike summative assessments such as standardized tests that occur infrequently and provide retrospective snapshots of learning, formative assessments are integrated into daily classroom activities and yield real-time, low-stakes feedback on student understanding. This could include data from quizzes, in-class exercises, practice tasks and digital learning platforms. As shown in the study (Li 2024), when incorporated into predictive models, these data can explain substantial variance in later performance, enabling early identification of students at risk of underperforming and providing teachers with actionable insights for timely, targeted instructional adjustments.

FROM PROMISE TO PITFALLS: ASSESSING PREDICTIVE BIAS

Beyond the promises and anticipated benefits, the risks of predictive analytics, especially its potential to perpetuate or even amplify existing inequalities, have become pressing concerns when applied to educational scenarios (Li 2023), as these predictions are often used to support high-stakes decisions related to students, such as admissions, grading and access to resources. In this section, we begin by introducing the theoretical foundations of fairness in predictive analytics, followed by a discussion on how the choice of fairness notion should be context-dependent. We then transition to the practical aspects, exploring how these theoretical concepts are translated into measurable fairness metrics to guide the evaluation and mitigation of bias in educational predictive models.

An Overview of Fairness Notions

In a broader sense, fairness in predictive analytics refers to a model's ability to generate predictions that are free from bias or discrimination against individuals or groups based on protected attributes such as gender, race or socioeconomic background (Li 2023). Within the general machine learning domain, a wide array of fairness concepts has been developed to articulate what constitutes unbiased predictions from different perspectives. These are often accompanied by formal metrics designed to assess the extent to which predictive outputs deviate from fairness principles – commonly referred to as predictive bias. At an abstract level, three major notions have commonly been discussed to frame fairness in predictive analytics (Caton 2024; Hardt 2016), namely, *group fairness*, *individual fairness* and *causal fairness*. *Group fairness* treats fairness as a statistical problem, examining associations or disparities between model outputs and sensitive attributes across different demographic groups using observed data. *Individual fairness*, however, is based on the principle that similar individuals should receive similar predictions, requiring a well-defined notion of similarity between individuals (Barocas 2023). In contrast, *causal fairness* conceptualizes fairness as a causal problem, focusing on whether and how sensitive attributes causally influence model predictions – either directly or indirectly – through specific pathways, often relying on counterfactual reasoning (Kusner 2017).

Notations. Before delving further into the discussion of fairness notions and their applications, we first introduce the necessary notations to ensure clarity and consistency in our analysis. Let $X \in R^{n \times d}$ denote the training features or independent variables, where n represents the number of training samples and d is the number of features per sample and Y denotes the target variable. In a typical prediction task, the goal is to identify a predictive function f that maps X to Y, such that $\hat{Y} = f(X)$, where $\hat{Y}$ closely approximates Y. Depending on the task, the target variable Y can be either categorical or numerical. In the case of binary classification, where $Y \in \{0,1\}$ such as identifying at-risk students, the predictive function may be defined as $\hat{Y} = f(X) = 1\{R(X) > t\}$ where $R(X)$ is a scoring function representing the probability of X falling into class 1, and t is the decision threshold. For regression tasks, where Y is numerical (for example, predicting students' test scores), the predictive function f might simply return $\hat{Y} = f(X) = R(X)$, where $R(X)$ directly provides the predicted numerical value. When fairness considerations are introduced, an additional dimension emerges: the protected attribute, denoted as A, which describes the demographic group membership, for example, if a binary gender attribute is used, $A \in \{0,1\}$ represents either females or males.

Individual Fairness is grounded in the principle that any two individuals who are similar with respect to a particular task should receive similar decisions, regardless of their group membership (Barocas 2023). The first formal definition of this idea is known as the *Lipschitz condition* (Dwork 2012). In the context of binary classification, the *Lipschitz condition* requires that the statistical distance between the predicted outcomes of two individuals should not exceed the distance between these individuals in the feature space, that is, $D_t(R(x_i), R(x_j)) < D_f(x_i, x_j)$, where $D_t(R(x_i), R(x_j))$ represents the distance in predicted outcomes between sample x_i and x_j and $D_f(x_i, x_j)$ is the similarity of the two individuals in the feature space. Building on this condition, another widely used fairness notion is *Consistency* (Castelnovo 2022), which evaluates how similar the prediction of an individual, that is, $\hat{y}_i$, is to the predictions of its k-nearest neighbours, that is, *consistency* $= 1 - \frac{1}{n}\sum_{i=1}^{n}\left|\hat{y}_i - \frac{1}{k}\sum_{xj \in kNN(x_i)}\hat{y}_j\right|$.

Group Fairness concerns how predictions vary across different groups defined by a protected attribute, in terms of different key aspects such as error rates. There are three fairness notions widely acknowledged as the foundations in motivating subsequent studies: *Independence*, *Separation* and *Sufficiency* (Castelnovo 2022; Barocas 2023). *Independence* requires the statistical independence between predictions and the protected attribute, that is, $R \perp A$. In the context of classification, this translates to equal likelihoods of receiving the same predicted class label across different groups, that is, $P(A = a) = P(A = b)$, which has also been widely known as *demographic parity* or *statistical parity*. In educational contexts, such as predicting student college admission, a difference in the proportions of male and female students predicted to be admitted indicates a bias in the form of *demographic disparity*. It's worth noting that *Independence* essentially seeks equal rates of being predicted as a specific label across all groups while ignoring the actual labels, which could lead to undesirable outcomes. For example, in a hiring setting, ensuring the same proportion of applicants is admitted from both groups might result in qualified applicants from one group being rejected at a higher rate than those from the other, potentially leading to reverse discrimination. Furthermore, it may increase the likelihood of admitting less-qualified applicants from underrepresented groups, which could inadvertently reinforce negative stereotypes if these applicants perform worse than their counterparts.

To address this limitation, *Separation* requires that predictions satisfy *independence* conditional on the ground truth of the target variable, that is, $R \perp A \mid Y$. In the context of binary classification, several fairness measures align with this concept: (i) *Predictive Equality*, which expects equal false positive rates (equivalent to equal true negative rates) across groups, formally defined as $P(Y = 0, A = a) = P(Y = 0, A = b)$, (ii) *Equal Opportunity* that expects equal true positive rates, which is equivalent to the equal false negative rates, that is, $P(Y = 1, A = a) = P(Y = 1, A = b)$, and (iii) *Equalized Odds*, which combines the previous two, requiring both equal true positive rates and equal false positive rates across different groups. Therefore, *Separation* essentially seeks equal error rates across groups. In a similar spirit to recall, *Sufficiency* requires the conditional independence of the ground truth target variable given predicted outcomes, that is, $Y \perp A \mid R$. One fairness criterion for binary classifiers that aligns with this notion is *Predictive Parity* (also known as the outcome test), which expects that the fraction of correct positive predictions is the same across groups, formally defined as $P(\hat{Y} = 1, A = a) = P(\hat{Y} = 1, A = b)$.

Causal Fairness differs from individual and group fairness by going beyond observed associations to uncover unfairness through examining the underlying causal relationships between variables. One of the most representative notions in this line of work is *counterfactual fairness* (Kusner 2017), which defines fairness as the extent to which a prediction would remain unchanged if an individual's demographic group membership were different, while all other factors remained the same. While this notion is theoretically compelling, implementing it in practice presents several challenges. It requires constructing causal models that accurately reflect the data-generating process, which often involves strong, hard-to-test assumptions about the relationships between variables. Moreover, specifying and validating these causal structures can be difficult in real-world settings where the true causal mechanisms are unknown or complex.

Contextualizing Fairness: Which Notion to Focus On and For Whom?

A central question underpinning fairness measurement is which notion of fairness should be applied and to whom it should apply. This raises several key considerations often involved in the discourse on fairness: (i) how group membership is defined and why certain attributes are considered protective; (ii) which fairness notion – individual, group or causal – is most appropriate given the context and how the chosen notion aligns with the practical and ethical goals of the educational task at hand.

Group Membership. From a legal perspective, protected attributes refer to characteristics or traits that are safeguarded by law to prevent discrimination. These typically include attributes such as race, gender, age, disability, sexual orientation, religion and national origin (Mehrabi 2021). Most existing fairness analyses are grounded in binary group membership based on a single demographic attribute (Li 2023; Baker 2021), such as male vs. female or Black vs. non-Black. While this approach offers a straightforward starting point for detecting disparities, advancing fairness requires a broader perspective that takes into account educational relevance and practices. Beyond focusing solely on legally protected attributes, fairness analysis should also consider attributes that, while not legally protected, may still serve as illegitimate sources of discrimination such as learning disabilities. Additionally, it is crucial to account for intersectionality, that is, how multiple, intersecting demographic attributes may compound bias in ways that a single-attribute analysis cannot capture (Gohar 2023). This more comprehensive approach allows for a deeper understanding of fairness and ensures that all forms of unfair treatment are addressed.

Selection of Fairness Notions. It has been widely acknowledged that satisfying all fairness notions simultaneously is not feasible (Castelnovo 2022; Kizilcec 2022). While existing studies often justify the adoption of specific fairness criteria under the overarching goal of promoting equity, the contextual relevance of these notions deserves further scrutiny. In compulsory education, where predictive decisions can have profound effects on foundational learning outcomes, the careful selection of fairness criteria is crucial. This selection should be guided not only by abstract ideals but also by the specific circumstances in which predictions are made, encompassing both the immediate decision-making context and the broader, long-term consequences of those decisions.

Instead of theoretically comparing how these notions differ and their potential deficiencies, we provide an example scenario to demonstrate the contextual relevance of selecting a specific fairness notion in practice. Consider a primary school setting where resources, such as remedial tutoring, are limited, and decisions must be made about which students should receive support. In this context, predictive analytics are used in a two-stage process: first to determine which students should be considered for more detailed screening and, second, to identify those in actual need of support. In the first stage, the goal is not to directly identify students in need of support, but to ensure all students, regardless of demographic characteristics like gender, race or socioeconomic status, have an equal chance of being selected for further assessment. In this case, *independence* fairness is particularly relevant, as it ensures that the probability of being selected is not influenced by attributes unrelated to educational need, fostering an equal opportunity for all students to be considered for limited interventions. In the second stage, predictive analytics are used to identify students who urgently need resources. However, bias may arise if certain groups face less accurate predictions, leading to unfair outcomes, such as misidentifying students who need support or excluding others who are in need. Here, fairness notions like *separation* and *sufficiency* become more relevant. *Separation* ensures that predictions are aligned with actual needs across groups, while *sufficiency* evaluates whether the proportion of students who genuinely need support is consistent among those predicted to need it.

Both fairness notions have potential shortcomings in this context. *Sufficiency* may inadvertently allow for biased predictions if they align with true outcomes, even if the model itself is discriminatory. For example, a biased model that rejects all Black students while accepting all White students could still satisfy sufficiency if the predictions match the true outcome distribution. On the other hand, *separation* could lead to unfairness if actual outcomes are inherently linked to group membership, as in the case of early literacy development, where forcing equalized odds might result in less accurate predictions for boys and girls. This scenario illustrates the importance of carefully selecting fairness criteria based on the specific context and objectives of the predictive model, taking into account both the immediate decision-making needs and the broader, long-term consequences.

Measuring Fairness: From Concept to Practice

Beyond recognizing the importance of prioritizing appropriate fairness notions, it is equally critical to emphasize the need for effectively measuring bias as a foundational step towards mitigating it. In education contexts, where predictive models are often used to support educators' decisions, such as allocating learning resources, identifying students in need of intervention or tailoring instruction, fairness metrics must be chosen with a clear understanding of both the nature of the task (for example, classification vs. regression) and how the outputs will be interpreted and acted upon by stakeholders. For instance, classification tasks may involve identifying whether a student is likely to need additional support, while regression tasks typically predict continuous outcomes such as test scores. Unlike in higher education where binary classification is often used, numerical scores hold greater significance in compulsory education. This is because, in compulsory education, numerical scores often serve as key indicators of students' academic progress, skill development and readiness for future learning stages (Kuncel 2007). The numerical nature of these scores enables educators to track students' progress over time with greater precision and to understand their relative performance within a cohort. In high-stakes testing scenarios, such scores carry even more significance, as they may influence critical decisions such as eligibility for special programmes. These scores often serve as benchmarks for academic success and have long-term implications for students' educational trajectories. Consequently, ensuring fairness in predictions of numerical scores becomes paramount, as even subtle biases can disproportionately impact students' opportunities and outcomes, particularly for those from vulnerable or underrepresented groups. In our view, predictions – whether categorical or continuous – should be seen as assistive tools rather than definitive decisions. Educators can use these outputs to support their professional judgement in both daily practices and long-term planning. Therefore, we believe fairness metrics must go beyond detecting disparities; they should provide interpretable, context-specific insights that genuinely help guide equitable decision-making.

Fairness Metrics for Classification Tasks. For the extensively studied binary classification tasks, a wide range of fairness metrics have been developed (Li 2023). Classical group fairness metrics, including *Demographic/Statistical Parity*, *Equal Opportunity* and *Equalized Odds*, are grounded in group-level comparisons of specific classification outcomes. These metrics assess fairness by examining whether individuals from different demographic groups receive similar rates of favourable or unfavourable outcomes (for example, whether a student will be admitted) or experience similar error rates (for example, false positives or false negatives). For example, *Demographic Parity* requires that the likelihood of receiving a positive prediction is equal across groups, corresponding to the *Independence* notion, while *Equal Opportunity* focuses on ensuring equal true positive rates. *Equalized Odds* further requires that both true positive and false positive rates be equal across groups. All these metrics implicitly assume the use of a fixed decision threshold to convert predicted probabilities into binary outcomes. This reliance on threshold-dependent decisions (as pointed out in Gardner 2019) can be very limited in educational settings, as there exist situations where educators and institutions may set different thresholds for different groups of students. To this end, more advanced metrics, such as *ABROCA (Absolute Between-ROC Area)* (Gardner 2019) and *MADD (Model Absolute Density Distance)* (Verger 2023), go beyond fixed thresholds by evaluating disparities across all possible decision boundaries. *ABROCA*, for example, quantifies the area between the ROC curves of the base and comparison groups, offering a threshold-independent measure of group-level differences in true and false positive rates, which can be considered as the more advanced threshold-independent version of *Equalized Odds*. This makes it especially valuable in educational contexts, where the optimal decision threshold is often ambiguous or varies depending on the specific application. *MADD*, calculated as absolute density distances point-by-point between the two density vectors, relaxes *Demographic Parity* without any classification threshold to quantify the model's predictive differences between groups.

Fairness Metrics for Regression Tasks. Compared to classification, fairness in regression tasks has received considerably less attention in the literature, despite the widespread use of continuous predictions in educational settings, such as forecasting students' standardized test scores or academic growth trajectories. This imbalance is perhaps unsurprising, as much of the predictive analytics research in education has predominantly focused on classification tasks. One notable exception is automated essay scoring, where regression models are often used to predict human-assigned scores. In this context, a few fairness metrics have been proposed, including *Standardized Mean Difference (SMD)*, *Overall Scoring Accuracy (OSA)*, *Overall Scoring Difference (OSD)* and *Conditional Scoring Difference (CSD)* (Litman 2021). Standardized Mean Difference (SMD) measures the average standardized signed error (i.e., prediction minus true score, normalized to z-scores using their respective means and standard deviation) for each subgroup defined by the sensitive attribute. This metric captures the extent to which predictions systematically overestimate or underestimate scores for different groups on average. While SMD provides subgroup-specific insights, Overall Scoring Accuracy (OSA), Overall Scoring Difference (OSD) and Conditional Scoring Difference (CSD) offer summary statistics that reflect the extent to which group membership explains variation in prediction errors. Rather than reporting outcomes separately for each subgroup, these metrics quantify disparities by regressing predicted outcomes on the sensitive attribute and computing the proportion of variance explained, that is, R^2. Specifically, OSA measures group disparities in prediction accuracy by regressing squared errors $\left(\hat{Y}-Y\right)^2$ on the sensitive attribute A; OSD is calculated by regressing signed errors $\hat{Y}-Y$ on A; and CSD is computed as the difference in R^2 values between two models: one that regresses signed prediction errors on both the sensitive attribute A and the actual score Y and one that regresses errors on Y alone. This difference isolates the variance in prediction errors attributable to the sensitive attribute after controlling for students' true proficiency.

The R^2-based approach offers the advantage of generalizability to categorical attributes with more than two groups. However, it also comes with limitations, most notably the assumption of linearity, which may oversimplify complex, nonlinear patterns of bias. Furthermore, while the R^2 values provide a summary measure of association, they offer limited actionable insights, such as which groups are most affected or how the disparities manifest across score ranges, thereby constraining the ability of educators and policymakers to design targeted fairness interventions. While specific fairness treatment received by each group can be further explored by averaging predictive performance metrics within that group, such as SMD, these summary statistics still risk masking important within-group variability or context-specific nuances. For example, a low average error might obscure systematically higher errors at certain score levels or among subpopulations within the same demographic group. Thus, there is a need to develop fairness metrics to better reflect such differences in predicted outcomes between groups. Beyond these four metrics focused on prediction errors or accuracy, a recent study also introduces the use of *Kolmogorov-Smirnov (KS) distance* to quantify dissimilarities between predicted score or true score distributions across groups (Li 2024). The KS distance is defined as the maximum difference between the empirical cumulative distribution functions (ECDFs) of the two groups, offering a non-parametric, threshold-independent measure of distributional disparity. This metric enables direct comparison of performance gaps between student groups in terms of both predicted and actual scores, highlighting whether performance disparities between different groups of students are amplified or mitigated by the model's predictions. This may be particularly relevant in contexts where predicted scores are directly used to make decisions, such as student admissions.

MITIGATING PREDICTIVE BIAS: FROM DATA TO DECISION

One natural question that arises once predictive bias is detected is why such bias occurs and where it originates. Answering this question can be the first step in developing solutions to further mitigate the bias. It is generally believed that the root of predictive bias lies in the data used for model training (Li 2025, 2023).

Mitigating Data Biases for Fairer Inputs

A variety of data-related biases have been defined to describe the diverse ways in which the composition of educational data can disadvantage certain groups of students. These biases are particularly concerning in the context of compulsory education, where predictive models based on biased data can reinforce and exacerbate inequalities during the critical early years of learning. These biases can disproportionately affect students who are already marginalized, including those from lower socioeconomic backgrounds, racial-ethnic minorities and gendered groups. Here, we introduce four types of data biases that have been widely documented and targeted for fairness enhancement (Li 2025): representation bias, stereotypical bias, proxy discrimination and labelling bias. These biases highlight various imbalances that may exist with respect to protected attributes and/or target variables in predictive models.

- *Representation bias* (Dominguez-Catena 2024) occurs when certain groups of children are unequally represented in the dataset. In compulsory education, examples may include under-representation of students from lower socioeconomic backgrounds, who may engage less with online learning platforms due to limited access to devices or home internet, leading to data gaps that diminish their presence in learning analytics.
- *Stereotypical bias* (Dominguez-Catena 2024) refers to the reinforcement of societal stereotypes through skewed patterns in the data. In compulsory education, this bias is likely more prevalent and susceptible to further amplification through biased predictions. For example, if models are trained on datasets that disproportionately associate males with a higher interest in STEM subjects than females, female students might be underrepresented in STEM programmes or have their potential underestimated, perpetuating stereotypes that could influence educational opportunities and outcomes.
- *Proxy discrimination* (Tschantz 2022) arises when non-sensitive attributes – such as parental education level or school attendance rates – are correlated with protected attributes like socioeconomic status, ethnicity or language background. In compulsory education, where children's backgrounds are often reflected in these non-sensitive proxies, such biases can inadvertently perpetuate inequalities. For instance, the number of books in a student's home might serve as a proxy for socioeconomic status, which could then skew educational outcomes if these non-sensitive features are included in predictive models. In contrast, higher education models are more likely to use self-reported data from students who have more autonomy over their backgrounds and educational decisions.
- *Labelling bias* (Jiang 2020) refers to the potential misalignment between the observed labels in the data (such as competency ratings, behavioural assessments or performance evaluations) and an unbiased ground truth. In compulsory education, teachers' subjective judgements are often a key source of labelling bias, influenced by implicit biases, limited interactions or inconsistent standards (Ready 2011). For instance, a teacher may rate a student's reading ability lower than it is due to preconceived notions about the student's socioeconomic or cultural background.

In compulsory education, these types of biases can have significant long-term effects on a child's educational trajectory. For instance, misrepresentations in the data due to under-representation or misperception of certain student groups can lead to the exclusion of those students from important educational interventions, support services or enrichment opportunities. Moreover, when predictive models reflect stereotypes that align with biased social norms, they can influence not only academic performance predictions but also the opportunities available to children, perpetuating cycles of disadvantage.

Therefore, effectively tackling these data biases carries even greater significance. Representation and stereotypical biases typically manifest through observable disparities in group distributions or associations with certain labels in the dataset and can often be detected and mitigated using quantitative techniques such as reweighing or resampling (Kamiran 2012). In contrast, labelling bias and proxy discrimination are more subtly embedded in the ways data are generated and interpreted. Methods for addressing these forms of bias often rely on optimization-based strategies that minimize the influence of spurious features or labels (Jiang 2020). These include learning data representations that preserve predictive abilities while reducing dependence on protected attributes (Zemel 2013) or applying label correction or smoothing techniques (Kamiran 2012),

Model-centric Interventions and Post-hoc Corrections

While addressing bias in training data is a critical first step, fairness can also be improved through model-centric and output-centric interventions. Model-centric approaches (or in-processing methods) intervene during training by incorporating fairness objectives into the model's optimization process. This includes methods such as fairness-constrained learning, where the loss function is regularized to balance predictive accuracy with group fairness metrics and adversarial debiasing, which encourages the model to learn representations that are informative for prediction but uninformative about protected attributes (Beutel 2017; Zhang 2018). Conversely, output-centric approaches (or post-processing methods) adjust the model's predictions after training to satisfy fairness constraints. These include threshold adjustments, probability calibration or reject option classification, which allow selective modification of outputs to reduce disparities across groups without retraining the model (Hardt 2016; Pleiss 2017). These methods can be valuable when retraining is impractical or when residual unfairness persists despite data pre-processing.

OPPORTUNITIES AND CHALLENGES

When predictive analytics is carefully audited and designed with fairness in mind, it holds great potential to support teachers in compulsory education by leveraging available – and increasingly rich – student data. As indicated by the recent study focused on standardized test performance prediction utilizing formative assessment performance (Li 2024), the integration of predictive analytics into compulsory education presents a valuable opportunity to enhance teaching effectiveness. Beyond forecasting students' academic performance for earlier interventions, predictive analytics can also be used to model qualitative input from teachers such as observation reports or from students such as writing responses, capturing rich, context-specific insights that are often underutilized (Fateen 2021; Urrutia 2022). These models can support teachers by identifying patterns not immediately visible in quantitative data, easing the burden of continuous monitoring and informing instructional adjustments. In addition to leveraging available administrative data, the integration of advanced technologies into compulsory education settings is expanding access to multi-modal data, including classroom audio and video, gesture recognition and eye-tracking (Aslan 2024; Chettaoui 2024). These diverse sources further extend the scope of predictive modelling. By integrating such varied data, systems afford the opportunities to obtain a more holistic view of student learning processes and engagement patterns. This fusion of data modalities enables predictive analytics to move beyond static indicators towards dynamic, real-time support tools that are tailored to each student's context and needs.

However, beyond these anticipated benefits, challenges remain, particularly around data collection, the ethical use of sensitive information and the risk of introducing or amplifying discrimination. Collecting high-quality and representative data in compulsory education settings is often constrained by privacy regulations and the need for parental consent. For example, despite multi-modal approaches such as through video or body movements demonstrated to effectively identify learners' affective states, the collection of such data can be particularly sensitive and may raise ethical concerns regarding surveillance and the long-term storage of children's information (Walker 2023). Moreover, as discussed in the earlier section on 'Data Availability', access to certain types of data, such as platform-derived interaction-level data, is very likely limited to certain families, schools, regions or countries due to disparities in technological infrastructure, policy constraints and varying levels of platform adoption. Predictive models trained on such data carry significant risks; they may reflect the experiences and behaviours of only a narrow segment of the population, thereby perpetuating or even exacerbating existing inequalities when applied more broadly. While considerable efforts have been made to measure and mitigate predictive bias, important questions remain. Notably, the use of demographic information, whether to evaluate fairness or to enhance it, continues to spark debate (Baker 2023). In addition, relatively limited attention has been given to predictive tasks focused on the continuous monitoring of students' progress. Such approaches often overlook the complexities involved in continuous educational measurements, which are especially critical in compulsory education settings. Furthermore, the fair and effective use of predictive analytics requires more than just technical solutions to detect and reduce bias. It also demands capacity building among educators, administrators and families, including efforts to enhance technology literacy, foster understanding of how predictive models work and raise awareness of potential sources of bias and their implications for different student groups. Ultimately, the responsible integration of predictive analytics into educational decision-making to support teaching and learning requires coordinated efforts from all stakeholders, including educators, families, researchers, policymakers and technology developers, to ensure that such tools are used in equitable and supportive ways.

REFERENCES

Afzal, A.a. (2023), 'Addressing the digital divide: Access and use of technology in education', *Journal of Social Sciences Review*, **3** (2), 883–95. doi:10.54183/jssr.v3i2.326

Albouy, V.a. (2009), 'Does compulsory education lower mortality?', *Journal of Health Economics*, **28** (1), 155–68. https://doi.org/10.1016/j.jhealeco.2008.09.003

Anderson, J.R.a. (1995), 'Cognitive tutors: Lessons learned', *The Journal of the Learning Sciences*, **4** (2), 167–207. https://doi.org/10.1207/s15327809jls0402_2

Andresen, M.A. (2009), 'Asynchronous discussion forums: Success factors, outcomes, assessments and limitations', *Journal of Educational Technology & Society*, **12** (1), 249–57. https://www.jstor.org/stable/jeductechsoci.12.1.249

Aslan, S.a. (2024), 'What is the impact of a multi-modal pedagogical conversational AI system on parents' concerns about technology use by young children?', *British Journal of Educational Technology*, **55** (4), 1625–50. https://doi.org/10.1111/bjet.13399

Baer, L.a. (2017), 'Unleashing the transformative power of learning analytics', in C. Lang, G. Siemens, A. Wise and D. Gašević (eds), *Handbook of learning analytics*, The Society for Learning Analytics Research, pp. 309–18. doi:10.18608/hla17.026

Baker, R.S.a. (2020), 'Predicting K–12 dropout', *Journal of Education for Students Placed at Risk (JESPAR)*, **25** (1), 28–54. https://doi.org/10.1080/10824669.2019.1670065

Baker, R.S.a. (2021), 'Algorithmic bias in education', *International Journal of AIED*, **32** (2022), 1052–92. https://doi.org/10.1007/s40593-021-00285-9

Baker, R.S.a. (2023), 'Using demographic data as predictor variables: A questionable choice', *Journal of Educational Data Mining*, **15** (2), 22–52. https://doi.org/10.5281/zenodo.7702628

Bakken, L.a. (2017), 'Early childhood education: The long-term benefits', *Journal of Research in Childhood Education*, **31** (2), 255–69. https://doi.org/10.1080/02568543.2016.1273285

Barocas, S.a. (2023), *Fairness and machine learning: Limitations and opportunities*. MIT Press.

Bastian, K.C.a. (2020), 'Is less more? Subject-area specialization and outcomes in elementary schools', *Education Finance and Policy*, **15** (2), 357–382. https://doi.org/10.1162/edfp_a_00278

Bayer, V.a. (2021), 'Learning analytics and fairness: Do existing algorithms serve everyone equally?', in I. Roll, D. McNamara, S. Sosnovsky, R. Luckin and V. Dimitrova (eds), *Artificial Intelligence in Education: 22nd International Conference, AIED 2021, Utrecht, The Netherlands, June 14–18, 2021, Proceedings, Part II*. Springer, Cham, pp. 71–75. https://doi.org/10.1007/978-3-030-78270-2_12

Beutel, A.a. (2017), *Data decisions and theoretical implications when adversarially learning fair representations*. Retrieved from arXiv preprint arXiv:1707.00075.

Bull, R.a. (2024), 'The impact of work-related wellbeing and workplace culture and climate on intention to leave in the early childhood sector', *Early Childhood Research Quarterly*, **69**, 13–24. https://doi.org/10.1016/j.ecresq.2024.06.002

Carmichael, C.a. (2014), 'Predictors of numeracy performance in national testing programs: Insights from the longitudinal study of Australian children', *British Educational Research Journal*, **40** (4), 637–59. https://doi.org/10.1002/berj.3104

Castelnovo, A.a. (2022), 'A clarification of the nuances in the fairness metrics landscape', *Scientific Reports*, **12**, 4209. https://doi.org/10.1038/s41598-022-07939-1

Caton, S.a. (2024), *Fairness in machine learning: A survey*. Association for Computing Machinery. doi:10.1145/3616865

Chettaoui, N.a. (2024), 'Using multi-modal data to cluster students' behavior within embodied learning context', *2024 15th International Conference on Information and Communication Systems (ICICS)*, 1–6. doi:10.1109/ICICS63486.2024.10638277

Darling-Hammond, L.a. (2020), 'Implications for educational practice of the science of learning and development', *Applied Developmental Science*, **24** (2), 97–140. https://doi.org/10.1080/10888691.2018.1537791

DeLuca, C.a. (2014), 'Assessment in early primary education: An empirical study of five school contexts', *Journal of Research in Childhood Education*, **28** (4), 441–60. https://doi.org/10.1080/02568543.2014.944722

Diffey, L.a. (2017), *Age requirements for free and compulsory education. 50-state review*. Education Commission of the States. https://www.ecs.org/wp-content/uploads/Age_Requirements_for_Free_and_Compulsory_Education-1.pdf

Dominguez-Catena, I.a. (2024), 'Metrics for dataset demographic bias: A case study on facial expression recognition', *IEEE Transactions on Pattern Analysis and Machine Intelligence*, **46** (8), 5209–26. doi:10.1109/TPAMI.2024.3361979

Dowley, M.a. (2022), 'Comparing student motivations for and emotional responses to national standardised tests and internal school tests: The devil in the detail', *Australian Journal of Education*, **66** (1), 92–110. https://doi.org/10.1177/000494412110618

Dwork, C.a. (2012), 'Fairness through awareness', *Proceedings of the 3rd Innovations in Theoretical Computer Science Conference*, pp. 214–26. https://doi.org/10.1145/2090236.2090255

Eccles, J.S. (1999), 'The development of children ages 6 to 14', *The Future of Children*, **9** (2), 30–44. https://pubmed.ncbi.nlm.nih.gov/10646256/

Essa, E.L.a. (2019), *Introduction to early childhood education*. Sage Publications.

Fancsali S.E.a. (2018), 'Using embedded formative assessment to predict state summative test scores', *Proceedings of the 8th International Conference on Learning Analytics and Knowledge*, pp. 161–70. https://doi.org/10.1145/3170358.3170392

Fateen, M.a. (2021), 'Predicting student performance using teacher observation reports', in *International Conference on Educational Data Mining*. https://eric.ed.gov/?id=ED615587

Feng, M.a. (2006), 'Predicting state test scores better with intelligent tutoring systems: developing metrics to measure assistance required', *International Conference on Intelligent Tutoring Systems*, pp. 31–40. https://doi.org/10.1007/11774303_4

Fischer, C.a. (2020), 'Mining big data in education: Affordances and challenges', *Review of Research in Education*, **44** (1), 130–60. https://doi.org/10.3102/0091732X20903304

Gardner, J.a. (2019), 'Evaluating the fairness of predictive student models through slicing analysis', *Proceedings of the 9th International Conference on Learning Analytics & Knowledge*, pp. 225–34. https://doi.org/10.1145/3303772.3303791

Geary, D.C. (2013), 'Early foundations for mathematics learning and their relations to learning disabilities', *Current Directions in Psychological Science*, **22** (1), 23–7. https://doi.org/10.1177/0963721412469398

Gohar, U.a. (2023), 'A survey on intersectional fairness in machine learning: Notions, mitigation and challenges', *Proceedings of the 32nd International Joint Conference on AI*, pp. 6619–27. https://doi.org/10.24963/ijcai.2023/742

Hardt, M.a. (2016), 'Equality of opportunity in supervised learning', *Proceedings of the 30th International Conference on Neural Information Processing Systems*, pp. 3323–31. doi:10.5555/3157382.3157469

Hecking, T.a. (2016), 'Investigating social and semantic user roles in MOOC discussion forums', *Proceedings of the Sixth International Conference on Learning Analytics & Knowledge*, pp. 198–207. https://doi.org/10.1145/2883851.2883924

Heffernan, N.T.a. (2014), 'The ASSISTments ecosystem: Building a platform that brings scientists and teachers together for minimally invasive research on human learning and teaching', *International Journal of Artificial Intelligence in Education*, **24**, 470–97. doi:10.1007/s40593-014-0024-x

Heller, S.S.a. (2012), 'Social-emotional development, school readiness, teacher–child interactions and classroom environment', *Early Education & Development*, **23** (6), 919–44. https://doi.org/10.1080/10409289.2011.626387

Huang, J.S.a. (2024), 'Unveiling the dynamics of learning behaviors in learning K–12 math: An exploration of an ASSISTments Dataset', *2024 IEEE Conference on Artificial Intelligence (CAI)*, pp. 1474–80. doi:10.1109/CAI59869.2024.00265

Hussain, M.a. (2018), 'Student engagement predictions in an e-learning System and their impact on student course assessment scores', *Computational Intelligence and Neuroscience*, 6347186. https://doi.org/10.1155/2018/6347186

Innovare SIP (2023), *Different types of data in education: A complete guide*. https://innovaresip.com/types-of-data-in-education/

Jiang, H.a. (2020), 'Identifying and correcting label bias in machine learning', *International Conference on Artificial Intelligence and Statistics*, pp. 702–12. https://arxiv.org/abs/1901.04966

Junker, B.W. (2006), 'Using on-line tutoring records to predict end-of-year exam scores: Experience with the ASSISTments project and MCAS 8th grade mathematics'. https://www.stat.cmu.edu/~brian/maryland2006/junker-assistments-submission.pdf

Kamiran, F.a. (2012), 'Data preprocessing techniques for classification without discrimination', *Knowledge and Information Systems*, **33**, 1–33. https://doi.org/10.1007/s10115-011-0463-8

Kizilcec, R.F.a. (2022), 'Algorithmic fairness in education', in W. Holmes and K. Porayska-Pomsta (eds), *The ethics of artificial intelligence in education*. Taylor & Francis, pp. 174–202. https://arxiv.org/abs/2007.05443

Kovanovic, V.a. (2021), 'Learning analytics for primary and secondary schools', *Journal of Learning Analytics*, **8** (2), 1–5. https://doi.org/10.18608/jla.2021.7543

Kuncel, N.R.a. (2007), 'Standardized tests predict graduate students' success', *Science*, **315** (5815), 1080–1. doi:10.1126/science.1136618

Kusner, M.J.a. (2017), 'Counterfactual fairness', *NeurIPS*. https://arxiv.org/abs/1703.06856

Larose, D.T.a. (2015), *Data mining and predictive analytics*. John Wiley & Sons.

Lee, O. (1995), 'Subject matter knowledge, classroom management, and instructional practices in middle school science classroom', *Journal of Research in Science Teaching*, **32** (4), 423–40. https://doi.org/10.1002/tea.3660320409

Li L.a. (2023), 'Moral machines or tyranny of the majority? A systematic review on predictive bias in education', *LAK23: 13th International Learning Analytics and Knowledge Conference*, pp. 499–508. https://doi.org/10.1145/3576050.3576119

Li L.a. (2024), 'Unveiling goods and bads: A critical analysis of machine learning predictions of standardized test performance in early childhood education', *Proceedings of the 14th Learning Analytics and Knowledge Conference*, pp. 608–19. https://doi.org/10.1145/3636555.3636920

Li L.a. (2025), 'When and how biases seep in: Enhancing debiasing approaches for fair educational predictive analytics', *British Journal of Educational Technology*, **56** (6), 2478–2501. https://doi.org/10.1111/bjet.13575

Litman, D.a. (2021), 'A fairness evaluation of automated methods for scoring text evidence usage in writing', *International Conference on Artificial Intelligence in Education*, pp. 255–67. https://doi.org/10.1007/978-3-030-78292-4_21

Mehrabi, N.a. (2021), 'A survey on bias and fairness in machine learning', *ACM Computing Surveys (CSUR)*, **54** (6), 1–35. https://doi.org/10.1145/3457607

Papamitsiou, Z.a. (2014), 'Learning analytics and educational data mining in practice: A systematic literature review of empirical evidence', *Journal of Educational Technology & Society*, **17** (4), 49–64. https://www.jstor.org/stable/jeductechsoci.17.4.49

Pardos, Z.A.a. (2014), 'Affective states and state tests: Investigating how affect and engagement during the school year predict end-of-year learning outcomes', *Journal of Learning Analytics*, **1** (1), 107–28. https://doi.org/10.18608/jla.2014.11.6

Patikorn, T.a. (2020), 'ASSISTments longitudinal data mining competition special issue: A preface', *Journal of Educational Data Mining*, **12** (2), i–xi. https://doi.org/10.5281/zenodo.4008048

Pazeto, T.a. (2020), 'Prediction of reading and writing in elementary education through early childhood education', *Psicologia Ciência e Profissão*, **40**, e205497. https://doi.org/10.1590/1982-3703003205497

Pleiss, G.a. (2017), 'On fairness and calibration', *Proceedings of the 31st International Conference on Neural Information Processing Systems*, pp. 5684–93. https://dl.acm.org/doi/10.5555/3295222.3295319

Ready, D.D.a. (2011), 'Accuracy and inaccuracy in teachers' perceptions of young children's cognitive abilities: The role of child background and classroom context', *American Educational Research Journal*, **48** (2), 335–60. https://doi.org/10.3102/0002831210374874

Ricciardi, C.a. (2021), 'School readiness skills at age four predict academic achievement through 5th grade', *Early Childhood Research Quarterly*, **57**, 110–20. https://doi.org/10.1016/j.ecresq.2021.05.006

Roberts, P.a. (2019), 'Early years teachers' perspectives on the effects of NAPLAN on stakeholder wellbeing and the impact on early years pedagogy and curriculum', *Australasian Journal of Early Childhood*, **44** (3), 309–20. https://doi.org/10.1177/1836939119855562

Rothbard, M.N. (1979), *Education: Free and compulsory*. Ludwig von Mises Institute.

Seidel, E.a. (2017), 'Using predictive analytics to target and improve first year student attrition', *Australian Journal of Education*, **61** (2), 200–18. https://doi.org/10.1177/0004944117712310

Stephens Jr, M.a. (2014), 'Compulsory education and the benefits of schooling', *American Economic Review*, **104** (6), 1777–92. https://www.aeaweb.org/articles?id=10.1257/aer.104.6.1777

Thompson, C. (2011), 'How Khan Academy is changing the rules of education', *Wired magazine*, 1–5. https://www.wired.com/2011/07/ff-khan/

Tschantz, M.C. (2022), 'What is proxy discrimination?', *Proceedings of the 2022 ACM Conference on Fairness, Accountability and Transparency*, 1993–2003. https://doi.org/10.1145/3531146.3533242

United Workers Union (2021), 'Exhausted, undervalued and leaving: the crisis in early education'. https://www.voced.edu.au/content/ngv%3A91207

Urrutia, F.a. (2022), 'Do written responses to open-ended questions on fourth-grade online formative assessments in mathematics help predict scores on end-of-year standardized tests?', *Journal of Intelligence*, **10** (4), 82. doi:10.3390/jintelligence10040082

Van Barneveld, A.a. (2012), 'Analytics in higher education: Establishing a common language', *EDUCAUSE learning initiative*, 1–11.

Verger, M.L. (2023), 'Is your model "MADD"?, A novel metric to evaluate algorithmic fairness for predictive student models', *16th International Conference on Educational Data Mining (EDM 2023)*. doi:10.5281/zenodo.8115785

Walker, K.L.a. (2023), 'Compulsory technology adoption and adaptation in education: A looming student privacy problem', *Journal of Consumer Affairs*, **57** (1), 445–78. https://doi.org/10.1111/joca.12506

Wood, S.G.a. (2016), 'Test anxiety and a high-stakes standardized reading comprehension test: A behavioral genetics perspective', *Merrill-Palmer Quarterly*, **62** (3), 233–51. doi:10.13110/merrpalmquar1982.62.3.0233

Yu, R.a. (2020), 'Towards accurate and fair prediction of college success: Evaluating different sources of student data', *International Conference on Educational Data Mining*. https://eric.ed.gov/?id=ED608066

Zemel, R.a. (2013), 'Learning fair representations', *International Conference on Machine Learning*, 325–33. https://dl.acm.org/doi/10.5555/3042817.3042973

Zhang, B.H.a. (2018), 'Mitigating unwanted biases with adversarial learning', *Proceedings of the 2018 AAAI/ACM Conference on AI, Ethics and Society*, pp. 335–40. https://doi.org/10.1145/3278721.3278779

8. When categories matter: attendance data practices in an upper secondary classroom

Fride Haram Klykken

INTRODUCTION

Systems for registering and managing attendance are digital companions in the daily lives of most teachers and students in formal education. The data registered in such systems have direct consequences for young people's completion of education, with high rates of school absenteeism and dropout considered indicators of future unemployment and health risks (Kearney and Childs 2023). Attendance data platforms are a mandatory component of many school systems' digital infrastructures (OECD 2024). As attendance data are used as a measure of school performance, it can be connected to data-based governance and the broader datafication of education, involving data collection and comparisons spanning individual, local, regional, national and international levels (Jarke and Breiter 2019; Selwyn 2016).

Digital technologies are often introduced with the intention of easing teachers' work and increasing schools' administrative efficiency. Meanwhile, research has shown how such visions stand in contrast to how school staff and students actually use and experience such systems (Frydenlund 2022; Selwyn et al. 2021). Furthermore, scholars have argued that data-producing technologies tend to complicate rather than simplify the activities they aim to streamline and that, consequently, there is a need to study such systems as situated in actual school environments (Hangartner et al. 2025; Pangrazio et al. 2023).

This chapter examines the relational complexity of attendance data in the daily life of an upper secondary classroom and is grounded in theoretical perspectives that foreground the material and spatial aspects of educational practice (Sørensen 2009). From this stance, the datafying processes of producing attendance data are considered a relational accomplishment involving the entanglement of humans and non-humans (Bodén et al. 2020). In line with the notion of *data practice*, our day-to-day engagements with data are understood as continually unfolding, while always being embedded within spatiotemporal constellations involving specific human and non-human relationships, bodies, actions, objects, ideas, networks, processes, systems and regulations (Decuypere 2021; Pangrazio et al. 2023; Sellar 2015; Smith 2018). Informed by this framework, the present chapter addresses how *attendance data practices* are constructed in the classroom.

The chapter presents empirical examples from a video ethnography conducted in a Norwegian upper secondary classroom, examining the activities related to the collection and use of attendance data and how they emerged through the daily interactions among students and teachers. The study shows how formal and informal attendance data-production routines engaged both students and teachers in attendance data practices related to the registration, monitoring and negotiation of absence data categories. As such, the process intended to improve and measure educational quality is intertwined with the pedagogical environment.

Thus, the chapter demonstrates how the attendance data measuring system itself became an integral part of the everyday classroom environment.

BACKGROUND

The Norwegian Context: Attendance Regulations and the Absence Limit

In Norway, pupils who have completed their compulsory ten-year lower secondary education have the right to access upper secondary school education. While not mandatory, the enrolment rates are high and in 2021, 98 per cent enrolled directly from lower to upper secondary school. A total of 84 per cent of the population had successfully completed upper secondary school before the age of 25 (UDIR 2023). Once enrolled, upper secondary students have the right to receive a certain number of hours of education and, simultaneously, a duty to attend school for a specific number of hours (Opplæringsforskrifta 2024).

Recording attendance and evaluating absence rates has a long history, with high international consensus on school absenteeism and dropout presenting key societal challenges (Fredriksson et al. 2023) and, in order to improve attendance rates, many countries operate with a required level of expected or obligatory attendance (Birioukov 2016; OECD 2024). This is also the case in Norway. In 2016, an absence limit was introduced to reduce dropout rates and increase school attendance and completion. After much debate, the ruling was furthered and updated with some amendments in 2025 (UDIR 2026).

The 2016 ruling states that if a student's absence exceeds 10 per cent in an individual subject, they risk failing to obtain an academic grade in that subject and, in turn, not completing upper secondary education. However, some absences are considered legitimate if they are documented and due to a valid reason, such as health issues, funerals or religious holidays. In these cases, the absences will be excused from counting towards the 10 per cent absence ceiling.

Schools are required to record data about students' absences (Opplæringsforskrifta 2024). The data is collected with the aim of safeguarding educational qualification processes by ensuring a sufficient basis for assessment and also to enable the schools to follow up on students at risk of dropout and intervene in school attendance issues as early as possible (Bergene et al. 2023). Teachers must register students' absences as a number of hours and days and also categorize the data according to the absence type. The student's total amount of absences is presented as hours and days on each student's final diploma. In certain cases, however, some absences can be removed from a student's final diploma if related, for instance, to long-term illness or to school arrangements and appointments with school staff (Kjeøy and Lysvik 2023; Opplæringsforskrifta 2024).

In the attendance registration system, absences are categorized using various codes, including 'documented' or 'undocumented absence'. A documented absence is granted if the student provides the school with documentation showing a legitimate reason for the absence. At the time this study was conducted (2018), absences placed in this category did not count towards the 10 per cent ceiling. An undocumented absence could additionally be recorded as either 'with' or 'without notice', depending on whether the student had notified the school about the absence (Thomas and Hennum 2020). Alongside their academic grades, each student receives grades for 'Order' and 'Conduct' (Good, Fair or Poor) on their final diploma

(Opplæringsforskrifta 2024). Since students are required to notify their schools about all types of absences, if a student fails to do so, the teacher may register a 'remark' (a negative note called 'anmerkning' in Norwegian) in the system. If such remarks accumulate, the student's grade in 'Order' may be lowered (Thomas and Hennum 2020).

As such, the ongoing handling, recording and categorization of absences are of high stakes for students. A high number of undocumented absences may jeopardize a student's chance of attaining a grade, which can hinder their completion of upper secondary education and, in turn, delay or hinder their attainment of vocational competence certificates or access to university studies (Bjørnset et al. 2018). Additionally, a high number of absences on the final diploma or a poor grade in 'Order' may deter future employers or reduce a student's opportunities for vocational training placement (Thomas and Hennum 2020).

In accordance with the 2016 ruling, a significant responsibility lies with the school and its teachers. If a student is at risk of exceeding the absence limit in one subject and, consequently, may not receive a grade for the final assessment in that subject, the school must provide the student (and, in some cases, parents or guardians) with written notification without delay. The student should be warned with enough time, allowing them the opportunity to improve their attendance and secure a grade. If the schools fail to notify in time, students have the right to receive a grade (UDIR 2026).

Norwegian upper secondary schools are required to use a dedicated digital administrative system for tasks related to absences, timetables, assessments and grades (Opplæringsforskrifta 2024). In addition to allowing teachers and students to manage attendance data, such administrative systems often feature automated actions that generate notifications (digital messages, emails and text messages) when a level of undocumented absences is reached in a subject. Currently, this represents the most commonly used type of adaptive system in Norwegian K–12 education (NOU 2023: 19, p. 34). A new administrative system was launched across upper secondary schools in Norway between 2018 and 2021 (Lindland 2022; Prøven 2023).

Research on Attendance Registration in Schools

Evaluations of the 2016 absence limit in Norway have indicated that both hourly and daily absences decreased following its introduction; however, they also reveal negative consequences for certain student groups, with the lower ceiling of 10 per cent causing more students to reach it (Bjørnset et al. 2018). Since the COVID-19 pandemic, the number of hourly absences has increased in Norway (UDIR 2025). Reports on the absence limit ruling have also highlighted an increased workload and time pressure on teachers and head teachers, as more time is now spent on registering absences and distributing notifications to students and parents (Kjeøy and Lysvik 2023). The requirement for students to document the reasons for legitimate absences has also led to increased pressure on the health system and doctors, as healthy pupils often request consultations long before they reach the 10 per cent ceiling, and to increased students' stress related to the cost of consultations and the time used to obtain documentation (Bjørnset et al. 2018). Furthermore, local interpretations and implementations of attendance registration rules and categories have been shown to vary between schools and among teachers (Bjørnset et al. 2018).

Internationally, attendance-based research has problematized prevailing data categories for following a simplistic logic of what it means to be physically 'present' or 'absent' in school (Bodén 2016). A research review by Birioukov (2016) critiques an overreliance on the dichotomy of absenteeism as 'excused' or 'unexcused', arguing that this approach provides only a partial understanding, with little effort to understand the reasons behind absenteeism (p. 347). Birioukov (2016) proposes instead the concepts of 'voluntary' and 'involuntary absenteeism' as part of a more holistic framework concerned with students' motivation, as well as the barriers that restrict access and abilities to enter education. In research on extended school non-attendance, Knage (2023) critiques another much-used binary of 'truancy' and 'school refusal' (without or with parental consent) and argues that both terms denote a negative narrative of the child's identity, positioning their individual behaviour as maladaptive rather than being sensitive to the case-by-case variety and complexities of the child's life circumstances. The dominant use of simplistic concepts reflects a societal desire for efficiency and neat labels (Birioukov 2016). Additionally, several studies have cautioned against the low quality of schools' attendance data, highlighting the weak association between attendance data recorded in the school's systems and students' self-reported absences (Keppens et al. 2019; Sandhaug et al. 2022). Moreover, the research field challenges a one-size-fits-all approach when defining and categorizing absences and many scholars stress the need for a more holistic approach and contextualized understanding of school absenteeism.

A study in Danish schools by Frydenlund (2022) demonstrates some of the complex work that teachers and students do to navigate the narrow categories given by regulations and administrative systems. The teachers described how they employed a range of contextualizing strategies to interpret and understand the reasons behind students' absences, which was a necessary step to make absences 'classifiable' before determining the appropriate attendance data category. As Frydenlund (2022) argues, the final registration in the system required the absence to be decontextualized, 'cutting away a plethora of complex issues', which made the final numbers seem clean and fair (Frydenlund 2022, p. 865). Furthermore, the study shows how the data was eventually recontextualized by social workers, who then used the 'clean' data to construct absence patterns with single causes.

Frydenlund's (2022) study also shows how the students contested and negotiated the meaning of their absences by providing alternative explanations and contexts. Other studies have also demonstrated how students navigate simplistic absence categories and rigid systems. For instance, a study by Thomas and Hennum (2020) shows how students' strategies included disputing the data and presenting their own version of the story through alternative contexts (whether real or fabricated), along with evidence and documents, with the aim of influencing how their absences were categorized. Student strategies have also been related to stress, for instance, as some students decide to attend school despite being unwell (Bjørnset et al. 2018).

Research by Moraiti et al. (2025) has detailed teachers' efforts, temporal solutions and 'workarounds' in the ongoing digital management of students' attendance data. Their study shows how, due to, for example, infrastructure breakdowns or delayed information from students, teachers had to postpone registrations and manually record attendance outside the system. Caught in the tension between 'control and care', the teachers often awaited more information on students' reasons for being absent, which involved the recurrent checking of emails and messages that could be sent through a variety of digital platforms and devices (Moraiti et al. 2025, p. 744). In some cases, it could take several days to determine the category for one single instance of absence.

Research on the performative agency of digital technologies in education has highlighted their sometimes unexpected and unintended influence on educational practice (Macgilchrist 2019; Selwyn et al. 2021). A study by Bodén (2017) demonstrates how computer software for absence administration can be understood as contributing to the agential production of school absenteeism. After a teacher registered a pupil as absent from their lesson, the software automatically generated and sent a text message to the pupil's parents. The study demonstrates how the text messages led to a range of affective responses. For some parents, receiving them created a feeling of calmness and control. Another parent, however, explained that the first time she received a text message about her daughter arriving late, she experienced nervousness and guilt, which led her to contact the teacher, who explained the text merely as 'information' (Bodén 2017, p. 411). The efficiency and one-way communication of the text messages thus produced distance (instead of closeness) between the school and the parents (p. 412). Moreover, the study demonstrates that neither the digital software nor the automated text messages were neutral resources with predetermined effects, but were entangled with multiple human and non-human agents to co-produce a wide range of emotions, relationships and school absenteeism practices, both inside and outside of the schools (Bodén 2016, 2017).

Adams and Thompson (2016) have argued that situations in which digital technologies break, unexpectedly disappear or act unpredictably, make our relationships with them visible (2016, p. 50). In line with this, studies of technology breakdowns have highlighted the more 'silent doings' of digital devices in educational settings (Alirezabeigi et al. 2020, p. 194) and show how teachers and school staff engage in repair practices when negotiating and mending systems to keep the school in working order (González López and Büchner 2024; Sørensen 2009). For instance, during the disruptions caused by the COVID-19 school closures, a variety of new attendance registration methods were generated, ranging from 'online roll calls', which resembled the traditional in-class practices, to a more disputed method of asking students' to click the 'Like'-button (Mörtsell 2022, p. 517). The study demonstrates how attendance rituals were re-negotiated within the affordances and limitations provided by digital platforms, teachers' differing practices and school policies (Mörtsell 2022).

THEORETICAL FRAMEWORK: A RELATIONAL MATERIALIST APPROACH TO DATA PRACTICE

To address how attendance data collection and use emerge in and shape classroom activities, this chapter takes a relational materialist approach that conceptualizes the performative effects of the ongoing entanglements of human and non-human actors (Bodén et al. 2020). Drawing on Science and Technology Studies (STS), Actor Network Theory (ANT) and sociomaterial theories, such frameworks have been shown to be fruitful in analysing how heterogeneous and spatiotemporal constellations of actors, relations and technological systems entangle and actively co-produce educational practices, sometimes generating unintended effects (Decuypere et al. 2021; Sørensen 2009).

Recognizing everyday actions as consequential, this stance considers everyday activities as both deeply embedded in the present, whilst simultaneously tied to power and knowledge by configuring the boundaries and possibilities for future ways of acting and being (Bodén et al. 2020; Klykken 2023b). This also counts for *data practices*, which Decuypere (2021) describes as 'the actions, performances and the resulting consequences, of introducing data-producing technologies in everyday situations' (Decuypere 2021, p. 67). Following a 'flat' understanding of the physical and the digital entails seeing both as equally materially present and consequential. As an enactment within the physical world, the creation of digital data is therefore not an act of abstract representation but a real and generative event. For instance, through human engagement with administrative school platforms, data points are generated, accumulated, communicated and acted upon, consequently causing new material relationships to be added to the world.

As such, when studying data practices, it is of interest to examine what the practices 'do', in other words, examining the processual specificities of how digital systems and interfaces 'emerge, develop and unfold' (Decuypere 2021, p. 69). Therefore, the key analytical focal point for this chapter is not to study intended and implied usage of attendance data, but to explore how attendance data practices are established in the classroom (Decuypere 2021), requiring an analytical mapping of embedded and entangled doings, as they take form in collective habits and activities in a broader environment.

METHODS AND MATERIALS

The chapter analyses empirical examples drawn from a video-based ethnography conducted in 2018 in a Norwegian upper secondary classroom, exploring material-discursive practices in day-to-day teaching situations (Klykken 2023a). Video-based ethnographic methods permit a close examination of the material, spatial and relational dimensions of everyday activities and were thus a suitable analytical tool for 'making the familiar strange' when investigating ordinary, taken-for-granted activities and routines in everyday situations (Delamont and Atkinson 2021).

The data collected consist of audiovisual recordings and field notes made during classroom activities and I followed one class and their teacher for a total of six weeks over a three-month period. The students were between 17 and 19 years old and in the last months of their second year (out of three) of upper secondary education.

In accordance with national ethical guidelines for research, I informed the participants about the study, emphasizing that consenting to participate was voluntary (Klykken 2025) and that I would anonymize participants' names and that personal data would not be shared (NESH 2021; NSD 2020).

The initial ethnographic analysis entailed searching for activities and 'ways of doing' that appeared normalized and legitimized within the teaching situations and the analytical process was aided by the engagement of relational materialist theoretical concepts (Delamont and Atkinson 2021; Klykken 2023a). After observing the recurring bodily orientation of students and teachers towards the recording and classification of absences, the analysis was further informed by the concept of data practice and the analytical question of how such practices are constructed and developed (Decuypere 2021). To examine this further, I looked for different types of attendance data relationships that emerged and stabilized within the ordinary classroom activities.

ANALYSIS: HOW STUDENTS AND TEACHERS NAVIGATE ATTENDANCE DATA

The following analytical mapping will present three empirical examples that foreground how *attendance data practices* can be understood as constructed and performed as part of ordinary classroom activities. As the teachers and students engaged with absences, three types of collective habits and relationships recurred, involving the processes of recording, monitoring and negotiating attendance data.

'Is she here? [Silence] Does anyone know?': Attendance Data Registration

The following situation took place early in the morning, at the start of the first lesson of the day. Some students had arrived early and were already engaging with their laptops. Other students had just arrived, sitting by their desks, still in their coats. The classroom had a sleepy atmosphere and while some students were talking quietly, most of the students were directing their attention towards the teacher. Standing in front of the classroom, the teacher was facing the students while looking at his laptop, which was placed on a high table. As one latecomer slipped through the door, the teacher began calling out names in quick succession. The students responded with similar immediacy, creating a continuous stream of names and responses:

T&S: Hilde!-Yes!-Tuva!-Yes!-Viktor!-Yes!-Åse! [Silence]
[The teacher looks up from the screen]
T: Åse? [Scans the classroom]
T: Is she here? [Silence] Does anyone know?
S: She is still sick, I think
T: OK (.) [Pauses briefly while interacting with the laptop]
T: Kristoffer! [Silence] Kristoffer?
S: Yes!
T: Ah, yes – good! You are here
Transcript codes: T: Teacher; S: Student; [Action]: Description of action; (.): Pause

The registration of attendance was part of the daily routine, typically conducted by the teacher reading aloud the names of each student at the start of the lesson, in front of the whole class, while accessing the digital administrative platform via a laptop. Various teachers employed distinct rhythms for their roll call routines, yet they all seemed to share the motivation to complete the registration as quickly as possible. The students were usually attentive and ready to respond immediately and thus also seemed to share an interest in facilitating the process.

In this type of situation, the administrative platform was not directly visible to anyone other than the teacher. Meanwhile, the interface of the technology can be understood as actively configuring the registration process. Teachers are required to locate the present-day timetable to view the online class list, before doing the roll call and registering absent students by checking the boxes next to the names according to the specific absence category. The listing of names thus renders tangible the materiality of the administrative platform's interface design and registration mechanisms. The roll call and registration routine also brought the students' voices to the fore by requiring them to respond to their own names, while also drawing attention to the silences that followed the names of absent students. Moreover, through this 'teacher–student–platform' interaction, data points were created in the school's administrative system and stored in each student's attendance profile.

Another morning, during the fieldwork, the teacher remained silent while engaging with his laptop for some time, before shutting down the laptop lid and announcing that the internet had 'broken down'. The teacher then started the lesson without taking the register. Any absences, therefore, in this case, had to be registered at a later point. As attendance is commonly recorded at the beginning of lessons, in cases where students arrive late or leave school early, it is not uncommon that records must be updated, either later in the lesson or during the day. As the literature has shown, teachers' digital work with registering attendance data can be prolonged, for instance, as they wait for messages from students before determining the final absence data category (Moraiti et al. 2025).

Meanwhile, research has also shown how the registration routines for late-arriving students are not always straightforward (Bjørnset et al. 2018; Selwyn et al. 2021), raising questions about, for instance, how late a student must be before the teacher registers someone as 'late', at what point does 'late' turn into 'absent' and in what situations and for what reasons do teachers exercise discretion? As studies have shown, rules and routines regarding such issues vary widely between schools and between teachers (Bjørnset et al. 2018).

To sum up, these *registration* processes can be understood as part of an attendance data practice, which is constructed and performed through recurring 'teacher–student–platform' interactions. This practice unfolded in everyday school situations through the relational entanglement of data-producing technologies and digital software interfaces (online class lists, ticking boxes), interweaving with traditional roll calls, teachers' and students' presence (their voices), silences (no response), latecomers, messages from students and the (un)available internet connection.

'It counts, I need to remove it': Attendance Data Monitoring

To follow up on the data registered on their attendance profiles, students had access to the same administrative platform used by teachers. As the fieldwork was conducted during the mid-to-late spring semester and as the second year drew to a close, with many courses completing their final assessments, some students seemed to be more attentive to their attendance records. The following interaction shows how a group of students monitored their attendance data during a lesson.

In this situation, five students were sitting together around a round table, each facing their own laptop while working on an assignment. At one moment, the schoolwork was interrupted when two of the students logged on to the administrative platform to check their attendance records:

S1:	I got two hours in History, but we were in the city with the Spanish class and the teacher said that she had talked to the History teacher.
S2:	For me, it just says: 'On an excursion with the Spanish class' (.) I didn't get it.
S1:	It counts. I need to remove it.

Transcript codes: S: Student; [Action]: Description of action; (.): Pause

In this excerpt, Student 1 discovered that she had received an undocumented absence for a school-organized field trip and she expressed concern since this absence was 'counting' towards the 10 per cent absence limit.

One by one, the other students at the same table also began checking their absences and comparing their attendance records:

S1: You have very little absence, right? Or- Is everything documented?
S3: I only have an absence in Geography?! [Surprised]
S4: Where are we supposed to look?
S1: Look where it says 'Absences per subject'
S3: I haven't gotten anything in Maths? Heh!
S5: You didn't get anything in Maths? Why did I get it?
S3: Emm (.) that must have been from another time.
S5: I have not got these as documented here hmm-
S4: I have an absence in Social Science that I'm not supposed to have
S2: I got one, but for me, it was the bus that drove past me (.) 'A notification about a lowered grade in Order will be sent'

Transcript codes: S: Student; [Action]: Description of action; (.): Pause

As they navigated the administrative platform while sitting together, the students compared their attendance data registrations in various subjects and examined closely how their absences were categorized. This activity caused both worry and surprise among the students. The students identified several instances of differing or wrongly registered absences. Students 1 and 2 received different categories for the same absence due to a field trip. This instance illustrates how attendance registration systems can be challenging when schedules change, as the student groups that make up classes can vary in different subjects, and timetables often need to be entered into the system well in advance.

Student 2 stated that she received an absence due to her bus not stopping and that she was soon to receive a notification about being at risk of a lower grade in Order. Meanwhile, Student 3 seemed surprised and perhaps relieved to have only one instance of absence. The inconsistencies between the school's recorded accounts and students' own reports of absences align with research showing the overall inconsistencies in school attendance records (Bjørnset et al. 2018; Keppens et al. 2019).

Student 4 asked the others about where on the platform she could find her absences, highlighting potential differences in students' often-taken-for-granted digital skills necessary to navigate the interfaces of administrative platforms.

Consequently, in this situation, the students actively and collectively *monitored* their attendance data. This 'student–student–platform' interaction can thus be understood as a type of attendance data practice which was constructed and performed through the relational entanglement of the registered absences (the data points and categories displayed in the system) and the systems' automated notifications, which interweaved with the students' responsibility to monitor the data (the absence limit ruling), their digital skills, the practicalities of navigating digital interfaces, and students' comparing data records, expressing emotions (worries and relief) and other issues (public transport and teachers' (mis)communication).

'Can I talk to you about absence?': Attendance Data Negotiation

During lessons, the students often requested to speak with the teacher regarding their absences and the following empirical example illustrates this. As explained earlier, this could be related to the fact that the fieldwork took place near the end of the term. As previously outlined, the potential consequences associated with undocumented absences on the final diploma, made minimizing them an important task for most students.

On this day, the class had four subsequent lessons with their lead teacher and the students continued their work on an individual project assignment. The teacher announced at the start of the day that he would prioritize giving tutorials but also make time for students wanting to talk to him about absences. The students then embarked on their projects and the teacher moved around in the classroom, offering guidance.

In the following interaction, the teacher was sitting with a student and had just finished a tutorial session, as another student approached the teacher hesitantly:

S6:	Can I talk to you (about absence)?
T:	Eh, yes. What do you need help with? Is it the assignment?
S6:	I am confused about getting a remark for an absence. We were in the classroom and I went out to fill my water bottle and then we came back in again.
T:	Yes, then I will help him first and then I'll help you with absence [Points to another student waiting at a nearby desk]

Transcript codes: [T]: Teacher; [S]: Student; [Action]: Description of action; (Word): Unclear

This situation illustrates how the lead teacher balanced teaching with administrative tasks related to attendance data. While prioritizing curricular, on-task guidance, the teacher made time for discussion on absence. The decision to do this during lessons may be linked to receiving a high number of requests from students towards the end of the term, but also due to the overall time pressure, which aligns with the reported increase in teacher workload following the introduction of the absence limit (Kjeøy and Lysvik 2023).

In the excerpt above, the student expresses concern that a 'remark' has been wrongly added to his attendance data profile. As explained previously, if a student fails to notify the school about an absence, it would be categorized as an undocumented absence without notice and the student may receive a remark. If the number of such remarks accumulates, the student could receive a lowered grade for Order on their final diploma. Hence, the student's hesitant approach could be interpreted as a sign of nervousness, reflecting the seriousness of what an undocumented absence without notice may mean for the student. Furthermore, this hesitancy could also be interpreted as an indication that it might not be easy for this particular student to raise this topic with the teacher. The situation above thus illustrates how the students also engaged in a careful balancing act, juggling on-task learning activities with their responsibilities for monitoring and managing their attendance data registrations, even though it took time away from working on their assignments.

When the students requested to talk to the teacher, they used phrases like 'I need to talk to you about absence' or 'I need to fix absence'. Expressions related to 'fixing' absence suggest that a registered attendance data point or category could, in a sense, be 'broken'. Hence, each instance of attendance data contestation can be understood as a type of digital disruption or technological breakdown (González López and Büchner 2024). In the above example, Student 6 explained to the teacher that he actually had been present during the lesson and initiated a meeting with the teacher about the absence. The conversation thus shows how the student began to address a registration error and negotiate with the teacher, thus asking him to review and adjust the registration of the absence in the school's administrative platform. Following this, the above example can be understood as illustrating how both teachers and students were drawn into attendance data repair activities.

Due to their personal nature, I was not present during the meetings when teachers and students talked about absences and, therefore, I do not know the actual topics of these conversations. Drawing from the literature (Kjeøy and Lysvik 2023), we can speculate that such meetings often concern the correction of a wrongly registered undocumented absence and/or the provision of a legitimate reason and any missing documentation. Alternatively, they could also concern alternative assessment arrangements – a right that students may have, for instance, when a prolonged absence results from health issues or difficult life circumstances (UDIR 2026). Additionally, it is important to acknowledge that absence-related requests may also serve as a socially safe or acceptable means for students to initiate one-to-one conversations with their lead teacher in the presence of others (for instance, peers, other teachers or the researcher). Consequently, it is possible that the topic of 'fixing' absence was used more creatively by students to 'mask' their requests, while intending to discuss related but more complex issues connected to underlying factors behind school absences, such as health issues, family or peer relationships or academic pressures (Hejl et al. 2025; Kjeøy and Lysvik 2023).

In the above instance, the student and the teacher engaged in *negotiation* and repair activities. As such, this type of attendance data practice can be understood as enacted and performed through 'student–teacher–platform' interactions. As students identified that a registered data point was incorrect or placed in the wrong category, thus in need of 'fixing' or adjustment, the processes of absence registrations and categorizations were re-initiated. The potentially 'broken' or 'contested' data registration thus intertwined with the students' and teachers' talks and meetings (student-teacher relationships), the teachers' and students' careful balancing of curricular work with attendance data management, the teachers' and students' responsibilities to monitor and manage the data (absence limit ruling and school regulations), students' school stress and family, peer and life circumstances.

DISCUSSION

This chapter examines how attendance data practices were enacted and developed in a Norwegian upper secondary classroom. The above analytical mapping suggests that the data-producing technologies, involving the digital administrative system as well as regulations, continued to entangle as part of the lessons long after the more formal attendance data registration events. The three empirical examples demonstrate how various types of attendance data practices were enacted within the ordinary activities of the classroom through processes related to the registration, monitoring, negotiation and repair of absence data categories.

The attendance data process did not end with the initial registration of (un)documented absences, but continued as the upper secondary students and teachers, in various ways, directed attention towards and engaged in a diverse set of constellations with attendance data.

As the analytical mapping shows, the data-producing technology was deeply entangled with the absence limit and attendance regulations and continued to be an active part of the broader pedagogical environment, embedded in the formal and informal routines, actions and talk through the teacher–student attendance monitoring and negotiation activities.

These processes align with the (re/de)contextualization processes outlined by Frydenlund (2022) understood as the continuous work teachers do to align with the official attendance data categories, eventually compressing complex issues into decontextualized and 'clean' absence codes. As such, while the schools' administrative platforms aim to make absence-related tasks and communication more efficient, this study supports existing research arguing that they, in contrast, add to teacher workload (Decuypere et al. 2021; Kjeøy and Lysvik 2024; Moraiti et al. 2025; Williamson et al. 2024)

The routines and activities connected to attendance data appeared so integrated and stabilized in the classroom that they were rendered almost invisible through their mundane repetition. Meanwhile, their consequences for daily teaching situations can be seen, for instance, in the teachers' attempts to complete the roll call process as quickly as possible, but also in the students' emotional and behavioural responses, the recurring student-teachers' meetings and repair work, and their overall demand on the time and attention of both teachers and students.

Another often-overlooked aspect of attendance data practices is the digital work of students. As this study demonstrates, for some students, navigating attendance data dashboards can be a challenge. The education system in Norway is highly digitalized (Kunnskapsdepartementet 2023) and assumes students have access to smartphones with internet connections, expecting them to notify schools right away if they are delayed. A study by Thomas and Hennum (2020) shows how the expectation of constant connectivity caused a fear of being disconnected as the students described stressful situations, for instance, when a phone was not accessible or the battery ran out just as their train failed to arrive on time (Thomas and Hennum 2020, p. 17).

The obligatory registration and management of attendance data place responsibilities on teachers, for instance, to accurately record data and categories, issue timely warnings to students and negotiate registrations and follow up with students who have high absences. Meanwhile, as shown, students are also held responsible, not only to be physically present in the classroom but also to engage in administrative activities, notify the school, secure and provide documentation and oversee and arrange meetings about their attendance data. The data production does, in this sense, recurrently bring teachers and students into each other's field of vision, thus generating student–teacher meetings, but also organizing them into practices of monitoring each other's attendance data work.

As shown, the students expressed concerns about receiving remarks and undocumented absences in their attendance data profile and initiated meetings with the teachers to correct, repair and update their data. The students can thus be intepreted as, to a degree, performing the logic of attendance data practices, by 'desiring' the right categories and 'fearing' the wrong ones. Following Decuypere et al. (2021), this can be understood as the working of a 'vigilant digital gaze', created for 'the exercise of (self)government' and as an effect of how each student 'sees data' and 'is seen by data' (Decuypere et al. 2021, p. 11).

Furthermore, as Smith (2018) has cautioned, the routinization of data use, combined with a generalized trust and belief in the functionality of such technologies, can, when accumulated, contribute to reducing our 'awareness of how data, as technology of government, structures social experiences' (Smith 2018, p. 2). Data practices can, in this way, make the norms, values, risks and power relationships embedded in these technologies invisible (Decuypere et al.

2021, p. 9), with one such risk being the collapsing of students' identities into specific 'data constructs' through the reductive processes of decontextualization (Knage 2023; Perrotta and Williamson 2018).

Meanwhile, when categories matter – as they do for most upper secondary students by potentially expanding or limiting their future employment or educational opportunities and overall life chances – students will (understandably) actively engage in data attendance practices and not only through compliance but also through resisting, disputing, negotiating and correcting data categories, whilst creatively learning from and interacting with loopholes in the systems, providing (real or invented) reasons, evidence and documents (Bjørnset et al. 2018; Thomas and Hennum 2020).

Currently, many researchers argue for the need for more data, suggesting that the solution lies in creating even more precise and nuanced data about individual students' absences (Kearney and Childs 2023). Researchers have also advocated for schools to undertake a more active analysis of the data they collect (Keppens et al. 2019). In the Nordic context, there have been calls for increased standardisation through clearer national guidelines on how to record, report and use attendance data (Sandhaug et al. 2022).

Meanwhile, several studies have highlighted the challenges in creating neutral or consistent classifications and concepts when defining and representing 'non-attendance' in education (Frydenlund and Strand 2024; Keppens et al. 2019; Kjeøy and Lysvik 2024; Knage 2023). This chapter can be seen as contributing to the field of research that highlights the relational complexity of attendance data and problematizes the belief in the possibility of high-quality, neutral measurement and classification of attendance (Frydenlund 2022; Perrotta and Williamson 2018).

CONCLUSION

As this chapter has shown, a range of *attendance data practices* were enacted in the upper secondary classroom, through the involvement of technologies (the administrative platform and its production and use of attendance data), regulations (the absence limit ruling), and the teachers' and students' (in)formal activities and responses. As students and teachers encountered and used data-producing technologies, these practices became intervowen with other classroom activities, ideas and relationships. Hence, while emerging as mundane and routinized, the attendance data practices were influential in the day-to-day pedagogical environment.

Understood as part of a larger school-launched system for educational quality, the data-producing system operated as a component in the larger attendance data constellation, and from a relational materialist perspective, were therefore an active contributor in the spatial and temporal ordering forces 'at work', participating in the production of everyday as well as future educational encounters and experiences (Klykken 2023a). As such, the chapter illustrates how a data-generating digital system, intended to measure and support educational quality, became an integrated part of the educational reality that it claims to measure (Perrotta and Williamson 2018). Hence, it is necessary to increase awareness that regardless of the measuring tool, it will always interweave with the world it measures and, therefore, exclude the possibility of neutral measurement processes.

ACKNOWLEDGEMENTS

The Trond Mohn Research Foundation financially supported the writing of this chapter through the EduTrust AI project (TMS2023TMT03).

REFERENCES

Adams, C. and T.L. Thompson (2016), *Researching a Posthuman World: Interviews with Digital Objects,* Palgrave Macmillan UK. https://doi.org/10.1057/978-1-137-57162-5

Alirezabeigi, S., J. Masschelein and M. Decuypere (2020), 'Investigating digital doings through breakdowns: A sociomaterial ethnography of a Bring Your Own Device school', *Learning, Media and Technology*, **45** (2), 193–207. https://doi.org/10.1080/17439884.2020.1727501

Bergene, A.C., K.S. Vika, B. Lynnebakke, M.N. Vonen, R.H. Lyckander and Ø. A. Samuelsen (2023), *Fravær som vekker bekymring: Skoleeieres og skolelederes inntrykk og forståelse av fraværssituasjonen i Skole-Norge* (NIFU report 2023:14). https://hdl.handle.net/11250/3087762

Birioukov, A. (2016), 'Beyond the excused/unexcused absence binary: Classifying absenteeism through a voluntary/involuntary absence framework', *Educational Review*, **68** (3), 340–57. https://doi.org/10.1080/00131911.2015.1090400

Bjørnset, M., N. Drange, H. Gjefsen, M.T. Kindt and J. Rogstad (2018), *In the absence limit's blind spot* (Fafo report 2018:41). https://www.fafo.no/publikasjoner/fafo-rapporter/i-fravaersgrensens-dodvinkel

Bodén, L. (2016), *Present absences: Exploring the posthumanist entanglements of school absenteeism*, Doctoral dissertation, Linköping University, Sweden. https://doi.org/10.3384/diss.diva-130460

Bodén, L. (2017), 'Going with the affective flows of digital school absence text messages', *Learning, Media and Technology*, **42** (4), 406–19. https://doi.org/10.1080/17439884.2017.1247859

Bodén, L., H. Lenz Taguchi, E. Moberg and C. Taylor (2020), 'Relational materialism', in G.W. Noblit (ed.), *Oxford Research Encyclopedia of Education*, Oxford: Oxford University Press, 1–20. https://doi.org/10.1093/acrefore/9780190264093.013.789

Decuypere, M. (2021), 'The topologies of data practices: A methodological introduction', *Journal of New Approaches in Educational Research*, **10** (1), 67–84. https://doi.org/10.7821/naer.2021.1.650

Decuypere, M., G. Emiliano and P. Landri (2021), 'Introduction: Critical studies of digital education platforms', *Critical Studies in Education*, **62** (1), 1–16. https://doi.org/10.1080/17508487.2020.1866050

Delamont, S. and P. Atkinson (2021), *Ethnographic Engagements: Encounters with the Familiar and the Strange*. London: Routledge. https://doi.org/10.4324/9780429056840

Fredriksson, U., M. Rasmusson, A. Backlund, J. Isaksson and S. Kreitz-Sandberg (2023), 'School absenteeism among students in Germany, Japan, Sweden and the United Kingdom: A comparative study using PISA data', *Nordic Journal of Comparative and International Education (NJCIE)*, **7** (1), 1–27. https://doi.org/10.7577/njcie.5034

Frydenlund, J.H. (2022), 'The dirty process of creating clean absence data: An ethnographic study', *Scandinavian Journal of Educational Research*, **67** (6), 853–69. https://doi.org/10.1080/00313831.2022.2070930

Frydenlund, J.H. and A.H. Strand (2024), 'Kampen om skolefraværet', *Norsk sosiologisk tidsskrift*, **8** (2–3), 1–6. https://doi.org/10.18261/nost.8.2-3.1

González López, A.E. and F. Büchner (2024), 'EdTech in a broken world: Breaking and repairing in Argentinian and German schools', *Postdigital Science and Education*, **6** (4), 1261–86. https://doi.org/10.1007/s42438-024-00490-4

Hangartner, J., D. Hürzeler and N. Aebli (2025), 'Everyday approaches to platform-mediated personalized learning in secondary schools', *Learning, Media and Technology*, **50** (4), 467–81. https://doi.org/10.1080/17439884.2024.2367051

Hejl, C., E.F. Nadine, H.R. Birner, N. Klaus and M. Thastum (2025), 'A review and qualitative synthesis of the voices of children, parents and school staff with regards to school attendance problems in the

Nordic countries', *Scandinavian Journal of Educational Research*, **69** (7), 1490–1504. https://doi.org/10.1080/00313831.2024.2434822
Jarke, J. and A. Breiter (2019), 'Editorial: the datafication of education', *Learning, Media and Technology*, **44** (1), 1–6. https://doi.org/10.1080/17439884.2019.1573833
Kearney, C.A. and J. Childs (2023), 'Improving school attendance data and defining problematic and chronic school absenteeism: The next stage for educational policies and health-based practices', *Preventing School Failure: Alternative Education for Children and Youth*, **67** (4), 265–75. https://doi.org/10.1080/1045988X.2022.2124222
Keppens, G., B. Spruyt and J. Dockx (2019), 'Measuring school absenteeism: Administrative attendance data collected by schools differ from self-reports in systematic ways', *Frontiers in Psychology*, **10**, 1–10. https://doi.org/10.3389/fpsyg.2019.02623
Kjeøy, I. and R.R. Lysvik, (2023), *Worrying school absence levels: A Scandinavian literature review* (Fafo report 2023:13). https://www.fafo.no/publikasjoner/fafo-rapporter/kunnskapsstatus-om-bekymringsfullt-fravaer-i-skolen
Kjeøy, I. and R.R. Lysvik (2024), 'Skulk, skolevegring eller bekymringsfullt fravær? Implikasjoner av begrepsbruk i skandinavisk forskning om fravær i skolen', *Norsk sosiologisk tidsskrift*, **8** (2–3), 70–85. https://doi.org/10.18261/nost.8.2-3.6
Klykken, F.H. (2023a), 'The teaching apparatus: A material-discursive entanglement of tasks and friendship in the upper-secondary classroom', *Critical Studies in Education*, **65** (1), 1–19. https://doi.org/10.1080/17508487.2023.2207607
Klykken, F.H. (2023b), *The teaching apparatus: Understanding the material entanglement of practices in the upper secondary classroom*, Doctoral dissertation, University of Bergen, Bergen. https://hdl.handle.net/11250/3062689
Klykken, F.H. (2025), 'Chapter 4: Informed consent in qualitative research: Lessons on relationality from a technologically dense classroom', in H. Busby (ed.), *Reframing Qualitative Research Ethics (Advances in Research Ethics and Integrity, Vol. 12)*, Leeds: Emerald Publishing, pp. 57–73. https://doi.org/10.1108/S2398-601820250000012004
Knage, F.S. (2023), 'Beyond the school refusal/truancy binary: Engaging with the complexities of extended school non-attendance', *International Studies in Sociology of Education*, **32** (4), 1013–37. https://doi.org/10.1080/09620214.2021.1966827
Kunnskapsdepartementet (2023), *Strategi for digital kompetanse og infrastruktur i barnehage og skole. 2023–2030.* Oslo: Kunnskapsdepartementet (Norwegian Ministry of Education and Research). https://www.regjeringen.no/no/dokumenter/strategi-for-digital-kompetanse-og-infrastruktur-i-barnehage-og-skole/id2972254/
Lindland, E. (2022), *Visma InSchool: troverdig visjon eller ren illusjon?*, Master's Thesis, University of Agder. https://hdl.handle.net/11250/3021562
Macgilchrist, F. (2019), 'Cruel optimism in edtech: When the digital data practices of educational technology providers inadvertently hinder educational equity', *Learning, Media and Technology*, **44** (1), 77–86. https://doi.org/10.1080/17439884.2018.1556217
Moraiti, K., B.R. Annika and M. Lundin (2025), 'Digital platform work reinforcing performativity: teacher responses to work intensification explored through trace ethnography', *Critical Studies in Education*, **66** (5), 73754. https://doi.org/10.1080/17508487.2024.2409661
Mörtsell, S. (2022), 'Sociomaterial explorations of attendance practices in "schooling without schools"', *Learning, Media and Technology*, **47** (4), 512–23. https://doi.org/10.1080/17439884.2022.2039939
NESH (2021), *Guidelines for Research Ethics in the Social Sciences and the Humanities.* National Committee for Research Ethics in the Social Sciences and the Humanities. https://www.forskningsetikk.no/globalassets/dokumenter/4-publikasjoner-som-pdf/nesh-guidelines-en-2024
NOU 2023: 19 (2023), *Learning: Lost in the Shuffle? Use of pupil and student data to enhance learning.* Oslo: Kunnskapsdepartementet (Norwegian Ministry of Education and Research). https://www.regjeringen.no/contentassets/c0471fcd36e8481a92b627f54a702c7e/en-gb/pdfs/nou202320230019000engpdfs.pdf
NSD (2020), *Norwegian Centre for Research Data: Data Protection in Research.* https://sikt.no/en/om-sikt/management-and-organisation
OECD (2024), *Education at a Glance 2024: OECD Indicators.* Paris: OECD Publishing. https://doi.org/10.1787/c00cad36-en

Opplæringsforskrifta (2024), *Regulations to the Education Act relating to Primary and Secondary Education and Training (FOR-2024-06-03-900).* Lovdata. https://lovdata.no/LTI/forskrift/2024-06-03-900

Pangrazio, L., N. Selwyn and B. Cumbo (2023), 'A patchwork of platforms: mapping data infrastructures in schools', *Learning, Media and Technology*, **48** (1), 65–80. https://doi.org/10.1080/17439884.2022.2035395

Perrotta, C. and B. Williamson (2018), 'The social life of Learning Analytics: cluster analysis and the "performance" of algorithmic education', *Learning, Media and Technology*, **43** (1), 3–16. https://doi.org/10.1080/17439884.2016.1182927

Prøven, H. (2023), *Når hver time telles*, Master Thesis, Norwegian University of Science and Technology (NTNU). https://hdl.handle.net/11250/3106501

Sandhaug, M., I. Palmu, S. Jakobsen, J. Strömbeck, M.-J. Nordby, P. Friberg, J. Berg, L. Fensbo, J. Sjöström and M. Thastu (2022), 'Recording, reporting, and utilizing school attendance data in Sweden, Finland, Denmark, and Norway: A Nordic comparison', *Orbis scholae*, **16** (2), 173–86. https://doi.org/https://doi.org/10.14712/23363177.2022.12

Sellar, S. (2015), 'Data infrastructure: a review of expanding accountability systems and large-scale assessments in education', *Discourse: Studies in the Cultural Politics of Education*, **36** (5), 765–77. https://doi.org/10.1080/01596306.2014.931117

Selwyn, N. (2016), '"There's so much data": Exploring the realities of data-based school governance', *European Educational Research Journal*, **15** (1), 54–68. https://doi.org/10.1177/1474904115602909

Selwyn, N., L. Pangrazio and B. Cumbo (2021), 'Attending to data: Exploring the use of attendance data within the datafied school', *Research in Education*, **109** (1), 72–89. https://doi.org/10.1177/0034523720984200

Smith, G.J. (2018), 'Data doxa: The affective consequences of data practices', *Big Data & Society*, **5** (1), 1–15. https://doi.org/10.1177/2053951717751551

Sørensen, E. (2009), *The Materiality of Learning: Technology and Knowledge in Educational Practice.* Cambridge: Cambridge University Press.https://doi.org/10.1017/CBO9780511576362

Thomas, P. and Ø. Hennum (2020), 'Absenteeism and the new 10% ruling in Norway: A case study', *Power and Education*, **12** (1), 1–22. https://doi.org/10.1177/1757743819850854

UDIR (2023), *The Norwegian Education Mirror 2022.* Utdanningsdirektoratet (Norwegian Directorate for Education and Training). https://www.udir.no/in-english/the-education-mirror-2022/

UDIR (2026), *Circular on the absence limit.* Utdanningsdirektoratet (Norwegian Directorate for Education and Training). https://www.udir.no/regelverk-og-tilsyn/skole-og-opplaring/rundskriv-om-fravarsgrensen/

UDIR (2025), *Fortsatt økt timefravær i videregående.* Utdanningsdirektoratet (Norwegian Directorate for Education and Training). https://www.udir.no/tall-og-forskning/statistikk/statistikk-videregaende-skole/analyser/2025/fortsatt-okt-fravar-videregaende/

Williamson, B., F. Macgilchrist and J. Potter (2024), 'Against contextlessness in Learning, Media and Technology', *Learning, Media and Technology*, **49** (3), 335–38. https://doi.org/10.1080/17439884.2024.2374266

PART IV

PEDAGOGICAL POSSIBILITIES AND CHALLENGES

9. Teacher development with learning analytics: a design narrative

Fabio Campos, Ha Nguyen, and June Ahn

INTRODUCTION

The growing adoption of human-centered design in learning analytics has spurred significant interest in how digital tools can be meaningfully integrated into educational settings. However, much of the existing literature focuses on either higher education or K–12 systems with established learning management infrastructures, leaving a critical gap in understanding how to develop and implement learning analytics in schools where such systems are absent (Ahn et al. 2019). This chapter draws from a seven-year design-research journey with Edsight, a visual analytics suite developed in collaboration with middle school mathematics teachers and instructional coaches in the USA. By embedding participatory design and iterative development, Edsight offers a unique perspective on how learning analytics can be tailored to meet the needs of educators working in diverse and often under-resourced school systems. Our work demonstrates that designing visual analytics for K–12 education requires approaches that align with existing teaching practices and routines and introduce innovative ways to support sensemaking, professional development and pedagogical decision-making.

In this chapter, we review the literature on human-centered learning analytics (Buckingham Shum et al. 2019), examine the specific challenges of applying these approaches in K–12 settings and detail the design and deployment of Edsight across three regions in the US. Through this, we propose three key design principles for learning analytics in K–12 education: fostering long-term research-practice partnerships; designing for actionable sensemaking; and embedding cultural forms into learning analytics tools. By articulating these principles, we aim to offer a roadmap for learning analytics scholars, designers and practitioners to support and enhance teaching and learning in non-platformized school environments. The story of how Edsight was developed, deployed and iteratively refined offers an empirical foundation for understanding how participatory design methodologies can be applied in long-term research-practice partnerships (Ahn et al. 2019). We present concrete design principles that can inform future developments and contribute to the growing field of human-centered learning analytics (Buckingham Shum et al. 2019). By exploring the affordances and limitations of leveraging *cultural forms* – recognizable constructs embedded in educators' routines (Horn 2013; Saxe 1999)—we provide insights into how learning dashboards can be designed to enhance, rather than disrupt, existing professional workflows and augment educators' *sensemaking*—the process through which individuals interpret data and make informed decisions (Campos et al. 2021).

This chapter serves as a guide for educators to implement learning analytics tools in real-world K–12 educational contexts. Teachers, instructional coaches and school leaders will find valuable takeaways on how analytics can be employed in solo or collaborative reflection and integrated into professional development cycles. Our findings emphasize the importance of designing tools that present data and actively support educators in interpreting and applying insights to improve classroom instruction (Klerkx et al. 2017). By detailing Edsight's iterative design process and its implementation across multiple school districts, we provide actionable strategies for educators looking to harness learning analytics in meaningful and sustainable ways. Finally, this chapter also serves as a practical example for researchers and practitioners navigating the complexities of co-designing Learning Analytics tools in the context of Research–Practice Partnerships (RPPs).

LITERATURE REVIEW

Learning Dashboards

Learning dashboards have emerged as pivotal tools in Learning Analytics, offering educators and students access to real-time, data-driven insights (Klerkx et al. 2017). Most importantly, the promise of these dashboards lies in their ability to aggregate, visualize and contextualize learning data, enabling informed decision-making to improve teaching and learning experiences. However, their effectiveness depends on their technical features and how well they align with their intended users' practices, routines, needs and values (Viberg et al. 2023). Research has shown that while dashboards can support teacher reflection and instructional decision-making, they often fall short in fostering deeper pedagogical insights and action (Duval 2011). The challenge is designing dashboards beyond static data representations (Ahn et al. 2019). Ultimately, for learning dashboards to fulfill their potential, they must bridge the gap between data and pedagogical inquiry, supporting educators in moving beyond awareness of classroom trends to deep, generative reflection and instructional improvement (Ahn et al. 2019; Li et al. 2025; Wise and Jung 2019).

Data Visualization

Data visualization is concerned with effectively representing complex information and transforming raw data into visual formats that facilitate comprehension, interpretation and decision-making (Islam and Jin 2019). Gestalt principles, for instance, further expand our understanding of how individuals perceive graphs, hierarchies and other relationships between data points. These cognitive theories inform the design of visualizations that maximize interpretability while minimizing cognitive load, ensuring that users can efficiently extract insights from the displayed data. In the context of learning analytics, data visualization plays a primary role in sensemaking, mainly when designed to align with the practices and needs of educators. Research has shown that effective visual analytics tools in educational settings must accommodate different levels of data literacy and attune to the complexities of the school as a living and ever-changing system.

Human-centered Learning Analytics Design

Human-centered design (HCD) approaches prioritize users' needs, experiences and contexts throughout the design and development of technological systems (Buckingham Shum et al. 2019). Rooted in cognitive science, human–computer interaction and participatory design,

HCD posits that tools should be developed *with*, rather than for, end users. HCD is particularly relevant in learning analytics, as data-driven tools must seamlessly integrate into educators' values, routines and decision-making processes to be genuinely effective.

One core principle of HCD is iterative design, where prototypes are developed, tested and refined in close collaboration with users. This process includes user interviews, low- and high-fidelity prototyping and participatory co-design sessions. By engaging educators early in the design cycle, learning analytics researchers can ensure that data representations and interface designs support meaningful sensemaking rather than simply providing information. Additionally, human-centered learning analytics (HCLA) frameworks emphasize designing for diverse stakeholders—teachers, coaches and administrators—who may have varying levels of data literacy and needs.

A crucial challenge in HCLA is addressing the social and organizational contexts in which these tools operate (Ahn et al. 2019; Buckingham Shum et al. 2019). Unlike commercial data dashboards that assume high technical proficiency, educational technologies must account for time constraints, pedagogical values and institutional structures that shape data interpretation and use. Leveraging cultural forms—recognizable artifacts, routines and visual metaphors—can help bridge this gap, allowing educators to engage with data in familiar and actionable ways.

Finally, researchers employing HCLA in complex educational environments—especially those of K–12 schools—may encounter numerous design tensions. Design tensions are conflicts or trade-offs that arise when designing software, products or experiences, where addressing one design goal may compromise another. These tensions often emerge due to competing user needs, technical constraints or contextual factors. Recognizing and taking advantage of—and not merely 'resolving'—the many tensions at a school or educational system (Tatar 2007) is at the core of HCLA. For example, the tensions between teachers and their school leaders regarding data privacy in a Learning Analytics (LA) platform may reveal how educators navigate transparency and confidentiality at the school and pave the way for design solutions that may exist beyond mere features (Ahn et al. 2019; 2021).

Learning Analytics and K–12 Schools

Learning analytics (LA) in K–12 education remains underdeveloped compared to its application in higher education, where robust learning management systems (LMS) provide a steady stream of student interaction data. In K–12 settings, the adoption of LA has been fragmented, with tools often designed for administrative monitoring rather than instructional decision-making (Paolucci et al. 2024). Most existing research focuses on higher education contexts, where students use digital platforms that generate vast structured data. In contrast, K–12 classrooms frequently rely on diverse, often disconnected data sources, ranging from student assessments and teacher observations to behavioral records and formative feedback (Wardrip and Herman 2018).

One significant gap in the LA literature is the absence of design principles that address the specific needs of K–12 educators. While LA dashboards in higher education are often built for self-regulated learning, teacher-facing tools in K–12 require a different design logic that prioritizes ease of use, rapid interpretation and actionable insights (Campos et al. 2024). Research has also overlooked the social and collaborative aspects of data use in schools, where instructional coaches, administrators and teachers work together to make sense of student data.

Without frameworks that acknowledge these collaborative decision-making processes, many LA tools fail to integrate effectively into school routines (Campos et al. 2021).

Another critical gap is the limited exploration of cultural and contextual factors influencing the adoption of LA in K–12 settings. Educators' engagement with data is shaped by institutional norms, professional values and varying levels of data literacy (Ahn et al. 2019; Campos et al. 2024; Viberg et al. 2023). Current LA research rarely examines how teachers make sense of data within these constraints. Addressing these gaps requires a shift toward human-centered, participatory approaches that align with the realities of K–12 teaching and learning environments.

Sensemaking with Learning Analytics

Sensemaking in learning analytics (LA) is a complex cognitive and social process through which individuals interpret data, derive meaning and make informed decisions (Campos et al. 2021). Rooted in cognitive psychology theories and information visualization, sensemaking involves more than simply reading charts or graphs—it requires users to contextualize data within their existing knowledge, experiences and goals (Dervin 1998). This process is particularly nuanced in educational settings, as teachers, instructional coaches and administrators must navigate multiple layers of meaning, connecting data representations to classroom realities, student behaviors and pedagogical strategies.

A key challenge in LA research is understanding how educators transition from awareness (recognizing that data exists) to actionable insight (using data to inform teaching practices; Wise and Jung 2019; Jivet et al. 2017; Li et al. 2025). Studies suggest that many LA tools fail at this juncture, as they primarily focus on data presentation rather than scaffolding users' interpretive processes. Effective sensemaking involves cognitive engagement and social interaction; educators often rely on discussions with colleagues, coaching sessions and institutional frameworks to interpret and validate data-driven insights. However, LA research has historically overlooked these collaborative processes, instead assuming an individualized model of data interpretation.

Another critical dimension of sensemaking is uncertainty. Data in education is often incomplete, ambiguous or subject to multiple interpretations. Rather than aiming for definitive answers, productive data use involves engaging in 'generative uncertainty'—a stance where educators explore patterns, ask critical questions and seek additional evidence before concluding (Nguyen et al. 2021). Ultimately, sensemaking in LA is not a passive process of receiving insights but an active, interpretive practice shaped by cognitive abilities, social interactions and institutional norms. Designing for meaningful sensemaking requires tools that facilitate inquiry, contextualize data and support educators in bridging the gap between representation and action.

DESIGNING AND DEPLOYING EDSIGHT

Context

Our research team is part of a more extensive network of Research–Practice Partnerships (RPPs) called PMR2: Practical Measures, Routines, and Representations (Jackson et al. 2016).

Established in 2016 with funding from the US National Science Foundation, PMR2 connects four RPPs, encompassing four universities and four school districts across different regions of the United States. The network is dedicated to helping middle school math teachers (grades 6–8) leverage data to promote student collaboration and discussion, fostering a deeper conceptual understanding of mathematics. In RPPs, district partners and researchers typically co-develop the research agenda and priorities (Coburn and Penuel 2016). In our case, the focus was on enhancing instructional practices and routines for math teachers and their instructional coaches, two key roles regularly engaging in classroom-level data sensemaking. While other K–12 educators, such as district leaders and subject specialists, also participate in our RPPs, their engagement with data falls beyond the scope of this analysis.

The PMR2 network focuses on designing and implementing Practical Measures (PMs)—short, formative assessments that capture key aspects of student learning experiences, such as engagement in mathematical discussions. These measures are integrated into instructional routines, allowing teachers and coaches to reflect on classroom interactions and make data-informed decisions. Rather than emphasizing static performance metrics, PMR2 prioritizes actionable insights that align with teachers' existing workflows. The initiative is deeply embedded in the principles of improvement science (Krumm et al. 2016), ensuring that design decisions are continuously refined through iterative feedback loops between researchers and educators.

In the PMR2 research network, PM data are gathered through student-facing surveys, each consisting of approximately eight questions. These surveys are administered by teachers at various points during a class session. For instance, after a whole-class discussion, students may complete a survey, often as an exit slip, reflecting on their experience. Example questions include, 'Were you comfortable sharing your thinking in today's whole-class discussion?' and 'Who talked the most in today's whole-class discussion?' (Figure 9.1). All survey questions use multiple-choice response formats. Responses are often collected electronically, while a smaller subset of classrooms utilizes paper-based surveys. Once collected, student responses are anonymized, processed and presented to educators through a dashboard that visualizes single- and multi-day 'classroom reports.'

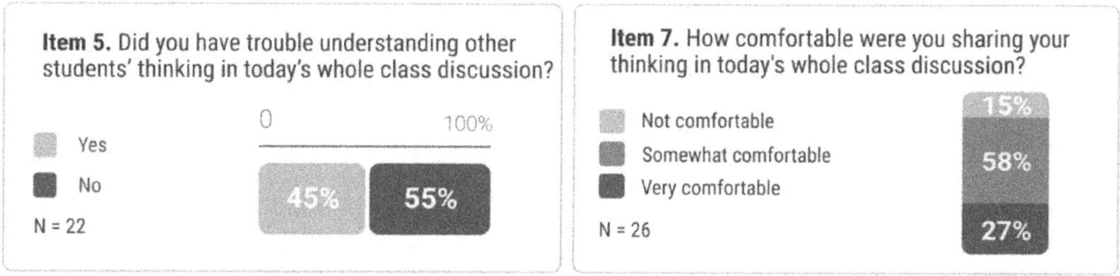

Source: Authors.

Figure 9.1 *Practical measures and their graphical representation*

Designing the Tool

Edsight was developed through a multi-year iterative process shaped by a commitment to human-centered design, deep collaboration with educators and an evolving understanding of how data can support instructional decision-making. From the outset, the goal was not just to build a learning dashboard to house PM data but to create a system meaningfully integrated into teachers' workflows to facilitate professional inquiry and respond to the realities of classroom practice.

A frequent observation from other RPP teams working with data is that while numerous tools exist for online data collection, whether through automated log data or online surveys and visualization and analysis, these tools often clash with established organizational routines or rigid district policy requirements (Farrell and Marsh 2016). Rather than imposing a rigid data framework, Edsight needed to be flexible, allowing teachers and instructional coaches to engage with data in ways aligned with their existing practices. This understanding led to a shift from purely performance-based analytics to a system emphasizing generative uncertainty, encouraging educators to question, interpret and act on data rather than merely consume it.

Our design process began in January 2017 and involved weekly meetings with a dedicated design team, including PMR2 researchers, designers, web developers and database programmers. Alongside these meetings, the broader PMR2 project team also convened weekly to coordinate project activities. This cross-team meeting has provided a space for collaborative decision-making on the dashboard application. As a result, our design process became an integral part of the initiative's weekly project management routines. As soon as prototypes were generated, our research design team engaged in successive user sessions, combining semi-structured interviews with think-aloud protocols (Van Someren et al. 1994), in which teachers, instructional coaches and district personnel used the tools and voiced their perceptions.

The initial prototypes relied on standard data representation techniques such as pie charts and bar graphs. Still, early user feedback revealed that these formats did not always support the inquiry educators needed. Through multiple iterations and design sessions, the team experimented with layered visualizations, longitudinal comparisons and interactive elements that allowed teachers to explore student data dynamically. The goal was not just to show what was happening in classrooms but to foster a sensemaking process—helping educators connect data to instructional decisions in meaningful ways. Figure 9.2 shows the first functional version of Edsight deployed to educators, with a simple 'report view' of PM data.

In the following subsection, we narrate the central design tensions faced when co-designing and deploying Edsight and describe how the design team managed said tensions.

Leveraging Design Tensions

The design tensions paradigm (Tatar 2007) is an approach to designing educational and technological systems that acknowledges the design process's inherent trade-offs and competing priorities. Instead of viewing design as a straightforward problem-solving activity, this paradigm frames it as balancing multiple, often conflicting, goals. Design tensions arise when different stakeholders—teachers, instructional coaches, administrators, students and policymakers—have diverse needs, constraints and expectations that must be negotiated in the context of learning analytics and educational tools.

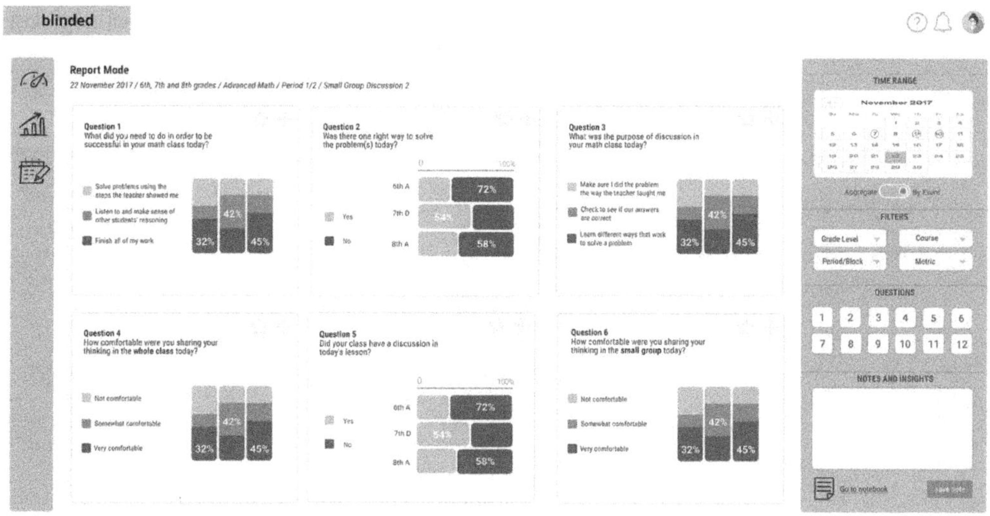

Source: Authors.

Figure 9.2 *Edsight, version 1: report view*

A myriad of such design tensions emerged throughout the development of Edsight. Each of these tensions was treated as an opportunity not just to disambiguate potential uses of the tool but, most importantly, to gain better insight into users' needs and contexts of use. First and foremost, our design team identified a tension between *flexibility* and *standardization*. From the start, the design team knew that a system like Edsight must be adaptable to different classroom contexts. Yet, consistency was also needed to ensure reliability and comparability across various schools and districts. Similarly, we noticed an ongoing trade-off between *providing immediate answers* and *fostering deeper inquiry*. Since dashboards offering quick, actionable data may discourage deeper sensemaking—while more open-ended systems might require additional training and support for educators to use them effectively (Campos et al. 2021)—we encouraged teachers and their coaches to reflect upon our data representations. We knew that teachers had limited time to engage with analytics and many had varying levels of experience with data interpretation. The design team addressed this by implementing a scaffolded approach, initially providing simple visualizations and gradually introducing more complex features as users became more comfortable.

Another type of design tension that emerged throughout the design process revolved around *privacy* versus *transparency*. The logic behind the PMR2 RPPs is based on teachers sharing data with their instructional coaches for professional development purposes. If teachers decided not to share their practical measures data—often due to a lackof trust, a perceived threat to their privacy or to avoid 'surveillance at the workplace,' as they frequently voiced—the whole workflow of the partnership could break. In one researcher's words: 'It could be a lost opportunity if half your teachers opted out of sharing that data.' To address this potentially harmful situation, the team designed, tested and iteratively refined a conversational data-sharing module in which teachers and coaches decide what, when and why data should

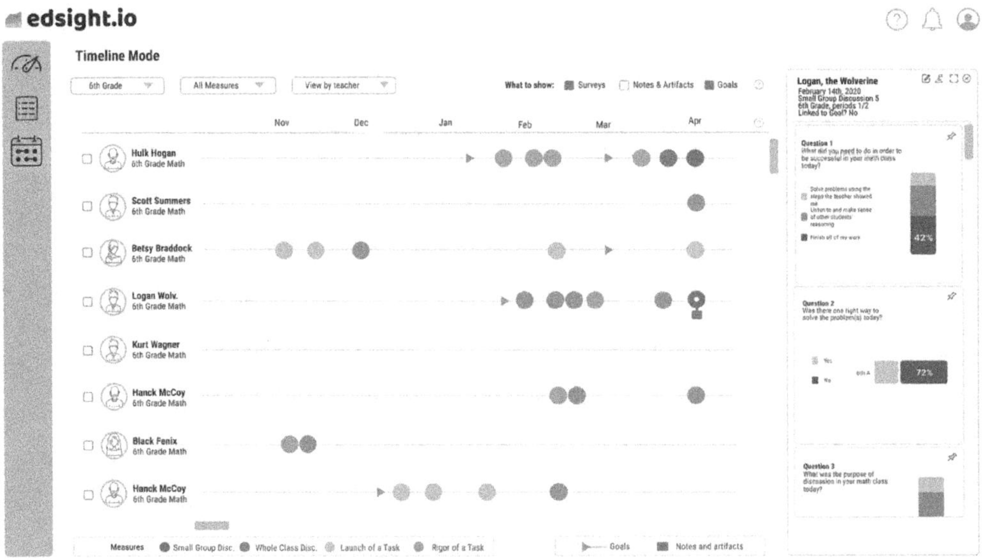

Source: Authors.

Figure 9.3 *Data-sharing module, where teachers and their coaches decide what will be shared*

be shared among peers (Figure 9.3). This is one concrete example of how such tension was leveraged into the tool's design for many years in the making.

Finally, we faced tensions between what *teachers and coaches needed* from the tool. Whereas teachers were often required to exclusively analyze their own data, coaches typically worked with groups of teachers. Moreover, teachers needed clear and well-grounded goals to pursue in their teaching endeavors, while coaches were the ones who needed to set such goals. To solve this puzzle, our team organized field trips to schools participating in the RPPs, where we followed educators through classes and coaching meetings and interviewed educators about their routines. In such trips, we also prototyped low-fidelity versions of new tools and modules to add to Edsight and tested them with educators in rapid design cycles at schools. On one such trip, our team started to attune to the most common cultural forms used by teachers and coaches at the school: binders, calendars and notebooks. Such observations sparked a new design insight that resulted in the second version of Edsight, launched in 2023 and a significant overhaul of the initial 2018 version (Figure 9.4).

LESSONS LEARNED

Edsight was designed to support teacher development by providing a structured yet flexible platform for engaging with data to enhance instructional practice and professional inquiry. Rather than simply presenting performance metrics, the tool was designed to encourage sense-making. It allowed teachers and their coaches to reflect on student learning trends, question

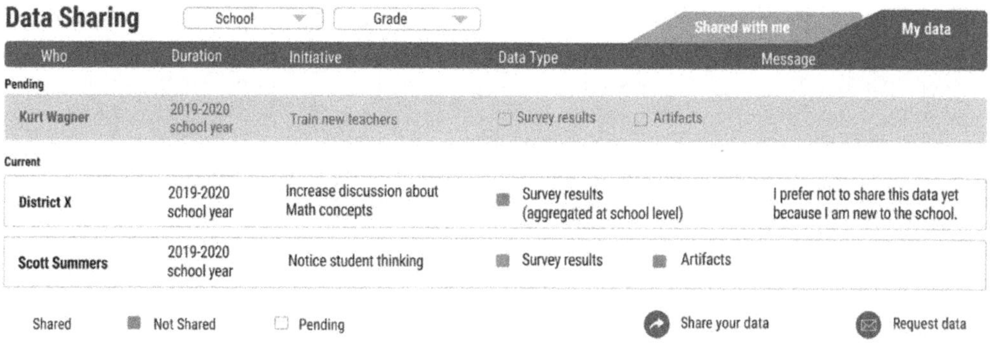

Source: Authors.

Figure 9.4 *Second deployment of Edsight, with views for coaches and teachers*

patterns and refine their teaching strategies based on actual classroom data. By embedding analytics into teachers' existing workflows—such as coaching cycles, collaborative planning and instructional goal-setting—Edsight becomes a tool for ongoing professional learning rather than a static reporting system. In this section, we present the main lessons learned throughout the various years of designing and refining Edsight with the direct input of K–12 educators.

This section summarizes the lessons learned after seven years of iterative development, deployment and redesign of Edsight. We focus on the four key overarching findings derived from intensive work with teachers, instructional coaches, school administrators and district-level personnel, mainly through semi-structured interviews, think-aloud sessions and site observations from 2017 to 2023.

Generative Uncertainty

One of the main theoretical concepts derived from the experience with Edsight is generative uncertainty (Nguyen et al. 2021), an interpretive stance in which educators engage with data not as a means to confirm pre-existing assumptions but as an opportunity to develop new inquiries that drive pedagogical improvement. Rather than treating data as a static representation of student performance, this approach encourages teachers and instructional coaches to navigate the ambiguity of information, question patterns, seek additional context and formulate the next steps beyond surface-level analysis.

In the context of learning analytics, generative uncertainty challenges the notion that dashboards should simply provide answers. Instead, it suggests that effective design should foster curiosity and deeper reflection. When teachers encounter unexpected data points, rather than dismissing them as anomalies or immediately searching for justifications, they should see them as starting points for exploration. This process often involves triangulating different sources of information, engaging in discussions with colleagues and considering broader classroom dynamics that explain the observed trends.

Designing for generative uncertainty requires careful attention to how data is represented. Visualizations that are too rigid or prescriptive may lead educators to superficial conclusions. On the other hand, representations that leave space for interpretation—such as time-series comparisons, layered contextual information or opportunities for qualitative input—can encourage richer engagement with the data. By fostering generative uncertainty, learning analytics tools move beyond simply tracking student performance and instead become instruments for professional inquiry, guiding educators toward meaningful instructional changes.

Sensemaking in the Context of Learning Analytics

The design and refinement of Edsight allowed the PMR2 research team to delve into how K–12 educators make sense of visual data available in learning dashboards. In this context, we learned that LA sensemaking is how educators interpret data, connect it to their experiences and use it to inform instructional decisions. It is not a passive act of reading visualizations but an active, iterative engagement with information that requires context, reflection and often peer collaboration. In tandem with the notion of generative uncertainty (Nguyen et al. 2021), effective sensemaking goes beyond merely identifying trends in student performance; it involves questioning why those patterns exist, considering multiple explanations and exploring potential responses that align with pedagogical goals.

Our design-research efforts showed that, for teachers and instructional coaches, sensemaking is deeply influenced by their prior knowledge, classroom dynamics and the broader institutional environment (Campos et al. 2021). When data is presented without context, educators may struggle to extract meaningful insights or misinterpret the information in ways that reinforce existing biases. This highlights the importance of designing learning analytics tools that support sensemaking rather than just data awareness (Jivet et al. 2017). Visualizations should display student performance metrics and provide educators with opportunities to layer their interpretations; compare across time and integrate qualitative insights from classroom observations or student interactions.

One potential risk of learning dashboards is the *overfitting* of narratives and plausible interpretations of data (Campos et al. 2021). Overfitting, a concept from statistics and machine learning, occurs when a prediction model fits too closely to the training data or existing patterns, reducing its ability to make accurate predictions with new data. In an in-depth study with 18 middle school mathematics educators, we found that educators were prone to over-normalize new evidence into familiar and plausible narratives, leading to repetitive or insubstantial interpretations. In our research, participants analyzed data reports while thinking aloud and responding to open-ended questions about how the data represented their practice, allowing researchers to explore contextual factors and interpretive processes. The research team developed a coding framework based on three dimensions—emotional, analytical and intentional—refining it through an iterative process to categorize educators' responses and strategies. In the final phase, the team systematically coded transcripts, ensured inter-rater reliability and conducted statistical analyses to compare differences between professional roles. In our findings, *overfitting* was evident in the high co-occurrence of causal attributions and lack of intentional responses, particularly among teachers who relied on past experiences to interpret data rather than engaging in deeper analysis or questioning. Emotional reactions, such as distrust in the data or its visualization, further contributed to this pattern, often resulting in no meaningful instructional action. These findings align with research showing that school data sensemaking can reinforce instructional practices, confirm biases or lead to ineffective experimentation (Farrell and Marsh 2016). This highlights the importance of careful design and computational choices for the LA community, as over-normalizing narratives can limit opportunities for deeper insights and meaningful change.

Cultural Forms in Learning Analytics Design

Cultural forms (Horn 2013; Saxe 1999) refer to the recognizable social and organizational structures, practices and symbols that shape how individuals engage with the world. In our research context, these forms can range from established routines like coaching cycles to physical artifacts such as notebooks, calendars or shared planning documents and serve as anchors for how information is interpreted and acted upon in educational settings. By leveraging cultural forms, learning analytics tools can be designed in ways that feel intuitive and meaningful to educators rather than imposing abstract or unfamiliar data representations (Campos et al. 2024).

In practice, designing with cultural forms means recognizing that data use does not happen in isolation but is embedded in the everyday activities and relationships of teachers, coaches and administrators. For instance, if teachers are accustomed to setting instructional goals through structured conversations with their coaches, an analytics dashboard that mirrors this process—by allowing goal-setting, reflection and collaborative annotations—can seamlessly integrate into existing workflows. Similarly, if schools rely on printed reports for discussions, a tool that generates printable summaries aligns more naturally with established habits than one that only offers interactive digital displays.

Incorporating cultural forms and other social signifiers into learning analytics design requires ensuring that they replicate existing practices and *enhance and evolve* them. Thoughtful design can use these forms to scaffold deeper engagement with data, supporting inquiry-driven practices rather than reinforcing routine compliance. By attuning to the cultural context in which data is used, learning analytics tools can foster more meaningful interactions, encourage adoption and ultimately lead to more effective data-informed decision-making.

Designing in Partnership for Learning Analytics

A key ingredient of the Edsight narrative is how it was designed in partnership with educators and school districts. Traditional learning analytics design often relies on existing theories, user interviews or feedback on analytics tools. However, our experience suggests that *designing in context*—within the workflow of partnership research—offers unique advantages over detached design approaches. This embedded method provides a deeper understanding of diverse users, real-world challenges and systemic factors like organizational, political and social dynamics that influence school adoption. Compared to decontextualized design, working closely with research and practice partners allows for richer insights into local conditions and design tensions. We see great potential in integrating design work within research–practice partnerships and improvement science models, as this approach captures nuanced contextual factors that traditional methods may overlook. Partnership-driven design values teachers' and instructional coaches' expertise and lived experiences, ensuring that learning analytics systems align with their needs, workflows and pedagogical goals. Rather than treating educators as end users who simply adopt pre-designed tools, this approach positions them as co-designers who actively shape the development process.

Designing a learning dashboard within a research–practice partnership (RPP) and improvement science (IS) framework revealed unforeseen complexities. While we initially relied on standard human-centered design (HCD) methods—such as empathy mapping, participatory design and iterative testing—the unique dynamics of RPPs and district-level pressures demonstrated the need for additional approaches. Developing learning analytics with the direct involvement of teachers, district leaders and instructional coaches requires integrating an extra layer of practice into the design process. Rather than operating separately from HCD, this RPP/IS design loop surrounds and informs it, ensuring that design decisions are grounded in the realities of district partnerships (Ahn et al. 2019). Successful partnerships, however, require ongoing dialogue and iterative refinement. These collaborative efforts also help bridge the gap between technical feasibility and practical usability, ensuring that a tool's data visualizations and interactions are intuitive and actionable.

One of the key benefits of designing in partnership is fostering a sense of ownership and trust among educators. This was the case, for instance, when concerns about trust and privacy arose within the project. When teachers and coaches see their contributions reflected in a tool's design, they are more likely to engage with it meaningfully and integrate it into their instructional practices. The design process moves beyond theoretical best practices by co-constructing learning analytics tools with those who will use them. It becomes a grounded, context-sensitive endeavor that ultimately leads to more effective and sustainable educational innovations.

CONCLUSION

Learning analytics design must be deeply human-centered, context-sensitive and grounded in long-term partnerships with K–12 educators. Practical tools go beyond usability and technical sophistication; they must align with teachers' workflows, pedagogical values and institutional realities to foster meaningful engagement with data. Generative uncertainty, sensemaking and cultural forms play critical roles in shaping how educators interpret and act on analytics, emphasizing the need for dashboards that prompt inquiry rather than passive information consumption. Designing in partnership ensures that learning analytics tools are not imposed but co-constructed, allowing for continuous adaptation and ownership among educators. Ultimately, learning analytics should not simply track student performance but empower teachers with insights that lead to deeper reflection, informed decision-making and sustainable pedagogical improvements.

Understanding learning analytics dashboards at the K–12 level is essential because these tools have the potential to bridge the gap between raw student data and meaningful instructional decisions. Unlike higher education, where learning analytics often focus on self-regulated learners and large-scale institutional insights, K–12 educators require dashboards that align with the complexities of classroom teaching, diverse student needs and district policies. Teachers, instructional coaches and administrators must be able to interpret data in ways that inform real-time pedagogical adjustments and long-term curriculum planning. For the learning analytics field, studying K–12 dashboards is crucial because it pushes the boundaries of human-centered design, ensuring that data visualization and interpretation are accessible to educators with varying levels of data literacy. Additionally, since K–12 environments often lack standardized data systems, researchers must develop solutions that integrate multiple sources of information while maintaining usability. Investing in research on K–12 dashboards also contributes to creating more equitable educational tools, ensuring that data is used not for punitive measures but to support differentiated instruction and student growth. By refining how dashboards are designed and implemented at the K–12 level, the learning analytics field can create technically robust models responsive to the realities of teaching and learning in diverse school settings.

REFERENCES

Ahn, J., F. Campos, M. Hays and D. DiGiacomo (2019), 'Designing in context: Reaching beyond usability in learning analytics dashboard design', *Journal of Learning Analytics*, **6** (2), 70–85.

Ahn, J., F. Campos, H. Nguyen, M. Hays and J. Morrison (April 2021), 'Co-designing for privacy, transparency and trust in K–12 learning analytics', *LAK21: 11th international learning analytics and knowledge conference,* pp. 55–65.

Buckingham Shum, S., R. Ferguson and R. Martinez-Maldonado (2019), 'Human-centred learning analytics', *Journal of Learning Analytics*, **6** (2), 1–9.

Campos, F.C., J. Ahn, D.K. DiGiacomo, H. Nguyen and M. Hays (2021), 'Making sense of sensemaking: Understanding how K–12 teachers and coaches react to visual analytics', *Journal of Learning Analytics*, **8** (3), 60–80.

Campos, F., H. Nguyen, J. Ahn and K. Jackson (2024), 'Leveraging cultural forms in human-centred learning analytics design', *British Journal of Educational Technology*, **55** (3), 769–84.

Coburn, C.E. and W.R. Penuel (2016), 'Research–practice partnerships in education: Outcomes, dynamics, and open questions', *Educational Researcher*, **45** (1), 48–54.

Dervin, B. (1998), 'Sense-making theory and practice: An overview of user interests in knowledge seeking and use', *Journal of Knowledge Management*, **2** (2), 36–46.

Duval, E. (February, 2011), 'Attention please! Learning analytics for visualization and recommendation', *Proceedings of the 1st international conference on learning analytics and knowledge*, pp. 9–17.

Farrell, C.C. and J.A. Marsh (2016), 'Contributing conditions: A qualitative comparative analysis of teachers' instructional responses to data', *Teaching and Teacher Education*, **60**, 398–412.

Horn, M.S. (February, 2013), 'The role of cultural forms in tangible interaction design', *Proceedings of the 7th international conference on tangible, embedded and embodied interaction*, pp. 117–24.

Islam, M. and S. Jin (November, 2019), 'An overview of data visualization', *2019 international conference on information science and communications technologies (ICISCT)*, pp. 1–7.

Jackson, K., E. Henrick, P. Cobb, N. Kochmanski and H. Nieman (2016), 'Practical measures to improve the quality of small-group and whole-class discussion' [White Paper]. https://bit.ly/2Kyhpx2

Jivet, I., M. Scheffel, H. Drachsler and M. Specht (2017), 'Awareness is not enough: Pitfalls of learning analytics dashboards in the educational practice', *Data-driven approaches in digital education: 12th European conference on technology enhanced learning (EC-TEL 2017),* pp. 82–96.

Klerkx, J., K. Verbert and E. Duval (2017), 'Learning analytics dashboards', in C. Lang, G. Siemens, A. Wise and D. Gašević (eds), *Handbook of learning analytics,* The Society for Learning Analytics Research, pp. 143–150.

Krumm, A.E., R. Beattie, S.R. Takahashi, C. D'Angelo, M. Feng and B. Cheng (2016), 'Practical measurement and productive persistence: Strategies for using digital learning system data to drive improvement', *Journal of Learning Analytics*, **3** (2), 116–38.

Li, Q., Y. Jung and A.F. Wise (2025), 'How instructors use learning analytics: The pivotal role of pedagogy', *Journal of Computing in Higher Education*, **38** (2026), 227–55.

Nguyen, H., F. Campos and J. Ahn (2021), 'Discovering generative uncertainty in learning analytics dashboards', in M. Sahin and D. Ifenthaler (eds), *Visualizations and dashboards for learning analytics*, Springer International Publishing, pp. 457–75.

Paolucci, C., S. Vancini, R.T. Bex II, C. Cavanaugh, C. Salama and Z. de Araujo, Z. (2024), 'A review of learning analytics opportunities and challenges for K–12 education', *Heliyon*, **10** (4), e25767.

Saxe, G.B. (1999), 'Cognition, development and cultural practices', *New Directions for Child and Adolescent Development*, **1999** (83), 19–35.

Tatar, D. (2007), 'The design tensions framework', *Human–Computer Interaction*, **22** (4), 413–51.

Van Someren, M., Y.F. Barnard and J. Sandberg (1994), *The think aloud method: A practical approach to modeling cognitive processes*. Academic Press.

Viberg, O., I. Jivet and M. Scheffel (2023), 'Designing culturally aware learning analytics: A value sensitive perspective', in O. Viberg and Å. Grönlund (eds), *Practicable learning analytics*, Springer International Publishing, pp. 177–92.

Wardrip, P.S. and P. Herman (2018), 'We're keeping on top of the students': Making sense of test data with more informal data in a grade-level instructional team', *Teacher Development*, **22** (1), 31–50.

Wise, A.F. and Y. Jung (2019), 'Teaching with analytics: Towards a situated model of instructional decision-making', *Journal of Learning Analytics*, **6** (2), 53–69.

10. Multi-case teacher inquiry to inform dashboard development

Merike Saar

INTRODUCTION

Learning Analytics Dashboards

Learning Analytics Dashboards (LADs) support human sense-making of learning situations by offering and visualising data about learners (Verbert et al. 2020). Although the research focus has shifted from visualisation and prediction techniques to multimodal data (Fernandez Nieto et al. 2022), theoretical underpinnings (Kaliisa and Dolonen 2023) and participatory design (Martinez-Maldonado et al. 2022; Wise and Jung 2019), large-scale application of such dashboards in authentic practice has not been achieved (Herodotou et al. 2019; Kaliisa et al. 2021). Also, despite the potential of LADs to inform teaching and learning, evidence about improved practice is scarce (Ferguson and Clow 2017; Knight et al. 2020; Rets et al. 2021).

In their study, Susnjak et al. (2022) state that technologies used in Learning Analytics (LA) research are 'heavy-duty in respect to design, development and maintenance of LADs' (p. 19), which might be one of the reasons for low adoption. Also, most research into LA and LADs has been conducted at the university level and compulsory education teachers and students are rarely in the loop. However, for LA adoption to be realised, teachers' needs and contexts should be central to LAD design processes as most school instruction is delivered face to face and data cannot be drawn from Learning Management Systems (LMS).

Another reason for low adoption might be the LADs' minimal alignment with learning theories (Gašević et al. 2016). That is why in-action data collection by teachers, especially in the context of innovation in teaching, should be considered an important source of information for LAD development. In addition, stringent ethics and data-protection requirements can both foster and limit the adoption of LADs, which is why more clarity is required about using students' data (Kollom et al. 2021).

Despite all these obstacles, research has shown the potential of LADs to affect learner outcomes (Susnjak et al. 2022). However, it is important that LADs have a theoretical foundation and meet stakeholders' needs in real life (Holstein et al. 2019), including usability in compulsory education (and face-to-face classrooms).

The purpose of this chapter is to contribute to the field through a multi-case teacher inquiry, where teachers collect and analyse data for decision-making about a classroom innovation (science-of-learning teaching practices). The case studies reveal what data teachers collected from their classrooms and how they analysed the data (without any specific LADs). From this information, we draw examples of what data and how compulsory education teachers would use to make decisions about innovations in their teaching practice.

Teacher Inquiry

Teacher inquiry (TI) refers to teachers' continuous professional development through investigation, reflection and change. It aims at developing habits of inquiry, data use and analysis among teachers (Avramides et al. 2015). It is also identified as a global twenty-first-century need for driving improvement in education, both for teachers and learners (Sergis and Sampson 2017). TI helps teachers become the learning professionals that society needs and can take several forms, such as Teacher Inquiry into Student Learning (Hansen and Wasson 2016), Teaching as Inquiry (Timperley et al. 2014), Japanese Lesson Study (Doig and Groves 2011; Murata 2011) or Action Research (Mertler 2021), which could be carried out either individually or, for example, in data teams (Schildkamp and Poortman 2015).

The fundamental difference between teaching and learning analytics is that the former is 'responsible for evaluating educational designs and deliveries by teachers to students', while the latter 'is concerned with analysing the interactions and results of students against those designs and deliveries' (Hoyos and Velásquez 2020, p. 2). Action research and TI differ from trial-and-error efforts by being 'more structured, more systematic and more sequential' (Mertler 2021, p. 11).

Although teachers analyse their teaching, especially when experimenting with innovative teaching methods, they often rely on their 'gut feeling', not data analysis. Several barriers, especially related to teachers' data literacy competencies (Mandinach 2012) and scarcity of teaching analytics (Saar et al. 2022a), deter teachers from engaging with inquiry to enhance learning. Learning Analytics research has focused on the digital data about learners, not teachers, from Learning Management Systems (LMS) and seldom from the physical classroom (Ndukwe and Daniel 2020).

Ebbeler et al. (2017) and Brown et al. (2017) emphasise that teachers need scaffolding in the research aspect of their inquiries and working with data. The current study aims to demonstrate how teachers can apply teaching analytics in the process of TI with the help of the Analytics Model for Teacher Inquiry (AMTI) (Saar et al. 2022b) and what changes such practices bring along in teachers' perceptions about their teaching and enhancing learning. The study also demonstrates how teachers would use data for decision-making about their teaching. This information can inform the development of LADs to foster the adoption of analytics and teacher inquiry.

METHODS

The study employs a multi-case study design (Yin 1981), involving 16 teachers from 15 Estonian schools. In total, 23 teachers (N=23) volunteered to participate in a teacher training course (from October 2022 to April 2023) to improve their teaching strategies and teacher inquiry skills. Sixteen teachers (14 female, 2 male) gave their consent to participate in the study, contributing their case study lesson plans and reflections about their interventions. Thirteen teachers managed to answer both surveys (pre and post), so teacher perceptions about the impact of the TI process are based on these 13 responses.

The teachers met once a month online for two hours to learn about teacher inquiry (using teaching analytics), novel science-of-learning (SoL) strategies (Beardsley 2020) (which the teachers applied in their intervention lessons between course meetings) and technologies for the application of these SoL strategies and data collection (for teaching analytics).

The teachers (N=16) implemented 24 interventions (Table 10.1) with 339 students (plus 104 students in control groups). Although the teachers included anonymised student data in their reflections, these data are not included in this chapter, as we focus on TI, and data from students were collected by teachers only to learn about the success of their interventions.

The Analytics Model for Teacher Inquiry (AMTI) (Saar et al. 2022b) was used for the teacher inquiry process. The AMTI is a process model for teachers that focuses on data collection and analysis, providing examples and explanations to teachers for easier application of inquiry steps in their work. Although all teachers follow the same steps and can plan their interventions together, it also enables TI application based on each teacher's needs and contexts.

This time, the interventions were planned collaboratively by teachers (of different subjects) within the Erasmus+ Illumine project, which was focused on research-based SoL strategies (Beardsley 2020) and digital tools for their implementation. In addition to applying novel teaching practices, the teachers were also guided to use teaching analytics to analyse the impact of the applied strategies on student engagement and outcomes. Despite co-design, teachers mostly applied the designed intervention plans individually, as they worked at different schools (only two teachers from the same school).

The SoL strategies introduced to the teachers were: retrieval practice or free recall (Karpicke and Blunt 2011); spaced practice, that is, alternating learning activities with active pauses and distractor activities to foster encoding into long-term memory (Kelley and Whatson 2013); distributed practice, which means distribution of learning on different days to enhance retention (Weinstein et al. 2018); and reframing or purposefully changing your mindset to face challenging learning situations (Crum et al. 2017).

Pre- and post-surveys, based on different survey instruments (subscales from SELFIE, TPACK, BALT 3, TERDS and TRPS) were carried out with the participating teachers to measure any possible change in their attitudes towards and skills in teacher inquiry, SoL strategies and the use of digital tools. The collected data were analysed using descriptive statistics

Table 10.1 *Data about the interventions*

Student ages	Subjects taught (no. of teachers)	SoL interventions	Data collected
7–12-year-olds: 139 13–18-year-olds: 200 Total: 339 Special needs: 14	English 4 French 1 Russian 1 Estonian (as a second language) 1 Mathematics 3 Informatics 1 History 1 Science 3 Music 1	Free recall 11 cases Distributed practice 4 cases Spaced learning 3 cases Reframing 6 cases	Student work or (self) test 12 Survey 5 Observation 5 Discussion 2

Source: Author.

and thematic analysis (Braun and Clark 2006). Teachers' case studies (intervention plans and reflections) were also analysed using thematic analysis.

RESULTS

Most teachers carried out one intervention where they collected and analysed data about the effects of the applied SoL strategy. One teacher implemented three different SoL strategies in three interventions, and six teachers implemented two different SoL strategies (either in one or several interventions). Of the four SoL strategies, teachers implemented free recall in 11 interventions, reframing in 6, distributed practice in 4 and spaced learning in 3 interventions (Table 10.1). The most popular data that teachers collected for their reflections were students' results (in 12 interventions), followed by surveys, observation data (both 5 times) and discussions (in two cases) (examples in Figures 10.1 and 10.2).

The main messages from teachers' reflections (from their intervention plans) are:

1. Although all participants considered the interventions very useful and eye-opening, many indicated a shortage of time for data analysis and a need for further training in it.
2. Teachers were satisfied that students' results improved: 'even two months later students remembered the material better'; 'even the weakest students passed the test at once (no need to retake)'.

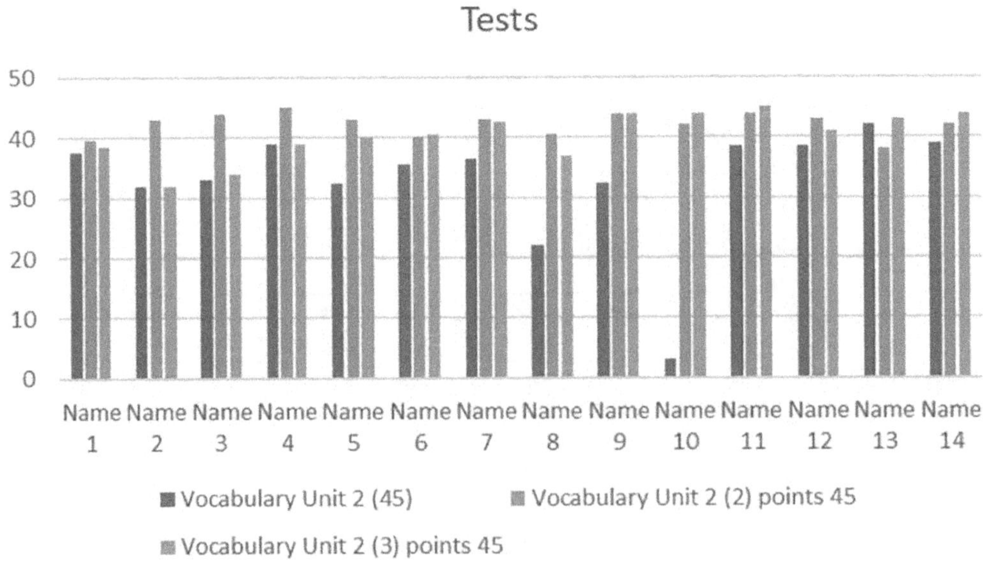

Source: Author.

Figure 10.1 *An example of teachers' data collection (the results of an immediate test, a week later and two weeks later)*

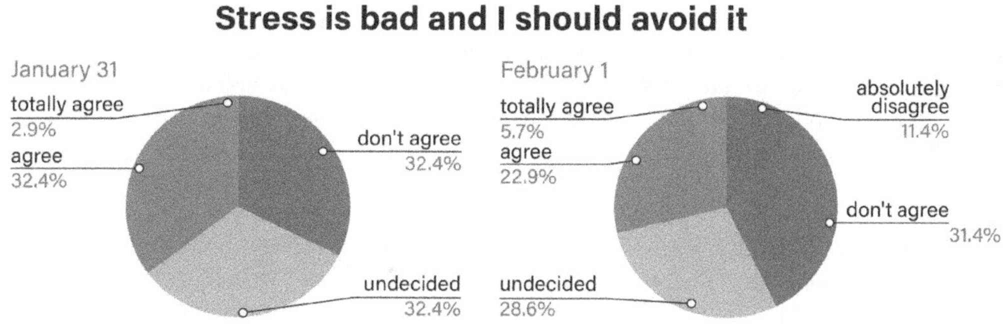

Source: Author.

Figure 10.2 *A survey about academic stress (reframing) after watching two stress-related videos*

3. Teachers liked that they could help learners become better at learning: 'I became inspired by the methods and by introducing them to learners'; 'I liked to teach learning strategies in addition to the subject material'.

The overall experience could be concluded with the following remark by a teacher: 'I thoroughly enjoyed the whole process and it certainly changed the way I teach'.

Of the three aspects of the multi-case study (SoL, digital tools and TI), teacher inquiry brought the greatest changes in teachers' practice. The survey results indicate that the lowest scores were initially linked to TI (which shows that teachers are not experienced in it). By the end of the project, eight teachers confirmed their increased experience with teacher inquiry, while three teachers said the rise was considerable. Using a five-point Likert scale, teachers' experience of carrying out TI increased from 2.70 to 3.56 (0.86). Sharing one's practice also increased, as the participating teachers reported gaining experience in sharing their teacher inquiry results at workshops or conferences: from 1.48 to 2.44 (0.96) and providing novel information to colleagues: from 1.70 to 2.63 (0.92).

As to their teaching practice, four teachers out of 13 reported weaker confidence, while six teachers improved their confidence in supporting and assessing students and providing feedback: from 3.37 to 4.06 (0.69). Confidence in using digital tools for teaching also slightly increased: from 3.48 to 3.88 (0.4). Seven teachers claimed to have improved their skills in using digital tools to help students enhance their learning and metacognitive skills: from 2.63 to 3.25 (0.62), while eight teachers became better at using digital tools for reflection and enhancing practice: from 2.81 to 3.50 (0.69). Teachers also became better at picking tools that enhance teaching (3.11 to 3.69; 0.58), learning (3.22 to 3.81; 0.59) and adapting digital tools for versatile teaching activities (3.0 to 3.56; 0.56). It is also important that six teachers felt that they are now more up to date with recent education-related research literature: from 2.93 to 3.56 (0.64).

As to the SoL strategies, the biggest changes emerged in using evidence-based strategies to raise student motivation: from 3.37 to 3.94 (0.57) and to create positive learning environments: from 3.59 to 4.11 (0.53). By the end of the six-month teacher inquiry cycle, out of 13 teachers, 12 picked retrieval practice as the SoL strategy most suitable for their daily practice. The participating teachers considered it important to learn about and implement research-based practices 'to understand what works and become confident to implement them', as well as to make the application of the strategies more conscious and systematic (as opposed to just randomly testing them out).

The most useful aspects of the collaborative TI for the participating teachers were the possibility to listen to others' experiences and the collaborative planning of the interventions. Teachers also reported that their students were excited to learn about and experiment with new strategies; that 'a learning teacher also inspires students' and that teacher inquiry should become a regular part of a teacher's profession, as it enhances evidence-based practice and provides a fuller picture of classroom realities.

The results reveal that the main perceived changes in teachers' practice, due to collaborative teacher inquiry, are linked to improved confidence and knowledge, a fuller picture of and better skills for evidence-based practice, and improved cooperation in the classroom. Although teachers claimed to have used some of these learning strategies to a certain extent before, thanks to teacher inquiry, their application of the SoL strategies became more conscious, systematic and consistent in enhancing learning. The requirement to collect and analyse data about the employed innovations helped teachers realise how the SoL strategies impacted their students. However, the teachers clearly stated that with the help of suitable LADs, the TI-process would have been less time-consuming and easier to carry out.

DISCUSSION

Organising teacher inquiry workshops for teachers with different backgrounds, subjects, contexts and needs might be challenging. Teacher inquiry is commonly implemented in data teams with teachers of the same school or subject. However, our case demonstrates the feasibility of collaborative teacher inquiry using the AMTI, especially when experimenting with innovative practices to enhance learning.

Making teacher inquiry a common practice requires LADs that teachers can easily use in face-to-face classrooms. It is important that each teacher can pick and focus on an inquiry topic relevant to their needs, although still following an established inquiry cycle (which makes collaboration possible). This, in turn, means that LADs have to *comply with varied contextual factors and teacher needs*. However, as Ndukwe and Daniel (2020) point out, the current implementation of dashboards does not adequately support teachers with the necessary data in a readily usable format. To improve the situation, teachers should be involved in LAD development throughout the process. Kaliisa et al. (2023) propose to engage LAD users through interviews, surveys and workshops. This study shows that educators' actual needs for LADs can also be drawn from their teacher inquiry practices.

In the current study, teachers were responsible for collecting data from their interventions, while no LAD was provided to them. Teachers mostly used students' (self)tests and survey results to guide their decisions about the impact the applied learning strategies had on student learning. In half of the cases, teachers used students' marks (for example, to compare immediate and later test results), which they had to manually insert from different testing systems (or paper tests) for such comparisons. So, teachers expect LADs to *enable automatic data retrieval*, for example, from varied testing environments or e-school systems.

Another issue is data interpretation, as teachers find it time-consuming even when analysing student surveys or test outcomes. Although Google Forms enabled teachers to see the visuals of their collected data, the actual interpretation remained rather superficial: teachers noticed the improved student results, but no further analysis was conducted (for example, into any differences in the results of slower/faster students). Also, seven out of 23 teachers in the study failed to do any analysis, even when they had collected data from their classrooms. They found it difficult and time-consuming to aggregate the collected data. Therefore, *in addition to visuals, LADs should offer some explanations*, as LA visualisations can be complicated to interpret for teachers, as stated by Kaliisa et al. (2021).

So, it is necessary to design tools and write algorithms that could easily analyse teacher-collected data and visualise it in ways that allow adequate understanding by teachers (Ndukwe and Daniel 2020). For example, the tools could enable fast data collection (or retrieval from other systems) about student engagement with the learning activities in a physical classroom, student mood when solving problems or the perceived effort put into their learning process. Rachmad (2022) recommends including student engagement, improvement in learning outcomes and student satisfaction (with the learning methods used) as necessary indicators to evaluate the impact of adaptive learning on engagement and learning outcomes. So, in addition to data collected automatically, LADs should also *offer short customisable surveys* (on students' perceived engagement, effort, mood etc.).

In the current study, the participants emphasised that using the introduced SoL strategies with students and collecting evidence about their possible effect on retention or academic stress helped teachers better understand the importance of their learning design and possibilities for implementing innovation to enhance learning. Although teachers managed data collection well, the analysis was perceived as time-consuming and often 'daunting'. Despite that, 16 out of 23 teachers finished their TI process (inspired by their colleagues' analyses) and expressed willingness to continue with TI. This demonstrates how TI can impact learning design and help adapt learning in a meaningful and evidence-based way, especially when carried out in data teams (Schildkamp and Poortman 2015). Therefore, it is crucial to combine learning and teaching analytics into dashboards or provide tools for teaching analytics that could be used in face-to-face instruction.

CONCLUSION

The findings of this study underscore the significant potential of teacher inquiry in enhancing teaching practices and informing the development of LADs. Despite the challenges associated with the large-scale application of LADs in face-to-face classroom settings, this research demonstrates that TI can bridge this gap by fostering evidence-based decision-making and increasing teachers' awareness of their instructional impact.

Through a multi-case inquiry, teachers were introduced to science-of-learning strategies and digital tools, which they adapted to their unique contexts. The collaborative nature of this inquiry not only improved teachers' skills in data collection and analysis but also highlighted the importance of using research-based strategies to enhance student learning outcomes. The study revealed that teachers' confidence and competence in using digital tools and implementing SoL strategies increased significantly, leading to more systematic and conscious application of these methods.

The results indicate that while teachers found the interventions valuable, they also faced time constraints and required further training in data analysis. The study emphasises the need for LADs that are user-friendly and capable of automatic data retrieval and interpretation to support teachers in their inquiry processes. By involving teachers in the development of LADs and ensuring these tools are tailored to their needs, the integration of teaching and learning analytics can be significantly improved.

However, we acknowledge that the number of teachers participating in the study was relatively small and homogeneous (from one country). Nevertheless, the aim was not to generalise the findings but to test the feasibility of in-action data collection and analysis by teachers to inform LAD development.

In conclusion, this research highlights the transformative impact of collaborative teacher inquiry on teaching practices and the critical role of well-designed LADs in supporting this process. The insights gained from teachers' experiences and reflections provide a valuable foundation for developing LADs that facilitate effective and efficient evidence-based teaching in face-to-face classrooms.

REFERENCES

Avramides, K., J. Hunter, M. Oliver and R. Luckin (2015), 'A method for teacher inquiry in cross-curricular projects: Lessons from a case study', *British Journal of Educational Technology*, **46** (2), 249–64. doi:10.1111/bjet.12233

BALT 3 [Beliefs about Learning and Teaching (BALT 3) instrument], in Darmawan, I.G.N., S. Vosniadou, M.J. Lawson, P. Van Deur and M. Wyra (2020), 'The development of an instrument to test pre-service teachers' beliefs consistent and inconsistent with self-regulation theory', *British Journal of Educational Psychology*, **90** (4), 1039–61. doi:10.1111/bjep.12345

Beardsley, M. (2020), *Science of Learning Concepts for Teachers (Project Illuminated)* (1st ed.). Retrieved from https://illuminated.pressbooks.com

Braun, V. and V. Clark (2006), 'Using thematic analysis in psychology', *Qualitative research in psychology*, **3** (2), 77–101.

Brown, C., K. Schildkamp and M.D. Hubers (2017), 'Combining the best of two worlds: A conceptual proposal for evidence-informed school improvement', *Educational Research*, **59** (2), 154–72. doi:10.1080/00131881.2017.1304327

Crum, A.J., M. Akinola, A. Martin and S. Fath (2017), 'The role of stress mindset in shaping cognitive, emotional and physiological responses to challenging and threatening stress', *Anxiety, Stress, & Coping*, **30** (4), 379–95. doi:10.1080/10615806.2016.1275585

Doig, B. and S. Groves (2011), 'Japanese lesson study: Teacher professional development through communities of inquiry', *Mathematics Teacher Education and Development*, **13** (1), 77–93.

Ebbeler, J., C.L. Poortman, K. Schildkamp and J.M. Pieters (2017), 'The effects of a data use intervention on educators' satisfaction and data literacy', *Educational Assessment, Evaluation and Accountability*, **29** (1), 83–105. doi:10.1007/s11092-016-9251-z

Ferguson, R. and D. Clow (March 2017), 'Where is the evidence? A call to action for learning analytics', in *LAK'17: Proceedings of the Seventh International Learning Analytics & Knowledge Conference,* ACM, pp. 56–65. https://doi.org/10.1145/3027385.3027396

Fernandez Nieto, G.M., K. Kitto, S. Buckingham Shum and R. Martinez-Maldonado (March, 2022). 'Beyond the learning analytics dashboard: Alternative ways to communicate student data insights combining visualisation, narrative and storytelling', *LAK22: 12th International Learning Analytics and Knowledge Conference*, pp. 219–29. doi:10.1145/3506860.3506895

Gašević, D., S. Dawson, T. Rogers and D. Gasevic (2016), 'Learning analytics should not promote one size fits all: The effects of instructional conditions in predicting academic success', *The Internet and Higher Education*, **28**, 68–84. doi:10.1016/j.iheduc.2015.10.002

Hansen, C.J. and B. Wasson (2016), 'Teacher Inquiry into Student Learning: The TISL heart model and method for use in teachers' professional development', *Nordic Journal of Digital Literacy*, **11** (1), 24–49. doi:10.18261/issn.1891-943x-2016-01-02

Herodotou, C., M. Hlosta, A. Boroowa, B. Rienties, Z. Zdrahal and C. Mangafa (2019), 'Empowering online teachers through predictive learning analytics', *British Journal of Educational Technology*, **50** (6), 3064–79. doi:10.1111/bjet.12853

Holstein, K., B.M. McLaren and V. Aleven (2019), 'Co-designing a real-time classroom orchestration tool to support teacher–AI complementarity', *Journal of Learning Analytics*, **6** (2), 27–52. doi:10.18608/jla.2019.62.3

Hoyos, A.A.C. and J.D. Velásquez (2020), 'Teaching analytics: Current challenges and future development', *IEEE Revista Iberoamericana de Tecnologias del Aprendizaje*, **15** (1), 1–9. doi:10.1109/RITA.2020.2979245

Kaliisa, R. and J.A. Dolonen (2023), 'CADA: A teacher-facing learning analytics dashboard to foster teachers' awareness of students' participation and discourse patterns in online discussions', *Technology, Knowledge and Learning*, **28** (3), 937–58. doi:10.1007/s10758-022-09598-7

Kaliisa, R., A. Gillespie, C. Herodotou, A. Kluge and B. Rienties (2021), 'Teachers' perspectives on the promises, needs and challenges of learning analytics dashboards: Insights from institutions offering blended and distance learning', in M. Sahin and D. Ifenthaler (eds), *Visualizations and Dashboards for Learning Analytics*, Springer, Cham, pp. 341–70. https://doi.org/10.1007/978-3-030-81222-5_16

Kaliisa, R., I. Jivet and P. Prinsloo (2023), 'A checklist to guide the planning, designing, implementation, and evaluation of learning analytics dashboards', *International Journal of Educational Technology in Higher Education*, **20** (1), 28. doi:10.1186/s41239-023-00394-6

Karpicke, J.D. and J.R. Blunt (2011), 'Retrieval practice produces more learning than elaborative studying with concept mapping', *Science*, **331** (6018), 772–75. doi:10.1126/science.1199327

Kelley, P. and T. Whatson (2013), 'Making long-term memories in minutes: A spaced learning pattern from memory research in education', *Frontiers In Human Neuroscience*, **7**, 589. doi:10.3389/fnhum.2013.00589

Knight, S., A. Gibson and A. Shibani (2020), 'Implementing learning analytics for learning impact: Taking tools to task', *Internet and Higher Education*, **45**, 100729. doi:10.1016/j.iheduc.2020.100729

Kollom, K., K. Tammets, M. Scheffel, Y.S. Tsai, I. Jivet, P.J. Muñoz-Merino … and T. Ley (2021), 'A four-country cross-case analysis of academic staff expectations about learning analytics in higher education', *The Internet and Higher Education*, **49**, 100788. doi:10.1016/j.iheduc.2020.100788

Mandinach, E. (2012), 'A perfect time for data use: Using data-driven decision making to inform practice', *Educational Psychologist*, **47** (2), 71–85. doi:10.1080/00461520.2012.667064

Martinez-Maldonado, R., D. Elliott, C. Axisa, T. Power, V. Echeverria and B. Shum (2022), 'Designing translucent learning analytics with teachers: An elicitation process', *Interactive Learning Environments*, **30** (6), 1077–91. doi:10.1080/10494820.2019.1710541

Mertler, C.A. (2021), 'Action research as teacher inquiry: A viable strategy for resolving problems of practice', *Practical Assessment, Research and Evaluation*, **26**, 19. doi:10.7275/22014442

Murata, A. (2011). 'Introduction: Conceptual overview of lesson study', in L.C. Hart, A.S. Alston and A. Murata, (eds), *Lesson Study Research and Practice in Mathematics Education*, SpringerDordrecht, pp. 1–12. https://doi.org/10.1007/978-90-481-9941-9_1

Ndukwe, I.G. and B.K. Daniel (2020), 'Teaching analytics, value and tools for teacher data literacy: A systematic and tripartite approach', *International Journal of Educational Technology in Higher Education*, **17**, 1–31. doi:10.1186/s41239-020-00201-6

Rachmad, Y. E. (2022), 'Adaptive Learning Theory', La Paz Costanera Publicaciones Internacionales, Edición Especial. https://osf.io/vfz38/overview

Rets, I., C. Herodotou, V. Bayer, M. Hlosta and B. Rienties (2021), 'Exploring critical factors of the perceived usefulness of a learning analytics dashboard for distance university students', *International Journal of Educational Technology in Higher Education*, **18**, 46. doi:10.1186/s41239-021-00284-9

Saar, M., L.P. Prieto and M.J. Rodríguez Triana (2022a), 'Classroom data collection for teachers' data-informed practice', *Technology, Pedagogy and Education*, **31** (1), 123–40. doi:10.1080/1475939X.2021.1989024

Saar, M., M.J. Rodríguez-Triana and L.P. Prieto (2022b), 'Towards data-informed teaching practice: A model for integrating analytics with teacher inquiry', *Journal of Learning Analytics*, **9** (3), 88–103. doi:10.18608/jla.2022.7505

Schildkamp, K. and C. Poortman (2015), 'Factors influencing the functioning of data teams', *Teachers college record*, **117** (4), 1–42. doi:10.1177/016146811511700

SELFIE [Self-reflection on Effective Learning by Fostering the Use of Innovative Educational Technologies]. European Education Area – europa.eu. https://education.ec.europa.eu/selfie/about-selfie

Sergis, S. and D.G. Sampson (2017), 'Teaching and learning analytics to support teacher inquiry: A systematic literature review', in A. Peña-Ayala (ed.), *Learning Analytics: Fundaments, Applications and Trends*, Springer, Cham, pp. 25–63. https://doi.org/10.1007/978-3-319-52977-6_2

Susnjak, T., G.S. Ramaswami and A. Mathrani (2022), 'Learning analytics dashboard: a tool for providing a tionable insights to learners', *International Journal of Educational Technology in Higher Education*, **19** (1), 12. doi:10.1186/s41239-021-00313-7

TERDS [The Teacher Educators' Researcherly Disposition Scale], in Tack, H. and R. Vanderlinde (2016), 'Measuring teacher educators' researcherly disposition: Item development and scale construction', *Vocations and Learning*, **9**, 43–62. doi:10.1007/s12186-016-9148-5

Timperley, H., L. Kaser and J. Halbert (2014), *A Framework for Transforming Learning in Schools: Innovation and the Spiral of Inquiry* (Vol. 234). Melbourne: Centre for Strategic Education.

TPACK [Technological Pedagogical Content Knowledge scale], in Schmidt, D.A., E. Baran, A.D. Thompson, P. Mishra, M.J. Koehler and T.S. Shin (2009), 'Technological pedagogical content knowledge (TPACK): The development and validation of an assessment instrument for preservice teachers', *Journal of Research on Technology in Education*, **42** (2), 123–49. doi:10.1080/15391523.2009.10782544

TRPS [Teachers Reflective Practices Scale]. In Gheith, E. and N. Aljaberi (2018), 'Reflective teaching practices in teachers and their attitudes toward professional self-development', *International Journal of Progressive Education*, **14** (3), 160–79. doi:10.29329/ijpe.2018.146.11

Verbert, K., X. Ochoa, R. De Croon, R.A. Dourado and T. De Laet (March, 2020), 'Learning analytics dashboards: The past, the present and the future', in *LAK'20: Proceedings of the Tenth International Conference on Learning Analytics & Knowledge*, ACM, pp. 35–40. https://doi.org/10.1145/3375462.3375504

Weinstein, Y., M. Sumeracki and O. Caviglioli (2018), *Understanding How We Learn: A Visual Guide* (1st ed.). London: Routledge. https://doi.org/10.4324/9780203710463

Wise, A.F. and Y. Jung (2019), 'Teaching with analytics: Towards a situated model of instructional decision-making', *Journal of Learning Analytics*, **6** (2), 53–69. doi:10.18608/jla.2019.62.4

Yin, R.K. (1981), 'The case study as a serious research strategy', *Knowledge*, **3** (1), 97–114. doi:10.1177/107554708100300

11. Understanding the interrelated nature of academic, social, and emotional competencies through learning analytics

Jae H. Paik, Igor Himelfarb, Seung Hee Yoo, Jongtak Lee, Hoyong Ha, and Yurim Park

UNDERSTANDING INTERRELATED NATURE OF ACADEMIC, SOCIAL AND EMOTIONAL COMPETENCIES THROUGH LEARNING ANALYTICS

Research over the past two decades has highlighted the significant positive impact of social-emotional competencies on academic success, school engagement and psychological well-being, including reductions in conduct problems and emotional distress such as stress, anxiety and depression (Durlak et al. 2011; Moazami-Goodarzi et al. 2021). This growing body of evidence has catalyzed a global movement to integrate social and emotional learning (SEL) into school systems worldwide (Weissberg et al. 2015). For instance, the Collaborative for Academic, Social and Emotional Learning (CASEL) framework outlines five key SEL skills—self-awareness, self-management, social awareness, relationship skills and responsible decision-making, which are incorporated as a part of K–12 education standards for more than half of US states (Greenberg 2023). Similarly, across Europe, SEL integration is being actively promoted through national policies and at the European Union level (Šćukanec Schmidt, Skledar Matijević and Anić 2023).

While research on the impact of SEL on educational outcomes across Africa remains largely underexplored, there is a growing recognition of SEL as a powerful tool for supporting mental health, particularly among youth experiencing trauma (Marsay et al. 2021). In Nigeria, for instance, SEL programs have shown promise in improving the emotional well-being of traumatized young people (Kim, Brown and Weiss-Yagoda 2017). Similarly, in the Democratic Republic of Congo, SEL has been embedded into a reading skills program to foster healing and enhance both academic performance and mental health outcomes for youth (Aber et al. 2016).

The urgency surrounding SEL has intensified in response to the rise in mental health concerns among youth worldwide in recent years (Racine et al. 2021; Zhao and Watterston 2021). According to the World Health Organization (WHO), one in seven adolescents (ages 10–19) experiences mental health disorders and suicide is the second leading cause of death in this age group globally (WHO 2024). In response, global organizations such as UNESCO, the World Bank and the WHO have issued a unified call to integrate SEL into all levels of education systems across the globe (Singh and Duralappah 2020). This integration must be widespread—in every classroom, after-school activities and summer programs—to ensure that every student is equipped for success in school, career and life (California Department of Education 2023).

Moreover, scholars are calling attention to the importance of prioritizing SEL within digital learning contexts (Topping et al. 2022). While educational technology has transformed how we assess, track and analyze student learning in core academic subjects such as math and literacy, SEL remains largely underexplored in the digital space (Joksimović et al. 2022; Poquet and de Laat 2021). This gap presents a critical opportunity in education as assessment is the hallmark of any effective learning program and SEL is no exception. SEL assessment can help identify students' strengths and areas of growth, enabling a student-centered approach to optimize learning. Without accurate assessment tools to measure social-emotional growth, educators and researchers are limited in their ability to provide timely feedback, personalized support or evaluate the effectiveness of the program.

Learning Analytics (LA) and Educational Data Mining (EDM) offer promising pathways for advancing our understanding of and support for SEL. By gathering large-scale and diverse data, it becomes possible to capture rich, continuous insights into students' emotional experiences, social interactions and school engagement patterns within digital learning, to name a few. For example, emotional awareness can be tracked through a daily log of reporting emotional states; self-management skills can be evaluated via interactive digital tasks; school engagement can be inferred from clickstream and assignment log files; and academic performance can be evaluated through skill-based and knowledge-mastery tasks across multiple time points. By combining these with other student behavioral and learning data, researchers can gain a deeper, student-centered understanding of how social-emotional competencies interact to shape their learning and psychological outcomes.

We argue that the development of sophisticated and refined predictive models that incorporate social-emotional competencies is crucial for understanding student behaviors and guiding personalized learning paths. We offer three recommendations for SEL-focused LA:

1. *Validating Social-emotional Dimensions*: Predictive models should prioritize dimensions rooted in the theoretical foundations of social and emotional development as well as learning sciences to ensure validity and relevance. Psychometric tests (for example, factor analysis, item response theory, reliability testing) should be conducted with diverse student samples to confirm the accuracy and cultural relevance of social-emotional assessments.
2. *Exploring Complex Relationships*: Predictive models should analyze the dynamic and interconnected relationships between students' social, emotional and academic engagement to identify key patterns and mechanisms that promote learning outcomes and well-being.
3. *Tracking Changes Over Time*: Temporal methods (for example, growth modeling, panel data and time-series analyses) are vital for understanding students' learning trajectories and their development, accounting for how these factors evolve (or stabilize) over time.

We illustrate these recommendations using data from South Korean elementary students collected through an online learning management system (LMS), demonstrating how incorporating digital assessment of social-emotional competencies can inform both research and practice.

INSIGHTS FROM SOUTH KOREAN LEARNING MANAGEMENT SYSTEM DATA

There is an urgent need to integrate SEL into K–12 digital learning environments in South Korea. Similar to the global trends, interest in building students' social-emotional competencies has grown in South Korea in recent years, driven by escalating mental health concerns (for example, depression, anxiety and stress) as well as behavioral challenges (for example, bullying and violence) (Do 2015; Lee and Bong 2017). Mental health issues have long been prevalent among South Korean adolescents, with suicide consistently the leading cause of death for individuals aged 13 to 17 since 2017 (Statistics Korea 2019). These challenges are perpetuated by societal pressures emphasizing academic achievement, deeply rooted in Confucian values that prioritize academic success over students' holistic development and well-being (Bae, Lee and Lee 2015; Park and Moon 2010). In fact, a cross-national survey of 36 countries ranked South Korea second in academic competence but 35th in social competence, prompting urgent calls among scholars for prioritizing SEL integration at the national level (Kim et al. 2010, cited in Lee and Bong 2017).

In response, the South Korean government shifted toward a more holistic approach to education. In 2015, the Ministry of Education introduced the Character Education Promotion Act (CEPA; Law #13004), mandating character education in the national K–12 curriculum. This law required the development of long-term strategies aimed at enhancing students' psychological and behavioral well-being, while maintaining academic rigor. More recently, the Ministry established a Mental Health Division to provide emotional and psychological support to address the mental health challenges that have been further exacerbated by the COVID-19 pandemic (Jeon 2023). These initiatives represent a significant step toward promoting SEL principles within the South Korean public-school system.

LA RESEARCH OVERVIEW

This chapter focuses on LA research using data collected through an LMS implemented in the Gyeongsangnamdo Province. Co-developed by the Provincial Office of Education and DataEum, a software company, the LMS serves a population of 408,757 K–12 students. The platform offers digital textbooks, instructional videos, teacher-generated activities, assessments and interactive learning tools.

We report findings from three studies conducted between 2022 and 2024 using LMS data: Study 1 (Paik et al. 2024a) and Study 2 (Paik et al. 2024b) analyzed behavioral and emotional data mined from 1,075 students in grades 3–6 during Spring 2022. Study 3 (Paik et al. 2025) examined two datasets from Fall 2023 and Spring 2024 from 116 and 196 students in grades 3–5, respectively.

Together, the three studies examined the following areas of learning:

- *Student Engagement*: Tracked using IMS Caliper Analytics Specifications (IMS Global Consortium, 2020) across the LMS' Forum, Assignment and Announcement portals (Studies 1 and 3).

- *Emotional Experiences*: Captured through daily Emotion Check-in logs, in which students reported their emotional states (Studies 1 and 2).
- *Social-emotional Competencies*: Measured using self-reports on Growth Mindset, Self-regulation Difficulties and Psychological Distress, along with a skill-based Emotion Knowledge task (Study 3).
- *Academic Performance*: Evaluated through embedded Literacy and Math assessments within the LMS (Study 3).

RECOMMENDATION 1: ASSESSING AND VALIDATING SOCIAL-EMOTIONAL DIMENSIONS

One of the most critical topics in LA is establishing the construct validity and reliability of the metrics used in digital learning environments (for example, Gašević, Dawson and Siemens 2015; Knight and Buckingham Shum 2017). As the field continues to grow, a key recommendation is to ensure that social, emotional and behavioral constructs (for example, school engagement and students' emotional experience) are measured in a theoretically grounded and psychometrically sound manner.

Assessing School Engagement through Behavioral Indicators (Study 1)

School engagement plays a vital role in learning across various educational settings, including online and traditional classrooms. Broadly defined, school engagement encompasses students' motivation and learning behaviors, which directly influence both academic performance and well-being (Martins et al. 2022). Learning analytics offers valuable tools for systematically exploring the dimensions of school engagement by analyzing a range of behavioral indicators left by students in online platforms. While school engagement has been studied extensively (Macfadyen and Dawson 2012; Fredricks, Blumenfeld and Paris, 2004), contemporary educators and researchers advocate for a multidimensional framework that reflects the complex and interrelated nature of student engagement (Martins et al. 2022; Redmond et al. 2018). In our LA research, we intentionally applied a multidimensional approach to identify latent patterns of engagement.

In Study 1 (Paik et al. 2024a), conducting Exploratory and Confirmatory Factor Analyses on a distinct subsample of 23 behavioral indicators extracted from the LMS yielded three latent engagement factors.

- *Behavioral Engagement*: reflected students' involvement with tasks, expectations and adhering to classroom rules such as assignment completion on time and engagement with announcements.
- *Social Engagement*: captured through non-graded social interactions with peers and teachers, such as 'likes' and comments, signaling students' efforts to foster relationships that enhance the overall collegial learning experience.
- *Cognitive Engagement*: represented by students' initiative and participation in knowledge-sharing behaviors, such as generating forum discussions and receiving 'likes' and comments from peers and teachers, indicating learning beyond minimum requirements.

This is one of the first studies to identify latent engagement dimensions for elementary-age students by extracting real-time behavioral indicators based on the IMS Calipers Analytics Specifications (IMS Global Consortium 2020). Interestingly, the engagement behaviors observed from Korean elementary students' digital learning align closely with well-established engagement frameworks developed for older students, particularly with US college students (Fredricks, Blumenfeld and Paris 2004; Redmond et al. 2018). These findings suggest potential generalizability of engagement frameworks in digital learning contexts, offering a promising direction for further LA research in K–12 education.

Assessing Emotional Experiences through Emotion Check-ins (Study 1 and Study 2)

Students' emotional experiences and competencies significantly influence their school engagement and academic achievement (Linnenbrink-Garcia, Rogat, and Koskey 2011; MacCann et al. 2020; Pekrun and Linnenbrink-Garcia 2012). Studies have shown that students who experience positive emotions (for example, enjoyment, interest) tend to engage and exert more effort when encountering challenges during learning (King et al. 2015), while students who experience negative emotions (for example, frustration, anxiety) tend to withdraw and disengage from learning (Hernandez et al. 2018). Other studies have shown that positive emotions (for example, enjoyment, pride) predict higher academic achievement, whereas negative emotions (for example, anger, anxiety, shame, boredom, hopelessness) predict lower academic achievement (Camacho-Morles et al. 2021; Pekrun et al. 2017). Furthermore, various aspects of emotional abilities (for example, emotion regulation) have been found to positively correlate strongly with school engagement (Fredricks, Blumenfeld and Paris 2004; Zhoc, King, and Chung 2020) and academic achievement (MacCann et al. 2020; Perera and DiGiacomo 2013). Despite the strong evidence linking emotion and learning, most LA research has largely overlooked elementary students' emotional experiences. Elementary-aged students undergo rapid and foundational emotional development, making them an especially important and intriguing area for LA research.

We gathered students' emotional data using the LMS's Emotion Check-in activity, where students were asked daily to voluntarily report on their emotional states. Upon logging into the platform, students were prompted with the following question, '*How are you feeling today?*' and were asked to report their emotions by selecting one emotion from a list that best fit their mood (see Figure 11.1). These emotional data were analyzed in conjunction with math assessments regularly administered within the platform.

Latent Class Analysis identified three distinct subclasses based on emotional reporting patterns: (1) those reporting both positive and negative emotions, (2) those reporting only positive emotions and (3) those who opted not to report emotions. Notably, significant differences in students' mathematics performance emerged across these subclasses. Students reporting both positive and negative emotions outperformed their peers, followed by those reporting only positive emotions, and students who opted not to report their emotions performed the lowest (see Figure 11.2). The frequency of participating in the Emotion Check-in activity and reporting Happy emerged as the strongest predictors of higher mathematics performance, while other predictors, such as reporting negative emotions (Sad and Angry), were identified as moderate predictors.

The potential academic benefits of negative emotions represent a novel contribution to the current literature, where negative emotions were often found to hinder cognitive processes and

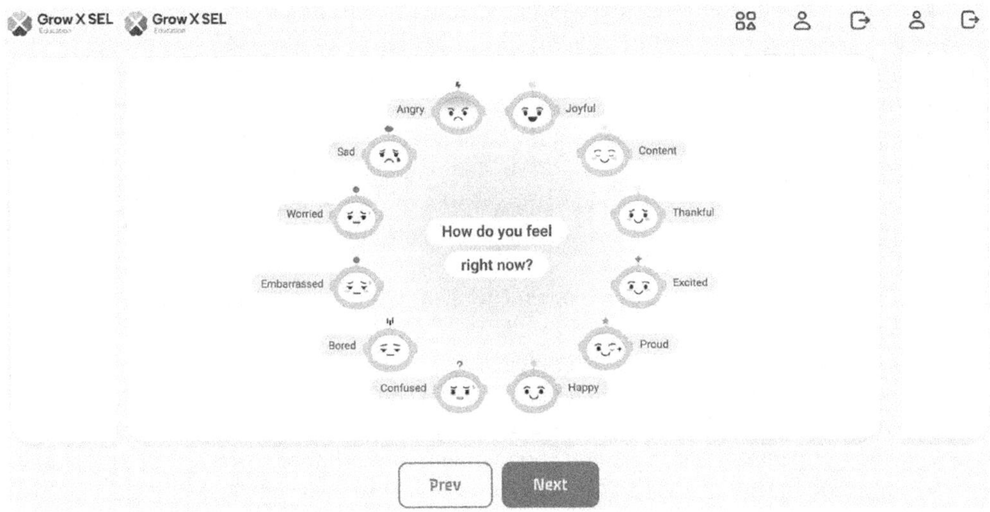

Source: Authors.

Figure 11.1 *Sample of emotion check-in activity*

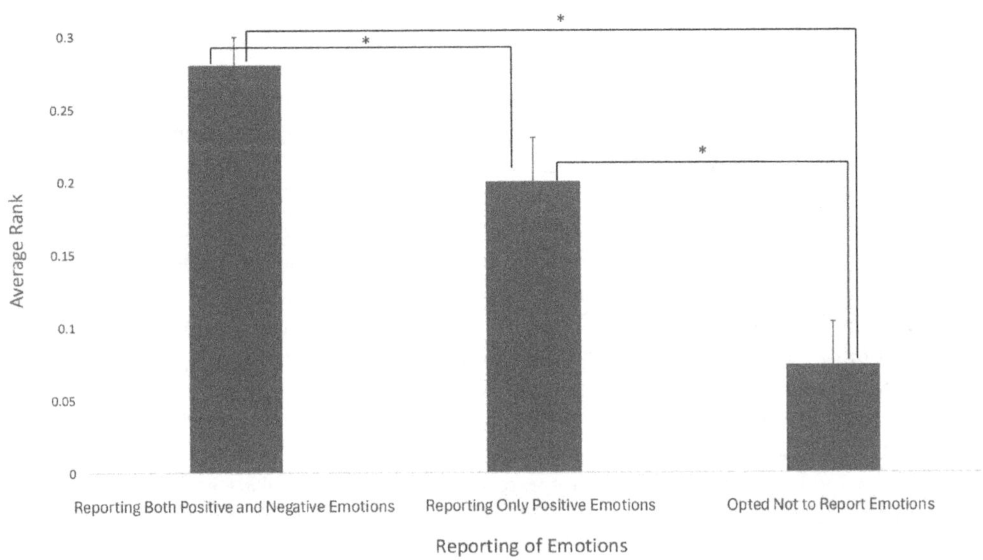

Source: Authors.

Figure 11.2 *Pairwise comparison of average rank in mathematics task across three latent emotional reporting classes*

motivation, in turn negatively impacting academic performance (Camacho-Morles et al. 2021; Pekrun et al. 2017). We posit that our unexpected finding suggests that the ability to navigate a range of emotions, including negative ones, may be a critical skill for facilitating effective self-monitoring and emotion regulation processes during learning. This interpretation aligns with research on emotional intelligence (Brackett, Rivers and Salovey 2011; Mayer and Salovey 1997). These findings also point to the potential benefits of self-awareness practices in the daily educational experience, namely, encouraging students to regularly reflect on and express their emotions in supporting their academic success.

One particularly promising direction for emotions in LA research involves 'sensor-free' affect detection methods (see D'Mello and Jensen 2022). These methods utilize supervised learning techniques to train intelligent tutoring systems to accurately discriminate students' affective states (for example, boredom, frustration, engaged concentration) based on features like body movements, gestures and facial expressions (Emotient 2014; Hutt et al. 2019; Pardos et al. 2014). Multimodal approaches for capturing students' emotional experiences in real time through learning analytics promise to provide a more comprehensive and nuanced understanding of how emotional data can be harnessed to support optimal student learning outcomes.

Assessing Social-emotional Competencies Using Digital Measures (Study 2)

Despite the growing recognition of the importance of social-emotional competencies for student success, there remains a lack of tools designed specifically for assessing these competencies in elementary-aged students (McKown 2019). Traditional methods of one-on-one paper-and-pencil evaluations are resource-intensive and difficult to scale, thereby hindering their ability to effectively reach all students. Study 2 explored methods for evaluating three key social-emotional competencies: Growth Mindset, Self-regulation Difficulties and Emotion Knowledge. These competencies were selected based on their positive impact on academic achievement, school engagement and psychological well-being and their potential to improve through targeted training (Brackett, Rivers and Salovey 2011; Burnett et al. 2020; Kim et al. 2020). Growth Mindset refers to the belief that abilities can improve through effort (Dweck 2007); Self-regulation Difficulties relate to challenges in managing thoughts, emotions and behaviors to achieve goals (McClelland et al. 2017); and Emotion Knowledge is the ability to recognize and understand emotions based on social cues (Izard 1971). We also measured Psychological Distress, which reflects emotional suffering and mental discomfort (Horwitz 2007), as a dependent variable in our predictive models (Study 3).

We developed measures for these competencies and evaluated their psychometric properties for South Korean elementary students (Paik et al. 2025). Self-report items were administered using Likert scales for Growth Mindset (for example, 'How possible is it for you to improve your talents in school?'), Self-regulation Difficulties (for example, 'I have trouble paying attention to the teacher') and Psychological Distress (for example, 'I worry about what will happen'). Emotion Knowledge was assessed through a skill-based format in which students selected the most appropriate emotional response from four options based on illustrated scenarios (for example, how a child might feel after disobeying a parent) (see Figure 11.3 for sample items). To ensure content validity, a team of US and Korean psychologists reviewed and adapted existing measures from educational and clinical research (DeVellis 2016; Kim and Park 2020).

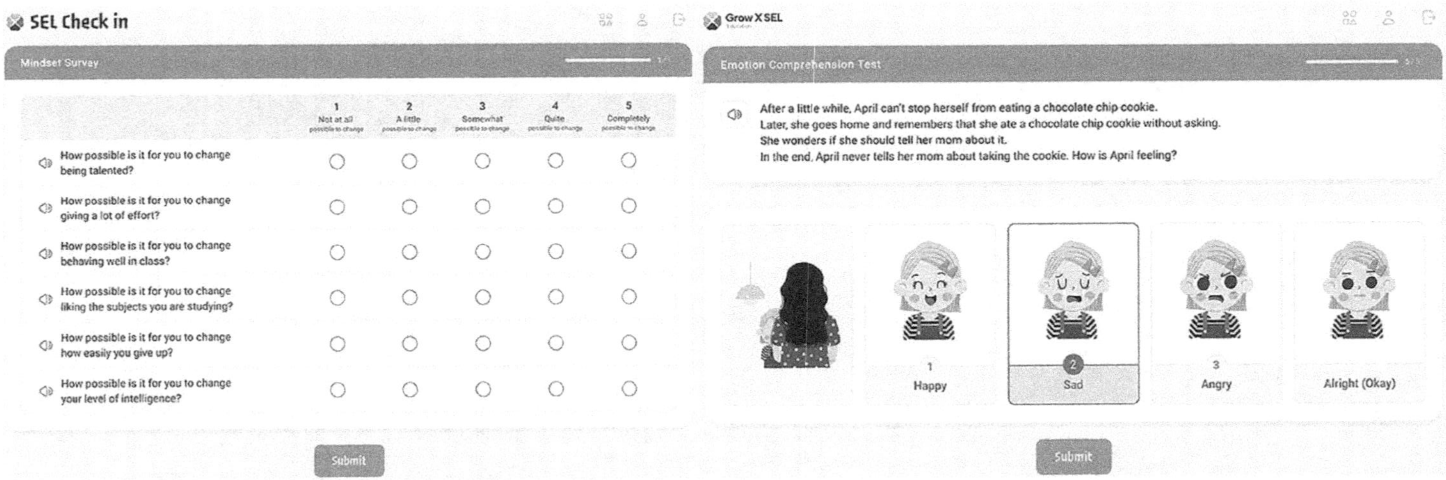

Source: Authors.

Figure 11.3 *Sample self-report and skill-based items for digital social-emotional assessment*

Confirmatory Factor Analysis conducted on the self-reported measures provided evidence of the validity of these measures, supporting their use in online settings. For the skill-based Emotion Knowledge task, Item Response Theory analysis illustrated strong item discrimination and validity. These findings highlight the potential for digital assessment as an effective tool for evaluating social-emotional competencies in a systematic and scalable way. The study also emphasized the importance of culturally adapting assessment tools to ensure relevance and accuracy across diverse educational contexts (Hecht and Shin 2015; Humphrey et al. 2011; Paik et al. 2022).

Key Takeaways

The studies presented here illustrate how advances in LA can be leveraged to collect and analyze data on elementary students' school engagement, emotional experiences and social-emotional competencies in digital environments. As research in this area continues to grow, refining these methods will be essential to enhance their scalability, reliability and validity across diverse student populations. The following two sections introduce predictive models that explore the complex relationships and temporal trajectories of these educational factors discussed thus far.

RECOMMENDATION 2: EXPLORING COMPLEX RELATIONSHIPS

The increasing use of digital learning data has facilitated advanced tracking of a wide variety of student behaviors and skills, allowing researchers to integrate multiple educational dimensions for more comprehensive analyses. Predictive modeling techniques, such as Hierarchical Multiple Regression, Structural Equation Modeling (SEM), Latent Growth Modeling, Bayesian Networks and Random Forests, play a crucial role in uncovering the complex relationships. These approaches support data-driven decision-making, providing insights into the role social-emotional competencies play in academic success, school engagement and psychological well-being.

Model 1: School Engagement as a Mediator Between Emotions and Academic Outcomes (Study 1)

Study 1 explored the relationships among school engagement behaviors, emotional experiences and academic performance in South Korean elementary students (Figure 11.4). Structural Equation Modeling (SEM) analysis revealed that both behavioral and social engagement positively predicted students' math performance. Additionally, students' reports of emotional states positively predicted these engagement dimensions. Importantly, this relationship was partially mediated by school engagement, where students' reporting of emotional experiences was shown to positively predict behavioral and social engagement, which in turn, were associated with better mathematics performance.

These findings emphasize the role of school engagement in driving academic performance, consistent with previous research across elementary and college students (Martins et al. 2022; Macfadyen and Dawson 2012). The mediation effect highlights how students' emotional

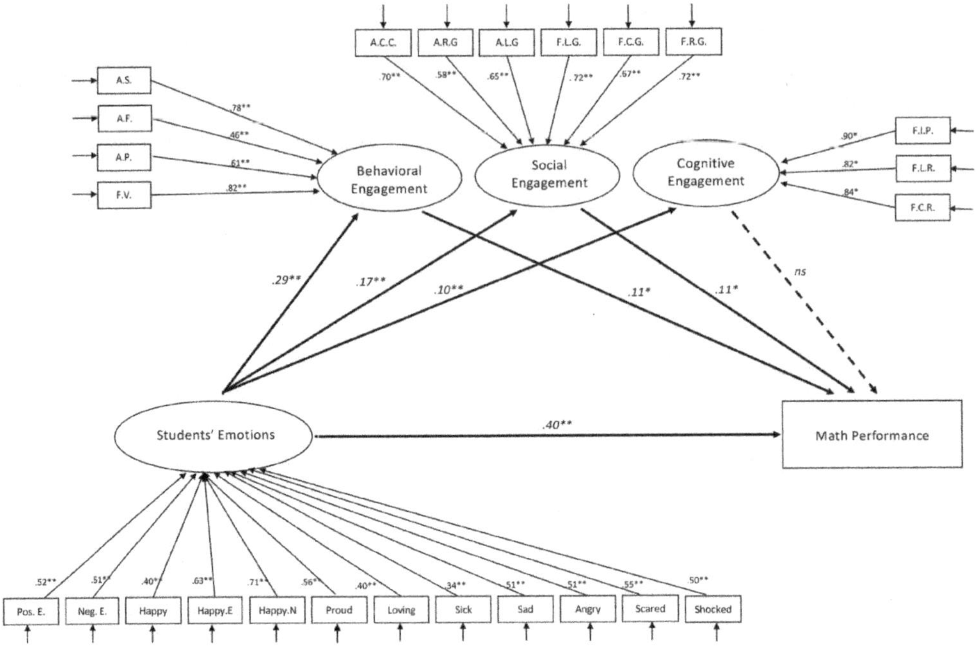

Note: $*p < 0.05$; $**p < 0.01$.
Source: Authors.

Figure 11.4 *Schematic diagram of the mediation effect path model for the role of school engagement (behavioral, social and cognitive) between students' emotions and math performance*

experiences may influence learning directly as well as indirectly through their engagement behaviors.

These findings support the need for nurturing emotional well-being and active participation in learning environments across different educational contexts, grade levels and subjects. Educators should intentionally cultivate both emotional awareness and active engagement to enhance students' academic achievement. Emotions serve as important social and cognitive cues, helping students navigate learning events more effectively, especially in their interactions with peers and teachers. School engagement is an active, effortful process, requiring students' sustained commitment of time, energy and cognitive resources (Krause 2005). For this reason, students must be equipped to effectively manage their emotional responses while directing their attention and cognitive efforts toward learning tasks to sustain engagement. Educators can support this by creating environments that encourage students to regulate their emotions as well as support behavioral and social engagement through goal settings and positive peer interactions.

Model 2: Social-emotional Competencies as Predictors of Academic Performance and Psychological Well-being (Study 2)

Study 2 used both SEM and Hierarchical Multiple Regression to examine how key social-emotional competencies—Growth Mindset, Self-regulation Difficulties and Emotion Knowledge—predict academic performance and Psychological Distress. SEM analysis showed that a higher Growth Mindset was associated with higher proficiency in both Literacy and Math, as well as lower levels of Self-regulation Difficulties. Conversely, greater Self-regulation Difficulties were linked to lower academic outcomes and greater Psychological Distress (see Figure 11.5). Additionally, results from a separate Hierarchical Multiple Regression analysis revealed that Emotion Knowledge positively predicted literacy and math performance, but did not show a measurable impact on Psychological Distress.

These findings further support the critical role of Growth Mindset, Self-regulation and Emotion Knowledge in promoting academic achievement (for example, Kim and Park 2021; MacCann et al. 2020). However, our study did not fully replicate previous research. Notably, we found no significant relationship between Growth Mindset and Psychological Distress among our South Korean students, which are in contrast with findings from the USA, where

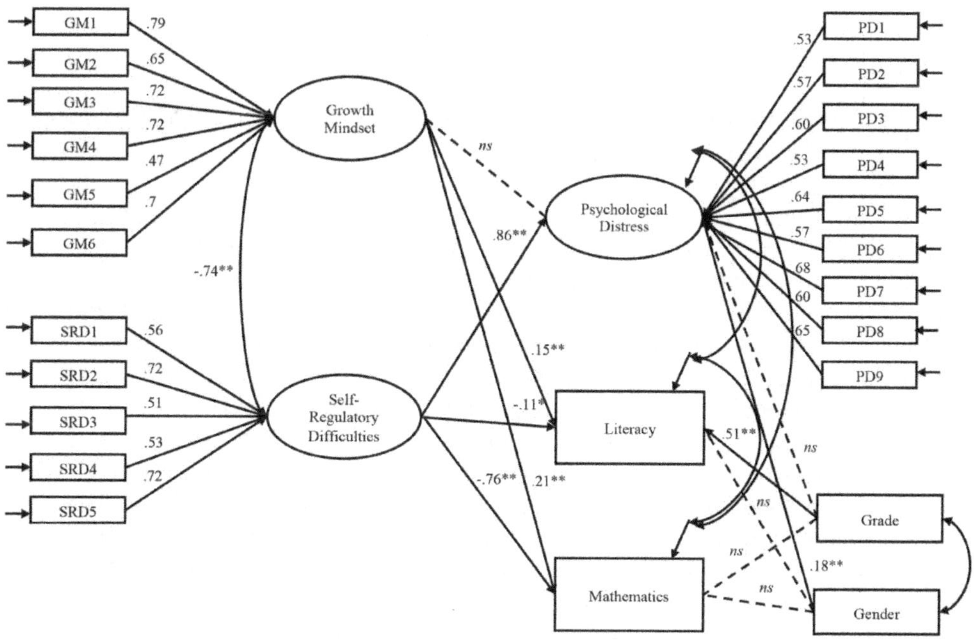

Note: *$p < 0.05$, **$p < 0.01$.
Source: Authors.

Figure 11.5 *Schematic diagram of the SEM model illustrating the predictive paths for students' emotional skills to achievement and psychological well-being*

a stronger Growth Mindset was related to lower Psychological Distress (Burnette et al. 2020). This raises an interesting question about how Growth Mindset may function differently depending on sociocultural values and norms, such as Confucian teachings about effort and perseverance, a topic previously explored by other scholars (for example, Yan, King and Haw 2021). Similarly, Emotion Knowledge did not predict lower Psychological Distress in our sample. Future research is needed to further investigate these relationships and explore how factors like grade, academic subjects, assessment methods and cultural differences may contribute to such relationships.

Key Takeaways

The predictive models presented provide insights into the complex, interrelated nature of social-emotional competencies, school engagement, academic achievement and psychological well-being. Future LA research should continue to refine these models, exploring how different social-emotional competencies interact across various educational contexts and developmental stages. Our findings allude to the importance of considering cultural, contextual and individual differences in shaping these models. Future studies should intentionally incorporate a diverse student population, including those from varied socio-economic, cultural and linguistic backgrounds, to examine the generalizability and applicability of these predictive models.

RECOMMENDATION 3: TRACKING CHANGES OVER TIME UTILIZING TEMPORAL LEARNING ANALYTICS

In Study 3, we applied temporal aspects of learning analytics (Paik et al. 2025) to explore whether students' engagement, as measured through learning behavioral indicators from the LMS's log files, changed systematically over the course of a semester. A latent growth model (LGM) with a Structural Equation Modeling (SEM) framework (LGM; Byrne and Crombie 2003; Duncan and Duncan 2004; Isiordia and Ferrer 2018) was considered to investigate the predictive trajectory of South Korean elementary students' engagement in online learning. Growth models, often conceptualized within the framework of multilevel modeling, treat time-dependent observations as nested within individuals (Raudenbush and Bryk 2002). LGM, an extension of traditional growth modeling, simultaneously estimates individual growth trajectories and their variability within a sample. This approach integrates latent variables to capture underlying growth patterns, allowing for the exploration of both individual- and group-level predictors of change over time. As such, LGM provides a comprehensive and robust means for examining the dynamic interactions in longitudinal data (McArdle and Bell 2000), offering key insights into the factors that may drive changes in student engagement.

Our analysis tracked student engagement at six time points from April to June 2024, representing the full span of an academic semester. Time-invariant predictors included Growth Mindset, Self-regulation Difficulties, Emotion Knowledge, academic performance in Math and Literacy, Grade and Gender. Our results indicated a positive linear growth pattern for student engagement, with intermittent spikes in engagement occurring between certain time intervals (between T1–T2, T3–T4 and T5–T6) (see Figure 11.6). This suggests that student engagement is not uniform but rather fluctuates in meaningful ways throughout the semester.

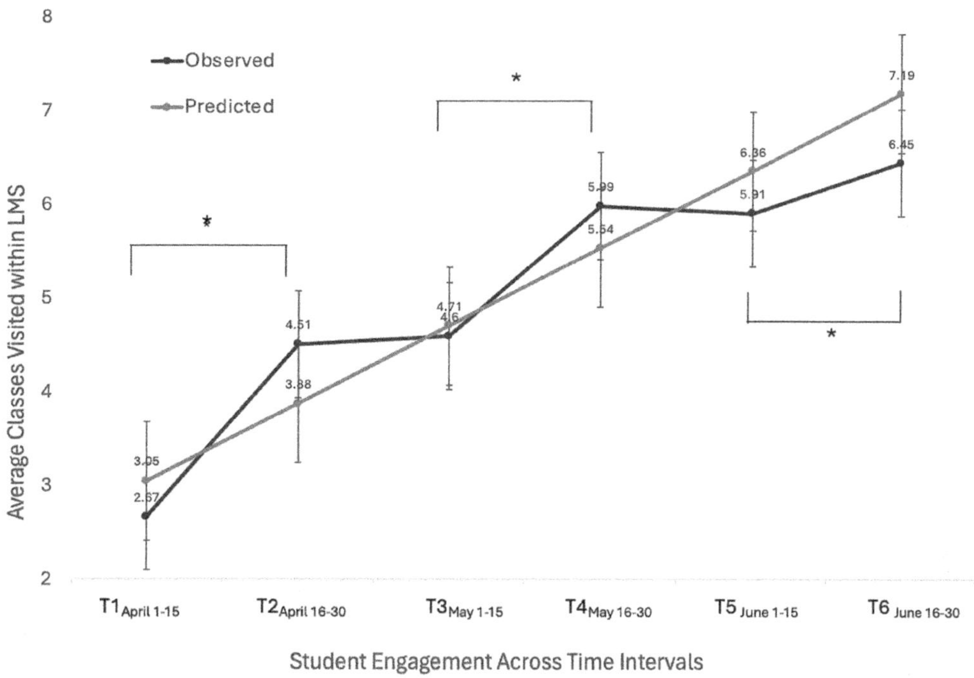

Note: *$p < 0.01$.
Source: Authors.

Figure 11.6 *Observed and predicted trends in student engagement, assuming linear growth*

This temporal variability suggests the importance of monitoring and supporting students at critical inflection points in the semester.

Students with higher levels of Growth Mindsets and Emotion Knowledge showed both higher initial engagement and greater increase throughout the semester, while those with greater Self-regulation Difficulties began the semester with lower initial engagement and slower growth (see Figure 11.7). Other predictors of engagement included math proficiency, grade level and gender, with students with higher math proficiency, older students and female students showing more pronounced initial engagement and growth across the semester.

These findings emphasize the importance of social-emotional competencies in sustaining student engagement within digital learning environments. Growth mindset interventions and emotional intelligence curricula may support students' academic success and overall well-being. Additionally, targeted strategies to strengthen self-regulation can help students maintain engagement and overcome obstacles more effectively. Personalizing learning environments to account for grade level, proficiency and gender differences is also crucial for ensuring that all students can engage meaningfully.

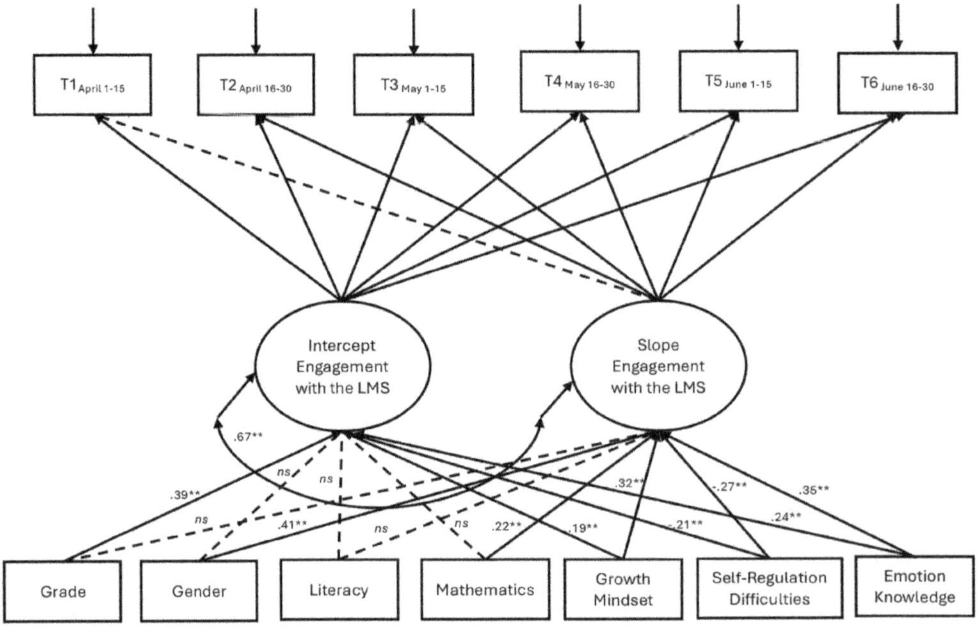

Note: $^{**}p < .01$.
Source: Authors.

Figure 11.7 Latent growth model of the change in student engagement

Temporal analyses are also effective in capturing the stability and consistency of student data. For example, in Study 2 presented in an earlier section, we examined the consistency of emotions students reported over time. Given that emotional states are highly context-specific and can change rapidly, it is uncertain whether the three distinct emotion reporting patterns observed in our sample were stable over time. To determine their stability, temporal analysis was used to examine Emotion Check-in data collected at five evenly spaced measurement points between March and July. Results indicated that students' emotion reporting patterns remained remarkably consistent over time (Paik et al. 2025).

Key Takeaways

This study demonstrates the powerful use of temporal predictive models in capturing both the evolving and stable nature of educational factors over time. By leveraging time-based data available through LA, these models offer richer insights than traditional static approaches. As illustrated, they can help uncover patterns of change and pinpoint key moments where interventions may be most needed or effective. This time-sensitive approach not only enhances our understanding of how educational factors influence learning, but also supports more targeted, data-driven interventions that are responsive to students' changing needs throughout their learning.

DISCUSSION AND FUTURE DIRECTIONS

In this chapter, we outlined strategies for leveraging LA and EDM to deepen our understanding of the complex interplay between academic, social and emotional learning. We focused on three recommendations (that is, validating social-emotional dimensions, exploring complex relationships and tracking changes over time) using concrete examples drawn from real-world implementation in South Korean elementary public schools using their primary LMS. The ability to collect and analyze a wide range of competencies has spurred increasing advocacy for the integration of social-emotional competencies into LA research (Joksimović et al. 2022; Buckingham Shum and Deakin Crick 2016). While this integration marks a significant advancement in educational research and practice, it is still in its infancy, with much potential yet to be explored. Expanding the scope of LA research and its practical applications will enable educators to design more responsive curricula and teaching strategies, capitalizing on important learning moments to support the full range of students' academic, social and emotional development.

As the field of LA continues to grow, researchers must harness its full potential by applying predictive models across diverse student populations, educational contexts and academic domains, ensuring that these models are generalizable and robust. As Dawson et al. (2019) have described, LA aims 'to understand the learning process as well as optimizing that process for all students across all contexts' (p. 454). Thus, collecting diverse student data and developing predictive models that are both inclusive and culturally sensitive are relevant and applicable across various educational settings worldwide.

One important subfield is multimodal learning analytics (MmLA), which collects rich contextualized student data from various students to offer richer insights into the learning process (Ochoa 2022; Ochoa and Worsley 2016). MmLA allows researchers to gather and analyze various metrics, such as video, logs, audio, gestures and biosensors, in tandem at high frequency to study the learning process in realistic, ecologically valid settings (Blikstein 2013). An exciting potential of MmLA lies in its ability to capture psychophysiological indicators as proxies for students' social and emotional experiences. For instance, current research is integrating data from micro-facial expressions, body language, self-reflective logs and physiological signals to gain a more comprehensive understanding of how emotional experiences affect student engagement and academic performance (Hutt et al. 2019; Pardos et al. 2014). Additionally, wearable devices such as smartwatches are being used to track physiological markers, allowing researchers to differentiate between high-stress and low-stress learning states (Ramakrishnan et al. 2019; Smets et al. 2018). This opens promising avenues for developing effective prevention and intervention strategies, such as supporting students experiencing anxiety in educational settings. While further research is needed to validate these methods, they demonstrate the immense potential of LA to address contemporary educational challenges.

Ultimately, the goal of LA and EDM is to generate actionable insights that improve the student learning experience. To achieve this, it is essential to integrate feedback and training mechanisms within the same platforms that collect student data. For example, incorporating emotional and behavioral training within digital learning environments can offer real-time support tailored to students' behaviors, skill sets, experiences and needs. A student displaying signs of distress might receive guidance on emotional regulation, while a student struggling with self-regulation could be prompted to practice mindfulness techniques during periods of low engagement. Additionally, tools such as digital planners could help students with a low Growth Mindset belief by helping them set and track achievable goals.

One key challenge in integrating LA research in the context of SEL is the lack of readily available educational technologies. Most existing EdTech platforms primarily target core academic subjects like literacy and mathematics (World Economic Forum 2016). Developing such sophisticated educational platforms designed to foster young students' SEL skills calls for a multidisciplinary effort, an area where LA research is well recognized (Ferguson 2012). We advocate for stronger partnerships between LA researchers, EdTech companies, educators and engineers to innovate evidence-based tools. An example is the Grow X SEL platform, created through partnerships between researchers, educators and EdTech engineers, which is currently being piloted with diverse student populations. The platform offers a comprehensive set of tools for assessing elementary students' social-emotional competencies, alongside many other features such as daily emotion reflections, instructional SEL videos, mindfulness exercises, games and lesson plans, all grounded in a theoretical framework. Designed for self-administration with minimal adult supervision by integrating X-BOT helper, the platform is scalable and adaptable, making it an effective tool for reaching larger student populations across various cultural and educational contexts.

Lastly, we acknowledge the importance of addressing the ethical concerns related to the regular collection of data on students' emotions and well-being. All studies presented in this chapter underwent review and approval by relevant institutional ethics boards, as well as by the participating school communities. In Korea, informed consent was obtained from parents or guardians, with assurances that all student responses would be confidential, used solely for research and program improvement purposes and reported only in aggregated form, never presented individually. Based on the current findings, we are actively collaborating with mental health professionals and educators in South Korea to develop informed practices that ultimately support and enhance student well-being. We believe this approach aligns with and is consistent with ethical principles that prioritize student privacy, respect the role of educational research and serve the best interests of the students. Going forward, continued ethical considerations must remain central to ensure that any social-emotional data gathered through platforms are used as a supportive tool aimed at serving students' well-being in a safe and respectful manner.

In conclusion, LA research is paving the way for innovative, efficient and validated methods to understand and integrate the multifaceted aspects of education. The ability to simultaneously track and analyze diverse student behaviors, knowledge and skills, once viewed as complex and resource-intensive, has become increasingly feasible through LA and EDM. Though the integration of social and emotional learning into LA is still in its early stages, it holds tremendous promise for providing a more holistic view of the learning process, not only fostering students' academic success, but also their overall well-being. As LA research continues to progress, the development of comprehensive SEL tools will ensure that education becomes more responsive to the unique needs and profiles of each student in addressing their social, emotional and cognitive development.

REFERENCES

Aber, J.L., C. Tubbs, C. Torrente, P.F. Halpin, B. Johnston, L. Starkey … and S. Wolf (2016), 'Promoting children's learning and development in conflict-affected countries: Testing change process in the Democratic Republic of Congo', *Development and Psychopathology*, **29** (1), 53–67. https://doi.org/10.1017/S0954579416001139

Bae, S.M., S.A. Lee and S.H. Lee (2015), 'Prediction by data mining, of suicide attempts in Korean adolescents: A national study', *Neuropsychiatric Disease and Treatment*, **11**, 2367–2675.

Blikstein, P. (2013), 'Digital fabrication and "making" in education: The democratization of invention', in J. Walter-Herrmann and C. Büching (eds), *FabLabs: Of Machines, Makers and Inventors*, Transcript Verlag, pp. 203–22. https://doi.org/10.14361/transcript.9783839423820.203

Brackett, M.A., S.E. Rivers and P. Salovey (2011), 'Emotional intelligence: Implications for personal, social, academic and workplace success', *Social and Personality Psychology Compass*, **5**, 88–103. https://doi.org/10.1111/j.1751-9004.2010.00334.x

Buckingham Shum, S. and R. Deakin Crick (2016), 'Learning analytics for 21st century competencies', *Journal of Learning Analytics*, **3** (2), 6–21. https://doi.org/10.18608/jla.2016.32.2

Burnette, J.L., L.E. Knouse, D.T Vavra, E. O'Boyle and M.A. Brooks (2020), 'Growth mindsets and psychological distress: A meta-analysis', *Clinical Psychology Review*, **77**, 101816 . https://doi.org/10.1016/j.cpr.2020.101816

Byrne, B.M. and G. Crombie (2003), 'Modeling and testing change: An introduction to the latent growth curve model', *Understanding Statistics*, **2** (3), 177–203.

California Department of Education (2023), *Social and Emotional Learning: Guidance and Resources for Supporting Social and Emotional Learning.* https://www.cde.ca.gov/eo/in/socialemotionallearning.asp

Camacho-Morles, J., G.R. Slemp, R. Pekrun, K. Loderer, H. Hou and L.G. Oades (2021), 'Activity achievement emotions and academic performance: A meta-analysis' *Educational Psychology Review*, **33** (3), 1051–95. https://doi.org/10.1007/s10648-020-09585-3

D'Mello, S.K. and E. Jensen (2022), 'Emotional learning analytics', in C. Lang, G. Siemens, A.F. Wise, D. Gašević and A. Merceron (eds), *Handbook of Learning Analytics,* Society for Learning Analytics Research, Vancouver, Canada, pp. 120–29. doi:10.18608/hla22.

Dawson, S., S. Joksimović, O. Poquet and G. Siemens (March 4, 2019), 'Increasing the impact of learning analytics', *LAK19: Proceedings of the 9th International Conference on Learning Analytics and Knowledge*, pp. 446–55. https://doi.org/10.1145/3303772.3303784

DeVellis, R.F. (2016), *Scale Development: Theory and Applications* (4th ed.), Sage Publications, Los Angeles.

Do, S.L. (2015), 'Social emotional learning and character education', Paper presented at the Annual Meeting of the Korean Educational Psychology Association, Seoul, Korea.

Duncan, T.E. and S.C. Duncan (2004), An introduction to latent growth curve modeling. *Behavior Therapy*, **35** (2), 333–63.

Durlak, J.A., R.P. Weissberg, A.B. Dymnicki, R.D. Taylor and K.B. Schellinger (2011), 'The impact of enhancing students' social and emotional learning: A meta-analysis of school-based universal interventions', *Child Development*, **82**, 405–32. https://doi.org/10.1111/j.1467-8624.2010.01564.x

Dweck, C.S. (2007), *Mindset: The New Psychology of Success*. Ballantine Books, New York, NY.

Emotient (2014), FACET: Facial expression recognition software. www.emotient.com .

Ferguson, R. (2012), *The State of Learning Analytics in 2012: A Review and Future Challenges,* Technical Report, Knowledge Media Institute, The Open University, UK. http://kmi.open.ac.uk/publications/pdf/kmi-12-01.pdf

Fredricks, J.A., P.C. Blumenfeld and A.H. Paris (2004), 'School engagement: Potential of the concept, state of the evidence', *Review of Educational Research*, **74**, 59–109. https://journals.sagepub.com/doi/abs/10.3102/00346543074001059

Gašević, D., S. Dawson and G. Siemens (2015), 'Let's not forget: Learning analytics are about learning', *TechTrends*, **59**, 64–71. https://doi.org/10.1007/s11528-014-0822-x

Greenberg, M.T. (2023), *Evidence for Social and Emotional Learning in Schools,* Learning Policy Institute. https://doi.org/10.54300/928.269

Hecht, M.L. and Y. Shin (2015), 'Culture and social and emotional competencies', in J.A. Durlak, C.E. Domitrovich, R.P. Weissberg, and T.P. Gullotta (eds), *Handbook of Social and Emotional Learning: Research and Practice*, The Guilford Press, New York, NY, pp. 50–64.

Hernandez, M.M., N. Eisenberg, C. Valiente, M.S. Thompson, T.L. Spinrad, K.J. Grimm … and D.E. Gal (2018), 'Trajectories of expression of negative emotion from kindergarten to first grade: Associations with academic outcomes', *Journal of Educational Psychology*, **110** (3), 324–37. https://doi.org/10.1037/edu0000213

Horwitz, A.V. (2007), 'Distinguishing distress from disorder as psychological outcomes of stressful social arrangements', *Health*, **11** (3), 273–89.

Humphrey, N., A. Kalambouka, M. Wigelsworth, A. Lendrum, J. Deighton and M. Wolpert (2011), 'Measures of social and emotional skills for children and young people: A systematic review', *Educational and Psychological Measurement*, **71** (4), 617–37. doi:10.1177/0013164410382896

Hutt, S., K. Krasich, C. Mills, N. Bosch, S. White, J.R. Brockmole and S.K. D'Mello (2019), 'Automated gaze-based mind wandering detection during computerized learning in classrooms', *User Modeling and User-Adapted Interaction* **29**, 821–67. doi:10.1007/s11257-019-09228-5

IMS Global Consortium (2020), *Caliper Analytics Specification: EdTech Final Release Version 1.2.* https://www.imsglobal.org/spec/caliper/v1p2~

Isiordia, M. and E. Ferrer (2018), 'Curve of factors model: A latent growth modeling approach for educational research', *Educational and Psychological Measurement*, **78** (2), 203–31.

Izard, C.E. (1971), *The Face of Emotion*. Appleton-Century-Crofts, New York, NY.

Jeon, D.H. (2023), *The Ministry of Education is establishing a new department in charge of mental health for school staff, and is pushing for organizational restructuring.* https://imnews.imbc.com/news/2023/society/article/6549004_36126.html

Joksimović, S., S. Dawson, A. Barthakur, O. Poquet, Y.E. Wang, F. Marmolejo-Ramos and G. Siemens (2022), 'Mapping the landscape of social and emotional learning analytics', in Y.E. Wang, S. Joksimović, M.O.Z. San Pedro, J.D. Way and J. Whitmer (eds), *Social and Emotional Learning and Complex Skills Assessment*, Springer, Cham, Switzerland, pp. 27–47. https://doi.org/10.1007/978-3-031-06333-6_3

Kim, E., M.M. Jackman, S.-H. Jo, J. Oh, S.-Y. Ko, C.L. McPherson, Y.-S.Hwang and N.N. Singh (2020), 'Effectiveness of the mindfulness-based OpenMind-Korea (OM-K) preschool program', *Mindfulness*, **11**, 1062–72. https://doi.org/10.1007/s12671-020-01337-2

Kim, H., L. Brown and J. Weiss-Yagoda (2017), *3EA Education in Emergencies: Evidence for Action Impact Report 2.1: IRC Healing Classrooms Remedial Tutoring Programming Improves Nigerien and Nigerian Children's Learning.* Global TIES for Children.

Kim, J. and Y. Park (2020), 'Cultural adaptation and validation of psychological scales: A Korean perspective', *Korean Journal of Psychology: General*, **39** (2), 123–40.

Kim, M.S. and S. Park (2021), 'Growth of fixed mindset from elementary to middle school: Its relationship with trajectories of academic behavior engagement and academic achievement', *Psychology in the Schools*, **58** (11), 2,175–88.

King, R.B., D.M. McInerney, F.A. Ganotice and J.B. Villarose (2015), 'Positive affect catalyses academic engagement: Cross-sectional, longitudinal and experimental evidence', *Learning and Individual Differences*, **39**, 64–72. https://doi.org/10.1016/j.lindif.2015.03.005

Knight, S. and S. Buckingham Shum (2017), 'Theory and learning analytics', in C. Lang, G. Siemens, A.F. Wise and D. Gašević (eds), *The Handbook of Learning Analytics*, Society for Learning Analytics Research, Vancouver, BC, pp. 17–22.

Krause, K.L. (2005), *Understanding and Promoting Student Engagement in University Learning Communities.* https://www.liberty.edu/center-for-academic-development/wp-content/uploads/sites/99/2019/10/Stud_eng.pdf

Lee, S.K. and M. Bong (2017), 'Social and emotional learning as a solution for adolescent problems in Korea', in E. Frydenberg, A.J. Martin and R.J. Collie (eds), *Social and Emotional Learning in Australia and the Asia-Pacific*, Springer, Singapore, pp. 233–51. https://doi.org/10.1007/978-981-10-3394-0_13

Linnenbrink-Garcia, L., T.K. Rogat and K.L.K. Koskey (2011), 'Affect and engagement during small group instruction', *Contemporary Educational Psychology*, **36** (1), 13–24. https://doi.org/10.1016/j.cedpsych.2010.09.001

MacCann, C., Y. Jiang, L.E.R. Brown, K.S. Double, M. Bucich and A. Minbashian (2020), 'Emotional intelligence predicts academic performance: A meta-analysis', *Psychological Bulletin*, **146** (2), 150–86. https://doi.org/10.1037/bul0000219

Macfadyen, L.P. and S. Dawson (2012), 'Numbers are not enough: Why e-Learning analytics failed to inform an institutional strategic plan', *Journal of Educational Technology and Society*, **15**, 149–63.

Marsay, G., K.A. Atitsogbe, A. Ouedraogo, H. Nsubuga, P. Pari, E.Y. Kossi, C.M. Park and V.S.H. Solberg (2021), 'The importance of social emotional learning skills in assisting youth to successfully transition into the professional world', *African Journal of Career Development*, **3** (1), a37. doi:10.4102/ajcd.v3i1.37

Martins, J., J. Cunha, S. Lopes, T. Moreira and P. Rosário (2022), 'School engagement in elementary school: A systematic review of 35 years of research', *Educational Psychology Review*, **34**, 793–849. https://doi.org/10.1007/s10648-021-09642-5

Mayer, J.D. and P. Salovey (1997), 'What is emotional intelligence?', in P. Salovey and D. Sluyter (eds), *Emotional Development and Emotional Intelligence: Educational Implications*, Basic Books, New York, NY, pp. 3–34.

McArdle, J.J. and R.Q. Bell (2000), 'An introduction to latent growth models for developmental data analysis', in T.D. Little, K.U. Schnabel and J. Baumert (eds), *Modeling Longitudinal and Multilevel Data: Practical Issues, Applied Approaches and Specific Examples*, Lawrence Erlbaum Publishers, Mahwah, NJ, pp. 69–108.

McClelland, M., J. Geldhof, F. Morrison, S. Gestsdóttir … and J. Grammer (2017), 'Self-regulation', in N. Halfon, C.B. Forrest, R.M. Lerner and E.M. Faustman (eds), *Handbook of Life Course Health Development*, Springer, Cham, Switzerland, pp. 275–98. https://www.ncbi.nlm.nih.gov/books/NBK543706/

McKown, C.M. (2019), 'Reliability, factor structure and measurement invariance of a web-based assessment of children's social-emotional comprehension', *Journal of Psychoeducational Assessment*, **37**, 435–49.

Moazami-Goodarzi, A., M. Zarra-Nezhad, M. Hytti, N. Heiskanen and N. Sajaniemi (2021), 'Training early childhood teachers to support children's social and emotional learning: A preliminary evaluation of Roundies program', *International Journal of Environmental Research and Public Health*, **18** (20), 10679. https://doi.org/10.3390/ijerph182010679

Ochoa, X. (2022), 'Multimodal learning analytics: Rationale, process, examples and direction', in C. Lang, G. Siemens, A.F. Wise, D. Gašević and A. Merceron (eds), *Handbook of Learning Analytics* (2nd ed.), SoLAR, Vancouver, BC, pp. 54–65. https://www.solaresearch.org/publications/hla-22/hla22-chapter6/

Ochoa, X. and M. Worsley (2016), 'Editorial: Augmenting learning analytics with multimodal sensory data', *Journal of Learning Analytics*, **3** (2), 213–19. https://doi.org/10.18608/jla.2016.32.10

Paik, J.H., S. Duh, C. Lopez and R. Rodriguez (2022), 'Emotion knowledge and theory of mind among Chinese preschoolers: A curriculum-based approach', *Early Education & Development Special Issue*, **33** (5), 764–85. https://doi.org/10.1080/10409289.2021.1995258

Paik, J.H., I. Himelfarb, S.H. Yoo, K. Yoo and H. Ha (2024a), 'The relationships among school engagement, students' emotions, and academic performance in an elementary online learning', *LAK '24: Proceedings of the 14th Learning Analytics and Knowledge Conference,* pp. 219–30. https://dl.acm.org/doi/10.1145/3636555.3636871

Paik, J.H., I. Himelfarb, S.H. Yoo, M.J. Kim and H. Ha (2024b), 'The role of students' reporting of emotional experiences in mathematics achievement: Results from the e-learning platform', Research paper presented at the American Educational Research Association, Pittsburgh, Pennsylvania, USA.

Paik, J.H., I. Himelfarb, S.H. Yoo, J.K. Lee, H. Ha and Y. Park (April 2025), 'Predictive models for examining the relationships among elementary students' social, emotional, academic and engagement factors over time'. A symposium paper presented at the Annual Meeting of the American Educational Research Association, Denver, Colorado, USA.

Pardos, Z.A., R.J.S.D. Baker, M. San Pedro, Sujith M. Gowda and Supreeth M. Gowda (2014), 'Affective states and state tests: Investigating how affect and engagement during the school year predict end-of-year learning outcomes', *Journal of Learning Analytics*, **1** (1), 107–28. doi:10.18608/jla.2014.11.6

Park, J.S. and J.W. Moon (2010), 'Factors affecting suicidal ideation of the middle and high school students in Korea', *Health Social Sciences*, **27**, 105–31.

Pekrun, R. and L. Linnenbrink-Garcia (2012), 'Academic emotions and student engagement', in S.L. Christenson, A.L. Reschly and C. Wylie (eds.), Handbook of Research on Student Engagement, Springer Science + Business Media, pp. 259–282. https://doi.org/10.1007/978-1-4614-2018-7_12

Pekrun, R., S. Lichtenfeld, H.W. Marsh, K. Murayama and T. Goetz (2017), 'Achievement emotions and academic performance: Longitudinal models of reciprocal effects', *Child Development*, **88** (5), 1653–70. https://doi.org/10.1111/cdev.12704

Perera, H.N. and M. DiGiacomo (2013), 'The relationship of trait emotional intelligence with academic performance: A meta-analytic review', *Learning and Individual Differences*, **28**, 20–33. https://www.sciencedirect.com/science/article/abs/pii/S1041608013001143

Poquet, O. and M. de Laat (2021), 'Developing capabilities: Lifelong learning in the age of AI', *British Journal of Educational Technology*, **52** (4), 1695–1708. https://doi.org/10.1111/bjet.13123

Racine, N., B.A. McArthur, J.E. Cooke, R. Eirich, J. Zhu and S. Madigan (2021), 'Global prevalence of depressive and anxiety symptoms in children and adolescents during COVID-19: A meta-analysis', *JAMA Pediatrics*, **175** (11), 1142–50. https://doi.org/10.1001/jamapediatrics.2021.2482

Ramakrishnan, A., A. Pardes, W. Lynch, C. Molaro and M.L. Platt (2019), 'A machine learning approach to identifying objective biomarkers of anxiety and stress', BioRxiv. https://doi.org/10.1101/745315

Raudenbush, S.W. and A.S. Bryk (2002), *Hierarchical Linear Models: Applications and Data Analysis Methods* (2nd ed.), Sage Publications, Thousand Oaks, CA.

Redmond, P., A. Heffernan, L. Abawi, A. Brown and R. Henderson (2018), 'An online engagement framework for higher education', *OLJ*, **22** (1), 183–204. https://doi.org/10.24059/olj.v22i1.1175

Šćukanec Schmidt, N., A. Skledar Matijević and Z. Anić (2023), 'Linking quality assurance and the social dimension of higher education', NESET report, Publications Office of the European Union. doi:10.2766/268811.

Singh, N.C. and A. Duralappah (eds) (2020), *Rethinking Learning: A Review of Social and Emotional Learning for Education Systems,* UNESCO/MGIEP.

Smets, E., E. Rios Velazquez, G. Schiavone, I. Chakroun, E. D'Hondt, W. De Raedt, J. Cornelis, O. Janssens, S. Van Hoecke, S. Claes, I. Van Diest and C. Van Hoof (2018), 'Large-scale wearable data reveal digital phenotypes for daily-life stress detection', *Npj Digital Medicine*, **1** (1), 67. https://doi.org/10.1038/s41746-018-0074-9

Statistics Korea (2019), *Causes of Death Statistics in 2018,* Ministry of Data and Statistics, Seoul, South Korea, pp. 1–4.

Topping, K.J., W. Douglas, D. Robertson and N. Ferguson (2022), 'Effectiveness of online and blended learning from schools: A systematic review', *Review of Education*, **10** (2), e3353. https://doi.org/10.1002/rev3.3353

Weissberg, R.P., J.A. Durlak, C.E. Domitrovich and T.P. Gullotta (2015), 'Social and emotional learning: Past, present and future', in J.A. Durlak, C.E. Domitrovich, R.P. Weissberg, and T.P. Gullotta (eds), *Handbook of Social and Emotional Learning: Research and Practice*, Guilford Press, New York, NY, pp. 3–19.

World Economic Forum (2016), *New Vision for Education: Fostering Social and Emotional Learning through Technology*, Geneva. http://www3.weforum.org/docs/WEF_New_Vision_for_Education.pdf

World Health Organization (2024), *Mental Health of Adolescents*, Geneva. https://www.who.int/news-room/fact-sheets/detail/adolescent-mental-health

Yan, Z., R.B. King and J.Y. Haw (2021), 'Formative assessment, growth mindset, and achievement: examining their relations in the East and the West', *Assessment in Education: Principles, Policy, and Practice*, **28** (5–6), 676–702. https://doi.org/10.1080/0969594X.2021.1988510

Zhao, Y. and J. Watterston (2021), 'The changes we need: Education post Covid-19', *Journal of Educational Change*, **22** (1), 3–12. doi:10.1007/s10833-021-09417-3

Zhoc, K.C.H., R.B. King, T.S.H. Chung and J. Chen (2020), 'Emotionally intelligent students are more engaged and successful: Examining the role of emotional intelligence in higher education', *European Journal of Psychology of Education*, **35**, 839–63. https://doi.org/10.1007/s10212-019-00458-0

12. Using learning analytics to explore pre-service teachers' lesson planning

Kjersti Nedland Røneid, Gleb Belokrys, and Kristin Børte

INTRODUCTION

Lesson planning is a core task in teaching and a key competence that pre-service teachers (PSTs) must develop during their education. It is in the planning process that important decisions are made about teaching and students' learning experiences (Mutton et al. 2011). When planning lessons, teachers set learning goals, choose appropriate instructional strategies, organise learning activities and learning environments, and adjust these to support the needs of specific groups or individual learners. Although there is extensive knowledge of how experienced teachers plan lessons, there is comparatively limited knowledge regarding how PSTs acquire and develop lesson planning skills throughout their teacher education (Krepf and König 2023; Lammert and Godfrey 2025; Zaragoza et al. 2023). A review on preparing teachers for lesson planning (Lammert and Godfrey 2025) revealed that most studies primarily describe PSTs' lesson planning practices, give little attention to teacher educators' influence, and provide little insight into innovations and designs aimed at enhancing PSTs' lesson planning skills. Improved understanding of how PSTs plan lessons, the choices they make in the learning design process, and how they plan activities tailored to learners' needs and aligned with the learning objectives is therefore crucial for improved teacher education and better training for PSTs.

The aim of this chapter is to investigate how learning analytics (LA) can provide teacher educators with insight into PSTs' lesson planning process, with the goal of informing instructional decisions in teacher education. In this chapter, we draw on research from three different research fields – lesson planning, learning analytics, and learning design – to explore the challenges and possibilities of using LA in teacher education. Learning analytics is defined by the Society for Learning Analytics Research as 'the measurement, collection, analysis, and reporting of data about learners and their contexts, for purposes of understanding and optimizing learning and the environments in which it occurs' (LAK 2011). Hence, learning analytics is the analysis of learning for learning in which both the data and analysis are digital (NOU 2023: 19 2023). Moreover, LA always involves a stakeholder such as learners, teachers, tutors, assistants, educational leaders, institutions, schools, policymakers, parents/guardians, edtech developers, or researchers – and they all use LA for different purposes. Here, we use LA for research purposes to explore possibilities for use in teacher education.

Previous research on learning analytics in teacher education has shown that LA can support teachers by identifying students at risk, tailoring teaching to students' needs (that is, providing more challenging/easier tasks), and provide information relevant for redesigning courses to improve students' learning (Oliva Córdova et al. 2021). Most research on LA is in higher education, and there are few studies on how teachers integrate LA into their teaching practice (Shibani et al. 2020). A systematic review on LA for learning design (Mangaroska and

Giannakos 2019) shows that most studies focused on topics such as design and management of learning scenarios/activities, students' learning behaviour and engagement, usefulness of LA tools, teachers' professional development, improved orchestration, students' self-reflection/self-assessment, and predictive modelling. However, there is little research on the use of LA for specific tasks such as lesson planning.

We report from the first iteration in a research and development project in Norwegian teacher education called ILUKS in which PSTs used a specific learning design tool, the ILUKS planner, to plan lessons during coursework and practicum placement. The ILUKS planner provides students with a framework for lesson planning including key components to consider such as student prerequisites, learning goals, content, activities, assessment, and learning resources. Moreover, it allows PSTs to plan a lesson and share a learning design with teacher educators, peers, or school mentors who then can provide feedback on the design. The ILUKS planner is developed to support PSTs' active learning when they learn how to plan lessons. Pedagogical and technical considerations are described in more detail in Børte and Lillejord (2024). In addition, the tool is designed to capture activity data from users that can be utilised by teacher educators to inform instructional decisions. We present an empirical example of how LA from the ILUKS planner can be used to inform teacher educators about PSTs' competence in lesson planning and identify topics they find challenging.

A variety of learning design tools have been developed for different purposes in education. Some are large learning management systems, some are e-learning platforms, and some are tools for lesson planning. The learning designer (Laurillard et al. 2018) and Pheobe, the pedagogical planner (Masterman 2008), are examples of research-based tools designed to support teachers' lesson planning and development of teaching content that can be shared and reused. Learning design research has offered pedagogical principles for developing tools that support design processes, proposed strategies to enhance teachers' planning, enabled resource sharing, and provided teaching tasks or lesson plans (Nguyen and Bower 2018). Despite these efforts, more knowledge is needed to understand and improve PSTs' planning practices (Lammert and Godfrey 2025). Moreover, few tools are created to aid PSTs in learning how to plan lessons (Børte and Lillejord 2024). By analysing activity data from the ILUKS planner, this study contributes insights into PSTs' planning trajectories. By revealing details in their planning process, we can identify what students struggle with and topics that need further attention in PSTs' training. It also contributes insight into the challenges and possibilities of LA when it is used to teach lesson planning. The chapter answers the following research question: *How can learning analytics inform teacher educators about pre-service teachers' lesson planning?*

We first present previous research on lesson planning and LA and explicate its potential relevance for teacher educators. Next, we situate our study within current research on learning design and tools, before describing how the learning design tool – the ILUKS planner – is designed and captures activity data from users.

BACKGROUND

Learning to Plan Lessons

All teachers engage in lesson planning, an activity that is at the core of their professional practice (Mutton et al. 2011). During planning, they make important decisions about teaching. Subject-specific knowledge and pedagogical considerations are integrated as they consider learning objectives, plan activities for students, which learning resources to use, and how to assess students' learning outcomes (Atjonen et al. 2024; Beckmann and Ehmke 2023; Zaragoza et al. 2024). Teacher education programmes provide pedagogical and practical learning opportunities for PSTs in lesson planning and teaching through on-campus activities and in-school placements (Hammerness et al. 2020). However, studies show a lack of coherence between stakeholders, and PSTs report difficulties with integrating theoretical knowledge into classroom teaching (Karlström and Hamza 2021; Morrison-Love and Patrick 2024).

Previous research on lesson planning has shown that PSTs differ from experienced teachers in how they plan their lessons. They tend to make decisions primarily based on subject-specific knowledge, thus excluding pedagogical concerns (Nilsson 2009; Şahin-Taşkın 2017). Whereas experienced teachers plan for the unforeseen, what Schön (1983) refers to as anticipatory reflection, PSTs' lack of experience makes it difficult to include flexibility in their planning practice and learning designs. As PSTs have limited knowledge of the students they will teach, they find it hard to incorporate situated and contextual factors when they plan and need feedback from either a school mentor while in practice or a university supervisor during coursework (Beckmann and Ehmke 2023; Mena et al. 2017). This support is also considered essential when learning to integrate assessment in teaching. Atjonen et al. (2022) found that PSTs tend to understand the pedagogical importance of including assessment strategies in teaching. However, to develop PSTs' conceptions of assessment and learn how to incorporate assessment into teaching, PSTs benefit from both coursework and support from mentors in authentic assessment practices (Atjonen et al. 2024; Xu and He 2019). Providing PSTs with the possibility to actively work with lesson planning, integrating practice-based knowledge and theoretical knowledge in the planning process, can support the integration of theoretical and practical knowledge necessary for their teaching (Canrinus et al. 2017; Jenset et al. 2018).

When learning to plan lessons, PSTs are usually provided with a lesson planning outline to support their planning process. These outlines are often presented linearly, from learning objective to assessment of learning outcome, and based on general didactical considerations. In Norway, templates often use the didactical, relational model developed by Bjørndal and Lieberg (1978) and bring three questions PSTs should answer when planning a lesson: (1) *what* (the students should do); (2) *how* (they should do it); and (3) *why* (they should do it). This linearity has been criticised for reducing PSTs' understanding of how different aspects play a part in lesson planning and does not reflect PSTs' planning process (John 2006; Karlström and Hamza 2021). The ILUKS planner was developed to counteract linearity and support PSTs when learning how to plan lessons (Børte and Lillejord 2024). It provides PSTs with the opportunity to work actively with lesson planning while receiving feedback from teacher educators in the process. Using a digital tool specifically designed to support students' learning process also provides opportunities for collecting useful data about PSTs' planning activities.

Learning Analytics for Teacher Education

There has been a significant increase in digital tools for collecting information in educational contexts; the quality of tools has improved, and huge amounts of data about learners' activities are generated. The objective of learning analytics is to support educators in teaching and learning processes by converting data into fruitful actions for learners (Ferguson 2012; Ifenthaler and Yau 2020).

Learning analytics is a multidisciplinary research field, dependent on data sources that effectively capture the complexity of a learning process. For example, monitoring students' learning environments to discover learning *patterns* related to engagement, trends, motivation, or learning strategies, *predict* learner behaviour such as failure, final grade, or drop out, or provide personalised feedback to guide future actions (*recommendations*) such as individualised feedback, pedagogical resources, or learning design. Such traces are often referred to as activity data (Samuelsen et al. 2019). Lockyer et al. (2013) suggest dividing analytics into two categories, checkpoint analytics and process analytics. The first provides information about, for example, students' location, access, downloads, and time spent on activities. The latter involves tracking student interactions, regarding how they engage with activities and interact with peers when using the tool. Student tracking data are mainly collected from Learning Management Systems (LMS), but these types of data are still underused as teachers lack data literacy to analyse and use them (Ifenthaler and Yau 2020). In the current study, process analytics were conducted to analyse the activity data from the ILUKS planner, providing a detailed understanding of PSTs' interactions with the tool.

In Norway, the Ministry of Education expects students in higher education to participate in high-quality teaching guided by knowledge-based practices (Meld.St. 16 2016–2017). With access to students' activity data, different stakeholders (students, teachers, researchers, teacher educators, or edtech developers) can better understand students' learning processes and potentially use LA systematically and intentionally to improve teaching quality (Gabbi 2022; Ministry of Education and Research 2022). It is, however, challenging to demonstrate the 'direct impact' of LA in research (Kluge 2021).

A review on how LA can be integrated in teacher education (Salas-Pilco et al. 2022) shows that previous research has focused on (1) how different types of behavioural data and statistics can be used to investigate students' learning behaviour, (2) documenting the effectiveness of activities, and (3) predicting learning outcomes and dropouts. LA has also been used to inform learning design by fostering a data-informed approach to instructional decisions (Mangaroska and Giannakos 2019; van Leeuwen et al. 2017). In Norway, the national Expert Group on LA (NOU 2023:19 2023) suggests introducing measures targeting PSTs and teacher education institutions to support their development of competencies in LA. Digital tools designed to support students' learning and collect activity data for the purpose of understanding learning processes can provide important information for teacher educators about their teaching. However, this entails that teacher educators understand the importance *of* and know *how* to use different types of data to develop teaching practices for their students (Ifenthaler and Yau 2021; Salas-Pilco et al. 2022).

Learning Design and Tools to Support Pre-service Teachers' Lesson Planning

The field of learning design emerged from research on educational technology and has been concerned with ways to support educators in designing effective learning experiences with the use of technology (Bennett et al. 2015; Mangaroska and Giannakos 2019; Wasson and Kirschner 2020). The term learning design has a broad meaning and includes researchers who focus their attention on 'facilitating practitioners in the sharing, modification, and reuse of their pedagogical plans' (Persico and Pozzi 2015, p. 233). According to Wasson and Kirschner (2020), learning design emphasises the goal of the activities, that is, the learning rather than the teachers' instruction. Research on learning design can be grouped into three different strands: (1) how learning designs can be represented; (2) different approaches to support sharing, reuse, and enactment of designs; and (3) the development of tools. Persico and Pozzi (2015) distinguish between different types of learning design tools. *Reflection tools and pedagogical planners* intend to support teachers' decision-making and reflect on pedagogical choices. *Authoring and sharing tools* can represent activities rooted in specific pedagogical models or allow representations or visualisations of activities or the flow of activities. *Repositories* provide teachers with a range of examples of, for instance, design ideas, best practices, or experience reports and delivery tools that are intended for developing learning activities for students. While the learning design field provides educators with supporting tools, methodologies, and representation when they design learning activities aimed to effectuate design processes and ease teachers' work (Mangaroska and Giannakos 2019), studies have shown substantial variations in how teacher educators use technology in their teaching (Uerz et al. 2024). Digital tools tend to be used for administrative tasks or communication, rather than to support PSTs' learning processes (Aagaard et al. 2025).

This chapter argues that an important competence for PSTs is learning how to plan lessons and design teaching and learning activities. For this purpose, digital tools such as learning design tools or pedagogical planners can be well-suited. However, existing tools do not support the learning process of lesson planning, allow feedback in the planning process or open for collecting activity data about the work conducted. Scholars have argued the importance of developing tools that effectively integrate LA to support teachers during the design phase (Amarasinghe et al. 2024; Hernandez-Leo et al. 2019; Persico and Pozzi 2015). Opportunities for PSTs to learn about lesson planning using digital tools are unexplored, and tools used for mentoring PSTs tend to be used as reflection tools post-teaching, rather than supporting PSTs in preparing and planning lessons (Nesje and Lejonberg 2022).

The ILUKS planner – A learning design tool for inquiry-based lesson planning

The ILUKS planner is aligned with pedagogical principles of student active learning and provides possibilities for PSTs to plan lessons, share designs, and give and receive feedback on learning designs. The tool can also serve as a digital infrastructure for an inquiry-based approach to developing and improving learning designs, supporting lesson planning as a professional activity. We use the term 'lesson planning' about the activities of PSTs who use the ILUKS planner to plan their lessons (Børte and Lillejord 2024) and the term 'learning design' to denote the product of the planning activity (Masterman and Manton 2011).

The ILUKS planner provides PSTs with a framework for lesson planning including key categories to consider, such as learning goals, content, activities, assessment, learning resources, and student prerequisites. The different categories constitute columns in the learning design tool and PSTs develop cards within the different columns before they choose cards to assemble into a learning design in the left column. As there are no mandatory fields or specific prescriptions to follow, the tool allows for flexible planning and composition of learning designs. The columns and cards can be moved and placed in any preferred order. In addition, PSTs can create as many cards as they want, and cards can be moved back and forth between the learning design column and the designated category allowing for switching cards and adding new cards to a design. Figure 12.1 shows the interface of the ILUKS planner with columns and cards in different columns. In each card, PSTs develop content, describe, for example, activities, and upload learning materials needed. Figure 12.2 gives an example of content created on a specific card. ILUKS provides an integrated feedback functionality when the learning design is shared. For instance, PSTs can choose to share their learning design and peers, university supervisors, or mentors in school can give feedback on a design during practice placement. The cards that are assembled in the learning design column (first column on the left, Figure 12.1) are available in a document view displaying the content of the cards chosen to be included in a particular learning design as well as given feedback. In this way, the tool supports feedback loops to refine and adjust learning designs.

As we wanted to track student activities when they plan lessons and research how PSTs go about their planning work, the ILUKS planner was designed to capture activity data from users. By tracking the PSTs' activities in the learning design tool, it may be possible to provide teacher educators with insights into how PSTs plan lessons. This information can be used to support teacher educators when making instructional decisions on how and what to teach PSTs about lesson planning.

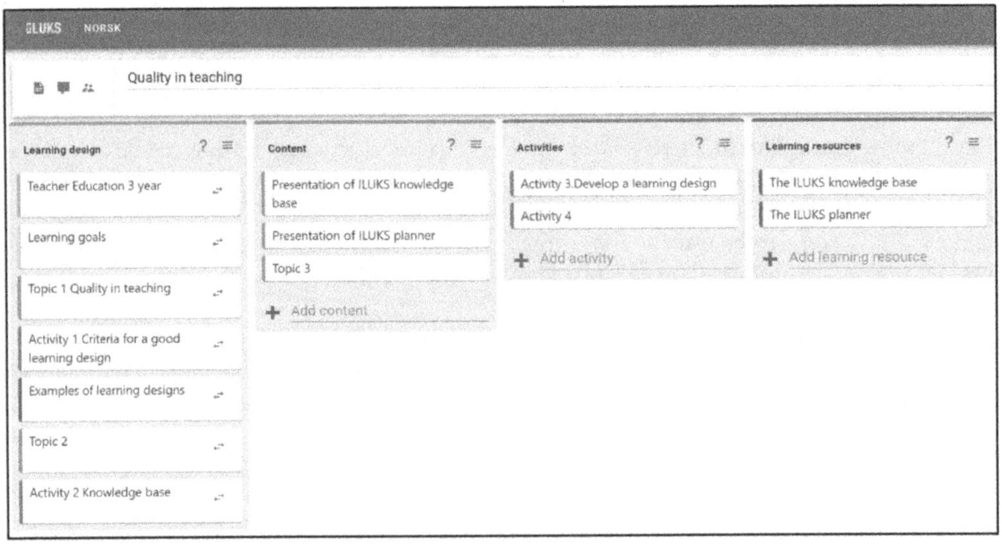

Source: Authors.

Figure 12.1 *Screenshot of the interface in the ILUKS learning design tool*

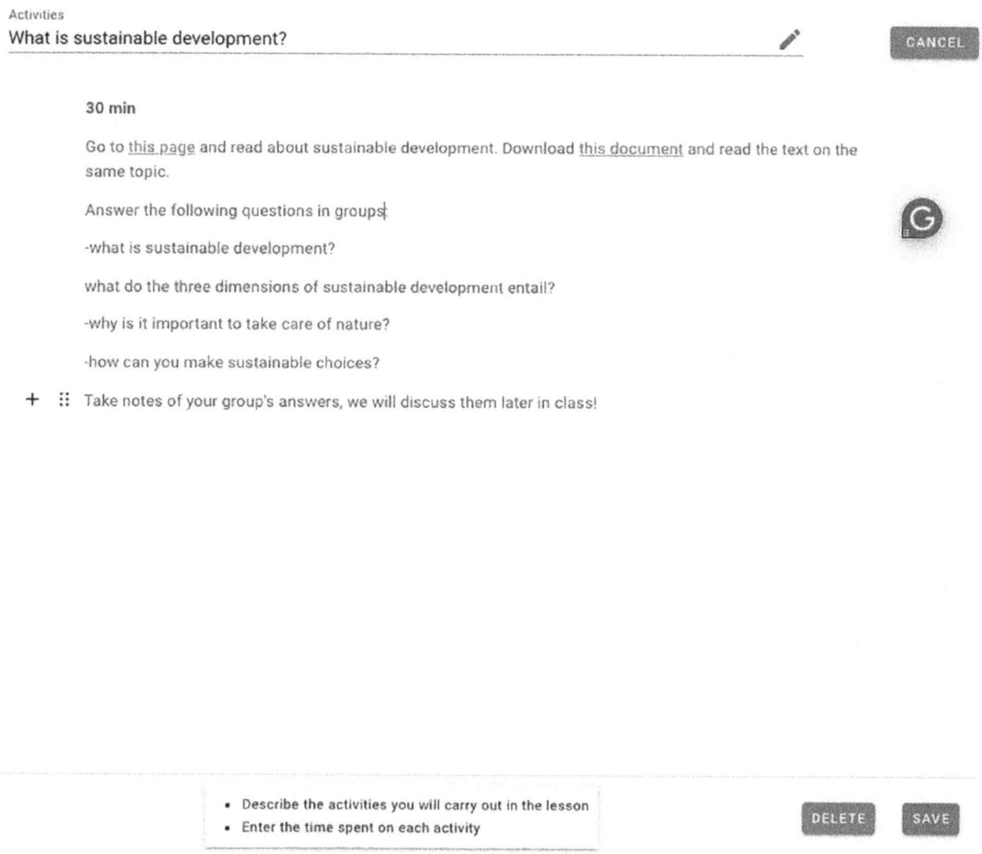

Source: Authors.

Figure 12.2 *Screenshot of an activity card with description*

METHOD

We report on data from a three-year research and development project called ILUKS, financed by the Norwegian Directorate for Higher Education and Skills. It follows the principles of Design-Based Research as described by Anderson and Shattuck (2012), facilitating iterative testing and refinement of educational interventions in authentic settings. A team of educational researchers, software developers, and a teacher educator designed and developed teaching seminars and a learning design tool, the ILUKS planner, to support PSTs' inquiry-based work when learning how to plan lessons. Here we report on the first evaluation in practice in which PSTs used the learning design tool to plan lessons during teaching seminars and practicum placements.

Context and Participants

The first evaluation in practice was conducted in a teacher education programme during the autumn semester in 2022. Due to COVID-19 restrictions, researchers presented the project at an online meeting for all third-year students and invited them to participate in three half-day, on-campus teaching seminars called 'Learning design for student active learning' and to use the ILUKS planner to plan lessons during practice placement. Eight PSTs volunteered to participate. The PSTs were enrolled in a five-year integrated master's programme in teacher education at a Norwegian university, where they studied to become secondary school teachers in the subjects of History, Norwegian and English language, social sciences, and STEM. The PSTs were all females in their mid-twenties with little teaching experience. During seminars, PSTs: (1) were introduced to the learning design tool and tested out its functionalities; (2) created learning designs; (3) shared learning designs with peers and teacher educators; and (4) updated learning designs based on feedback. The PSTs used the ILUKS planner to plan lessons they were going to teach during practicum placement, and shared and received feedback on their designs from school mentors prior to teaching in class.

Data and Analysis

The data material consists of activity data from 19 different learning designs developed by the eight PSTs. These data include system logs that were extracted from the ILUKS planner and describe the PSTs' use of the ILUKS planner: how and when PSTs create and update their learning designs, and how they revise after feedback. After each revision, a snapshot of the document is saved, with additional information about who made the changes and when they were made. This way, the activity data provides a complete history of document changes for analytical purposes. Data were stored as an immutable graph with version history preservation and anonymised during log analysis. In addition, the learning designs were extracted (*pdf) to allow for a qualitative analysis of the content.

To explore which types of LA could provide meaningful insights into the PSTs' planning process, we conducted multiple analyses focusing on the planning process and their interaction with the tool. Our aim was not only to interpret the data but to assess which types of analyses generated the most valuable insights for teacher educators. First, we carried out descriptive statistics to present how PSTs, on average, compose a learning design. Second, we analysed log data generated from the use of the ILUKS planner, including timestamped records of actions, navigation, and feedback patterns, to understand how they, individually, engaged with the tool. Third, we carried out a qualitative content analysis of the learning designs. The object of this analysis was to cross-check and contextualise findings from the log data related to what kind of content (learning goals, activities, etc.) PSTs describe on different types of cards.

Ethical Considerations

When conducting LA research, ethics must be considered carefully. The growing possibility of collecting large amounts of data about learners leads to the possibilities of designing pedagogical interventions based on the analysis of data captured. At the same time, the amount of data leads to challenges for stakeholders related to data access, transparency, consent, security, data ownership, and interpretation of the data (NOU 2023:19 2023). This study is approved by the Norwegian Agency for Shared Services in Education and Research (SIKT) and follows the European Union's General Data Protection Regulation (GDPR). When the PSTs opened the digital learning design tool, a pop-up message appeared on the screen, asking for permission to collect activity data for research purposes. It was voluntary for the PSTs to accept this. All informants gave informed consent to participate in the research by signing a written consent form. They also confirmed the collection and use of activity data in the ILUKS tool. None of the participants withdrew from the study.

RESULTS

Findings from the analysis of activity data allowed us to reveal how PSTs go about planning a lesson and identify their individual planning patterns. We present findings on (1) how PSTs compose an average learning design, (2) the trajectory of PSTs' planning processes, (3) which cards PSTs do not use in their learning designs, and (4) which cards PSTs receive feedback on from teacher educators.

Composition of an Average Learning Design

The PSTs mainly used the ILUKS planner to plan for single or subsequent double lessons of about 45 or 90 minutes. The lessons were often stand-alone lessons in which PSTs did not know whether they would teach the next lesson in the same subject next week. Topics and guidelines for the lessons were provided by school mentors. When PSTs planned a lesson and assembled different cards into a learning design, the learning designs consisted of, on average, 12.5 different cards, as shown in Table 12.1. Most cards in a learning design are *activity cards*, in which PSTs describe the activities their students are expected to do while in class and the activities they as teachers will perform. After *activity cards*, the most frequent cards included in a learning design are *content cards*, followed by the *learning resources cards* describing the content students are going to learn and the different types of learning resources the PSTs will use during teaching. 8.5 of the 12.5 cards are created in these three columns.

Table 12.1 *Composition of an average learning design*

Type of cards	Number of cards
Learning goal	1.7
Student prerequisites	1.6
Content	2.4
Learning resources	2
Activities	4.1
Assessment	0.7
Total	12.5

Source: Authors.

When dragging and dropping cards into a learning design, PSTs can choose which cards to include for a particular lesson. This means that if they plan similar lessons on the same topic for different groups of students, they can choose the cards they need for one learning design and adapt the design by switching some of the cards, so that the design can be tailored to a different group of students. The average number of cards PSTs create for a learning design is 13.7, indicating that they mainly create the cards they plan to use in a particular lesson. There are variations in the number of revisions it takes to plan a lesson. Revisions are snapshots of the document after any action by the owner that results in a change in the document. This includes document creation, document name change, card creations, descriptions of content, change of card order in columns, moving cards between columns, and deleting cards. The lowest number of revisions is 21 and the highest number is 349 revisions, with the median being 87. Nine out of 19 learning designs have between 78 and 89 revisions before the learning design is assembled.

Pre-service Teachers' Planning Trajectory

The analysis of PSTs' planning trajectory reveals their individual planning patterns. It shows that the PSTs' planning process is dynamic, as they move back and forth between columns to develop cards. Figure 12.3 shows the individual planning pattern for all the 19 learning designs. While the ILUKS planner provides movable columns in the following order: (1) Learning goals; (2) Student prerequisites; (3) Content; (4) Learning resources; (5) Assessment; and (6) Activities, the PSTs do not necessarily plan their lessons in this order or use this sequence when composing their learning designs.

There are, however, commonalities between the PSTs' planning processes. In 13 out of 19 learning designs, PSTs started their planning by creating a *learning goal card* where they are asked to describe the learning goals and/or the skills students should achieve after the lesson. In four of the learning designs, the PSTs started their planning process by creating a *student prerequisites card*. In this card, the PSTs are asked to provide information on the year level, study programme, and other relevant prerequisites of the students they are going to teach.

As the PSTs continued their planning, the most frequently created second card was a *student prerequisites card* (eight designs), followed by a *content card* (four designs). The last card in their planning process was most often an *activity card* (eight designs), followed by a *content card* (five designs) describing the subject and academic content the students should acquire during the lesson. The analysis reveals that PSTs find it important to establish certain essential conditions of the lesson to be taught before planning and describing content and activities. However, the content analysis of the learning designs shows that PSTs tend to copy and paste competency goals directly from the curriculum, without adjusting them to the learning goals of their specific lesson. Additionally, the PSTs' descriptions of student prerequisites were often limited to short introductions like year level or duration of lesson, rather than more details about the students or class that could influence their teaching. This may be explained by the limited knowledge PSTs have about their students during practicum, and that they have not learned how to operationalise competency goals from the national curriculum in their own teaching.

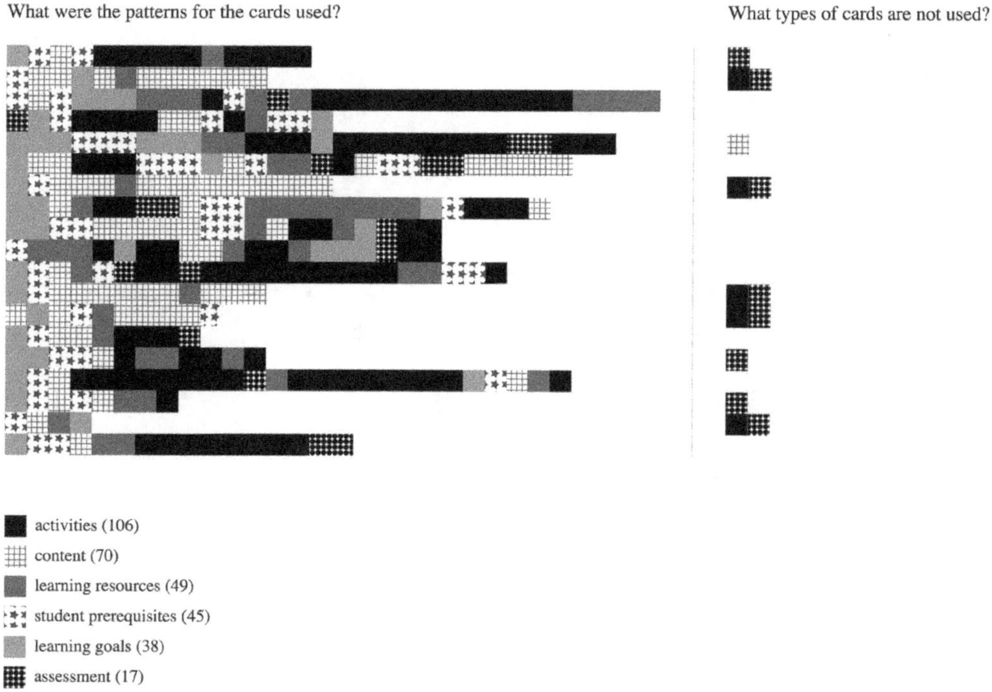

Source: Authors.

Figure 12.3 Pre-service teachers' planning patterns

Missing Cards

The possibility to include selected cards in a learning design allows PSTs to tailor the planning process to their individual preferences and pedagogical intentions. The activity data allow us to track which kind of cards the PSTs create, and which cards they decide not to include in their learning design. In 13 of the 19 learning designs, one or more types of cards are skipped and not included in the design. Figure 12.4 gives an overview of the types of cards that are missing in a particular learning design. In six of the learning designs, *activity cards* have not been included. However, the analysis of the PSTs' planning trajectory reveals that *activity cards* were created when planning, but for some reason, the PSTs decided not to include them in the learning design. Cross-checking with the content analysis reveals that the PSTs did describe activities but included the description in other types of cards, that is, *content cards*. This indicates that PSTs find it challenging to distinguish between the different didactical categories used in the tool.

Another interesting finding is that 11 of the 19 learning designs lack a card on assessment. The activity data show that some of the PSTs have created an *assessment card* during their planning process but not included it in the learning design. However, the content analysis reveals that the PSTs have not included any information in any card about how they would

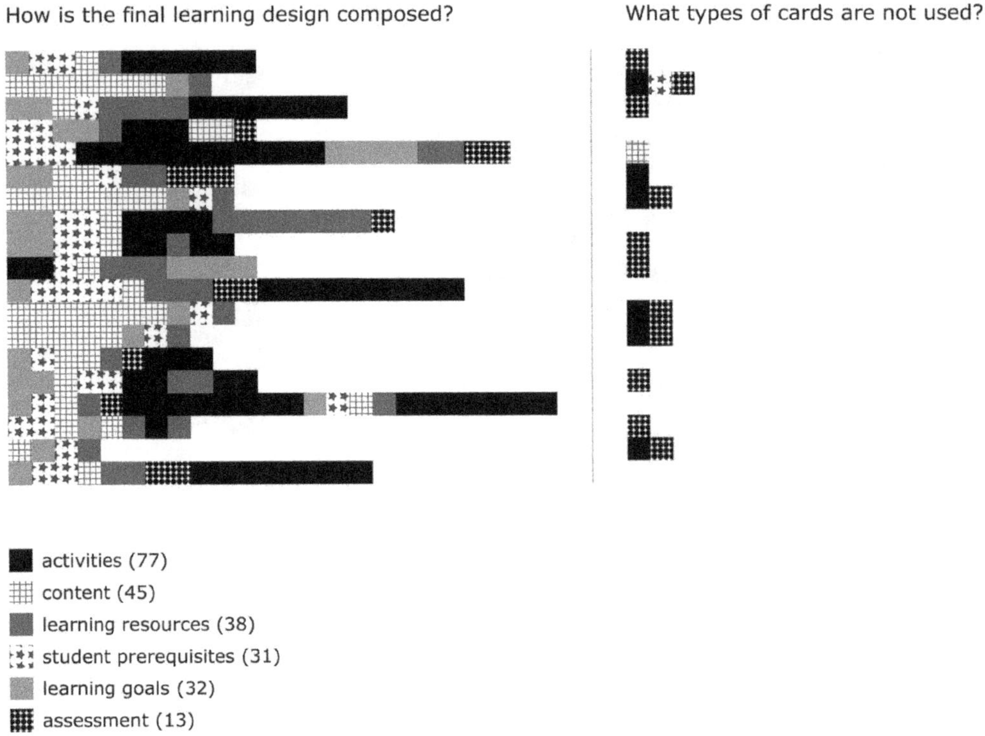

Source: Authors.

Figure 12.4 Composition of final learning design, including missing cards

work with assessment during their lesson. While 'plenary summarising in class' is listed as an activity on an *activity card*, students are not specific about how this could contribute to assessing students' learning outcomes. This indicates that the PSTs have little knowledge about assessment (assessment literacy) and how to integrate assessment (formative) into their own teaching.

Feedback on Learning Designs

In the ILUKS tool PSTs can share a learning design in which university supervisors and school mentors (or peers) can give feedback, either on individual cards, and/or as a general comment on the learning design. During practicum PSTs shared their learning design with school mentors prior to teaching in class. Table 12.2 shows an overview of how many comments (feedback) were provided on the different types of cards. Most feedback was provided on *activity cards* (51 comments) and *content cards* (27 comments). These cards are also most frequently used in their learning designs (77 *activity cards*, 45 *content cards*).

We then analysed the activity data in terms of what the PSTs updated in their learning designs after feedback was provided by university supervisors or school mentors. Figure 12.5

Table 12.2 *Feedback in learning designs*

What type of cards received feedback	Total number of comments related to specific cards
Learning design	15
Activities	51
Content	27
Learning resources	16
Student prerequisites	21
Learning goals	13
Assessment	9

Source: Authors.

illustrates the six different types of cards in addition to the learning design document in which feedback could be provided. The arrows show the direction to which cards were updated next after receiving feedback. The numbers on the arrows show how many updates were conducted after each comment for all designs. We could not identify a consistent pattern between which item in the learning design the feedback was provided, and where the PSTs did their (next) revision. In fact, very few of the PSTs revised cards after feedback. Changes were made in 51 corresponding cards out of a total of 160 comments. To illustrate, there are 9 comments on *assessment cards*, but none of the PSTs later revised *assessment cards*. Instead, they made changes on *learning goal cards*, *activity cards*, *student prerequisite cards*, and to the learning design document.

The qualitative content analysis of *assessment cards* and related feedback revealed two issues. First, that the PSTs tended to describe assessment in short sentences, for example 'walk around and see how the students are doing when working on tasks' and 'look at the students while they work and see if they have questions'. Second, the feedback from supervisors on *assessment cards* tended to have a reflective form, often posed as a question where the PSTs were encouraged to reflect on how their teaching and assessment practices could be related to students' learning, rather than actual suggestions of how to integrate assessment into their lessons. The content analysis provides important contextualisation that could explain why the PSTs have not updated their *assessment cards* and chose to do other revisions instead. Hence, it is impossible with the available activity data to establish whether revisions responded to the feedback provided.

DISCUSSION: CHALLENGES AND POSSIBILITIES OF USING LEARNING ANALYTICS IN TEACHER EDUCATION

This chapter presents an empirical example of how LA can provide insights into PSTs' lesson planning process. Among the advantages of LA is the possibility to handle large data sets. However, smaller data sets allow for the identification of patterns that can reveal students' individual challenges. Our study presents activity data from 19 learning designs (N=19),

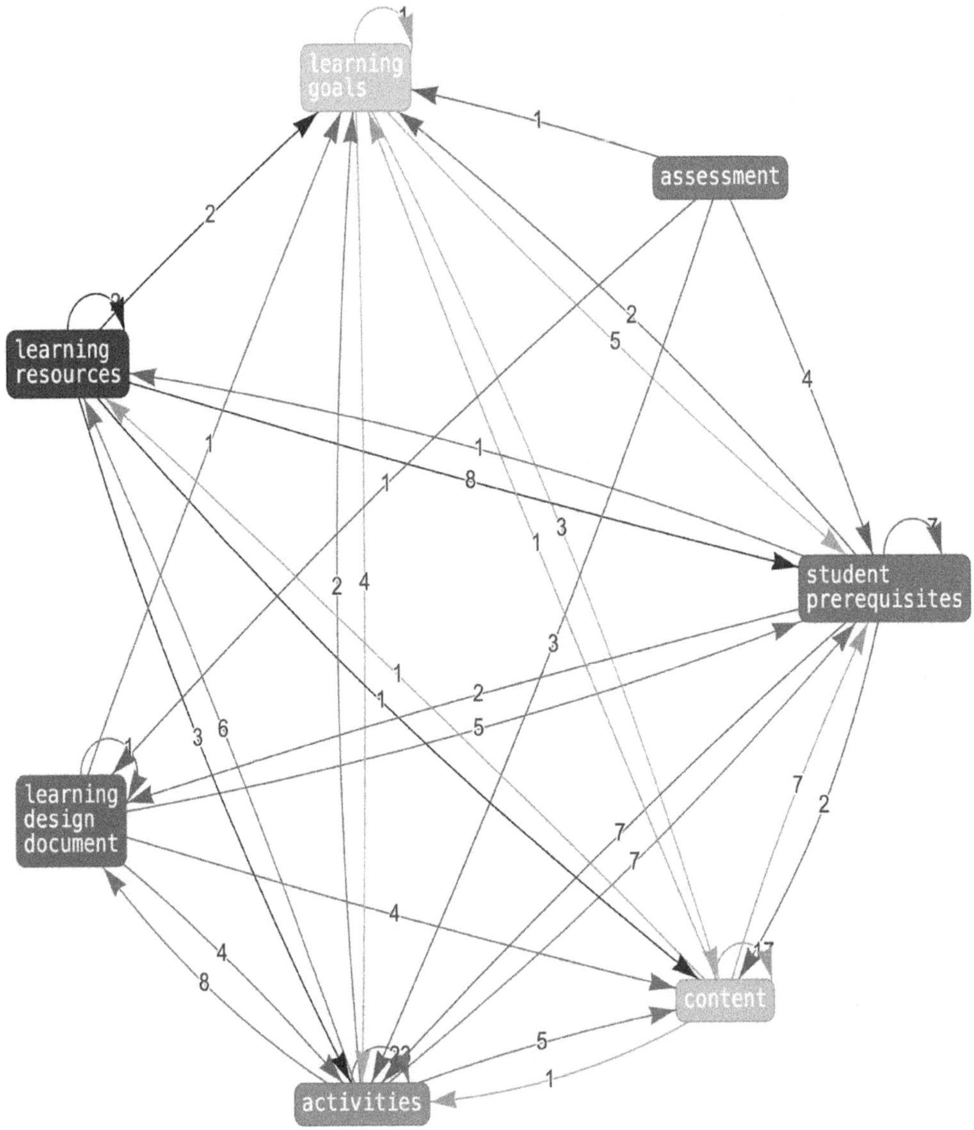

Source: Authors.

Figure 12.5 *Update of learning design after feedback*

intended to provide teacher educators with relevant insights for teaching PSTs how to plan lessons and the challenges they face.

First, the activity data allows us to track the individual pre-service teacher's planning trajectory. By identifying where PSTs start their planning process, which types of cards they create in what order, and which cards they include in a typical learning design, teacher educators get information about students who could need a closer follow-up in their lesson planning. While the ILUKS planner was developed to counteract a linear approach to lesson planning (John 2006), we cannot be sure of how the tool impacted the PSTs' planning process. The results show that the PSTs have a dynamic planning pattern, indicating that the learning design tool facilitates such a process. Rather than 'forcing' students into a linear approach through standardised lesson planning formats, the ILUKS planner fulfils a need for providing PSTs with 'empirically grounded models of planning that are realistic and useful in future practice' (Karlström and Hamza 2021, p. 667). As the tool provides PSTs with the opportunity to receive feedback directly in the learning design tool during planning, it supports the concept of active collaboration with school mentors during the planning process itself, rather than serving as a reflection tool post-planning, as Nesje and Lejonberg (2022) showed in their last review that most mentoring tools do. This way, the tool facilitates theory–practice integration in lesson planning and serves as an example of how digital tools can be integrated into pedagogical practices, which Uerz et al. (2024) and Aagaard et al. (2025) reported to be challenging. We found that it is important for the PSTs to establish conditions for the lesson, to start their planning with learning goals or student prerequisites. However, the content analysis reveals that PSTs find it difficult to operationalise competency goals from the national curriculum as these are copied directly as learning goals. The PSTs also find it difficult to make pedagogical considerations related to student prerequisites as only short descriptions of the year, level, and/or study programme are provided, indicating limited insight into what student prerequisites entail, an important aspect to consider when planning lessons. This confirms findings, reported by Beckmann and Ehmke (2023), that it is difficult for PSTs to include situational and contextual factors when planning a lesson. In addition, school mentors need to systematically give feedback, orally or through the tool, to provide the specific information needed, and at the same time model feedback practices to broaden PSTs' assessment literacy, as Atjonen et al. (2022) pointed out.

Second, the analysis reveals what components are included in a typical learning design. This also gives us insight into what kind of components are lacking. The activity data allows us to identify 'missing cards' in designs, but more importantly, it allows for investigating whether a missing card was part of the planning activity or not. The activity data did not provide information about the specific content of cards. However, the qualitative content analysis revealed that in most designs, the PSTs had not included cards on assessment, nor had they created *assessment cards*. This could indicate that they did not plan any form of assessment (formative or summative) during their lectures while in practicum. However, the content analysis did reveal that some students had described formative assessment as an activity without explicating it as such. This may entail: (1) that PSTs lack assessment literacy and do not have enough knowledge about assessment and how, in particular, formative assessment can support students' learning; (2) that PSTs while in practicum may not see it as their task to plan or conduct assessment in the relatively short time frame they are teaching during practicum; and (3) that assessment is a topic that should receive greater attention in PSTs' training to make them more aware of how assessment can be integrated in teaching. Atjonen et al. (2024) and Xu and He (2019) found that exposing PSTs to authentic opportunities of assessment during practicum benefited their understanding of assessment.

Third, the activity data provides information about the feedback pattern. Where (on which type of cards) do PSTs receive feedback on in their learning designs and what do they revise after receiving feedback? Our analysis shows that feedback was provided most frequently on the *activity card*, indicating that this is at the core of lesson planning and a concern for school mentors, and that several students could benefit from a follow-up on planning activities in lessons. However, the challenges related to planning activities and what PSTs are struggling with cannot be disclosed without an analysis of the actual feedback they received on the different activities. While system logs do not provide information about what the actual feedback is, they give important information about trajectories and the course of action after feedback is provided; for instance, the fact that assessment is missing from most designs – nine comments were tied to the *assessment cards* in different designs, and none of the PSTs appeared to make revisions on *assessment cards*. This reveals that we need more knowledge about how PSTs understand and integrate assessment in lessons, and how teacher educators can support their development of assessment literacy (Atjonen et al. 2024; Xu and He 2019). However, in order to provide information that is accurate enough to act upon, it needs to be contextualised and combined with qualitative content analysis of the learning designs and the feedback provided. Our analysis could not establish whether PSTs were able to utilise feedback from teacher educators (theory and practice-based knowledge) when they worked on planning lessons.

Limitations and Recommendations for Future Research

This study is small scale, with a homogeneous group of participants and thus provides insight into a particular group of PSTs and their individual planning patterns. Findings are therefore not generalisable but offer an understanding of the possibilities of using LA to inform teacher educators' instructional decisions. Moreover, we cannot be certain whether the use of ILUKS influenced the PSTs' planning patterns, or whether subject didactics influenced their planning process. However, the study contributes important understandings about how PSTs plan a lesson and how activities, learning resources, and assessment are integrated into a learning design to reach a learning goal. More research is needed on how PSTs plan lessons and how they understand and develop assessment literacy and include it in learning designs.

CONCLUDING REMARKS

While there are firm beliefs about the potential of learning analytics and that it can provide important and necessary knowledge about students' learning processes that can inform teachers' teaching, activity data and system logs do not give us the complete picture of PSTs' lesson planning process. Still, it provides some interesting, new insights into PSTs' lesson planning. We believe that by combining different types of data and different types of analysis such as content analysis and LA, we could acquire an even better understanding of how PSTs learn to plan lessons and provide teacher educators with actionable knowledge for better support in training. The present tool provides information to researchers about the PSTs' lesson planning. A relevant feature for further research is the development of a dashboard for teacher educators visualising the planning work and learning design. Information on PSTs' lesson planning during teaching can support teacher educators directly with actionable knowledge on both their own instruction and PSTs' learning.

REFERENCES

Aagaard, T., S. Amdam, I. Nagel, K. Vika, J.K. Andreasen, C. Pedersen and F.M. Røkenes (2025), 'Teacher preparation for the digital age: Is it still an instrumental endeavor?', *Scandinavian Journal of Educational Research*, **69** (3), 651–65. https://doi.org/10.1080/00313831.2024.2330927

Amarasinghe, I., K. Michos, F. Crespi and D. Hernandez-Leo (2024), 'Learning analytics support to teachers' design and orchestrating tasks', *Journal of Computer Assisted Learning*, **40** (6), 2416–31. https://doi.org/10.1111/jcal.12711

Anderson, T. and J. Shattuck (2012), 'Design-Based Research: A decade of progress in Educational Research', *Educational Researcher*, **41** (1), 16–25. https://doi.org/10.3102/0013189X1142881

Atjonen, P., S. Pöntinen, S. Kontkanen and P. Ruotsalainen (2022), 'In enhancing preservice teachers' assessment literacy: Focus on knowledge base, conceptions of assessment, and teacher learning' [Original Research], *Frontiers in Education*, **7**, 891391. https://doi.org/10.3389/feduc.2022.891391

Atjonen, P., K. Sini, R. Päivi and S. Pöntinen (2024), 'Pre-service teachers as learners of formative assessment in teaching practice', *European Journal of Teacher Education*, **47** (2), 267–84. https://doi.org/10.1080/02619768.2024.2338840

Beckmann, T. and T. Ehmke (2023), 'Informal and formal lesson planning in school internships: Practices among pre-service teachers', *Teaching and Teacher Education*, **132**, 104249. https://doi.org/10.1016/j.tate.2023.104249

Bennett, S., S. Agostinho and L. Lockyer (2015), 'Technology tools to support learning design: Implications derived from an investigation of university teachers' design practices', *Computers and Education*, **81**, 211–20. https://doi.org/10.1016/j.compedu.2014.10.016

Bjørndal, B. and S. Lieberg (1978), *Nye veier i didaktikken? en innføring i didaktiske emner og begreper.* Oslo: Aschehoug.

Børte, K. and S. Lillejord (2024), 'Learning to teach: Aligning pedagogy and technology in a learning design tool', *Teaching and Teacher Education*, **148**, 104693. https://doi.org/10.1016/j.tate.2024.104693

Canrinus, E.T., O.K. Bergem, K. Klette and K. Hammerness (2017), 'Coherent teacher education programmes: Taking a student perspective', *Journal of Curriculum Studies*, **49** (3), 313–33. https://doi.org/10.1080/00220272.2015.1124145

Ferguson, R. (2012), 'Learning analytics: drivers, developments and challenges', *International Journal of Technology Enhanced Learning*, **4**, 304–17. https://doi.org/10.1504/IJTEL.2012.051816

Gabbi, E. (2022), 'About or with teachers? A systematic review of learning analytics interventions to support teacher professional development', *Qwerty – Open and Interdisciplinary Journal of Technology, Culture and Education,* **18** (2), 88–109. https://doi.org/10.30557/QW000053

Hammerness, K., K. Klette, I.S. Jenset and E.T. Canrinus (2020), 'Opportunities to study, practice, and rehearse teaching in teacher preparation: An international perspective', *Teachers College Record*, **122** (11), 1–46. https://doi.org/10.1177/016146812012201108

Hernandez-Leo, D., R. Martinez-Maldonado, A. Pardo, J.A. Muñoz-Cristóbal and M.J. Rodríguez-Triana (2019), 'Analytics for learning design: A layered framework and tools', *British Journal of Educational Technology*, **50** (1), 139–52. https://doi.org/10.1111/bjet.12645

Ifenthaler, D. and J.Y.-K. Yau (2020), 'Utilising learning analytics to support study success in higher education: A systematic review', *Educational Technology Research and Development*, **68** (4), 1961–90. https://doi.org/10.1007/s11423-020-09788-z

Ifenthaler, D. and J.Y.-K. Yau (2021), 'Supporting teaching staff through data analytics: A systematic review', *ASCILITE 2021 Conference Proceedings: Back to the Future*, pp. 37–41.

Jenset, I.S., K. Klette and K. Hammernes (2018), 'Grounding teacher education in practice around the world: An examination of teacher education coursework in teacher education programs in Finland, Norway, and the United States', *Journal of Teacher Education*, **69** (2), 184–97. https://doi.org/10.1177/0022487117728248

John, P.D. (2006), 'Lesson planning and the student teacher: re-thinking the dominant model', *Journal of Curriculum Studies*, **38** (4), 483–98. https://doi.org/10.1080/00220270500363620

Karlström, M. and K. Hamza (2021), 'How do we teach planning to pre-service teachers – a tentative model', *Journal of Science Teacher Education*, **32** (6), 664–85. https://doi.org/10.1080/1046560X.2021.1875163

Kluge, A. (2021), *Læring med digital teknologi. Teorier og utviklingstrekk*. Oslo: Cappelen Damm.

Krepf, M. and J. König (2023), 'Structuring the lesson: an empirical investigation of pre-service teacher decision-making during the planning of a demonstration lesson', *Journal of Education for Teaching*, **49** (5), 911–26. https://doi.org/10.1080/02607476.2022.2151877

LAK (2011), *What is Learning Analytics?* https://www.solaresearch.org/about/what-is-learning-analytics/

Lammert, C. and V.C. Godfrey (2025), 'How are elementary teachers prepared for lesson planning? A critical scoping review', *Cogent Education*, **12** (1), 2498867. https://doi.org/10.1080/2331186X.2025.2498867

Laurillard, D., E. Kennedy, P. Charlton, J. Wild and D. Dimakopoulos (2018), 'Using technology to develop teachers as designers of TEL: Evaluating the learning designer', *British Journal of Educational Technology*, **49** (6), 1044–58. https://doi.org/10.1111/bjet.12697

Lockyer, L., E. Heathcote and S. Dawson (2013), 'Informing pedagogical action: Aligning learning analytics with learning design', *American Behavioral Scientist*, **57** (10), 1439–59. https://doi.org/10.1177/0002764213479367

Mangaroska, K. and M. Giannakos (2019), 'Learning analytics for learning design: A systematic literature review of analytics-driven design to enhance learning', *IEEE Transactions on Learning Technologies*, **12** (4), 516–34. https://doi.org/10.1109/TLT.2018.2868673

Masterman, E. (2008), 'Activity theory and the design of pedagogic planning tools', in L. Lockyer, S. Bennett, S. Agostinho and B. Harper (eds), *Handbook of Research on Learning Design and Learning Objects: Issues, Applications, and Technologies*, Hershey, PA: Information Science Publishing, pp. 209–27.

Masterman, E. and M. Manton (2011), 'Teachers' perspectives on digital tools for pedagogic planning and design', *Technology, Pedagogy and Education*, **20** (2), 227–46. https://doi.org/10.1080/1475939X.2011.588414

Meld.St. 16 (2016–2017), *Kultur for kvalitet i høyere utdanning*. https://www.regjeringen.no/no/dokumenter/meld.-st.-16-20162017/id2536007/?ch=2

Mena, J., P. Hennissen and J. Loughran (2017), 'Developing pre-service teachers' professional knowledge of teaching: The influence of mentoring', *Teaching and Teacher Education*, **66**, 47–59. https://doi.org/10.1016/j.tate.2017.03.024

Ministry of Education and Research (2022), *Læringsanalyse – noen sentrale dilemmaer. Delrapport fra ekspertgruppen for digital læringsanalyse*. https://www.regjeringen.no/contentassets/e1d6eec14bf34762ba01230e81cdc191/no/pdfs/f-4476-b-rapport-digital-laeringsanalyse.pdf

Morrison-Love, D. and F. Patrick (2024), 'Supporting student teachers to integrate theory, research, and practice: Developing the Adaptive Subject Pedagogy Model', *Research in Science and Technological Education*, **42** (3), 595–617. https://doi.org/10.1080/02635143.2022.2116422

Mutton, T., H. Hagger and K. Burn (2011), 'Learning to plan, planning to learn: The developing expertise of beginning teachers', *Teachers and Teaching: Theory and Practice*, **17**, 399–416. https://doi.org/10.1080/13540602.2011.580516

Nesje, K. and E. Lejonberg (2022), 'Tools for the school-based mentoring of pre-service teachers: A scoping review', *Teaching and Teacher Education*, **111**, 103609. https://doi.org/https://doi.org/10.1016/j.tate.2021.103609

Nguyen, G. and M. Bower (2018), 'Novice teacher technology-enhanced learning design practices: The case of the silent pedagogy', *British Journal of Educational Technology*, **49** (6), 1027–43. https://doi.org/10.1111/bjet.12681

Nilsson, P. (2009), 'From lesson plan to new comprehension: exploring student teachers' pedagogical reasoning in learning about teaching', *European Journal of Teacher Education*, **32** (3), 239–58. https://doi.org/10.1080/02619760802553048

NOU 2023:19 (2023), *Læring, hvor ble det av deg i alt mylderet? Bruk av elev- og studentdata for å fremme læring*. https://laringsanalyse.no/nyheter/lenke-til-nou-202319-laering-hvor-ble-det-av-deg-i-alt-mylderet-bruk-av-elev-og-studentdata-for-a-fremme-laering/

Oliva Córdova, L., A. García-Cabot and H. Amado-Salvatierra (2021), 'Learning analytics to support teaching skills: A systematic literature review', *IEEE Access*, **9**, 58351–63. https://doi.org/10.1109/ACCESS.2021.3070294

Persico, D. and F. Pozzi (2015), 'Informing learning design with learning analytics to improve teacher inquiry', *British Journal of Educational Technology*, **46** (2), 230–48.

Şahin-Taşkın, Ç. (2017), 'Exploring pre-service teachers' perceptions of lesson planning in primary education', *Journal of Education and Practice*, **8**, 57–63.

Salas-Pilco, S.Z., K. Xiao and X. Hu (2022), 'Artificial intelligence and learning analytics in teacher education: A systematic review', *Education Sciences*, **12** (8), 569. https://www.mdpi.com/2227-7102/12/8/569

Samuelsen, J., W. Chen and B. Wasson (2019), 'Integrating multiple data sources for learning analytis - review of literature', *Research and Practice in Technology Enhanced Learning,* **14** (11), 1–20 https://doi.org/10.1186/s41039-019-0105-4

Schön, D.A. (1983), *The Reflective Practitioner: How Professionals Think in Action*. New York: Basic Books.

Shibani, A., S. Knight and S. Buckingham (2020), 'Educator perspectives on learning analytics in classroom practice', *The Internet and Higher Education*, **46**, 100730. https://doi.org/10.1016/j.iheduc.2020.100730

Uerz, D., M. van Zanten, K. de Korte, M. Volman and M. Kral (2024), 'Teaching teachers to teach with technology: Teacher educators' practices', *Teachers and Teaching*, **30** (4), 471–88. https://doi.org/10.1080/13540602.2024.2342862

van Leeuwen, A., M. van Wermeskerken, G. Erkens and N. Rummel (2017), 'Measuring teacher sense making strategies of learning analytics: a case study', *Learning: Research and Practice*, **3** (1), 42–58. https://doi.org/10.1080/23735082.2017.1284252

Wasson, B. and P.A. Kirschner (2020), 'Learning design: European approaches', *TechTrends*, **64** (6), 815–27. https://doi.org/10.1007/s11528-020-00498-0

Xu, Y. and L. He (2019), 'How pre-service teachers' conceptions of assessment change over practicum: Implications for teacher assessment literacy' [Original Research], *Frontiers in Education*, **4**, 145. https://doi.org/10.3389/feduc.2019.00145

Zaragoza, A., T. Seidel and R. Santagata (2023), 'Lesson analysis and plan template: scaffolding preservice teachers' application of professional knowledge to lesson planning', *Journal of Curriculum Studies*, **55** (2), 138–52. https://doi.org/10.1080/00220272.2023.2182650

Zaragoza, A., T. Seidel and J. Hiebert (2024), 'Exploring preservice teachers' abilities to connect professional knowledge with lesson planning and observation', *European Journal of Teacher Education*, **47** (1), 120–39. https://doi.org/10.1080/02619768.2021.1996558

13. Teaching Learning Analytics as formative assessment for pre-service teachers: report from a first trial

Cathrine Edelhard Tømte and Maria Wasmuth Grønvold

INTRODUCTION – LEARNING ANALYTICS IN TEACHER EDUCATION

In Norway, both students and teachers have access to their own digital devices for teaching and learning, known as 1:1 coverage (Bocconi et al. 2013; Munthe et al. 2022). The use of digital devices in schools generates various types of data, such as students' interactions with digital learning resources (Selwyn 2023). These data may be further adapted into Learning Analytics (LA) (Gašević et al. 2016). LA can guide teachers by measuring, collecting, analysing and reporting data about learners and their contexts. This data can be visualised in dashboards, providing teachers with information on students' progress, understanding of concepts, subjects and engagement (Kaliisa et al. 2023). The information provided from the dashboards may help teachers to further align their pedagogical support to students (Berková et al. 2024; Oliva-Córdova et al. 2021). Students, on the other hand, can receive feedback on their progress and learning outcomes from the software in use (Andriamiseza et al. 2023).

As teacher educators, we need to prepare future teachers to handle this school environment that is highly influenced by digital technologies, to be prepared for a shifting landscape of newer technologies, and to critically assess the possibilities and challenges that digital technologies may allow for when it comes to teaching and learning. This capacity is central to developing teachers' professional digital competence (PDC) (Pedersen et al. 2024). LA forms an opportunity for teachers to align their teaching with students' pedagogical needs. The present chapter aims to explore how teacher trainers can introduce possibilities and challenges that come with LA to their pre-service teachers. To further operationalise LA's pedagogical potential and constraints, we align it with formative assessment, here understood as to produce, interpret, respond to data (Stanja et al. 2023). To our knowledge, research is limited as regards the use of LA in teacher education, and even less is known about how to introduce pre-service teachers to concepts such as LA in general, or LA and formative assessments.

In this chapter, we therefore ask: *How do teacher trainers introduce LA as formative assessment to pre-service teachers?* The remaining part of the chapter includes a brief review of previous studies on formative assessment and LA, followed by a presentation of the research context, method and data. The latter comprises a presentation of the development of a lesson plan on LA and formative assessment, the first trial of it, and the pre-service teachers' responses to the assignment. Findings from the trial of the lesson plan and its assignment will inform an overall discussion on how teacher trainers can prepare pre-service teachers to adapt and adopt LA as part of being capable of meeting schools' needs for new and updated competencies and knowledge deriving from the introduction of new digital technologies and newer pedagogical developments.

PREVIOUS STUDIES

Teachers' Professional Digital Competence and LA

Teachers' professional digital competence (PDC) significantly impacts their use of digital technologies in teaching (Heine et al. 2023; Masoumi and Noroozi 2025). There are several conceptualisations of teachers' PDC (see, for example, Fernández-Batanero et al. 2022; Skantz-Åberg et al. 2022), and key areas include technical and pedagogical competencies (Skantz-Åberg et al. 2022). Professional training in PDC is crucial for teacher education programmes, which have emphasised PDC in general, but not directly addressed LA (Arstorp et al. 2024; Howard and Tondeur 2023; Pedersen et al. 2024).

Preparing pre-service teachers to integrate LA into their teaching may be crucial for the development of their PDC. In addition, pre-service teachers would also need training in data literacy and visualisation skills to effectively interpret and act on the feedback from dashboards, as part of their LA and PDC training (Berková et al. 2024; Broos et al. 2017; Rodda 2023). However, this integration needs to be further developed and aligned with PDC conceptualisations in use within the teacher education programmes. To our knowledge, research is still limited on these matters, but there are some studies that touch upon related issues that may be worth looking at. Here we will report on some of them. While the first two studies (Krull and Leijen 2015; Oliva-Córdova et al. 2021) address university teachers' need to familiarise themselves with LA, the third takes a closer look at LA and teacher education (Salas-Pilco et al. 2022).

Krull and Leijen (2015) analysed the possibilities for performance-based evaluation of pre-service teachers' teaching skills in their field practice by using LA. When analysing the literature, they looked for how applying LA in pre-service teacher education required reliable performance-based indicators to model teaching competencies. They found no formal procedures for defining these indicators, relying instead on expert ratings of teaching quality. Existing assessment matrices for teaching competence were context-sensitive and needed adaptation across countries. To avoid overcomplicating the evaluation process, the study recommended focusing on essential teaching competencies through core practices (Krull and Leijen 2015). Nonetheless, Krull and Leijen do not look to competence frameworks that highlight teachers' PDC, where there might be some indicators that may align with teaching competencies as regards LA, for example, data literacy. In a systematic review on LA and its link to the teaching skills carried out in university practice, Oliva-Córdova and colleagues organised their findings into three dimensions: the purposes of LA; teaching competencies; and teaching practices in higher education (Oliva-Córdova et al. 2021). The first dimension revealed that LA had been applied for various purposes in higher education (HE), spanning from monitoring and analysis, evaluation and feedback, adaptation, personalisation, recommendations and reflection. The second dimension, on teacher competences on LA in HE, Oliva-Córdova and colleagues underscore that while technology is continuously evolving, many tools can be used in educational work, and teachers need to stay tuned to provide students with the best teaching and learning experience. The authors also suggest that teachers'

PDC include appropriate knowledge and use the tools provided by technology for their professional practice (Oliva-Córdova et al. 2021). Another suggestion was to further study the role of teachers in HE as designers of innovative technology-enhanced learning activities for deep student learning, including the capabilities and benefits that LA can provide for teaching. They conclude by suggesting that there is a need for educational institutions to provide teachers with ongoing training and the means to receive continuing education in the use of digital technologies in general and the possibilities and constraints that come with LA for teaching and learning (Oliva-Córdova et al. 2021). Taking a closer look at LA in teacher education, Salas-Pilco and colleagues conducted a systematic review including 30 studies addressing Artificial Intelligence (AI) and LA in teacher education (Salas-Pilco et al. 2022). They reviewed, analysed and discussed how AI and LA were integrated into teacher education based on the studies' goals, participants, data sources and the tools used to enhance teaching and learning activities. They found that the studies under review focused on the behaviours, perceptions and digital competence of pre-service teachers and schoolteachers regarding the use of AI and LA in their teaching practices. Moreover, the data sources in use were behavioural data, discourse data and statistical data; and most studies used machine learning algorithms. Interestingly, fewer studies reviewed by Salas-Pilco and colleagues addressed ethical concerns (Salas-Pilco et al. 2022).

Formative Assessment and LA

In their study, Stanja and colleagues (2023) explored how LA could be integrated into formative assessment practices for students in higher education, further elaborating on how to understand students' conceptions using learning analytics (Stanja et al. 2023). Based on their review of existing assessment tools in biology and computer science education, they suggested that LA can improve the ability to stimulate students' conceptions. In addition, they highlighted the need for further development of techniques for unstructured text and multimodal data analysis to better support this process of developing students' concepts (Stanja et al. 2023). Zhang et al. (2023) reviewed 63 studies on the use of LA in formative assessment for learning. The analysis revealed a significant increase in LA in formative assessment research over the past decade, covering various disciplines, methods and learning environments. While their review may inform LA implementation in higher education, it also emphasises the need for further research (Zhang et al. 2023). Taking another perspective on LA and formative assessment, Andriamiseza and colleagues (2023) found that formative assessment helped teachers to adapt their behaviour based on feedback. They explored software allowing for LA in a HE context and found that the tools in use allowed for the improvement of teaching quality by analysing substantial amounts of data. Sequences in the tool involved students answering a question, voting with a confidence level and rationale, peer grading and re-answering the question. Results showed benefits when around 50 per cent of first votes are correct and when peers reward rationales linked to correct answers. Confidence levels and the number of peer evaluations did not significantly affect outcomes, and self-grading was inaccurate. These findings lead to recommendations for improving formative assessment practices (Andriamiseza et al. 2023). Berková and colleagues (2024) introduced a visual dashboard with block diagrams and use cases for application development in assessment. They interviewed eight university teachers who reported the usefulness of a simple, user-friendly dashboard, the semaphore method for score scaling and features like colour coding and comparison of teacher evaluations with student self-assessments (Berková et al. 2024).

To sum up, the studies referred to here all emphasise the importance of LA in enhancing teaching practices and evaluating teaching competencies. Each study addressed the need for teachers to develop digital competence, although to varying extents. Formative assessments were most likely explored through evaluation, feedback and the analysis of teaching practices. Furthermore, Krull and Leijen (2015) focus specifically on pre-service teachers' field practice, while Oliva-Córdova et al. (2021) and Salas-Pilco et al. (2022) have a broader scope, including higher education and AI applications.

Oliva-Córdova et al. (2021) and Andriamiseza et al. (2023) explicitly addressed PDC, whereas Krull and Leijen (2015) and Salas-Pilco et al. (2022) do so more implicitly. The primary research gap identified across these studies is the lack of formal procedures for defining reliable performance-based indicators for LA in education. Additionally, there is a need for more explicit integration of PDC frameworks that highlight essential competencies such as data literacy. Ethical considerations related to the use of AI and LA in teaching practices also require further exploration. Salas-Pilco et al. (2022) note the lack of focus on ethical concerns in the studies reviewed, which was not directly addressed in the other studies. Based on these findings, the present chapter aims to further elaborate on how LA may be included in PDC training for pre-service teachers as part of their teacher education programme.

Professional Digital Competence (PDC) in Teacher Training

Pre-service teachers' PDC is to be developed across several areas of knowledge and learning areas and includes both general digital competence as well as subject-specific PDC and professional knowledge and skills (Kelentrić et al. 2017; Pedersen et al. 2024). Moreover, teacher education programmes offer various digital learning activities on campus and in practice, so that pre-service teachers can develop their PDC and gain relevant experience in the educational use of digital technologies. Pre-service teachers are also to learn about how ethical and legal issues, such as copyright and privacy issues, are affected by digital technologies (Kelentrić et al. 2017; Gudmundsdottir et al. 2020). As noted, there are various conceptualisations of PDC across teacher education institutions. In Norway, one framework known as the Professional Digital Competence Framework (PDCF), introduced in 2017 by the government, has gained ground across teacher education institutions (Andreasen et al. 2022; Arstorp et al. 2024; Pedersen et al. 2024; Aagaard et al. 2025). The framework comprises seven PDC areas: (1) Subjects and basic skills; (2) School in society; (3) Ethics; (4) Pedagogy and subject didactics; (5) Leadership of learning processes; (6) Interaction and communication; and (7) Change and development. Under each area, seven to ten learning outcomes are listed (Kelentrić et al. 2017). Due to the advancements of digital technologies, including generative AI, the framework was renewed in 2024. The present version has kept the seven areas but further developed the learning outcomes. For example, in area 4 (Pedagogy and subject didactics), learning outcomes now include to 'plan, conduct, reflect on teaching and learning in digital environments; critically assess and utilize artificial intelligence, learning analytics, adaptive learning tools; use digital resources to promote each student's desire to learn, participation, motivation' (Kelentrić et al. 2024). The development of pre-service teachers' PDC, when aligned with the PDCF framework, is thus to address LA, with adaptive learning as key features. To our knowledge, in Norway, fewer teacher trainers have implemented teaching about LA and adaptive learning directly (Pedersen et al. 2024; Aagaard et al. 2025), which makes our trial serve as one of the first of its kind.

RESEARCH CONTEXT: AN ELECTIVE COURSE ON TEACHERS' PDC WITHIN A TEACHER EDUCATION PROGRAMME

The empirical grounding of this study is an elective course in PDC for pre-service teachers, including 30 ECTS, offered by a teacher education programme at a university in Norway. The course includes five mandatory assignments, one of which involves LA and formative assessment. Pre-service teachers were in their 6th semester when entering the course. The course had been offered about four times since 2019. In previous rounds, LA in its broadest sense had been introduced to students in more traditional manners, such as lectures and group work, but without aligning any mandatory assignment. In the course evaluations from previous years, students reported that they did not really see the potential that comes with LA, nor how they could benefit from LA in their own teaching. This formed the backdrop of the development of a new lesson plan and a new mandatory assignment where we wanted students to understand and communicate to peers the possibilities and constraints when adapting LA to formative assessment in schools. The lesson plan and the assignment on LA and formative assessment were thus included for the first time in spring 2024. Here we will report from this first trial.

DATA, METHOD AND ANALYTICAL APPROACH

The data include responses from 13 pre-service teachers to the lesson plan and mandatory assignment, as well as reflections and notes from the teachers responsible for developing and testing the lesson. The authors behind the chapter were the teachers in the course. Additionally, responses from a small open-ended survey (Neuert et al. 2021) conducted after the pre-service teachers completed the assignment serve as data for this chapter. The study was reported and approved by the governmental agency responsible for data protection services for research. The pre-service teachers' responses were originally written in Norwegian and have been translated into English by the authors. We asked students for permission to use the data from the course for future research after their course completion and final grading.

A reflexive thematic analysis (RTA) approach was employed for the analysis (Braun and Clarke 2021). RTA is theoretically flexible, enabling an interpretative approach to qualitative data analysis and facilitating the identification and examination of patterns or themes within a dataset (Braun and Clarke 2021). It also recognises the potential influence of researchers' own experiences, biases and perspectives and how these may shape the interpretative process (Byrne 2022). In this study, our design of the lesson plan and the assignment was informed by our roles as teachers. Furthermore, our analysis of the survey responses – capturing students' perceptions of the lesson plan and assignment – may have been influenced by this dual role as both educators and researchers. Byrne (2022) suggests that the researcher's role may be shaped by such contextual factors, including the nature of the dataset, the theoretical assumptions underpinning the analysis and the researcher's analytical skills and resources (Braun and Clarke 2021; Byrne 2022).

While the development of the lesson plan, assignment and the assessment are analysed in a reflexive manner, we took an inductive approach to analysing the responses from the qualitative data collected through the small post-assignment survey, which comprised four open-ended questions. The aim was to explore students' perceptions of a trial lesson and its associated assignment. Three overarching themes emerged from the responses: (1) Perceptions of Content and Format where the students reflected on the subject-specific content and the structure of the assignment; (2) Engagement with Academic Concepts, here the responses highlighted how students approached activating and communicating key academic concepts (learning analytics and formative assessment) to peers unfamiliar with the material; and (3) Group Dynamics and Peer Learning, here students discussed the challenges and opportunities related to group collaboration and their understanding of peer learning.

Findings from the survey and reflections related to the design and implementation of the lesson plan will be outlined in the next sections.

RESULTS – TEACHING ABOUT LEARNING ANALYTICS AND FORMATIVE ASSESSMENT

The development of the lesson plan was built on the social-cultural theory of learning and its assumptions that learning is enhanced through active participation in knowledge development and co-constructed in social settings (Säljö 2006). Taking this approach, we as teachers based the development of the lesson plan on the assumption that learning occurs through linguistic, social and cultural collaboration, particularly in problem-solving scenarios (Säljö 2006). Thus, we assumed that pre-service teachers' learning developed as an interplay between individual, social and cultural activities. With this as a point of departure, the final version of the lesson plan included two sessions and an assignment, one session followed by another with only a short break of 15 minutes. The lesson plan included a mix of teacher-led instruction, discussions and problem solving, followed by a mandatory group-based multimodal assignment. In the following, we will elaborate on the various elements comprising the lesson plan and the assignment.

Designing a Lesson Plan with an Assignment

The first section of the lesson plan was dedicated to introducing pre-service teachers to LA and connecting LA to formative assessment. As preparation, pre-service teachers were to familiarise themselves with the subject syllabus that targeted conceptualisations of data and what constitutes data literacy (Pangrazio and Selwyn 2019). Pre-service teachers were exposed to theoretical and practical approaches, including discussing their own perceptions. In the second hour, pre-service teachers were to familiarise themselves with the dashboards available in the software used by schools. Based on their trials of the software, they were to develop their own lesson plans on how to adapt their teaching with the support from LA. The idea behind this was to have students take an overall perspective on their own teaching and to reflect on how they could integrate LA and formative assessments. Their draft version of lesson plans was presented to all in class and reviewed by peers and teachers, allowing for a joint reflection.

The last part of the second section included an introduction to the mandatory group-based multimodal assignment. We, as teachers, outlined the idea behind the assignment as we want the pre-service teachers to be capable of explaining to peer pre-service teachers what LA is and how LA can be used as formative assessment in schools. Their explanations were to be delivered as a poster and a video-recorded talk show. In other words, two untraditional academic genres comprised the multimodal assignment. We described the poster as a genre where aggregated information about a topic is communicated via text in various fonts and colours, photos and illustrations (Wallengren Lynch 2018) and the talk show as a type of 'infotainment' (Savolainen 2022). In the assignment text, we also provided pre-service teachers with some more detailed information about the procedures. This text is extracted in Box 13.1.

BOX 13.1 PROCEDURAL INFORMATION

Create a poster in A3 size, where you address definitions of LA, and how LA may align with formative assessment. Formative assessment is also to be defined. The poster should include suggestions on how learning analytics can be used in formative assessment. Use relevant curriculum. The learning poster should be on one page. Use images, text, and QR codes.

Create a video where you reflect on the content of the poster. The reflections should be tied to relevant literature. The video should include the poster, your own recorded comments, and a reference list at the end of the film. The film is submitted as an MP4 in Canvas.

The intended audience for the poster and the video is your peers/future teacher colleagues.

In the following paragraphs, we will outline more of the rationale behind why we, as teachers, chose this multimodal approach.

Development of a Multimodal Assignment

Designing new assignments can be time-consuming, and it is important that the assessments serve as integral parts of the course and avoid functioning as mere 'add-ons' (Jacobs 2013, cited in Cartner and Hallas 2020, p. 134). This highlights the connection between meaningful, authentic tasks and assessments, learner engagement, interaction, collaboration and the construction of knowledge through peers and digital resources (Cartner and Hallas 2020, p. 142). Here, we designed the assignment to be applicable to pre-service teachers' future teaching roles, making them try out how to communicate new concepts in a multimodal manner (Ceallaigh and Connolly 2024). In the assignment, we also provided pre-service teachers with opportunities to create, experience and engage in peer assessment. As noted, based on the work from the lesson in which a key feature included making the pre-service teachers activate their learning in diverse ways, by discussing the content, interpreting it and further adopting and adapting it to their own teaching, we designed the mandatory assignment as a group-based multimodal delivery (Meijer et al. 2020).

Pre-service teachers were to familiarise themselves with LA as a phenomenon, to identify which school resources include LA, to reflect on how LA can be applied as formative assessment and to consider privacy and ethical dimensions. Furthermore, pre-service teachers were to discuss, share experiences and reflections from data collection, analysis and planning of adapted teaching and to communicate their understandings in the form of a learning poster and a talk show (Box 13.1).

We also wanted the pre-service teachers to further 'digest' this new topic by providing them with an assignment that further aligned with pre-service teachers' real world experience. We therefore designed it so that pre-service teachers were to present the topic to peer pre-service teachers outside this course, in a playful learning manner (Boysen et al. 2022). Furthermore, the assignment was to be delivered as a poster and the video-recorded talk show as group work (Rees et al. 2015). While there is always a risk of uneven performance among members in group works (Silseth and Gilje 2019), we as teachers decided that in this assignment all members of a group were to get a joint grade. The assignment was guided by the following questions: What is learning analytics? What are the pedagogical opportunities for teachers and pre-service teachers? What are the challenges? How can we use LA in formative assessment?

Pre-service teachers had two weeks to work on the assignment. During this period, teachers and pre-service teachers met twice to discuss their progress. First, teachers helped pre-service teachers understand the genres of 'poster' and 'talk show'. We then allocated time for pre-service teachers to present initial drafts of their posters and storyboards for the talk show. Peers and teachers provided feedback on these drafts, which pre-service teachers used to revise and finalise their work. The feedback covered their understanding of LA and formative assessments, the genres and the technical aspects of producing their final submissions.

Assessment Criteria as a Joint Effort between Teachers and Pre-service Teachers

As multimodal assignments were quite new to the pre-service teachers, we invited them to discuss the assessment criteria. In so doing, we as teachers presented an initial draft of assessment criteria, based on the overall guidelines on assessment procedures from the university and with some additional criteria that addressed the multimodal dimensions. There is a risk that pre-service teachers may use assessment criteria as a recipe (Bell et al. 2013, p. 774), which again may hinder them from understanding the overall rationale of learning behind the assignment (Ross et al. 2020, p. 301). Nonetheless, studies also suggest that professionally written assessment criteria can contribute to increasing transparency in the assessment process (Price 2005, p. 215) and help the pre-service teachers get started with the task and create good structure in their work (Ross et al. 2020, p. 295). With this in mind, pre-service teachers responded to the initial draft version as being 'too open', making it hard to understand what was expected from them to get a good grade. They argued that since this type of assignment was new to them, they were afraid of misunderstanding what we were 'looking for' when assessing their deliveries of assignments. Based on discussions, teachers and pre-service teachers thus agreed upon a set of criteria that framed the multimodality characteristics of the assignment in a slightly more detailed manner than its initial version. A key take-away from the discussions and joint development of assessment criteria was that pre-service teachers obtained a more substantial understanding of the assignment. The last version of the assessment criteria is listed in Table 13.1.

Table 13.1 Assessment rubric for multimodal assignment (poster and talk show) on LA and formative assessment

Criteria	Basic (E/D)	Satisfactory (C)	Good/Excellent (B/A)
Task requirements and use of sources	• Investigates the topic superficially, using limited resources. • Barely meets task requirements (length, visible poster, clear speech, etc.). • Citation is present but with errors.	• Investigates the topic and uses relevant sources. • Meets task requirements (length, poster size, clear speech, etc.). • Mostly accurate citation and reliable source evaluation.	• Thorough investigation using a wide range of relevant sources, demonstrating strong knowledge of literature. • Fully meets task requirements (length, poster size, clear speech, etc.). • Accurate citation from both literature and media.
Content and understanding of the topic	• Limited understanding of Learning Analytics and Formative Assessment. • Little reflection on practical application in schools.	• Sufficient understanding of Learning Analytics and Formative Assessment. • Shows some reflection on practical application in schools.	• Excellent understanding of Learning Analytics and Formative Assessment. • Reflects deeply on practical application in schools.
Poster design	• Unorganised layout, minimal relevant information, does not follow A3 format. • Layout, colours and media elements (videos, QR codes) add little value.	• Organised, contains relevant information, follows A3 format. • Layout, colours and media elements satisfactorily enhance the presentation.	• Well-organised, visually appealing, contains contemporary information, follows A3 format. • Layout, colours and media elements (videos, QR codes) significantly enhance the presentation.
Talk show presentation	• Lacks structure and clear communication. • Poor time management (less than 5 or more than 8 minutes). • Roles are assigned, but some pre-service teachers contribute minimally.	• Structured, content is satisfactorily communicated. • Time is mostly well utilised (5–8 minutes). • Roles are defined and all pre-service teachers contribute satisfactorily to the academic conversation.	• Well structured, content is clearly communicated. • Time is efficiently utilised (5–8 minutes). • Each student masters their role and all contribute excellently to the academic conversation.

Source: Authors.

Pre-service Students' Responses to the Trial (Lesson on LA and the Formative Assessment)

The stepwise approach as described above included practical testing along with diverse types of dialogue towards a new topic, namely, LA and how LA may connect with formative assessment. This approach made pre-service teachers learn about LA in general, and about LA and visual dashboards in formative assessments in particular. When assessing the pre-service teachers' deliverables from the four groups, one group was rewarded with an A, and the rest received two Bs and one C. We believe that showing the results from the assessment in this way demonstrates that pre-service teachers worked quite well with the assignment and did their best to get satisfactory results based on their achievements. Moreover, as we had a joint discussion about the grading procedure and had a shared understanding of the assessment criteria, pre-service teachers also accepted their results without any further discussion. By including pre-service students in the grading procedure, they may also have achieved a better understanding of the assignment itself.

As noted, through a small survey including four open-ended questions conducted after they had completed the assignment, we asked about their opinions on the trial lesson and the assignment. Three overall responses formed their feedback. The first related to their perception of the subject-specific content and the format of the assignment; the second on how to activate the academic content (LA and formative assessment) and manage to communicate the key features to peer students unfamiliar with the content (LA and formative assessment). Lastly, they addressed challenges and opportunities as regards how to proceed as a group and what constitutes peer learning. We will elaborate on their feedback in more detail in the next paragraphs.

Getting started – Perceptions of the assignment

The pre-service teachers reported that they first had problems in understanding the assessment criteria. They found the assignment to be too open, and they did not really understand how to get started, as noted by this student:

> Overall, things went well, but most of the challenges were due to unclear criteria at the beginning. It was a bit difficult to get started since the task was very open-ended. We had to get a solid overview of the topic before we could figure out what was relevant to include in the assignment. (Student 4)

It may also be that they simply needed some time to familiarise themselves even more with concepts of LA and formative assessment before they could proceed with the assignments, the poster and the talk show video: 'We addressed this by focusing on the academic aspects first and then looking for opportunities to incorporate creativity within that framework' (Student 2). Nevertheless, they considered it useful to be included in the development of the assessment criteria and argued that this helped them to further understand what was expected from them:

> The process helped answer some of the questions I had about the assignment, while at the same time it raised new ones. I believe that involving pre-service teachers in creating assessment criteria can be a useful approach for certain tasks, and it might help them understand how to approach the assignment. (Student 1)

Moreover, some pre-service teachers underscored that it helped them to understand how much time they should allocate and how to proceed with this type of assignment that involves various media.

Taking a student-active approach towards learning about LA and formative assessment

All pre-service teachers mentioned that they felt that the student-active approach, including group work, peer assessment and the multimodal assignment, helped them in their learning: 'I really enjoyed working in such a practical way. It was exciting to be creative and fun to have an outlet for that creativity' (Student 2). They also highlighted that this way of working helped to deepen their understanding of LA and formative assessment: 'I feel that what I learned the most about was learning analytics and the many advantages, disadvantages and challenges it brings' (Student 1). They also highlighted that the delivery format of their assignments, although hard to grasp initially, still served as an engaging way of learning: 'I learned what learning analytics is in a more engaging way and it was great to work together as a team throughout the process of creating an informative video' (Student 5).

Collaboration and peer learning

Pre-service teachers highlighted the value of working together in teams and sharing their work in progress with peers. They reported it as motivating to get feedback on their initial work in progress: 'It was nice to get feedback that our work looked good and suggestions for any potential changes' (Student 2). They also considered peer assessment to be useful for their further progress: 'It helps highlight things you might not have noticed yourself, and valuable feedback did contribute to improving the assignment. Overall, we worked well together and it seemed like everyone was equally motivated' (Student 4).

Findings suggest that student-active approaches, including group work and multimodal assignments, can effectively engage pre-service teachers with concepts such as LA and formative assessment. Collaborative work is crucial for developing a joint understanding of the concept. By adding a multimodal approach to their collaboration in a somewhat playful manner, we as teacher trainers modelled ways of teaching in schools and prepared them for future professional learning communities. The trial demonstrated that group assignments led to solid final products and helped pre-service teachers familiarise themselves with LA and its pedagogical potential.

DISCUSSION AND CONCLUSION

The study explored how LA may be integrated into teacher education to prepare pre-service teachers for their future work in schools. We asked: *How can teacher trainers introduce LA as formative assessment to pre-service teachers?* Student-active approaches and collaborative work can enhance the learning experience and help pre-service teachers understand and apply LA in formative assessment. Professional training in PDC and LA is essential for teachers and pre-service teachers to realise the pedagogical potential of LA (Pedersen et al. 2024). Oliva-Córdova and colleagues (2021) highlight in their paper that barriers, primarily related to teachers' data literacy skills, may hinder their participation in activities and research aimed at improving teaching practices, and they highlight the need for these competencies in schools. They argue that staff at school, including teachers and school leaders, need to expand their PDC to include ethics, LA technologies and data handling procedures (Oliva-Córdova et al. 2021). Moreover, data literacy is highlighted as central to the actual PDC. Further, they suggest equipping teachers with various resources to work and learn how to use LA in their pedagogical work and to teach and evaluate their pre-service teachers appropriately. While Oliva-Córdova and colleagues do not mention student-active approaches as a way of solving this, our study supports that such pedagogical approaches may have additional value in this context. While Oliva-Córdova and colleagues performed their study in schools, ours has been in a teacher education context. Nonetheless, we find their recommendations for schools also relevant to teacher education. As teacher trainers, we must prepare pre-service teachers for their work in schools, and their PDC forms a key element in this respect (Skantz-Åberg et al. 2022; Pedersen et al. 2024; Aagaard et al. 2025).

Based on the assumptions that learning is enhanced through active participation in knowledge development and co-constructed in social settings (Säljö 2006), we thus developed a lesson plan including a mandatory assignment to get pre-service teachers to learn about LA and formative assessment and their interrelationships.

Limitations, Implications and Future Research

The chapter thus reports from the first trial of the lesson and its assignment on LA and formative assessment, with only a limited number of participating pre-service teachers involved. Nonetheless, we believe that the results from our trial provide some indications that this somehow complex pedagogical approach, including group work, peer reviews and multimodal assignments, new to both the teachers and the students, may have some merits in getting the pre-service teachers involved in complex areas of knowledge, such as LA in general, and in the context of LA and formative assessment. Future studies may further develop this approach or supplement it with other innovative pedagogical approaches, with more systematic research designs.

The integration of Learning Analytics (LA) and formative assessment in teacher education has several important implications for pre-service teachers and their trainers. First, pre-service teachers need to develop strong data literacy skills to effectively interpret and utilise data from LA. This includes understanding how to collect, analyse and apply data to improve teaching practices and student outcomes. Second, by using LA, pre-service teachers can gain insights into their teaching effectiveness and areas for improvement. This helps them refine their teaching strategies and better meet the needs of their pre-service teachers. Third, LA allows pre-service teachers to tailor their instruction to individual student needs, promoting differentiated learning and ensuring that all pre-service teachers receive the support they need to succeed. Moreover, engaging with LA encourages pre-service teachers to reflect on their teaching practices and make data-driven decisions. This reflective practice is crucial for continuous professional growth.

That said, the integration of LA and formative assessment in teacher education may also have some implications for teacher trainers. For example, trainers need to incorporate LA and formative assessment into the teacher education curriculum. This includes providing training on data literacy, assessment strategies and the use of digital tools; to our knowledge, this is currently not the case, at least not at our university. Furthermore, professional development is essential for trainers to stay updated with the latest advancements in LA and formative assessment. This ensures they can effectively train pre-service teachers and support their growth.

In addition, trainers must address ethical concerns related to the use of LA, such as data privacy and the responsible use of AI. This is crucial for ensuring that pre-service teachers understand the ethical implications of their data practices. To our knowledge, little is known about how teaching about LA in general, and formative assessment is being played out in teacher education institutions. Future research may therefore find merit in further exploring these dimensions in teacher education, especially when it comes to issues related to privacy for the students. Moreover, we need more empirical evidence on the pedagogical potential and limitations when addressing LA in assessment practices, and on how we may address these quite complex topics in an engaging manner to in-service teachers.

REFERENCES

Aagaard, T., S.H. Amdam, I. Nagel, K.S. Vika, J.K. Andreasen, C. Pedersen and F.M. Røkenes (2025), 'Teacher preparation for the digital age: Is it still an instrumental endeavor?', *Scandinavian Journal of Educational Research*, **69** (3), 651–65. https://doi.org/10.1080/00313831.2024.2330927

Andreasen, J.K., C.E. Tømte, I. Bergan and V.B. Kovac (2022), 'Professional digital competence in initial teacher education: An examination of differences in two cohorts of pre-service teachers', *Nordic Journal of Digital Literacy*, **17** (1), 61–74. https://doi.org/10.18261/njdl.17.1.5

Andriamiseza, R., F. Silvestre, J.-F., Parmentier and J. Broisin (2023), 'How learning analytics can help orchestration of formative assessment? Data-driven recommendations for technology-enhanced learning', *IEEE Transactions on Learning Technologies*, **16** (5), 804–19. https://doi.org/10.1109/TLT.2023.3265528

Arstorp, A.T., A.D. Olofsson and J.O. Lindberg (2024), 'Professional digital competence in teacher education – where are we, where are we headed and how to get there?', *Teachers and Teaching*, **30** (4), 395–9. https://doi.org/10.1080/13540602.2024.2379845

Bell, A., R. Mladenovic and M. Price (2013), 'Students' perceptions of the usefulness of marking guides, grade descriptors and annotated exemplars', *Assessment and Evaluation in Higher Education*, **38** (7), 769–88. https://doi.org/10.1080/02602938.2012.714738

Berková, K., M. Chalupová, F. Smrčka, M. Musil and D. Frendlovská (2024), 'A design of the panel for the progress and formative self-assessment detection in the learning analytics', *Education and Information Technologies*, **29**, 16441–67. https://doi.org/10.1007/s10639-024-12496-3

Bocconi, S., P. Kampylis and Y. Punie (2013), 'Framing ICT-enabled innovation for learning: The case of one-to-one learning initiatives in Europe', *European Journal of Education*, **48** (1), 113–30. https://doi.org/10.1111/ejed.12021

Boysen, M.S.W., M.C. Sørensen, H. Jensen, J. Von Seelen and H.M. Skovbjerg, (2022), 'Playful learning designs in teacher education and early childhood teacher education: A scoping review', *Teaching and Teacher Education*, **120**, 103884.

Braun, V. and V. Clarke (2021), *Thematic analysis: A practical guide*. Sage Publications.

Broos, T., L. Peeters, K. Verbert, C. Van Soom, G. Langie and T. De Laet (2017), 'Dashboard for actionable feedback on learning skills: Scalability and usefulness', in P. Zaphiris and A. Ioannou (eds), *Learning and collaboration technologies. Technology in education. LCT 2017. Lecture Notes in Computer Science* (Vol. 10296). Springer, Cham, pp. 190–200. https://doi.org/10.1007/978-3-319-58515-4_18

Byrne, D. (2022), 'A worked example of Braun and Clarke's approach to reflexive thematic analysis', *Quality and Quantity*, **56** (3), 1391–1412.

Cartner, H. and J. Hallas (2020), Aligning assessment, technology, and multi-literacies. *E-learning and Digital Media*, **17** (2), 131–47. https://doi.org/10.1177/204275301989973

Ceallaigh, T.Ó. and C. Connolly (2024), 'Navigating transformative assessment and feedback in teacher education: Unveiling challenges and innovative practices', *European Journal of Teacher Education*, **47** (2), 197–203.

Fernández-Batanero, J.M., M. Montenegro-Rueda, J. Fernández-Cerero and I. García-Martínez (2022), 'Digital competences for teacher professional development: A systematic review', *European Journal of Teacher Education*, **45** (4), 513–31.

Gašević, D., S. Dawson, T. Rogers and D. Gašević (2016), 'Learning analytics should not promote one size fits all: The effects of instructional conditions in predicting academic success', *The Internet and Higher Education*, **28**, 68–84.

Gudmundsdottir, G.B., H.H. Gassó, J.C.C. Rubio and O.E. Hatlevik (2020), 'Student teachers' responsible use of ICT: Examining two samples in Spain and Norway', *Computers and Education*, **152**, 103877. https://doi.org/10.1016/j.compedu.2020.103877

Heine, S., M. Krepf and K. König (2023), 'Digital resources as an aspect of teacher professional digital competence: One term, different definitions – a systematic review', *Education and Information Technologies*, **28** (4), 3711–38. https://doi.org/10.1007/s10639-022-11321-z

Howard, S.K. and J. Tondeur (2023), 'Higher education teachers' digital competencies for a blended future', *Educational Technology Research and Development*, **71**, 1–6. https://doi.org/10.1007/s11423-023-10211-6

Kaliisa, R., I. Jivet and P. Prinsloo (2023), 'A checklist to guide the planning, designing, implementation and evaluation of learning analytics dashboards', *International Journal of Educational Technology in Higher Education*, **20** (1), 28.

Kelentrić, M., K. Helland and A.-T. Arstorp (2017), *Professional digital competence framework for teachers (PfDK).* https://www.udir.no/in-english/professional-digital-competence-framework-for-teachers/

Kelentrić, M., K. Helland and A.-T. Arstorp (2024), *Rammeverk for lærerens profesjonsfaglige digitale kompetanse.* Utdanningsdirektoratet. https://arstorp.dk/onewebmedia/Kelentric%20PfDK%20rammeverk%202024.pdf

Krull, E. and Ä Leijen (2015), 'Perspectives for defining student teacher performance-based teaching skills indicators to provide formative feedback through learning analytics', *Creative Education*, **6**, 914–26. https://doi.org/10.4236/ce.2015.610093

Masoumi, D. and O. Noroozi (2025), 'Developing early career teachers' professional digital competence: a systematic literature review', *European Journal of Teacher Education*, **48** (3), 644–66. https://doi.org/10.1080/02619768.2023.2229006

Meijer, H., R. Hoekstra, J. Brouwer and J.W. Strijbos (2020), 'Unfolding collaborative learning assessmentliteracy: A reflection on current assessment methods in higher education', *Assessment & Evaluation in Higher Education*, **45** (8), 1222–40.

Munthe, E., O. Erstad, M.B. Njå, S. Forsström, Ø. Gilje, S. Amdam … and S.B. Hagen (2022), 'Digitaliseringi grunnopplæring; kunnskap, trender og framtidig kunnskapsbehov', Kunnskapssenter for utdanning, Universitetet i Stavanger.

Neuert, C., K. Meitinger, D. Behr and M. Schonlau (2021), 'The use of open-ended questions in surveys', *Methods, Data, Analyses: A Journal for Quantitative Methods and Survey Methodology*, **15** (1), 3–6. https://nbnresolving.org/urn:nbn:de:0168-ssoar-73172-3

Oliva-Córdova, L.M., A. Garcia-Cabot and H.R. Amado-Salvatierra (2021), 'Learning analytics to support teaching skills: A systematic literature review', *IEEE Access*, **9**, 58351–63. https://doi.org/10.1109/ACCESS.2021.3070294

Pangrazio, L. and N. Selwy (2019), '"Personal data literacies": A critical literacies approach to enhancing understandings of personal digital data', *New Media and Society*, **21** (2), 419–37. https://doi.org/10.1177/1461444818799523

Pedersen, C., T. Aagaard, S. Daus, I. Nagel, S.H. Amdam, K.S. Vika … and J.K. Andreasen (2024), 'Profiling teacher educators' strategies for professional digital competence development', *Teachers and Teaching*, **30** (4), 417–36. https://doi.org/10.1080/13540602.2024.2336612

Price, M. (2005), 'Assessment standards: the role of communities of practice and the scholarship of assessment', *Assessment and Evaluation in Higher Education*, **30** (3) 215–30. https://doi.org/10.1080/02602930500063793

Rees, E.L., P.J. Quinn, B. Davies and V. Fotheringham (2015), 'How does peer teaching compare to faculty teaching? A systematic review and meta-analysis', *Medical Teacher*, **38** (8), 829–37. https://doi.org/10.3109/0142159X.2015.1112888

Rodda, A. (2023), 'Student-centered design and evaluation of a learning analytics dashboard', in R. Jallouli, M.A. Bach Tobji, M. Belkhir, A.M. Soares and B. Casais (eds), *Digital economy. Emerging technologies and business innovation. ICDEc 2023. Lecture Notes in Business Information Processing* (Vol. 485), Springer, Cham, pp. 67–80. https://doi.org/10.1007/978-3-031-42788-6_5

Ross, J., J.S. Curwood and A. Bell (2020), 'A multimodal assessment framework for higher education', *E-Learning and Digital Media*, **17** (4), 290–306. https://doi.org/10.1177/2042753020927201

Salas-Pilco, S.Z., K. Xiao and X. Hu (2022), 'Artificial intelligence and learning analytics in teacher education: A systematic review', *Education Sciences*, **12** (8), 569. https://doi.org/10.3390/educsci12080569

Savolainen, R. (2022), 'Infotainment as a hybrid of information and entertainment: A conceptual analysis', *Journal of Documentation*, **78** (4), 953–70. https://doi.org/10.1108/JD-08-2021-0169

Säljö, R. (2006), *Læring som kulturelle redskaper. Om læreprosesser og den kulturelle hukommelsen.* Cappelen Damm Akademisk.

Selwyn, N. (2023), '"There is a danger we get too robotic": An investigation of institutional data logics within secondary schools', *Educational Review*, **75** (3), 377–393. https://doi.org/10.1080/00131911.2021.1931039

Silseth, K. and Ø. Gilje (2019), 'Multimodal composition and assessment: a sociocultural perspective', *Assessment in Education: Principles, Policy and Practice*, **26** (1), 26–42. https://doi.org/10.1080/0969594X.2017.1297292

Skantz-Åberg, E., A. Lantz-Andersson, M. Lundin and P. Williams (2022), 'Teachers' professional digital competence: An overview of conceptualisations in the literature', *Cogent Education*, **9** (1), 2063224. https://doi.org/10.1080/2331186X.2022.2063224

Stanja, J., W. Gritz, J. Krugel, A. Hoppe and S. Dannemann (2023), 'Formative assessment strategies for students'–conceptions: The potential of learning analytics', *British Journal of Educational Technology*, **54** (1), 58–75. https://doi.org/10.1111/bjet.13288

Wallengren Lynch, M. (2018), 'Using conference poster presentations as a tool for student learning and development', *Innovations in Education and Teaching International*, **55** (6), 633–39. https://doi.org/10.1080/14703297.2017.1286999

Zhang, K., R. Yılmaz, A.B. Ustun and F.G.K. Yılmaz (2023), 'Learning analytics in formative assessment: A systematic literature review', *Journal of Measurement and Evaluation in Education and Psychology*, **14** (Special Issue), 359–81. https://doi.org/10.21031/epod.1272054

14. EssayCritic: enhancing student essays with locally trained AI feedback

Anders Mørch and Irina Engeness

INTRODUCTION

This chapter presents a study on EssayCritic, a locally trained artificial intelligence (AI)-based writing tool developed to support students in secondary education with formative feedback during the essay writing process. The primary purpose of this study is threefold: (1) to introduce the rationale and design of EssayCritic as a content-based feedback tool aligned with curriculum goals; (2) to investigate how students interact with EssayCritic in an authentic classroom setting; and (3) to examine how the feedback supports students' writing development, particularly through collaborative learning.

Unlike general-purpose AI tools, EssayCritic is designed to detect missing or underdeveloped themes in student essays on specific topics and stimulate discussion and revision. The chapter draws on empirical data from a design-based case study in a Norwegian upper secondary school, using both qualitative and quantitative methods to assess how the tool mediates student learning. The findings are situated within broader debates on the educational use of AI, addressing both the promises and limitations of deploying language models for formative assessment in writing tasks.

Educational institutions have been in turmoil since the introduction of ChatGPT at the end of November 2022, as knowledge acquisition, effective teaching and meaningful learning experiences are its foundational building blocks. We are in a time of AI-integrated tool exploration, during which the challenges and opportunities of using generative AI (GenAI) in classrooms and teacher education programmes are put to the test, rendering older educational tools and resources obsolete. AI has existed in education for a long time, and research has led to gradual improvements in adaptive technology for student learning. Recent innovations in deep learning and large language models (LLMs) have sparked significant advancements in the field, leading to a new generation of AI tools that can assist students in writing more quickly by generating text for them. However, completing an assignment in a shorter time is not necessarily better for learning (Mørch et al. 2023; Reiser 2002). If misused, AI tools will prevent the acquisition of important learning skills, such as writing, and replace them with mathematical methods and GenAI. These methods and tools conflict with the notion that knowledge is constructed through a rigorous process of human learning, which includes making mistakes and learning from them in an iterative and gradual effort, as emphasised in constructivist and sociocultural learning theories (Piaget 2000; Vygotsky 1978).

Interaction Metaphors: Human–AI Interaction

Creating comprehensive metaphors to describe human interactions with AI (i.e. interaction metaphors) is important to explain the technology to end users but challenging because of the nature of AI itself. Explaining how a generative AI tool functions must consider the underlying mechanisms rooted in the long evolution of the developments of artificial neural networks, which spans 80 years, during which several 'AI springs' and 'AI winters' have occurred. In brief, the underlying architecture is stimulated by the biology of the brain and includes the mathematical model of the neuron (McCulloch and Pitts 1943), backpropagation for training neural networks (Rumelhart et al. 1986), deep learning using models such as the Boltzmann machine and autoencoders to achieve unsupervised learning (Hinton and Salakhutdinov 2006). More recently, generative adversarial networks (GANs) (Goodfellow et al. 2014) and transformer models (Vaswani et al. 2017) have advanced natural language processing (NLP) tasks. The mathematical and computational complexity of AI makes it challenging to explain its workings without the use of technical jargon and concepts related to sub-symbolic cognitive processing (Smolensky 2012). To address this challenge, we adopted a technique from human-computer interaction (HCI): using understandable metaphors to approximate human-AI interactions.

Thus, we suggest incorporating interaction metaphors to make the AI technology more relatable and easier for users to comprehend (Kim and Maher 2020), such as how a driver's manual helps ordinary drivers understand how to operate a car by focusing on practical instructions instead of the technical details of the car's mechanics. Here are three proposed interaction metaphors that draw parallels to commonly used tools in popular media and policy discussions, aiming to capture interest or provide critique:

- *Calculator metaphor*: Just as a calculator assists with arithmetic operations while maintaining the necessity for mathematical understanding, AI tools such as ChatGPT function as 'textual calculators' (Lodge et al. 2023), automating the writing process through higher-level operations.
- *Steroids metaphor*: Like how steroids can enhance existing skills in sports, AI tools such as ChatGPT enhance users' current knowledge or capacities in a way that society at large disapproves of, as these are artificial skill enhancers (Elstad 2023). If there is no foundational skill to build upon, the tool's benefits are limited.
- *Power drill metaphor*: A power drill enables rapid drilling through wood and metal, making it invaluable for securing bolts and nails in solid materials. However, if misused, such as when used without supervision in a sloyd room in a school, it poses risks. Likewise, allowing students unrestricted access to ChatGPT in a writing class could lead them to bypass developing essential writing skills by simply using the tool to generate assignment responses. Proper guidance from instructors on how to engage with ChatGPT in a meaningful way is crucial to preventing this scenario.

These metaphors help illuminate both the potential benefits and risks associated with integrating AI tools, such as ChatGPT, into educational settings. These metaphors are revisited at the end of the chapter when we discuss the findings from the study.

In this chapter, we introduce EssayCritic, an AI tool that predates today's GenAI. It combines rule-based logic and machine learning techniques, such as decision tree learning and latent semantic analysis, using a training dataset significantly smaller than those employed in LLMs (Mørch et al. 2017). We advocate for viewing AI as a writer's assistant, and EssayCritic is designed to enhance creativity through contextual feedback rather than automate the writing process. From an educational perspective, it is crucial to provide students with essential learning opportunities. We achieve this by helping learners externalise and systematise their ideas collaboratively. Additionally, AI-based writing assistants can help students who struggle with writing or lack motivation to get started.

EssayCritic AI System

EssayCritic is an essay writing assistant that was developed in Hong Kong and Norway by the authors and their colleagues over a ten-year period (2004–2015) in a series of design-based research experiments of system building (three iterations of user interface design and machine learning algorithm tuning), empirical research and theory building (Cheung et al. 2007). The latest version (EssayCritic-3) is trained with a supervised machine learning technique, which means that the training data were annotated by humans – in our case, teachers and researchers – in a workshop (Engeness and Mørch 2016; Mørch et al. 2017). The training data included sample essays, the textbook utilised by the teachers, and other relevant texts compatible with the textbook, which researchers found on the internet. Our findings indicate that EssayCritic can stimulate students who struggle or lack motivation to complete writing tasks. This is at odds with the current informal observations with ChatGPT that indicate a widening gap between struggling and high-achieving students in terms of how they incorporate ChatGPT outputs into their own texts. The findings from EssayCritic can shed light on this discrepancy.

While generative AI systems like ChatGPT are general-purpose, EssayCritic is a specialised AI system. Instead of using an LLM for text interaction, EssayCritic employs a specialised language model (SLM) to provide automated feedback upon request on the specific essay topics aligned with the teacher's learning objectives. Compared with ChatGPT, its 'knowledge base' is small, limiting its language comprehension and generative capabilities. However, EssayCritic has significant advantages, such as reducing the carbon footprint associated with LLMs by enabling localised data training and processing, which we examine further in this chapter with an empirical example. Figures 14.1 and 14.2 illustrate the EssayCritic user interface.

Research Questions

In this chapter, we address the following research questions (RQs) that pertain to EssayCritic:

1. How do students interact with EssayCritic during their writing process?
2. How does EssayCritic support the development of students' writing skills?

The remainder of this chapter is organised as follows: First, we present a literature review that provides the rationale for the RQs. We then present our methods and research design, which combines quantitative and qualitative data collection and analysis. Next, we present and analyse the results of an educational design experiment. We discuss our findings by comparing them with those reported in the literature. Finally, we summarise our findings and provide practical recommendations, drawing on our interaction metaphors.

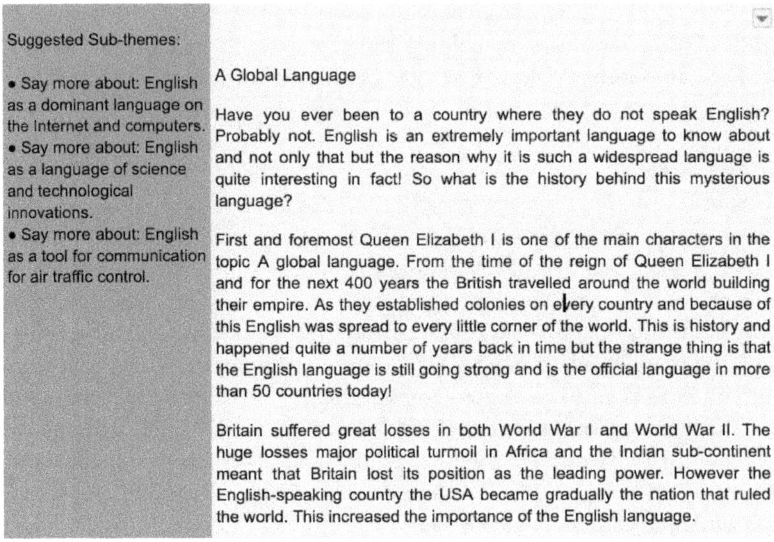

Source: Authors.

Figure 14.1 EssayCritic is trained on texts about English as a global language and this screen image shows its critique mode (suggested subthemes)

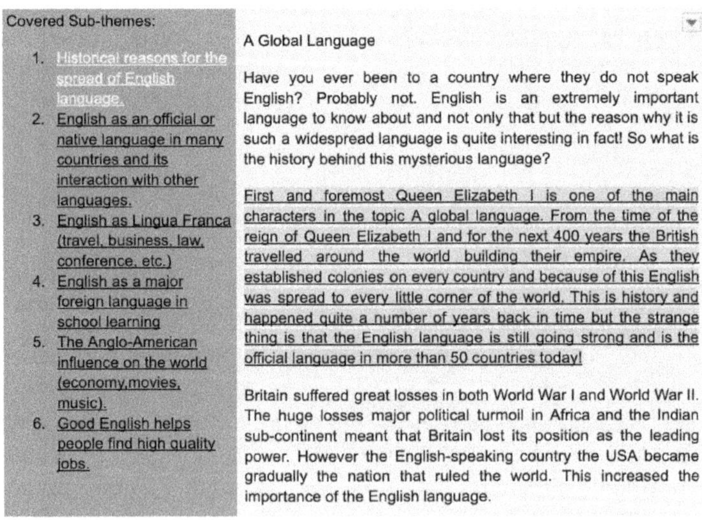

Source: Authors.

Figure 14.2 EssayCritic is trained on texts about English as a global language and this screen image shows its praise mode (covered subthemes)

LITERATURE REVIEW

Research and innovation in enhancing the writing skills of English as a foreign language (EFL) and English as a second language (ESL) learners have progressed significantly over the past 20 years. A wide range of automated writing evaluation (AWE) systems has emerged, which can broadly be divided into form-based feedback systems and content-based feedback systems. This distinction is crucial for understanding the pedagogical aims of each type of tool and for positioning the contribution of our work.

Form-based systems such as Project Essay Grader (PEG) consist of a set of features, or variables, that predict human ratings (Page 2003). Typical examples of such variables include sentence length, use of higher-level vocabulary and grammar. These systems aligned reasonably well with human scoring but offered little support for creativity or critical thinking (Dikli 2006). Later tools, including e-rater and Criterion, incorporated more advanced NLP algorithms to generate detailed feedback on surface features. This marked a shift from high-stakes testing to formative support in classrooms, but critiques remained that such tools primarily emphasised mechanical aspects of writing (Dikli 2006). Contemporary AWE tools such as Grammarly, Pigai and CriterLiuion continue this trajectory. These tools offer real-time feedback, focusing on grammar, vocabulary and organisational features, and have been shown to improve writing proficiency, particularly in ESL and EFL contexts (Ding and Zou 2024). For example, Grammarly is known for its usability and strength in error detection, while Criterion includes holistic scoring capabilities. Nonetheless, these systems – though useful – often fail to support deeper engagement with content or the development of thematic coherence and argumentation (Shadiev and Feng 2024).

By contrast, content-based feedback systems are designed to help learners improve the substance of their writing. For example, Intelligent Essay Assessor (IEA) was among the first to automate feedback by using NLP techniques like latent semantic analysis to compare student texts with pre-scored examples (Foltz et al. 1998). Contemporary tools and prototypes such as Wordcraft, which integrates a LaMDA-based large language model, demonstrate how AI can support idea generation, narrative development and stylistic variation (Yuan et al. 2022). However, Wordcraft and similar systems are typically optimised for creative writing and not directly embedded in classroom assessment practices.

This conceptual space is where EssayCritic makes its contribution. Developed prior to the emergence of LLMs, EssayCritic is a locally trained content-based feedback system designed specifically for educational contexts. Rather than functioning as a general-purpose writing assistant, it is aligned with assignment-specific learning objectives and offers formative feedback by identifying missing themes and concepts relevant to the curriculum (Engeness and Mørch 2016; Mørch et al. 2017). In this section, we present EssayCritic not to report findings – which are discussed in the results and discussion sections – but to highlight its design rationale and pedagogical novelty.

Technically, EssayCritic relies on a specialised language mode trained on essays, textbooks and related materials drawn from local schools. This approach ensures alignment with educational goals, enhances transparency, and supports equitable deployment. It also decreases reliance on energy-intensive infrastructure commonly associated with LLM-based tools, such as data centres, contributing to more sustainable AI research and development when servers operate on local machines (Schwartz et al. 2020; Schick and Schütze 2021).

While LLM-based systems such as ChatGPT (Barrot 2023) offer impressive capabilities for fluency and stylistic refinement in text production, they are not primarily designed for providing persistent, curriculum-aligned feedback. They also introduce risks such as 'template rigidity', vague responses, or ethical concerns related to privacy, accessibility and data misuse (Hopfenbeck et al. 2023; Brown et al. 2020). Moreover, their general-purpose nature means they often require significant teacher scaffolding to be pedagogically meaningful in specific classroom settings.

Furthermore, ethical issues related to data privacy, algorithmic biases and the potential misuse of AI-generated content challenge the implementation of GenAI tools in educational settings (Hopfenbeck et al. 2023). For example, it is easy for students to ask the system to generate texts instead of receiving tailored feedback to stimulate their own writing processes, which, in the past, required students to 'game the system' (Cheung et al. 2007). Moreover, the lack of teacher training on how to effectively integrate these tools into classroom practices remains a significant barrier to their integration (Asiri and Khadawardi 2024).

In summary, while AWE tools have made notable advancements, form-based tools tend to focus primarily on surface-level accuracy and content-based tools on short-term writing enhancements. By contrast, tools like EssayCritic highlight how locally trained AI systems can deliver more content-focused, formative feedback and foster collaborative learning within specific curricular contexts, spanning a broader educational context. The following sections will explore how such a system functions in practice, how theory has informed its intended use, and the unique educational value it can provide alongside traditional AWE tools.

METHODS

This chapter reports findings from the second phase of a broader design-based research project investigating the use of AI-generated formative feedback in secondary education. While the project involved three phases of data collection and system refinement, only Phase Two is presented in detail here, as it is the phase most relevant to our research questions about how students interact with EssayCritic and how the tool supports writing development. Phase Two focused on one target class (n=24 students) and one comparison class (n=24 students), both of whom worked on multiple drafts of an English essay assignment. The target class used EssayCritic and worked on multiple drafts for 4.5 hours, while the comparison class used peer feedback over the same period. These students were not participants in Phase One, which involved training the EssayCritic model, or Phase Three, which focused on post-intervention interviews.

Data collection of student work in target and control classes was conducted at an upper secondary school in Norway, which has emphasised the use of assessment for learning as a central approach to developing teaching practices (Black and Wiliam 2009). A total of 125 students, aged 16–17 years, from five classes were asked to write an essay during an English lesson on the topic 'English as a Global Language', following a rubric provided by the teachers. This task was based on previously studied materials and information from a chapter in the textbook *Passage* (Burgess and Sørhus 2009). The essay assignment was crafted in collaboration with five teachers and two researchers. The students were tasked with writing a 300- to 400-word essay on how English spread worldwide, highlighting the main reasons for its global adoption.

To provide context and rationale for choosing the second phase as the focus for our study, we briefly describe Phases One and Three. Phase One involved the collection and annotation of essays used to train EssayCritic, and 50 essays from three classes that were graded between 4 and 6 (on a scale of 0 to 6) were selected and coded using supervised machine learning. Phase Three consisted of interviews with students and teachers following the intervention. These interviews were aimed at gathering qualitative insights and feedback about the experience and effectiveness of the different methods used during the study. In addition to two teachers, an independent teacher graded the essays afterwards.

Furthermore, we used Vygotsky's (1978) sociocultural theory to inform our research, especially the idea of cultural tools that aid cognitive development. We applied this framework to explore how interacting with EssayCritic, profiled as a feedback tool aligned with the curriculum, encouraged peer dialogue, reflection and text revision. This approach informed both our video analysis and our understanding of student learning in the target class. We focused our analysis on how students used it collaboratively to create meaning and improve their writing.

Three groups of four students who volunteered were recorded on video, and an additional camera captured the teachers' movements. Two experienced teachers moved around the classroom to answer students' questions. The researchers did not intervene in the group activities. Nine hours of video data were recorded and transcribed. Field notes were also taken during class observations (Derry et al. 2010) to provide additional context for the video data.

To address our RQs, both qualitative and quantitative methods were used. The methods were combined using the embedded design approach (Creswell and Plano Clark, 2011). This mixed-methods design implies that one form of data was incorporated within a larger design framework. In our case, qualitative (process) data were the main data source, supported by quantitative (outcome) data. We focused our analyses on examining the target students' learning processes and outcomes.

Quantitative Methods

A paired *t* test was used to analyse the grade improvement and the improvement in the number of subthemes from the pretest to the post-test. Cohen's *d* (Cohen 1992; Field 2013) was calculated to evaluate the effect size of the improvements. We used an independent *t* test (Cohen et al. 2011; Field 2013) to calculate the statistical differences between the pretest and post-test results, and between the numbers of pretest and post-test subthemes in both classes.

The quantitative part of the study focused on two main measures: (1) the students' overall essay grades and (2) the number of relevant subthemes covered in their texts. Two experienced teachers, who did not teach the classes, assigned grades on a 1–6 scale using a shared rubric. This rubric evaluated argument quality, structure, content relevance and language use, in line with the assignment's learning objectives.

To further capture content development over time, we also analysed the number of subthemes present in each version of the essays. These subthemes were explicitly linked to the assignment rubric and the formative feedback suggestions provided by EssayCritic. This allowed us to track not only general improvement in writing quality but also the degree to which students incorporated targeted content into their final drafts.

The grading and subtheme analysis together formed the basis for comparing essay development between the initial version (v1) and the revised version (v3) submitted for grading in both the target class using EssayCritic and the control class using peer feedback.

Qualitative Methods

Video and audio recordings of group interactions were qualitatively analysed using interaction analysis techniques (Jordan and Henderson 1995), focusing on dialogue sequences and turns. Each interaction episode was preceded by a description of the classroom context to understand the learning conditions. Approximately 30 student interaction episodes were initially reviewed, shaping a narrative (Derry et al. 2010) that guided the final selection of extracts. In this study, the analysis of student learning adopted a Vygotskian perspective (Vygotsky 1978), highlighting the importance of social interactions, cultural tools and teacher interventions in cognitive development. Vygotsky posits that through dialogue with peers and instructors, students articulate thoughts, challenge ideas and build on each other's knowledge within their zones of proximal development, advancing towards learning goals set by teachers and the curriculum.

The qualitative analysis focused on how students collaboratively engaged with the content-based feedback provided by EssayCritic at distinct stages of the writing process. We structured our analysis around three key stages: (1) initial engagement with the tool; (2) interpretation and negotiation of feedback; and (3) integration of feedback into final drafts. This structure mirrors the pedagogical progression of the essay assignment and corresponds to observed patterns of student activity in the classroom.

From the initial set of 30 video-recorded episodes, three episodes were selected – each aligned with one stage of the writing process – for detailed analysis. These excerpts were chosen because they functioned as critical incidents (Derry et al. 2010): they reflect moments of cognitive shift, peer co-regulation, or strategic reorientation in response to feedback. For each excerpt, we provide a contextual description followed by line-by-line interactional data to show how students made sense of and acted upon the feedback. This allowed us to trace the process by which the content-specific suggestions from EssayCritic were socially interpreted and transformed into new writing actions.

In this study, EssayCritic was used as a cultural tool to mediate the students' learning. The automated feedback guided the students' revisions and deepened their understanding of the essay topic 'English as a Global Language'. The students learned not just from the automated feedback but also through interpreting and discussing this feedback with their classmates. As such, EssayCritic functioned as a bridge between the students' prior knowledge and the more advanced understanding they could achieve collaboratively, which is a hallmark of the Vygotskian theory (Vygotsky 1978).

ANALYSIS OF THE RESULTS

Quantitative Analysis

We compared the outcomes of the first and third versions of the students' essays, treating version 1 as a pretest and version 3 as a post-test. In total, 96 essays were graded by three teachers on a scale of 1 to 6, providing quantitative data for this study. The inter-rater reliability (Cohen's kappa) between the classroom teachers and the independent teacher in grading the student essays was calculated (see Table 14.1).

Table 14.1 *Cohen's kappa values for the inter-rater reliability between the classroom teachers and the independent teacher in grading pretest and post-test essays in the target class*

Class	Cohen's kappa, pretest	Cohen's kappa, post-tests
Target class	0.226	0.229

Source: Authors.

Table 14.2 *Average pretest and post-test grades in the target class and observed group*

-	Average pretest grade (essay v1)	Average post-test grade (essay v3)	Difference	Paired *t* test	Cohen's *d*
Target class	2.79; M = 2.79 SD = 0.88	4.79; M = 4.49 SD = 1.41	2	$t(24) = -7.62$ $p < 0.000$	2.26 large effect
Observed target group	2.75	4.5	1.75	-	-

Source: Authors.

On the basis of a scale ranging from 0.2 to 1.0 (Field 2013), Cohen's kappa results suggest a fair level of inter-rater reliability between the classroom teachers' and the independent teacher's evaluations. The pretest and post-test results are presented in Table 14.2.

The paired *t* test (Cohen et al. 2011) revealed a significant difference in the average grades between the pretest and post-test in the target class. In addition, Cohen's *d* values (Cohen 1992; Field 2013) exceeded 1.0, which is considered substantial according to Plonsky and Oswald (2014), and demonstrated a large effect size.

Qualitative Analysis

Beginning of the learning process: In Extract A from Table 14.3, the students are at the initial stage of the writing process. Four students are seated around a table with their laptops open. They have just uploaded their first drafts to EssayCritic and are in the process of receiving feedback from the system.

In Extract A, the students experienced difficulties in understanding how to receive feedback. The four girls (Molly, Christine, Sofie and Eline) are wondering if they should log on to EssayCritic, upload their essays, and receive feedback (lines 1–17). Eventually, Eline gets her feedback and starts presenting it to the group while the other students are still in the process of receiving their feedback from EssayCritic (lines 18–24).

In this extract, the students reveal their need to comprehend the operational aspects (usability) of EssayCritic to effectively leverage its feedback, as they are surprised by the comments they received. The initial challenges they faced underscore the importance of understanding the technology before fully engaging in academic tasks productively. Throughout their exchanges, the students demonstrated the value of peer support in mastering a new writing

Table 14.3 *Extract A – beginning of the learning process*

No.	Speaker	Response
1.	Molly:	Christine, have you logged on EssayCritic?
2.	Christine:	No, not yet
3.	Sofie:	I have logged on
4.	Molly:	Shall we click on the 'Assignment'?
5.	Christine:	Shall we upload our essays?
6.	Eline:	Yes
7.	Sofie:	Who is going to be number one?
8.	Molly:	I would like to be number three
9.	Sofie:	I would like to be number two
10.	Molly:	One of you should be number one *(pointing at Eline and Christine)*
11.	Sofie:	Eline, would you like to share your comments?
12.	Eline:	Where do I find them?
13.	Sofie:	They are there *(pointing at the screen).*
14.	Molly:	Who is going to start?
15.	Sofie:	I have written just about historical reasons
16.	Eline:	*(turning her PC to the group)*: I think these are the comments *(pointing at the screen)*
17.	Molly:	Yes, these are the comments
18.	Eline:	So, my comments are (*reads aloud adaptive feedback from EssayCritic*): Say more about English as a dominant language on the Internet. Say more about English as a language of Science and technological innovations. Say more about English as a language of communication for air traffic controllers.
19.	Molly:	How did you get these comments?
20.	Sofie:	You must scroll up and click on that one *(pointing at the screen)*
21.	Molly:	OK, wow!
22.	Sofie:	You have three suggestions, and I have six!
23.	Molly:	No, one, two, three, four… six too!
24.	Sofie:	OK, so, what are we going to do?

Source: Authors.

aid, which facilitates collaboration and encourages a collective approach to overcoming technological hurdles (for example, Sofie tells Molly how she finds her feedback in lines 20 and 21). Their experience highlights the significance of implementing user-friendly interfaces in educational technologies to ensure that the focus remains on the learning process rather than on technological tools, a key principle of human–computer interaction. These insights are of utmost relevance to today's more advanced LLM-based AI tools, emphasising the broader educational imperative to equip students not only with the content knowledge but also with the skills to navigate and leverage digital tools for academic success.

Middle of the learning process: The students have uploaded their drafts and received feedback from EssayCritic. They are in the process of presenting their feedback to the group and discussing it as we show in Extract B in Table 14.4.

The students in Extract B are engaged in presenting their feedback from EssayCritic and discover that all of them have received feedback to elaborate on the role of the internet in spreading the English language. Having discussed this feedback, they pointed out that it is also important to mention the role of science and air traffic communications in spreading the language. These topics were prompted by feedback on the suggested subthemes. Finally, Sofie summarises that the main goal of the essay is to elaborate on the use of the English language as it is used today in their lives and explain the reasons for its use (line 20). In doing so, the students demonstrated the development of their shared understanding based on personal perspectives in which they were engaged.

The students' discussion showcases a dynamic process of collaborative learning, where automated feedback plays a pivotal role in shaping their conceptual understanding. By actively engaging with the feedback from EssayCritic, they not only refined their ideas about the necessary subthemes, such as the role of the internet, science and air traffic communications in spreading the English language, but also deepened their comprehension of the assignment's objectives for them. This interaction highlights their ability to synthesise various personal inputs and collaboratively clarify the main goal of their essay, which was to articulate how English is utilised today and the underlying reasons for its widespread use. Through this dialogue, oscillating between personal and shared perspectives, the students exemplified their growing capacity to integrate feedback into a cohesive understanding of their task in the form of an essay, ultimately advancing their academic skills and collaborative problem-solving abilities.

Final stage of the learning process: The students have uploaded their second drafts and received feedback from EssayCritic. They are in the middle of their discussion of the feedback they received before working on their final drafts, which will be submitted to the teacher for grading. Their conversation is reproduced in Extract C in Table 14.5.

In Extract C, the students are actively discussing the feedback they received on their second drafts from EssayCritic, indicating a collaborative effort to refine their essays based on the feedback while improving their understanding and presentation of the topic. This dialogue not only addresses specific content changes (that is, the suggested subthemes obtained from EssayCritic in Extract B) but also significantly contributes to the students' understanding of how to develop a well-structured essay. The students focused on ensuring that their essays covered all suggested subthemes, exploring how to sequence the themes by organising them with an introduction and conclusion. For example, Sofie emphasised the importance of topic sentences in each paragraph. She outlined her essay's structure, which included an introduction, the historical spread of English through colonies and its contemporary significance with technology. This information was not provided by EssayCritic but by the teacher in an introduction to the assignment.

In summary, the students' discussion shows how feedback from EssayCritic deepened their understanding of creating essays that consist of a set of ideas from parts of a pre-defined topic area and defined in a curriculum. The dialogue illustrates the students' collaborative effort to grasp the topic and complete the assignment. This shared understanding is reflected in both their group interactions (different perspectives superimposed) and individually written essays (interpretations of shared understanding).

Table 14.4 *Extract B – middle of the learning process*

No.	Speaker	Response
1.	Molly:	*(to Eline)* Could you please zoom out? *(reading from Eline's screen)* Write about English as a dominant language on the Internet. I have the same comment!
2.	Sofie:	Me too! Why do we have the same comments?
3.	Molly:	I think it's because the Internet is a new thing
4.	Sofie:	I think it's important to write about it here because the Internet is such a big part of our life
5.	Molly:	We have focused only on writing about the historical reasons for the spread of English language
6.	Eline:	I haven't written about the Internet either
7.	Sofie:	My whole text is about the historical reasons!
8.	Eline:	I have mentioned three subthemes
9.	Molly:	We can start with the Internet because neither of us said anything about it
10.	Sofie:	I have mentioned the Internet only in two sentences in the whole text. I have written how it influences the world through spreading music and movies. It's only two lines at the very bottom of my text *(showing her screen to Eline)*
11.	Molly:	Eline has already covered many subthemes, good!
12.	Sofie:	Eline, if you could just go back to your subthemes. I think we should talk about the Internet and computers, because they are so essential today.
13.	Molly:	Yes, the new generations use the Internet. The older generations didn't use the Internet that much. So, that's one thing. And it says we have to say more about English as a language of Science. I think it's the same as computers and the Internet because…
14.	Sofie:	Eline, I think you should say something about Science and the Internet because they are so important today. And I don't know why they have air traffic controllers…
15.	Molly:	Air traffic controllers?
16.	Sofie:	Yeah, it's like airplanes and stuff.
17.	Molly:	Air traffic, we don't know anything about it at all.
18.	Sofie:	I think it's because we have international flights and when they are up in the air, you should speak English to them.
19.	Molly:	So, I will have to write a new paragraph about air traffic controllers.
20.	Sofie:	No, I think you should write about how you use English today, where we use it, and you offer some reasons for this use.
21.	Eline:	I think we can write about how Norwegian air traffic controllers talk to British airlines
22.	Sofie:	Yes and other airlines as well.
23.	Molly:	Yes, because it's International. We can write about how English is used today. It's used for air traffic, on the Internet…
24.	Sofie:	In Science and everywhere…
25.	Eline:	Yes, you are right.

Source: Authors.

DISCUSSION

We organised our empirical findings into three stages of the students' writing process: (1) understanding the technology; (2) collaborative meaning making through dialogue; and (3) refining the content and structure of their essays. These stages originated from a socioculturally informed interaction analysis and are closely aligned with our research questions.

First, the analyses of the group interactions revealed patterns of the students' learning prompted by the feedback from EssayCritic. At the start of the writing process, the students emphasised the need to understand the usability of EssayCritic to make sense of its feedback. Their initial struggles highlight the importance of mastering the technology before fully engaging with it in the process of meaning making. Peer support, as advocated by a Vygotskian (1978) perspective, plays a crucial role, as students collaboratively help each other navigate the tool, such as when Sofie assisted Molly (lines 20 and 21, Table 14.3). This experience underscores the value of user-friendly educational technologies that prioritise learning over technical features and highlights the broader need to equip students with competencies to understand how to use advanced digital tools for academic success. The first stage, understanding technology, primarily addresses RQ1 (How do students interact with EssayCritic during their writing process?). Students initially focused on navigating the system and interpreting its feedback. Their struggles with usability demonstrated how peer support was essential for enabling productive engagement with the tool.

In the middle of the writing process, the students engaged in domain-specific collaborative learning content using feedback from EssayCritic to refine their understanding of the assignment as a process of meaning making through dialogue. The feedback helped them identify key subthemes, such as the role of the internet, science and air traffic communications in spreading English, and clarified the essay's objective of explaining how and why English is widely used today. This interaction demonstrated the students' abilities to synthesise feedback, build on each other's suggestions, collaboratively define their goals and enhance their academic skills and problem-solving abilities within the scope of the assignment. The second stage, collaborative meaning making, responds to both RQ1 and RQ2. Students discussed EssayCritic's suggestions, elaborated on missing subthemes, and collectively developed their ideas. This illustrates how the feedback tool facilitated conceptual development through social interaction.

In the final stage, the students collaboratively analysed the feedback on their second drafts from EssayCritic, using it to refine their essays and enhance their understanding of both the content and essay organisation. They addressed specific content suggestions, such as subthemes, while combining this with information from the teacher, such as discussing strategies for organising the text by introductions, conclusions and arguments. Therefore, the automated feedback was a catalyst for improving their essay content, and the students followed up with additional information provided by the teacher to address the related topic of essay organisation. By addressing these aspects together, the students might improve their understanding of how to write a good text.

The third stage, refining content and structure, directly addresses RQ2 (How does EssayCritic support the development of students' writing skills?). Students used EssayCritic's content-based feedback – combined with teacher guidance – to reorganise their texts, integrate relevant subthemes and improve argumentative clarity. This stage reveals how the tool

Table 14.5 Extract C – final stage of the learning process

No.	Speaker	Response
1.	Sofie:	*(to Eline)* How many words do you have now?
2.	Eline:	I have 450 words.
3.	Sofie:	I have 560 words
4.	Christine:	469 words
5.	Sofie:	I have 100 words more than you…
6.	Molly:	441.
7.	Sofie:	I should work on the structure of my text. Shall we read our texts to each other so we can say something about the structure?
8.	Molly:	Yes, that would be helpful.
9.	Sofie:	It's good to have a topic sentence in each paragraph. So, the first one I have: Introduction, and then I have why and when English spread around the world. And then I have about the colonies, the colonies in America and Africa and what happened in Australia. Then I have about our society today with the technology and stuff and how English is used today…
10.	Molly:	What did you write in your conclusion?
11.	Sofie:	I have the following *(reading from the screen)*: Although English has been removed from the colonies around the world, its legacy is still there. In some colonies, several rival tribes in Africa were put together and this led to many conflicts as they didn't speak the same language. Then English speaking was compromised. In America the majority speaks English today, English is spoken in Canada, in Australia. Today you cannot go anywhere without hearing English.
12.	Molly:	I should adjust my structure. I start with how English is spread, for example in Australia from a few people to 19 million in a few years. Then I say about how it is important in communication and then I go back to the new generations and the old generations.
13.	Sofie:	I think you should mention old generations and new generations before communications, what is your communication part about?
14.	Molly:	It's about everything. English is very important for communication, everywhere you go in the world, you find people speaking English. For example, if you are in the plane and you want to ask the airhostess for something, you usually speak English. It's not only used for communication, but in social networks and on the Internet, but where do we learn English?
15.	Sofie:	How is your structure, Eline?
16.	Molly:	I believe I should start with history.
17.	Sofie:	Yes, why and how English spread around the world, first to Ireland, America, Africa and other colonies. The to Australia and New Zealand and how English affects us today.
18.	Molly:	I will write a paragraph about schools and…
19.	Sofie:	And modern technology and scientists and stuff like that.

No.	Speaker	Response
20.	Molly:	Then I can talk about movies. Yes, and the last thing will be about, it can be about technology and what?
21.	Sofie:	I don't know. Eline, how is your structure?
22.	Eline:	I have written about the history and where we use English today
23.	Sofie:	I think you have covered most of it. Which subthemes do you still need to cover? *(Sofie and Eline are looking at the screen)* OK, it's the Internet and air traffic. And I think in the part why we need it today, you can put it in there, like you need it because you can find English everywhere on the Internet and you must know English to get a job or something or to read websites and stuff like that.
24.	Eline:	I believe I have written about that…
25.	Sofie:	I think you should use other words for the program to think you have covered it. Because I have talked about air traffic control, and it still thinks I don't have it.
26.	Eline:	OK, I will do it.

Source: Authors.

supported higher-order writing development. In contrast to form-based AWE tools such as PEG or Grammarly, which primarily focus on grammar, sentence length and mechanics (Dikli 2006; Ding and Zou 2024), EssayCritic supports deeper learning goals by promoting content elaboration and peer engagement. Our findings suggest that integrating a content-specific tool like EssayCritic into classroom instruction can help shift the focus from writing outcomes to the writing process itself, thereby cultivating skills such as reflection, analysis and dialogue.

Students in the target class showed grade improvement from their first to their final draft, indicating the potential effectiveness of EssayCritic's content-directed feedback. This feedback, particularly during the middle stages of writing, fostered a shared understanding of the assignment and enhanced collaborative, analytical and problem-solving skills – an often overlooked aspect in educational technology studies. Such automated assistance may help shift the focus of essay composition from outcomes to the process itself, encouraging deeper engagement and reflection when students are encouraged to share their ideas and automated feedback with peers. Aligning with Vygotsky's perspective (1978), we emphasise the collaborative nature of learning. Students initially reflect on automated feedback, and then work with peers to interpret and integrate suggestions. EssayCritic's feedback promoted collaboration, encouraging the students to refine ideas and deepen their understanding. Feedback on subthemes such as the historical spread of English prompted the students to explore complex topics together, providing distinct advantages over grammar-focused feedback in enhancing collaborative learning. These findings align with Vygotsky's (1978) view of learning as socially mediated and scaffolded. EssayCritic served as a scaffold, helping students articulate and refine ideas in collaboration with their peers.

EssayCritic fills a gap in previous research by prioritising content-directed feedback in collaborative settings, thus fostering higher-order skills and conceptual understanding through AI-mediated dialogue, as identified by Barrot (2023). Barrot notes that GenAI can enhance coherence, organisation, and style, surpassing mere surface corrections. EssayCritic supports incremental, iterative learning, allowing students to revise and improve their essays over time in response to feedback and dialogue (human and automated), aligning with the characteristics of effective AWE tools that were indicated by Rahimi et al. (2024).

As highlighted in the students' initial struggles with using EssayCritic, mastering the tool's usability is a prerequisite for interpreting and applying its feedback successfully. Hopfenbeck et al. (2023) stress that inadequate teacher training in integrating automated feedback tools can limit their pedagogical impact. Therefore, fostering AI literacy among students and educators is essential in today's technology-rich learning environments, enabling students to engage critically with automated feedback. AI literacy refers to the ability to understand, interpret and use AI in a competent and critical manner. This implies that individuals have: (1) a fundamental understanding of how AI works; (2) a fundamental understanding of the applications and implications of AI; and (3) the ability to critically evaluate AI systems and their outputs. EssayCritic is a good tool for addressing these recommendations.

Finally, the metaphors presented earlier – calculator, steroids and power drill – remain relevant as interpretive tools to illustrate the educational potential and limitations of AI systems like EssayCritic. These metaphors reinforce the importance of guided use and critical engagement to ensure meaningful learning outcomes. These metaphors can help contextualise the recommendations for EssayCritic. We argue that the usability of a complex system such as an AI tool can best be understood through interaction metaphors of everyday tools. As an AI-based feedback tool, we propose that EssayCritic can be understood through the following calculator, steroids and power drill metaphors, highlighting its educational potential and limitations:

- *Calculator Metaphor*: Like a calculator streamlines arithmetic, EssayCritic automates technical aspects of writing, such as identifying subthemes as higher-level abstractions. It does not replace the understanding of writing fundamentals such as argumentation but allows students to focus on these as higher-level skills, acting as a 'textual calculator' that aids essay refinement through generating content suggestions, fostering engagement and reflection.
- *Steroids Metaphor*: Much like steroids enhance an athlete's skills, EssayCritic enhances students' writing by providing targeted feedback. However, it requires a foundational skill level to be effective. Students who lack writing skills, AI literacy, or prerequisite domain knowledge might find the feedback less impactful, as they may struggle to interpret, understand, or apply it.
- *Power Drill Metaphor*: EssayCritic, similar to a power drill, accelerates writing and revision when used properly. Without proper guidance, such as clear teacher instructions, it might lead to dependency on feedback and an inability to transfer the skills to other situations, potentially hindering the development of higher-order writing skills and causing more harm than the aid it provides.

In summary, these metaphors address the usability problems mentioned at the beginning regarding the use of the AI tool by shifting the issue to a different level of abstraction and bringing a relatable tool into focus for comparison. They collectively highlight the dual nature of EssayCritic, which enables student learning when integrated thoughtfully into instruction to enable meaningful engagement, collaboration and skill development. This is aligned with the sociocultural framework that informed the study.

CONCLUSIONS, LIMITATIONS AND FURTHER WORK

In conclusion, our findings underscore the potential of EssayCritic, powered by SLMs, as an effective writing assistant for use in classroom practices in EFL. By fostering collaborative problem-solving and analytical abilities that take advantage of AI-aided academic writing support, EssayCritic promotes students' collaborative problem solving, small group reflection and idea development. One significant advantage of SLMs is their reduced carbon footprint compared with those of large models (LLMs), making them environmentally sustainable.

However, our study has some limitations. It focused on a single high school and age level (10th grade) and had a small sample size, limiting the generalisability of its results. The assessment relied primarily on video-recorded observations and student grades, lacking qualitative insights into the students' subjective experiences or long-term outcomes. In addition, interactions between EssayCritic's feedback and other forms of feedback, such as teacher input, were not explored, leaving gaps in understanding the comprehensive role of feedback in the writing process, which is an aspect aligned with the Vygotskian framework we adopted and explored in previous works (Engeness and Mørch 2016; Mørch et al. 2017).

Future research should address these limitations by expanding the participant base to include diverse backgrounds, levels and disciplines in order to broaden the applicability of our findings. Longitudinal studies can evaluate EssayCritic's long-term impacts on writing development and skills transferability. Usability studies focusing on AI literacy and training for both students and teachers are crucial for optimising the utilisation of EssayCritic and similar tools. Finally, customising generic GenAI tools such as ChatGPT to function as a writing assistant, in effect simulating EssayCritic, through a local configuration can maintain the small carbon footprint of an SLM while simultaneously providing the flexibility and generalisability of an LLM. It is vital to strike a balance between generality and specialisation, considering the perspectives of all stakeholders to ensure optimal usage. By taking these steps, we can ensure the effective and responsible implementation of AI writing aids across diverse learning environments, fostering efficiency and critical engagement with new educational technologies.

REFERENCES

Asiri, A.S. and H.A. Khadawardi (2024), 'Teachers' perceptions of electronic corrective feedback and its impact on EFL learners' uptake', *Arab World English Journal*, Special Issue on CALL, (10), 204–18.

Barrot, J.S. (2023), 'Using ChatGPT for second language writing: Pitfalls and potentials', *Assessing Writing*, **57**, 100745.

Black, P. and D. Wiliam (2009), 'Developing the theory of formative assessment', *Educational Assessment, Evaluation and Accountability*, **21** (1), 5–31.

Brown, T.B., B. Mann, N. Ryder, M. Subbiah, J. Kaplan, P. Dhariwal … and D. Amodei (2020), 'Language models are few-shot learners', arXiv preprint arXiv:2005.14165.

Burgess, R. and T.B. Sørhus (2009), *Passage. English for general studies programme, first year.* Oslo: Cappelen Damm, pp. 60–115.

Cheung, W.K., A.I. Mørch, K.C. Wong, C. Lee, J. Liu and M.H. Lam (2007), 'Grounding collaborative learning in semantics-based critiquing', *International Journal of Distance Education Technologies*, **5** (2), 40–55.

Cohen, J. (1992), 'A power primer', *Psychological Bulletin*, **112** (1), 155–59.

Cohen, L., L. Manion and K. Morrison (2011), *Research methods in education.* London & New York: Routledge, pp. 535–704.
Creswell, J.W. and V.L. Plano Clark (2011), *Designing and conducting mixed methods research* (2nd ed.). Thousand Oaks, CA: Sage Publications, pp. 53–143.
Derry, S.J., R.D. Pea, B. Barron, R.A. Engle, F. Erickson, R. Goldman … and M.G. Sherin (2010), 'Conducting video research in the learning sciences: Guidance on selection, analysis, technology, and ethics', *The Journal of the Learning Sciences*, **19**, 3–53.
Dikli, S. (2006), 'An overview of automated scoring of essays', *The Journal of Technology, Learning, and Assessment*, **5** (1).
Ding, L. and D. Zou (2024), 'Automated writing evaluation systems: A systematic review of Grammarly, Pigai, and Criterion with a perspective on future directions in the age of generative artificial intelligence', *Education and Information Technologies*, **29** (11), 14151–203.
Elstad, E. (2023), *Teacher meets ChatGPT.* Universitetsforlaget.
Engeness, I. and A.I. Mørch (2016), 'Developing writing skills in English using content-specific computer-generated feedback with EssayCritic', *Nordic Journal of Digital Literacy*, **11** (2), 118–35.
Field, A. (2013), *Discovering statistics using IBM SPSS statistics.* Thousand Oaks, CA: Sage Publications, p. 79, pp. 368–88.
Foltz, P.W., W. Kintsch and T.K. Landauer (1998), 'The measurement of textual coherence with latent semantic analysis', *Discourse Processes*, **25** (2–3), 285–307.
Goodfellow, I., J. Pouget-Abadie, M. Mirza, B. Xu, D. Warde-Farley, S. Ozair, A. Courville and Y. Bengio (2014), 'Generative adversarial nets', *Advances in Neural Information Processing Systems*, **27**, 2672–80.
Hinton, G.E. and R.R. Salakhutdinov (2006), 'Reducing the dimensionality of data with neural networks', *Science*, **313** (5786), 504–7.
Hopfenbeck, T.N., Z. Zhang, S. Sun, P. Robertson and J.A. McGrane (2023), 'Challenges and opportunities for classroom-based formative assessment and AI: A perspective article', *Frontiers in Education*, **8**, 1270700.
Jordan, B. and A. Henderson (1995), 'Interaction analysis: Foundations and practice', *Journal of the Learning Sciences*, **4**, 39–103.
Kim, J. and M.L. Maher (2020), 'Conceptual metaphors for designing smart environments: Device, robot, and friend', *Frontiers in Psychology*, **11**, 198.
Liu, Y. (2023), 'A comparison of automated corrective feedback and traditional corrective feedback: A review study', *The Educational Review*, **7** (9), 1365–68.
Lodge, J.M., S. Yang, L. Furze and P. Dawson (2023), 'It's not like a calculator, so what is the relationship between learners and generative artificial intelligence?', *Learning: Research and Practice*, **9** (2), 117–24.
McCulloch, W.S. and W. Pitts (1943), 'A logical calculus of the ideas immanent in nervous activity', *The Bulletin of Mathematical Biophysics*, **5** (4), 115–33.
Mørch, A.I., I. Engeness, V.C. Cheng, W.K. Cheung and K.C. Wong (2017), 'EssayCritic: Writing to learn with a knowledge-based design critiquing system', *Educational Technology, and Society*, **20** (2), 216–26.
Mørch, A.I., E.E. Flø, K.T. Litherland and R. Andersen (2023), 'Makerspace activities in a school setting: Top-down and bottom-up approaches for teachers to leverage pupils' making in science education', *Learning, Culture and Social Interaction*, **39**, 100697.
Page, E.B. (2003), 'Project essay grade: PEG', in M. Shermis and J. Burstein (eds), *Automated essay scoring: A cross-disciplinary perspective.* New York: Routledge, pp. 43–54.
Piaget, J. (2000), *The psychology of the child.* New York: Basic Books, pp. 13–16.
Plonsky, L. and F.L. Oswald (2014), 'How big is "big"?, 'Interpreting effect sizes in L2 research', *Language Learning*, **64** (4), 878–912.
Rahimi, M., J. Fathi and D. Zou (2024), 'Exploring the impact of automated written corrective feedback on the academic writing skills of EFL learners: An activity theory perspective', *Education and Information Technologies*, **30** (3), 1–45.
Reiser, B.J. (2002), 'Why scaffolding should sometimes make tasks more difficult for learners', in G. Stahl (ed.), *Proceedings of the Conference on Computer Support for Collaborative Learning: Foundations for a CSCL Community*, International Society of the Learning Sciences, pp. 255–64.

Rumelhart, D.E., G.E. Hinton and R.J. Williams (1986), 'Learning representations by back-propagating errors', *Nature*, **323** (6088), 533–6.

Schick, T. and H. Schütze (2021), 'It's not just size that matters: Small language models are also few-shot learners', arXiv preprint arXiv:2102.11952.

Schwartz, R., J. Dodge, N.A. Smith and O. Etzioni (2020), 'Green AI', *Communications of the ACM*, **63** (12), 54–63. https://doi.org/10.1145/3381831

Shadiev, R. and Y. Feng (2024), 'Using automated corrective feedback tools in language learning: A review study', *Interactive Learning Environments*, **32** (6), 2538–66.

Smolensky, P. (2012), 'Subsymbolic computation theory for the human intuitive processor', in S.B. Cooper, A. Dawar and B. Löwe (eds), *How the world computes* (Vol. 7318). Berlin, Heidelberg: Springer, pp. 675–85.

Vaswani, A., N. Shazeer, N. Parmar, J. Uszkoreit, L. Jones, A.N. Gomez, Ł. Kaiser and I. Polosukhin (2017), 'Attention is all you need', *Advances in Neural Information Processing Systems*, **30**, 5998–6008.

Vygotsky, L.S. (1978), *Mind in society: The development of higher psychological processes.* Cambridge, MA: Harvard University Press.

Yuan, A., A. Coenen, E. Reif and D. Ippolito (2022), 'Wordcraft: Story writing with large language models',*Proceedings of the 27th International Conference on Intelligent User Interfaces (IUI '22)*, Association for Computing Machinery, pp. 841–52.

15. Adaptive learning in primary mathematics: teachers' practices and insights

Kjetil Egelandsdal

INTRODUCTION

In recent years, a growing number of adaptive learning systems (ALS) have become available in education. These are software applications that adjust instruction to the individual learner's pace and level, based on data gathered during task-solving. At the core of such systems are data-driven algorithms that tailor educational content and activities to learners' prior knowledge and skills. This personalisation is particularly relevant in mathematics education, where student progression often varies significantly. ALS are therefore often welcomed as tools for differentiation, especially in classrooms with wide variation in student ability.

While the technological potential of ALS has been well documented, particularly in higher education (Martin et al. 2020), far less attention has been paid to the experiences and practices of teachers, especially in primary schools (see Moltudal, Krumsvik and Høydal 2022 for such a study). As key agents in implementing educational technologies, teachers play a critical role in aligning these systems with curriculum goals and classroom realities.

This chapter presents findings from a study of Multi Smart Øving, an ALS developed for primary school mathematics by the Norwegian publisher Gyldendal. Based on an adaptive engine designed by the US company Knewton, Multi Smart Øving was launched in 2016 and, by 2019, had reached 188,000 pupils and 9,822 teachers – over 40 per cent of all primary school pupils in Norway. At the time of the study, it was the only adaptive learning system implemented at scale in Norwegian primary schools, making it a significant case for examining how teachers respond to and use adaptive technology in mathematics instruction.

Although ALS offer automated, individualised learning paths, their design often prioritises independent, self-paced student work and minimises external intervention – a logic rooted in efficiency and personalisation (Kabudi, Pappas and Olsen 2021). This stands in contrast to sociocultural theories of learning, which emphasise guidance, interaction, and social mediation. The present study is informed by a sociocultural perspective on learning (Vygotsky 1978), in which learning is understood as a mediated activity involving tools, signs, and collaboration with others. Central to this view is the concept of the zone of proximal development (ZPD), the space between what a learner can do independently and what they can achieve with guidance. Scaffolding within this space is considered vital for effective learning (Wood, Bruner and Ross 1976). The tension between the independent logic of ALS and sociocultural models of instruction forms a key analytical lens in this chapter.

In addition, the study draws on perspectives that frame teaching as a design activity (Laurillard 2012). Teachers do not simply implement pre-built technologies – they actively shape learning environments by deciding how tools, tasks, and interactions are used in the classroom. From this perspective, teachers are not just passive users of technology, but professionals who make informed pedagogical decisions that guide students' learning. This role becomes particularly significant when working with ALS, whose algorithmically determined pathways may or may not align with teachers' instructional goals or students' actual learning needs.

Despite the growing adoption of ALS, few empirical studies have examined how teachers interact with these systems in everyday classroom practice: how they interpret system-generated data, intervene in automated tasks, and assess the pedagogical fit of the technology. Teachers play a pivotal role as mediators between students and technology, shaping the classroom integration of adaptive tools and influencing their impact on learning. Understanding their perspectives is therefore essential for ensuring that ALS are meaningful in diverse school contexts.

To address this gap, this chapter examines how teachers utilise and perceive an ALS in primary mathematics education. The study employed a mixed-methods approach, including semi-structured interviews (N=7 teachers), focus groups (n1=4 teachers, n2=2 teachers), classroom observations, and a large-scale national survey involving 1,008 teachers. By centring the teacher perspective, the chapter contributes to the broader discourse on adaptive learning by illuminating how ALS are integrated into classroom practice and exploring their implications for teaching and learning.

The research question guiding the chapter is:

How do teachers experience and use an adaptive learning system (ALS) in primary mathematics education?

SYSTEM DESCRIPTION

The adaptive learning system (ALS) examined in this chapter is grounded in principles of learning analytics, drawing on large datasets from student interactions to dynamically adapt content. It presents students with a sequence of mathematics tasks that continuously adjust to their performance – whether they answer correctly or incorrectly, and how they perform over time. These data feed into a recommender algorithm, a type of predictive model also used by platforms like Netflix or Amazon, to suggest the next task. These algorithms analyse patterns in user behaviour to anticipate what might be most relevant or beneficial, and in the context of learning, they tailor task selection to match the student's current level and progress. This approach reflects what Brusilovsky and Peylo (2003) describe as skill-based personalisation through adaptive task sequencing.

Unlike intelligent tutoring systems, which rely on detailed learner models to deliver individualised feedback and instructional support (Kulik and Fletcher 2016), adaptive systems based on learning analytics take a different approach. These systems analyse large datasets generated by student interactions – such as response accuracy, time on task and behavioural patterns – to inform the sequencing and personalisation of learning tasks (Misiejuk and Wasson 2017; Samuelsen, Chen and Wasson 2019). ALS in this study follows this model, employing a task-based adaptation strategy rather than offering deep conceptual scaffolding.

As a result, the system emphasises the first two of Sonwalkar's (2008) adaptive functions – (1) sequencing content and (2) generating personalised learning paths based on individual task performance – while offering only limited support for the third: formative feedback that fosters conceptual understanding. It is designed to function with minimal teacher intervention, relying on undisturbed student activity to infer proficiency levels and generate task recommendations through its recommender engine.

To characterise the design of this system more precisely, we can draw on the framework proposed by Vandewaetere, Desmet and Clarebout (2011), which identifies three core dimensions of adaptive learning environments. Within this typology, ALS in this study can be described as follows:

- *Source of adaptation*: Student activity within the system ('learner');
- *Goal of adaptation*: Customisation of content and tasks ('content');
- *Path of adaptation*: A recommender system.

The system operates with two dashboards, one for students and one for teachers. The student dashboard offers visual indicators of progress, such as completion bars and gamified feedback like stars. The teacher dashboard provides an overview of both individual and group performance, helping teachers identify students who are struggling and, if needed, manually adjust task levels. Despite these options, the system is intended to function with minimal teacher intervention, as it relies on undisturbed student activity to diagnose proficiency and chart learning trajectories.

The vendor explicitly frames ALS as a tool for practice, not for instruction. Teachers are advised to introduce topics through other methods before assigning tasks in ALS. The system is best used for exercises to reinforce previously taught skills. Teacher training materials recommend limiting student use to about 60 minutes per week and assigning more exploratory or collaborative tasks outside the system, especially for students who demonstrate high mastery (Egelandsdal et al. 2019). The system itself only accommodates tasks with single correct answers and does not support open-ended problem-solving, reflection or group collaboration. The vendor has voiced concerns about overuse of the system and emphasises the importance of balancing its use with broader pedagogical strategies.

This positioning introduces tensions when the system is implemented in classroom practice. By design, ALS assumes that the most effective learning occurs when students solve tasks independently. It penalises external assistance by interpreting it as interference, potentially conflicting with sociocultural learning theories that emphasise social interaction and scaffolding within the zone of proximal development (Vygotsky 1978; Wood, Bruner and Ross 1976).

The system's limited capacity for formative feedback and conceptual support shapes the types of learning it best supports. While effective for procedural fluency and consolidation, it does not explain why an answer is correct or incorrect, detect conceptual misunderstandings, or prompt metacognitive reflection. In this sense, it optimises for efficient, individualised practice over deep, conceptual understanding.

Consequently, ALS should not be viewed as a comprehensive instructional tool, but as a supplementary resource that must be carefully integrated into broader teaching strategies. Teachers play a crucial role in interpreting the system's data, supplementing its limitations, and ensuring that learning remains within a purposeful, pedagogically grounded context.

METHODS

The research project employed a sequential mixed-methods design, characterised by the systematic collection of both qualitative and quantitative data across multiple phases. In such designs, findings from each phase inform the planning and execution of subsequent phases (Johnson and Christensen 2016; Teddlie and Tashakkori 2009). The study comprised three phases:

- Phase 1: Semi-structured interviews with teachers.
- Phase 2: Classroom observations of teaching with ALS.
- Phase 3: An online survey of teachers informed by findings from the previous phases.

Data from interviews and observations were thematically coded in NVivo, while survey data were analysed separately using descriptive statistics and comparative analysis in SPSS.

Interviews

Thirteen teachers from nine schools participated in semi-structured interviews. Seven interviews were conducted individually, and two were group interviews (n1=4, n2=2). All interviews were conducted at the participants' schools. The interviews explored how teachers used and experienced ALS, its functionality, the purposes for which it was found useful, and its perceived strengths and weaknesses.

Interview data were thematically analysed using NVivo software to identify key themes and patterns, following the six-phase approach outlined by Braun and Clarke (2006). The excerpts included in the chapter are representative of the analytical categories developed through this process and were selected to reflect patterns in teachers' accounts.

Observations

A total of 11 hours of classroom observation were conducted with eight student groups across six schools, covering all grades except Year 3. Observations focused on the practical implementation of ALS, how students interacted with the system, and the role of teachers during these sessions. Observational data were thematically analysed alongside interview data to explore recurring patterns and enrich the qualitative analysis.

Survey

An online survey was distributed to all teachers using ALS via the publisher's email network, reaching 9,822 teachers. A total of 1,008 teachers responded to the survey.

The survey was developed based on the findings from the interviews and observations and consisted of two parts:

1. *Quantitative section*: Multiple-choice questions rated on a five-point Likert scale to capture teachers' experiences with ALS.

2. *Qualitative section*: Two open-ended questions inviting teachers to share suggestions for improving the system and to describe their experiences in more detail.

Survey responses were analysed using descriptive statistics and mean comparisons in SPSS to identify trends and insights.

RESULTS

Levels and Usage Patterns

Primary education in Norway includes students aged 5 to 13, spanning 1st to 7th grade. Survey results show a relatively even distribution of users of ALS across grade levels (see Figure 15.1), with a slight underrepresentation in the 1st and 2nd grades. Notably, the system is utilised in diverse instructional settings, including special education (28 teachers) and introductory classes for minority language students (3 teachers).

A majority of teachers (66 per cent) report that ALS plays a significant role in their mathematics instruction, while 19 per cent disagree (N=1,006). On average, teachers allocate approximately 30 minutes weekly for using the system in the classroom and 30 minutes for homework (N=1,008). In the interviews, some teachers say that they use the system exclusively for homework.

Using ALS for Homework

Teachers emphasise that ALS provide manageable, personalised tasks for students. Features like timed assignments encourage equitable engagement and reduce reliance on parental support, particularly benefiting students in multicultural classrooms. One teacher noted:

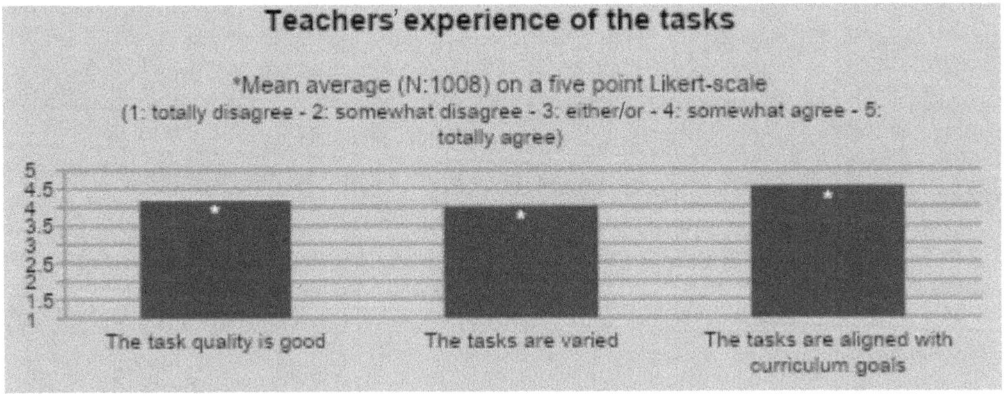

Source: Author.

Figure 15.1 *Teachers' experience of the tasks in ALS*

> With our student group, where at least half are non-native speakers, it's not always easy for them to get help at home. The adaptive learning system provides homework that they can manage independently, which is invaluable.

However, several of the teachers say that parents have expressed concerns about limited insights into their children's progress due to the system's interface, which displays only correct or incorrect answers. Additionally, some students face barriers such as insufficient access to digital devices or internet connectivity, prompting teachers to provide alternative assignments or facilitate homework at school.

Other challenges include students rushing through tasks or misusing the system by idling or pressing random buttons to complete timed activities. Teachers address these issues by monitoring task completion rates, accuracy, and time spent, identifying behaviours such as prolonged time spent on minimal progress (for example, 30 minutes for two tasks).

Integration with Other Educational Materials

The majority of teachers (82 per cent, N=831) use a textbook series that aligns with ALS, developed by the same vendor. These integrate system activities with textbook chapters, employing the platform for practice and assessment following topic coverage. Ten per cent (N=97) use other textbooks, while 8 per cent (N=80) do not follow a specific textbook-based curriculum.

For teachers without a textbook structure, ALS is used selectively, often targeting foundational areas such as number sense and arithmetic operations. These teachers generally have broader access to digital resources and expertise in using various mathematics tools, enabling flexible approaches to instruction.

Equipment Accessibility in the Classroom

Eighteen per cent of teachers report limited access to digital devices as a barrier to using ALS, while 65 per cent encounter no such issues (N=1,006). Device availability significantly impacts efficiency: students with personal devices maximise their time on the platform, while those sharing devices or logging in during class lose valuable working time.

Alignment with Curriculum and Task Quality

As shown in Figure 15.1, a substantial majority (95 per cent) of teachers believe the exercises (tasks) in ALS align well with curriculum competency goals, with 88 per cent rating them as good. However, 7 per cent express dissatisfaction with task quality, and 11 per cent disagree with the assertion that the exercises are sufficiently varied (N=1,008).

The observations consistently show that many tasks in ALS for intermediate grades require students to write down their calculations outside of the programme (see Figure 15.2). If students lack the opportunity to do this or simply don't bother, some tasks become very difficult to solve using mental maths alone. Certain tasks also require additional tools, such as a calculator, and the programme provided notifications when these tools were needed. In one class where students were working on telling time, the teacher opted to let them use an analogue clock as a supplementary tool.

Source: Author.

Figure 15.2 *Students doing calculations outside the adaptive system*

Various tools were used for writing down calculations: whiteboards, paper, workbooks, split screens with note-taking software and frozen screens that allowed students to write directly on them. Even when opportunities for calculations were provided by the teacher, we sometimes observed that students failed to do so, even for tasks that obviously required it. Some students started recording their work after being reminded by the teacher of its importance, while others expressed that they simply didn't want to. The drawback of not writing down calculations for tasks that require it is that students often provide many incorrect answers, which affects the system's adaptation, resulting in overly simplified tasks being assigned to them.

Practice and Learning

The survey shows that most teachers (94 per cent) find ALS useful for providing students with practice in fundamental mathematics. Additionally, the majority (84 per cent) see also that the system is useful for developing students' mathematical understanding.

Several teachers interviewed emphasise that students do not necessarily learn something new in ALS, and that other activities and conversations with the teacher are essential for developing students' conceptual understanding and mathematical reasoning. However, they highlight the importance of the practice provided by the system for the students' learning. One teacher explains it like this:

> Learning something new means that you didn't know it before. So if you can do something, it means you already knew it. By definition, you won't learn something new, but you'll gain confidence in it, and you'll, so to speak, reflect in new ways and see connections and combinations. In mathematics, it's essential to automate, practice, and repeat. I think the adaptive learning system provides the practice they need.

This is primarily attributed to the fact that students complete more tasks in the adaptive system than they would in a traditional workbook. Teachers view this practice as critical for students to build confidence and automate their approaches to solving various types of tasks. Many teachers observe that students have improved since starting with the system and claim that this improvement is evident in their assessment tools. This progress is attributed both to the exercises within the programme itself and to the way the programme streamlines practising, allowing teaching time to be used for other activities that help develop students' mathematical understanding.

Adaptivity

In the survey, 75 per cent of teachers reported that the adaptivity of ALS is an important reason for using the programme, while 5 per cent stated that this claim does not apply to them (N=1,006). Additionally, 82 per cent agreed that the system successfully identifies gaps in students' mathematical competence, whereas 10 per cent disagreed with this statement (N=1,008). Furthermore, 78 per cent believe that the system provides tailored tasks that gradually help students progress to a higher level, while 10 per cent disagreed with this statement (N=1,008).

Regarding the adaptation for different student groups in ALS, 77 per cent of teachers feel that low-performing students are provided with tasks suited to their skill level, 90 per cent believe this is true for average-performing students, and 78 per cent for high-performing students (N=1,008).

Most teachers interviewed are satisfied with the adaptivity of the system, but some challenges were noted. In some instances, teachers observe what they call a 'kangaroo effect', where students oscillate between levels – receiving tasks they can master, moving up to more difficult ones, failing, and then being demoted, leading to boredom and loss of focus. Some teachers also find that it takes a long time for the programme to identify students' levels, particularly for low-performing students, which can be demotivating. For example, one teacher noted that low-performing students may need to solve numerous tasks before the programme accurately assesses their level, which some students find overwhelming. Teachers also mentioned cases where low-performing students receive overly simple tasks, causing frustration and disengagement.

Teachers have the option to manually adjust students' levels or move them between chapters. Some use this feature effectively for both low- and high-performing students, though it can be less effective if advanced students encounter unfamiliar topics. Overall, teachers appreciate the programme's differentiation, which allows students to quickly move past tasks they have mastered.

Challenges also arise from students' behaviour. Some guess answers, skip steps, or rely on mental calculations, which disrupt the programme's adaptivity. Conversely, when parents help too much with homework, students may face tasks that are too advanced when working independently. Teachers address this by advising parents to let students work on their own and focusing their own support on encouraging reflection rather than providing answers.

Teachers support students in three main ways: (1) interpreting tasks; (2) guiding how to set up calculations; and (3) providing answers. Observations showed teachers primarily used the first two approaches. Some teachers, however, lack understanding of how the programme's algorithm works, particularly regarding how students' first attempts influence adaptivity. The vendor advises teachers to provide answers only after the first attempt.

Misunderstanding tasks can also lead to students being stuck at overly simple levels, requiring unnecessary repetition. Some students, when unable to solve a task, opt to do nothing rather than use the 'Give up' feature. Peer assistance was also observed as a potential source of error for the programme's adaptivity.

Student Motivation

Teachers generally regard ALS as engaging, with 83 per cent noting students are motivated by the platform's 'star feature', and 88 per cent reporting that students enjoy working on it (N=1,006, see also Figure 15.3). The system is also considered effective in fostering mathematical interest (76 per cent) and a sense of mastery (82 per cent) (N=1,008, see also Figure 15.4).

These findings are echoed in our interviews, where the teachers report that students are motivated by the variety of tasks in ALS, which also helps them stay engaged for longer periods compared to working with a maths textbook. One teacher observed that students who are restless and struggle with concentration tend to calm down more easily when working in ALS. The sessions we observed lasted 20, 45, or 60 minutes. In sessions longer than 45 minutes, it appeared that students' concentration and motivation for the tasks declined. The youngest students seemed the most motivated to work in the programme. At the higher grade levels, students showed less enthusiasm when engaging with the tasks and appeared to care less about

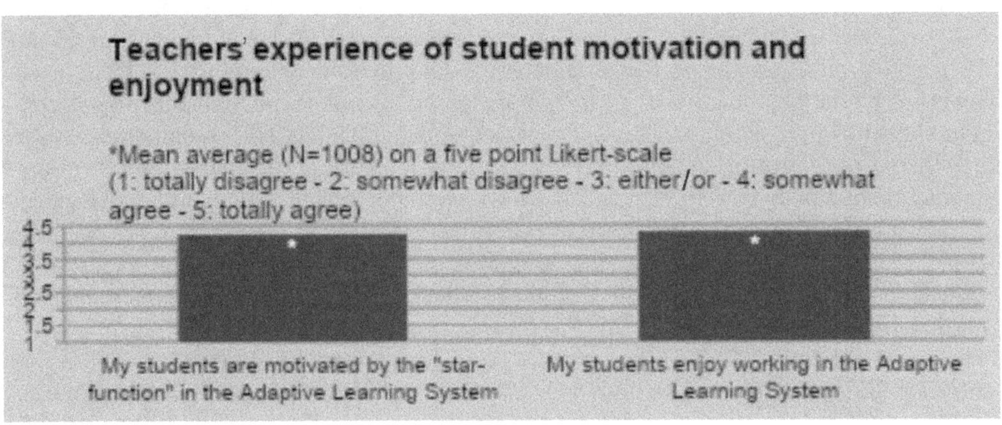

Source: Author.

Figure 15.3 *My students' motivation: reward and enjoyment*

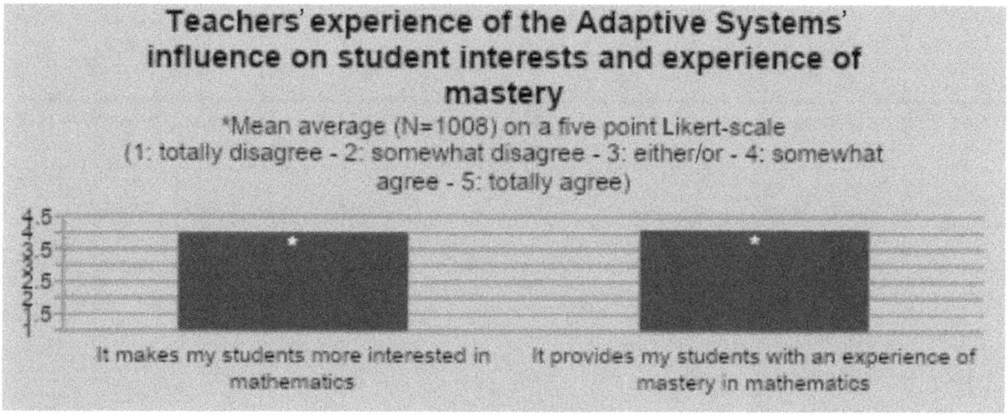

Source: Author.

Figure 15.4 *My students' motivation: interest and mastery*

stars as rewards. We also see this tendency in our survey results, where the teacher's experience of student motivation with the reward system seems to diminish in higher grade levels (see Table 15.1).

Some teachers experience that their students focus excessively on earning stars, misunderstanding the system's educational intent. Nonetheless, the independence of the star system from task difficulty and learning progress is also praised, as it allows students of varying skill levels to feel equally rewarded. One teacher explained:

> In my class, some students are at the first-grade level while others are at the third, yet they can earn the same number of stars. This keeps them motivated.

Classroom Management

We observed few challenges related to students working on simpler tasks than the rest of the class in MSØ. However, there were some exceptions. One such exception involved groups where classroom management was weak or absent, either because teachers rarely took charge of how students worked or because the teachers were less present due to students working in separate rooms. This resulted in a clear divide within the groups between students who worked with focus and those who did not engage in productive activities. Some students worked diligently in MSØ, while others started chatting with one another on various digital platforms or 'goofing around' with nearby peers. Some students did not bother to answer the tasks correctly but simply clicked through them, while others chose not to engage with the programme at all. For instance, one student who was tasked with shooting at ducks representing the correct numbers in a maths problem decided to indiscriminately shoot at every duck they saw. In these environments, it seemed that students working on tasks at a lower level than the majority were more vulnerable, and we observed instances where students made disparaging comments about the level of tasks their peers were working on.

Table 15.1 Compare means analysis of the relationship between student motivation and grade level

Grade level	Statistic	My students are motivated by the 'star function'	My students enjoy working in ALS
1. grade	Mean	4.6024	4.6386
1. grade	N	83	83
1. grade	Standard Deviation	.69738	.57548
2. grade	Mean	4.6765	4.4118
2. grade	N	102	102
2. grade	Standard Deviation	.54794	.73596
3. grade	Mean	4.4354	4.3243
3. grade	N	147	148
3. grade	Standard Deviation	.85262	.80150
4. grade	Mean	4.3851	4.3219
4. grade	N	148	146
4. grade	Standard Deviation	.75163	.73283
5. grade	Mean	4.2393	4.3620
5. grade	N	163	163
5. grade	Standard Deviation	.89466	.71856
6. grade	Mean	3.9346	4.1234
6. grade	N	153	154
6. grade	Standard Deviation	1.15664	.86567
7. grade	Mean	3.8380	4.1341
7. grade	N	179	179
7. grade	Standard Deviation	.93105	.74495
Total	Mean	4.2462	4.2995
Total	N	975	975
Total	Standard Deviation	.92252	.76670

Source: Author.

Another exception was a group of students who appeared to have a competitive attitude towards mathematics. In this group, we observed that some students refrained from working in MSØ when faced with tasks they could not solve. Their teacher noted that certain students hesitate, move away, and lower their screens slightly to hide the tasks they are working on during class. She perceives this as stemming from students feeling that they cannot achieve the same level of success as their peers, observing others advancing while they struggle to keep up. This becomes particularly apparent when working in MSØ, where tasks with correct and incorrect answers are adapted to each student's level.

DISCUSSION

Balancing Functionality, Adaptivity, and Teacher Input

The study reveals both the technical capabilities and pedagogical constraints of adaptive learning tools. Most teachers expressed confidence in the system's ability to identify and address gaps in students' knowledge. The adaptive engine was particularly effective for students performing at or near grade level, as it provided tailored practice aligned with their current skill level. However, for students performing significantly below expected levels, the system often alternated between tasks that were too basic or too difficult. In these cases, teachers frequently had to intervene manually to adjust levels and realign content with student needs.

Student motivation also played a crucial role. Learners who were less confident in mathematics often struggled to stay engaged, limiting the system's ability to adapt effectively. Many teachers observed that the system required a high number of similar tasks to register progression, which could feel demotivating or repetitive for some students. These findings highlight the need for pedagogical flexibility in adaptive systems and reinforce the importance of teacher judgement in supporting motivation and progress.

Key points:

- The adaptive tool was effective for most students but required manual adjustments for those with significant learning gaps.
- Student motivation affected the tool's effectiveness and the quality of adaptability.
- A balance must be maintained between algorithmic decisions and teacher input.

The Scaffolding Problem

A major concern from a sociocultural standpoint is the system's lack of scaffolding. ALS provides tasks within the student's current level of competence but offers little structured support for conceptual growth. This approach aligns with Vygotsky's (1978) concept of the zone of proximal development (ZPD) and the scaffolding model (Wood, Bruner and Ross 1976), which emphasise the distinction between what a student can achieve independently and what they can accomplish with guided support (see Figure 15.5). While the system excels at tailoring tasks to a student's individual zone, it lacks robust mechanisms for the kind of social and instructional support often required to advance students into new learning territory. Teachers and parents are discouraged from assisting students while using the system, as doing so may cause the algorithm to overestimate the student's competence and assign tasks that are too difficult.

Despite this limitation, 78 per cent of teachers reported that ALS offered adaptive tasks that helped students progress gradually towards higher levels of competence. By operating within each student's existing capabilities, the system can foster a sense of flow – where learners experience challenge and success in balance (Csikszentmihalyi 2008). However, this form of progression does not inherently support conceptual breakthroughs or movement beyond what the student can already do independently.

Teachers reported that real conceptual development occurred only when ALS were combined with whole-class instruction, small-group work, or targeted support.

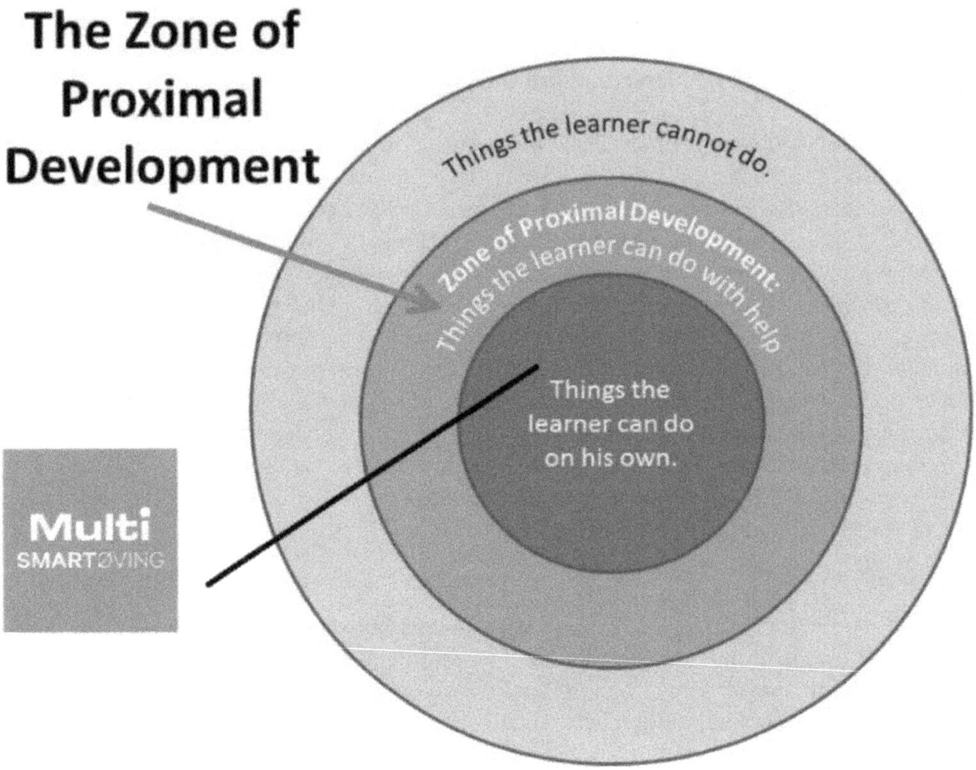

Source: Author.

Figure 15.5 *Students working in ALS relative to Vygotsky's model for development*

Key points:

- ALS assigns tasks tailored to students' independent capabilities, making it most effective as a practice tool for topics already introduced in class.
- Teachers and parents are discouraged from assisting students working in ALS to avoid disrupting adaptivity.
- While the system provides optimal challenges for students, its ability to support learning new concepts remains limited, emphasising the importance of alignment with broader instructional contexts.

Teachers as Designers and Pedagogical Mediators

A central finding of the study is the importance of the teacher's role in shaping how ALS functions in practice. While the system supports procedural learning and individual practice, it does not provide conceptual explanations or scaffolded support. Teachers therefore act as pedagogical mediators – interpreting system feedback, providing context, and supplementing the tool with instruction.

This mediating role reinforces the argument made earlier about the limitations of systems that prioritise individual performance without scaffolding. While ALS adapts to students' current level, it is the teacher who provides the necessary support to move students beyond it. In this way, teachers compensate for the system's lack of alignment with sociocultural learning principles by designing learning environments that foster guided participation and conceptual growth (Rogoff 1990).

This design orientation aligns with the view of teaching as a design-based activity (Laurillard 2012), where educators actively shape learning environments through iterative decisions about tools, content, and pedagogy. Teachers made decisions about when to use ALS, how to interpret its data, and how to embed it within larger learning trajectories. These teachers did not expect the system to teach for them; rather, they saw it as a tool that could free up time for more targeted instruction and offer additional data to inform their teaching.

Key points:

- Teachers mediated and adapted the system to align with pedagogical goals.
- ALS was considered most effective when integrated into a broader instructional design.
- Adaptive tools can reduce teacher workload and free up time for higher-value teaching tasks.

The Role of ALS in Teaching

The findings show that ALS is typically not used in isolation. Most teachers (82 per cent) used it alongside a related textbook series from the same publisher, suggesting that the tool is integrated into an established pedagogical framework. Only 8 per cent reported not using any printed materials, and these teachers tended to use ALS for foundational skills, such as arithmetic and number sense.

While some teachers saw ALS as a potential replacement for traditional exercise books – particularly because it enabled students to complete more tasks in less time – others noted that it lacked transparency in student reasoning. Unlike paper-based tasks, digital responses do not capture students' problem-solving strategies. This limitation was seen as a barrier to formative assessment unless teachers actively monitored system use and supplemented it with written tasks and discussion.

As Kynigos (2019) points out, many ALS tend to reinforce traditional instructional approaches, emphasising problem-solving with clear-cut correct or incorrect answers. These platforms are generally most effective for practising basic skills. However, fostering deeper learning, conceptual understanding, creativity, and innovation requires educators to incorporate additional experiences – such as practical applications, collaborative activities and opportunities for creative problem-solving – that go beyond the capabilities of adaptive systems.

Key points:

- ALS complements textbooks and is often embedded within an existing pedagogical framework.
- Efficiency gains do not replace the need for transparency in student thinking.

- ALS primarily supports efficient practice in fundamental skills but does not foster the development of deep understanding or creative exploration.

Homework: Equity, Engagement, and Access

The use of ALS for homework was widely appreciated by teachers, particularly for its ability to differentiate tasks and reduce the need for parental support. Time-based assignments, rather than a fixed number of tasks, allowed students to work at their own pace and helped ensure a more equitable workload across diverse learners. Teachers observed that this format supported fairness and autonomy, especially for students who typically struggled with standardised homework.

At the same time, several challenges emerged. A minority of students faced barriers to completing digital homework due to limited access to devices or stable internet at home. While relatively rare, such issues raised concerns about digital inequality and the risk of social stigma. Some schools responded by offering additional time for students to complete ALS homework at school or by assigning alternative tasks. However, these solutions placed additional demands on teacher planning and school infrastructure.

According to the teachers, parents also raised concerns about reduced visibility into their children's homework when digital tools like ALS were used. Because the system operates independently and revolves around the correctness of answers, parents felt they had less insight into their child's effort, progress, or areas of difficulty. This concern underscores the importance of maintaining transparency in digital learning systems and ensuring open communication with families.

Key points:

- ALS supports differentiated, time-based homework that promotes equity and reduces reliance on parents.
- Access to digital devices and the internet remains a barrier for some students.
- The lack of transparency in task-solving remains a critical consideration when integrating adaptive tools into homework assignments.

Equipment and Infrastructure in Schools

Although adaptive learning systems are increasingly integrated into classroom practice, many teachers reported challenges related to the availability and management of digital equipment during school hours. In particular, 18 per cent of teachers indicated that limited access to individual devices – such as tablets or laptops – impeded the consistent and effective use of ALS.

In classrooms where students shared devices, instructional time was lost to equipment setup, device login, and navigating technical issues. Teachers noted that even brief delays caused by software glitches or network instability disrupted student engagement and lesson flow. These inefficiencies made it difficult to implement adaptive tools seamlessly as part of the school day and placed additional pressure on teachers to manage both pedagogical and technical responsibilities.

Moreover, some teachers reported that using shared devices reduced opportunities for spontaneous, flexible use of ALS during lessons, for instance, when a student needed immediate practice on a particular topic. The lack of one-to-one device access limited the potential for integrating adaptive learning into formative instruction or targeted support within a single lesson.

Key points:

- Limited access to individual devices during school hours reduces the flexibility and effectiveness of ALS' use.
- Shared equipment setups increase time spent on logistics, reducing available learning time.
- Technical issues and inconsistent infrastructure create barriers to seamless integration of adaptive tools in everyday instruction.

Formative Assessment

A valuable feature of ALS is the overview it provides of students' competencies at the class and individual levels. This study shows that it is essential for teachers to interpret these overviews within the context of the learning goals and the types of tasks embedded in the system. ALS evaluates students based on their performance on specific tasks, focusing on procedural skills. As a result, the data provided by the systems does not fully capture the breadth of students' mathematical competencies, including areas like collaboration, creativity, or critical thinking. Teachers should be aware that such systems highlight certain skills while potentially overlooking others, offering only a partial view of students' overall abilities. Most teachers in our study seem to be aware of this.

The role of teachers, therefore, is to go beyond the statistics provided by the system and conduct their own investigations into the students' mathematical competencies, using formative assessments to inform and guide future teaching (Black and Wiliam 1998; Hattie and Timperley 2007). ALS can complement this process, but they cannot replace the need for ongoing teacher involvement.

Thus, while ALS can inform teaching and provide valuable feedback, it should not be regarded as comprehensive tools. A holistic approach that includes diverse tasks designed to promote deeper understanding is essential for addressing the full range of students' learning needs.

Key points:

- ALS provide useful competency overviews, but these are limited to the evaluation of correct/incorrect answers and do not account for the full range of students' mathematical abilities.
- Teachers must contextualise data with their own assessments to fully understand student learning.
- Adaptive systems support formative assessment but cannot replace it.

Motivation and Reward Systems

Some teachers have raised concerns that the reward systems can encourage students to rush through tasks. Since rewards are given only for correct answers, rather than for effort or progress, students may focus on answering quickly instead of carefully working through problems. This approach reflects behaviourist principles of operant conditioning, where positive reinforcement, such as digital rewards or points, is used to strengthen desired behaviours like task completion or correct responses (Slavin 2018). The challenge arises when students receive rewards without necessarily demonstrating mastery, as there are no penalties for incorrect answers or for abandoning tasks prematurely. This can result in students rushing through tasks, getting answers right without truly engaging with the material, and accumulating rewards without acquiring meaningful learning. Consequently, the adaptive system may present a skewed view of a student's competencies. This issue is particularly pronounced for students who are not intrinsically motivated and prefer simpler tasks (Lepper, Corpus and Iyengar 2005). These students may quickly collect rewards, but fail to deepen their understanding of the material, hindering their academic growth.

However, some educators appreciate that the reward system is based directly on correct answers, rather than on progress or mastery. This design helps ensure that students working at different levels can still earn the same rewards, preventing lower-performing students from feeling demotivated by comparisons to their peers.

A critical concern for reward-based systems is their potential to undermine intrinsic motivation (Deci, Koestner and Ryan 1999; Lepper, Corpus and Iyengar 2005). Intrinsically motivated students are already driven by an internal desire to engage with the content, making external rewards unnecessary and, in some cases, detrimental. The reward system may shift students' attention away from the learning process towards the external goal of earning rewards, eroding their intrinsic interest in the subject matter and, over time, decreasing their overall motivation to engage with the content (Harackiewicz, Smith and Priniski 2016).

To mitigate this, teachers can foster more intrinsic motivation by helping students recognise the value of their progress and emphasising the importance of sustained effort in learning. Encouraging students to see beyond the rewards and focus on their growth and understanding can be an effective strategy.

Ultimately, the effectiveness of reward systems in adaptive learning environments hinges on how students perceive these incentives and how they are embedded within the broader classroom context. Although many students report enjoying the use of rewards, such systems may function primarily as weak extrinsic motivators. Compared to more tangible incentives, such as physical prizes, digital stars and points are often perceived as less valuable and are therefore less likely to distract from the learning process. However, this perceived lower value may also lead to a gradual decline in student interest, which may benefit or hinder student engagement depending on how the rewards interact with individual motivation. Providing teachers with greater autonomy over the timing and delivery of rewards could offer a more flexible and responsive approach, allowing the system to better accommodate the diverse motivational profiles and learning needs of students.

Key points:

- Reward systems in ALS reflect behaviourist principles of operant conditioning, using external reinforcement to increase desired behaviours.
- Reward-based systems may encourage surface-level engagement, such as rushing through tasks to earn points.
- Teacher autonomy in managing rewards could help adapt the system to diverse student needs.

Classroom Management and Culture

Our observations suggest that weak classroom management can lead to disruptions and non-academic use of digital tools, which in turn causes distractions and insecurity for students who are otherwise motivated to engage with ALS. This aligns with prior studies that highlight the crucial role of classroom management in regulating students' digital activities (Johler et al. 2022). While classroom management is important in all settings, digital environments amplify both the opportunities and risks for students to divert their attention to non-academic tasks. Teachers must therefore possess strong digital and pedagogical skills to effectively manage potential challenges and use digital tools in a manner that supports the learning objectives (Moltudal et al. 2019; Moltudal, Krumsvik and Høydal 2022).

Additionally, we found that competitive classroom environments may hinder some students from engaging with adaptive learning platforms. Fear of answering incorrectly and receiving simpler tasks can discourage these students from participating. Teachers reported that some students avoided engaging with the system because they feared being placed on easier levels compared to their peers. In more learning-oriented classrooms, where collaboration and self-paced learning were emphasised, these challenges were not as pronounced.

Key points:

- Weak classroom management leads to distractions and non-academic use of digital tools.
- In competitive environments, students may avoid using adaptive learning tools due to fear of easier task levels or incorrect answers.
- A strong classroom management approach can help foster a collaborative, learning-focused environment and reduce students' anxiety about performance levels.

CONCLUSION

This chapter has examined how primary school teachers use and experience an adaptive learning system (ALS) in mathematics instruction. Drawing on a sociocultural perspective and conceptualising teaching as a design-based activity, the study highlights the teacher's role in mediating between the algorithmic structure of ALS and the pedagogical aims of the classroom.

Findings show that teachers widely valued ALS as a tool for differentiation, procedural practice, and time-efficient monitoring. It allowed for more personalised learning pathways by assigning tasks that matched students' current levels, and many teachers appreciated the insights it provided into student progress. However, these benefits were most evident for students working at or near grade level. Those with significant difficulties or advanced abilities were more likely to experience mismatches in task complexity, requiring manual adjustment and additional support.

A key limitation of the system lies in its focus on individual task completion and binary assessments of correctness. While it supports independent practice, ALS offers little scaffolding or formative feedback. As such, it tends to reinforce traditional models of learning that privilege correctness and repetition over collaboration, exploration, or creative thinking. Students who are less intrinsically motivated may disengage or game the system to earn rewards, while those ready for deeper learning may not be sufficiently challenged.

These limitations point to a broader tension in the use of adaptive technologies: between systems optimised for efficiency and data collection, and pedagogical approaches grounded in guided participation and conceptual development. From a sociocultural standpoint, learning occurs not only through individual task execution but also through interaction, support, and challenge within the learner's zone of proximal development.

Importantly, ALS did not replace the need for teacher intervention – on the contrary, its value often depended on how teachers interpreted the system's outputs, contextualised its data and integrated it into their broader instructional designs. Teachers who were most successful in using the system adopted a designer stance: treating it as one resource among many, not a stand-alone solution. This aligns with the view of teaching as a design-based profession, where educators make iterative decisions about tools, content, and interactions to meet students' needs.

Ultimately, the success of adaptive learning systems depends as much on the pedagogical judgement of teachers as on the technical quality of the tools themselves. ALS can be valuable additions to the educational toolkit – particularly for practising basic skills and tracking individual progress – but their potential is only fully realised when they are used critically, thoughtfully, and in alignment with broader educational goals. Their role is not to replace the teacher, but to extend the teacher's capacity to support diverse learners in meaningful ways.

ACKNOWLEDGEMENTS

The research findings presented in this book chapter are based on the Adaptive Learning in Mathematics (ALMAT) project, funded by the Centre for the Science of Learning & Technology (SLATE) at the University of Bergen. This project culminated in two final reports: (1) *Adaptiv læring i matematikk: Empirisk rapport om Multi Smart Øving i grunnskolen* (Egelandsdal et al. 2019), and (2) *Adaptive Learning in Mathematics: Situating Multi Smart Øving in the Landscape of Digital Technologies for Mathematics Education* (Kynigos 2019). In particular, the chapter draws on the empirical findings from the first report, on teachers' use of and experiences with adaptive learning.

REFERENCES

Black, P. and D. Wiliam (1998), 'Inside the black box: Raising standards through classroom assessment', *Phi Delta Kappan*, **80** (2), 139–44.

Braun, V. and V. Clarke (2006), 'Using thematic analysis in psychology', *Qualitative Research in Psychology*, **3** (2), 77–101. https://doi.org/10.1191/1478088706qp063oa

Brusilovsky, P. and P. Peylo (2003), 'Adaptive and intelligent web-based educational systems', *International Journal of Artificial Intelligence in Education*, **13**, 156–8.

Csikszentmihalyi, M. (2008), *Flow: The psychology of optimal experience*. Harper Perennial Modern Classics.

Deci, E.L., R. Koestner and R.M. Ryan (1999), 'A meta-analytic review of experiments examining the effects of extrinsic rewards on intrinsic motivation', *Psychological Bulletin*, **125** (6), 627–68. https://doi.org/10.1037/0033-2909.125.6.627

Egelandsdal, K., M. Smith, C.S. Hansen, I.J. Ness and B. Wasson (2019), *Adaptiv læring i matematikk: Empirisk rapport om Multi Smart Øving i grunnskolen* (SLATE Research Report No. 2019-4). Centre for the Science of Learning and Technology (SLATE), p. 68. https://hdl.handle.net/1956/21354

Harackiewicz, J.M., J.L. Smith and S.J. Priniski (2016), 'Interest matters: The importance of promoting interest in education', *Policy Insights from the Behavioral and Brain Sciences*, **3** (2), 220–7. https://doi.org/10.1177/2372732216655542

Hattie, J. and H. Timperley (2007), 'The power of feedback', *Review of Educational Research*, **77** (1), 81–112. https://doi.org/10.3102/003465430298487

Johler, M., R.J. Krumsvik, H.E. Bugge and N. Helgevold (2022), 'Teachers' perceptions of their role and classroom management practices in a technology-rich primary school classroom', *Frontiers in Education*, **7**, 841385. https://doi.org/10.3389/feduc.2022.841385

Johnson, R.B. and L. Christensen (2016), *Educational research: Quantitative, qualitative, and mixed approaches* (6th ed.). Sage Publications.

Kabudi, T., I.O. Pappas and D.H. Olsen (2021), 'AI-enabled adaptive learning systems: A systematic mapping of the literature', *Computers and Education: Artificial Intelligence*, **2**, 100017. https://doi.org/10.1016/j.caeai.2021.100017

Kulik, J.A. and J.D. Fletcher (2016), 'Effectiveness of intelligent tutoring systems: A meta-analytic review', *Review of Educational Research*, **86** (1), 42–78. https://doi.org/10.3102/0034654315581420

Kynigos, C. (2019), *Adaptive learning in mathematics: Situating Multi Smart Øving in the landscape of digital technologies for mathematics education* (SLATE Research Report No. 2019-3). Centre for the Science of Learning and Technology (SLATE), p. 35. https://hdl.handle.net/1956/21352

Laurillard, D. (2012), *Teaching as a design science: Building pedagogical patterns for learning and technology*. Routledge.

Lepper, M.R., J.H. Corpus and S.S. Iyengar (2005), 'Intrinsic and extrinsic motivational orientations in the classroom: Age differences and academic correlates', *Journal of Educational Psychology*, **97** (2), 184–96. https://doi.org/10.1037/0022-0663.97.2.184

Martin, F., Y. Chen, R.L. Moore and C.D. Westine (2020), 'Systematic review of adaptive learning research designs, context, strategies, and technologies from 2009 to 2018', *Educational Technology Research and Development*, **68**, 1903–29. https://doi.org/10.1007/s11423-020-09793-2

Misiejuk, K. and B. Wasson (2017), *State of the field report on learning analytics* (SLATE Report No. 2017-2). https://hdl.handle.net/1956/17740

Moltudal, S.H., R.J. Krumsvik and K.L. Høydal (2022), 'Adaptive learning technology in primary education: Implications for professional teacher knowledge and classroom management', *Frontiers in Education*, **7**, 830536. https://doi.org/10.3389/feduc.2022.830536

.Moltudal, S., R.J. Krumsvik, L. Jones, O.J. Eikeland and B. Johnson (2019), 'The relationship between teachers' perceived classroom management abilities and their professional digital competence', *Designs for Learning*, **11** (1), 80–98. https://files.eric.ed.gov/fulltext/EJ1235526.pdf

Rogoff, B. (1990), *Apprenticeship in thinking: Cognitive development in social context*. Oxford University Press.

Samuelsen, J., W. Chen and B. Wasson (2019), 'Integrating multiple data sources for learning analytics: Review of literature', *Research and Practice in Technology Enhanced Learning*, **14** (1), 11. http://doi.org/10.1186/s41039-019-0105-4

Slavin, R.E. (2018), *Educational psychology: Theory and practice* (12th ed.). Pearson.

Sonwalkar, N. (2008), 'Adaptive individualization strategies in e-learning design: A review of the models', *International Journal on E-Learning*, **7** (3), 401–25.

Teddlie, C. and A. Tashakkori (2009), *Foundations of mixed methods research: Integrating quantitative and qualitative approaches in the social and behavioral sciences*. Sage Publications.

Vandewaetere, M., P. Desmet and G. Clarebout (2011), 'The contribution of learner characteristics in the development of computer-based adaptive learning environments', *Computers in Human Behavior*, **27** (1), 118–30. https://doi.org/10.1016/j.chb.2010.07.038

Vygotsky, L.S. (1978), *Mind in society: The development of higher psychological processes*. Harvard University Press.

Wood, D., J.S. Bruner and G. Ross (1976), 'The role of tutoring in problem solving', *Journal of Child Psychology and Psychiatry*, **17** (2), 89–100. https://doi.org/10.1111/j.1469-7610.1976.tb00381.x

16. Operationalising science competencies to support teachers' formative assessment and instruction with Inq-ITS AI

Janice D. Gobert, Amy Adair, Jessica A. Owens, and Rachel Dickler

INTRODUCTION

Students struggle with Science, Technology, Engineering and Mathematics (STEM) competencies worldwide; for example, American students rank much lower than students from other countries, that is, namely, 16th in science and 28th in maths (OECD 2023). In order to improve students' science competencies, important in an increasingly technological society, twenty-first-century skill frameworks (OECD 2018) and the Next Generation Science Standards (NGSS 2013), adopted by the majority of the states in the USA have outlined the scientific competencies (referred to as practices in the NGSS) that students need to participate in fully in an increasingly technological society. Specifically, the NGSS states that students must be able to engage in authentic science, including: form questions, develop and use models, plan and carry out investigations, analyse and interpret data, construct explanations and communicate findings. Further, and important to the present chapter, teachers must provide instruction on these competencies, as well as assess, support students' learning, and report on their progress on each of these. However, assessing and supporting students on these competencies is a near impossible task for teachers for a plethora of reasons, namely: there are few resources for instruction, assessment and progress monitoring and reporting (Martinez-Maldonado et al. 2015) that capture the complexities of the NGSS (2013); science inquiry competencies are complex (Kuhn 2005); there is a wide range of competencies exhibited by students within science classrooms (Kuhn et al. 1992); and class sizes in the USA can be large.

In this chapter, we argue that it is necessary that teachers be given rigorous, actionable, formative data in real time to support their instruction of science competencies, extended by twenty-first-century frameworks (OECD 2018) and the NGSS (2013), when it is most optimal for student learning (Koedinger and Corbett 2006). These data, in turn, can be used to support students' learning of competencies (that is, practices) that then can be applied in new contexts to address problems the world faces, for example, climate change, future pandemics, etc. (Harris et al. 2016). Further, we argue that in order to provide teachers with actionable data, each of the practices needs to be rigorously operationalised, and teachers must know which types of support to apply, for whom, and when and how to apply these different types of support.

Here, we describe how we rigorously operationalised the practices outlined in the NGSS (2013) into their respective sub-components and into actionable and pedagogically meaningful formative data and information used to support teachers' instruction aligned to NGSS and, in turn, students' learning. We argue that fine-grained, rigorous assessments of students' competencies are critical to teachers' instruction of science practices. Then, further on in the chapter, we provide a description of Inq-ITS, our student platform, and Inq-Blotter, our corresponding teacher platform, and summarise how the system was developed to support teachers in science instruction.

Some Key Foundations and Presuppositions Underlying American Science Frameworks

Prior to the development of the NGSS (2013), there was an articulated need to conceptualise and, in turn, organise science education by aligning curriculum, instruction, and assessment to reflect the underpinnings of deep understandings of science content and practices (NRC 2007). Seminal reports describing this goal include *Science for All Americans* (AAAS 1989; 1993) and *Taking Science to School* (NRC 2007), which both utilised the term 'learning progressions'. In these documents, learning progressions, described as foundational to the goal of aligning curriculum, instruction, and assessment, are defined as 'how students' understandings of ideas and skills might grow over time' and as 'pathways of increasingly sophisticated levels of thinking and ability that students demonstrate in a particular topic or content area over time', respectively.

Subsequent to the AAAS and NRC (2007) reports, a growing body of research on learning progressions (Jin et al. 2025) has yielded some key presuppositions and tenets. Those important to the present chapter are as follows. First, learning progressions assume that certain knowledge or skills are required a priori to understand and develop more sophisticated scientific ideas, but second, that this progression is not developmental in nature, that is, it is not necessarily age-related (Duncan and Hmelo-Silver 2009; Duschl et al. 2011; NRC 2007). Third, that the multiple, possible progressions or pathways exhibited by students may be context-dependent (Black et al. 2011). Lastly, learning progressions describe the types of difficulties students exhibit at the beginning of a progression (for a concept or skill; Duschl et al. 2011) and identify the knowledge and skills that students should be able to demonstrate by the end of the progression (Duncan and Hmelo-Silver 2009), and between the two ends are 'stepping stones' (Smith et al. 2010) along the learning progression to the targeted learning goal. In our system, we refer to these stepping stones as sub-components of science competencies (to be described later).

Prior Work on Learning Progressions for Curriculum, Instruction, and Assessment

Learning progressions have been described as potentially beneficial to education in many ways, including in 'providing a common framework at multiple levels (for example, from classroom- to state- and national) … to improve the overall coherence of the system' (National Research Council 2006). With respect to the AAAS's (1989; 1993) and the NRC's (2007) goal of aligning *curriculum*, *instruction*, and *assessment*, learning progressions have been promoted as a guide to develop *curricula* for 'science content and scientific inquiry practices' (Songer et al. 2009; Wiser et al. 2012), and, in turn, to support standards (for example, Foster and Wiser 2012). With respect to supporting *instruction*, learning progressions have been promoted for many purposes: as road maps for teaching (Alonzo 2011; Black et al. 2011; Furtak 2012); to address common learning difficulties (Furtak 2012); to inform interactions with students (Berland and McNeill 2010; Furtak 2012; Shea and Duncan 2013) and inform in-class discussions on-the-fly (Furtak 2012); and to adapt instruction to meet student learning needs (Corcoran et al. 2009; Furtak et al. 2014) so as to close the gap between students' current understanding and the desired learning goal (Alonzo 2011). Lastly, as regards teachers' *assessment*, learning progressions are described as having the potential to help teachers get a sense of the terrain of students' ideas (Jin et al. 2019b; Lobato and Walters 2017), make sense of patterns in students' written work (Sikorski et al. 2009), anticipate students' responses (Furtak 2012), categorise and analyse students' ideas (Furtak and Heredia 2014; Furtak et al. 2015), monitor students' progress (Liu and Jackson 2019), identify indicators of learning (Alonzo 2011), diagnose students' understanding (Corcoran et al. 2009; Yin et al. 2013), and structure their assessments (Alonzo et al. 2012; Furtak et al. 2014; Yin et al. 2013) to provide evidence of student learning (Black et al. 2011; Furtak 2012). Researchers have noted the value of learning progressions as a means to validating assessments (Duncan and Rivet 2013; Gotwals and Songer 2013) for both formative and summative assessment use (Black et al. 2011).

Implementation Research on Learning Progressions

Studies addressing the implementation of learning progressions in science classrooms have shown some positive research findings. For example, they can broaden the teachers' scope of students' ideas (Furtak et al. 2015) and can be useful for teachers who have weak formative assessment practices (Furtak 2012). However, implementation research on learning progressions also revealed multiple problems. Specifically, some teachers were sceptical about learning progressions, especially when they were not involved in developing them (Furtak and Heredia 2014). Some teachers were not able to use learning progressions to inform instructional strategies (Bianchini et al. 2014), nor did their use change teachers' design or enactment of formative assessment activities (Furtak et al. 2016) as was envisioned by researchers' intentions (Alonzo and Elby 2019; Furtak et al. 2014). Some studies showed that teachers were not able to move beyond the knowledge available in the learning progressions, and instead used them as oversimplified starting places for student thinking; however, other studies found that teachers adopted finer-grained information rather than the levels specified in the learning progression (Alonzo and Elby 2019).

These negative findings from learning progressions implementation research are largely due to two issues. First, some researchers expressed concerns about the coarse grain-size (Jin et al. 2019a; Harris et al. 2016), that is, the lack of specificity of learning progressions (Shea and Duncan 2013) as a possible barrier for teachers. Second, it was suggested that teachers' strong didactic orientations towards content teaching present a barrier for teachers (Covitt et al. 2018). This is particularly critical to NGSS, which deliberately seeks to orient teachers away from a content-only focus, which tends to default to rote instruction and inert knowledge (Bereiter and Scardamalia 1985 [2013]).

THE DESIGN OF INQ-ITS AND INQ-BLOTTER TO SUPPORT TEACHERS' FORMATIVE ASSESSMENT AND INSTRUCTION OF INQUIRY PRACTICES

Our work on developing technology-based resources, namely Inq-ITS and Inq-Blotter, we believe, addresses the coarse grain-size (Jin et al. 2019a; Harris et al. 2016) or lack of specificity of learning progressions (Shea and Duncan 2013) cited by others, and also mitigates the implementation issues related to teachers' orientation towards a 'content-first' instructional approach (Covitt et al. 2018). In short, our solution supports teachers' assessment and instruction of NGSS-based curricula so that students' learning needs, described by NGSS, can be realised (NGSS 2013).

In our development work on Inq-ITS (Inquiry Intelligent Tutoring System) and its corresponding teacher dashboard, Inq-Blotter (Gobert 2019; Gobert and Sao Pedro 2016; Gobert et al. 2016, 2017, 2019 January, 2023; Sao Pedro 2015, 2016), we operationalised the sub-components underlying science practices (NGSS 2013) as a way to unpack these for teachers' formative assessment and, in turn, instruction of science for the full range of competencies exhibited by students, including those in the messy middle (Gotwals and Songer 2010). Specifically, to address issues related to grain-size, we developed a technology-based platform and authentic, simulation-based activities that have the technical capacity to assess students' inquiry competencies and their respective sub-practices (Gobert et al. 2016, 2017). To address issues related to teachers' content-first orientation towards science instruction, we developed a multi-function teacher dashboard, Inq-Blotter (Gobert et al. 2019 January, 2023), to accompany Inq-ITS that could provide teachers with: (1) real-time, fine-grained, formative data on students' competencies on the sub-components of the NGSS practices (2013); (2) actionable alerts to identify who was struggling and in what specific ways (at the sub-component level); and (3) TIPS (Teacher Inquiry Practice Supports: Adair et al. 2020, 2022; Dickler 2021; Dickler et al. 2021a, 2021b, 2021c) to guide their real-time instruction of science. Operationalising each practice into its respective sub-components of each of the NGSS (2013) practices was necessary so that we could, in turn, send teachers via Inq-Blotter, actionable alerts, and TIPS on their students' struggles with the NGSS practices and sub-components, as this level of specificity is important to instruction. Next, we describe how this was done.

The Evidence-Centered Design framework (ECD, henceforth; Mislevy et al. 2012), a framework that is used to unpack and specify all aspects of the assessment process from start to finish, was used to design assessment tasks for Inq-ITS that would elicit students' competencies on the NGSS practices in an authentic manner that captures them in the context in which they are developing (Mislevy et al. 2012). ECD has been used for a wide variety of assessment tasks, including science inquiry tasks and science ITSs (for example, Clarke-Midura et al. 2012; Mislevy 2013; Shute 2011). ECD is particularly useful given the ill-defined nature of science inquiry (cf. Kuhn 2005), and it permitted us to design a system and tasks, including simulations, that elicit and collect evidence (in the form of log file data) of students' proficiencies at inquiry practices (Gobert and Sao Pedro 2017) as they engage in rich, authentic inquiry tasks with simulations aligned to NGSS (2013), such as forming questions, collecting data (with simulations), analysing and interpreting data, and communicating findings.

A key first step to developing Inq-ITS activities was to break down the NGSS science practices into more concrete, appropriately grain-sized sub-practices. These were created by reviewing the NRC (2006; 2007) and NGSS frameworks (NGSS 2013), interviewing teachers, conducting think-aloud studies with students using hands-on and virtual materials, and reviewing relevant research on students' difficulties with inquiry at the middle school and early high school levels (Gobert and Sao Pedro 2017). Example sub-skills for key practices are as follows:

- *Asking Questions* (NGSS Practice 1) entails formulating a testable question, which requires students to be able to distinguish independent (manipulable) variables from dependent (outcome) variables and posit a relationship between them (Gobert et al. 2012).
- *Planning and Carrying out Investigations* (NGSS Practice 3) entails collecting controlled data and data to enable the supporting or refuting of testable questions specified (Sao Pedro et al. 2013a).
- *Analysing and Interpreting Data* (NGSS Practice 4) entails interpreting the relationship between the independent and the dependent variable, and linking the interpretation back to the original testable question (Gobert et al. 2018).
- *Constructing Explanations* (NGSS Practice 6) entails forming a claim based on the data collected and warranting the claim by selecting appropriate evidence (data trials collected) that backs up the claim (Gobert et al. 2018).
- *Communicating Findings* (NGSS Practice 8) entails describing the results of the investigation in a claim-evidence-reasoning (McNeill and Krajcik 2011) open response format against which several sub-skills are checked (Li et al. 2017b, 2017c, 2019).

Based on the sub-component breakdown, formative assessment activities were developed with a similar look and feel that combine simulations that represent science phenomena with representational tools that elicit students' thinking processes and related actions as they complete a full end-to-end experiment. The simulations and representational tools provide the data streams over which our algorithms can score students' inquiry practices. Each activity provides students with a goal aligned to a specific NGSS Disciplinary Core Idea and content misconception (Gobert and Sao Pedro 2017), marrying the content and practices as envisioned by the NGSS (NGSS Lead States 2013).

As students work, the assessment algorithms assess students' competencies at the sub-practice level and also capture what kinds of difficulties students have with inquiry competencies at the sub-practice level, and then communicate those difficulties to the teacher with Inq-Blotter's succinct, formative and actionable alerts (Gobert and Sao Pedro 2017). These visual representations of students' progress, especially those that capture the specific sub-components of students' competencies, can be essential for classrooms that are designed to support students with learning difficulties. Learning goals for these students are required to be both specific and measurable (Hedin and DeSpain 2018). Because the Inq-ITS reports provide data at the sub-component level, teachers can be assured they are focusing on specific and measurable learning goals that best support their students' needs.

Inq-ITS Components

There are many core features of the two systems, including a *no-install, cross-platform* software base that runs over the web without any configuration and works on standard browsers with PCs, Macs, iPads and Chromebooks; a *lightweight Learning Management System* (LMS) that organises and manages access to the lab/assessment activities and teacher support materials; a *scalable logging infrastructure* enabling us to log students' interactions with simulations and tools; a rigorous *testing infrastructure* so we can 'run' simulated students to check that our logging, assessment, and scaffolding mechanisms are working properly before implementation; a robust *inquiry activity authoring architecture* with which we have developed 45+ simulation engines for NGSS for middle school Physical, Life, and Earth Science; *representational tools* that elicit students' thinking and enable assessment of inquiry practices; *inquiry assessment algorithms* for automatically scoring competencies for asking questions, planning and carrying out investigations, analysing/interpreting data, and warranting claims. Our algorithms were built and validated using middle school student data (Sao Pedro et al. 2010, 2012, 2013a, 2013b, 2014; Gobert et al. 2012, 2013, 2015; Moussavi et al. 2015, 2016a, 2016b; Moussavi 2016a, 2016b, 2018), and are robust across inquiry activities with diverse students and match human coders with high precision (84 to 99 percent; Sao Pedro et al. 2012, 2013a, 2013b, 2014); *scaffolds and pedagogical agents* hypothesising/question asking (Gobert et al. 2012), planning and carrying out investigations (Sao Pedro et al. 2013b), analysing and interpreting science data (Gobert et al. 2018), and warranting claims with evidence (Li et al. 2017a, 2017b, 2019; Gobert, Li & Dickler 2019), which have been shown to support robust transfer across topics and over long periods of time (Gobert et al. 2024a); *automated scoring of written Claim, Evidence, and Reasoning (CER)* using a variety of techniques including regular expressions and LLMs (Adair 2024), allowing us to identify students who are competent at inquiry but not good at describing what they know in words (false positives) and students who are simply parroting what they have read or heard but are not competent at conducting inquiry (false negatives; Gobert 2016); and *teacher reports*, including a class performance report with all sub-components for all practices, an assignment report, individual student detail, a lab report (to see all students' work), and a downloadable report.

Inq-Blotter Components

Inq-Blotter has the following components and features, enabling formative assessment and instruction of the practices (NGSS 2013). A *fully integrated, secure, cloud-based platform*, usable without any software installation that allows teachers to handle student accounts, view reports of students' work and assessments, and assign/preview labs; *Actionable alerts for inquiry practices across all 160+ Inq-ITS activities*; *Alert contextual information* allowing teachers to see information about students' challenges on a particular practice and its sub-components or skills; *Continually updated alerts that* appear automatically when students struggle during their investigations, which get resolved when the teacher marks them as "resolved", after helping a student, or automatically if the student's skill level in question improves without teacher help; *Class-wide alerts, which can be configured by the teacher from a settings menu,* fire when a large portion of the students in the class are having difficulty with a particular aspect of inquiry (that is, hypothesising, collecting data, or analysing data, etc.). Once such an alert is fired, a detailed alert screen is presented to the teacher that contains: (1) a visualisation and text description of how many students are struggling; and (2) a sorted list of students having the most difficulty. Given that it was found that teachers' strong didactic orientations towards content teaching presented a barrier to learning progression (LP)-based assessment practices (Covitt et al. 2018), a result we have also found in our earliest studies with

Inq-Blotter, we added TIPS (Teacher Inquiry practice Supports) (described below; Gobert 2019; Dickler 2021; Dickler et al. 2021a, 2021b, 2021c; Adair et al. 2020) to provide teachers with instructional supports for how they can help students when certain alerts are triggered by our assessment algorithms.

SUMMARY OF STUDIES ON INQ-ITS WITH INQ-BLOTTER

In our development of a dashboard to accompany Inq-ITS, we hypothesised that, by providing real-time alerts based on fine-grained data as to which students are struggling and on what specific sub-components for each science practice, teachers would be better equipped to support students in their developing competencies for each science practice (NGSS 2013). These data were borne out; that is, in a number of studies conducted both in class and in remote settings, we showed that the alerts helped teachers provide support to their students on the practices for which they were struggling, as evidenced by significant improvements demonstrated by the students who received help from their teachers compared to students who did not receive support (Dickler et al. 2019, 2021c). Providing further evidence of the benefits of Inq-Blotter's fine-grained alerts, Dickler et al. (2021c) showed that students who were helped by their teacher in response to an alert on their first Inq-ITS lab activity performed significantly better on their second Inq-ITS lab activity on the same topic with a different goal when compared to students who were not helped by their teacher on their first lab activity. Moreover, students who received help from their teacher in response to Inq-Blotter alerts on their first lab activity also did better on their third activity compared to students who were not helped.

As a next step, we analysed teachers' discourse collected in the studies above to examine whether it was focused on helping students with the science competency they were struggling with, and if so, what kind of support (orienting, conceptual, procedural, or instrumental help on the science competency; see Table 16.1), or whether the teachers' help focused on the scientific content addressed in the lab. Important to the current chapter, we found that the students' improvement on the science practices was largely dependent on the types of support that they received from their teacher. That is, students who did not improve on the science practices either received support on the scientific content in the lab rather than support on the science practice or received lower-level types of support on the science practices (Dickler et al. 2021c, 2021b; Gobert et al. 2024b); whereas for those students who showed improvement

Table 16.1 *Example of TIPS for the sub-practice of collecting controlled trials*

Type	TIPS
Orienting	'Let's take a look at your data. What data have you collected?'
Conceptual	'Remember, you should be running controlled trials. Controlled trials are when you only change one variable at a time'.
Procedural	'Which variable is the one that you should be changing?'
Instrumental	'You should only change the red dye'.

Source: Authors.

on subsequent activities, their teachers typically integrated more types of support directed at the science practices, such as procedural support (see Dickler et al. 2021c, 2021b for details).

Because these findings illustrated how the type of support mattered to students' improvement, we determined that there was a need for instructional supports to be embedded directly into the Inq-Blotter dashboard alerts so that the alerts could not only notify teachers of the difficulty the student was experiencing, but also provide guidance on how to support that student on the practices rather than on the content, as per the NGSS (2013). This work is also aligned and motivated by research that showed that teachers' tendency to be content-focused in their science instruction is an impediment to implementing instruction (Covitt et al. 2018) that is expected by more current frameworks such as the NGSS (2013). Thus, to help teachers provide support on the science inquiry practices assessed by Inq-ITS and alerted by Inq-Blotter, we developed the Teacher Inquiry Practice Supports (TIPS; Adair et al. 2020). TIPS are instructional supports that provide teachers with instructional strategies once they receive an alert about a student or a set of students. Within each alert, teachers can click through four levels of increasingly targeted suggestions for how to guide students on the practices, including: *orienting* TIPS (that is, helping direct student attention towards the practice of difficulty); *conceptual* TIPS (that is, explaining key components of the practice of difficulty); *procedural* TIPS (that is, outlining the steps involved in the practice of difficulty), and *instrumental* TIPS (that is, telling the student the exact steps needed to move forward). For example, if a student is failing to collect controlled trials (a fine-grained sub-practice of NGSS Practice 3: Planning and Carrying Out Investigations and a common type of difficulty with data collection; Chen and Klahr 1999) using the simulation in Inq-ITS, then a teacher would receive an alert stating, 'Paul is changing too many variables at once'. Table 16.1 shows the set of TIPS that the teacher would receive alongside this alert and could use to support their student in collecting controlled trials.

To develop the text of the TIPS messages, we analysed the teachers' discourse from the previous study (Dickler et al. 2019) to identify the high-quality discourse, that is, the support that the teachers provided to their students that led to students' improvement on the practices in subsequent investigations (Adair et al. 2020). For example, in our study presented in Dickler et al. (2019), students completed an Inq-ITS lab testing the effect of red dye on the redness of flower petals. When a student began to struggle with developing a hypothesis in the lab, the teacher received an alert on Inq-Blotter regarding that student's difficulty. To address the student's difficulty, the teacher said: 'So you have the red dye, right? Is that your independent or your dependent variable? … Is that what you're changing or what you're measuring?' In this example, the teacher intertwines two types of support by orienting the student to the type of variables to consider (that is, independent and dependent variables) and hinting at the conceptual definitions (that is, the independent variable is what the experimenter changes, and the dependent variable is what the experimenter measures). Further, the student who received this support from the teacher improved on their hypothesising competencies when assessed on a subsequent activity in Inq-ITS. Because of this improvement, we used the content of this support (as well as other high-quality supports that led to student improvement) to construct the TIPS messages for that practice, which would then be embedded in the future design iterations of the Inq-Blotter alerts.

Since the TIPS are based on high-quality supports that have been shown to improve students' competencies (Dickler et al. 2019; Adair et al. 2020), we hypothesised that the alerts coupled with TIPS (that is, alerts that simultaneously notify teachers of their students' difficulties and provide them guidance for how to support their students on those difficulties) could be effective at supporting teachers in supporting their students on the practices. In other words, we suspected that these TIPS could help teachers along a pedagogical learning progression in terms of refining their pedagogical content knowledge for inquiry (Magnusson et al. 1999), as evidenced by their use of more sophisticated combinations of higher-level inquiry supports in their discourse with their students.

To better understand how the TIPS could support teachers in their formative assessment and instructional discourse, we used Epistemic Network Analysis (ENA; Shaffer et al. 2016) to compare the discursive patterns of support from one teacher, Mrs. A, and to explore how those patterns differed when she was using the dashboard alerts without TIPS followed by with TIPS (Adair et al. 2022). Findings from this study showed that Mrs A. did in fact benefit from having TIPS available within the dashboard alerts, as evidenced by her more frequent usage of high-level inquiry supports (that is, conceptual and procedural supports) when addressing her students' difficulties upon receiving an alert (Adair et al. 2022). The ENA also revealed that Mrs A. interwove more sophisticated combinations of the different support types (for example, orienting, conceptual, etc.) when she received alerts with TIPS vs. the alerts without TIPS. The graphs of the subtracted networks (see Figure 16.1), which were generated using the ENA Web Tool (version 1.7.0; Marquart et al. 2018), show that conceptual and procedural supports co-occurred more often with the other types of inquiry support on Day 2 than on Day 1 (as evidenced by the stronger connection, or thicker lines, between the different support types, or nodes). That is, when responding to alerts with TIPS, the teacher used and integrated more of the different types of inquiry support than she did when responding to alerts without TIPS, demonstrating greater complexity of support appropriate for the sophistication of the practices.

Further, when asked about her usage of the TIPS in an informal follow-up interview, Mrs A. stated, 'In general it was helpful to remind me to not jump straight to giving kids the answer. I had a few kids surprise me. They figured things out on their own using the TIPS more often than I thought they would' (Mrs A. personal communication 2021). These results are promising evidence that TIPS can be an effective way to support teachers in growing their

Source: Authors.

Figure 16.1 *Discursive Support Networks Day 1 (without TIPS; left) vs. Day 2 (with TIPS; right)*

pedagogical content knowledge for inquiry (Magnusson et al. 1999; Yang et al. 2018) as well as their informal formative assessment practices (Ruiz-Primo and Furtak 2006), which are essential for fostering students' science inquiry learning. Moreover, this study shows how a computational method, such as ENA, can help researchers pinpoint empirical evidence of a teacher's learning progression of their pedagogical performance, such as in this case, where the teacher more richly integrates various types of inquiry support over time with help from fine-grained, real-time alerts of students' difficulties combined with instructional support from TIPS.

CONCLUSIONS

As stated earlier, our 'sub-component' approach to unpacking the NGSS practices is key to supporting teachers so they can better support their students' developing science competencies. Our Inq-ITS lab-based activities provide assessments that trigger alerts and, in turn, TIPS; these assessments leverage learning analytics (Kubsch et al. 2022) and produce formative data on students' competencies in science practices, alerts as to who is struggling in what specific ways, and TIPS as to how to support students, all in real time, and at scale. In our work described here, we have chosen not to specify a learning progression per se for each of the NGSS practices (as some have done; see Jin et al. 2025).

We have chosen this approach for a number of reasons. First, there are many studies suggesting that teachers are not well equipped (yet) to effectively implement LPs (see our earlier review of these). Second, there is no consistency across researchers' views of LPs, and some propose that there are multiple possible progressions or pathways that students exhibit; thus, their learning is not likely to progress in lock-step fashion, with some students in the 'messy middle' (Gotwals and Songer 2010), as we have also found (Li et al. 2017a). Lastly, some students' performance on tasks could be context-dependent (Black et al. 2011). Furthermore, there is variation in what districts expect at the end of each grade level, which can depend on a variety of factors (for example, Tyler and Britton 2018), and we have found a great deal of variation in the way that teachers integrate the practices with the science content in their classrooms, which is corroborated by other recent literature as well (for example, Park et al. 2022).

In our work described here, we sought to operationalise the sub-components underlying each of the practices (NGSS 2013) and then design technology-based resources at a fine-grained level of specificity to support different pedagogical practices. For formative assessment purposes, our reports serve to support standards (NGSS 2013) and structure assessment (Alonzo et al. 2012; Furtak et al. 2014; Yin et al. 2013) by providing teachers with rigorous indicators of students' competencies (Alonzo 2011) that can serve to diagnose students' difficulties and understanding (Corcoran et al. 2009; Yin et al. 2013). In addition, our whole class reports make it easier to address common learning difficulties and change whole class instruction on the fly (Furtak 2012), as well as adapt instruction to meet individual students' needs (Corcoran et al. 2009; Furtak et al. 2014) or do differentiated instruction. Our alerts support instruction (Foster and Wiser 2012) by permitting teachers to monitor students (Liu and Jackson 2019) in real time during instruction, and our TIPS (Teacher Inquiry Practice Supports) embedded in the alerts inform interactions with students in the classroom and provide conceptual guidance for students' ideas (Berland and McNeill 2010; Furtak 2012; Shea and Duncan 2013). Further, our teacher dashboard, Inq-Blotter, along with its alerts and TIPS, has been used by teachers and administrators in actionable and creative ways to understand how students are progressing on these practice-centred learning targets and, in turn, inform instruction that has led to demonstrable student growth on the scientific practices needed for inquiry, as described earlier, and in other work (Dickler et al. 2021c, 2021b; Dickler 2021). Instead of being 'locked in' to a specific learning progression, teachers can use the data, alerts, and TIPS in a way that suits the goals of their individual classrooms and students, varying them as needed instructionally throughout the school year. While the NGSS documents (2013) provide high-level guidance on the expectations of students at the end of large grade bands (for example, expectations for Grades 6–8 vs. Grades 9–12; see Appendix F in NGSS 2013), these are not specified at the level that is actionable for teachers in designing lessons and understanding their students' progress throughout a full school year.

Inq-Blotter is unique in both its capacity to provide alerts based on formative assessment data and its capacity to support teachers in monitoring students (Liu and Jackson 2019) in real time. Inq-Blotter's alerts and the addition of TIPS provide real-time technological support for assessment conversations (Duschl and Gitomer 1997; Ruiz-Primo and Furtak 2007), both closing the formative assessment loop and orchestrating learning (Prieto et al. 2011; Berland and McNeill 2010; Furtak 2012; Shea and Duncan 2013) on a whole class level when the teacher gets an alert that many students are struggling with the same practice, for differentiated instruction to small groups of students who are struggling with the same practice, or to an individual student who is at risk of falling behind their peers. One teacher said, 'Inq-Blotter provides a crystal ball to know exactly when and how each student is struggling as they work. Before I used your system, I thought that students were poor at interpreting data, but using your reports and alerts, I know now that many students are collecting confounded data that cannot be interpreted' (N. Foote, personal communication, 2017). An instructional coach succinctly described the benefits of our alerting dashboard as follows:

> Before, when I was in the classroom, students would raise their hands. I'd have to go over... spend time orienting. That means I'd have to read over their work, look to see where they are in their work, and make that assessment. And that will take time. But now, using Inq-ITS, I get that information right from the dashboard. I can see exactly what they're struggling with. I know exactly what to do to get them on track. I'm able to get to many more students in the classroom than I was prior to using it. (M. Castronova, personal communication 2025; NSTA TV Film Series 2025)

ACKNOWLEDGEMENT

This research was funded by the National Science Foundation (IIS- 1902647 & IIS-1629045) and by the SBIR program of the IES/US Dept. of Education (ED-IES-15-C-0018, ED-IES-16-C-0014). Any opinions, findings, etc., expressed are those of the authors and do not necessarily reflect those of the fundings agencies.

REFERENCES

Adair, A. (2024), *AI-driven assessment and scaffolding for mathematical modeling and explanations during science investigations.* Doctoral dissertation, Rutgers The State University of New Jersey, School of Graduate Studies. ProQuest Dissertations Publishing.

Adair, A., R. Dickler and J. Gobert (2020), 'Supporting teachers supporting students: Iterative development of TIPS in a teacher dashboard', in M. Gresalfi and I.S. Horn (eds), *14th International Conference of the Learning Sciences, Volume 3*, International Society of the Learning Sciences, pp. 1969–70.

Adair, A., J. Owens and J. Gobert (2022), 'Using epistemic network analysis to explore discourse patterns across design iterations of a teacher dashboard', in C. Chinn, E. Tan, C. Chan and Y. Kali (eds), *16th International Conference of the Learning Sciences – ICLS 2022*, International Society of the Learning Sciences, pp. 297–304. https://dx.doi.org/10.22318/icls2022.297

Alonzo, A.C. (2011), 'Learning progressions that support formative assessment practices', *Measurement: Interdisciplinary Research and Perspectives*, **9**, 124–9. doi:10.1080/15366367.2011.599629

Alonzo, A.C. and A. Elby (2019), 'Beyond empirical adequacy: Learning progressions as models and their value for teachers', *Cognition and Instruction*, **37** (1), 1–37.

Alonzo, A.C., T. Neidorf and C.W. Anderson (2012), 'Using learning progressions to inform large-scale assessment', in A.C. Alonzo and A.W. Gotwals (eds), *Learning progressions in science*, Sense Publishers, pp. 211–40.

American Association for the Advancement of Science (AAAS) (1989), *Science for all Americans,* Oxford University Press.

American Association for the Advancement of Science (AAAS) (1993), *Benchmarks for science literacy.* Oxford University Press.

Bereiter, C. and M. Scardamalia (1985 [2013]), 'Cognitive coping strategies and the problem of inert knowledge', in S. Chipman, J. Segal and R. Glaser (eds), *Thinking and learning skills* (Vol. 2), Routledge, pp. 65–80.

Berland, L.K. and K.L. McNeill (2010), 'A learning progression for scientific argumentation: Understanding student work and designing supportive instructional contexts', *Science Education*, **94** (5), 765–93.

Bianchini, J.A., N. Yestness, K.J. Nilsen, J. Kim, L.M. Hammond, S. Carpenter, T. Irish, S.D. Parker and A.R. Berkowitz (2014), *Learning progression-based teaching strategies in environmental science: Teachers' successes and struggles in implementation*, NARST Annual International Conference, Pittsburgh, PA.

Black, P., M. Wilson, M. and S.Y. Yao (2011), 'Road maps for learning: A guide to the navigation of learning progressions', *Measurement: Interdisciplinary Research Perspective*, **9** (2–3), 71–123.

Castronova, M. (2025), 'Personal communication.

Chen, Z. and D. Klahr (1999), 'All other things being equal: Acquisition and transfer of the control of variables strategy', *Child Development*, **70** (5), 1098–1120.

Clarke-Midura, J., J. Code, C. Dede, M. Mayrath and N. Zap (2012), 'Thinking outside the bubble: Virtual performance assessments for measuring complex learning, in M.C. Mayrath, J. Clarke-Midura, D.H. Robinson and G. Schraw (eds), *Technology-based assessments for 21st century skills: Theoretical and practical implications from modern research*, Information Age Publishers, pp. 125–48.

Corcoran, T., F.A. Mosher and A. Rogat (2009), 'Learning progressions in science: An evidence-based approach to reform', CPRE Research Report #RR-63, Consortium for Policy Research in Education.

Covitt, B.A., K.L. Gunckel, B. Caplan and S. Syswerda (2018), 'Teachers' use of learning progression-based formative assessment in water instruction', *Applied Measurement in Education*, **31** (2), 128–42.

Dickler, R. (2021), *An intelligent tutoring system and teacher dashboard to support students on mathematics in mathematics and science inquiry.* Publication No. 28643659. Doctoral dissertation, Rutgers The State University of New Jersey, School of Graduate Studies. ProQuest Dissertations Publishing.

Dickler, R., A. Adair, J.D. Gobert, H. Hussian-Abidi, J. Olsen, M. O'Brien and M.A. Sao Pedro (2021a), 'Examining the use of a teacher alerting dashboard during remote learning', in I. Roll, D. McNamara,

S. Sosnovsky, R. Luckin and V. Dimitrova (eds), *International conference on artificial intelligence in education*, Springer, Cham, pp. 134–38.

Dickler, R., J.D. Gobert, A. Adair and J. Olsen (2021b), *Using a teacher dashboard to support students remotely on science inquiry.* Conference presentation, Society for Text and Discourse, virtual.

Dickler, R., J.D. Gobert and M.A. Sao Pedro (2021c), 'Using innovative methods to explore the potential of an alerting dashboard for science inquiry', *Journal of Learning Analytics*, **8** (2), 105–22.

Dickler, R., J.D. Gobert and M.A. Sao Pedro (2019), *Using epistemic network analysis to characterize teacher discourse in response to an alerting dashboard.* Conference presentation, Society for Text and Discourse, New York, NY.

Duncan, R.G. and A.E. Rivet (2013), 'Science learning progressions', *Science*, **339** (6118), 396–7.

Duncan, R.G. and C.E. Hmelo-Silver (2009), 'Learning progressions: Aligning curriculum, instruction, and assessment', *Journal of Research in Science Teaching: The Official Journal of the National Association for Research in Science Teaching*, **46** (6), 606–9.

Duschl, R.A. and D.H. Gitomer (1997), 'Strategies and challenges to changing the focus of assessment and instruction in science classrooms', *Educational Assessment*, **4** (1), 37–73. doi:10.1207/s15326977ea0401_2

Duschl, R., S. Maeng and A. Sezen (2011), 'Learning progressions and teaching sequences: A review and analysis', *Studies in Science Education*, **47** (2), 123–82.

Foote, N. (2017), Testimonial about Inq-ITS in Front Page with James Earl Jones Film Series.

Foster, J. and M. Wiser (2012), 'The potential of learning progression research to inform the design of state science standards', in A.C. Alonzo and A.W. Gotwals (eds), *Learning progressions in science*, Sense Publishers, pp. 435–459.

Furtak, E.M. (2012), 'Linking a learning progression for natural selection to teachers' enactment of formative assessment', *Journal of Research in Science Teaching*, **49** (9), 1181–1210.

Furtak, E.M. and S.C. Heredia (2014), 'Exploring the influence of learning progressions in two teacher communities', *Journal of Research in Science Teaching*, **51**, 982–1020. doi:10.1002/tea.21156

Furtak, E.M., D. Morrison and H. Kroog (2014), 'Investigating the link between learning progressions and classroom assessment', *Science Education*, **98**, 640–73.

Furtak, E.M., J. Thompson and B. Van Es (2016), *Formative assessment and noticing: Toward a synthesized framework for attending and responding during instruction.* Presented at the Annual Meeting of the American Educational Research Association, Washington, D.C. doi:10.13140/RG.2.1.3471.1443

Furtak, E.M., K. Kiemer, R. Swanson, V. de León and R.K. Circi (2015), *Learning progressions, formative assessment, and professional development: Results of a longitudinal study.* NARST Annual International Conference, Chicago, IL.

Gobert, J.D. (2016, May 13), 'Op-Ed: Educational data mining can enhance science education', *US News World Report.* https://www.usnews.com/news/articles/2016-05-13/op-ed-educational-data-mining-can-enhance-science-education

Gobert, J.D. (2019), 'Inq-Blotter: Designing Supports for Teachers' Real Time Instruction'. Awarded from the National Science Foundation (NSF-IIS-1902647).

Gobert J.D. and M.A. Sao Pedro (2016), 'Inq-Blotter - A Real Time Alerting Tool to Transform Teachers' Assessment of Science Inquiry Practices'. Awarded August 2016 from the National Science Foundation (NSF-IIS-1629045).

Gobert, J.D. and M.A. Sao Pedro (2017), 'Digital assessment environments for scientific inquiry practices', in A.A. Rupp and J. P. Leighton (eds), *The Wiley handbook of cognition and assessment: Frameworks, methodologies, and applications,* John Wiley & Sons, pp. 508–534.

Gobert, J.D., H. Li and R. Dickler (2019), 'Dusting off the messy middle: Comparing students' science investigation competencies with their writing competencies', presented at the *3rd International Conference on AI + Adaptive Education.*

Gobert, J.D., H. Li, R. Dickler and C. Lott (2024a), 'Can AI-based scaffolding promote students' robust learning of authentic science practices?', in X. Zhai and J. Krajcik (eds), *Uses of artificial intelligence in STEM education*, Oxford University Press pp. 250–268. doi:10.1093/oso/9780198882077.003.0012

Gobert, J.D., M.A. Sao Pedro and C.G. Betts (2023), 'An AI-based teacher dashboard to support students' inquiry: Design principles, features, and technological specifications', in N. Lederman, D. Zeidler and J. Lederman (eds), *Handbook of research on science education*, Routledge, pp. 1011–1044.

Gobert, J.D., M.A. Sao Pedro, C. Betts and R.S. Baker (2017, February), *Inquiry skills tutoring system (child patent for additional claims to Inq-ITS).* US Patent no. 9,564,057 (issued).
Gobert, J.D., M.A. Sao Pedro, C. Betts and R.S. Baker (2019, January), *Inquiry skills tutoring system (child patent for alerting system).* US Patent no. 10,186,168 (issued).
Gobert, J.D., M.A. Sao Pedro, J. Raziuddin and R.S. Baker (2013), 'From log files to assessment metrics: Measuring students' science inquiry skills using educational data mining', *Journal of the Learning Sciences*, **22** (4), 521–63.
Gobert, J.D., M.A. Sao Pedro, R.S. Baker, E. Toto and O. Montalvo (2012), 'Leveraging educational data mining for real-time performance assessment of scientific inquiry skills within microworlds', *JEDM-Journal of Educational Data Mining*, **4** (1), 111–43.
Gobert, J.D., R. Dickler and A. Adair. (2024b), 'Using an AI-based dashboard to help teachers support students' learning progressions for science practices', in H. Jin, D. Yan and J. Krajcik (eds), *Handbook of research on science learning progressions*, Taylor & Francis Group. https://doi.org/10.4324/9781003170785
Gobert, J.D., R. Moussavi, H. Li, M.A. Sao Pedro and R. Dickler (2018), 'Real-time scaffolding of students' online data interpretation during inquiry with Inq-ITS using educational data mining', in A.K.M. Azad, M. Auer, A. Edwards and T. de Jong (eds), *Cyber-physical laboratories in engineering and science education*, Springer, pp. 191–217.
Gobert, J.D., R.S. Baker and M.A. Sao Pedro, (2016, June), *Inquiry skills tutoring system.* US Patent no. 9,373,082 (issued).
Gobert, J.D., Y.J. Kim, M.A. Sao Pedro, M. Kennedy and C.G. Betts (2015), 'Using educational data mining to assess students' skills at designing and conducting experiments within a complex systems microworld', *Thinking Skills and Creativity*, **18**, 81–90.
Gotwals, A.W. and N.B. Songer (2010), 'Reasoning up and down a food chain: Using an assessment framework to investigate students' middle knowledge', *Science Education*, **94** (2), 259–81.
Gotwals, A.W. and N.B. Songe (2013), 'Validity evidence for learning progression-based assessment items that fuse core disciplinary ideas and science practices', *Journal of Research in Science Teaching*, **50** (5), 597–626.
Harris, C.J., J.S. Krajcik, J.W. Pellegrino and K.W. McElhaney (2016), *Constructing assessment tasks that blend disciplinary core ideas, crosscutting concepts, and science practices for classroom formative applications,* SRI International. https://www.sri.com/wp-content/uploads/2021/12/constructing_assessment_tasks_2016.pdf
Hedin, L. and S. DeSpain (2018), 'SMART or not? Writing specific, measurable IEP goals', *TEACHING Exceptional Children*, **51** (2), 100–110.
Jin, H., C. Delgado, M.I. Bauer, E.C. Wylie, D. Cisterna and K.F. Llort (2019a), 'A hypothetical learning progression for quantifying phenomena in science', *Science & Education*, **28** (9), 1181–208.
Jin, H., J.N. Mikeska, H. Hokayem and E. Mavronikola (2019b), 'Toward coherence in curriculum, instruction, and assessment: A review of learning progression literature', *Science Education*, **103** (5), 1206–34.
Jin, H., D. Yan and J. Krajcik (eds) (2025), *Handbook of research on science learning progressions.* Routledge.
Koedinger, K. and A. Corbett (2006), 'Cognitive tutors: Technology bringing learning sciences to the classroom', in R. Sawyer (ed.), *The Cambridge handbook of the learning sciences*, Cambridge University Press, pp. 61–77,
Kubsch, M., B. Czinczel, J. Lossjew, T. Wyrwich, D. Bednorz, S. Bernholt … and N. Rummel (2022, August), 'Toward learning progression analytics: Developing learning environments for the automated analysis of learning using evidence centered design', *Frontiers in Education*, **7**, 981910.
Kuhn, D. (2005), *Education for thinking.* Harvard University Press.
Kuhn, D., L. Schauble and M. Garcia-Mila (1992), 'Cross-domain development of scientific reasoning', *Cognition and Instruction*, **9** (4), 285–327.
Li, H., J.D. Gobert and R. Dickler (2017a), 'Dusting off the messy middle: Assessing students' inquiry skills through doing and writing', in E. André, R. Baker, X. Hu, M. Rodrigo and B. du Boulay (eds), *Artificial intelligence in education. AIED 2017.* Lecture Notes in Computer Science (Vol. 10331), Springer, Cham, pp. 175–87.

Li, H., J.D. Gobert and R. Dickler (2017b), 'Automated assessment for scientific explanations in on-line science inquiry', in A. Hershkovitz and L. Paquette (eds), *Proceedings of the 10th International Conference on Educational Data Mining*, EDM Society, pp. 214–19.

Li, H., J.D. Gobert and R. Dickler (2017c), *Analyzing the sub-skills underlying students' scientific claims, evidence, and reasoning during inquiry.* Presented at the 27th Annual Meeting of the Society for Text and Discourse, Philadelphia, PA.

Li, H., J.D. Gobert and R. Dickler (2019), 'Evaluating the transfer of scaffolded inquiry: What sticks and does it last?', in S. Isotani, E. Millán, A. Ogan, P. Hastings, B. McLaren and R. Luckin (eds), *Artificial intelligence in education*, Springer, Cham, pp. 163–68.

Liu, L. and T. Jackson (2019), 'A recent review of learning progressions in science: Gaps and shifts', *The Educational Review, USA*, **3** (9), 113–26.

Lobato, J. and C.D Walters (2017), 'A taxonomy of approaches to learning trajectories and progressions', in J. Cai (ed.), *Compendium for research in mathematics education*, The National Council of Teachers of Mathematics, pp. 74–101.

Magnusson, S.J., H. Borko and J.S. Krajcik (1999), 'Nature, sources, and development of pedagogical content knowledge for science teaching' in J. Gess-Newsome and N.G. Lederman (eds), *Examining pedagogical content knowledge,* Springer Dordrecht, pp. 95–132.

Marquart, C.L., C. Hinojosa, Z. Swiecki, B. Eagan and D.W. Shaffer (2018), *Epistemic network analysis* (Version 1.7.0) [Software]. http://app.epistemicnetwork.org

Martinez-Maldonado, R., A. Claphan and J. Kay (2015), 'Deploying and visualizing teacher's scripts of small group activities in a multi-surface classroom ecology: A study-in-the-wild', *Computer-supportive Cooperative Work*, **24**, 177–221, doi:10.1007/s10606-015-9217-6

McNeill, K.L. and J.S. Krajcik (2011), *Supporting grade 5–8 students in constructing explanations in science: The claim, evidence, and reasoning framework for talk and writing.* Pearson.

Mislevy, R.J. (2013), 'Evidence-centered design for simulation-based assessment', *Military Medicine*, **178** (10), 107–14.

Mislevy, R.J., J.T. Behrens, K.E. DiCerbo and R. Levy (2012), 'Design and discovery in educational assessment: Evidence centered design, psychometrics, and data mining', *Journal of Educational Data Mining*, **4** (1), 11–48.

Moussavi, R., M. Kennedy, M.A. Sao Pedro and J.D. Gobert (2015), 'Evaluating a scaffolding design to support students' data interpretation skills within a simulation-based inquiry environment', presented at the Annual Meeting of the American Education Research Association.

Moussavi, R., J.D. Gobert and M.A. Sao Pedro (2016a), 'The effect of scaffolding on the immediate transfer of students' data interpretation skills within science topics', in *Proceedings of the 12th International Conference of the Learning Sciences* (pp. 1002–6).

Moussavi, R., M.A. Sao Pedro and J.D. Gobert (2016b), 'Evaluating the efficacy of real-time scaffolding for data interpretation skills', presented at the Annual Meeting of the American Education Research Association.

Moussavi, R. (2018), *Design, development, and evaluation of scaffolds for data interpretation practices during inquiry* [Doctoral dissertation]. Worcester Polytechnic Institute.

National Research Council (2006), *Systems for state science assessment.* National Academies Press. https://doi.org/10.17226/11312

National Research Council (2007), *Taking science to school: Learning and teaching science in grades K–8.* National Academies Press. https://doi.org/10.17226/11625

National Research Council (2012), *A framework for K–12 science education: Practices, crosscutting concepts, and core ideas.* National Academies Press.

NGSS Lead States (2013), *Next Generation Science Standards: For states, by states.* National Academies Press.

NSTA TV Film Series (2025, March), *Inq-ITS: Real AI in Real time – Apprendis LLC & Rutgers Graduate School of Education* [Video]. National Science Teachers Association.

OECD (2018), *The future of education and skills: Education 2030 the future we want* [Position paper]. OECD Publishing.

OECD (2023), *PISA 2022 results (volume I).* OECD.

Park, S., V. Kite, J.K. Suh, J. Jung and A. Rachmatullah (2022), 'Investigation of the relationships among science teachers' epistemic orientations, epistemic understanding, and implementation of

Next Generation Science Standards science practices', *Journal of Research in Science Teaching*, **59** (4), 561–84.
Prieto, L.P., M. Holenko Dlab, I. Gutiérrez, M. Abdulwahed and W. Balid (2011), 'Orchestrating technology enhanced learning: A literature review and a conceptual framework', *International Journal of Technology Enhanced Learning*, **3** (6), 583–98.
Ruiz-Primo, M.A. and E.M. Furtak (2006), 'Informal formative assessment and scientific inquiry: Exploring teachers' practices and student learning', *Educational Assessment*, **11**, 205–35.
Ruiz-Primo, M.A. and E.M. Furtak (2007), 'Exploring teachers' informal formative assessment practices and students' understanding in the context of scientific inquiry', *Journal of Research in Science Teaching*, **44** (1), 57–84.
Sao Pedro, M.A. (2015), 'Inq-Blotter: Revolutionizing how teachers identify and support students needing help during inquiry', SBIR Phase I, awarded by IES program.
Sao Pedro, M.A. (2016), 'Recognizing how teachers identify and support students needing help during inquiry', SBIR Phase II, awarded by IES program.
Sao Pedro, M.A., R.S.J.D. Baker and J.D. Gobert (2012), 'Improving construct validity yields better models of systematic inquiry, even with less information', in *User Modeling, Adaptation, and Personalization: 20th International Conference*, Springer, pp. 249–60.
Sao Pedro, M.A., R.S.J.D. Baker and J.D. Gobert (2013b), 'What different kinds of stratification can reveal about the generalizability of data-mined skill assessment models', In *Proceedings of the Third International Conference on Learning Analytics and Knowledge*, ACM, pp. 190–4.
Sao Pedro, M.A., R.S.J.D. Baker, J.D. Gobert, O. Montalvo and A. Nakama (2013a), 'Leveraging machine-learned detectors of systematic inquiry behavior to estimate and predict transfer of inquiry skill', *User Modeling and User-Adapted Interaction*, **23** (1), 1–39.
Sao Pedro, M.A., R.S.J.D. Baker, O. Montalvo, A. Nakama, A. and J.D. Gobert (2010), 'Using text replay tagging to produce detectors of systematic experimentation behavior patterns', in R. Baker, A. Merceron and P. Pavlik (eds), *Proceedings of the 3rd International Conference on Educational Data Mining*, EDM, pp. 181–90.
Sao Pedro, M.A., J.D. Gobert and C.G. Betts (2014, June), 'Towards scalable assessment of performance-based skills: Generalizing a detector of systematic science inquiry to a simulation with a complex structure, in *International Conference on Intelligent Tutoring System*, Springer, pp. 591–600.
Shaffer, D.W., C. Collier and A.R. Ruis (2016), 'A tutorial on epistemic network analysis: Analyzing the structure of connections in cognitive, social, and interaction data', *Journal of Learning Analytics*, **3** (3), 9–45. https://doi.org/10.18608/jla.2016.33.3
Shea, N.A. and R.G. Duncan (2013), 'From theory to data: The process of refining learning progressions', *Journal of the Learning Sciences*, **22** (1), 7–32.
Shute, V.J. (2011), 'Stealth assessment in computer-based games to support learning', *Computer Games and Instruction*, **55** (2), 503–24.
Sikorski, T.R., V. Winters and D. Hammer (2009, June), *Defining learning progressions for scientific inquiry.* Conference presentation. Learning Progressions in Science (LeaPS) Conference, Iowa City, IA.
Smith, C.L., M. Wiser and D.W. Carraher (2010, March), *Using a comparative, longitudinal study with upper elementary school students to test some assumptions of a learning progression for matter.* Conference presentation, Annual Meeting of the National Association for Research on Science Teaching, Philadelphia, PA.
Songer, N.B., B. Kelcey and A.W. Gotwals (2009), 'How and when does complex reasoning occur? Empirically driven development of a learning progression focused on complex reasoning about biodiversity', *Journal of Research in Science Teaching*, **46** (6), 610–31.
Tyler, B. and T. Britton (2018), *Developing district plans for NGSS implementation: Preventing detours and finding express lanes on the journey to implement the new science standards.* WestEd.
Wiser, M., C.L. Smith and S. Doubler (2012), 'Learning progressions as tools for curriculum development: Lessons from the Inquiry Project', in A.C. Alonzo and A.W. Gotwals (eds), *Learning progressions in science*, Brill, pp. 357–403.

Yang, Y., X. Liu and J.A. Gardella Jr (2018), 'Effects of professional development on teacher pedagogical content knowledge, inquiry teaching practices, and student understanding of interdisciplinary science', *Journal of Science Teacher Education*, **29** (4), 263–82.
Yin, Y., M.K. Tomita and R.J. Shavelson (2013), 'Using formal embedded formative assessments aligned with a short-term learning progression to promote conceptual change and achievement in science', *International Journal of Science Education*, **36**, 531–52.

PART V

PROMOTING IMPLEMENTATION

17. Navigating learning analytics: challenges, opportunities, and recommendations

Marte Blikstad-Balas

SETTING THE STAGE: WHY SHOULD WE CARE ABOUT WHAT HAPPENS IN NORWAY?

Norway has been a frontrunner when it comes to digital technology in education, with decades of high curricular ambitions aimed at developing students' digital competence, and a technological infrastructure where most schools have 1:1 access. Since 2006, digital competence has been an integrated part of the curriculum in all school subjects at all levels (Erstad 2006). However, we also know that the uptake of digital hardware and software varies greatly between teachers, and that it has been up to each teacher individually to develop good teaching practices drawing on digital technology (Blikstad-Balas and Klette 2020; Kongsgården and Krumsvik 2016; Kure, Brevik and Blikstad-Balas 2023). This means that even within the same school, there may be great variation in how the teachers actually use the digital infrastructure and digital tools they have available. Teacher education has not been able to prioritise the development of the teacher candidates' digital skills. Instefjord and Munthe (2017) identified that only 35% of Norwegian teacher educators considered themselves to be good role models when it comes to the use of digital technology in teaching. In an analysis of the emphasis on digital competence in teacher education curricula, they also found that preparing teachers for technology use did not have a prominent position in teacher education (Instefjord and Munthe 2016). The Teaching and Learning International Survey (TALIS) shows that the main area in which Norwegian teachers have a strong need for professional development is the successful uptake of digital technology in their teaching (Throndsen, Carlsten and Björnsson 2019). Access alone has not been enough to promote good use of digital technologies in ways that support learning in specific subjects.

During the global COVID-19 pandemic, Norway's view of itself as a digital frontrunner took a severe hit: while schools were able to transition from physical to digital education overnight due to a good digital infrastructure, it became evident that not all teachers and students were prepared to capitalise on access to technology and adapt their teaching to a digital format with online teaching. Studies have found that many Norwegian students spent their days solving individual tasks alone on their learning platform, and they had minimal guidance from their teachers (Blikstad-Balas 2023; Blikstad-Balas et al. 2022). In other words, students were asked to use technology for individual tasks, rather than for real-time collaboration. The consequences of the rather long period of digital, individual schooling on digital platforms are increased inequality (Blikstad-Balas 2023; Vennerød-Diesen et al. 2024).

Norway should be interesting to anyone who is concerned with digitalisation, as the discrepancy between the high digital hopes of becoming the best country in the world to adopt technology in education (Klausen 2023) and the actual, documented practices is evident. The Norwegian context serves as a good example of how providing each student with their own digital device and having high curricular ambitions are not the same as actually increasing or systematically developing their digital competence or using technology in ways that improve learning. This essential point is established even before we start the discussion on learning analytics – and as we will soon see, it will have severe implications also for that discussion.

The issue in Norway, and many other school systems, is not really whether we should digitalise education and adopt digital technologies in schools and higher education. We already have, and it is difficult to imagine a student in any grade going through an entire school day with zero use of digital technology. Even if the students are not using specific apps in the classroom, a majority of the communication between the school and the home is digital, through different digital platforms and systems. Thus, the question is not whether we should collect digital data on students' actions, as this is also done every single day. The big questions are not about digitalisation per se, but about what roles technology and learning analytics can play in supporting students' learning, and what aspects of the teachers', students', administrators' and school owners' everyday actions we want technology to support, change, or even challenge. These questions are relevant every time a student logs into any kind of digital platform, app, or device – across countries.

LEARNING ANALYTICS IN EDUCATION – AN EXPERT ASSESSMENT

In 2021, the Norwegian Ministry of Education and Research appointed an Expert Group to assess what they called 'digital learning analytics' in primary and secondary education and training, as well as in tertiary education and higher education. The Expert Group consisted of experts in education, ethics, technology and law,[1] and I was the appointed Chair of it. In their mandate, the Expert Group was asked to provide the Norwegian Ministry of Education and Research with a better basis for decisions regarding learning analytics and adaptive tools. It should also advise on the need for regulation and input to policy development.

The Expert Group was asked to deliver a so-called Official Norwegian Report (hereafter, ONR). This is a formal report commissioned by the government or a ministry to investigate and provide research-based recommendations on various societal issues. The main purpose of an ONR is to present knowledge and discuss possible actions or strategies for addressing public issues. The findings and recommendations in an ONR report typically lead to further political discussions and may result in a parliamentary white paper. ONRs cover a wide range of topics, from climate and environment to education and social policies. They play a crucial role in shaping public policy in Norway.

The ONR on learning analytics was the first national report looking into the use of students' digital data for learning purposes. It should be noted that the Expert Group was asked to consider pedagogical, ethical, and legal issues as well as data protection considerations. These issues are often discussed in isolation, and the Expert Group behind ONR 2023:19 was the first to be explicitly tasked to discuss these issues in a more holistic way.

In addition to assessing pedagogical and ethical issues, as well as legal issues and issues concerning data protection, the mandate stated that the Expert Group should advise on the need for the development of legislation for the different levels of the educational system. Further, the work should include an assessment of future opportunities relating to learning analytics, and input on how good learning analytics practices could be developed in accordance with ethical and pedagogical standards and applicable legislation. The group delivered two reports, one interim report looking into dilemmas in learning analytics (see Wasson et al. 2024 for an English account of the interim report), and the final ONR 2023: 19, available in Norwegian and English versions. An explicit premise for the work of the Expert Group is that learning analytics can never be seen solely as a technological phenomenon. Learning analytics is understood as the analysis of learning for learning, and this is a process. As the group explains, there cannot be 'an obvious, static path from the collected data to fulfilling the ambition of enhanced learning' (ONR 2023: 19, p. 12). The group also points out that while they see the human aspects of using technology as the most decisive, there is also a risk associated with failing to consider the technological potential and opportunities that learning analytics offers. Thus, the report aimed to explore and discuss both the potential and perils of learning analytics and provide policy recommendations about the use and potential of it.

It can be challenging to separate discussions about learning analytics from broader discussions on digitalisation in general. A main reason for this is that the term 'learning analytics' in itself is rarely used in the Norwegian education systems, and even the few people who actually use data from different applications and processes to inform their teaching going forward (in line with definitions of learning analytics), may not label what they do as drawing on learning analytics – perhaps due to a lack of awareness of what constitutes learning analytics in the first place. Interestingly, the Expert Group identified a related term that may be overused, namely 'adaptivity'. While adaptivity in a learning analytics context has a very specific meaning, the Expert Group found many teachers and school leaders in their work who would label any kind of adaptation (also happening outside a digital process) as 'adaptive learning' or 'adaptivity' (ONR 2023: 19). For example, they would refer to it as adaptivity if a teacher chose to change a task, a text or even the instructional format for one or more of their students. Thus, an important discovery in the ONR is that the concept of learning analytics plays a marginal role in the everyday discourse of teachers and school leaders.

DILEMMAS IN LEARNING ANALYTICS: THE INTERIM REPORT

As in all questions regarding education, there is no easy yes or no answer to whether learning analytics can or even should play a central role in teaching in classrooms, and under what circumstances this would be desirable. The interim report (Wasson et al. 2024) presents four central dilemmas that are intended to capture the essence of the possibilities and challenges in the adoption of learning analytics. I will briefly mention them here as a backdrop for the upcoming recommendations on learning analytics provided in the final report from the Expert Group.

The first dilemma concerns the very difficult balance between the ever-existing need for information about the learning process and the unquestionable and fundamental right students have to data protection and privacy. Teachers have always needed information about their students' learning, but prior to digitalising everyday school activities, it was much clearer what information students were providing – and perhaps also for what purposes. Key issues here revolve around how much information we need about each student's learning process, when students should be allowed to 'opt out' (or even better, 'opt in') from being monitored, and how we can ensure that we follow up each student based on actual information about their competences and needs while at the same time following principles of data minimisation.

This dilemma also concerns the blurring of boundaries between the school day and students' private lives, as all their digital learning environments are with them at all times through their phones or laptops, and communication between the school and the student is no longer bound by physical presence in the same room. Further, this dilemma asks questions about whether we can know that the information we get from learning analytics provides an accurate picture of students' learning, and specifically, the Expert Group addresses the risk that the information we get from learning analytics is based on students' actions and efforts, not a valid assessment of their achievement or subject competence.

The second dilemma concerns the gap between the generally agreed-upon view on learning as a sociocultural and collective endeavour, and the tendency of learning analytics to emphasise individuals' personal learning trajectories. A main critique of learning analytics is that it is reductionist and only captures, at best, a limited glimpse of students' actual learning. There is a concern that learning analytics may prioritise individual and quantifiable results, in selected and measurable subject areas, greatly narrowing the educational mission. If we want learning analytics to provide data about more than drill and practice and narrow learning goals, we need learning analytics that actually underpins an active and exploratory approach to learning where there is room to try and fail and improve over time. This probably means a very different kind of learning analytics than the majority available at scale today.

The third dilemma is about where decisions on learning analytics should be made, namely, the issue of centralisation versus autonomy. Which decisions about learning analytics should be centralised, and which decisions should always be made close to each local context and those providing and assessing the data? Today, many schools, colleges, universities and municipalities spend a great amount of time and effort assessing the soundness and legality of different technologies that enable learning analytics. The same questions are addressed over and over again in these legal assessments, and centralisation could make these decisions better and in a more time-efficient way. However, central decision-making on particular legality and the General Data Protection Regulation (GDPR) compliance of different digital technologies and apps may give the impression that these products have been 'approved' by central authorities once and for all, regardless of actual use. Another big issue is whether developing a central digital ecosystem in the public sector would benefit the largest actors and hinder innovation and new technologies that lack the infrastructure to take part in a more centralised and standardised ecosystem.

Finally, the fourth dilemma concerns the huge gap between the competence we have on learning analytics in the Norwegian system (from each student to their teacher to school owners, municipalities, and universities) and the competence that good use of learning analytics actually requires. Or, as phrased in Wasson et al. (2024, p. 276), 'the significant gap between competence needs and competence realisation'. As of now, the necessary competence to use learning analytics in education in beneficial ways is lacking at all levels. Here, the Expert Group discusses the competence demands of existing digital tools on the market, as well as the risks we are all running if the competence gap is not closed – it could mean that we get bad and misguided use of learning analytics, but also that we miss the opportunity to get better insight into students' learning through good use of it.

ASSESSMENT OF POTENTIAL

Before discussing selected parts of the actual assessment of potential and challenges of learning analytics, I would like to list the eight general requirements that the Expert Group highlighted as being essential in order for any added value of learning analytics to be realised, and to ensure that learning analytics can appropriately enhance learning and improve teaching and instruction (ONR 2023: 19, p. 68).

1. The data on student learning must be relevant and of good quality.
2. There must be good management systems for privacy and data security that are adapted to the use of artificial intelligence.
3. Information on data processing must be clearly communicated to students and parents.
4. Information from the analytics must be presented in a comprehensible manner.
5. Information from learning analytics must be viewed in connection with other relevant information about learning and teaching.
6. Teachers and instructors must have sufficient and relevant competence.
7. It must be possible to adapt the use of learning analytics to the unique nature of the subject, professional judgement, and local conditions.
8. Sufficient time, resources, and capacity must be provided in order to follow up on data gained from the analyses.

The discussion in the Expert Group's final report identifies potential benefits of learning analytics that I will briefly highlight here. It should be noted that in the actual final report, the preconditions of each potential benefit are also discussed (ONR 2023: 19, Chapter 7). The three main identified benefits of learning analytics across both primary and secondary education, as well as higher education are:

1. Learning analytics can provide insight for students about their own learning. As stated in the report: 'Learning analytics that provide pupils with greater insight based on relevant and qualitatively good data, where they also receive the necessary assistance to interpret and understand the data, can support schools in their formative task that involves having pupils reflect on their own learning and understand their own learning processes' (ONR 2023: 19, p. 69). Through insight into their own learning process, students can become more aware of how they learn and reflect better on what they could do to develop further, which is essential for developing self-regulation. We also link this kind of insight to being better equipped to make choices about instruction, thus potentially providing better conditions for pupil participation.
2. Learning analytics has the potential to support adapted and inclusive education. Different students have different needs and, in order to meet these, teachers require knowledge about how students learn and what they are able to do, as well as areas where they struggle and typical misconceptions. Systematic use of digital traces can be used to inform teachers' work when adapting their instruction to each student. The Expert Group finds that 'teachers and instructors would have much better opportunities to adapt their instruction if they have the sufficient and relevant information to assess their own teaching' (ONR 2023: 19, p. 78).

3. Learning analytics can support educational quality development over time. Schools and higher education institutions need to base their quality development on actual insight into their own work, and here the Expert Group sees potential for using learning analytics for data-supported quality development.

ASSESSMENT OF CONCERNS

Stakeholders like teacher unions, student unions, students' parents' organisations, and other interest groups have voiced some concerns about learning analytics, and, in the final report, the Expert Group reports on a widespread concern across stakeholders when it comes to particularly one issue: Learning analytics could draw more attention to the aspects of a school subject that 'can be counted and measured'. This resonates well with concerns in the field of educational research, where several researchers are worried about how learning analytics may diminish the educational mission and only count what is easily counted (Selwyn 2019). In the Norwegian curriculum, the concept of competence is very broadly defined, as competence is understood as 'the ability to acquire and apply knowledge and skills in order to master challenges and solve problems in both known and unknown contexts and situations' (Norwegian Ministry of Education and Research 2017, Chapter 2.2). It also emphasises the ability to reflect upon your own learning and the value of critical thinking. In the market-driven development of learning analytics, the Expert Group finds it very likely that developers and suppliers will prioritise measuring and assessing what is easily measurable, neglecting pretty much everything else.

Another concern is that, due to the market-driven development, only the majority language in Norway (Norwegian Bokmål) and some key school subjects that have a larger number of hours per year (like mathematics and L1) will be prioritised, at the expense of less-used languages and smaller subjects (like arts and crafts, physical education). It has already been documented that students who need resources in the Norwegian minority standard (Norwegian Nynorsk) or Sámi languages do not have that access in their digital resources. A purely market-driven development may lead to very uneven and unfair access to learning analytics, which again will hinder good use.

Learning analytics may lead to less varied and more individualised working methods, even though the national curriculum in Norway (as in many other countries) specifically asks for more inquiry-based and exploratory, open-ended approaches. The Norwegian Association of Graduate Teachers reported to the Expert Group that they are concerned that guidelines supporting and encouraging more use of these in education would implicitly also require choosing digital formats over analogue formats more often. This is a concern the Expert Group shares. In addition, there is concern that an increased use of individual methods, which we already see in highly digitalised classrooms (Blikstad-Balas and Klette 2020; Gilje, Bjerke and Thuen 2020), would place significant demands on both teachers' professional competence and the accessibility of relevant teaching aids. It also worries the Expert Group that more and more, schools and universities are obtaining licences for different pedagogical and technical solutions as a 'package deal' and bundle, where educational institutions get access to a package rather than buying the exact products they want or need – greatly reducing teachers' access to relevant tools in a challenging school economy. For instance, it is unlikely that a Spanish teacher would get their preferred app to practise Spanish vocabulary from provider

A, if the school has already signed up for a total all-subjects package (including Spanish) from provider B. The Expert Group sees it as essential that teachers and instructors should have the possibility to choose freely what learning analytics solutions to use across different providers.

Yet another big concern regards the link between learning analytics systems and what they actually measure, and the aims for student learning listed in the national curriculum in grades 1–13. Or, in other words, who gets to break down the curriculum, interpret different learning aims, and decide how they should be measured. In Norway, the national curriculum lists different broad competence aims, and it is common for different providers of textbooks and digital learning resources to signal what area of the curriculum they are addressing and what specific learning aims. But, with the broad competence concept mentioned earlier, it is not possible to assume that only one method of measuring and developing students' competencies is sufficient. A supplier will seldom deliver more than a few concrete suggestions for how one or more competence aims can be measured or worked on, which is understandable (the alternative would be an enormous, never-ending amount of content, which would probably not be very user-friendly). To make it even more complex, students in Norway have a right to take part in decisions about *how* they show their competence; thus, there should always be a possibility to choose between different ways, and there should also be a possibility to develop competence over time. Learning aims are not something you should do and move on from, which is often what we see in different digital learning solutions. As explained in the report (ONR 2023: 19, p. 82):

> Competence aims should function as targets for a competence that pupils should have the opportunity to develop over time, and pupils develop different knowledge and skills along the way towards reaching these objectives. Therefore, these are not things that can simply be ticked off a list as each is completed. We believe there is a risk that the sector will continue to view them in this way if individual modules involving resources with a functionality for learning analytics are directly linked to specific competence aims. In addition, the competence aims for a subject are related to each other, and to the introductory parts of the curriculum. It is thus beneficial for pupils' learning to work in larger contexts rather than just one individual competence aim after the other.

What makes this issue even more complex is that a clear link between what the curriculum asks for and what a specific digital resource is trying to develop is identified as a clear expectation from the educational practitioner. Teachers want to know what part of the curriculum and which parts of the learning aims different apps and learning aids are addressing. However, in addition to the problems discussed above, the broad learning aims cannot be directly measured; they have to be broken down into a number of smaller and measurable aims. This may lead to a very narrow and black-boxed version of the curriculum, where no one in reality has insight into what aspects of the curriculum each student has actually worked with over time. Here, the Expert Group has a clear standing (ONR 2023: 19, p. 83):

> The Expert Group believes that instead of linking parts of the teaching materials and analyses to specific competence aims, they should describe the areas of knowledge and skills in a subject that the analytics in question could help develop. We believe it is essential to develop methods of linking the learning analytics to the content in a way that promotes rather than narrows teachers' didactic reflection and their work on the what, how and why aspects of learning. As with all other learning resources brought into the classroom, teachers must always determine which specific competence aims the learning resource would be relevant for.

Linking all the different resources to specific learning aims in a very competitive market could be interpreted as an incentive to 'link as much content as possible', simply to show how much a specific provider is offering. The Expert Group warns that linking to national curricula will benefit the big actors who already promise things like 'covering the entire curriculum' and provide 'everything you need in all subjects', at the expense of smaller actors who may have developed very good solutions that are only relevant to a very small portion of a school subject.

Another big concern that should not surprise anyone familiar with learning analytics is the concern that what is meant to provide support for students and teachers' decision making and inform this decision making actually becomes the decision. The Expert Group fears that some teachers may accept recommendations and evaluations from the system without making their own assessment, even though it is essential that they do. There is also a worry that learning analytics that could be used to support the teacher when planning their lessons (for example, an adaptive test showing low scores) could also be used as a summative competence assessment of the same students later on in time, which would be very problematic. As the final report states, a number of digital resources today actually offer results or overviews of students' academic answers, 'but it is not made clear whether this is intended as a basis for adapting instruction or as a measurement of what the pupil has done' (ONR 2023: 19, p. 85). This is troublesome, as students should always be aware of whether data collected from their learning process is intended to give insight on progress along the way, or if these data are used to document their competence at a later point. The Expert Group says clearly that suppliers should always state which of these two objectives any resource will help to achieve.

Misleading data is always a concern when it comes to learning analytics, and in the final report, the Expert Group discusses a number of ways data could systematically provide the wrong picture of students' actions, competencies and needs. In short, the claim in the final report is that the data that is easy to get, for example, how much time a student spends on something or what they choose when encountering pre-defined answers to choose from, may not at all be the data that best provides insight into their learning. One of the students (in Grade 9) that the Expert Group talked to in order to map students' perspectives explained this well: 'It's ok that you can see what we've answered, but not how much time we spent on it. We may make mistakes, take breaks, and so on. So that would be completely wrong' (ONR 2023:19, p. 86). As stated in the report, the problem is often not that the data itself is providing incorrect information, but rather that it is hard to reach good conclusions about learning based on the available data – unless such a relationship has been demonstrated through research and testing.

Monitoring and increased stress are also concerns related to the use of learning analytics. Students reported to the Expert Group that they may feel uneasy when educational institutions gather, share and analyse data from their activities on digital devices. This flow of information can influence the trust and relationship between teachers and students. Numerous students expressed that ongoing data collection makes them feel like they are constantly being evaluated, which increases pressure and stress for many young people. Several of the students the Expert Group consulted expressed that you should, as a student, be able to 'make mistakes without someone seeing them' and remembering them (ONR 2023: 19, p. 88). Fear that our actions are being monitored or that our information might be used without our knowledge can lead us to modify our behaviour. Students may start reconsidering what they write, who they interact with, and how they act in digital environments. This self-censorship, driven by the fear of surveillance, is known as the 'chilling effect', and the Expert Group saw several concrete examples of this effect. One that is mentioned in the final report (p. 88) is students who used an app to train vocabulary when learning a foreign language. Rather than using the app to practise, students would write down everything elsewhere so as not show their teachers how often and when they practised. The experience of constant assessment can easily feel like constant surveillance, something that is not in line with most countries' educational ambitions.

Finally, the random and planless use of data is seen as a main challenge with learning analytics. Large amounts of data are being collected every day in classrooms (and when students visit educational digital platforms outside classrooms), but for what purposes is unclear at best. For pedagogical as well as ethical and legal reasons, it is a highly questionable practice to gather data with undetermined purposes – and it also seems at odds with the data minimalisation principle of the GDPR.

SUMMING UP: FOUR MAIN POLICY RECOMMENDATIONS

The four main recommendations of The Expert Group are explained in detail in the final report, but here I will share a brief overview.

First of all, the Expert Group recommends clarifying the legal basis for learning analytics at all educational levels. The purpose of this recommendation is to clarify when the processing of personal data in learning analytics is lawful – which today often is quite unclear – and to ensure better predictability.

Second, the Expert Group recommends 'developing a data protection *code of conduct* in primary and secondary education and training' (ONR 2023: 19, p. 13). The goal of this recommendation is to strengthen pupils' and students' data protection, facilitate good data protection practices, increase awareness about data protection, and enhance competence regarding data protection.

Third, the Expert Group recommends establishing frameworks for good learning analytics in primary and secondary education and training. The ambition behind this recommendation is to strengthen the free choice of pupils and teachers when choosing technologies supporting learning analytics, and to provide a better basis for pedagogical decisions regarding learning analytics to enhance learning.

Finally, the Expert Group recommends developing broad guidelines for good and justifiable learning analytics in higher education, to 'facilitate good data protection practices and justifiable learning analytics that promote student learning and increase the quality of education' (ONR 2023: 19, p. 13).

DISCLOSURE STATEMENT

While the Expert Report is a result of collaborative work and represents the view of the entire Expert Group, this chapter is my own prioritised account of particularly interesting aspects of the Expert Report I chaired. While I do not think that anyone in the Expert Group would object to my narrative in this chapter, I am certain other experts would have written it slightly differently and perhaps given more weight to other issues. This is also why I highly recommend reading the report in its entirety if you found this chapter interesting.

ACKNOWLEDGEMENT

I would like to thank all the participants in the Expert Committee for their hard work. Thank you, Monica, Barbara, Einar, Ann-Tove, Michail, Hedda, Malcolm, Per Henning and Eirin for all the discussions, fruitful disagreements and your ability to compromise. For me, what characterises true collaboration is when someone is able to put aside their personal conviction for the benefit of the group – and we all had to do that often. I would also like to thank our wonderful secretariat, Hilde Hultin, Jon Lanested, Øystein Baste, Øyvind Bjerkestrand and Helle Kristin Jensen.

NOTE

1. The members of the group were Monica Andreassen (teacher and advisor), Einar Duenger Bøhn (professor), Ann-Tove Eriksen (Norwegian Directorate of Higher Education and Skills), Michail Giannakos (professor), Hedda Birgitte Huse (Norwegian Directorate for Education and Training), Malcolm Langford (professor), Eirin Oda Lauvset (lawyer and data protection officer), Per Henning Uppstad (professor) and Barbara Wasson (professor). I functioned as the Chair of the Expert Group.

REFERENCES

Blikstad-Balas, M. (2023), 'The fragility of the Norwegian policy response: How relying on digital infrastructure and local autonomy led to an increase in inequality in education', in F. Reimers (ed.), *Schools and Society During the COVID-19 Pandemic: How Education Systems Changed and the Road Ahead*, Springer, pp. 131–47.

Blikstad-Balas, M. and K. Klette (2020), 'Still a long way to go: Narrow and transmissive use of technology in the classroom', *Nordic Journal of Digital Literacy*, **15** (1), 55–68.

Blikstad-Balas, M., A. Roe, C.P. Dalland and K. Klette (2022), 'Homeschooling in Norway during the pandemic: Digital learning with unequal access to qualified help at home and unequal learning opportunities provided by the school', in F. Reimers (ed.), *Primary and Secondary Education During COVID-19: Disruptions to Educational Opportunity During a Pandemic*, Springer, pp. 177–201.

Erstad, O. (2006), 'A new direction? Digital literacy, student participation and curriculum reform in Norway', *Education and Information Technologies*, **11**, 415–29.

Gilje, Ø., Å. Bjerke and F. Thuen (2020), *Gode eksempler på praksis: rapport – Undervisning i en-til-en-klasserommet* [*Good Examples of Practice: One-to-one Classroom Teaching*]. Universitetet i Oslo: FIKS.

Instefjord, E. and E. Munthe (2016), 'Preparing pre-service teachers to integrate technology: An analysis of the emphasis on digital competence in teacher education curricula', *European Journal of Teacher Education*, **39** (1), 77–93.

Instefjord, E. and E. Munthe (2017), 'Educating digitally competent teachers: A study of integration of professional digital competence in teacher education', *Teaching and Teacher Education*, **67**, 37–45.

Klausen, S.W. (2023), 'Why are Norwegian education authorities digitising education? An analysis of political arguments in policy documents', *Nordic Journal of Digital Literacy*, **18** (4), 246–64.

Kongsgården, P. and R.J. Krumsvik (2016), 'Use of tablets in primary and secondary school: A case study', *Nordic Journal of Digital Literacy*, **11** (4), 248–70.

Kure, A.E., L.M. Brevik and M. Blikstad-Balas (2023), 'Digital skills critical for education: Video analysis of students' technology use in Norwegian secondary English classrooms', *Journal of Computer Assisted Learning*, **39** (1), 269–85.

Norwegian Ministry of Education and Research (2017), 'Core curriculum – values and principles forprimary and secondary education'. Report. https://www.regjeringen.no/contentassets/53d21ea2bc3a4202b86b83cfe82da93e/core-curriculum.pdf

Official Norwegian Report (ONR) (2023), 'Learning - Lost in the shuffle? Use of pupil and student data to enhance learning', Norwegian Ministry of Education and Research, NOU 2023: 19. https://www.regjeringen.no/en/documents/nou-2023-19/id2982722/

Selwyn, N. (2019), 'What's the problem with learning analytics?', *Journal of Learning Analytics*, **6** (3), 11–19.

Throndsen, I., T.C. Carlsten and J.K. Björnsson (2019), 'TALIS 2018: Første hovedfunn fra ungdomstrinnet [TALIS 2018: First main findings from lower secondary school].' Report.

Vennerød-Diesen, F.F., C. Pedersen, M.F. Persson, P.L. Andersen and J. Ljunggren (2024), 'Et bevis på at man trenger skolen, egentlig' ['Proof that you need school, really']. 'Delrapport 2: Koronapandemiens langsiktige konsekvenser for elever på ungdomstrinnet [Report 2: The Covid Pandemic's long-term consequences for students in lower secondary school].'

Wasson, B., M. Giannakos, M. Blikstad-Balas, P.H. Uppstad, M. Langford and E.D. Bøhn (2024), 'Implementing learning analytics in Norway: Four central dilemmas', *Journal of Learning Analytics*, **11** (2), 268–80.

18. Implementing learning analytics and adaptive learning in Norwegian schools: lessons learned

Barbara Wasson and Cecilie J.S. Hansen

INTRODUCTION

Much of the research on learning analytics (LA) and adaptive learning (usually AI systems) takes place in universities or research institutions; moving this research from the laboratory to implementation (or deployment) in actual schools raises several technical, ethical, and legal complexities. While many of these complex issues are context dependent (for example, European educational systems must comply with the General Data Protection Regulation[1] (GDPR)), most will be a challenge in any country when deploying LA and AI applications. Thus, experience from the Norwegian AVT (Activity data for Assessment and Adaptivity) project will provide insight into some of the complexities those implementing such systems might encounter.

AVT was an R&D project that, among other things, highlighted opportunities and shed light on the challenges faced by the Norwegian education sector when it comes to using students' activity data for learning analytics. Activity data is the information that is created when a student completes tasks in a learning application (for example, an answer, how long the student took to answer, whether the answer is right or wrong). In AVT, activity data from multiple vendors (providers of learning applications) was used to generate visualisations of student and class learning activity and progress across the different learning applications being used in a single classroom, and to make recommendations for the student and/or teacher. The visualisations were presented in MittFagkart,[2] a learning analytics dashboard (LAD). Schwendimann et al. (2016) define LADs as 'displays that aggregate different indicators about learner(s), learning process(es) and/or learning context(s) into one or multiple visualisations' (p. 37).

Some of the applications used in the Norwegian classrooms were adaptive learning applications that tailor the learning path of the student based on their interaction with the tool (for example, the next task a student encounters is based on an analysis of their answer to a previous task and perhaps on data about other students' learning paths). AVT did not intervene in the individual applications but integrated data from the different applications for a more insightful and in-depth picture of students' learning. Furthermore, AVT[3] turned out to be a driving force for the development of national common solutions, guidelines, norms, and infrastructure. The insights gained in the project should be of interest to researchers, developers, school leaders, teachers and policymakers.

This chapter begins with an introduction to the AVT project, including the results and highlighting the range of complexities that were encountered, along with the project's participation in the Norwegian Data Protection Authority's Regulatory Sandbox, before concluding with lessons learned.

ACTIVITY DATA FOR ASSESSMENT AND ADAPTIVITY (AVT)

Integrating multiple learning applications in classrooms presents challenges for teachers in monitoring student progress. Learning analytics dashboards (Verbert et al. 2013; Schwendimann et al. 2016; Kaliisa et al. 2024), which collect and analyse student activity data, offer a potential solution. This approach, however, raises significant technical, ethical, and legal considerations regarding student data privacy and usage. The Norwegian AVT (Activity data for Assessment and Adaptivity) project (2017–2019 and 2019–2025) explored this approach, revealing substantial technical, ethical and legal hurdles in implementing learning analytics and adaptive learning systems in schools. During the eight-year period, 59 vendors (suppliers of learning applications), 159 schools and 3 municipalities were involved in one way or another. This section describes two periods of the AVT project, focusing on the main activities and outcomes of each period.

AVT Period 1 (2017–2019)

The AVT project was instigated in 2017 by the Department of Education, Oslo Municipality (UDE) and funded by KS, the Norwegian organisation of municipalities, with the Centre for the Science of Learning & Technology (SLATE), University of Bergen as a research partner. During the first period, AVT aimed to investigate the possibilities for sharing activity data between the different providers of digital tools in schools, and to use this data to develop a learning analytics framework that: (1) structures the student data and provides an infrastructure to manage secure data flow between providers; (2) provides a subject model of topics within mathematics; and (3) provides a conceptual model that describes the components needed for learning analytics (Morlandstø et al. 2019; Wasson et al. 2019). The framework was evaluated by selected schools in the municipality and by participating EdTech vendors. This R&D enabled the project to gain experience and test solutions for further work on learning analytics in compulsory education, and supported UDE's original vision that the vendors could make use of each other's data to support their own application's decision-making (for example, if two vendors had tasks that addressed the same competence goal, they could share data about the student regarding their performance on that task). While this was shown to be technically and legally possible through the AVT-HUB (see Figure 18.1), which 'provides quality assurance of the coding and decoding of raw data (that is, the pupils' activity in the digital tools and assessment of their competence) based on national standards for the field … making sure privacy and data integration follow national and international standards and regulations' (Wasson et al. 2019, p. 3), the vendors did not seem to know what to do with data from another vendor.

During interviews with the vendors, it became clear that (a selection of results as reported in Wasson et al. 2019, pp. 4–5):

- Learning analytics is seen by the vendors as an opportunity for providing individually tailored (adaptive) learning activities where digital tools can support the teacher's teaching and assessment practices.

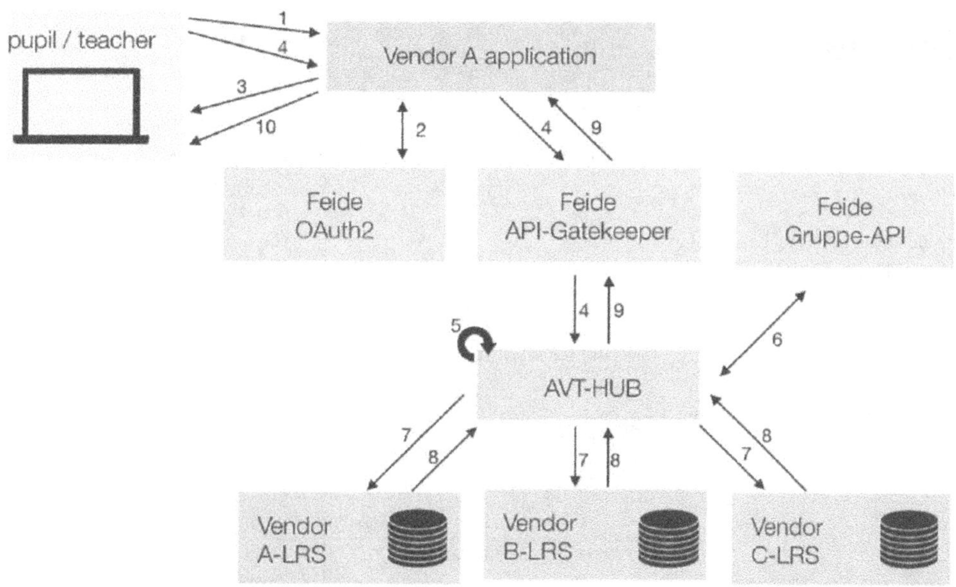

Source: Wasson et al. (2019, figure 2).

Figure 18.1 *Integration of vendor data*

- To provide adaptivity, the pupil's achievement must be identified so that the tasks can be adapted to the pupil. The possibilities for identifying goal achievement are dependent on various factors, such as a common taxonomy and the quality of the tool.
- Sharing data with other vendors is seen as challenging due to the competitive nature of the sector, as well as seeing how to use each other's data.
- It has been important for the vendors to participate in the project. It provided a platform for dialogue with other vendors and with Oslo Municipality (UDE); it offered an opportunity to share their expertise and experiences, and to start developing new versions of their technologies.

In 2018–2019, ten teachers and two school leaders were interviewed (divided over four groups) about the use of learning applications with learning analytics in practice, and their thoughts and wishes regarding opportunities and challenges with learning analytics. The focus group data were analysed using Malterud's (2012) systematic text condensation, a multi-phased method involving transcription, thematic identification and code group division with subcategories (see Figure 18.2). Text fragments (meaning units) from the transcribed interviews, related to the identified themes, were extracted using NVivo, labelled with codes and compiled into a condensate (presented in full in Morlandstø et al. 2019) that ensures it reflected the participants' own statements.

Figure 18.3 presents a summary of what the teachers wanted to know about their students' learning and learning progression.

Identified themes	Codes	Sub-codes
1. Increased individual adaptation for teaching 2. Increased learning outcomes for students 3. Better quality for assessment	Use of learning analysis, tools and tasks	1. The teacher 2. Learning 3. Learning outcomes 4. The market 5. School development 6. Adapted learning 7. The tool 8. Visualisation 9. Assessment 10. Adaptivity
	About the AVT project	1. Incentives 2. Technology 3. Opportunities
	About the data	1. Data quality 2. Data sharing and linking 3. Ethics and GDPR 4. What data
	About the learning analytics	1. What is LA? 2. Own LA?

Source: Translated version of tables 1 and 2 from Mørlandstø et al. (2019).

Figure 18.2 Identified themes from the interviews

Teachers wanted information about individual students, groups, and the entire class. They were interested in knowing what discipline topics had been addressed by the tasks in the different applications (for example, Geometry, 3D representations), if the answer was correct or a wrong answer, if the student had misconceptions, and about their progression through the learning applications. Other issues of interest for the teachers were the competence goals and the strategies students were using to solve tasks, the number of activities related to each competence goal, and student progression. In the interviews, they also talked about the possibility of knowing more about the tasks/activity (that is, which task, difficulty level) and which type of tasks the students had trouble with (for example, word problems, simulations), and what competence gaps an individual student, group, or the class had. The teachers were especially interested in competence gaps at both the individual and class level. This was explained as being helpful to direct teaching and focus attention. Another issue brought up by the teachers was an interest in getting recommendations for new assignments suitable for an individual or group of students. Interestingly, the teachers worried about the privacy rights of the students, mentioning issues such as which data was being used, where it came from, and for how long such data would be stored.

The results of the interviews with the teachers not only impacted the design of the MittFagkart interface but also provided input on the types of recommendations that the teachers were interested in, thus informing the kinds of algorithms needed in the LAD application. The types of desired recommendations are both general about a student or a class and specific about a vendor task/activity, for example:

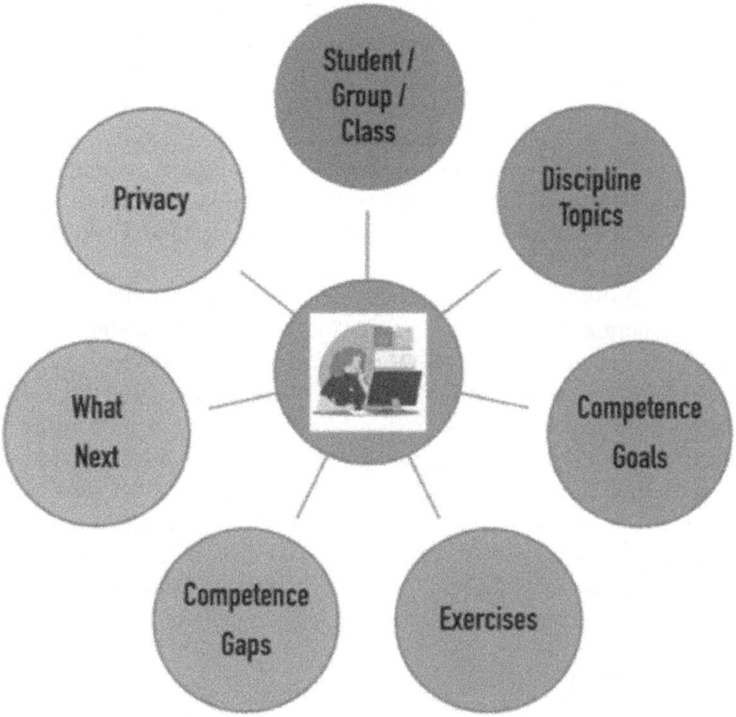

Source: Authors.

Figure 18.3 What teachers want to know about their students

- which *competence goal* to work on (for a class/an individual student/a group);
- which *subject area and topics* need attention (for example, class needs to work on algebraic expressions);
- which *topics are difficult* (for example, 3D geometry);
- what misconceptions does the class seem to have;
- what types of tasks is a student having difficulty with (for example, multiple choice, video, text);
- what learning application should the class work on to address some competence gap (for example, application x from vendor y); and
- which specific task/activity should a student work on to address a misconception (for example, capital 5 in application x from vendor y).

The conclusions of the first period of AVT were that the learning analytics framework contributes to how learning analytics can be used: (1) to identify a learner's or class level; (2) to link to relevant learning resources with the intention of supporting learners in their learning activities and teachers in their practice; and at the same time (3) to help vendors to develop higher quality learning materials (Morlandstø et al. 2019). Furthermore, the framework contributed to the national discussion around improving the quality of assessment in schools and personalising students through learning analytics and served as a point of reference for both school owners and vendors across the country when procuring and developing digital learning resources, respectively.

Recommendations for period 2 (summarised from Morlandstø et al. 2019 and Wasson et al. 2019, p. 5) were that there was a need for (1) more work on a domain model within a subject area that links topics to the competence goals defined in the Norwegian national curriculum, (2) further specification of a national standard for activity data (xAPI)[4] and that (3) vendors make available APIs for searching metadata[5] for items and tasks in the applications. Furthermore, SLATE should (4) develop a centralised dashboard for pupils, teachers, and eventually parents/guardians that should contain visualisations of aggregated data showing achievement levels for the various topics, competence gaps, and recommended items for further work, and (5) carry out more research to identify the opportunities and challenges that activity data and learning analytics bring into schools, and finally, (6) clarify which organisation(s) should have ownership of the various solutions so that further development and maintenance are ensured.

AVT Period 2 (2019–2025)

The second AVT period aimed to carry out R&D to further develop the framework for LA and AI in schools. In subsequent years, the focus shifted to exploring how AVT components could be part of a national ecosystem for access and use of learning resources. With its goal of leveraging student data for LA and AI, the project was selected as one of the first four cases to participate in the Norwegian Data Protection Authority's Regulatory Sandbox. The mission of the Sandbox is 'to stimulate privacy-enhancing innovation and digitalisation',[6] and the project was given valuable insight into the regulation and laws related to the use of student data for LA and AI applications (Datatilsynet 2022). Finally, with the release of the Large Language Model (LLM)-based chatbots in November 2022, the possibility of using AI for tagging vendor items to the national curriculum was tested for a set of tasks from one of our vendors.

Thus, the main outputs from AVT period 2 include:

- Fagkart, the domain maps based on the Norwegian national curriculum (for maths, Norwegian, and English);
- central API and specification of xAPI format for activity data (available in GitHub);
- Fagkartkoder, a tool for vendors to tag their tasks/activities against Fagkart;
- MittFagkart, an LAD application that visualises what data has been collected about a student and provides an overview of a student's progression (views of teachers, students, and parents);

- a procurement and payment model;
- an ecosystem for student data exchange, AVT, and national components;
- testing of generative AI for tagging of assignments; and
- extension of the international standard xAPI.

This section briefly introduces some of these main outputs.

Fagkart

Fagkart is a subject map (sometimes called a domain model) that structures the topics (for example, algebra or geometry) in a subject (for example, mathematics) and their relationship to the Norwegian national curriculum. The topics in the subject maps were extracted from GREP,[7] the Ministry of Education's national database for the subjects (for example, mathematics, Norwegian, science, etc.) and their curricula in the compulsory education.

The national curriculum is presented as a set of competence goals to be achieved at the end of specific grades. For example, the mathematics curriculum covers the knowledge areas: Numbers and Number Sense; Algebra; Geometry; Statistics and Probability; and Functions. Figure 18.4 shows parts of a subject map for the Norwegian math curriculum (in Norwegian), where the circles represent the topics and the links show a relationship between topics in the curriculum. Some of the topics under Algebra are addition, algebraic expressions, equations, likeness, communicative, polynomial, coherence, modelling, problem-solving etc. Topics can be shared by two or more knowledge areas. For example, Geometry and Algebra share measurement, algorithms and patterns, among others, while Numbers and Number Sense and Algebra share numbers, calculation strategies, equality and inequality, etc. An example of a curriculum goal at the end of 2nd grade is 'organise numbers, quantities and shapes based on properties, compare them and reflect on whether they can be organised in multiple ways', and at the end of 8th grade is 'create and explain mathematical expressions with numbers, variables, and constants related to practical situations'.

A Fagkart enables the vendors to tag their tools at a finer granularity than the competence goal (a requirement for applications being used in Norwegian schools), which enables better learning analytics and decision-making.

Fagkartkoder

The Fagkartkoder (Fagkart coder) is a tagging tool used to link vendors' tasks or activities to a Fagkart through a generated *Subject Map ID*, which is a set of parameters that include skills, core elements, cross-curricular themes, knowledge area, topics, competency class, verb, learning objective set (level) and learning objective context. The *subject map ID* can be added to the activity data that a digital learning application generates when a student responds to tasks and activities. This enables more fine-grained learning analytics on the activity data.

MittFagkart

MittFagkart is an Open Learner Model (OLM) LAD application for teachers, students, and parents that was developed in period 2 of the AVT project. An OLM supports assessment, promotes student metacognitive activities such as reflection, planning, and monitoring, and allows a learner to take greater control and responsibility for their learning (Bull and Kay 2010) or teachers to gain insight into the progression of an individual student or the class. In order to identify what teachers would like to know about their students, ten teachers and

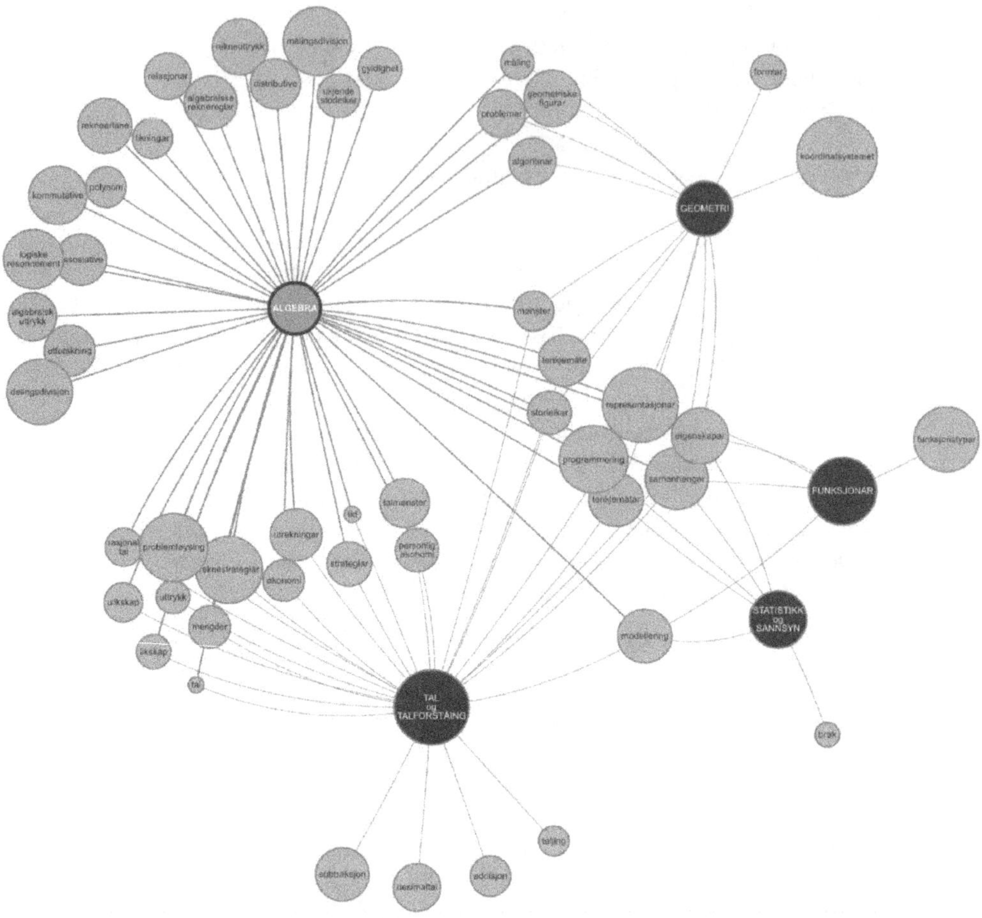

Source: Authors.

Figure 18.4 *A section of the Fagkart for mathematics, with Algebra expanded one level*

two school leaders were interviewed. The results of the interviews fed the design of the MittFagkart interface and enabled the identification of the type of algorithms needed to make desired recommendations. This subsection describes the results of the interviews, the design work, and the MittFagkart application.

Design of the MittFagkart interface

MittFagkart visualises student activity data across digital tools used in Norwegian classrooms, aiming to provide teachers and learners with a comprehensive overview of student learning and progress (Bull and Kay 2010; Bull and Wasson 2016). Its user-centred design (Ovchinnikova 2021) was informed by a systematic literature review identifying effective OLM visualisations to display student progress (such as skill meters, concept maps, tree maps, and word clouds) and involved users (teachers) throughout the entire development process to ensure the final prototype met their needs and preferences.

The user-centred design included all phases from establishing the requirements (for example, the interviews described above), through three iteration cycles of prototypes, and the evaluation of a final prototype (see Ovchinnikova 2021 for details). The final design was used for the user interface in the MittFagkart application[8] (see Figure 18.5).

The screenshot shown in Figure 18.5 shows a teacher (Lærer) view of an individual student (elever), Alexander Andersen (not a real name) and his progress towards five competence goals in algebra using data from two vendor tools. This visualisation shows the average score of the tasks that have been associated with each competence goal, the number of tasks (Oppgaver: #; for example, the first one has 12 tasks), and the number of tries (forsøk) on the tasks (for example, the first one had 24 tries on the 12 tasks). It also indicates that this is information from one student (elever: 1). The teacher can choose to view the entire class (choosing which class under the menu item Klasse if they have more than one class) or an individual student (as shown in Figure 18.5). They can choose the discipline (fag) they want to view, the grade level (trinn), and can make choices in the menus (on the right of the figure) to either look at all the competence goals for the chosen discipline and grade, or zoom in on an area/several areas in the discipline (through menu item Områder i fagkart) and/or a particular competence goal (kompetansemål) or verb. The teacher can also choose to see the data from all the vendors or choose only one vendor. The items that can be selected in the menus are steered by the previous choices made by the user. In the student (elev) profile, a student can only see visualisations built on their own data. In the parent/guardian (Foresatt) profile, they see information about the number of learning activities from which data about their child/children has been collected. They can choose if they do not want their children's data to be used for improving the algorithm. This feature is required by law as parents have the right to exclude their children's data for improving algorithms. For example, this message informs them and gives them a button to click to exclude the data from algorithm improvement:

> We have registered 7,708 of your children's learning activities. An anonymised version of the collected data is used to improve the algorithms that make recommendations. Click here if you do not want your children's data to be used for this.

DATA PROTECTION AUTHORITY'S REGULATORY SANDBOX

AVT was selected for participation in the inaugural round of the Norwegian Data Protection Authority's Regulatory Sandbox, which was established 'to promote the development of artificial intelligence solutions that, from a data protection perspective, are both ethical and responsible' (Datatilsynet 2022, p. 5). For the AVT project, the participation was an opportunity to explore legal, regulatory, and ethical issues related to the use of student data for learning analytics and adaptive learning in schools (from Datatilsynet 2022, p. 5):

1. *Legal basis.* Whether the legal basis for the processing of pupil activity data meets the requirements of the General Data Protection Regulation (GDPR). If not, what will it take to ensure compliance?

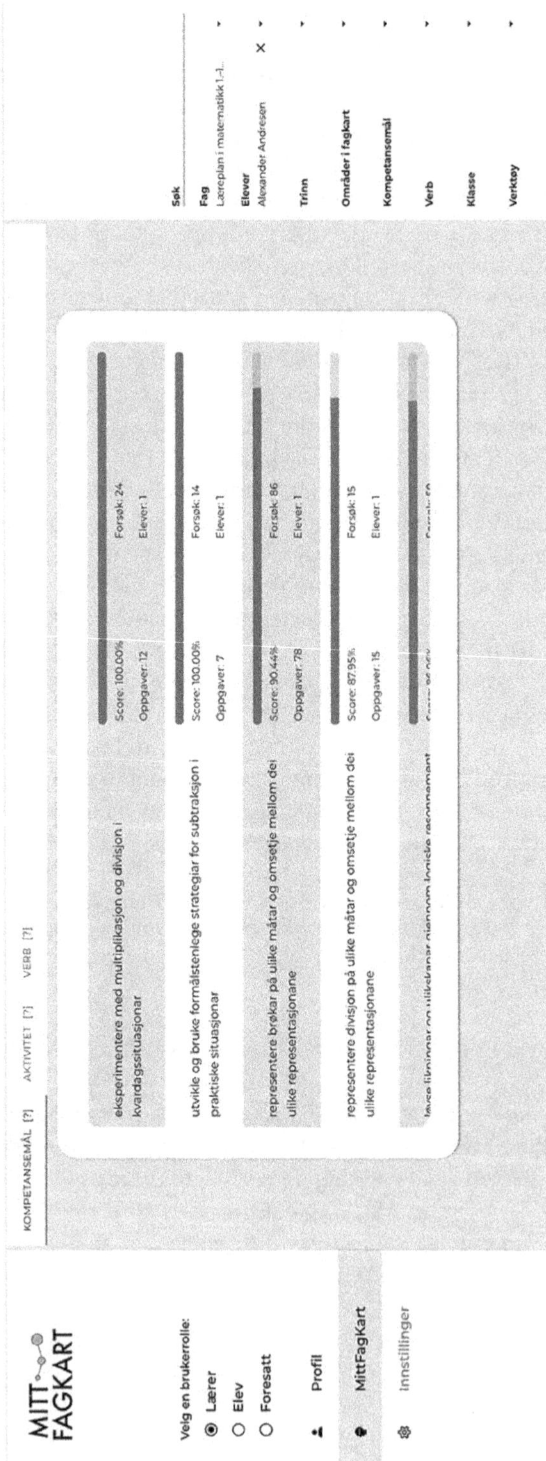

Source: Authors.

Figure 18.5 *A screenshot of the MittFagkart application*

2. *Pupil privacy.* What are the consequences of the learning analytics system on the protection of the pupils' personal data? What do the parties responsible have to keep in mind to ensure that the pupils' privacy is protected?
3. *Transparency.* How can information about the learning analytics system be given to its users (teachers, pupils and parents)? What do they have to be informed about, and what should they be informed about?

To use student data for processing (for example, for learning analytics or in an AI algorithm), the data controller (for example, in AVT's case, the Education Department in Oslo Municipality) needs to have a legal basis for its use in the GDPR and a country's educational laws. A summary of the results from the Sandbox (Datatilsynet 2022) show that there was a disagreement as to whether the legal basis for processing student data was a 'legal obligation' (AVT view) using a supplementary basis in the Norwegian education legislation to support this view, or 'in the public interest' (Data Protection Authority view) as the supplementary basis in the Norwegian law is not as strong as it should be on this issue. The data controller must make the final choice. The third issue, transparency, is with regard to the legal obligation to explain what data and how it is used to all relevant stakeholders, such as the students (including all ages from primary to high school students), teachers, parents, school leaders etc. The discussions ranged from which linguistic and visualisation tools might be relevant for helping with the explanation, although no concrete examples were developed (most of the time in the Sandbox went to the legal aspects and the DPIA).

Finally, during the time in the Sandbox, a preliminary data protection impact assessment (DPIA) was developed for MittFagkart,[9] as required by the European GDPR, mapping the potential impact of MittFagkart on the protection of personal data and which measures should be undertaken to mitigate the identified risks. From this work, where many stakeholders were engaged in dialogue, three main risks were identified: 'the risk of altered behaviour (cool-down effect), the risk of incorrect personal data in the system, and the risk of the technology causing the pupils unwanted stress' (Datatilsynet 2022, p. 3). In addition, three other potential risks were highlighted (and should be monitored): 'risks associated with special categories of personal data, the processing of third-party data, and where to draw the line towards an automated decision-making system' (ibid.). This last risk was also a major discussion point in the Norwegian expert group on learning analytics, appointed by the Norwegian Ministry of Education and mandated to investigate the relevant pedagogical, ethical, legal and privacy issues with the use of learning analytics in schools, and to make recommendations to the government (Ekspertgruppen for digital læringsanalyse 2022; NOU 2023; Wasson et al. 2024).

The results of AVT's participation in the Sandbox provided valuable insight and input to relevant stakeholders who are working to strengthen the privacy of students in their learning work and provided insight into how infrastructure and guidelines can make it easier for both suppliers and school owners to comply with the regulations.

LESSONS LEARNED

There are a plethora of interesting challenges that were encountered when working with the implementation of learning analytics and artificial intelligence in Norwegian schools during the two periods of the AVT project. It was an extremely rich learning experience. The challenges ranged from issues about the data and its use, access to data, data standards, regulation, and infrastructure. This section shares reflections on these challenges and the lessons we learnt.

Data Issues: What Data? Who Owns the Data? Can You Use the Data?

One of the first issues that arises in the use of student data for learning analytics and artificial intelligence is 'What data?', 'Who owns the data?' and 'Can you use the data?', as you need to know who to ask for both access to the data and permission to process the data. Data is complex. In learning analytics, we are generally using data that is generated by a student interacting with a digital tool, referred to as activity data or trace data, grades, demographic data, assessment data, context data etc. There is also metadata, which is data about data that provides descriptive information about data and its context. For example, when you take a picture, the metadata that is recorded might be what camera you used, the location you were in when you took the picture, the time the picture was taken etc. In AVT, we were interested in the activity data students generated while working with the digital tools in school.

In Norway, the ownership of student data generated in schools is a nuanced issue. The general principle is that the municipality (or the owner of a private school) owns the data on behalf of the student. However, the students themselves (or their parents/guardians if the student is a minor) have legal rights regarding their data, including the right to access, correct, and in some cases, delete their data. During the later years of the AVT project, some vendors began to claim that they owned the metadata about the students' interactions. For example, the answer to a question and data about whether it is right or wrong belonged to the municipality, but the vendors claimed ownership of the metadata, such as the time of answering, how long it took to answer, how many attempts to answer etc. Thus, a major lesson learned is to have a clear overview of what data and metadata are under discussion and their ownership.

Regulations: Do You Have the Right Data to Do the Analytics?

In Europe, the General Data Protection Regulation (GDPR) regulates children's personal data, and the school owner is the *data controller* (for example, in Norway, this will be a municipality or private school owner). The data controllers are responsible for ensuring that data processing complies with the Norwegian Personal Data Act (Personopplysningsloven) and the GDPR. As shown in the results of the Sandbox (Datatilsynet 2022), this includes (1) having a legal basis for processing the data, (2) implementing appropriate security measures (including where and how long the data can be stored), and (3) providing information to the students and parents/guardians, at their level, about what data is collected and how the data is processed and its consequences. An ethical question that arose in discussion with students is who has the right to see the analysis of their data; they were not too keen on teachers seeing that they used six attempts to solve a task or were doing their homework at midnight; neither were they interested in their parents having too much insight into everything they are doing at school; basically, they did not want to feel like they were under surveillance.

The data controller can make a data processing agreement (a legal contract) with a data handler (or data processor) to process the data on behalf of the data controller and in accordance with the law. For example, all vendors having applications in Norwegian schools need to have a data processing agreement, including SLATE for the MittFagkart application (a research prototype). As illustrated with the Sandbox work, it is also necessary to have a Data Protection Impact Assessment (DPIA) for each tool.

Furthermore, the data controller has to act in accordance with the law and respect the rights of the data subjects (and their parents/guardians if they are minors). Legally, data subjects have the right to know what data a school holds about them (access), the right to have inaccurate or incomplete data corrected (rectification), in some cases have their data deleted (right to be forgotten) and have the right to object to certain types of data processing.

Thus, the lesson learned is that you need to understand how the legal landscape applies to your situation for having access to and processing student data: the laws and the rights of the data subjects must be respected.

Laws: Clarification and Strengthening of Laws

Another lesson learned is that the education laws in a given country are probably not up to date with the current needs for clarification on the use of student data and digital tools. During AVT's work over the years, it was highlighted that there is a clear need to clarify and strengthen the existing educational laws in Norway with regard to the use of student data for learning analytics and artificial intelligence. This was a recognition made in the final AVT report (Datatilsynet 2022) from the Sandbox, where it is stated that 'The Ministry of Education is currently working on a new education act, which will not be ready until 2023, at the earliest. The education sector, therefore, currently has a unique opportunity to clarify how schools can contribute to the development of educational AI tools (p. 3). There were several opportunities where AVT project members brought this to attention, including the work of the expert group on learning analytics (NOU, 2023), direct input to the Ministry by the project owner, KS, and in several webinars, etc.

Practicalities: Do You Have Access to the Data? Is it in the Right Format?

There were many practical issues related to accessing and using data that we had not anticipated – these were valuable lessons that arose. As MittFagkart was not operating in a lab but was to be used in schools, the first issue was that access to data in real time from the schools was not possible given the digital infrastructure in Norway. This led to several decisions about the architecture and functionality of MittFagkart that were not in alignment with providing real-time updates as desired by teachers. The second issue was the bottleneck that arose with the vendors tagging their applications to the Fagkart. Most of the vendors only tagged their tasks/activities to the competence goals (which are very complex and not fine-grained), and, as a result, no real meaningful learning analytics could be undertaken. There were several reasons for this including: (1) time and competence, many vendors are SMEs and just did not have the time to do the tagging or the personnel, it was recommended that someone with pedagogical competence (or domain competence) carry out the tagging; (2) motivation, as this was an R&D project, it was not clear that their time investment would pay off in the long run as it was uncertain if the Fagkart would be maintained beyond the lifetime of the project; and (3) they were not convinced of the necessity. The third issue encountered was access to data in the chosen standard xAPI (chosen independent of AVT – by Standards Norway). Only three of the vendors provided data tagged and in xAPI format. By providing the Fagkart coding tool, we tried to mitigate the difficulty of having the data in xAPI format. Finally, the fourth practical issue that arose was accessing the data from the vendors that were willing to share their data with us. Even if there was agreement, it was not always the case that they could program the API that allowed us to access the data on an agreed schedule. Thus, if you are interested in carrying out R&D in school settings, there is a need to really investigate the bottlenecks that can arise when working with professionals in their everyday work practice.

Data Standards for Integration

AVT had a vision of using data from multiple vendors and integrating the data for learning analytics. Another of the lessons learned is that this is not that easy. As Samuelsen et al. (2021) explain:

> Integration of multiple data sources, an important dimension of scalability, has the potential to provide rich insights within LA. Using a common standard such as the Experience API (xAPI) to describe learning activity data across multiple sources can alleviate obstacles for data integration. Despite their potential, however, research indicates that standards are seldom used for [the] integration of multiple sources in LA. (p. 1)

Early experience in the project confirmed this (Morlandstø et al. 2019), thus the xAPI standard, as selected by Standards Norway, was chosen for the project. As mentioned earlier, it was difficult to receive the data from the participating vendors in the required format and tagged as we requested.

However, the AVT project served as a case study (Samuelsen 2023) to investigate the scalability of learning analytics, focusing on data integration across data sources. More specifically, the xAPI learning activity data standard was investigated. Research (literature study and stakeholder interviews) identified deficiencies in xAPI, particularly regarding consistent descriptions of contextual data. A conceptual solution for more consistent data descriptions in xAPI was developed to address this (Samuelsen et al. 2021) and subsequently implemented as a technical solution in the form of an extension to xAPI. This extension was validated through user testing with Norwegian Edtech experts familiar with AVT and xAPI, who performed data description tasks and provided feedback, as detailed in Samuelsen et al. (2021) and Samuelsen (2023).

GenAI: A Future Solution for Tagging?

As described earlier, one of the bottlenecks for the technical side of AVT was to have the vendors tag their data. The lesson learned was that even providing help (for example, the Fagkart tagging tool, and even paying for a domain expert to tag all the tasks in one of the vendor's applications) may not be enough. Thus, with the release of the generative AI chatbots at the end of 2022, we experimented with using ChatGPT-4 to tag one of the vendor's individual tasks to the Fagkart. The tagging was done with the following parameters: 'knowledge area', 'competence goal', 'competence class', 'area in subject map' and 'verb', and compared to what a pedagogical expert had originally tagged. The first experiments showed that automatic tagging can be a good approach to experiment with further, both to (1) suggest classifications (as shown for the tag 'knowledge area' where 27 of the 28 suggested by ChatGPT-4 matched the human pedagogical expert's classification), and (2) to narrow down the number of possible alternative values from which a pedagogical expert can choose (for example, we had ChatGPT-4 suggest five potential competence goals from the 95 possible, and in almost all cases the originally selected competence goal was one of the five suggested). Both these have the potential to reduce time and other resources for the vendors.

CONCLUSIONS

The AVT project, initiated in 2017 with the ambitious goal of integrating student data across learning tools from different vendors, to later integrate AVT concepts into a national learning analytics ecosystem, concluded after an eight-year journey marked by significant learning and contributions.

The Data Protection Agency sums it up well:

> The sandbox project is completed, but the exploration of artificial intelligence in schools has only just begun. The AVT project is blazing the trail in a field that will only become more important in the future. The project's contributions in the sandbox have shed light on an area the Data Protection Authority does not have previous experience with. The opportunities are endless, and the importance of a sober, ethical approach could not be clearer. The AVT project has taken its responsibilities seriously and is now likely to build the foundation for a better education of our children in the time to come. (Datatilsynet 2022, p. 3)

AVT has been a collaborative endeavour, and, while perhaps premature for the Norwegian school sector's readiness for learning analytics and artificial intelligence at the time, it yielded valuable insights from educators, vendors, school leaders, parents, students, and authorities, shaping both policy and practice. Hopefully, our lessons learned give insights useful for others embarking on such a journey.

ACKNOWLEDGEMENTS

The authors would like to thank KS for funding the project, and UDE Oslo Kommune for inviting SLATE as a research partner. In particular, we thank Lene Karin Wiberg (KS) for her excellent leadership and vast knowledge and Brian Jørgensen (UDE) for his insights and creativity. In addition, we thank SLATE contributions from master's student Maria Ovchinnikova for her excellent work on the MittFagkart learning analytics dashboard, our gifted head developer at SLATE Gleb Belokrys, and Jeanette Samuelsen, PhD, who brought her expertise on interoperability to AVT.

NOTES

1. https://gdpr-info.eu/
2. https://fagkart.no/#/
3. https://www.ks.no/fagomrader/digitalisering/laringsanalyse-i-skolen/dette-er-laringsanalyse-i-skolen/ (KS site) and https://slate.uib.no/projects/ks-fou-prosjekt-174018-laeringsanalyse (SLATE site); both in Norwegian.

4. https://github.com/Utdanningsdirektoratet/ns4180/blob/master/utdanningsrammeverk.md
5. According to the standard: Learning Technology – Metadata for learning resources NS 4180.
6. https://www.datatilsynet.no/en/regulations-and-tools/sandbox-for-artificial-intelligence/
7. https://www.udir.no/om-udir/data/kl06-grep/ (in Norwegian).
8. A demo version is available here: https://fagkart.no/demo/#/profile
9. https://www.ks.no/contentassets/4aef2834b79a4daea2b839f7e5b58753/Utkast-DPIA-for-MittFagkart-v09-310821.pdf

REFERENCES

Bull, S. and J. Kay (2010), 'Open learner models', in R. Nkambou, J. Bourdeau and R. Mizoguchi (eds), *Advances in Intelligent Tutoring Systems*, Berlin: Springer-Verlag, pp. 301–22. https://doi.org/10.1007/978-3-642-14363-2_15

Bull, S. and B. Wasson (2016), 'Competence visualisation: Making sense of data from 21st-century technologies in language learning', *ReCALL* **28** (2), 147–65. https://doi.org/10.1017/S0958344015000282

Datatilsynet (2022), 'AVT. Exit report from the sandbox project AVT - Activity data for assessment and adaptation'. https://www.datatilsynet.no/en/regulations-and-tools/reports-on-specific-subjects/reports/the-avt-project-activity-data-for-assessment-and-adaptation/

Ekspertgruppen for digital læringsanalyse (2022), 'Læringsanalyse – noen sentrale dilemmaer: Delrapport fra ekspertgruppen for digital læringsanalyse' [Learning analysis – some key dilemmas: Interim report from the expert group for digital learning analytics]. Kunnskapsdepartementet. https://www.regjeringen.no/no/dokumenter/laringsanalyse-noen-sentrale-dilemmaer/id2916747/

Kaliisa, R., K. Misiejuk, S. López-Pernas, M. Khalil and M. Saqr (2024), 'Have learning analytics dashboards lived up to the hype?', *The 14th Learning Analytics and Knowledge Conference (LAK '24), March 18–22, 2024, Kyoto, Japan*. ACM. https://doi.org/10.1145/3636555.3636884

Malterud, K. (2012), 'Systematic text condensation: A strategy for qualitative analysis', *Scandinavian Journal of Public Health*, **40** (8), 795–805. https://doi.org/10.1177/1403494812465030

Morlandstø, N.I., C.J.S. Hansen, B. Wasson and S. Bull (2019), 'Aktivitetsdata for vurdering og tilpasning: Sluttrapport. SLATE Research Report 2019-1', pp. 1–89. Centre for the Science of Learning & Technology (SLATE), University of Bergen. https://hdl.handle.net/1956/20825

NOU (2023), 'Learning: Lost in the shuffle? Use of pupil and student data to enhance learning', Official Norwegian Reports, NOU 2023: 19 (Translation from Norwegian), Norwegian Ministry of Education and Research. https://www.regjeringen.no/en/dokumenter/nou-2023-19/id2982722/

Ovchinnikova, M. (2021), 'An open learner model dashboard for adaptive learning', Master of Information Science Thesis, Department of Information Science and Media Studies and Centre for the Science of Learning & Technology (SLATE), University of Bergen. https://hdl.handle.net/11250/2760243

Samuelsen, J. (2023), 'Towards learning analytics scalability: Enriching Context Descriptions Across Data Sources', Doctoral Dissertation, Department of Information Science and Media Studies and Centre for the Science of Learning & Technology (SLATE), University of Bergen.

Samuelsen, J., W. Chen and B. Wasson (2021), 'Enriching context descriptions for enhanced LA scalability: a case study', *Research and Practice in Technology Enhanced Learning*, **16**, 6. https://doi.org/10.1186/s41039-021-00150-2

Schwendimann, B.A., M.J. Rodriguez-Triana, A. Vozniuk, L.P. Prieto, M.S. Boroujeni, A. Holzer … and P. Dillenbourg (2016), 'Perceiving learning at a glance: A systematic literature review of learning dashboard research', *IEEE Transactions on Learning Technologies*, **10** (1), 30–41. https://doi.org/10.1109/TLT.2016.2599522

Verbert, K., E. Duval, J. Klerkx, S. Govaerts and J.L. Santos (2013), 'Learning analytics dashboard applications', *American Behavioral Scientist*, **57** (10), 1500–9. https://doi.org/10.1177/0002764213479363

Wasson, B., M. Giannakos, M. Blikstad-Balas, P.H. Uppstad, M. Langford and E.D. Bøhn (2024), 'Implementing learning analytics in Norway: Four central dilemmas', *Journal of Learning Analytics*, **11** (2), 268–80. https://doi.org/10.18608/jla.2024.8241

Wasson, B., N.I. Morlandstø and C.J.S. Hansen (2019), 'Summary of SLATE Research Report 2019-1: Activity Data for Assessment and Activity (AVT)', Centre for the Science of Learning & Technology (SLATE), University of Bergen. https://hdl.handle.net/1956/20187

19. Bridging the data divide in Swedish school education: challenges and opportunities in data standards

Italo Masiello and Zeynab (Artemis) Mohseni

INTRODUCTION

The use of digital technology leads to data generation that can be collected and analysed for commercial and/or improvement purposes, among many others. This is true, for example, for simple data generated by a refrigerator, to indicate to the owner when it is time to buy eggs, as well as aggregated data about world events, which, once analysed, can indicate to the trader which stocks to sell or buy at the stock market. Data is today a vital resource that opens up a technological revolution (Perez 2002). Indeed, data is inexpensive, can be recycled for many purposes simultaneously and across different domains, and processes and procedures can be made more efficient through the use of data analysis (Klingenberg et al. 2019). Within the domain of education, too, digital platforms or applications collect a wide range of data on students, both in the classrooms and outside. Educational data, such as text, grades, quizzes, timestamps and online behavioural data in connection to the use of digital learning platforms or digital learning materials (DLMs), is constantly collected, whether students or their caregivers are aware of it. That data can then be analysed to provide support for decision-making to students, teachers, or both (Masiello et al. 2024). For public health reasons, the COVID pandemic has contributed to an upsurge of digital technologies in education, and therefore, also of educational data generation. The pandemic has also served as an opportunity to rethink how education is administered and organized, and how educational data in primary and secondary education specifically can be utilized to provide value to primary users – teachers and students (Masiello et al. 2023a). The purpose of formal education has always been to improve the facilitation of learning, and learning analytics is poised to help reach this goal.

Learning analytics (LA) is the measurement, collection, analysis, and reporting of data about students and their contexts, for the purposes of understanding and optimizing learning and the environments in which it occurs, as defined in 2011 by the Society for Learning Analytics Research.[1] LA can be used by students, their caregivers, teachers, school principals, and education leaders when analyses of the same datasets represent different aspects of utility – micro, meso and macro (Drachsler 2023). For example, LA dashboards can visualize data at the micro level, focusing on the needs of individuals, such as students and instructors within a specific course or subject. The meso level looks at a broader scope, covering multiple courses or subjects and providing relevant LA information for school principals and students' caregivers. The macro level offers a comprehensive overview, allowing for insights into a number of schools for education leaders.

In contemporary educational settings, the management and utilization of data at lower education levels are typically dispersed across multiple stakeholders, both public and private entities (Aguerrebere et al. 2022), such as schools, municipal authorities, and educational technology (EdTech) providers. To enable the effective use of such data, a robust framework is required to ensure that the data is well defined, structured, and semantically harmonized across all stakeholders (Facile et al. 2022), thereby facilitating interoperability. The importance of standardizing data is universally acknowledged, particularly in terms of enhancing data quality and sharing mechanisms (Facile et al. 2022). However, efficient, reliable and secure manipulation of educational data necessitates the integration of student data stored across disparate systems and by different stakeholders into a unified and coherent dataset. This integration should represent a comprehensive view of students' academic progress and digital platforms' usage patterns.

Sweden is recognized as a digitally advanced nation with a robust educational infrastructure, including strong digital support for primary and secondary schools (Masiello et al. 2023b). It is worth noting that Sweden's education system includes public and independent schools, each with distinct approaches. Public schools are managed by municipalities and are funded by governmental tax revenue. They follow a national curriculum to ensure equal access and comprehensive education for all students, regardless of socio-economic status. While a few private schools with tuition fees still exist, the more common model is that of independent schools, which are also publicly funded. The independent schools are privately owned – typically by corporations or cooperative organizations – but receive government funding and are required to follow the same national curriculum as municipal schools. More importantly, both school systems report students' and staff's personal data to the public authorities and essentially follow the same rules. However, independent schools do not have the same duties as municipal schools have in archiving obligations, open-data requirements and freedom-of-information principles. Despite these differences, Sweden's education system prioritizes equality and high standards, aiming to minimize disparities and prepare students for global competitiveness while fostering personal development and citizenship. The Swedish education system has widely adopted digital technologies across all systems and levels. Already in the 1980s, personal computers were frequently adopted in the classroom (Winman et al. 2018). More recently, driven by national strategies introduced in 2017 to enhance digital competence among students and teachers (Regeringen 2017), digital learning platforms or DLMs are part of every primary and secondary school. Key advancements include one-to-one computing, integration of programming and computational thinking into the curriculum, and extensive use of digital tools like DLMs, virtual reality and online resources. Sweden's comprehensive IT infrastructure ensures high connectivity and availability of digital devices in schools. Investments in digital transformation have fostered personalized learning and data-informed approaches, empowering teachers to tailor instruction and monitor student progress. However, challenges persist, such as ensuring equitable access to technology, addressing gaps in teacher training for digital skills, and tackling privacy concerns. The Swedish National Agency for Education (Skolverket) continues to spearhead initiatives to bridge these gaps. Sweden exemplifies a leading model in integrating digital innovation within education, emphasizing student-centred learning while navigating the complexities of a rapidly evolving technological landscape.

In this study, we implement a previously developed technical framework (Mohseni et al. 2024a) incorporating a data pipeline that leverages a reliable national data infrastructure. The implementation has been applied in a number of schools. This study is guided by the following question: How can the organization and structuring of educational data facilitate interoperability between DLMs and educational institutions? How can the implementation be brought up to scale?

BACKGROUND

Data Standards

Educational institutions collect extensive data on students and their activities, but these datasets often vary in volume, complexity, and heterogeneity (Mohseni et al. 2022). Differences in parameters such as location, time, subject, and activity can make it challenging to utilize these datasets strategically, especially as they are often dispersed across various digital platforms (Nissenbaum 2019). This challenge is particularly pronounced in lower education levels (Aguerrebere et al. 2022).

While fields like clinical research have successfully implemented data standards (Richesson and Krischer 2007; Tsueng et al. 2023), such standards are lacking for data collection, processing and analysis in primary and secondary education (Hernández-Leal et al. 2021). Hernández-Leal et al. (2021) proposed a framework for integrating high school data across Latin America, but did not address crucial issues like data standardization. Similarly, Ocheja et al. (2023) emphasized the integration of diverse DLMs using Blockchain of Learning Logs but neglected standardization, a key element for effective data integration. As mentioned earlier, all independent and municipal schools must comply with the same rules on data sharing and the protection of students' personal information as set forth by law. However, especially independent schools owned by private corporations do not have the same obligation of public transparency. This difference in data sharing and absence of data standardization in the Swedish school systems has led to data lock-in, hindering efficient information flow across the educational value chain (Hylén and Karlén 2019). Data standards define the data to be collected, its structure, and storage protocols (Gal and Rubinfeld 2019), thus improving portability and interoperability (Lemley 2002). Although data standards do not mandate data sharing, they enable it by providing the necessary infrastructure (Contreras and Reichman 2015). The Swedish National Agency for Education introduced the SS 12000[2] standard in 2018 to enhance interoperability between digital systems in schools, covering processes like scheduling, attendance, and grade reporting. Supported by the Swedish EdTech Industry, the SS 12000 standard focuses on the format and structure of data rather than its content, enabling smoother platform integration. SS 12000's core principle is active data retrieval, where systems request data instead of receiving it passively. For instance, if System A needs data from System B, it must actively retrieve the data. This approach allows data producers to control data availability and sharing, facilitated by access codes or keys. The Swedish EdTech Industry illustrates this with a scenario, Figure 19.1, which demonstrates how the standard can be applied. In this scenario, a municipality manages multiple IT systems (for example, Systems A, B, C) to support various administrative and educational processes. Basic data, housed in System A, is shared with other systems (B and C), which handle functions such as attendance, grades, and exam results. This exchange of data is essential for ensuring compliance with national regulations and for maintaining communication with national authorities such as the Swedish National Agency for Education, Central Statistics Sweden, the Swedish Council for Higher Education, and the Swedish Board of Student Finance.

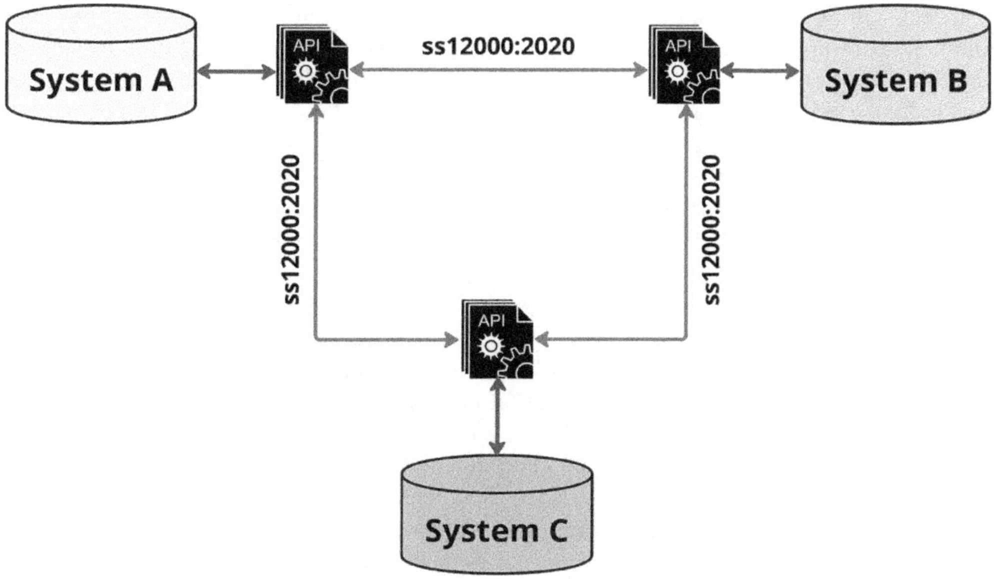

Source: Figure reproduced from the Swedish EdTech Industry under the CC 4.0.

Figure 19.1 *Example with the standard SS 12000:2020*

The standardized format in SS 12000 simplifies data flow (illustrated by the lighter gray arrows in Figure 19.1) across various systems. Each provider ensures that their application programming interfaces (APIs) comply with the standard, while users decide which data to transfer. This uniform data format aids in integrating and updating systems across the educational landscape.

Despite SS 12000's advantages, its adoption in Swedish schools remains limited due to the diversity in data sharing of the school systems, of digital tools and the proprietary data formats used by many EdTech providers. These factors make it difficult to integrate EdTech data with municipal systems, limiting the ability to create a comprehensive view of student progress.

Data Pipelines

The integration of data pipelines is increasingly critical for organizations to facilitate data-informed decision-making, reporting and the development of machine learning (ML) and deep learning models (Goodhope et al. 2012; Jovanovic et al. 2021). The efficacy of these applications depends fundamentally on the integrity and quality of data (Cai and Zhu 2015). For stakeholders to utilize data effectively, they must possess the capabilities for accurate collection, storage, and analysis of high-quality datasets. The process of integrating data from diverse sources to derive meaningful insights is inherently complex (Batini et al. 2015), further complicated by the challenges of big data's volume, velocity, and variety (Kaisler et al. 2013).

Recent studies underscore the necessity of robust data pipelines (Ghosh Chowdhury et al. 2020). A data pipeline comprises a sequence of processes from data ingestion to storage, where each step's output feeds into the next (Raman et al. 2013). These systems automate data flow, reducing manual interventions and enabling streamlined procedures for data extraction, transformation, validation, and loading (Jovanovic et al. 2021). Additionally, they enhance throughput by minimizing bottlenecks, handling both streaming and batch data concurrently (Munappy et al. 2020). Adrian et al. (2021) exemplified this by adapting the Public Health Surveillance framework (McNabb et al. 2002) into a data pipeline for efficient data processing.

Implementation Science

The technical framework was implemented into the schools following an implementation science approach, which is a research framework used to lay the groundwork for exploring teaching and learning processes in schools (Albers and Pattuwage 2017). Implementation science in education is associated with promising and lasting changes (Albers and Pattuwage 2017) by improving the evidence of what works best, how and why. The methods of implementation science ensure that education changes are executed to ensure that the implementation process accounts for local variables and other contextual factors in schools in order to scale up and succeed in any setting (Nordstrum et al. 2017). The process of implementation unfolds over a series of stages with different implementation activities at each stage (more in the Methods section). Besides, there are also common components of successfully implemented programmes, that is, implementation drivers (competency, organization and leadership) (Fixsen et al. 2013). The stages and drivers are derived from long-lasting successful programmes and a review of the implementation research literature (Fixsen et al. 2005). The process can span over a period of two to four years.

This study is part of a larger study (Masiello 2023a) that was approved by the Swedish Ethical Advisory Board (Der 2021-06400-01, with supplementary records Dir 2022-06055-02). The larger study had the aim of understanding how the systematic professional development of teachers and school principals to use DLM and LA dashboards could allow for sustained improvements in teaching practices and student outcomes. As such, implementation science also guides, among others, the integration of the technical framework into school activities. The basic idea is that teachers can gain deeper insights into student performance and preferences by consulting LA dashboards, to potentially target pedagogical intervention more specifically. However, it is important to acknowledge that the implementation of these advanced techniques presents considerable challenges for teachers. Teachers must first attain data literacy, defined as the capability to utilize data for informed decision-making, enabling them to apply insights derived from these sophisticated analytical methods (Kippers et al. 2018). In the context of educational data, it is imperative to ensure robust student privacy and data security while preserving data that is both pertinent to enhancing student learning outcomes and valuable for refining pedagogical strategies. Employing a data pipeline can facilitate the generation of secure, enriched datasets for various stages of the learning analytics cycle, safeguarding student privacy and reducing the need for manual intervention (Tsoni et al. 2022).

This study adopts our technical solution leveraging a drive-based data pipeline alongside a novel data standard framework and customized scripts tailored to each stakeholder. The proposed approach should facilitate the integration of anonymous, low-risk data into a learning analytics cycle, providing a structured pathway for researchers and developers to enhance interoperability and manage data transfer, analysis and visualization for various stakeholders. The implementation science research framework should also ensure the results of the integration of the technical solution in the respective school environments.

METHODS

In this study, we applied our technical solution containing a data pipeline by employing a trustworthy Swedish warehouse – the Swedish University Computer Network (SUNET).[3] Data pipelines usually comprise four core components: (1) heterogeneous data sources; (2) sequential data processing stages; (3) a centralized repository; and (4) data visualization through an integrated dashboard interface. This architecture enables efficient data transfer from source applications to a centralized data warehouse, where each processing stage generates outputs that serve as inputs for the subsequent stage. The pipeline ultimately visualizes data outputs via a multi-element dashboard system, facilitating comprehensive data insights. In our case, ensuring data security, privacy, and ethical integrity was crucial, as we handled student-related educational data of children between the ages of 11 and 13. We addressed these concerns and ensured data compartmentalization through the SUNET Simple Storage Service (S3).[4] Each stakeholder's dataset was isolated in separate S3 instances. This service, known for its high accessibility and scalable storage capabilities, was compatible with various cloud-based database platforms, including Amazon Relational Database Service[5] (RDS), Microsoft Azure SQL Database,[6] Cloudman[7] and IBM Db2 on Cloud.[8]

A major challenge was the integration of student data from heterogeneous sources, critical for a holistic analysis of students' academic performance and engagement metrics. In this study, EdTech providers managed data concerning DLM interactions, such as quiz results, number of attempts, timestamps and user engagement metrics. Conversely, municipal authorities maintained data on student identities, attendance and academic records. The absence of a standardized data format significantly hindered the merging of these datasets, posing substantial obstacles to achieving interoperability. Therefore, we developed a script to (1) reformat data according to the defined API data standard; (2) merge and integrate data from municipalities and EdTech providers stored in the S3 drives; and (3) hash the formatted data. Such technical solutions and data standards are novel in Sweden, especially if meant to support a network of stakeholders in the processes of standardization, anonymization, management, transport, analysis and visualization of educational data.

According to the Active Implementation Framework – used in the larger study of which this study is part – four stages were common: Exploration (assessing needs, creating readiness etc.); Installation (selecting and training practitioners/participants etc.); Initial Implementation (introducing changes, improvement cycles etc.); and Full Implementation (new practices adopted, etc.) (Fixsen et al. 2013). The stages could run over a period of two to four years and did not necessarily constitute a linear process. All the data collected during the larger project are presented in our previous publication (Nordmark et al. 2024). In this chapter, we limit the explanation of the methods pertinent to this study.

During the Exploration stage, we assessed the needs of all the actors involved in the project, including the needs of the system administrators responsible for the data, both at the municipalities and EdTech providers (34 teachers, three school principals, four EdTech providers represented by four system administrators and four managers, and four municipal system administrators). We also examined the data sources of all the stakeholders and the key data components needed for the LA dashboards. At the Installation stage, we started to build the implementation capacity by initiating meetings with all the system administrators and data-protection officials to discuss the data available, how to move it, where to move it, and which data to move through the pipeline. Subsequently, we acquired the necessary technical infrastructure, storage, and resources to achieve the data move. In parallel, informed consent was collected from both guardians and students. During the Initial Implementation stage, we started a series of workshops with 29 teachers to co-design the LA dashboards in compliance with design-based research (Mohseni et al. 2023a). We went through a series of cumulative iterations of the dashboard with each workshop and group of participating teachers. When the beta version of the LA dashboard was complete, we ran workshops to train the teachers to read the dashboard and understand which datasets were used for each visualization comprising the LA dashboard, making it as transparent as possible. At stage four, Full Implementation, the LA dashboard should have been tested in classrooms to reach the partial objective of the larger study, that is, understand how the use of the LA dashboard could allow for sustained improvements in teaching practices and student outcomes.

RESULTS

Data standardization and the data pipeline were developed in parallel during stages 2 and 3 of the project implementation process, that is, the stages of Installation and Initial Implementation.

Data Standardization

To enable the integration of data from municipalities and EdTech providers, we developed a data standard, encompassing key features such as student attendance and final grades (provided by three different and distinct data sources) and learning activities like assignments, quizzes and timestamps from four different DLMs. The data standard comprised 14 tables, as outlined in Figure 19.2, and shown in detail in Mohseni et al. (2024a). Each table was identified by an orange header, with primary features in dark blue and primary keys, indicating table interrelations, in light blue. The focus remained on commonly shared attributes across datasets.

The content of the tables made up the name of each: 'Student', 'Teacher', 'Class', 'School', 'Homework', 'Language', 'Course', 'Subject', 'Lesson', 'Quiz', 'Question', 'Answer', 'Attendance' and 'FinalGrade'. These 14 tables were selected to collect data that could be used to analyse learning by correlating students' activities, attendance, and academic performance. This enabled the grouping of students by performance, evaluating achievements across classes and schools, and identifying challenging lessons or assignments.

Figures 19.1, 19.2 and 19.3 illustrate hierarchical relationships among an example of tables, such as from 'Teacher' to 'Class' to 'School', from 'Lesson' to 'Course' to 'Subject', and from 'Question' to 'Quiz'. These relationships can be summarized as follows:

- Teacher–Class: A many-to-many relationship, indicating that multiple teachers can be linked to multiple classes.

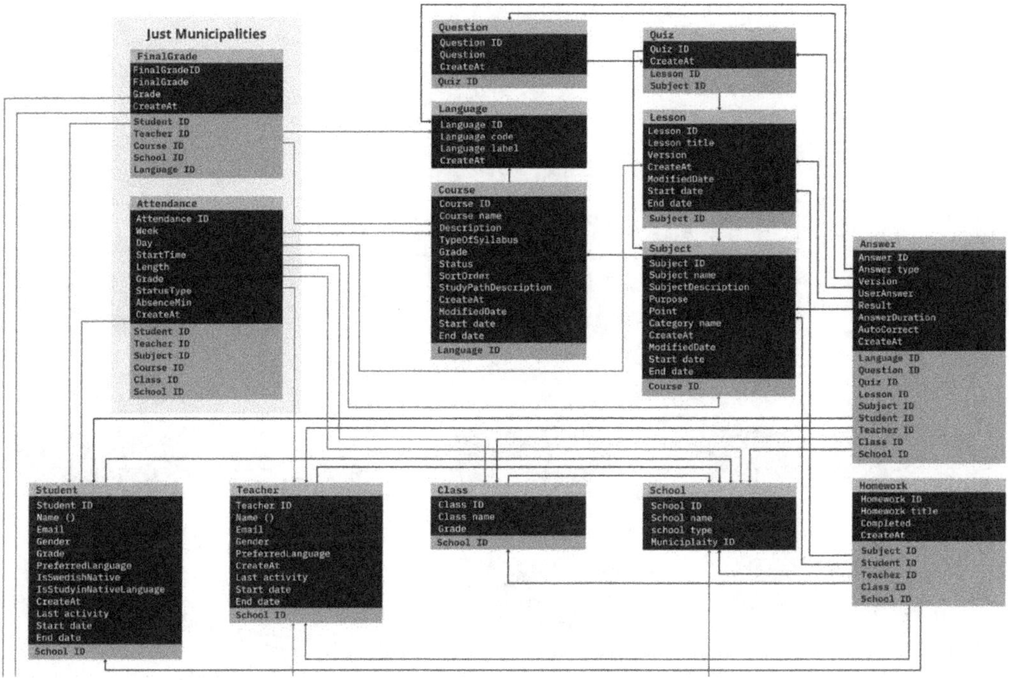

Source: Figure reproduced under the CC 4.0 from Mohseni et al. (2024a).

Figure 19.2 *Fourteen tables making up the data standard*

- Class–School: A many-to-one relationship, where many classes belong to a single school.
- Lesson–Course: A many-to-many relationship, where multiple lessons (for example, Multiplication, Division) can be part of multiple courses (for example, Mathematics grade 5, Mathematics grade 6).
- Course–Subject: A many-to-one relationship, indicating that many courses are affiliated with a single subject (for example, Mathematics).
- Question–Quiz: A many-to-many relationship, where multiple questions can be associated with multiple quizzes.

'Homework' and 'Quiz' represent components of student assignments across lessons. Since EdTech providers lack access to final grades and attendance data, municipalities are responsible for populating the 'Attendance' and 'FinalGrade' tables shown above in Figure 19.2.

The steps of the pipeline were successfully tested with four EdTech providers and five schools, demonstrating a functional technical framework for primary education data. This progress required extensive collaboration and dialogue among all stakeholders.

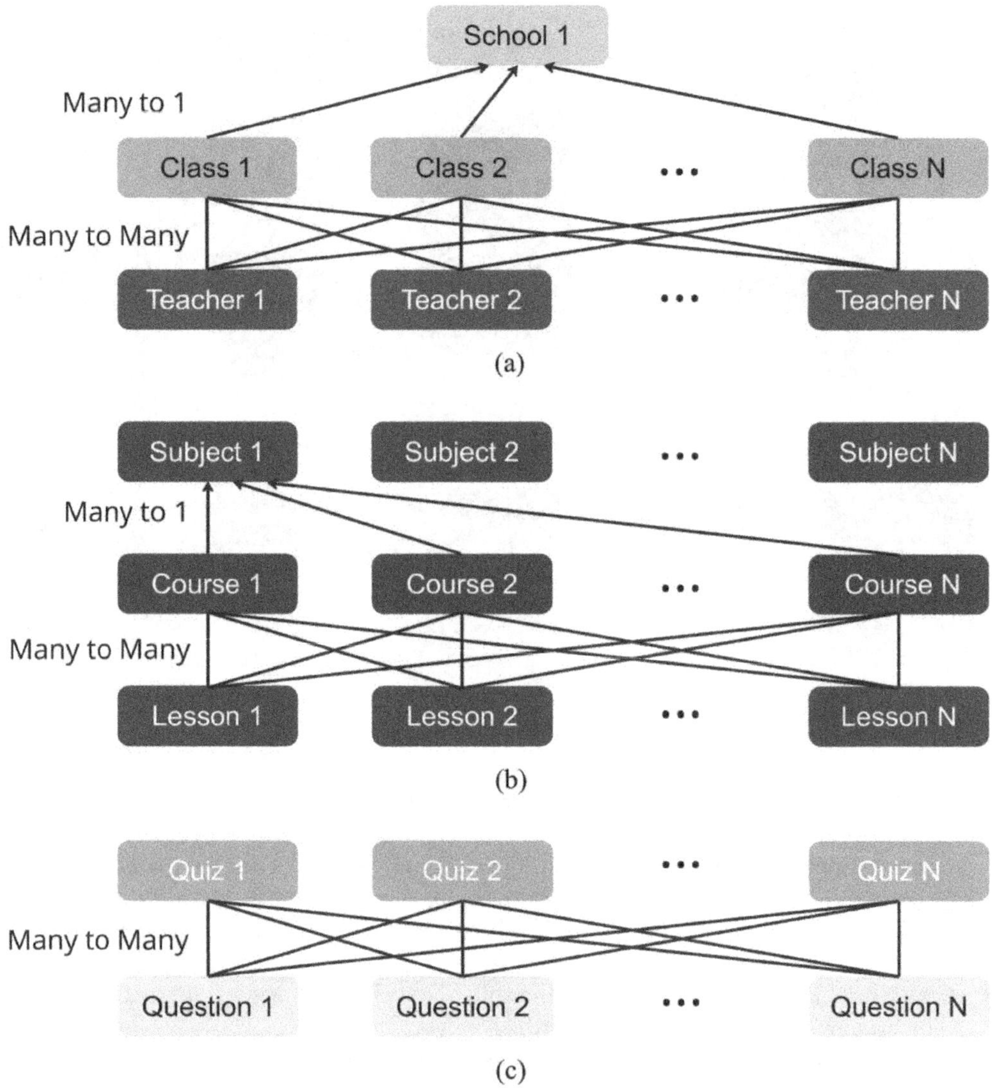

Source: Figure reproduced under the CC 4.0 from Mohseni et al. (2024a).

Figure 19.3 *Example of the hierarchical relationship of the tables: (a) school, class, and teacher; (b) subject, course, and lesson; and (c) quiz and question*

Data Pipeline

Figure 19.4 illustrates the seven sequential steps of the technical framework, providing detailed information about the data pipeline (Mohseni et al. 2024a). Data from each stakeholder was

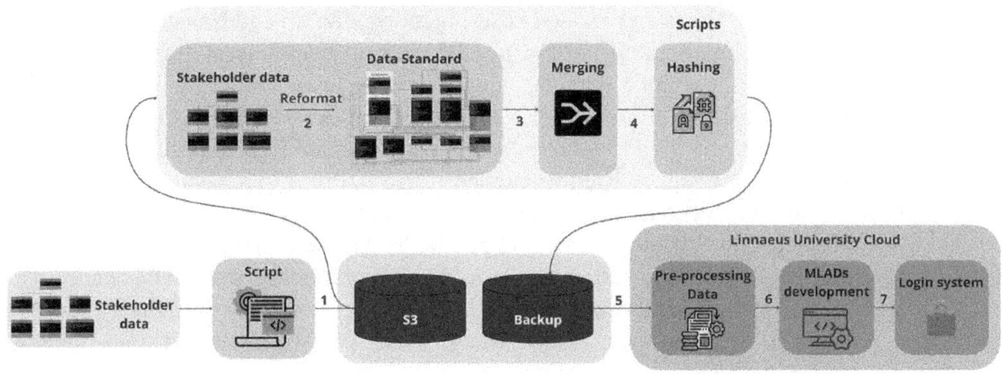

Source: Figure adapted under the CC 4.0 from Mohseni et al. (2024a).

Figure 19.4 The seven steps of the technical solution in detail

uploaded and stored to respective S3 instances (1), where scripts were applied for data standardization (2), merging (3) and hashing (4). The hashed data was then stored in the SUNET drive, with original data removed from S3 to anonymize data handling. To support data preprocessing (5), analysis, and visualization through developed Multiple Learning Analytics Dashboards (MLADs) (6), a virtual machine was deployed at the university's cloud, allowing stakeholders to access tailored dashboards through a secure login (7).

An explanation of each step follows:

1. Data Storage: S3 instances facilitated secure data uploads in compliance with the General Data Protection Regulation (GDPR), accessible by stakeholders such as teachers and municipalities. Some stakeholders faced challenges in regularly uploading data due to time constraints. Customized Python[9] scripts automated these uploads, reducing dependency on diverse APIs.
2. Data Standardization: Despite the simplicity of the proposed standard presented in the previous section, stakeholders struggled with data formatting due to limited expertise and resource constraints. Customized Python scripts were provided by us to each stakeholder to ensure compliance with the standard.
3. Data Merging: A script merged data across S3s to create a comprehensive view of student progress, utilizing students' email addresses and names for accurate matching.
4. Data Hashing: Data encryption was implemented using Fernet[10] from the cryptography library, ensuring only hashed data was accessible to the development team. Pseudonymized data was securely stored as a backup, with access restricted to essential administrative purposes, such as removing records of students who leave the project or move to another school. Teachers could access the hashed codes in line with GDPR Article 6.1.C. When integrating data from an EdTech provider that used an alternate hashing method, a matching process was conducted to ensure compatibility with our approach.

5. Data Pre-processing: This step included cleaning, normalizing, and transforming hashed data, enhancing data quality and computational efficiency for analysis. It involved eliminating missing values, correcting errors, and performing feature extraction.
6. MLAD Dcvelopment: Pre-processed data was then used to create MLADs, tailored to different aspects of utility and therefore different stakeholders. This was donc through a Human-centred Design approach (Mohseni et al. 2023a). Prototyping and scenario-based frameworks gathered feedback, emphasizing stakeholders' involvement to refine dashboard requirements and utility (Mohseni et al. 2023b; Mohseni 2024).
7. Login System: A secure login system was also developed to allow stakeholders access to their specific dashboard using usernames and hashed passwords. Despite the limitations of password-based systems, such as the risks of weak passwords or theft, this method ensured controlled access.

Implementation

At the Exploration stage, the interviews with the teachers revealed several key findings related to this part of the project; among others, while digital infrastructure is mostly reliable, some schools still struggle with internet connectivity, and teachers view digital transformation as exciting but not well integrated. Additionally, managing devices like tablets and laptops was time-consuming, and there was a mixed level of familiarity with learning analytics among teachers. Interviews with school principals acknowledged the pandemic's role in accelerating digital tool adoption in education. They emphasized the need for strategic collaboration at all levels to effectively integrate digital tools to enhance LA and improve student outcomes, highlighting a holistic view of technology's evolving role in education. Meetings with the various system administrators revealed that data competencies were heterogeneous, displaying a need for support, especially for the municipal system administrators.

At the Installation stage, by meeting with the system administrator and data-protection officials, we uncovered a very broad disparity in dataset structures. No data standards were used. In addition, we discussed the vulnerabilities with GDPR compliance issues, especially related to user data collection. That led to delayed deployment of the LA dashboard due to ethical and security compliance. Once the technical infrastructure was in place with the SUNET system, we developed scripts to collect data that each stakeholder could use.

At the Initial Implementation stage, the researchers co-designed the LA dashboards together with the teachers. When it was possible to match the data between the EdTech providers and municipalities, we were able to show visualizations for which teachers could easily recognize their data source, making the visualizations transparent and trustworthy. However, it was also at this stage that we realized that we were not always getting enough data to show reliable analytics. Combining data from DLMs and school systems proved difficult for a number of reasons related to different datasets: (1) students used a login system at the start of the day, which ideally should have granted access to all the DLMs students use throughout the day. However, a data-anchor was missing between different datasets, which resulted in a significant amount of data that could not be matched for analysis; (2) data that could be used for analysis were too little; (3) machine learning predictions were therefore unreliable; (4) important pieces of information from DLM were not present, which led to impractical exercises from the teachers to understand the relation between a score and its significance for possible improvements; (5) DLMs' data were not updated weekly, even though we kept reminding of this for accuracy reasons; (6) DLMs were used for practice and not as the main learning resource; and (7) because of all of the above, teachers could not derive insights from the LA dashboard, which led to ignoring them until accuracy would be restored in the next iterations.

However, stage 4, that is, Full Implementation, was never reached. The project funds were depleted, and we were not able to test new LA dashboard iterations in the classrooms for real-world testing.

DISCUSSION

The implementation of the data standardization process and data pipeline described in this study highlights both the achievements and the challenges encountered when integrating heterogeneous datasets from different educational stakeholders. By developing a 14-table data standard (Figure 19.2) and creating a robust data pipeline (Figure 19.4), we successfully demonstrated the possibility of integrating data from municipalities and EdTech providers, thus the possibility of enabling in the future better insights into student learning activities and performance. In addition, with our implementation, we want to put a spotlight on Sweden's digital maturity and align it with broader Nordic and European approaches to data privacy and interoperability in education, like those driven by the European EdTech Alliance.[11] Swedish education operates under robust GDPR frameworks (Swedish Data Protection Act 2018:218[12]), ensuring secure data practices across public and private education providers. This legal landscape emphasizes the protection of student and teacher data, reflecting the high regional priority on ethical data use. The Swedish Data Protection Authority fined a municipality for using facial recognition technology to monitor student attendance, marking Sweden's first penalty under GDPR (European Data Protection Board 2022). This case underscores the importance of compliance with data-protection regulations in educational settings. However, several limitations related to data consistency, stakeholder engagement and privacy concerns were identified in this project. This reflects broader trends observed in recent literature (Aguerrebere et al. 2022; Karademir et al. 2024; Masiello et al. 2024). Further refinement is needed to fully realize the potential of the LA dashboard for improvement in teaching practices and student outcomes. Both achievements and limitations are discussed below.

Key Achievements

The development of the educational data standard for primary and secondary contexts was a pivotal achievement. This has to be understood in light of existing, or ready-to-use, digital systems. We know that data standardization is critical to ensuring interoperability between different systems (Drachsler and Greller 2012). Drachsler and Greller (2012) highlight that without standardized data formats, LA systems struggle to produce meaningful, comparable analytics across different contexts. By focusing on commonly shared attributes such as student attendance, academic performance and learning activities, our hierarchical table relationships (for example, teacher-to-class, lesson-to-course) provide a solution that bridges municipal data and DLM data from already-in-use systems. By linking student performance on assignments to specific lessons and activities, our approach enables the identification of learning patterns that can inform teaching practices and support the development of adaptive learning technologies. This aligns with research on how complex, relational datasets can support personalized learning experiences (Liu et al. 2017).

Moreover, our solution aligns with open-data architecture models seen in a new initiative such as the IMS Global Learning Consortium,[13] which aims to provide a similar framework for data exchange. Many of the LA dashboard solutions present in the current literature present the use of a single resource that collects most or all educational data to be analysed for a specific research or educational purpose (Mohseni et al. 2024b). This exposes a lack of integration between the administrative systems and the various digital products making up the teaching and learning ecosystem. It is the interoperability of the various systems that enables us to better understand what could possibly impact student outcomes. This gains greater importance in the Swedish education context. Sweden's unique model of public and independent schools further necessitates standardized data processes. The coexistence of privately managed and municipal schools requires a unified framework to facilitate seamless data exchange and interoperability. Unlike some European counterparts, Sweden has been pioneering in integrating these frameworks through initiatives like the Swedish EdTech Industry's work on IT standards[14] and testbeds,[15] ensuring transparency and equity.

The deployment of the data pipeline (Figure 19.4) further ensured that this integrated data could be processed and analysed efficiently. The pipeline facilitated secure data uploads and pre-processing, making it easier for teachers and other stakeholders to access useful learning analytics. The development of a data pipeline capable of integrating, anonymizing and analysing data aligns with the increasing demand for data-informed decision-making in education, as described by Ifenthaler and Schumacher (2016). Their work emphasizes the importance of LA dashboards in providing teachers with actionable insights to tailor instruction and support student learning. Our solution also went as far as to deploy MLADs that provided utility for various stakeholders, as shown in one of our publications (Mohseni et al. 2024a). The use of hashing and encryption to ensure compliance with the GDPR is particularly important given the growing concerns over data privacy in educational contexts (Tsoni et al. 2022). This approach aligns with best practices for secure data handling in education, as discussed in recent studies on GDPR compliance in learning analytics (Teasley 2018).

Our approach attempted to promote a data-informed decision-making process, which, as emphasized in the Installation and Initial Implementation stages, may be crucial for improving student outcomes in an increasingly digital educational landscape. In fact, we facilitated the co-design of the LA dashboard according to design-based research, where a number of iterative meetings for development resulted in the visualization of elements chosen by the teachers and school principals (Mohseni et al. 2023b). Working with this stakeholder by showing which piece of data leads to a specific visualization, like, for example, a line graph or a prediction about whether a student will succeed in completing a subject, generates a sense of trust and transparency of the data. This is an important step towards data-informed decision-making, as research has demonstrated (Utterberg Modén 2021). Our integration of data from multiple datasets and diverse stakeholders allows for a partial analysis of student progress and performance at the individual level, contributing to teachers' data literacy, which is important for using the LA dashboard effectively (Kippers et al. 2018).

Challenges and Limitations

Despite the technical achievements, several challenges emerged, particularly regarding data collection, consistency and stakeholder engagement, which are echoed across the current body of research. For example, the inconsistent data upload from some stakeholders, as well as missing or incomplete data, irregular updates of data – despite frequent reminders to the EdTech providers – hampered the reliability of machine learning predictions, making it difficult to produce actionable insights in real time. The absence of key information from DLMs, such as timestamps or detailed breakdowns of quiz scores, further complicated the ability to provide teachers with clear insights for data-informed decision-making. In addition, data gaps due to irregular student login behaviour and irregular use of the DLMs not promoted by the teachers mirror, together with inconsistent data upload, the issues discussed by Klein et al. (2019), who found that inconsistent data entry often hampers the reliability of LA systems and their trustworthiness. The same authors also point out the fact that unclear visualizations lead to teachers ignoring the LA dashboard, which is also the case in our study, where the participating teachers could not derive valuable insight from them and decided to use the LA dashboard only after updating it with accurate visualizations. These challenges underscore the need for more seamless data collection mechanisms, as has also been recommended in other sectors (Holmström et al. 2024).

One significant challenge was the heterogeneity of data competencies among stakeholders, including system administrators. The municipal system administrators struggled with the technical aspects of data formatting, requiring us to provide customized Python scripts for data uploads and standardization. While this mitigated some challenges, it highlighted the need for continued training and support to ensure stakeholders, like municipal system administrators, can actively participate in the implementation. This result of our research is not found or discussed openly in the literature.

An additional challenge relates to compliance with the GDPR. Studies have documented the delays and complications associated with implementing GDPR-compliant systems in educational settings, particularly when dealing with cross-organizational data sharing for automated decision-making (Labadie and Legner 2023) or data-informed decision-making (Mandinach and Abrams 2022). Although we took steps to ensure data privacy through hashing and encryption methods, delays in meeting GDPR requirements contributed to the slow deployment of the LA dashboards. This underlines the importance of addressing legal and ethical issues early in the project planning phase to prevent such delays in the implementation process. Moreover, the Nordic emphasis on digital inclusivity and sustainability underpins the development of systems that bridge public and private data repositories. Such systems exemplify regional aspirations for collaborative data ecosystems that serve diverse educational needs without compromising individual privacy. Lessons from this project of Sweden's municipal-system integration can inform European efforts towards harmonizing education data standards under GDPR compliance while fostering innovation in learning analytics.

A major limitation of this chapter is the fact that we could not test the co-developed LA dashboard based on the described pipeline on a larger scale. The above challenges delayed the onset of the fourth stage, that is, the Final Implementation, and subsequently also the termination of the project funds.

Implications for Future Work

The mixed familiarity with learning analytics among teachers and the time-consuming management of digital devices, as revealed during the Exploration stage, indicate that while there is excitement about digital transformation, more effort is needed to integrate DLMs and LA dashboards effectively into everyday teaching practices. Current research underscores that while teachers are generally positive about the potential of learning analytics, they often lack the time, training, and institutional support needed to fully leverage these tools in their teaching practice (Nordmark et al. 2024). A human-centred design approach, as we used for developing the MLADs, should continue to be the focus in future iterations to ensure that the dashboards meet the needs of all users. Furthermore, additional support structures, including professional development and technical assistance, are necessary to improve stakeholder engagement and data quality.

To improve data collection consistency and reliability, future efforts should focus on refining the data entry process, perhaps through automatic logging mechanisms within the current data systems. This would reduce the reliance on manual input by system administrators and teachers and decrease the risk of incomplete data. A further step could involve exploring the use of adaptive learning systems that provide continuous feedback loops between student performance and learning activity, creating a richer dataset for analysis.

CONCLUSIONS

In conclusion, our development of a data standard and pipeline to integrate educational data from municipalities and EdTech providers represents an important step forward and a solid foundation for creating a more connected and data-informed educational landscape. However, the challenges of data consistency, stakeholder engagement, and GDPR compliance reflect broader trends in the literature, suggesting that more work is needed to refine these systems and ensure their successful adoption. Future efforts should focus on improving data collection processes, providing greater support for teachers and addressing legal and ethical issues early in the implementation process, ensuring that LA can reach its full potential in enhancing student learning outcomes.

ACKNOWLEDGEMENTS

This work is supported by the Swedish Research Council for Health, Working Life and Welfare (FORTE), grant number 2020-01221 and Växjö Komen, grant number 2020/3209-5.1.1.

NOTES

1. https://www.solaresearch.org/about/what-is-learning-analytics/
2. https://www.sis.se/standardutveckling/tksidor/tk400499/sistk450/ss-12000/
3. https://www.sunet.se/om-sunet
4. https://wiki.sunet.se/pages/viewpage.action?pageId=18612359

5. https://aws.amazon.com/rds/
6. https://azure.microsoft.com/en-gb/free/sql-database/
7. https://cloudian.com/blog/s3-compatible-storage/
8. https://cloud.ibm.com/catalog/services/db2
9. https://www.python.org/about/
10. https://cryptography.io/en/latest/fernet/
11. https://www.edtecheurope.org/
12. https://gdprhub.eu/Data_Protection_in_Sweden
13. https://www.imsglobal.org/home
14. https://swedishedtechindustry.se/wp-content/uploads/2022/10/Standarder-for-datadrivna-processer-i-skolan-2019.pdf
15. https://swedishedtechindustry.se/edtest/

REFERENCES

Adrian, V., I.R. Sari and H.G. Hikmahrachim (2021), 'Establishing Data Warehouse to Improve Standardize Health Care Delivery: A Protocol Development in Jakarta City', *1st Virtual Conference on Implications of Information and Digital Technologies for Development.* Computers and Society. https://arxiv.org/abs/2108.09736v1

Aguerrebere, C., H. He, M. Kwet, M.-J. Laakso, C. Lang, C. Marconi, D. Price-Dennis and H. Zhang (2022), 'Global Perspectives on Learning Analytics in K12 Education', in C. Lang, G. Siemens, A.F. Wise, D. Gašević and A. Merceron (eds), *The Handbook of Learning Analytics* (2nd ed.) SoLAR, pp. 223–231. https://solaresearch.org/wp-content/uploads/hla22/HLA22_Chapter_22_Aguerrebere.pdf

Albers, B. and L. Pattuwage (2017), *Implementation in Education: Findings from a Scoping Review.* https://doi.org/10.13140/RG.2.2.29187.40483

Batini, C., A. Rula, M. Scannapieco and G. Viscusi (2015), 'From Data Quality to Big Data Quality', *Journal of Database Management (JDM)*, **26** (1), 60–82. https://doi.org/10.4018/JDM.2015010103

Cai, L. and Y. Zhu (2015), 'The Challenges of Data Quality and Data Quality Assessment in the Big Data Era', *Data Science Journal*, **14,** 1–10 . https://doi.org/10.5334/dsj-2015-002

Contreras, J.L. and J.H. Reichman. (2015), 'Sharing by Design: Data and Decentralized Commons', *Science*, **350** (6266), 1312–14. https://doi.org/10.1126/science.aaa7485

Drachsler, H. (2023), *Towards Highly Informative Learning Analytics.* Open Universiteit. https://doi.org/10.25656/01:26787

Drachsler, H. and W. Greller (2012), 'The Pulse of Learning Analytics Understandings and Expectations from the Stakeholders', *Proceedings of the 2nd International Conference on Learning Analytics and Knowledge*, pp. 120–29. https://doi.org/10.1145/2330601.2330634

European Data Protection Board (2022), *Facial Recognition in School Renders Sweden's First GDPR Fine.* https://www.edpb.europa.eu/news/national-news/2019/facial-recognition-school-renders-swedens-first-gdpr-fine_sv

Facile, R., E.E. Muhlbradt, M. Gong, Q. Li, V. Popat, F. Pétavy, R. Cornet, Y. Ruan, D. Koide, T.I. Saito, S. Hume, F. Rockhold, W. Bao, S. Dubman and B. Jauregui Wurst (2022), 'Use of Clinical Data Interchange Standards Consortium (CDISC) Standards for Real-world Data: Expert Perspectives From a Qualitative Delphi Survey', *JMIR Medical Informatics*, **10** (1), e30363. https://doi.org/10.2196/30363

Fixsen, D., K. Blase, A. Metz and M.V. Dyke (2013), 'Statewide Implementation of Evidence-based Programs', *Exceptional Children*, **79** (3) 213–30. https://doi.org/10.1177/001440291307900206

Fixsen, D., S. Naoom, K. Blase, R. Friedman and F. Wallace (2005), *Implementation Research: A Synthesis of the Literature,* University of South Florida, Louis de la Parte Florida Mental Health Institute, National Implementation Research Network.

Gal, M. and D.L. Rubinfeld (2019), *Data Standardization* (SSRN Scholarly Paper 3326377), Social Science Research Network. https://doi.org/10.2139/ssrn.3326377

Ghosh Chowdhury, A., M. Illian, L. Wisniewski and J. Jasperne (2020), 'An Approach for Data Pipeline with Distributed Query Engine for Industrial Applications', *2020 25th IEEE International Conference on Emerging Technologies and Factory Automation (ETFA)*, *1*, 1005–8. https://doi.org/10.1109/ETFA46521.2020.9212050

Goodhope, K., J. Koshy, J. Kreps, N. Narkhede, R. Park,J. Rao and V.Y. Ye (2012), 'Building LinkedIn's Real-time Activity Data Pipeline'. *IEEE Data Engineering Bulletin*. https://www.semanticscholar.org/paper/Building-LinkedIn%27s-Real-time-Activity-Data-Goodhope-Koshy/259ca60b03a1101f1ef44e6ccbfabe843bfe78d4

Hernández-Leal, E., N.D. Duque-Méndez and C. Cechinel (2021), 'Unveiling Educational Patterns at a Regional Level in Colombia: Data from Elementary and Public High School Institutions', *Heliyon*, **7** (9), e08017. https://doi.org/10.1016/j.heliyon.2021.e08017

Holmström, J., A. Kostis, E. Galariotis, D. Roubaud and C. Zopounidis (2024), 'Stalled Data Flows in Digital Innovation Networks: Underlying Mechanisms and the Role of Related Variety', *Industrial Marketing Management*, **121**, 16–26. https://doi.org/10.1016/j.indmarman.2024.06.007

Hylén, J. and J. Karlén (2019), *Standarder för datadrivna processer i skolan*. https://swedishedtechindustry.se/wp-content/uploads/2022/10/Standarder-for-datadrivna-processer-i-skolan-2019.pdf

Ifenthaler, D. and C. Schumacher (2016), 'Student Perceptions of Privacy Principles for Learning Analytics', *Educational Technology Research and Development*, **64** (5), 923–38. https://doi.org/10.1007/s11423-016-9477-y

Jovanovic, P., S. Nadal, O. Romero, A. Abelló and B. Bilalli (2021), '*Quarry*: A User-centered Big Data Integration Platform', *Information Systems Frontiers*, **23** (1), 9–33. https://doi.org/10.1007/s10796-020-10001-y

Kaisler, S., F. Armour, J.A. Espinosa and W. Money (2013), 'Big Data: Issues and Challenges Moving Forward', *46th Hawaii International Conference on System Sciences*, pp. 995–1004. https://doi.org/10.1109/HICSS.2013.645

Karademir, O., D. Di Mitri, J. Schneider, I. Jivet, J. Allmang, S. Gombert, M. Kubsch,K. Neumann and H. Drachsler (2024), 'I Don't Have Time! But Keep Me in the Loop: Co-designing Requirements for a Learning Analytics Cockpit with Teachers', *Journal of Computer Assisted Learning*, **40** (6) 2681–99. https://doi.org/10.1111/jcal.12997

Kippers, W.B., C.L. Poortman, K. Schildkamp and A.J. Visscher (2018), 'Data Literacy: What do Educators Learn and Struggle with During a Data Use Intervention?', *Studies in Educational Evaluation*, **56**, 21–31. https://doi.org/10.1016/j.stueduc.2017.11.001

Klein, C., J. Lester, H. Rangwala and A. Johri (2019), 'Technological Barriers and Incentives to Learning Analytics Adoption in Higher Education: Insights from Users', *Journal of Computing in Higher Education*, **31** (3), 604–5. https://doi.org/10.1007/s12528-019-09210-5

Klingenberg, C.O., M.A.V. Borges and J.A.V. Antunes Jr (2019), 'Industry 4.0 as a Data-driven Paradigm: A Systematic Literature Review on Technologies', *Journal of Manufacturing Technology Management*, **32** (3), 570–92. https://doi.org/10.1108/JMTM-09-2018-0325

Labadie, C. and C. Legner (2023), 'Building Data Management Capabilities to Address Data Protection Regulations: Learnings from EU-GDPR', *Journal of Information Technology*, **38** (1), 16–44. https://doi.org/10.1177/02683962221141456

Lemley, M.A. (2002), *Intellectual Property Rights and Standard-setting Organizations* (SSRN Scholarly Paper 310122), Social Science Research Network. https://doi.org/10.2139/ssrn.310122

Liu, D. Y.-T., K. Bartimote-Aufflick, A. Pardo and A.J. Bridgeman (2017), 'Data-driven Personalization of Student Learning Support in Higher Education', in A. Peña-Ayala (ed.), *Learning Analytics: Fundaments, Applications, and Trends: A View of the Current State of the Art to Enhance e-Learning*, Springer International Publishing, pp. 143–69. https://doi.org/10.1007/978-3-319-52977-6_5

Mandinach, E.B. and L.M. Abrams (2022), 'Data Literacy and Learning Analytics', in C. Lang, G. Siemens, A.F. Wise, D. Gašević and A. Merceron (eds), *Handbook of Learning Analytics* (2nd ed.), Society for Learning Analytics Research (SoLAR), pp. 196–204. https://www.solaresearch.org/publications/hla-22/hla22-chapter19/

Masiello, I., D.L. Fixsen, S. Nordmark, Z. Mohseni, K. Holmberg, J. Rack, M. Davidsson, T. Andersson-Gidlund and H. Augustsson (2023a), 'Digital Transformation in Schools of Two Southern Regions of Sweden through Implementation-informed Approach: A Mixed-methods Study Protocol', *PLOS ONE*, **18** (12), e0296000. https://urn.kb.se/resolve?urn=urn:nbn:se:lnu:diva-126167

Masiello, I., Z. Mohseni and S. Nordmar (2023b), 'Trends and Issues of Digital Learning in Sweden', in Y.-F. Lee and L.-S. Lee (eds), *Trends and Issues of Promoting Digital Learning in High-digital-competitiveness Countries: Country Reports and International Comparison*, pp. 311–47, Technological and Vocational Education Research Center (TVERC), National Taiwan Normal University, Taiwan and K–12 Education Administration (K12EA), Ministry of Education, Taiwan. https://urn.kb.se/resolve?urn=urn:nbn:se:lnu:diva-126015

Masiello, I., Z. Mohseni, F. Palma, S. Nordmark, H. Augustsson and R. Rundquist (2024), 'A Current Overview of the Use of Learning Analytics Dashboards', *Education Sciences*, **14** (1), 82.

McNabb, S.J., S. Chungong, M. Ryan, T. Wuhib, P. Nsubuga, W. Alemu, V. Carande-Kulis and G. Rodier (2002), 'Conceptual Framework of Public Health Surveillance and Action and its Application in Health Sector Reform', *BMC Public Health*, **2** (1), 2. https://doi.org/10.1186/1471-2458-2-2

Mohseni, Z. (2024), *Development of Visual Learning Analytic Tools to Explore Performance and Engagement of Students in Primary, Secondary, and Higher Education*, Doctoral dissertation, Linnaeus University Press. https://doi.org/10.15626/LUD.532.2024

Mohseni, Z., R.M. Martins and I. Masiello (2022), 'SBGTool v2.0: An Empirical Study on a Similarity-based Grouping Tool for Students' Learning Outcomes', *Data*, **7** (7), 98. https://doi.org/10.3390/data7070098

Mohseni, Z., I. Masiello and R.M. Martins (2023a), 'Co-developing an Easy-to-Use Learning Analytics Dashboard for Teachers in Primary/Secondary Education: A Human-centered Design Approach', *Education Sciences*, **13** (12), 1190. https://urn.kb.se/resolve?urn=urn:nbn:se:lnu:diva-125814

Mohseni, Z., I. Masiello and R.M. Martins (2023b), 'Towards a Teacher-oriented Framework of Visual Learning Analytics by Scenario-based Development, 12–17', *18th European Conference on Technology Enhanced Learning (EC-TEL 2023).* https://urn.kb.se/resolve?urn=urn:nbn:se:lnu:diva-125545

Mohseni, Z., I. Masiello and R.M. Martins (2024a), 'A Technical Infrastructure for Primary Education Data that Contributes to Data Standardization. *Education and Information Technologies*, **29**, 21045–61. https://doi.org/10.1007/s10639-024-12683-2

Mohseni, Z., I. Masiello, R.M. Martins and S. Nordmark (2024b), 'Visual Learning Analytics for Educational Interventions in Primary and Secondary Schools: A Scoping Review', *Journal of Learning Analytics*, **11** (2), 91–111. https://doi.org/10.18608/jla.2024.8309

Munappy, A.R., J. Bosch and H.H. Olsson (2020), 'Data Pipeline Management in Practice: Challenges and Opportunities', *Product-Focused Software Process Improvement: 21st International Conference, PROFES 2020, Turin, Italy, November 25–27 2020, Proceedings*, pp. 168–84. https://doi.org/10.1007/978-3-030-64148-1_11

Nissenbaum, H. (2019), 'Must Privacy Give Way to Use Regulation?', in M.X. Delli Carpini (ed.), *Digital Media and Democratic Futures*, University of Pennsylvania Press, p. 345. https://www.pennpress.org/9780812295894/digital-media-and-democratic-futures/

Nordmark, S., H. Augustsson, M. Davidsson, T. Andersson-Gidlund, K. Holmberg, Z. Mohseni (Artemis), J. Rack and I Masiello (2024), 'Piloting Systematic Implementation of Educational Technology in Swedish K–12 Schools – Two-Years-In Report', *Global Implementation Research and Applications*, **4** (3), 309–23. https://doi.org/10.1007/s43477-024-00130-w

Nordstrum, L.E., P.G. LeMahieu and E. Berrena (2017), 'Implementation Science: Understanding and Finding Solutions to Variation in Program Implementation', *Quality Assurance in Education*, **25** (1), 58–73. https://doi.org/10.1108/QAE-12-2016-0080

Ocheja, P., B. Flanagan, H. Ogata and S.S. Oyelere (2023), 'Visualization of Education Blockchain Data: Trends and Challenges', *Interactive Learning Environments*, **31** (9), 5970–94. https://doi.org/10.1080/10494820.2022.2026406

Perez, C. (2002), *Technological Revolutions and Financial Capital: The Dynamics of Bubbles and Golden Ages*. Edward Elgar Publishing.

Raman, K., A. Swaminathan, J. Gehrke and T. Joachims (2013), 'Beyond Myopic Inference in Big Data Pipelines', *Proceedings of the 19th ACM SIGKDD International Conference on Knowledge Discovery and Data Mining*, pp. 86–94. https://doi.org/10.1145/2487575.2487588

Regeringen (2017), *Nationell digitaliseringsstrategi för skolväsendet 2017–10–19*. https://www.regeringen.se/4a9d9a/contentassets/00b3d9118b0144f6bb95302f3e08d11c/nationell-digitaliseringsstrategi-for-skolvasendet.pdf

Richesson, R.L. and J. Krischer (2007), 'Data Standards in Clinical Research: Gaps, Overlaps, Challenges and Future Directions', *Journal of the American Medical Informatics Association*, **14** (6), 687–96. https://doi.org/10.1197/jamia.M2470

Teasley, S.D. (2018), 'Learning Analytics: Where Information Science and the Learning Sciences Meet', *Information and Learning Sciences*, **120** (1/2), 59–73. https://doi.org/10.1108/ILS-06-2018-0045

Tsoni, R., V. Zorkadis and V. Verykios (2022), 'A Data Pipeline to Preserve Privacy in Educational Settings', *Proceedings of the 25th Pan-Hellenic Conference on Informatics*, pp. 138–42. https://doi.org/10.1145/3503823.3503850

Tsueng, G., M.A.A. Cano, J. Bento, C. Czech, M. Kang, L. Pache, L.V. Rasmussen, T.C. Savidge, J. Starren, Q. Wu, J. Xin, M.R. Yeaman, X. Zhou, A.I. Su, C. Wu, L. Brown, R.S. Shabman and L.D. Hughes (2023), 'Developing a Standardized but Extendable Framework to Increase the Findability of Infectious Disease Datasets', *Scientific Data*, **10** (1), 99. https://doi.org/10.1038/s41597-023-01968-9

Utterberg Modén, M. (2021), *Teaching with Digital Mathematics Textbooks: Activity Theoretical Studies of Data-driven Technology in Classroom Practices*. Doctoral dissertation, Göteborg Universitet. https://gup.ub.gu.se/publication/309262

Winman, T., M. Spante, S. Willermark, L. Svensson and U. Lundh Snis (2018), *Digitaliseringen i skolan: Möjligheter och utmaningar*. Skolverket. http://urn.kb.se/resolve?urn=urn:nbn:se:hv:diva-12878

20. The paradoxes of AI promises in schools: Insights from a multi-sited ethnography

Katarina Sperling and Linnéa Stenliden

INTRODUCTION

> What is perhaps most striking is that AI, for the first time, enables each student to have a 'private tutor' who tailors their pedagogy to the student's individual conditions – a teacher who also has unlimited time and is available around the clock. (…) Because AI enables large-scale analysis and pattern recognition, it would be possible, by collecting and analysing data from thousands of students, to identify patterns and connections in learning processes that would otherwise be impossible to detect. (AI kommissionen 2025, p. 97)

In late 2024, the Swedish AI Commission first presented its *Roadmap for Sweden*, aiming to inspire Sweden to collectively embrace the shared challenge and opportunity presented by AI development (AI commission [AI kommissionen] 2025). Although the commission was prevented from making specific statements about AI in compulsory education, the report reflects *techno-solutionist* ideas (Morozov 2013) about how AI has the potential to automate and improve teaching and education at large. Similar narratives underpin an international discourse that has been ongoing for nearly a decade (Facer and Selwyn 2021; Holmes and Tuomi 2022; Linderoth et al. 2024; Luckin et al. 2016; Tuomi 2018). In fact, claims about AI as something that will disrupt and transform education are so common that they are often accepted as facts. In this chapter, we try to demystify some of these claims, drawing on the findings of a multi-sited ethnography in Swedish primary and secondary schools (Sperling 2024). More specifically, we discuss AI promises related to the *automation* and *augmentation* of teachers' work and point to less discussed ethical dilemmas that arise from introducing AI technologies into schools. We use the term *f(ai)th* to describe the unchallenged trust in AI, as this trust seems to persist even when various AI technologies repeatedly fail to meet the expectations of teachers and to deliver on the claimed promises.

In the remainder of the chapter, we elaborate on the long-standing promises of automation and augmentation in relation to AI and learning analytics. To illustrate how these promises influence teaching practice, we present the key findings from the multi-sited ethnography conducted in Swedish primary and secondary classrooms. Based on a cross-analysis of the findings, we then discuss two main takeaways: the AI symmation paradox and emerging ethical dilemmas. Given that the current promises of AI as something that can automate and augment the work of teachers are highly questionable, we conclude by proposing avenues for approaching AI beyond that of simply accepting it on f(ai)th. These propositions relate to teachers' abilities to reflect on, engage with, and, when necessary, resist AI. We conceptualised these abilities as teachers' ethical knowledge or professional judgement, *phronesis*, as imperative parts of teachers' AI literacy.

PROMISES OF AUTOMATION AND AUGMENTATION

While there is no universally accepted definition of AI, it is generally understood as the ability of computers or other machines to exhibit or simulate intelligent behaviour. It also refers to the field of study concerned with this concept (Oxford English Dictionary, n.d.). However, the meaning of 'simulating intelligent behaviour' has evolved since AI was first coined in 1956 (McCarthy et al. 2006). Once cutting-edge AI technologies are integrated into mainstream applications, they often cease to be classified as AI, turning AI into a vague and fluid concept (Korseberg and Elken 2025). This fluidity is reflected in Lucy Suchman's description of AI as a *floating signifier* (2023, p. 3), a term intentionally kept vague to preserve its influence. At the same time, the claimed opportunities of AI in education related to *automation* and *augmentation* have been influential in shaping educational AI systems, and have persisted for over 50 years since the establishment of AI in education as a research field (du Boulay 2022; Luckin et al. 2022; Molenaar 2022). *Automation* suggests that AI could take over tasks traditionally performed by teachers, such as attendance-taking using facial recognition, or offering *personalised learning* through, for example, intelligent tutoring systems (ITS) or AI-powered chatbots (Holmes and Tuomi 2022; Rensfeldt and Rahm 2023). *Personalised learning*, often used in educational settings, refers to a pedagogical approach that adapts to the individual needs, strengths, and interests of learners (Boninger et al. 2019). This method is frequently touted as a more efficient form of learning, often seen as the 'holy grail' in educational AI and other EdTech circles because it is imagined to deliver individualised teaching en masse (Facer and Selwyn 2021; Nemorin et al. 2023). Personalised learning relates to automation in that it replaces the teacher, both in terms of instruction and assessment (Cukurova et al. 2019).

Augmentation, on the other hand, reflects ideas that teachers, rather than being replaced, are becoming better teachers and making more informed decisions through advanced AI-based data analysis (Holmes and Tuomi 2022). Augmentation is often manifested through learning analytics (LA) systems that leverage AI to measure, predict, and analyse students' learning processes (Siemens 2013). Here, AI is expected to enhance, rather than replace, teachers' work by providing data, suggesting actions, and predicting outcomes based on this data. Knox et al. (2020) describe this as a kind of 'precision science for education' that is said to offer teachers guidance in areas where they may otherwise be working 'blindly'. The promises of automation and augmentation through data-driven AI reflect a broader trend towards data-driven schooling (Mandinach 2012; Nouri et al. 2019; Schildkamp et al. 2017; Selwyn 2022). Continuous collection, analysis, and visualisation of student data – such as performance, engagement and motivation – become central educational activities expected to enhance the management of student populations, including monitoring their behaviours, attitudes, and academic performance (Nemorin et al. 2023; Williamson et al. 2023).

While automation and augmentation have long influenced the development of educational AI, it is only in the past five years – accelerated by the global COVID-19 pandemic – that a broader range of AI technologies has transitioned from research labs into the global EdTech market (Williamson et al. 2021). This shift has increased the presence of AI in schools. The latest generation of AI technologies now includes software that diagnoses students' attention spans, analyses their emotions, uses patterns to predict grades and dropout risks, and even employs facial recognition for classroom monitoring (Holmes 2023).

At present, the use of AI in classrooms has become increasingly associated with generative AI, such as ChatGPT (Miao and Holmes 2023; Williamson 2024). The increasing adoption of AI in schools highlights how commercial interests are gradually influencing not only educational policy and governance (Eynon and Young 2021; Gulson and Witzenberger 2022; Komljenovic 2021; Williamson 2019), but also teachers' work and their professional knowledge. However, *how* AI affects teachers' work is still poorly understood, as scientific contributions, particularly studies coming from the educational sciences, are scarce. The research studies informing this chapter aim to fill this knowledge gap, adding to an improved understanding of the implications of AI for the teaching profession. The findings are based on three different fieldworks conducted in Swedish primary and secondary schools between 2020 and 2024 (Sperling 2024; Sperling et al. 2022;, 2023; Stenliden and Sperling 2024). Before describing these fieldworks, some words about how AI was approached need to be mentioned. As illustrated above, AI arises from the convergence of various complex factors. These include the advancement of AI in controlled research environments, shifts in technological approaches, the emergence of related overlapping research fields, the expansion of a multi-million-dollar EdTech industry, the growing interest in AI within educational policy and governance, and social and material conditions pertinent to teachers' practices. As AI emerges from the relations between numerous influencing factors in constant change, it has been conceptualised *relationally* as something constructed through the relationships between people and technology, between the social and the material (Bearman and Ajjawi 2024; Fenwick and Edwards 2010; Latour 2007). This means understanding AI not primarily on the inherent qualities of the technology per se, nor as an arrangement of neat 'tools' that can be employed in various manners by teachers, yielding different outcomes, but as an effect from the relational bonds between humans and technology (Bearman and Ajjawi 2024).

THE MULTI-SITED ETHNOGRAPHY

To move beyond the promises of AI, beyond f(ai)th in its future benefit, has meant getting access to different classrooms in different locations and taking part in the daily lives of teachers as they interact with three distinct AI technologies. The participation varied from spending entire school days in classrooms to only observing lessons where the AI technology was present. Swedish primary and secondary schools, which provide the educational context in this chapter, are characterised by a high level of computer accessibility and adoption of EdTech (Rensfeldt and Player-Koro 2020), as well as by neo-liberalism and marketisation (Bjorklund et al. 2006; Dahlstedt and Fejes 2019). Although Sweden ranks among the countries in the world with the highest levels of access to computers in classrooms as part of a longstanding political strategy (Nissen and Stenliden 2023), AI in Swedish education was largely overlooked until 2023, when ChatGPT was released to a broader audience. Today, much of the conversation about AI in Swedish education, as elsewhere, is centred around large language models (LLMs) as manifested in AI chatbots (Swedish National Agency for Education [Skolverket] 2023). This is also reflected in Swedish EdTech companies, which are seeing a growing interest in AI (Swedish EdTech Industry 2024).

Data Production

As mentioned, the chapter draws on a multi-sited ethnography conducted in Swedish primary and secondary schools. It comprises three fieldworks, each with a comprehensive set of data. Fieldwork I (see Sperling et al. 2022; Stenliden and Sperling 2024) was based on a Swedish innovation and research project in which a machine learning-based ITS was tried out by 22 teachers and more than 250 primary school students. Fieldwork II focused on the development of a commercial Learning Management System (LMS) enhanced with AI and Learning Analytics (LA), specifically designed for K–12 education. This LMS supported lesson planning, classroom management and the visual tracking of student wellbeing and classroom observations conducted in a primary and upper secondary school (see Sperling et al. 2023). Fieldwork III extended the work from Fieldwork II by advancing the co-design process further into the development of a wellbeing app for students. Created by the same EdTech company behind the LMS, the app was developed in close collaboration with a Swedish upper secondary school. It was implemented school-wide as part of the school's engagement in a professional development programme on data-driven school improvement. The primary aim of this study was to explore how AI became embedded in school practices, with particular attention to its impact on teachers' work (see Sperling 2024). The data produced from all different fieldworks are primarily observations in schools, interviews and video-recorded meetings (Table 20.1).

It is important to note that during the period of Fieldworks I and II (from 2020 to November 2022), the use of AI in education remained largely underexplored, particularly within Swedish K–12 schools. Identifying concrete examples of implemented AI technologies in classrooms proved surprisingly difficult. The technologies that were eventually selected for study – a

Table 20.1 Summary of data production

Data Production	Explanation
Fieldwork I (ITS)	Participation in research and development project as a team member Classroom observations in four classrooms in three schools Seven in-depth interviews of 45–90 minutes (three teachers from two schools and four members of the project team)
Fieldwork II (LMS)	Around 90 hours of classroom observation in six classrooms in two schools Thirteen in-depth interviews (three representatives from the EdTech company, eight teachers, one principal, one representative from the local school authority) Participation in two introductory meetings Observations from one workshop with 30 students Observations from one workshop with 15 teachers Observations from one workshop with teachers and EdTech provider Observations at an EdTech trade show
Fieldwork III (Wellbeing app)	Seventeen video-recorded meetings with five teachers/form tutors Four audio/video-recorded interviews with two teachers, one development teacher/strategist, and the school principal Two visits with fieldnotes

Source: Authors.

machine learning-based Intelligent Tutoring System (ITS), a Learning Management System (LMS) incorporating AI and Learning Analytics (LA), and later, a wellbeing app – were all in active stages of development. Fieldwork II was underway when, in November 2022, OpenAI publicly released the first version of the AI chatbot ChatGPT. This release marked a turning point, significantly intensifying how AI was being introduced and implemented in educational settings. At the same time, the rapid introduction of AI chatbots into schools reinforced the relevance of findings concerning the promises and ethical implications of AI in education.

Analytical Work

Actor-Network Theory (ANT) (Latour 2007; Law 2019), serving as both a theoretical and methodological orientation, was employed to approach AI relationally, as something constructed through the relationships between people and technology. Using ANT made it possible to move beyond the promises often associated with AI, instead embracing the uncertainty, complexity, and contradictions inherent in such explorations. Accordingly, the analytical focus was placed on the interaction between teachers, students, and various AI technologies, specifically, a machine learning-based Intelligent Tutoring System (ITS), a Learning Management System (LMS) enhanced with learning analytics, and a wellbeing app. Additionally, the analytical work has been influenced by *ethno-drama* (Saldaña 2005), *Thinking Through Comics* (Laurier and Sabeti 2023), and *Visual Network Analysis* (Venturini 2010), each different modes of representation. For a detailed presentation of the theoretical and methodological approaches, see Sperling (2025).

Main Findings: Compensatory Work and Non-action

The findings from the partial studies collectively illustrate how AI is enacted as a multifaceted, negotiated, data-driven technology in the making. As detailed, teachers co-produced AI promises of automation and augmentation through different kinds of work, which can be referred to as *compensatory*. The studies also highlight how not only teachers and students but also commercial interests and policy initiatives influence this co-production. Thus, in contrast to many common descriptions of AI technologies as time-saving, efficient, smart disruptive and transformative, findings from the multi-sited ethnography demonstrate that for AI to be introduced and materialised in school settings, teachers must contribute significant labour and use their professional expertise and ethical judgement. Yet, paradoxically, the expertise sustaining the promises of AI is being undermined in this process. As elaborated upon in Stenliden and Sperling (2024), the extra workload teachers have to accommodate to compensate for the AI technology requires various forms of action: adaptation, experimentation, compensation and confirmation. These actions highlight that the co-production, in the study formulated as *symmation*, between teachers and technology required different strategies and competencies from teachers. With *symmation*, we mean that something that may have looked like automation and/or augmentation when an AI technology was introduced in a classroom emerged instead as a result of a 'sym-' or a 'with' (see Wagener-Böck et al. 2023, p. 137). Teachers had to tailor their teaching and monitor their students' progress to counteract the misalignment of 'personalised' content and be creative and experiment with different solutions to keep students on track and motivated. Teachers also needed to monitor the automated insights delivered by the learning analytics dashboards and use their professional know-how when taking actions on data by either confirming or rejecting the learning analytics. In the study related to a wellbeing app (Sperling 2024), teachers had to rely on their professional knowledge and judgement, as the presented data turned out to be inaccurate, incomplete, and ultimately a very poor indicator of students' wellbeing. Still, teachers treated the collected data as true, acted in ways that supported the technology promises, and continued to express their trust in AI, albeit in some future version of it. An important finding was therefore that teachers' added work seemed to be justified as long as there was a continued faith in AI – a f(ai)th – to improve and transform education. Here, the most problematic result is the disjunction between, on the one hand, promises currently made about AI, and the actions taken by teachers in response to the shortcomings or misalignments of the technologies in question on the other. The findings also highlight several dilemmas introduced by the AI technologies, particularly related to increasing teachers' workload and the undermining of their professional knowledge, as well as the risks of negatively influencing teacher-student relationships. Other dilemmas relate to how student data was collected for commercial purposes without being sufficiently problematised by the participating schools.

At the same time, the findings from the conducted studies show that how AI and education come into being is not fixed or predictable. Some teachers *resisted* co-producing the AI promises in different ways; for example, by not complying with the extra work or the necessary data collection. Teachers' non-actions or resistance suggest not only that they can refrain from being mobilised by technology to act in certain ways but that, as they resist or withdraw, the AI promises fade. This also implies that there is still space, at least to a degree, to rethink and redo AI in school settings so teachers can act in ways that align with their values and that allow them to respond to the needs of their students. The analysis across the findings from the entire ethnographic study points to what may be considered the most problematic outcome of this research: the disconnect between, on the one hand, the promises currently made about AI in education, and on the other, the actions taken by teachers in response to the shortcomings or misalignments of these technologies, what we refer to as the *symmation paradox*. This disconnect also highlights deeper educational dilemmas, notably the often-invisible labour of teachers and the gradual erosion of teacher-student relationships. These issues will be discussed in the following sections.

THE SYMMATION PARADOX

The contradictions that arise when teachers co-produce what may appear to be automation or augmentation in education can be understood as a paradox. The paradox lies in the fact that, in order to create or effectively interact with AI systems, teachers must actively engage with and apply their deep understanding of pedagogy, content and the learning environment. This time-consuming engagement contradicts the very notion of automation, which is meant to reduce human input, yet in practice, it requires significant human involvement and professional judgement to ensure the technology works as humans expect it to. So, while in the future AI might offer the promise of reducing workload or enhancing education, the reality is that these different technologies still depend heavily on the teachers' expertise to function well, which means teachers continue to play a central role in the process. Teachers' actions are instrumental for AI technologies to function as desired and not the other way around. This resonates with what Langdon Winner (1978, p. 229) termed 'reverse adaptation', in which human ends are adapted to the characteristics of the available means. Winner argued that automation through technology, rather than enhancing our self-determination and choice, reduces our autonomy by changing the way we think and do things. Across the partial studies, we have found that rather than the technology adapting to the social world of the teachers, the teachers adapted their social worlds to the technologies. This adaptation was in turn dependent on teachers' professional knowledge, particularly in cases where the technology was not acting in desirable ways – for example, when presenting erroneous answers to exercises (Sperling et al. 2022) or presenting data that teachers could not act upon (Sperling 2024). While adapting to the technology, the teachers had to question their own professional knowledge. The underlying promises of the AI technologies therefore both challenged and undermined their role as teachers. This reflects a contradiction that can be understood as a paradox of *symmation*: to co-produce what might look like automation or augmentation, teachers must use their professional knowledge. The concept of symmation suggests that classroom practice is not an individual endeavour but rather a collective one, grounded in the idea of sym (from the Greek sún [σύν], meaning 'with' or 'together'). Therefore, what is often attributed to technology – such as automation or augmentation through AI in schools – is, in reality, a product of co-production through acts of symmation involving students, teachers and machines (Wagener-Böck et al. 2023, p. 137). However, the paradox lies in the fact that teachers' professional knowledge is simultaneously challenged and undermined by the discourse surrounding AI, suggesting that AI can automate or augment the role of the teacher. This, in turn, implies that as teachers' pedagogical judgement is eroded by AI systems, their ability to uphold the promises of these technologies will be increasingly compromised.

Today, generative AI is sparking what we may see as the most recent EdTech utopia (Bearman et al. 2023), where narratives about replacing teachers with technology are gaining traction. Such narratives, already proposed in the past (Papert 1980; Petrina 2004; Skinner 1968), suggest that expert teachers may no longer be necessary to oversee educational processes, a view further supported by commercial incentives:

> [But] I do think AI will dramatically affect education, because the AI is an extremely knowledgeable teacher. It will be very patient, will be almost always correct, and can tailor the lessons specifically to the child. It will be like each child has Einstein for a teacher. So, it will be something quite profound. (Musk as cited in VivaTechnology 2024)

With continuous propositions from influential tech giants like Elon Musk, we need to remind ourselves about the symmation paradox as the notion of automating teachers' work while requiring that the work of teachers is often concealed under labels such as 'collaborating', 'assisting' or 'helping'. The argument is that, if properly implemented, AI can alleviate the burden on teachers from tasks that are repetitive or administrative, allowing them to dedicate more time to each student. Such statements are very common, both from research authorities within the field (for example, Luckin 2023), as well as from international organisations (for example, World Economic Forum 2024). In Sweden, scholars have suggested that AI can also help address the anticipated future shortage of teachers (Huss 2024). Automation and augmentation are perhaps most clearly reflected in the visions outlined in the government-initiated AI Commission Report, as stated at the beginning of this chapter. However, if we look more closely into what this type of 'help' or 'assistance' entails in practice, it requires reducing teachers' work and complex relationships, and a context-dependent profession, into a variety of many different interlinked competencies, to smaller tasks and decisions, some of which are deemed less important than others. While such reduction actually risks diminishing teachers' essential competencies (Miao and Cukurova 2024), it is also very likely that 'automated' tasks will require added work for teachers; the result of symmation. Put differently, based on our empirical findings, it is likely to assume that teachers will end up doing additional work to ensure that the intended relief from their workload in specific tasks is effective! Moreover, rather than transforming and innovating educational practice, the AI promises of automation and augmentation seem to be different ways of doing more of what is already done. Accordingly, the introduction of AI in the educational context might lead to increased demands, where teachers do more work than previously. This is exemplified by Neil Selwyn (2025): 'If teachers can create student feedback at the touch of a button, then perhaps they should be providing feedback on multiple drafts of *every* piece of writing that a student produces?' As narratives about the automation and augmentation of teachers continue to be promoted, often by those outside the teaching profession, it is important to remain sceptical and to critically examine the symmation processes taking place in classrooms.

EMERGENT DILEMMAS

The symmation paradox not only reflects a contradiction but also describes an emergent and immediate ethical dilemma rarely raised in the context of AI ethics. While AI is positioned as a means of reducing teachers' workload, it actually contributes to more labour by requiring them to manage, interpret and troubleshoot these technologies. This and the fact that the necessary added work of teachers required to sustain AI is rarely articulated, acknowledged, or valued as essential – either by technology developers or by the teachers themselves – is problematic. Second, it is inherently problematic when teachers' professional knowledge is being undermined by technology. This undermining emerges, for example, when colour codes and numerical values or mathematical exercises contradict teachers' judgement, potentially altering the dynamics between students and teachers (Sperling 2024). This dilemma also encompasses teachers diminishing or dismissing their own competence by disregarding it as 'gut feelings', whereas this intuitive knowledge has in fact been built over years of meaningful exchanges with their students (Stenliden and Sperling 2024). Related to the symmation paradox, where teachers' competencies are being undermined, is the question of trust. As shown in the studies, the AI technologies instilled uncertainty about whether the students were truly being honest, which risks negatively affecting the relationship between students and teachers. In one of the studies (Stenliden and Sperling 2024), the teacher had to disregard some of the student responses, stating 'so they don't always understand exactly what they're filling in, either', which suggests that rather than providing novel insights about students and their learning, the technologies could not properly capture the anticipated data and therefore introduced contradictions about student responses. However, ignoring certain responses might limit opportunities for feedback, growth, or deeper understanding, and make students feel their input is undervalued, potentially impacting their engagement and motivation. Hence, as trust is fundamental in the teacher–student relationship, when AI technology forces teachers to ignore student input, it undermines this trust.

The encountered ethical dilemmas also reflect previously raised concerns around privacy, misinformation, and protection from harm vis-à-vis students (Lupton and Williamson 2017;

Selwyn 2022). Such concerns also relate to how student data are collected as part of research and development projects for commercial purposes. As discussed in previous studies on the data collection by platforms like Google Classroom (Decuypere et al. 2021; Hillman et al. 2020), EdTech providers are increasingly processing larger volumes of personal data from school children under a less stringent enforcement regime compared to government-mandated organisations (Day et al. 2024; Livingstone et al. 2024). This situation creates a power imbalance between EdTech companies and schools, ultimately placing student information in contexts that are not primarily focused on educational needs nor under democratic control, and putting educational institutions into locked-in situations where, for example, an AI platform company makes it difficult for its users to quit their services (Komljenovic et al. 2025). As dilemmas continue to arise with the rapid adoption of different AI technologies in schools, it seems important to emphasise the ethical dilemmas of AI specific to educational settings, and to encourage the development of teachers' abilities to reflect on, engage with, and, when necessary, resist AI. We propose that such abilities correspond to what can be conceptualised as teachers' ethical knowledge or professional judgement – *phronesis* (Bornemark 2020; Kinsella and Pitman 2012) – and should be an imperative part of teachers' AI literacy (Sperling et al. 2024).

MOVING BEYOND F(AI)TH WITH AI LITERACY AND PHRONESIS

Education has always been central to the general adoption, use and dissemination of technology, and as such, education is also where desired futures are often imagined (Rahm 2019; 2023). This often means that policymakers, researchers and EdTech providers reframe the problems of education and suggest technological solutions in response rather than addressing the 'real' problems in education, which certainly exist (Bacchi 2009; Linderoth et al. 2024). To advance the discussions around AI and education beyond pseudo-problems and beyond f(ai)th therefore requires a deeper, scientifically founded, and critical understanding of how AI comes into being in school settings, including more research related to the mundanity of ethical dilemmas related to AI and education. While we may currently be in a period of AI hype (Nemorin et al. 2023; Cerratto Pargman et al. 2024), it is also reasonable to assume that AI will increasingly engage teachers and impact their work in unforeseen ways. It is therefore important that teachers actively engage in the conversation about AI and education, as well as support children and young people to be prepared for a society where AI is ubiquitous. This motivates the acquisition of a set of competencies also referred to as *AI literacy*.

AI Literacy

AI literacy can still be considered an emergent concept, stemming from the computer science domain (Long and Magerko 2020; Sperling et al. 2024) and with strong connections to data literacy. These connections are particularly visible in various national AI curricula, which focus on the technological dimensions of AI technologies, including techniques like machine learning and natural language processing (Miao and Shiohira 2022). At the same time, it is argued that AI technologies often operate autonomously and can adapt to their context, enabling them to make decisions and take actions based on predictions. Therefore, understanding the role of AI ethics and the potential impact on employment and sustainable development has been identified as pivotal parts of AI literacy (Holmes et al. 2022). While many current definitions of AI literacy often fall short in suggesting how this understanding may facilitate learners to examine AI and its impact critically, we would like to argue that AI literacy can serve the purpose of fostering a critical and conscious mindset, asking for what purpose and in whose interests AI technologies are being introduced in society. By asking critical questions, the future-making of AI can move beyond f(ai)th and beyond aspirations of the past; aspirations associated with the automation and augmentation of teachers' work.

Ethical Judgement: Phronesis

Passionate teachers have always been at the forefront of integrating technology in education (Selwyn 2017). Still, the teaching workforce is frequently held responsible for the slow adoption of or resistance to digital technologies in schools, including AI-based technologies. Teachers' resistance has been explained as a matter of an aversion to algorithms (Dietvorst et al. 2015), confirmation biases (Nazaretsky et al. 2021), poor understanding of the analytics (Tsai and Gasevic 2017; Wolff et al. 2016), or a lack of trust in AI EdTech (Nazaretsky et al. 2022; Viberg et al. 2025). We would like to argue that teachers' resistance or non-adoption is not necessarily a matter of 'bad' attitudes or incompetence, but of professional values and professional discernment, that is, *phronesis* (Bornemark 2020).

An increasing number of researchers argue that many of the current theories of teacher expertise are missing out on this special form of knowledge related to reasoning and judgement (Brookfield 2018; Burbules 2019; Ellett 2012; Kinsella and Pitman 2012; Koutsikouri et al. 2023; Kristjánsson 2005; Yacek and Jonas 2025). As proposed by Koutsikouri et al. (2023), phronesis is in fact an aspect of professional knowledge that cannot be automated or augmented through AI. Such knowledge relates to the not-knowing, for example, emotions, sensory perception, experience and intuition, allowing teachers to grasp complexities and everyday classroom dilemmas and act in ways that are appropriate for the situation at hand. In the context of AI, phronesis therefore represents the part of teachers' professional knowledge that is necessary in order to resist harmful applications of AI and to interact with AI technology using sound scepticism in a way that is aligned with the educational needs of students. Understanding and exploring teachers' phronesis in relation to AI, both when interacting with AI in educational settings and teaching about AI, can provide new insights into what AI ethics mean in educational practice. Teachers' phronesis can also inform the development and enactment of AI in ways that are aligned with the needs, as well as with the values, of teachers and students. A better understanding of teachers' phronesis in relation to AI could potentially also influence the development of ethical guidelines and the development of AI-based technologies that do not add to workloads, undermine teachers' professional knowledge or create ethical dilemmas concerning the students.

REFERENCES

AI kommissionen (2025), *Färdplan för Sverige* (Slutbetänkande No. SOU 2025:12). https://www.riksdagen.se/sv/dokument-och-lagar/dokument/statens-offentliga-utredningar/ai-kommissionens-fardplan-for-sverige_hdb312/html/

Bacchi, C. (2009), *Analysing policy*. Pearson Higher Education AU.

Bearman, M. and R. Ajjawi (2024), 'When I say … artificial intelligence', *Medical Education*, **58** (11), 1273–5.
Bearman, M., J. Ryan and R. Ajjawi (2023), 'Discourses of artificial intelligence in higher education: A critical literature review', *Higher Education*, **86** (2), 369–85.
Bjorklund, A., M.A. Clark, P.-A. Edin, P. Fredricksson and A.B. Krueger (2006), *The market comes to education in Sweden: An evaluation of Sweden's surprising school reforms*. Russell Sage Foundation.
Boninger, F., A. Molnar and C.M. Saldaña (2019), 'Personalized learning and the digital privatization of curriculum and teaching', National Educational Policy Center White Paper.
Bornemark, J. (2020), *Horisonten finns alltid kvar: Om det bortglömda omdömet*. Volante.
Brookfield, S. (2018), 'Transformative learning and the awareness of white supremacy', *Phronesis*, **7** (3), 63–9.
Burbules, N.C. (2019), 'Thoughts on phronesis', *Ethics and Education*, **14** (2), 126–37. https://doi.org/10.1080/17449642.2019.1587689
Cerratto Pargman, T., E. Sporrong, A. Farazouli and C. McGrath (2024), 'Beyond the Hype: Towards a Critical Debate About AI Chatbots in Swedish Higher Education', *Högre Utbildning*, **14** (1), 74–81.
Cukurova, M., C. Kent and R. Luckin (2019), 'Artificial intelligence and multimodal data in the service of human decision-making: A case study in debate tutoring', *British Journal of Educational Technology*, **50** (6), 3032–46.
Dahlstedt, M. and A. Fejes (eds) (2019), 'Market forces in Swedish education', in *Neoliberalism and market forces in education*, Routledge, pp. 1–12.
Day, E., K. Pothong, A. Atabey and S. Livingstone (2024), 'Who controls children's education data? A socio-legal analysis of the UK governance regimes for schools and EdTech', *Learning, Media and Technology*, **49** (3), 356–70. https://doi.org/10.1080/17439884.2022.2152838
Decuypere, M., E. Grimaldi and P. Landri (2021), 'Introduction: Critical studies of digital education platforms', *Critical Studies in Education*, **62** (1), 1–16.
Dietvorst, B.J., J.P. Simmons and C. Massey (2015), 'Algorithm aversion: People erroneously avoid algorithms after seeing them err', *Journal of Experimental Psychology: General*, **144** (1), 114–26.
du Boulay, B. (2022), 'Artificial intelligence in education and ethics', in O. Zawacki-Richter and I. Jung (eds), *Handbook of open, distance and digital education*, Springer, pp. 93–108.
Ellett, F.S. (2012), 'Practical rationality and a recovery of Aristotle's 'phronesis' for the professions', in E.A. Kinsella and A. Pitman (eds), *Phronesis as professional knowledge*, SensePublishers, pp. 13–33. https://doi.org/10.1007/978-94-6091-731-8_2
Eynon, R. and E. Young (2021), 'Methodology, legend, and rhetoric: The constructions of AI by academia, industry, and policy groups for lifelong learning', *Science, Technology, & Human Values*, **46** (1), 166–91. https://doi.org/10.1177/0162243920906475
Facer, K. and N. Selwyn (2021), 'Digital technology and the futures of education: Towards "non-stupid' optimism", Background paper for the Futures of Education initiative, UNESCO Education Sector.
Fenwick, T. and R. Edwards (2010), *Actor-network theory in education*. Routledge.
Gulson, K.N. and K. Witzenberger (2022), 'Repackaging authority: Artificial intelligence, automated governance and education trade shows', *Journal of Education Policy*, **37** (1), 145–60. https://doi.org/10.1080/02680939.2020.1785552
Hillman, T., A.B. Rensfeldt and J. Ivarsson (2020), 'Brave new platforms: a possible platform future for highly decentralised schooling', *Learning, Media and Technology*, **45** (1), 7–16. https://doi.org/10.1080/17439884.2020.1683748
Holmes, W. (2023), 'The unintended consequences of artificial intelligence and education', Executive Summary, Education International Research.
Holmes, W., J. Persson,I.-A. Chounta, B. Wasson and V. Dimitrova (2022), *Artificial intelligence and education: A critical view through the lens of human rights, democracy and the rule of law,* Council of Europe.
Holmes, W. and I. Tuomi (2022), 'State of the art and practice in AI in education', *European Journal of Education*, **57** (4), 542–70. https://doi.org/10.1111/ejed.12533
Huss, J. (2024), Professorn: AI lösning när lärarbristen ökar. *Vi Lärare*. https://www.vilarare.se/nyheter/ai/professorn-ai-raddningen-nar-lararbristen-okar/
Kinsella, E.A. and A. Pitman (2012), *Phronesis as professional knowledge: Practical wisdom in the professions* (Vol. 1), Springer Science and Business Media.

Knox, J., B. Williamson and S. Bayne (2020), 'Machine behaviourism: Future visions of "learnification" and "datafication" across humans and digital technologies', *Learning, Media and Technology*, **45** (1), 31–45.

Komljenovic, J. (2021), 'The rise of education rentiers: digital platforms, digital data and rents', *Learning, Media and Technology*, **46** (3), 320–32. https://doi.org/10.1080/17439884.2021.1891422

Komljenovic, J., K. Birch, S. Sellar, A. Bergviken Rensfeldt, J. Deville, C. Eaton, L. Gourlay, M. Hansen, N. Kerssens, A. Kovalainen, P.-L Nappert, J. Noteboom, L. Parcerisa, J.P. Pardo-Guerra, S. Poutanen, S. Robertson, D. Tyfield and B. Williamson (2025), 'Digitalised higher education: key developments, questions, and concerns', *Discourse: Studies in the Cultural Politics of Education*, **46** (2) 276–92. https://doi.org/10.1080/01596306.2024.2408397

Korseberg, L. and M. Elken (2025), 'Waiting for the revolution: how higher education institutions initially responded to ChatGPT', *Higher Education*, **89**, 953–68. https://doi.org/10.1007/s10734-024-01256-4

Koutsikouri, D., L. Hylving, S. Lindberg and J. Bornemark (2023), *Seven elements of phronesis: A framework for understanding judgment in relation to automated decision-making, Proceedings of 56th Hawaii International Conference on System Sciences.*

Kristjánsson, K. (2005), 'Smoothing it: Some Aristotelian misgivings about the phronesis-praxis perspective on education', *Educational Philosophy and Theory*, **37** (4), 455–73. https://doi.org/10.1111/j.1469-5812.2005.00135.x

Latour, B. (2007), *Reassembling the social: An introduction to actor-network-theory.* Oxford University Press.

Laurier, E. and Sabeti, S. (2023), *Thinking through comics.* University of Manchester. https://aspect.ac.uk/wp-content/uploads/2024/01/Thinking-Through-Comics-Method-Report.pdf

Law, J. (2019), 'Material semiotics'. http://www.heterogeneities.net/publications/Law2019MaterialSemiotics.pdf

Linderoth, C., M. Hultén and L. Stenliden (2024), 'Competing visions of artificial intelligence in education: A heuristic analysis on sociotechnical imaginaries and problematizations in policy guidelines', *Policy Futures in Education*, **22** (8), 1662–78.

Livingstone, S., K. Pothong, A. AtabeyL. Hooper and E. Day (2024), 'The Googlization of the classroom: Is the UK effective in protecting children's data and rights?', *Computers and Education Open*, **7**, 100195. https://doi.org/10.1016/j.caeo.2024.100195

Long, D. and B. Magerko (2020), 'What is AI literacy? Competencies and design considerations', *roceedings of the 2020 CHI Conference on Human Factors in Computing Systems (CHI'20).* https://doi.org/10.1145/3313831.3376727

Luckin, R. (2023, July 14), 'Yes, AI could profoundly disrupt education. But maybe that's not a bad thing', *The Guardian.* https://www.theguardian.com/commentisfree/2023/jul/14/ai-artificial-intelligence-disrupt-education-creativity-critical-thinking

Luckin, R., K. George and M. Cukurova (2022), *AI for school teachers.* CRC Press.

Luckin, R., W. Holmes, M. Griffiths and L.B. Forcier (2016), *Intelligence unleashed: An argument for AI in education.* Pearson. https://static.googleusercontent.com/media/edu.google.com/en//pdfs/Intelligence-Unleashed-Publication.pdf

Lupton, D. and B. Williamson (2017), 'The datafied child: The dataveillance of children and implications for their rights', *New Media & Society*, **19** (5), 780–94.

Mandinach, E.B. (2012), 'A perfect time for data use: Using data-driven decision making to inform practice', *Educational Psychologist*, **47** (2), 71–85.

McCarthy, J., M.L. Minsky, N. Rochester and C.E. Shannon (2006), 'A proposal for the Dartmouth Summer Research Project on Artificial Intelligence, August 31, 1955', *AI Magazine*, **27** (4), 12–14.

Miao, F. and M. Cukurova (2024), *AI competency framework for teachers* (No. ED/577/1; p. 52), UNESCO. https://doi.org/10.54675/ZJTE2084

Miao, F. and W. Holmes (2023), *Guidance for generative AI in education and research* (Nos. 978-92-3-100612–8), UNESCO. https://doi.org/10.54675/EWZM9535

Miao, F. and K. Shiohira (2022), *K–12 AI curricula: A mapping of government-endorsed AI curricula,* UNESCO Education Sector.

Molenaar, I. (2022), 'Towards hybrid human-AI learning technologies', *European Journal of Education*, **57** (4), 632–645. https://doi.org/10.1111/ejed.12527

Morozov, E. (2013), *To save everything, click here: The folly of technological solutionism*. PublicAffairs.

Nazaretsky, T., M. Ariely, M. Cukurova and G. Alexandron (2022), 'Teachers' trust in AI-powered educational technology and a professional development program to improve it', *British Journal of Educational Technology*, **53** (4), 914–31.

Nazaretsky, T., M. Cukurova, M. Ariely and G. Alexandron (2021), 'Confirmation bias and trust: Human factors that influence teachers' attitudes towards AI-based educational technology', *AI for blended learning: Empowering teachers in real classrooms co-located with 16th European Conference on Technology Enhanced Learning (ECTEL 2021)*.

Nemorin, S., A. Vlachidis, H.M. Ayerakwa and P. Andriotis (2023), 'AI hyped? A horizon scan of discourse on artificial intelligence in education (AIED) and development', *Learning, Media and Technology*, **48** (1), 38–51. https://doi.org/10.1080/17439884.2022.2095568

Nissen, J. and L. Stenliden (2023), 'How computers entered Swedish classrooms: The importance of educating digital citizens', in J. Hallström and M. J. de Vries (eds), *Programming and computational thinking in technology education: Swedish and international perspectives*, Brill, pp. 13–37. 10.1163/9789004687912_002

Nouri, J., M. Ebner, D. Ifenthaler, M. Saqr, J. Malmberg, J. Khalil, J. Bruun, O. Viberg, M. Conde-González and Z. Papamitsiou (2019), 'Efforts in Europe for data-driven improvement of education: A review of learning analytics research in six countries', *International Journal of Learning Analytics and Artificial Intelligence for Education*, **1** (1), 8–27.

Oxford English Dictionary (n.d.), 'Artificial intelligence'. https://www.oed.com/dictionary/artificial-intelligence_n?tab=meaning_and_use#38531565

Papert, S. (1980), *Mindstorms: Computers, children, and powerful ideas*. Basic Books.

Petrina, S. (2004), 'Sidney Pressey and the automation of education, 1924–1934', *Technology and Culture*, **45** (2), 305–30.

Rahm, L. (2019), *Educational imaginaries: A genealogy of the digital citizen* (Vol. 214). Linköping University Electronic Press. https://www.diva-portal.org/smash/record.jsf?pid=diva2%3A1281888&dswid=5120

Rahm, L. (2023), 'Education, automation and AI: A genealogy of alternative futures', *Learning, Media and Technology*, **48** (1), 6–24.

Rensfeldt, A.B. and C. Player-Koro (2020), '"Back to the future": Socio-technical imaginaries in 50 years of school digitalization curriculum reforms', *Seminar.net*, **16** (2), 20.

Rensfeldt, A.B. and L. Rahm (2023), 'Automating teacher work? A history of the politics of automation and artificial intelligence in education', *Postdigital Science and Education*, **5**, 25–43. https://doi.org/10.1007/s42438-022-00344-x

Saldaña, J. (2005), *Ethnodrama: An anthology of reality theatre*. Rowman Altamira.

Selwyn, N. (2017). *Education and technology: Key issues and debates (2nd ed.)*. Bloomsbury Publishing.

Schildkamp, K., C. Poortman, H. Luyten and J. Ebbeler (2017), 'Factors promoting and hindering data-based decision making in schools', *School Effectiveness and School Improvement*, **28** (2), 242–58. https://doi.org/10.1080/09243453.2016.1256901

Selwyn, N. (2022), '"Just playing around with Excel and pivot tables": The realities of data-driven schooling', *Research Papers in Education*, **37** (1), 95–114. https://doi.org/10.1080/02671522.2020.1812107

Selwyn, N. (2025, March 20), 'More work for teacher: The ironies of GenAI as a labour-saving technology', *Critical Education Technology*. https://criticaledtech.com/2025/03/20/more-work-for-teacher-the-ironies-of-genai-as-a-labour-saving-technology/

Siemens, G. (2013), 'Learning analytics: The emergence of a discipline', *American Behavioral Scientist*, **57** (10), 1380–1400.

Skinner, B. (1968), *The technology of teaching*. Appleton-Century-Crofts.

Skolverket (2023, September 5), *AI i skolan – risker och möjligheter*. Skolverket. https://www.skolverket.se/om-oss/aktuellt/nyheter/nyheter/2023-09-05-ai-i-skolan---risker-och-mojligheter

Sperling, K. (2024), 'The fading of f(AI)th: Tracing the technological promises of a wellbeing app in K–12 education', in C. Herodotou, S. Papavlasopoulou, C. Santos, M. Milrad, N. Otero, P. Vittorini, R. Gennari, T. Di Mascio, M. Temperini and F. De La Prieta (eds), *Methodologies and intelligent systems for technology enhanced learning, 14th International Conference* (Vol. 1171), Springer Nature Switzerland, pp. 103–15. https://doi.org/10.1007/978-3-031-73538-7_10

Sperling, K. (2025), *Beyond f(AI)th: The introduction and materialisation of artificial intelligence in schools* (Vol. 22). Linköping University Electronic Press. https://doi.org/10.3384/9789180759052

Sperling, K., C.-J. Stenberg, C. McGrath, A. Åkerfeldt, F. Heintz and L. Stenliden (2024), 'In search of artificial intelligence (AI) literacy in teacher education: A scoping review', *Computers and Education Open*, **6**, 100169. https://doi.org/10.1016/j.caeo.2024.100169

Sperling, K., L. Stenliden, J. Nissen and F. Heintz (2022), 'Still w(AI)ting for the automation of teaching: An exploration of machine learning in Swedish primary education using actor-network theory', *European Journal of Education*, **57** (4), 584–600. https://doi.org/10.1111/ejed.12526

Sperling, K., L. Stenliden, J. Nissen and F. Heintz (2023), 'Behind the scenes of co-designing AI and LA in K–12 Education', *Postdigital Science and Education*, **6**, 321–41 https://doi.org/10.1007/s42438-023-00417-5

Stenliden, L. and K. Sperling (2024), 'Breaking the magic of automation and augmentation in Swedish classrooms', *Nordisk Tidsskrift for Pedagogikk Og Kritikk*, **10** (1). https://doi.org/10.23865/ntpk.v10.6174

Suchman, L. (2023), 'The uncontroversial "thingness" of AI', *Big Data & Society*, **10** (2), 20539517231206794. https://doi.org/10.1177/20539517231206794

Swedish EdTech Industry (2024), *Funkar edtech? Edtechbarometern 2024*. https://swedishedtechindustry.se/wp-content/uploads/2024/05/SwedishEdtech-branschrapport-2024.pdf

Tsai, Y.-S. and D. Gasevic (2017), 'Learning analytics in higher education – Challenges and policies: A review of eight learning analytics policies', *LAK17: Proceedings of the Seventh International Learning Analytics and Knowledge Conference*, pp. 233–42.

Tuomi, I. (2018), *The impact of artificial intelligence on learning, teaching, and education*. European Union. https://op.europa.eu/es/publication-detail/-/publication/5cb8eee3-e888-11e8-b690-01aa75ed71a1

Venturini, T. (2010), 'Diving in magma: how to explore controversies with actor-network theory', *Public Understanding of Science*, **19** (3), 258–73. https://doi.org/10.1177/0963662509102694

Viberg, O., M. Cukurova, Y. Feldman-Maggor, G. Alexandron, S. Shirai, S. Kanemune, B. Wasson, C. Tømte, D. Spikol, M. Milrad, R. Coelho and R.F. Kizilcec (2025), 'What explains teachers' trust in AI in education across six countries?', *International Journal of Artificial Intelligence in Education*, **35**, 1288–1316. https://doi.org/10.1007/s40593-024-00433-x

Viva Technology (2024, May 23). *Everything you always wanted to know about Elon Musk - VivaTech 2024* [Video]. YouTube. https://www.youtube.com/watch?v=TJnBqCL98Y8

Wagener-Böck, N., F. Macgilchrist, K. Rabenstein and A. Bock (2023), 'From automation to symmation: Ethnographic perspectives on what happens in front of the screen', *Postdigital Science and Education*, **5** (1), 136–51. https://doi.org/10.1007/s42438-022-00350-z

Williamson, B. (2019), 'Policy networks, performance metrics and platform markets: Charting the expanding data infrastructure of higher education', *British Journal of Educational Technology*, **50** (6), 2794–2809.

Williamson, B. (2024), 'The social life of AI in education', *International Journal of Artificial Intelligence in Education*, **34** (1), 97–104. https://doi.org/10.1007/s40593-023-00342-5

Williamson, B., F. Macgilchrist and J. Potter (2021), 'Covid-19 controversies and critical research in digital education', *Learning, Media and Technology*, **46** (2), 117–27. https://doi.org/10.1080/17439884.2021.1922437

Williamson, B., F. Macgilchrist and J. Potter (2023), 'Re-examining AI, automation and datafication in education', *Learning, Media and Technology*, **48** (1), 1–5.

Winner, L. (1978), *Autonomous technology: Technics-out-of-control as a theme in political thought*. MIT Press.

Wolff, A., D. Gooch, J.J.C. Montaner, U. Rashid and G. Kortuem (2016), 'Creating an understanding of data literacy for a data-driven society', *The Journal of Community Informatics*, **12** (3), 9–26.

World Economic Forum (2024, April 28), *The future of learning: How AI is revolutionizing education 4.0*. https://www.weforum.org/agenda/2024/04/future-learning-ai-revolutionizing-education-4-0/#:~:text=Integrating%20AI%20into%20education%20can%20streamline%20administrative%20tasks%2C,educators%20can%20thrive%2C%20creating%20a%20richer%20learning%20experience

Yacek, D.W. and M.E. Jonas (2025), '*Phronesis* in teacher education: a critical reexamination', *European Journal of Teacher Education*, **48** (4), 722–38. https://doi.org/10.1080/02619768.2023.2253495

Index

5Es (efficacy, effectiveness, ethics, equity and environment)
- current situation and next steps 59–60
- dimensions of impact 54
- expanded model and its implementation 56–7, 59
- framework 53–5
- nurturing evidence mindset with 58–9
- points of overlap with EdTech impact frameworks 54
- and science of learning 55–6

academic achievement
- digital tools used to predict 81
- emotional experiences influencing 141
- incoming knowledge as predictor of 25
- recommendations for enhancement 146
- school engagement as mediator between emotions and 145–6
- social-emotional competencies as predictors of 147–8
- social-emotional competencies impacting 143
- societal pressures emphasizing, in South Korea 139
- student data 79

adaptive coaching 30, 31

adaptive learning
- GDPR Article 22's automated decisions in context of 71–4
- implementing in Norwegian schools
  - AVT 260–267
  - context 259
  - Data Protection Authority's regulatory sandbox 267, 269
  - lessons learned 269–73
  - summary and conclusions 273
- and personalized learning 2–3, 71, 72
- reasons for needing handbook on 2–3

adaptive learning systems (ALS)
- central premise 24
- challenges of 28, 31
- components
  - domain module 22–3
  - instructor module 23
  - learner module 23
  - from standalone to modularized 23–4
- conceptualization 21, 210
- design priorities 210
- evolution of 21–2
- examples of 21, 22
- functioning of
  - how to adapt (knowledge tracing) 25–7
  - machine learning models 27
  - probabilistic models 26
  - statistical models 26
  - what to adapt 24–5
  - when to adapt 25
- future recommendations 31
- integration
  - barriers to 224–5
  - into broader teaching strategies 212, 223, 228
  - into classroom practice 211, 224
  - into established pedagogical framework 223
  - with GenAI 29–31
  - with other educational materials 215
- optimizing adaptivity by integration with GenAI 29, 31
  - adaptive coaching 30
  - authoring tools 29–30
  - enhanced knowledge tracing 30, 31
- personalized learning in 21–2, 25–6, 210, 211–12, 214, 227
- in primary mathematics
  - adaptivity 217–18
  - alignment with equipment and task quality 215–16
  - balancing functionality, adaptivity, and teacher input 221
  - classroom culture 227
  - classroom management 219–20, 227
  - context 210–211
  - description 211–12
  - equipment accessibility in classroom 215
  - equipment and infrastructure in schools 224–5
  - equity, engagement, and access in relation to homework 224
  - formative assessment 225
  - integration with other educational material 215
  - levels and usage patterns 214
  - methods 213–14
  - motivation and rewards systems 225–6
  - practice and learning 216–17
  - results 214–21

results discussion 221–7
role of ALS in teaching 223–4
scaffolding problem 221–2
student motivation 218–19, 220
summary, conclusion, and limitations 227–8
teachers as designers and pedagogical mediators 222–3
using for homework 214–15
role in teaching 223–4
valued as tool for differentiation 210, 217, 227
AI (artificial intelligence)
allowing for development of new tools 36–7
EssayCritic's system 193
human–AI interaction 191–3
hybrid approach 37, 46–7
and learning analytics 296, 298–300
MMLA data pipelines using different techniques 47
MMLA system leveraging advanced models 45
new tools enabling insights in learning and group work 46
promises in schools
AI literacy and phronesis 303–4
context 295
emergent dilemmas 302–3
multi-sited ethnography 297–300
related to automation and augmentation 296–7
symmation paradox 300–302
in relation to data protection 64–5, 74, 259, 264, 267, 269
using computer vision and NLP as central to MMLA system 41
see also GenAI (generative artificial intelligence)
AI-based writing tool *see* EssayCritic
AI literacy 206, 207, 295, 303–4
algorithmic decisions
balance with teacher input 221
and GDPR's right to explanation
Article 22 automated decisions 71–4
derived from right of access, boundaries of 67–71
legal debate on 65–7
as seemingly limited 65
summary and conclusion 74
and social vulnerability 14, 16
algorithmic fairness *see* fairness
ALS *see* adaptive learning systems (ALS)
American science frameworks 231
attendance data practices
background
attendance regulations and absence limit 97–8
research on attendance registration in schools 98–100
context 96–7
methods and materials 101
monitoring 103–4
negotiation 105–6
process, discussion on 106–8
registration 102–3
students' digital work as overlooked aspect of 107
summary and conclusion 108
theoretical framework 100–101
augmentation
as approach to modular ALS 24
of teachers' work, AI promise related to 295, 296–7, 299
aspirations 304
paradox of 300–302
automated feedback 29, 193, 198, 201, 203, 205–6
automated writing evaluation (AWE) 195, 196, 205–6
automation of teachers' work 295, 296–7, 299, 300–302, 304
AVT (activity data for assessment and adaptivity)
context 259
lessons learned 269–73
period 1 (2017–2019) 260–264
period 2 (2019–2025) 264–7
regulation 267, 269, 270–271
summary and conclusions 273

Bayesian knowledge tracing (BKT) 23, 27, 30, 31
behavioral engagement 140, 145, 146
bias measurement 86–8
bias mitigation
of data biases for fairer inputs 88–90
model-centric and post-hoc corrections 90
recommendations for 91

calculator metaphor 192, 206
care
about Norway's issue 248–9
to be taken over LA's use in schools 18
and control, teachers caught in tension between 99
given to data representation 122
over auditing of predictive analytics 90
over selection of fairness criteria 85, 86
taken to balance curricular work with attendance data management 105, 106
caregivers 276
causal fairness 83, 84–5
children
e-safety 13–14

forms of bias related to 89
and MMLA 47
preparing for society where AI is ubiquitous 303
protection under GDPR 14–15, 65, 270
right to privacy 13
and science of learning 55
use of data-driven approaches 79
use of EdTech 51
vulnerability of
age differentials 12–13, 17
as dynamic 17
legal perspective 14–15
sociological perspective 15–18
see also consent
children's data
concerns over collection of 10–11
controllers of 270–271
EdTech providers processing large volumes of 303
legal agreements related to 17
long-term storage of 91
MittFagkart's handling of 267
and transparency 12
use in schools 13–14
Children's Online Privacy Protection Act (COPPA) 13–14, 15
China 11
classroom integration 211, 224
classroom management 219–20
and culture 227
cognitive engagement 80, 116, 140, 146
collaboration
in education 37
group 181, 212
in MMLA study 36, 38–9, 45, 46–7
with peers 59, 122, 186, 205
PSTs' views on 181, 186
with school mentors 171
social and cultural 181
strong classroom management approach helping to foster 227
see also teacher development; teacher inquiry (TI)
collaborative activities
and ALS in teaching 223
of science students 38–9, 45, 46–7
collaborative learning
and EssayCritic 191, 193, 196, 197, 198, 200, 201, 203, 205–6, 207
focus on, in MMLA study 35, 36
future research area 45
collaborative problem-solving (CPS)
EssayCritic promoting 207
facets in MMLA system 43–4
students enhancing abilities in 201
competencies *see* learning analytics (LA): understanding interrelated nature of competencies through
compulsory education
mitigating data biases for fairer inputs 88–90
predictive analytics in
context 77–8
data availability 79–80
emerging use of 82
key tasks in current practices 81–2
mitigating predictive bias 88–90
opportunities and challenges 90–91
promises of 78–82
risks 82–8
selection of fairness notions 85–6
significance of numerical scores 86
successful examples of ALS in 22
consent 10–11, 12–13
informed 17, 152, 164–5, 282
parental 11, 15, 90–91, 99, 152
to participation 128
and processing of pupils' personal data in educational context 64
voluntary 101
constitutive vulnerability 14, 17, 18
cultural forms 113, 115, 120, 123

data-driven instruction 230–240
data literacy
AI literacy with strong connection to 303
as challenge for ALS 28
definition 280
as important to effective use of LA dashboard 288
many educators lacking formal training in 3
need to accommodate different levels of 114, 115, 116, 124–5
and PDC 179, 186–7
PSTs need for training in 177, 187
teachers' competencies in, as barrier 128, 160, 186
data pipelines
components of 281
integration of 279–80
MMLA, using different AI techniques 41, 47
in primary and secondary education
achievements 288, 290
as drive-based 280–281
implementation of 284–6, 287
limitation 289
successful testing of 283
data practices 96
relational materialist approach to 100–101
see also attendance data practices

data protection
AI in relation to 64–5, 74, 259, 264, 267, 269
importance of compliance with regulation 287
as LA challenge 65, 250
lack of research on, in context of schools 12
and LADs 127
and Norwegian Data Protection Authority's regulatory sandbox 267, 269
and Norwegian Expert Group 249, 256
transparency as problem raised by deployment of AI 64
see also GDPR (General Data Protection Regulation)
data standards/standardization
for integration 272
in Swedish school education
achievements 287, 290
background 278–9
challenges 289, 290
with data pipeline 280–281, 285
at implementation stage 286
reformatting data according to 281
results 282–4
tables of 283, 284, 287
and usability of ALS 28
data visualization 114, 124–5, 276, 281
datafication of education, sociomaterial perspective on 96–108
analysis 101–6
background 97–100
context 96–7
methods and materials 101
study discussion 106–8
summary and conclusion 108
theoretical framework 100–101
decisional vulnerability 14, 16, 18
deep knowledge tracing (DKT) 27, 31
design-based research 163, 193, 196, 282, 288
see also learning analytics (LA): design narrative
digital learning materials (DLMs) 276, 277–8, 280, 281, 282, 286–7, 289, 290

Edsight
designing and deploying
context 116–17
data-sharing module 120
design of tool 118
leveraging design tensions 118–20
second deployment 121
version 1: report view 119
lessons learned from deployment
cultural forms in LA design 123
designing and deploying 120–121
designing in partnership for LA 123–4
generative uncertainty 121–2
sensemaking with LA 122–3
nature of 113
PMR2 (Practical Measures, Routines, and Representations) 116–17, 118, 119, 122
EdTech (educational technology)
5Es
current situation and next steps 59–60
expanded model 56–7, 59
framework 53–5
nurturing evidence mindset with 59–60
and science of learning 55–6
and AI technologies 296–7, 298, 301, 303, 304
context 51–2
evaluation frameworks 52–3
evidence mindset 57–9
impact frameworks
multi-dimensional 52–3
points of overlap with 5Es model 54
quality indicators for products 52–3
limitations and implications 59–60
recommendation for 152
Swedish companies 297–8, 303
Swedish industry 278–9, 288
Swedish providers 279, 281–2, 283, 285–6, 287, 289, 290, 298, 303
educational data
in connection to digital learning platforms 276
and data-related biases 88
development of standard 287, 290
LA dashboards 280, 288
in primary and secondary education 276, 281, 287
requirements of efficient, reliable and secure manipulation of 277
upsurge in generation of 276
educational data mining (EDM) 11, 21, 138, 151–2
educational settings
complications with implementing GDPR-compliant systems in 289
cultural forms as anchors for information in 123
dispersal of management and utilization of data at lower education levels in 276–7
impact of ChatGPT 191
importance of compliance with data protection regulations in 287
integration of AI tools into 192, 196, 299, 303, 304
interest in integration of digital tools into 113
personalized learning as often used in 296
platforms designed to support formal 80
predictive analytics in context of 77
purpose of MMLA system in 41

recommendations for effective visual analytics tools in 114
role of school engagement in 140
sensemaking as nuanced in 116
supporting for anxious students in 151
survey to integrate cultural and contextual information in 44–5
widespread use of continuous predictions in 87
effectiveness
of ALS 22, 24, 28, 31, 225
of deep knowledge tracing models 27
as dimension of impact 53, 54
and Edtech 52, 54, 57
and evidence mindset 58
of learning dashboards 114
measuring 52
product 58
and science of learning 55, 56
teaching 90, 187
efficacy
of ALS 28
of data pipelines 279
as dimension of impact 54
and Edtech 52, 54, 57
and science of learning 55, 56
emotional experiences
assessing through emotion check-ins 140, 141–3
capturing insights into students' 138
impact of students' reporting of 145
and multimodal learning analytics 151
English as a foreign language (EFL) 195, 207
English as a second language (ESL) 195
environment
as dimension of impact 53, 54
and EdTech 54
and science of learning 55–6
equity
of ALS and homework 224
as dimension of impact 53, 54
and Edtech 54, 288
and evidence mindset 58
and science of learning 55–6
see also fairness
ESSA (Every Student Succeeds Act) evaluation framework 52, 53, 56
EssayCritic
AI system 192–3
beginning of learning process 199–200, 203
combining rule-based logic and machine learning techniques 192
designed to enhance creativity through contextual feedback 192–3
final stage of learning process 201, 203–5
interaction metaphors 191–2, 206
literature review 195–6
as locally-trained AI-based writing tool 191
methods 196–7
qualitative 198
quantitative 197
middle of learning process 201, 202, 203
purpose of 191
research question pertaining to 193
results
discussion 203–6
qualitative analysis 199–202
quantitative analysis 198–9
study conclusions, limitations and future research 207
user interface 194
ethics
as challenge in China 11
as challenge of predictive analytics in compulsory education 90–91
as dimension of impact 53, 54
and Edtech 54, 59
ethical judgements (phronesis) 304
and evidence mindset 58
fairness as ethical responsibility 78
and gathering data with undetermined purposes 256
literature review 13
within LLM-based systems 196
MMLA facing challenges 47
pertaining to LA 3, 12, 18
and AI in teaching practices 179, 188
conducting research 164–5
and education in Norway 249–50, 260, 267, 269, 270, 273
in relation to LADs 127, 286, 289
in relation to regular collection of student's socio-emotional data 152
and science of learning 55–6
and students' right to see analysis of their data 270
in Sweden 281, 286, 287
and AI in education 295, 299, 302–4
see also fairness
ethnography *see* multi-sited ethnography; video-based ethnography
evaluation
Edtech 51, 52–3, 54, 57
impact 51, 54, 57
multidimensional 52–3
of MMLA system
human 45–6
initial 40
technical 45

Every Student Succeeds Act (ESSA) evaluation framework 52, 53, 56
evidence
and 5Es model 53–4, 56, 59
Edtech's impact 51, 52–3, 54, 57, 60
empirical, and functioning of ALS 24–5
holistic building of 59–60
evidence-based decision-making 133
evidence-based Edtech impact framework 54
evidence-based strategies
to create positive learning environment 131
to raise student motivation 131
supporting diverse learners 55
evidence-based teaching practice 132, 134
evidence-based tools 152
evidence-centered design framework (ECD) 233
evidence mindset 56, 57–8, 60
nurturing with 5Es 58–9
explainability *see* GDPR (General Data Protection Regulation): right to explanation of algorithmic decisions

Fagkart (subject map) 264, 265, 266, 271
Fagkartkoder (tagging tool) 264, 265, 271, 272
fairness
contextualizing 85–6
as ethical responsibility 78
measuring 86–8
mitigating data biases for 88–90
model-centric and output-centric interventions 90
notations 83
notions
independence, separation, sufficiency 84–6
overview 83–5
selection of 85–6
types of 83–5
theoretical foundations 83–5
fairness measurement
metrics for classification tasks 86–7
metrics for regression tasks 87–8
Finland 11
formative assessments
and adaptive learning systems 223, 225
definition 176
design of Inq-ITS and Inq-Blotter to support 233–6, 240
and learning analytics 178–9, 187–8
and learning progressions 232
limitations, implications and future research 187–8
platforms supporting 80
practical measures as 117
and predictive analytics 82, 90
PSTs' responses to trial of 185–6
research context 180
research question pertaining to 176–7, 186–7
student-active approach towards learning about 186
teaching about 181–6
and TIPS 238–9

GDPR (General Data Protection Regulation)
and AVT 267, 269
compliance of different digital technologies and apps 251
data minimalization principle of 256
European educational systems as bound to comply with 259
and Norwegian data controllers 270–271
origins 64–5
providing same high level of data protection to all in EU/EEA 65
regulation of children's personal data 270
right to explanation of algorithmic decisions
automated decisions 71–4
derived from right of access, boundaries of 67–71
legal debate on 65–7
summary and conclusion 74
in Swedish school education 285, 286, 287, 288, 289
GenAI (generative artificial intelligence)
comparison with Essay Critic 193, 205–6
conceptualization 29, 36
data pipelines using 47
ethical issues challenging implementation in educational settings 196
future recommendation 207
integrating with ALS 29–30, 31
and job replacement narratives 301
as possible future solution for tagging 272–3
preventing acquisition of important learning skills 191
underlying architecture 192
use of AI in classrooms associated with 297
generative uncertainty 116, 118, 121–2
GIFT (Generalized Intelligent Framework for Tutoring) 24
group fairness 83, 84, 86–90
group membership 83, 84, 85, 86, 87

homework
parents helping too much with 217–18
use of ALS for 215–16
equity, engagement, and access 224
human-centred design (HCD) 114–15, 124, 286, 290
human-centred learning analytics (HCLA) 115

ILUKS planner 158, 159, 160
as learning device tool for inquiry-based lesson planning 161–3
limitations and opportunities 171, 172
method 163–5
results 165–6, 168
screenshot of activity card 163
screenshot of interface 162
impact
and 5Es toolkit 59
EdTech frameworks
and evidence mindset 57–9
on learning 51
multidimensional evaluation 52–3, 57
points of overlap with 5Es model 54
recommendations for 30
systematic review 51
five dimensions of 53–4
in expanded model 56–7
and holistic evidence-building 59
implementation science 280–281
individual fairness 83–4, 87
Inq-Blotter
components of 235–6
design of, to support teachers' formative assessment 233–4, 235–6, 239–40
with Inq-ITS, summary of studies on 236–9
summary and conclusions 239–40
Inq-ITS
components of 234–5
design of, to support teachers' formative assessment 233–5
with Inq-Blotter, summary of studies on 236–9
summary and conclusions 239–40
interaction metaphors 191–2, 206

K–12 education
AI promises in
AI literacy and phronesis 303–4
context 295
emergent dilemmas 302–3
multi-sited ethnography 297–300
related to automation and augmentation 296–7
symmation paradox 300–302
deployment of LA in 11–13, 17–18
design principles for LA in 113, 115–16
and LADs 124–5
monitoring applications in context of 13
see also primary and secondary education
knowledge tracing
Bayesian 23, 27, 30, 31
categorization of
machine learning models 27
probabilistic models 26
statistical models 26
concept of 25–6
enhanced 30, 31
types of model 27

LA *see* learning analytics (LA)
labelling bias 89–90
LADs *see* learning analytics dashboards (LADs); multiple learning analytics dashboards (MLADs)
large language models (LLMs)
and AI in Swedish education 297
carbon footprint 207
combined with large multimodal models 36
comparison with Essay Critic 193, 195–6, 207
and computer vision 41
GIFT's use of 24
as having transformative potential for ALS 22
lack of common sense 31
multimodal 29
release of chatbots based on 264
use in MMLA system 41–2, 45
use of generative
in educational settings 29, 30, 191
as embodied pedagogical agents 30
for knowledge tracing tasks 30
law *see* legalities and law
learning analytics dashboards (LADs)
about 127
data visualization at micro level 276
definition 259
at K–12 level 124–5
in Norwegian schools *see* MittFagkart (LAD)
as solution to monitoring student progress 260
in Swedish primary and secondary education
achievements 288
aim of study 280
challenges and limitations 289
future work implications 290
implementation 286–7
methods 282
and teacher inquiry 128, 132–4
teachers needing to monitor automated insights delivered by 299
see also multiple learning analytics dashboards (MLADs)
learning analytics (LA)
and AI 296, 298–300
ALS system based on principles of 211–12
data protection as challenge for 65
definitions 2, 157, 276
design narrative
context 113–14

design principles for K–12 education 113, 115–16
Edsight 116–20
embedding cultural forms into 113, 115, 123
human-centred design 114–15
lessons learned 121–4
literature review 114–16
research-practice partnerships 113–14, 116–17, 118, 119–20, 123–4
sensemaking with 116, 122–3
summary and conclusion 124–5
and formative assessments 178–9, 187–8
GDPR Article 22's automated decisions in context of 71–4
human-centred 115
implementing in Norwegian schools
AVT 260–267
context 259
Data Protection Authority's regulatory sandbox 267, 269
lessons learned 269–73
summary and conclusions 273
introducing to PSTs as formative assessment
assessment as joint effort with teachers 183–4
collaboration and peer learning 186
context 176–7
data, method, and analytical approach 180–181
designing lesson plan with assignment 181–2
development of multimodal assignment 182–3
formative assessments 179
limitations, implications and future research 187–8
previous studies 178–80
professional digital competence 179–80
research context 180
responses to trial lesson 185–6
student-active approach towards learning about 186
summary and conclusion 186–7
teaching about 181–6
navigating
assessment of concerns 253–6
assessment of potential 252–3
in context of Norway 248–9
dilemmas in 250–251
in education, expert assessment 249–50
policy recommendations 256
objective 160
as part of EdTech 51
and professional digital competence 177–8, 186
reasons for needing handbook on 2–3
in schools
consent problem 10–11
context 10
literature review 11–13
paucity of research on 13, 17
recommendations for 18
understanding interrelated nature of competencies through
assessing and validating social-emotional dimensions 138, 140–145
context 137–8
exploring complex relationships 138, 145–8
insights from South Korean learning management system data 138–40
LA research overview 139–40
study discussion and future research directions 151–2
use of temporal LA 138, 148–50
using to explore pre-service teachers' lesson planning
background 159–63
challenges and possibilities 169–72
context 157–8
limitations and future research recommendations 172
method 163–5
results 165–9
summary and conclusion 172
see also teacher education: learning analytics
learning dashboards 114, 118, 122, 124
learning design
composition of average 165–6, 171
feedback on 168–9, 171–2
update 170
LA used to inform 160
PSTs' difficulty with including flexibility in 159
study limitations and future research recommendations 172
study method and results 163–72
to support PSTs' lesson planning 161–3
systematic review on LA for 157–8
teacher inquiry impacting 133
learning design tools 158, 161
see also ILUKS planner
learning management system (LMS)
comparison with EdTech 57
comparison with LA 115
designed for K–12 education, development of 298–9
digital data about learners from 128
lightweight, as Inq-ITS component 235

South Korean, insights from data 139–40, 141, 148, 151
student tracking data collected from 160
as type of learning design tool 158
learning progressions
for curriculum, instruction, and support 231–2
definition 231
implementation research 232
lack of specificity of 232, 233
as potentially beneficial to education 231
prior work on 231–2
learning strategies *see* science of learning (SoL): strategies
legal perspective
protected attributes 85
on vulnerability 14–15
legalities and law
Character Education Promotion Act 139
clarification and strengthening of 271
and consent 11
on consent 15, 17
experts in 249
on GDPR's right to explanation 65–71
Article 22 automated decisions 71–4
lack of discussion on 12
Law of Disuse 27
legal basis for processing children's data 267, 269, 270–271
legal basis for processing pupil activity 256
Norwegian assessment in relation to LA in education 249–50, 251, 256
period of education required for children 78
student data 264, 271, 278
on use of children's data 13, 17, 264
lesson plan
with assignment
designing 181
mandatory 187
multimodal approach 182–3, 184
data, method, and analytical approach 180–181
development of 181
presentation on development of 176
research context 180
lesson planning
background
LA for teacher education 160
learning design and tools to support 161–3
learning to plan lessons 159
challenges and possibilities 168–9
context 157–8
ILUKS planner for inquiry-based 161–3
limitations and future research recommendations 172
method 163
context and participants 164
data and analysis 164
ethical considerations 164–5
results
composition of average learning design 165–6
feedback on learning designs 168–9, 170, 171–2
missing cards 167–8, 171
pre-service teachers' planning trajectory 166–7
summary and conclusion 172
locally trained model *see* EssayCritic

machine learning (ML)
comparison with GenAI 29
and data pipelines 47, 279
deep learning and transfer learning as developments in 21
definition 27
in Essay Critic 192, 193, 197
and fairness 83
inconsistent data upload hampering reliability of 286, 289
intelligent tutoring system 298–9
overfitting as concept from 122
and predictive analytics 77
techniques 23, 192
machine learning models 5, 21, 27
MittFagkart (LAD) 259, 262, 264, 265–6
data access issue 271
data protection impact assessment developed for 269, 271
design of interface 266–7
need for data processing agreement 270
screenshot of application 268
section for mathematics 266
MMLA *see* multimodal learning analytics (MMLA)
modular ALS
approaches
augmentation 24
GIFT 24
evolution of 23
monitoring applications (MA) 10, 13
multi-sited ethnography 297
analytical work 299
compensatory work and non-action 299–300
context 295
data production 298–9
multimodal assignment
assessment criteria and rubric for 183–4
development of 182–3
introduction to 181–2
and student-active approach 186

multimodal learning analytics (MMLA) 10
  background 37
    collaboration, persistence and optimal learning moments 37–8
    gaps 38
  and emotional experiences 151
  increasing use in educational contexts 10, 35
  methodological approach
    context 38–9
    design approach 39–40
  study research aims 36
  system
    challenges 36, 47
    current 40–42
    design 46
    effectiveness 46
    human evaluation 45–6
    inferring learning constructs 42–4
    next steps for 47
    survey approaches 44–5
    technical evaluation 45
multiple learning analytics dashboards (MLADs) 285–6, 288, 290
  see also learning analytics dashboards (LADs)

Next Generation Science Standards (NGSS) 230–237, 239–40

optimal learning moments 38, 47

participatory design 113, 114, 124, 127
PDC *see* professional digital competence (PDC)
pedagogical challenges 221, 224
  teachers as mediators 222–3, 227, 228
peer learning 181, 186
personalization techniques 25–7
personalized learning (PL)
  and adaptive learning 2–3, 71, 72
  in ALS 21–2, 25–6, 210, 211–12, 214, 227
  complex, relational datasets supporting 288
  conceptualization 21–2, 296
  digital transformation investment fostering 277
  in mathematics education 210, 211–12, 214–15, 227
  for meaningful student engagement 149
  misalignment of content 299
  platforms supporting 80
  predictive models guiding 138
  relation to augmentation 296
  skill-based, through adaptive task sequencing 211
personalized technologies 16–17, 23
phronesis 295, 303, 304
policy recommendations 256
power drill metaphor 192, 206
pre-service teachers (PSTs)
  introduction of LA as formative assessment to
    assessment as joint effort with teachers 183–4
    collaboration and peer learning 186
    context 176–7
    data, method, and analytical approach 180–181
    designing lesson plan with assignment 181–2
    development of multimodal assignment 182–3
    formative assessments 179
    limitations, implications and future research 187–8
    previous studies 178–80
    professional digital competence 179–80
    research context 180
    responses to trial lesson 185–6
    summary and conclusion 186–7
    taking student-active approach 186
  using LA to explore lesson planning
    background 159–63
    challenges and possibilities 169–72
    context 157–8
    limitations and future research recommendations 172
    method 163–5
    results 165–9
    summary and conclusion 172
predictive analytics
  in compulsory education
    context 77–8
    continuous monitoring 82
    data availability 79–80
    key tasks in current practices 81–2
    mitigating predictive bias 88–90
    opportunities and challenges 90–91
    promises of 78–82
    risks 82–8
  conceptualization 77
  in educational settings 77
  fairness
    contextualizing 85–6
    measuring 86–8
    mitigating data biases for 88–90
    model-centric and output-centric interventions 90
  fairness notions
    overview 83–5
    selection of 85–6
predictive bias
  assessing 82–8
  concept 83

mitigating 88–90, 91
predictive modeling
in compulsory education 77, 78–80, 82, 86, 88–91
incorporating social-emotional competencies 138, 140–150, 151
primary and secondary education
background
data pipelines 279–80
data standards 278–9
implementation science 280–281
context 276–8
learning analytics in
benefits of 252–3
digital 249
methods 281–2
policy recommendations 256
results
data pipeline 284–6
data standardization 282–4
implementation 286–7
study discussion 287
achievements 287–8
challenges and limitations 289
implications for future work 290
summary and conclusion 290
technical infrastructure 277, 282, 284–6
see also K–12 education
primary mathematics *see* adaptive learning systems (ALS): in primary mathematics
probabilistic models 23, 26
professional digital competence (PDC) 176
and data literacy 186–7
elective course on 180
and learning analytics 177–8, 186
in teacher training 179–80
proxy discrimination 89–90
PSTs *see* pre-service teachers (PSTs)

reflexive thematic analysis (RTA) 180
regulation
data protection, importance of compliance with 287
emotion 141, 143, 150
EU 64–5
in Norway
attendance 97–8, 107
regulatory sandbox 264, 267, 269
for use of correct data 270–271
privacy 91, 269
self-regulation difficulties 140, 143, 147, 148, 149, 151–2
see also GDPR (General Data Protection Regulation)
reinforcement learning 27, 31
relational approach to AI 297, 299
relational complexity
of attendance data 96, 108
of data-producing technologies 103
of registered absences 104
relational materialist approach to data practice 100–101, 108
relational, vulnerability as 15, 17
representation bias 89
research-practice partnerships (RPPs) 113–14, 116–17, 118, 119–20, 123–4
reward systems 219, 225–6

scaffolding
in ALS
automatic and adaptive 25
precise 30
problem of 221–2, 223, 227
and zone of proximal development 210, 212, 221
and LA tools 116
in LLM-based systems 196
teachers' need for 128
school absence
analysis 101–6
background 97–100
context 96–7
methods and materials 101
study discussion 106–8
summary and conclusion 108
theoretical framework 100–101
school engagement
assessing through behavioral indicators 140–141
emotional experiences influencing 141
as inferred from clickstream and assignment log files 138
mediation effect path model 146
as mediator between emotions and academic outcomes 145–6
positive impact of social-emotional competencies on 137
and social-emotional competencies 143
schools
equipment and infrastructure in 224–5
moral obligation and fiduciary duty to act as guardians 10
reasons for needing handbook on LA in 2–3
use of children's data in 13–14
science education
AI frameworks for 35
American 231
context 37
MMLA system
current 40–42

design 46
discussion 46–7
evaluation 45–6
future research areas 47
inferring learning constructs 42–4
survey approaches 44–5
study design 39–40
study method 38–9
see also STEM education
science of learning (SoL) 133–4
and 5Es 55–6
and evidence mindset 57
as guiding framework for educational impact 51
interventions 129
and strategies 130
teachers' reflections on 130–131
next steps for 58, 59–60
strategies
benefits of 133
and interventions 130
teachers' application of 131–2
teachers introduced to 128–9
SEL *see* social and emotional learning (SEL)
self-improving systems 31
sensemaking
in context of learning analytics 122–3
and dashboards 119
design for 115
Edsight designed to encourage 120–121
goal to foster process of 118
with learning analytics 116
roles regularly engaging in 117
skills
21st Century 7, 230
ALS as not highlighting all 225
data literacy 186, 187
digital 104, 131, 200, 227, 248, 277
foundational 80, 81, 223–4
higher-order 205, 206
and learning progressions 231
lesson planning 157
social and emotional learning 137, 138, 147, 152
sub-skills for key practices 234, 235
teacher inquiry 128, 129, 132, 133
teaching 177, 227
writing 191, 192, 195, 203–5, 206, 207
social and emotional learning (SEL)
benefit of developing 152
challenge of integrating LA research in context of 152
importance of prioritizing within digital learning contexts 138
key skills 137
movement to integrate into schools worldwide 137
recommendations for LA focused on 138
urgent need to integrate into K–12 digital learning environments in South Korea 139
social-emotional competencies
assessment using digital measures 140, 143–5, 152
importance in sustaining student engagement within digital learning environments 149
increasing advocacy for integration into LA research 151
positive impacts of 137
predictive models incorporating 138
as predictors of academic performance and psychological well-being 147–8
status of, in South Korea 139
social engagement 140, 145, 146
social vulnerability 14, 16–17, 18
socio-digital vulnerability 14, 16, 18
sociomaterial perspective *see* datafication of education, sociomaterial perspective on
South Africa 11
South Korea *see* learning analytics (LA): understanding interrelated nature of competencies through
specialised language model (SLM) 193, 195, 207
statistical models 26
STEM education
and American science frameworks 231
context 230–231
Inq-ITS and Inq-Blotter
design of, to support teachers' formative assessment 233–6
summary of studies on 236–9
learning progressions for curriculum, instruction, and assessment
implementation research 232
prior work on 231–2
summary and conclusions 239–40
stereotypical bias 89
steroids metaphor 192, 206
student-active approach 186, 187
student data
AI
collection for commercial purpose, as dilemma 300, 303
continuous collection, analysis, and visualisation of 296
collaboration in relation to 115
ethical issues 55, 267, 269, 270
integration
across learning tools from different vendors 273

with feedback and training mechanism 151–2
from heterogeneous sources, as challenge 281
into unified and coherent dataset 277
and learning analytics dashboards 124
and multimodal learning analytics 151
in Norway
AVT 260, 264–5, 267–8, 269, 270, 271, 273
collection of, as done every day 249
dilemmas in relation to 250–251
general requirements for 252–3
legalities and law 264, 271
misleading 255
ownership of 269
policy recommendations for 256
random and planless use of 256
regulation 267, 269, 270–271
report looking into use of 249–50
right to protection of 251
and predictive analytics 82, 90
temporal analysis as effective in capturing stability and consistency of 150
uncertainty around use of in schools 2
see also children's data
student engagement
and affective states 143
current research 151
and emotions 141
latent factors 140–141
latent growth model of change in 150
observed and predicted trends in 149
recommendations for 151–2
temporal analysis 148–50
student motivation 131, 140, 141–2, 193, 218–19, 220, 221, 225–6

teacher development
collaboration and iterative design 115, 118
collaboration with peers 122
collaborative aspects of data use in schools 115–16
collaborative decision-making 116, 118
collaborative efforts 124
collaborative planning 121
collaborative processes 116
collaborative reflection 113, 123
context 113–14
Edsight
designing and deploying 116–20
lessons learned 121–4
nature of 113
literature review
data visualization 114
human-centred LA design 114–15
LA and K-12 in schools 115–16
learning dashboards 114
sensemaking with LA 116
math teachers leveraging data to promote student collaboration 117
summary and conclusion 124–5
teacher education
and digital competence 248
learning analytics 176–7
and AI 178
challenges and possibilities of using 157, 169–72
future research areas 188
goal of informing instructional decisions in 157
integration 160, 186–7
previous research findings 157–8
teacher education programmes
PDC in 177, 179–80, 186
purpose of 159
using GenAI in 191
teacher inquiry practice supports (TIPS) 233, 236–40
teacher inquiry (TI)
bringing greatest changes in teachers' practices 131
as collaborative 129, 132, 133–4
introduction to 128
and learning analytics dashboards 128, 132–4
methods 128–30
results 130–132
study discussion 132–3
summary and conclusion 133–4
teacher perspectives on ALS
balancing with functionality and adaptivity 221
conclusion 227
context 210–211
methods 213–14
results 214–21
study discussion 221–7
teacher trainers 176–7, 179–80, 186–8
teacher training 186–8
addressing gaps in, as challenge 277
ALS materials 212
course to improve teaching strategies 128–9
EdTech 57
inadequate, in integrating automated feedback tools 206
lack of 196
professional digital competence in 179–80
teachers
and AI promises 295–304
concerns of 2
as designers and pedagogical mediators 222–3

handbook as providing support for 3
joint effort with PSTs 183–4
professional digital competence and LA 177–8
role as mediators between students and technology 211
shaping learning environments 210–211
teaching analytics
methods 128–30
recommendations for 133
results 130–132
summary and conclusion 133–4
temporal analysis 138, 148–50
TIPS *see* teacher inquiry practice supports (TIPS)
transparency
absence of, as hindering LA 65
in ALS 223, 224
of decision-making system 72
in EdTech 59, 288
EssayCritic enhancing 195
in Norwegian Data Protection regulatory sandbox 269
versus privacy, as design tension 119
as problem raised by AI use 64, 65
in schools 12, 115, 278
and written assessment criteria 183

United States (US)
college students compared with Korean students 141, 143, 147–8
Edsight 113
ESSA evaluation framework 52, 53, 56
intelligent tutoring systems 80
learning analytics in schools 12
legislation 13–14
Next Generation Science Standards 230
PMR2 funded by 117
science education 231
SEL skills 137
Uruguay 11–12

video-based ethnography
analysis 101–6
background 97–100
context 96–7
methods and materials 101
study discussion 106–8
summary and conclusion 108
theoretical framework 100–101
vulnerability of children
digitally mediated learning raising concerns regarding 18
as dynamic, relational and constantly developing 17
legal perspective 13–14
sociological perspective 15–17
types of 14, 16–18

zone of proximal development (ZPD) 210, 212, 221–2, 228